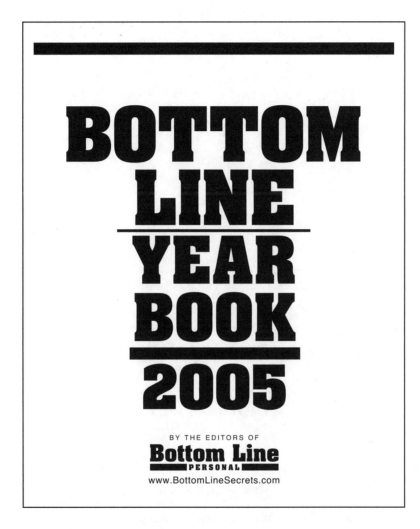

BOTTOM LINE YEAR BOOK 2005

BY THE EDITORS OF

Bottom Line
PERSONAL

www.BottomLineSecrets.com

Contents

PART FOUR: YOUR LEISURE

14 • THE SAVVY TRAVELER

15 • HAVING FUN

16 • AUTOMOTIVE KNOW-HOW

17 • TAKING CARE OF HOME AND FAMILY

18 • BETTER WAYS

PART FIVE: YOUR LIFE

19 • BUSINESS AND CAREER SMARTS

20 • KIDS, COLLEGE AND MORE

21 • SAFE AND SECURE

1

Health News

Breakthrough Therapies For Heart Disease, Cancer —and Varicose Veins

Sophisticated radiologic treatments—like high-speed computed tomography (CT) scans —now are being used both as an alternative to traditional surgery and as a new diagnostic tool for a number of common ailments.

Typically administered by interventional radiologists, these treatments are available at most medical centers across the US.*

Three leading experts discuss these new therapies below…

CANCER TREATMENT
Jeff Geschwind, MD

When surgical removal of a malignancy of the liver, kidneys, bone or other organs is not

*Interventional radiologists specialize in minimally invasive treatments that use image-guided techniques. To find such a specialist in your area, consult the Society of Interventional Radiology (800-488-7284, *www.sirweb.org*).

an option, due to the size or location of the tumor, patients may now receive a new therapy called *radiofrequency ablation.*

What's involved: An interventional radiologist uses an ultrasound to locate the tumor. A needle is then placed through the skin directly into the malignancy. A radiofrequency current is emitted through the needle to burn away the tumor without damaging any surrounding tissue. The treatment typically takes one to three hours and can be performed as an outpatient procedure, without general anesthesia.

Typical cost: $13,000 to $20,000.

Important: Radiofrequency ablation is only appropriate for the smaller malignancies—that

Jeff Geschwind, MD, associate professor of radiology, oncology and surgery at Johns Hopkins University School of Medicine, and director of cardiovascular and interventional radiology at The Johns Hopkins Hospital, both in Baltimore.

Heiko Schöder, MD, assistant attending physician at Memorial Sloan-Kettering Cancer Center and assistant professor of radiology at Weill Medical College of Cornell University, both in New York City.

Sheldon Sheps, MD, cardiologist and emeritus professor of medicine at Mayo Medical School in Rochester, MN.

is, tumors no larger than 3 to 4 centimeters (cm) in diameter. This procedure is not a cure for cancer but can be used to help control it.

VARICOSE VEINS

Approximately 25% of all American women and 10% of American men suffer from varicose veins. These will occur when a vein's emptying mechanisms malfunction, resulting in reflux (the pooling of blood), most often in the legs or pelvis. Besides being unsightly, varicose veins also can lead to chronic pain.

A new image-guided technique called *vein ablation,* done with radiofrequency or laser heat, now makes it easier to destroy varicose veins without surgery or the injection of chemical solutions.

What's involved: Guided by ultrasound, the radiologist threads a small catheter into the varicose vein. The laser is then fired briefly, which heats and seals the vein. The treatment takes less than an hour, and the patient is up and walking 20 minutes later.

Typical cost: $2,000 to $3,000 per leg.

Another new technique uses image-guided therapy to eliminate varicose veins in the pelvis. Some 9 million American women suffer from unexplained chronic pelvic pain.

Known as *pelvic congestion syndrome,* this condition has traditionally been very difficult to diagnose and thought to be untreatable. Doctors now believe that many of these cases are caused by varicose veins in the pelvis.

A *venogram* allows doctors to identify varicose veins in the pelvis. During this procedure, a catheter is inserted and threaded through the affected vein, and an X-ray dye is injected to highlight the vein. An X ray is then taken. Next, small steel coils are implanted to block blood flow through the abnormal vein. This causes the varicose veins to shrivel and disappear.

Typical cost: $7,000.

MALIGNANCY DETECTION
Heiko Schöder, MD

A new technology, known as PET-CT fusion, allows doctors to pinpoint the precise location of cancer cells in the body (for all types of cancer) without having to rely on additional imaging procedures and examinations. The positron emission tomography (PET) locates the small

lesions, and the CT scan then precisely pinpoints them.

What's involved: The patient first undergoes a CT scan, a computer-enhanced X-ray study that produces two-dimensional images. Then the patient undergoes a PET scan. For this test, a radioactive substance called a "tracer" is injected into a vein. The patient next is placed inside a ring-shaped PET scanner, which detects radiation and records sites of high activity, where cancer is likely to be present. The two tests take about one-half hour to perform. Afterward, the radiologist "fuses" the results of a PET scan with the detailed anatomical images of a CT scan.

Typical cost: $2,000 to $4,000 for both.

A study at Memorial Sloan-Kettering Cancer Center found that the use of combined scans improved accuracy by 42% when diagnosing the location of tumors of the head and neck.

CORONARY ARTERY DISEASE
Sheldon Sheps, MD

A new five-minute, noninvasive imaging test known as an *electron beam CT* (EBCT) heart scan assesses the amount of calcium in your coronary arteries. Because calcium is a major component of arterial plaque, a high coronary calcium level indicates significant plaque buildup in the blood vessels.

What's involved: A cardiologist or radiologist uses the recently developed ultrafast-CT scanner that provides detailed pictures of your heart. The procedure exposes the patient to relatively low levels of radiation.

Typical cost: $400.

A heart scan provides a quick and accurate assessment of heart attack risk without the potential risks associated with an angiogram, in which a catheter is used to inject a dye into the heart that can be seen on X rays.

Beware of Hidden Carcinogens

Christopher J. Portier, PhD, director of the environmental toxicology program at the National Institutes of Environmental Health Sciences in Research Triangle Park, NC. The National Toxicology Program, part of the National Institutes of Health, publishes the biennial *Report on Carcinogens.*

Every two years, the federal government publishes their *Report on Carcinogens* (ROC), a list of all environmental substances that are either known—or appear likely—to cause cancer. The ROC does not calculate the odds that an individual exposed to these substances will get cancer. Nor does it offer ways to offset cancer risks.

Common carcinogens to avoid…

ESTROGENS

Every woman is exposed to various forms of the hormone estrogen. This includes the natural form secreted by the ovaries and fat tissue, as well as, in some cases, the estrogens used in birth control pills, hormone replacement therapy (HRT), vaginal creams, etc.

Estrogens are carcinogenic. And, the greater a woman's exposure, the greater her risk for uterine and breast cancer. In rare cases, men must take estrogen to treat prostate cancer. They are also at increased risk for breast cancer.

Women cannot reduce their exposure to natural forms of estrogen. Those who began menstruating at an early age (before age 11) or had a late onset of menopause (after age 55) will naturally have greater estrogen exposure—and should be sure to get regular Pap smears, mammograms and other screening tests.

The use of HRT is controversial. The drugs clearly are beneficial for reducing menopausal symptoms. However, long-standing claims that HRT helps reduce heart disease have not been borne out by research. Furthermore, HRT may increase the risk for blood clots, strokes and other problems.

The FDA requires that estrogen drug labels, including those on birth control pills, warn about possible cancer risks.

It is not yet clear if estrogen-like compounds found in soy increase cancer risk. More research is under way.

To protect yourself: Every woman should talk to her doctor about the risks versus benefits of taking supplemental estrogen.

IQ

IQ, the abbreviation for *2-amino-3-methylimidazo [4,5-f] quinoline,* belongs to the chemical family called *heterocyclic amines,* which are produced by high-heat cooking. Cooked foods with the highest IQ levels include grilled, broiled or fried beef or fish.

Animal studies suggest that exposure to IQ may bring on cancers of the mammary gland, liver and small intestine. Some human studies suggest that people who eat the most grilled, broiled or fried foods have a higher risk for breast and colorectal cancers.

To protect yourself: Cook your foods more slowly at lower heats. Avoid or reduce the frequency of high-heat grilling and broiling. Do not blacken or char food.

METHYLEUGENOL

Methyleugenol is a naturally occurring substance found in many essential oils, including those in basil, nutmeg and cinnamon. It is used as a flavoring agent in many packaged foods. The words "natural flavoring" on a label may mean the product contains methyleugenol.

Other sources: Insect strips or traps…and baked goods, such as gingersnaps.

Animal studies suggest that long-term exposure to methyleugenol triggers DNA damage that increases the risk for liver cancer. We aren't sure if humans face the same risk—but nearly everyone is exposed to the chemical on a daily basis.

To protect yourself: Research is under way to determine the carcinogenic levels of methyleugenol. It is still unknown whether dangerous levels of methyleugenol are emitted from insect traps. Using less basil, cinnamon and nutmeg when preparing food may be helpful.

RADON

Radon—a colorless, odorless gas produced by the breakdown of uranium in soil and water —is one of the most dangerous carcinogens to which the US public is regularly exposed. The Environmental Protection Agency (EPA) estimates that one in 15 American homes has elevated radon levels. As many as 22,000 lung cancer deaths are believed to be caused by radon each year.

Radon seeps into homes through cracks or other foundation openings. Since it's nine times denser than air, it tends to accumulate in basements or first-floor areas.

To protect yourself: Test your indoor radon levels. These levels should not exceed 4 picocuries per liter (pCi/L), according to the EPA. Radon testing kits are available at hardware stores for less than $20. The most common type is a small charcoal canister that's placed in the lowest part of the house for at least 48 hours, then mailed to a laboratory for analysis.

When radon levels are high, radon mitigation should be performed by a professional.

ULTRAVIOLET LIGHT

We've known for a long time that different types of ultraviolet light—mainly the ultraviolet A (UVA) and ultraviolet B (UVB) radiation produced by the sun and indoor tanning beds—are likely carcinogens.

Exposure to UV light causes cell damage that will increase the risk for skin cancer, including melanoma, as well as non-Hodgkin's lymphoma. The more exposure, the greater the risk.

In 1994, the American Medical Association passed a resolution calling for a ban on tanning equipment—and yet up to 28 million Americans still use tanning beds. What's more, approximately one-third of Americans spend excessive amounts of time in the sun.

To protect yourself: Avoid the use of any tanning equipment, as well as excessive sun exposure. I drive a convertible, but I always wear a hat or other protective clothing…and I apply SPF 15 or higher sunscreen before going outdoors for extended periods.

WOOD DUST

Approximately 600,000 Americans—mainly furniture makers, carpenters and mill workers—are exposed to hazardous levels of wood dust. Also at risk are people who work with wood in their spare time or who compost bark and other wood-containing organic material in the yard or garden.

Exposure to wood dust has been shown to increase lung cancer risk. It also increases the risk for Hodgkin's disease and cancers of the nasal cavities and paranasal sinuses.

To protect yourself: Wear a paper mask whenever you're cutting or sanding wood. The masks, available at hardware stores and home centers, cost about 10 cents each and can dramatically reduce the amount of dust that gets into the lungs or nasal cavities.

Skin Cancer: Debunking the Myths

Barney J. Kenet, MD, a dermatologist specializing in skin cancer. Dr. Kenet is a dermatologic surgeon at New York–Presbyterian Hospital/Cornell Medical Center in New York City, and is coauthor (with Patricia Lawler) of *Saving Your Skin—Prevention, Early Detection, and Treatment of Melanoma and Other Skin Cancers* (Four Walls Eight Windows).

Everyone knows that excessive sun exposure is dangerous, yet up to 50% of people over the age of 65 are diagnosed with melanoma or some other type of skin cancer.

Why? Even health-savvy individuals remain confused about the best ways to adequately protect their skin.

Most dangerous myths…

Myth #1: A beach umbrella keeps you safe from the sun.

Reality: When you're at the beach, a large percentage of ultraviolet (UV) light bounces off the sand onto your skin, even when you're beneath an umbrella. Water and snow have the same reflective effect.

When boating or sitting beneath a beach umbrella, apply a sunscreen to all the exposed areas, including your face and neck—even if you're wearing a brimmed hat. When skiing, apply sunscreen to your face and neck.

Myth #2: Sunscreen with a sun-protection factor (SPF) of 45 is three times more effective than SPF 15.

Reality: Most doctors recommend using a sunscreen with an SPF of at least 15. A higher SPF will not give you much additional protection. A sunscreen with an SPF of 45 is only about 5% more protective than an SPF 15 sunscreen. The higher-rated sunscreen doesn't last any longer, either.

All sunscreens need to be reapplied every two hours—and whenever you're exposed to water. This includes "waterproof" sunscreens, which provide some protection while swimming but still must be reapplied.

Make sure your sunscreen is labeled "broad spectrum"—meaning it blocks both ultraviolet A (UVA) and ultraviolet B (UVB) rays. Look for titanium dioxide or Parsol 1789 in the listing of ingredients.

Myth #3: Sunscreen provides complete sun protection.

Reality: While sunscreen is essential, there are other steps you also should take. The most important is to minimize sun exposure between 10 am and 4 pm, when the sun's rays are most intense. Hit the beach in the early morning or late afternoon instead.

To protect the commonly neglected areas, be sure to wear…

●UV-protective lip balm with an SPF of 15 or higher.

●A hat with a three-inch brim. Baseball caps don't protect the ears or the back of the neck—common skin cancer sites, especially for golf and tennis players.

●UV-protective sunglasses. UV exposure can cause cataracts.

●Sun-protective clothing. UV rays can pass through many fabrics, including cotton. If you hold a garment up to a light and can see the shape of the bulb shining through, it's not providing adequate sun protection.

Many companies now offer lightweight, tightly woven garments designed for comfort and maximum protection. *Example:* Solumbra 30+ SPF sun protective clothing (800-882-7860, *www.sunprecautions.com*).

If you will be outdoors and don't have special clothing, be sure to wear sunscreen under your shirt.

Myth #4: Family history is the best indication of skin cancer risk.

Reality: A family history of skin cancer *is* a major risk factor—but the most important factor is your own skin type. People who have light-colored skin and eyes (blue or green) and freckles are at highest risk for all types of skin cancer and sun-related skin damage, such as wrinkles.

People with many moles, freckles and spots have the next-highest cancer risk, followed by individuals with a family history of skin cancer. If you have any of these risk factors, you need to carefully monitor your sun exposure.

When skin is exposed to sunlight, it increases the body's production of *melanin,* the main skin pigment. This results in tanning, in which a brown color is imparted to the skin. The more difficult it is for you to tan, the more vulnerable you are to skin cancer.

If you're dark-skinned, tan easily, don't have many moles and have no family history of skin cancer, your risk is low but you should still protect yourself from the sun.

Myth #5: Building a "base" tan protects against sunburn.

Reality: There is no such thing as a "safe" tan. UV exposure increases lifetime risk of skin cancer and other skin damage. Rather than expose yourself to those pre-vacation rays, protect yourself by following the rules described in this article.

Myth #6: "Self-tanning" products help protect against sunburn.

Reality: Self-tanning products are perfectly safe and are a good way to appear tan without any sun exposure. However, the dyes in these products do not offer UV protection. Some of these products do contain sunblock—but this provides only two hours of protection following application.

Myth #7: Melanoma occurs only where the skin has been exposed to the sun.

Reality: Sun exposure is just one of the potential causes of melanoma. For unknown reasons, cancerous moles can also develop under the arm, between the buttocks or toes or on the bottom of the foot. If you have a mole, spot or freckle *anywhere* on your body that shows a sudden change in size, shape or color, get it checked by a dermatologist.

Myth #8: Melanoma is always deadly.

Reality: When limited to the top layers of the skin, melanoma has a cure rate of 100%. That's why it's important to do a monthly self-exam of all skin surfaces, using a full-length and a handheld mirror.

You should also get screened annually by a dermatologist (twice a year, if you have skin cancer risk factors). During the screening, the doctor should use *epiluminescence microscopy* (ELM). This new technique, which involves examining moles with a handheld microscope, detects melanoma earlier than ever.

Acrylamide: A Tasty Risk

George M. Gray, PhD, executive director of the Harvard Center for Risk Analysis, Harvard School of Public Health, Boston.

When Swedish scientists reported in April 2002 that french fries, potato chips and other starchy foods contained extremely high levels of *acrylamide,* a potential carcinogen, the findings made headlines throughout the world. Some of the foods analyzed had up to *600 times* more acrylamide than the Environmental Protection Agency permits in a glass of water.

Nearly all foods contain some acrylamide, but starchy foods contain the most. This compound is also formed by chemical reactions produced during high-heat cooking, such as roasting and deep frying.

Although the initial reports were alarming, researchers have now put the risk into context. Acrylamide does increase cancer risk in laboratory animals—but only when its consumed in extremely large doses. You would have to eat *tens of thousands* of french fries or other cooked starchy foods to get a hazardous amount.

Bottom line: Eat a varied diet rich in fruits, vegetables and other healthful foods. Reduce your intake of chips and other snack foods, which, of course, will decrease your intake of acrylamide—as well as salt, fat and other ingredients that we know are unhealthy.

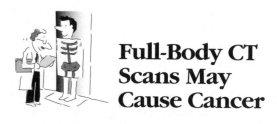

Full-Body CT Scans May Cause Cancer

While the heavily advertised full-body computed tomography (CT) scans can detect some cancers at an early stage, every pass of the X ray increases risk of premature death from radiation-induced cancer by one in 800—greater than the risk caused by one year of smoking.

Also: Most "findings" turn out to be insignificant, but patients have to undergo invasive testing to find this out.

Bottom line: Never get a full-body scan unless your physician recommends one for a specific reason.

Everett M. Lautin, MD, FACR, a radiologist at Lenox Hill Hospital and former professor of radiology, Albert Einstein Medical College, both in New York City.

Cancer Cure?

Experimental vaccines made from patients' own tumors can stimulate the immune system to destroy deadly cancers.

New finding: In 18 of 22 lung cancer patients studied, the vaccine stimulated immune response and caused fewer side effects than conventional cancer treatments.

Journal of Clinical Oncology, 330 John Carlyle St., Suite 300, Alexandria, VA 22314.

Aspirin May Reduce Pancreatic Cancer Risk

In the largest study yet to examine the link between aspirin and cancer of the pancreas, women who took aspirin just once a week had a 43% lower chance for pancreatic cancer than those who did not take any aspirin. Researchers have yet to identify the mechanism for this beneficial effect. Other studies have indicated that aspirin may curb pancreatic cancer risk in men as well.

Kristin E. Anderson, PhD, MPH, associate professor, division of epidemiology, School of Public Health, University of Minnesota, Minneapolis.

Out-of-Body Cancer Therapy

Doctors have treated cancer for the very first time by removing a patient's liver, bombarding it with high-dose radiation, then reimplanting it in the body. This experimental technique protects nearby healthy organs from the damaging effects of radiation.

New Scientist, Reed Business Information Limited, 151 Wardour St., London.

A New Way to Look at Cancer Statistics

Cancer-survival statistics are better than they have been reported.

Reason: Cancer data in the traditional statistical method include patients who received advanced treatment and patients who received treatment as many as 20 years in the past. A new statistical method separates the groups. When this new method is used, survival rates for the group receiving current treatments improve significantly.

Example: Breast cancer patients have a 71% chance of surviving for 15 years after diagnosis under the new method, versus only 58% under the old one.

Hermann Brenner, MD, MPH, epidemiologist, German Centre for Research on Aging, Heidelberg, and developer of the new statistical method, published in *The Lancet.*

Triglycerides: Too-Often Overlooked Culprit in Heart Disease

Daniel Rader, MD, director of the Preventive Cardiovascular Medicine and Lipid Clinic, department of medicine, University of Pennsylvania School of Medicine, located in Philadelphia.

If you get your cholesterol levels checked regularly, you no doubt know the difference between the "bad" form of cholesterol (low-density lipoprotein, or LDL) and the "good" form (high-density lipoprotein, or HDL). But there's another type of blood lipid that deserves equal attention—triglycerides.

Here's what you should know…

WHAT ARE TRIGLYCERIDES?

Triglycerides, which circulate in the bloodstream, are fats that have been digested and are ready to provide energy to muscle cells or be deposited in fatty tissues. Like cholesterol, triglycerides do not float freely in the blood but are attached to larger molecules known as lipoproteins.

In a recent analysis of 17 studies comprised of over 46,000 men and approximately 11,000 women, it was found that elevated triglycerides significantly increased the risk for heart disease during the next decade—by 14% for men and 37% for women—even after other factors, such as smoking, obesity and high blood pressure, were taken into account.

According to the most recent guidelines published by the National Heart, Lung and Blood Institute, a normal triglyceride level is less than

150 milligrams per deciliter (mg/dl)...border-line-high is 150 to 199...high is 200 to 499...and very high is 500 or above.

Important: If your triglyceride level is very high (especially if it's above 1,000 mg/dl), there is a more immediate risk for acute pancreatitis, a sudden inflammation that can be deadly.

ELEVATED TRIGLYCERIDES

Like high cholesterol, elevated triglyceride levels tend to run in families.

Certain medications can also increase triglyceride levels. They include estrogen (even the low-level hormones found in birth control pills)...steroids, such as *prednisone* (Deltasone) or *cortisone* (Cortone)...beta-blockers, such as *propranolol* (Inderal) or *atenolol* (Tenormin)...and diuretics. *Tretinoin* (Retin-A), which is often prescribed for skin conditions, can trigger particularly steep increases in triglycerides.

Triglyceride levels may also be elevated by diseases, such as type 2 (adult-onset) diabetes and kidney failure.

LIFESTYLE CHANGES

To lower your triglyceride level, follow these proven strategies...

●**Cut back on carbohydrates.** Although the amount and type of fat is critical for cholesterol, the key factor for triglycerides is carbohydrates. When digested carbohydrates pass through the liver, they are believed to stimulate the release of triglycerides.

The simple carbohydrates—sugar and refined starches—are broken down most quickly and have the strongest effect on triglyceride levels. Avoid pastries, candies, white bread and pasta. Beverages that contain sugar are particularly bad. Eliminate soft drinks, and substitute fruit for fruit juice. A single orange contains approximately half the sugar of an eight-ounce glass of orange juice.

Alcohol has the same effect as sugar. Scale back to no more than one drink a day.

●**Get enough exercise.** If you now have a sedentary lifestyle, any increase in activity may be helpful. Take a walk at lunchtime...use the stairs...garden instead of watching television.

More is better. You'll probably see a much bigger drop in triglycerides if you get at least 30 minutes of aerobic exercise (brisk walking, jogging, swimming or bike riding) at least three times a week.

●**Lose weight, if necessary.** Being obese is strongly linked to elevated triglycerides. To determine if you are overweight, calculate your body mass index (BMI).

Formula: Multiply your weight in pounds by 703, and divide this by your height (in inches) squared. If the result is 25 or above, you may need to lose weight. For a BMI calculator, visit the National Heart, Lung and Blood Institute Web site at *www.nhlbisupport.com/bmi.*

DRUG TREATMENT

If lifestyle changes don't lower your triglyceride level to 150 or below within six months, you may need medication...

●**Fibrates.** *Gemfibrozil* (Lopid) and *fenofibrate* (Tricor) are the most effective medications. These drugs lower triglycerides by as much as 50%—and raise HDL cholesterol by up to 20%.

Side effects: Mild gastrointestinal problems (stomach upset, nausea, diarrhea).

●**Niacin.** It's almost as effective as fibrates. An over-the-counter B vitamin, niacin must be taken in large doses of 1,000 to 2,000 milligrams (mg) daily and should be used only under a doctor's supervision. Niacin also raises HDL.

Side effects: Hot flashes—a flushing which spreads upward from the chest to the face...stomach upset...and ulcer.

Note: An extended-release prescription form of niacin, *Niaspan,* has fewer side effects.

●**Statins.** They may be prescribed if LDL cholesterol also needs lowering. Statins reduce triglycerides, but not as much as fibrates or niacin. The more potent statins, such as *simvastatin* (Zocor) and *atorvastatin* (Lipitor), are most effective.

Side effects: Mild gastrointestinal difficulties (constipation, gas, cramps). In rare cases, muscle pain may occur.

●**Fish oil.** Fish oil supplements also lower triglycerides. However, this treatment requires a high dose (six to nine 1,000-mg capsules per day). Check with your doctor before taking this dose. Fish oil capsules are usually added only when drugs aren't effective.

Side effects: Fishy odor on the breath and stomach upset.

Heart Disease Risk Can Be Predicted by Your Fingers

Men with osteoarthritis (OA) in any finger joint are 40% more likely to die of heart disease than ones without finger OA, however, the association was not statistically significant for women.

Possible reason: High levels of fat found in heart disease patients' blood may speed the breakdown of bone cartilage—leading to the development of OA.

Mikko Haara, MD, University of Kuopio, Finland, and the leader of a 16-year study of 7,000 people, published in *Annals of the Rheumatic Diseases*.

Easier Cholesterol Control

Twice-yearly injections of a new vaccine raised HDL ("good" cholesterol) by 40% in animal studies. If it's successful in humans, it could be a convenient, less-expensive alternative to statin drugs, which are typically taken twice daily for life.

Arteriosclerosis, Thrombosis, and Vascular Biology, American Heart Association Journals, 7272 Greenville Ave., Dallas, TX 75231.

New Cholesterol-Lowering Drug

A new drug lowers cholesterol in patients who do not get good results with statins.

Ezetimibe (Zetia) inhibits the absorption of cholesterol through the intestinal wall. When taken alone, ezetimibe lowers LDL ("bad") cholesterol by 18%, about half the maximum response to a statin. When taken with a statin, ezetimibe causes an additional 24% drop in LDL cholesterol. Ezetimibe is typically used when LDL levels are not lowered sufficiently. Diarrhea was the only side effect experienced by patients taking the drug.

Robert H. Knopp, MD, professor of medicine and director of the Northwest Lipid Research Clinic, University of Washington, Seattle.

Don't Stop Taking Low-Dose Aspirin Once You Start

For many, daily doses of 81-milligram (mg) aspirin help protect against heart attack and stroke. But if you stop taking it after establishing a routine, a rebound effect can make heart trouble more likely. Discuss this with your physician if he/she asks you to stop using aspirin before a surgical procedure. If you do stop for that reason, find out how soon afterward you can start taking aspirin again.

Robert Bonow, MD, chief, division of cardiology, Northwestern Memorial Hospital, Chicago.

If You're Having a Heart Attack...

Chew an aspirin tablet if you think you may be having a heart attack. Do not just swallow the aspirin—chewing the aspirin gets it to work nearly twice as fast, bringing a quicker beneficial effect on your blood's clotting.

Richard O'Brien, MD, spokesperson for the American College of Emergency Physicians and an emergency physician at Moses Taylor Hospital, Scranton, PA.

Angioplasty Is Better Than Drugs

Emergency angioplasty is better than clot-busting drugs for treating heart attack.

New finding: Angioplasty, which uses balloon dilation and wire mesh devices known as stents to clear arteries and keep them open, can cut a patient's risk for death and other complications—including stroke or another heart attack—by 40% more than clot-busting drugs, such as *streptokinase* (Streptase).

If you or a loved one suffers a heart attack: Ask the treating physician about emergency angioplasty.

Henning Rud Andersen, MD, associate professor of cardiology, Skejby University Hospital, Aarhus N, Denmark.

Improved Angioplasty

A new type of catheter restores blood flow through completely blocked arteries more efficiently. Angioplasty is successful 50% of the time. The new catheter—Frontrunner, which is from LuMend, Inc.—was successful in clearing blockages in 75% of patients at one heart institute. The FDA-approved Frontrunner has jaw-like projections at the front. It is inserted into a blocked artery, and the jaws break open the blockage. The procedure usually takes 30 to 60 minutes and is generally covered by insurance.

Robert K. Strumpf, MD, director, interventional cardiology, Arizona Heart Institute and Hospital, Phoenix.

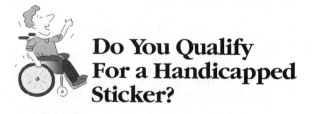

Do You Qualify For a Handicapped Sticker?

You may qualify for a vehicle handicapped sticker and not know it. You generally are eligible if you need walking assistance from a person or a device, such as a cane or a wheelchair…can't walk 200 feet without resting…are restricted by respiratory problems…have a serious cardiac condition…or are severely limited due to arthritic, neurological or orthopedic conditions. Apply for stickers and removable window placards at your local Department of Motor Vehicles. Your physician must sign the form.

Cost: Free in some states and up to $25 per application in others.

Jim Miller, editor of *Savvy Senior,* a syndicated newspaper question-and-answer column for senior citizens, Norman, OK, *www.savvysenior.org.* He is also author of the book *Savvy Senior* (Hyperion).

Surprising Stroke Risks Even Doctors Overlook

Gregory W. Albers, MD, professor of neurology and neurological sciences at Stanford University Medical Center and director of the Stanford Stroke Center. He also is chairman of the American College of Chest Physicians' expert panel for both stroke and atrial fibrillation, cochairman of the National Stroke Association's Stroke Center Network and chairman of the American Heart Association's Metro Stroke Task Force.

Stroke is the second most common cause of brain damage (after Alzheimer's disease) and the third most common cause of death (after heart attack and cancer).

Most of us know that risk of stroke can be reduced by controlling high blood pressure and cholesterol, eating a well-balanced diet and exercising on a regular basis. But it is what you may *not* know about this disabling disorder that could save your life.

Often overlooked stroke risks…

PREHYPERTENSION

Until just recently, blood pressure less than 140/90 was considered normal. However, studies now indicate that a reading higher than 120/80 raises the risk for stroke and should be treated with a combination of exercise, diet and medication, if needed.

What you may not know: Although diuretics, beta blockers and ACE inhibitors have long been utilized to lower blood pressure, recent research reveals that a newer class of antihypertensive medication, called angiotensin II receptor blockers (ARBs), may provide unique protection against stroke.

Recent study: An ARB known as *losartan* (Cozaar) reduced stroke risk by an additional 25% over the beta blocker *atenolol* (Tenormin). Several large trials are under way to further study ARBs. If the results are as promising as this preliminary one, ARBs could become the antihypertensive medication of choice for preventing stroke.

Bonus: ARBs cause fewer side effects than other blood pressure medications.

Self-defense: If you take blood pressure–lowering medication, ask your physician if an ARB would be appropriate for you.

ATRIAL FIBRILLATION

This heart rhythm disturbance affects 2 million Americans. With atrial fibrillation (AF), the upper chambers of the heart quiver rapidly or irregularly and fail to pump efficiently.

What you may not know: Each year, up to 70,000 strokes are caused by AF. During AF, some patients experience a racing heart, palpitations or a fluttering in their chest, dizziness and/or shortness of breath. For other patients, the first symptom of AF may be a stroke.

Self-defense: To determine if you may have AF, put your index finger on your wrist and check your pulse for an irregular or random rhythm. AF can be confirmed with a routine electrocardiogram (EKG).

If you are diagnosed with AF, your doctor may prescribe an antiarrhythmic medication, such as *digoxin* (Lanoxin) or *amiodarone* (Cordarone), or a type of electric shock, known as cardioversion, to correct the arrhythmia.

However, the recurrence rate for AF is high with these therapies. It is usually preferable to choose a treatment that prevents blood clots, rather than focusing on the heart rhythm disturbance. Lifetime use of anticoagulants can reduce stroke risk in AF patients by 68%.

The most frequently prescribed anticoagulant, *warfarin* (Coumadin), is extremely effective at preventing clots and reducing stroke risk in people with AF. Unfortunately, it has a narrow "therapeutic index"—slightly too much in your system can cause bleeding...slightly too little will permit stroke.

Warfarin also interacts with other drugs, supplements and even foods.

Example: Vitamin K, found in the leafy greens and margarine, counteracts the effects of warfarin.

Because warfarin interferes with so many common substances, people taking it need to undergo monthly blood tests...and physicians must adjust the dosage frequently. As a result, less than half of AF patients who should take Coumadin actually do.

Good news: The new anticoagulant called *ximelagatran* (Exanta) promises to revolutionize stroke and blood clot prevention. Early data suggest that it's as effective as warfarin for preventing stroke, causes less bleeding, has no known food, drug or alcohol interactions, and blood doesn't have to be tested regularly for coagulation. If the additional tests are positive, Exanta will go to the FDA for approval and may be available to patients sometime in 2005.

LEG PAIN

Just as atherosclerosis can narrow blood vessels to the heart and brain, it also can block arteries in the extremities, causing peripheral artery disease (PAD). Leg pain—especially in the calves—is the chief symptom. Known as intermittent claudication, the pain typically begins with walking and ends when you stop. PAD affects up to 20% of Americans who are age 65 or older.

What you may not know: If you have PAD, you also may have atherosclerosis elsewhere in the body, such as the heart or the brain. This puts you at increased risk for stroke. What's more, you also can have "silent," or asymptomatic, PAD. Risk factors for PAD are the same as those for cardiovascular disease—high blood pressure, high cholesterol, diabetes and age.

Self-defense: PAD is easily and painlessly diagnosed with an ankle brachial index test, which measures the ratio of blood pressure in the arm and ankle. If you're diagnosed with PAD, your physician might prescribe an antiplatelet medication, such as aspirin or *clopidogrel* (Plavix). Moderate exercise to reduce leg pain and blood pressure or cholesterol-lowering medications also may be recommended.

SLEEP APNEA

This disorder occurs when breathing is temporarily interrupted during sleep. An estimated 24% of men and 9% of women suffer from significant sleep apnea.

What you may not know: People with sleep apnea are three to six times more likely to suffer a stroke. Their blood pressure increases dramatically during the night, which can raise the risk for atherosclerotic blockages of the carotid—or neck—arteries, a chief cause of stroke.

In one recent study involving men ages 45 to 77, more than 21% of patients with sleep apnea had calcified plaques, which block blood flow, in their carotid arteries. Only 2.5% of the healthy control patients had calcified plaques.

Self-defense: Obesity is the leading risk factor for sleep apnea...and loud snoring and excessive daytime sleepiness are telltale signs. If you suspect you may have sleep apnea, consult your physician about diagnosis and the best treatment options.

Caution: It's important for AF patients who have symptoms of sleep apnea to undergo sleep apnea screening. Mayo Clinic researchers recently reported that AF is twice as likely to recur in patients with untreated sleep apnea.

Do You Know the Symptoms of a Ministroke?

Nearly four out of five primary care physicians recently surveyed could not identify the typical symptoms of a ministroke. Transient ischemic attack (TIA) occurs when an artery to or in the brain becomes blocked. Symptoms include numbness or weakness in the face, arm or leg, especially on one side...visual difficulties in one or both eyes...confusion or trouble speaking...trouble walking...and dizziness.

Self-defense: Anyone who experiences these symptoms needs to get to a hospital immediately. Treating the TIA risk factors, such as high blood pressure and cholesterol, can prevent a full-blown stroke.

S. Claiborne Johnston, MD, PhD, director, Stroke Service, University of California, San Francisco.

One-Minute Stroke Diagnosis

Jane H. Brice, MD, MPH, assistant professor of emergency medicine, University of North Carolina–Chapel Hill School of Medicine.

Stroke researchers have recently devised a simple three-step test to tell if someone has suffered a stroke...

1. Ask the person to show his/her teeth. The "smile test" helps to determine one-sided facial weakness.

2. Have the person close his eyes and raise his arms straight out in front of his body. Stroke victims usually cannot raise both arms to the same height.

3. Ask the person to repeat a simple sentence, such as "Don't cry over spilled milk." Listen for slurring.

This three-step test should not be used as a substitute for appropriate medical evaluation and can miss some types of strokes. However, if you or someone you know shows *any* of the symptoms described above, call 911 immediately.

Spotting stroke symptoms early is critical. Potentially lifesaving clot-busting drugs must be given within the first three hours of the onset of stroke.

The Migraine/Stroke Link

The migraines that are preceded by an aura increase ischemic stroke risk fivefold. Auras, which affect about 15% of all migraine sufferers, happen up to one hour before the headache strikes. An aura will typically include bright or flashing dots or other sensory disturbances. The reason for the association between migraines and stroke is unknown.

If you suffer migraines with auras: See your doctor for treatment and for a plan to reduce your risk for stroke.

Neil R. Poulter, MD, professor of preventive cardiovascular medicine, Imperial College, London. His study of 286 women was published in the *Journal of Neurology, Neurosurgery and Psychiatry*.

A New Brain-Saving Cocktail

An experimental therapy that combines alcohol and caffeine decreased stroke-related brain damage by up to 80% in laboratory animals that received the injection. The drug cocktail blocks chemical changes that cause stroke-related cell death. The treatment is now being tested on humans.

Stroke, American Heart Association Journals, 7272 Greenville Ave., Dallas TX 75231.

Taking a Break May Save Your Life

Desk jobs put you at risk for life-threatening deep vein thrombosis (DVT), which is a blood clot that forms in the leg and can travel up to the lungs. The condition has long been known to occur during long-distance air travel, but new research also links DVT to sitting at a desk for extended periods.

Self-defense: Be sure to take a short break every 30 to 60 minutes or so by getting up and walking around.

Richard Beasley, MD, director, Medical Research Institute of New Zealand, Wellington.

Diabetes Indicators

Bad breath and bleeding gums may be signs of diabetes. Because people with diabetes have decreased salivary flow and reduced ability to fight infection, bacteria grow more rapidly in the pockets around teeth. This makes them more susceptible to receding gums, oral infections and periodontal disease. Bad breath is the result of fermented bacteria in the mouth, sinuses or pharynx.

Self-defense: If you notice bleeding gums, bad breath or any other symptoms of diabetes, such as increased thirst, fatigue or frequent urination (especially at night), see your doctor.

Craig W. Valentine, DMD, dentist in private practice, Lakeland, FL, and spokesperson, Academy of General Dentistry, Chicago.

Coffee May Help Prevent Diabetes

Four to five cups of caffeinated coffee a day can cut diabetes risk by 30%. Drinking more has no added benefit. Decaffeinated coffee has only a slight effect. Tea has none. Other caffeinated beverages, such as cola, were not studied.

Caution: Additional study is required before researchers can recommend coffee to protect against diabetes.

Frank B. Hu, MD, PhD, associate professor of nutrition and epidemiology at Harvard School of Public Health, Boston, and the leader of a study of more than 100,000 people, presented at a meeting of the American Diabetes Association.

Possible Cause of Alzheimer's

Alzheimer's disease may be linked to excess copper. A defect in the mechanism that balances copper in the body may raise blood levels of the mineral, creating toxic amounts in the brain.

Self-defense: Limit your intake of copper to 1.5 to 3 milligrams (mg) a day.

Examples: Two ounces of liver or four medium oysters contain about 2.5 mg of copper. And, three ounces of lobster contains 1.6 mg of copper.

The defect that permits excess copper to accumulate in the brain can be detected with a blood test.

Rosanna Squitti, PhD, researcher, department of neuroscience, AFaR-Fatebenefratelli Hospital, Rome.

Common Drugs Fight Alzheimer's

Nonsteroidal anti-inflammatory drugs such as *ibuprofen* and *naproxen* seem to help clear up brain lesions caused by plaque buildup in Alzheimer's patients. These drugs bond to and help to break up the plaque, which also prevents new lesions from forming. All this suggests that anti-inflammatories may be useful in lowering a person's chance of developing Alzheimer's, but more research is needed.

Gary Small, MD, director of the Memory Clinic and Center on Aging at the University of California, Los Angeles, and leader of a study of Alzheimer's plaque buildup in brain tissue, reported in *Neuroscience.*

Memory Lapses— Causes and Treatments

Stress triggers the release of cortisol, which can affect memory. *Phosphatidylserine,* 100 to 300 milligrams (mg) a day, can stop some of cortisol's effects. Sleepiness, another cause of memory problems, can be counteracted by natural light, exercise and 1 to 3 mg of timed-release *melatonin* one to two hours before going to bed. Hidden hypothyroidism, yet another culprit,

can be detected by a doctor and treated with medication.

Linda Knittel, health writer for *Let's Live,* 11050 Santa Monica Blvd., Los Angeles 90025. She is author of *The Soy Sensation* (McGraw-Hill).

Help for Headaches

Robert B. Daroff, MD, professor of neurology and associate dean at Case Western Reserve University School of Medicine in Cleveland. He also is the chief of staff and senior vice president for academic affairs at the University Hospitals of Cleveland and president of the American Headache Society.

When their patients complain of headaches, most doctors simply pull out their prescription pads.

Fortunately, researchers have recently discovered many new approaches to preventing and treating this all-too-common condition.

Headache specialist Dr. Robert Daroff helped organize a gathering of hundreds of prominent headache researchers who discussed new scientific findings during the American Headache Society's annual meeting in Chicago. *The latest developments...*

BETTER MIGRAINE DETECTION

Fewer than half of the estimated 30 million Americans who suffer from migraines receive an accurate diagnosis. Patients—and their doctors—often mistake it for a tension or sinus headache. Because the treatments that may be effective for these conditions are not effective for migraines, a missed diagnosis often leads to unnecessary discomfort and frustration.

Headache experts have no trouble recognizing migraines. That's primarily because they typically will take an hour to evaluate each new patient. Primary care physicians don't have the time—or, in some cases, the expertise—to properly identify migraine symptoms.

New study: Researchers at Albert Einstein College of Medicine in New York City gave a simple survey to 443 patients who had a history of headaches. *More than 90% of those who* answered "yes" to two of three key questions were found to have migraines...

●**Has a headache limited your activities** for one or more days in the last three months?

●**Are you nauseated** when you have a headache?

●**Does light bother you** when you have a headache?

Implication: This three-question test provides a quick and accurate guideline that can help primary care physicians to make a proper diagnosis.

This test is not a perfect diagnostic tool. For example, some patients who answer "yes" to two of the questions may turn out to have an underlying disease, such as cancer.

Caution: Patients as well as physicians frequently confuse migraine with chronic sinusitis. *Don't believe it.* Migraine symptoms—intense pain along with nausea and/or visual disturbances, such as auras, in the absence of fever—are almost never caused by sinus infections.

HERBS AND HEADACHES

Nearly half of all Americans use herbal remedies on occasion. This includes ginkgo biloba for memory...ginseng for energy...echinacea for colds...St. John's wort for depression...garlic supplements for heart health, etc. What most people don't realize is that some of these common herbs can actually trigger headaches or interact with conventional headache treatments.

New study: University of Utah researchers identified the herbal products that are most commonly utilized in the US. *The researchers then scoured the scientific literature and identified the following possible side effects and/or potential drug interactions...*

Ginkgo biloba, ginseng, echinacea, St. John's wort and garlic supplements interfere with liver enzymes that break down the migraine drug *sumatriptan* (Imitrex) and the tricyclic antidepressants *amitriptyline* (Elavil) and *nortriptyline* (Aventyl), which are also commonly used for migraine prevention and treatment.

Possible result: Dangerous drug levels can accumulate in the bloodstream.

Combining herbs with drugs may also make treatments less effective, causing your doctor to prescribe unnecessarily high doses.

Ginkgo biloba may even cause headaches in some people.

Implication: Patients undergoing treatment for migraines or cluster headaches should *not* use ginkgo biloba, ginseng, echinacea, St. John's wort or even garlic supplements without being supervised by a physician.

BOTOX AND HEADACHES

Because over-the-counter (OTC) analgesics taken at the onset of a headache do not always relieve symptoms, some patients take these drugs daily. But the long-term daily use of such medication increases the risk for side effects, such as gastric irritation or bleeding.

In addition, daily use of OTC or prescription drugs can also cause severe *rebound* headaches —chronic daily headaches that happen when a medication wears off.

New study: Researchers at Kaiser Permanente in San Diego gave injections of *botulinum toxin* (Botox), the popular antiwrinkle treatment, to 271 headache patients who failed to get relief from standard treatments. Patients in the study were given injections every three months, for a period of six to 15 months.

At the conclusion of the study, 80% of participants said their headaches were less frequent, less intense or both. About 95% reported no side effects. This study, the largest to date on Botox and headaches, confirms the results of previous studies.

Most patients receive 30 small injections per treatment, usually in areas of the scalp where pain is present.

Implication: Botox reduces the frequency of headaches and is a good choice for sufferers who don't get relief from other methods. The use of Botox for headaches is still experimental, so insurance will not pay for it.

BENEFITS OF COUNSELING

The debilitating pain of migraines can affect emotional as well as physical health. It's common for people who get frequent migraines to feel misunderstood or frustrated by friends and colleagues who fail to appreciate the degree of their discomfort. Although doctors routinely treat physical symptoms, they often don't give sufficient attention to the emotional components of chronic headache pain.

New study: Researchers at Ohio University gave more than 100 migraine patients a battery of psychological and neurological tests. Nearly one-third of them were found to have mood or anxiety disorders, with depression being the most common diagnosis, followed by generalized anxiety disorder.

People who suffer frequent migraines understandably get depressed and anxious, but migraines are not the cause. It is possible that there's a third, underlying factor—possibly an imbalance in serotonin or other neurotransmitters—that triggers migraine headaches as well as mood disorders.

Implication: Migraines as well as other kinds of chronic pain are frequently accompanied by depression and/or anxiety. Patients who are depressed tend to experience even more pain. They're also less likely to pursue positive coping strategies, such as exercise or healthful dietary changes.

All migraine patients should consider seeing a therapist for psychotherapy and/or medication to help them cope with the psychological stress associated with migraine headaches.

Back Attack: When to See the Doctor

Carol Hartigan, MD, rehabilitation expert at the New England Baptist Hospital, Boston.

People suffering a "back attack" should be checked out if one or more of these conditions applies…

●**It is a result of significant trauma,** such as from a bad fall.

●**Fever is present.**

●**Legs or feet are weak, numb or tingly.**

●**You have a personal history of cancer.**

●**You are over age 50.**

●**It doesn't improve after four weeks.**

If you don't meet any of these conditions, chances are that a doctor won't do much for you. Time often is the only effective treatment for back pain. Some people sing the praises of massage or other therapy—but they most likely would have gotten better on their own. Treated or not, a back problem usually resolves within six weeks.

I advise against bed rest, since immobility can aggravate inflammation. Exercise acts as a natural anti-inflammatory. I recommend starting mild aerobic exercise as soon as possible—but no tennis or other high-impact, variable activity.

If you are able to take *ibuprofen* (Advil or Motrin), it can reduce pain and inflammation.

Ice the area with a bag of frozen vegetables or a body-conforming ice pack. Do this for 15 minutes every few hours for the first 24 hours to reduce inflammation. After several days, applying heat before activity may help.

Amazing Advances in Joint-Replacement Surgery

Andrew A. Shinar, MD, assistant professor of orthopedic surgery and director of the Joint Replacement Center at Vanderbilt University Medical Center, Nashville.

Physicians used to discourage all adults younger than age 65 from having joint-replacement surgery. It was thought that artificial joints would last only about 10 years and you would require subsequent surgery if you had decades of life ahead of you.

That's no longer true. The materials used now in artificial joints are very durable and can last 20 years or more.

Though most people have few or no complications, joint-replacement surgery isn't free of risks. Patients must take an active role to ensure that the new joints stay trouble-free.

Dr. Andrew Shinar, who performs about 300 joint-replacement surgeries per year at Vanderbilt University's Joint Replacement Center, answers some questions below…

●**Who should consider joint-replacement surgery?** Each year, as many as 400,000

Americans undergo joint-replacement surgery to relieve pain, stiffness and immobility. Most suffer from osteoarthritis, the gradual breakdown of cartilage and bone. Joint replacement also is an option for those who have been injured or who have severe rheumatoid arthritis or other conditions affecting the joints.

Joint replacement is most successful in large joints like hips, knees and shoulders. It is less effective in the small hand joints, though this is improving.

There's never a rush to undergo surgery. It's often possible to control discomfort with over-the-counter analgesics, exercise and other lifestyle approaches. Artificial joints may wear out, so it's better to delay the procedure if possible.

Patients usually opt for surgery if they have persistent, severe joint pain or have trouble with daily activities, such as walking, climbing stairs, getting out of a chair, etc. The patient—not the surgeon—decides when "enough is enough."

●**What are prosthetic joints made of?** Usually metal (titanium or cobalt chrome), plastic or a combination. The "ball" of an artificial hip joint, for example, typically is made of metal, while the "socket" is made of hard plastic.

A newer plastic—cross-linked polyethylene—is incredibly durable. It shows virtually no wear after 10 years.

A new approach—ceramic-on-ceramic joints—seems to have very impressive wear characteristics, but we don't yet have long-term data.

●**What causes replacement joints to wear out?** Abrasion. The parts move against each other, which causes them to wear over a long period of time. These newer, harder materials should eliminate such problems.

●**What does the surgery involve?** The patient is given a general, spinal or epidural anesthetic. I usually recommend an epidural—it offers better pain control after surgery.

The surgeon then makes an incision. Minimal incision hip replacement requires only a three- to five-inch incision, versus the standard 10- to 12-inch incision in standard hip replacement.

In all joint-replacement procedures, the surgeon removes the damaged bone and tissue, keeping healthy bone and tissue intact, and then implants the new joint.

Younger patients will often receive custom-made, "pressed-fit" implants—precise parts that are essentially banged into place. Surrounding bone gradually grows into the implant and gives additional support.

Older patients, who have more fragile bones, cannot always withstand the force that is necessary for pressed-fit implants. An alternative is to cement the joint to the bone. Some surgeons use this approach with all of their patients because cementing will give the implant immediate strength and speeds recovery. However, it can complicate subsequent procedures should the artificial joint need to be replaced.

Most people leave the hospital after two or three days, regardless of the technique or the type of joint being replaced.

●**What happens after surgery?** You want to get the joint moving as soon as possible. Your surgeon probably will arrange for you to meet with a physical therapist, who will design an appropriate exercise plan.

●**What else can I do to improve my recovery?** If you smoke, quit right away. Smoking delays the growth of new blood vessels in the bone surrounding the new joint. It can prevent the bone from growing into the artificial joint. Smoking also causes surgical incisions to heal more slowly.

●**What are the biggest risks of joint-replacement surgery?** Infection is one. Bacteria readily colonize on foreign material in the body, including artificial joints. The resulting infection can loosen the joint.

After replacement surgery, inform your dentist or doctor that you have an artificial joint. You may need to take antibiotics prior to any dental work or other invasive procedures for two years after the joint replacement.

Also, if you get any kind of infection (urinary, skin, etc.), get treatment immediately.

Dislocation is another risk. The moving parts in prosthetic joints can separate or dislocate. This is common in hip replacements.

Increasing muscle strength helps prevent dislocations. It's also important to avoid combination movements that cause the hip to move in two directions at once. Examples are crossing your legs at the knee or leaning to the side to pick up something.

Blood clots can form, but this is rare and usually not life-threatening. Your physician will give you blood-thinning medicine before, during and after the surgery to prevent this.

It is also important to flex your feet and calves several times a day. Keep doing it for at least three months after the operation. It pumps blood through the veins and helps prevent clotting. Also avoid taking long car or plane trips.

●**How successful are the results?** Some results are remarkable. With the new minimally invasive hip-replacement procedure, motivated patients can return to office work in as little as two weeks. I have had similar results with unicondular knee replacement, which is one-half of a total knee.

With other procedures, you can resume normal activities six to eight weeks after surgery, though certain activities may be restricted. For example, if you have hip- or knee-replacement surgery, high-impact activities, such as running or basketball, may never obtain your doctor's approval. You probably can swim, play golf, walk or ride a bike comfortably. With shoulder replacement, you may be able to lift light loads but should avoid playing tennis.

●**Will the artificial joint set off airport alarms?** Yes. Security devices are more sensitive than they used to be. Ask your surgeon to give you a card that explains you have an artificial joint. It will help you get through checkpoints more quickly.

Osteoporosis Drug Warning

Osteoporosis drugs can cause potentially serious vision problems.

Recent study: In rare cases, people taking the *bisphosphonate* osteoporosis drugs, such as *alendronate* (Fosamax) or *risedronate* (Actonel), developed inflammation of the eye.

If this eye condition progresses unchecked, it could lead to blindness. Tell your doctor immediately if you experience eye redness or pain, blurred or lost vision, headache or sensitivity to light while taking an osteoporosis drug. Alternative treatments for fragile bones include a diet that's rich in calcium and vitamin D, and weight-bearing exercises.

Frederick W. Fraunfelder, MD, assistant professor of ophthalmology, Casey Eye Institute, Oregon Health and Science University, Portland.

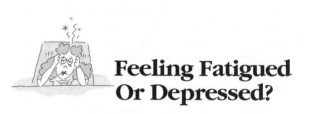

Feeling Fatigued Or Depressed?

If you feel unusually fatigued or depressed, get your blood calcium levels checked out. About 100,000 Americans—primarily women—have *hyperparathyroidism,* a condition which leaves too much calcium in the blood and not enough in the bones. It is caused by overactive parathyroid glands in the neck. Other symptoms include nausea, headaches, muscle weakness and constipation. Treatment may involve removing the parathyroid glands, medication to strengthen bones and/or working with your doctor to determine optimal calcium intake.

Sundeep Khosla, MD, professor of medicine at the Mayo Medical School in Rochester, MN.

Do-It-Yourself Skin Strategies for Looking Younger

Nicholas Lowe, MD, clinical professor of dermatology, UCLA School of Medicine, and senior lecturer in dermatology, University College, London, England. He is coauthor of *Skin Secrets—The Medical Facts Versus the Beauty Fiction* (Collins & Brown).

Antiaging creams for your skin are virtually becoming a reality, as the fine line between cosmetics and skin medications continues to blur. Here are ways to keep your skin young and supple, whether you're male or female, and no matter what your age.

● **Apply full-spectrum sunscreen every morning.** While some skin types are more prone to wrinkles than others, the way your skin ages has less to do with your genes than with the amount of sunlight your skin is exposed to.

Up to 80% of skin damage is ascribed to the ultraviolet rays of the sun—both ultraviolet B (UVB) rays, which are the primary cause of sunburn and skin cancer, and ultraviolet A (UVA) rays, which are largely responsible for the damage that is associated with aging.

Unlike UVB rays, UVA rays can penetrate your skin even on cloudy days. That's why the most important way to keep your skin young is to apply full-spectrum sunscreen (which absorbs both UVA and UVB rays) of SPF-15 or higher every morning.

Women should apply it right after bathing, then let the sunscreen dry before putting on makeup. Men should apply right after bathing and shaving.

This sunscreen rule holds even if you don't plan to be outdoors for very long.

Reason: Sun damage can occur even while driving your car—UV rays go right through your windshield.

Breakthrough: It's never too late to start this regimen. Researchers have found that by protecting your skin this way on a daily basis, you can actually begin to reverse sun damage that has already occurred.

● **Apply topical antioxidant cream.** Most skin damage is caused by the toxic effect of free radicals—rogue molecules created during the natural cell oxidation process. These molecules are missing a crucial electron, and so they try to grab an electron from wherever they can, often tearing apart healthy cells in the process. When exposed to sunlight or some other toxin, such as secondhand cigarette smoke, the production of free radicals accelerates.

To fight off these vicious free radicals, your body comes equipped with it's own all-natural antioxidants, which have extra electrons that can be given up to neutralize the rogue molecules. You can get added protection by taking

supplements of the antioxidant vitamins A, C and E. Unfortunately, while a daily multivitamin pill provides antioxidant protection to much of your body, only about 1% of dietary vitamins make it through to your skin.

Better solution: Apply a topical antioxidant cream to your skin about 10 minutes before your sunscreen.

Example: SkinCeuticals Topical Vitamin-C Skin Firming Cream.

● **Try using a retinoid cream.** I advise my patients not to waste their money on the expensive skin creams now sold in better department stores. They do not provide any special benefits to their skin. On the other hand, the topical retinoid *tretinoin* (a vitamin A derivative)—available by prescription under the brand names Retin-A, Renova and Avita—can reverse many signs of sun damage, including finely crisscrossing lines, areas of whitish pebbling, spider veins in the cheeks and rough, dull, uneven or yellowish skin tone. It can also generate new collagen, a fibrous tissue protein, making the dermis (the layer beneath your epidermis, or outer skin) plumper and firmer.

I recommend using either a 0.05% formulation of tretinoin or an even milder cream containing 0.025%. Apply the cream either every other night or every third night. It should be applied to your face and any other body parts you're concerned about, preferably about 30 minutes after washing. Within four to six months, you'll start to see significant improvement in your fine wrinkles, along with a clearer, smooth skin surface and a generally brighter, rosier complexion.

Tretinoin is best used at night—because it's degraded by sunlight and it makes your skin more sensitive to ultraviolet light.

Warning: Tretinoin can be irritating to the skin, although after two to six weeks, your skin should develop resistance to the worst signs of irritation, such as becoming red, flaky or itchy.

● **To moisturize your face, use a glycolic acid cream.** A cream containing glycolic acid in the range of 5%—such as NeoStrata Ultra Moisturizing Face Cream—will moisturize and protect your skin, and will also help reverse the drying effects of retinoid creams. Glycolic acid stimulates the synthesis of new skin tissue and inhibits the effect of free radicals. I recommend applying one of these skin moisturizers every morning, and—if you're also applying a tretinoin cream—again in the evening, on those nights when you're not using the tretinoin. Follow the same rule of applying it to a clean face, about 30 minutes after washing.

Note: If your doctor prescribes a stronger glycolic acid cream, he/she will probably recommend using it only at night.

●**Use as few different makeup products as possible**—to minimize your chances of developing contact dermatitis, a skin condition marked by inflammation, redness, itching or broken skin. This condition, sometimes called allergic dermatitis, is actually caused by chemical irritation, rather than an allergic reaction. The more chemicals your skin is exposed to, the greater chance irritation will occur.

●**Drink alcohol in moderation.** Heavy consumption of alcohol (more than one drink a day for women, or one or two drinks a day for men) dilates the blood vessels, leading to the formation of spider veins in your cheeks. It also exacerbates rosacea—a skin condition marked by flushing, lumpiness, red lines and a swollen, red nose.

●**Avoid cigarette smoke.** Smoking cigarettes will cause widespread free-radical damage to your skin, causing it to age prematurely. The act of smoking also causes fine lines to develop around the lips. As previously noted in this article, however, even exposure to someone else's cigarette smoke will accelerate the activity of toxic free radicals in your skin, leading to skin damage.

Stem-Cell Transplants For Blindness

Stem-cell transplants for eyes can cure some cases of blindness. If blindness is the result of a cornea damaged by certain diseases or chemical or heat burns and a relative has compatible tissue, surgeons can remove tissue containing stem cells from the donor eye…remove damaged tissue in the patient's blind eye…then attach the donor tissue. The new tissue should grow over the blind eye's cornea and restore sight. See an eye surgeon for more information.

Richard S. Fisher, PhD, director, corneal disease program, National Eye Institute, National Institutes of Health, Bethesda, MD.

Can Earwax Removal Help Hearing Loss?

Earwax removal via a syringe can improve hearing—but not always. In a new study of more than 100 patients who visited a doctor for earwax removal, two-thirds did *not* experience better hearing after the procedure. However, in patients who did benefit, hearing improved significantly, by up to 35 decibels. Patients who do not benefit from earwax removal may be hearing impaired. They should see an audiologist for testing.

David Memel, MD, senior teaching associate, division of primary health care, University of Bristol, England.

Help for Teeth and Gums

Nonsurgical treatment for periodontal disease can save teeth and make extractions unnecessary.

Recent study: Aggressive cleaning, known as root planing and scaling, plus antibiotic treatment for two weeks made 87% of surgeries and extractions unnecessary. The benefits lasted for five years.

If you have periodontal disease, ask your dentist about alternatives to surgery.

Walter J. Loesche, DMD, PhD, Marcus Ward Professor of Dentistry Emeritus, University of Michigan School of Dentistry, Ann Arbor, and leader of a study of 90 patients with periodontal disease, published in The Journal of the American Dental Association.

The Truth About Fluoridated Water

The rewards of fluoridated water seem to outweigh the risks. The addition of fluoride to the public water supplies has reduced tooth decay by as much as 70%, according to the National Institutes of Health. Fluoride strengthens the enamel in children's tooth buds—developing teeth that have not yet erupted—which helps prevent decay.

Caution: Too much fluoride can cause mottling or discoloration of teeth, but this rarely happens. Levels of fluoride in drinking water— one part per million gallons—are safe.

Many very young children don't drink enough fluoridated water or drink nonfluoridated bottled or well water. Talk to your doctor about giving your child supplements.

Also: Ingesting fluoride has no real benefit for adults because their teeth and enamel are already fully formed.

Alan Winter, DDS, Park Avenue Periodontal Associates, 532 Park Ave., New York City 10021.

Asthma Breakthrough

A new medication reduces asthma attacks by more than 50%. *Omalizumab* (Xolair) also allows patients to reduce use of inhaled corticosteroids, which can cause side effects. The drug, which is injected once or twice a month, is for patients with moderate to severe allergic asthma that can't be adequately controlled by other drugs.

Caution: Patients given omalizumab in clinical trials had slightly higher cancer rates than placebo patients, but the difference was not statistically significant. Patients with a personal or family history of cancer should discuss risks with their doctors.

Thomas Casale, MD, chief of allergy and immunology and director of clinical research at Creighton University in Omaha.

SARS Self-Defense

Deborah Lehman, MD, infectious disease specialist at Cedars-Sinai Medical Center in Los Angeles.

Severe acute respiratory syndrome (SARS) continues to spread. At last count, the virus had killed more than 774 people in more than two dozen countries, and still no cure has been found.

SARS is believed to be caused by a new type of coronavirus. Other coronaviruses cause the common cold. This virus can be spread in two ways—by breathing airborne droplets exhaled by an infected person...or by touching an infected surface and then touching your mouth, nose or eyes. Some viruses can live on such surfaces as elevator buttons and doorknobs for more than three hours.

To reduce your chances of contracting SARS or other respiratory viruses...

●**Wash your hands with warm water and plain soap** as often as possible—especially before eating, after shaking hands or handling money, and after touching any public surface, including countertops, fold-down trays in airplanes, armrests and handrails.

●**Use waterless sanitizing products,** such as Purell Instant Hand Sanitizer (available as an alcohol-based gel or wipe) or Lever 2000 Anti-Bacterial Moisturizing Wipes, when you don't have access to soap and water.

●**Carry your own pen and don't share it.** Avoid pens used in the pharmacy, supermarket, bank and all other public places.

●**Encourage people to cover their mouths when coughing or sneezing** and dispose of tissues promptly.

●**Avoid unnecessary travel to areas endemic for SARS,** including China, Hong Kong and Singapore.

Mad Cow Protection

Meat eaters who are concerned about contracting the human form of mad cow disease can minimize their risk by eating only the boneless muscle meats, such as boneless sirloin or roast, or hamburger ground from such cuts.

Even better: Eat beef that is labeled "organic." This certifies that the cattle have not consumed any animal byproducts in which the disease agent could be found. Avoid products that could contain the mad cow protein, such as beef brains, any cuts containing spinal bone and all processed beef—including pre-ground hamburger, hot dogs and sausage.

Marion Nestle, PhD, MPH, professor of nutrition, food studies and public health at New York University, New York City.

Keep Mercury Levels Down

To minimize your mercury exposure from canned tuna, eat only the chunk light tuna instead of albacore or solid white tuna. Chunk light tuna is darker than albacore and comes from smaller types of tuna, which tend to contain less mercury.

UC Berkeley Wellness Letter, 632 Broadway, New York City 10012.

Don't Be Fooled by Food Labels

Franca B. Alphin, MPH, RD, assistant clinical professor, student health dietitian, Duke University, Durham, NC.

By now, most everyone has heard about the FDA's recent ruling requiring food manufacturers to disclose the amount of trans fatty acids contained in food products on their "Nutrition Facts" panels. These chemically altered oils, which extend the shelf life of packaged foods, increase heart disease risk. The only problem is that the ruling does not take effect until January 2006.

Until then, manufacturers are free to use this harmful ingredient without clearly labeling it as "trans fat" or listing the amount that has been added to the product. Most chips, crackers and baked goods are loaded with trans fat.

Without the new labeling, it's impossible for consumers to know the exact content of food products. To protect yourself, limit intake of food products that list "hydrogenated" or "partially hydrogenated" ingredients on the label. These are code words for trans fat.

Whenever it is possible, choose foods with labels that clearly state no trans fat is present. Health food stores typically stock such products. Frito-Lay, which sells snacks and chips in grocery stores, also has removed trans fat from its products.

Beware: If you do buy foods that contain trans fat, make sure it does not appear among the top five ingredients. These ingredients add the most content (by weight) to the product. You owe it to yourself to find a more healthful alternative.

Choose Rye Bread Over Wheat

Rye breads are more healthful than wheat breads. Starches in rye bread break down more slowly than those in wheat bread, and so do not produce high insulin spikes. Researchers believe that repeated high post-meal insulin spikes, caused by high intake of carbohydrates, may increase risk of developing insulin resistance and type 2 diabetes.

Self-defense: Replace wheat bread with rye in your daily meals.

Hannu Mykkanen, PhD, professor of nutrition, University of Kuopio, Finland.

Is Microwaving In Plastic Safe?

Clair Hicks, PhD, professor of food science, University of Kentucky, Lexington.

You can microwave plastics with recycling codes that indicate they are safe for your microwave. Plastic containers labeled number 1 (*polyethylene terphthalate*) and number 5 (*polypropylene*) can be used. Number 6 (*polystyrene*) may be microwaved only if it is covered with a barrier film, such as a microwave-safe plastic wrap. Most baby bottles and their disposable liners are safe to microwave. Anything that is labeled *nylon, dual ovenable* or *microwave safe* also can be put in the microwave.

Don't microwave plastic containers labeled number 2 (*high-density polyethylene*)...3 (*polyvinyl chloride*)...4 (*low-density polyethylene*)... or 7 (which is made of other resins).

Also: Don't microwave plastic wrap or plastic bags—except for those specifically labeled *microwave safe*. Wax paper and paper towels are fine to use in the microwave.

Better: Glass or ceramic bowls made for the microwave—they will usually have a plastic top with a steam vent.

Safe Ways to Kill Deadly Germs

Kimberly M. Thompson, ScD, associate professor of risk analysis and decision science at Harvard University School of Public Health in Boston. She is the coauthor of *Overkill—How Our Nation's Abuse of Antibiotics and Other Germ Killers Is Hurting Your Health and What You Can Do About It* (Rodale).

The infectious diseases that make the headlines, such as severe acute respiratory syndrome (SARS), pose very little risk to most Americans. You're far more likely to get sick from microbes that already live in your own home.

Examples: A kitchen sponge can harbor 7 billion organisms...and a "clean" cutting board might have 62,000 bacteria per square inch.

The Centers for Disease Control and Prevention estimates that food-borne microbes *alone* cause 76 million illnesses a year. We can't even begin to estimate how many people get sick, or die, from bacteria and viruses in the home.

Many families automatically reach for antibacterial products or heavy-duty cleaners. *But don't overdo it.* Antibacterial products can weaken your resistance to harmful bacteria, which may ultimately increase your risk of getting sick.

Smart idea: Use an antibacterial soap after handling raw meat—probably the most common source of household infection—or if anyone in your home is sick or has a compromised immune system due to chronic illness.

Otherwise, plain soap and water are fine for hand-washing, and homemade natural cleaners can be just as effective as cleaning products that contain harmful chemicals.

KITCHEN

The sink is the most germ-ridden space in the house—and often contains more fecal matter (from washing meats) and E. coli bacteria than the average toilet.

Rinse the sink with hot water after every use. Clean it twice a week with a scouring powder, such as Ajax or Comet. Disinfect it weekly with a mild bleach solution—one tablespoon of bleach mixed with one cup of hot water. *Also...*

• **Replace sponges once or twice a month,** and run them through the dishwasher each time you use it. Sponges are the perfect breeding ground for harmful germs.

• **Stock up on dishtowels...**and change them every other day to prevent germs from passing among members of the family. Washing them in hot water and running them through the drier will kill bacteria and viruses.

• **Use separate cutting boards for meats, poultry and seafood**—and scrub them with dish detergent, such as Joy or Dawn, and hot water after each use. Clean all plastic cutting boards in the dishwasher.

BATHROOM

Even if you wear gloves when cleaning the toilet or bathtub, it is a good idea to wash your hands afterward. This eliminates bacteria from water that may get on your hands as you take off the gloves. *Also…*

●**Clean the bathtub at least once weekly** with scouring powder or a solution made with one-half cup of bleach and one gallon of water.

●**Sweep the bathroom floor at least once weekly** and clean with a basic cleaner, such as Lysol, or a solution made with one gallon of hot water…two tablespoons of borax…one teaspoon of dish detergent…and five drops each of patchouli and lavender essential oils. These oils contain effective natural disinfectants.

●**Wipe the bathroom sink and counters after every use.** Once a week, use a disinfectant made with one-quarter cup distilled white vinegar and one-half teaspoon of dish detergent in two cups of warm water. The bathroom sink is a bacterial hot spot because germs on your hands can spread to faucets.

●**Disinfect the toilet bowl, seat and outer surfaces weekly** with a commercial cleaner or with a solution made with one-half cup of baking soda…one-half cup of borax…one-quarter cup of distilled white vinegar…one teaspoon of dish detergent…three drops of sweet orange essential oil…and two drops of patchouli essential oil. Let it soak for an hour, scrub, then flush. Wipe and disinfect the handle daily because it's frequently touched by unwashed hands.

●**Close the toilet lid when you flush.** During flushing, bacteria disperse into the air and can land on any surface that's within six feet—including toothbrushes.

WASHING MACHINE

If there are young children in your household, every time you wash dirty underwear, millions of fecal bacteria are deposited on the inner surfaces of the washing machine—and can spread to the next load. Every few weeks, disinfect the machine by running it empty, using hot water and adding one-half cup of bleach.

TELEPHONES

Many bacterial illnesses are transmitted just by touching the telephone and then touching your eyes, nose or mouth. Wipe all phone surfaces every two weeks with a cotton ball that's moistened with rubbing alcohol or spray with a natural antibacterial.

To make: Combine one tablespoon of borax …one cup of hot water…one cup of distilled white vinegar…one-half teaspoon of dish detergent…one-half teaspoon of sweet orange essential oil…and one-quarter teaspoon each of rosemary and lavender essential oils.

DOORKNOBS

Disinfect them at least once a month with some rubbing alcohol or the natural antibacterial spray described above. Wipe them off daily when someone in your family is sick with a cold or flu. Doorknobs are great locations for bacteria to be transferred from the hands of a sick person to other members of the family.

Other spots to disinfect frequently: Refrigerator handles, light switches and bannisters.

The Cold Truth About Hot Tubs

Hot tubs can make you sick—sometimes *very* sick. The bacteria that thrive in such steamy places can cause hot-tub lung, a stubborn infection accompanied by a wet cough, shortness of breath and fever or chills. Soaking in a hot tub also can lead to skin infections, gastrointestinal upsets and Legionnaire's disease, a type of pneumonia.

How to protect yourself: Outdoor hot tubs are less risky than indoor ones (the germ-laden mist disperses faster)—but the only way to stay completely safe is to stay out of hot tubs. Germs may be present even if hot tubs are cleaned according to manufacturers' instructions.

Also beware: High temperatures stress the body. Hot tubs are not recommended for pregnant women or people with high blood pressure, diabetes or heart or lung problems.

Gwen Huitt, MD, assistant professor of pulmonary medicine, National Jewish Medical and Research Center, and assistant clinical professor of infectious diseases, University of Colorado Health Sciences Center, both in Denver.

2

Doctors, Drugs and Hospitals

Important Medical Tests Doctors Don't Tell You About

The special screening tests—for discovering heart disease, aneurysms, lung cancer and ovarian cancer—could save your life. But there's a good chance that your physician won't order them because insurance companies rarely pay for them.

Reason: Insurance companies typically pay for tests only when you have been diagnosed with a particular condition or when there is a high likelihood that you might have it. With some exceptions, such as mammograms, insurance rarely pays for screening tests aimed at early detection.

Ask your doctor if you should have any of the following tests, even if you have to pay for them yourself. They are available at most diagnostic and medical centers around the country. Ask your doctor for a referral.

These tests aren't appropriate for everyone, but early research suggests that they could be lifesavers for those with key risk factors...

CHOLESTEROL TEST

Traditional cholesterol tests only measure HDL ("good") cholesterol and triglycerides. The formula used to calculate levels of harmful LDL cholesterol isn't always accurate. This partly explains why half of people who have heart attacks have cholesterol levels that appear normal.

Better: Expanded cholesterol tests measure LDL specifically, giving more accurate readings. About 40 million American adults have hidden heart disease. Expanded cholesterol tests could identify 95% of these patients before a heart attack occurs.

The tests also look at individual HDL and LDL particles and determine how helpful—or harmful—they are likely to be.

Leo Galland, MD, director of the Foundation for Integrated Medicine in New York City. He has held faculty positions at The Rockefeller University and Albert Einstein College of Medicine, both in New York City, and is author of *Power Healing* (Random House).

Example: HDL protects against heart disease, so high levels are desirable. But some people who appear to have high levels actually have a subtype of HDL that isn't very helpful. Also, though all LDL particles are bad, the smaller ones are more dangerous than the bigger ones. These kinds of differences just aren't detectable with the conventional tests—but they can be detected with the expanded tests.

Who should consider them: Patients with mildly elevated cholesterol levels—200 to 230 milligrams per deciliter (mg/dl)—who smoke or who have cardiovascular risk factors, such as heart problems, high blood pressure or a family history of heart disease.

Cost: $75 to $175.

ANEURYSM TEST

Aneurysms are bulges in artery walls. They can be deadly when they rupture, killing 80% to 90% of people who have ruptured aneurysms. About 30,000 Americans die from this annually.

Better: An aneurysm scan uses an ultrasound wand to detect aneurysms in the abdominal aortic arteries. It's the only noninvasive test that allows doctors to identify aneurysms before they rupture. Surgery to repair aneurysms can increase survival rates to 99%.

Who should consider it: Anyone over age 60 who has cardiovascular risk factors, such as high blood pressure, or who smokes…as well as anyone over age 50 who has a family history of heart disease.

Cost: $60 to $200, depending on the extent of the scan.

HEART DISEASE TEST

Current methods for detecting heart disease risk, such as checking blood pressure, miss up to 75% of patients who later on develop heart problems.

Better: The electron beam tomography, or EBT, heart scan is the first direct, noninvasive way of identifying atherosclerosis, the primary risk factor for heart disease. The patient lies in a doughnut-shaped machine while the electron beams map out calcium deposits in the arteries. The buildup of calcium indicates the presence of plaque—fatty deposits that hamper blood flow to the heart and increase risk of blood clots. The patients who are found to have early signs of heart disease can take the appropriate steps—such as lowering cholesterol, controlling blood pressure, stopping smoking, etc.—to prevent problems from progressing.

Drawback: Calcium deposits don't always indicate an elevated risk of heart attack. The deposits may be harmless. On the other hand, a person who has a clear scan could actually have dangerous levels of plaque.

Patients with high calcium levels also may have to take a follow-up stress test. If this test is positive, the patient may have to undergo an angiogram—an invasive procedure. If the angiogram shows no heart disease, the patient has undergone these extra tests unnecessarily. Still the EBT is considered useful because traditional tests don't catch most heart problems.

Who should consider it: All men over age 45 and women over age 55. If you have heart disease risk factors—smoking, a family history of heart disease, etc.—consider having an EBT 10 years sooner.

Cost: About $400.

LUNG CANCER TEST

Lung cancer rarely causes symptoms until it reaches an advanced stage. The five-year survival rate is about 15%. Conventional X-rays may fail to detect early-stage tumors.

Better: The spiral CT scan can detect cancerous tumors as small as one grain of rice. Eighty percent of lung cancers spotted in scanning studies were caught at a potentially treatable stage.

Drawbacks: The test can result in false-positives—findings that indicate cancer when none is present. This could lead to unnecessary and risky lung biopsies. The false-positive rate improves when patients have follow-up scans.

Who should consider it: Smokers as well as former smokers age 50 and over who have smoked at least one pack daily for 10 years or two packs daily for five years.

Cost: $200 to $450.

OVARIAN CANCER

More than 14,000 American women die from ovarian cancer every year. It is now the deadliest of female cancers. Like lung cancer, it often has no symptoms until it reaches an advanced stage of development.

Better: An ultrasound device inserted into the vagina allows doctors to inspect the ovaries for any malignant changes. University of Kentucky researchers used this test on 23,000 women. Twenty-nine showed cancerous ovarian tumors, 76% of which were detected at an early, more treatable stage. Typically, only 25% of ovarian cancers are caught early.

Drawback: The test isn't able to differentiate between malignant and benign growths—so positive test results could result in unnecessary procedures.

Who should consider it: Women age 45 and older with risk factors, such as a family history of ovarian, breast or colon cancer...or a history of fertility or hormone-replacement treatment...or who never have been pregnant.

Cost: About $250.

How to Stay in Touch With Your Doctor

Daniel Z. Sands, MD, MPH, assistant professor of medicine, Harvard Medical School, and coauthor of national guidelines on doctor-patient electronic communications.

After a doctor's appointment, patients almost always have some follow-up questions—about the lab results, symptoms, referrals, etc. But busy physicians receive up to 75 phone messages per day. The doctors just don't have time to answer them all.

Daniel Z. Sands, MD, explains how to stay in touch between office visits...

●**Rely on the doctor's assistant.** Nurses, physician's assistants and nurse practitioners can handle almost all questions. If you call the assistant, he/she is more likely than the doctor to call back the same day.

●**Call in the morning.** Afternoons are the busiest times in doctors' offices.

●**Write down what you want to say.** Limit it to *one* issue per message or conversation.

You might also try e-mail. If your doctor is willing to field questions via e-mail, put your name and patient identification number in the subject line. That way, your doctor knows the message is from a patient. Keep the message short—and use e-mail only for medical issues.

Because regular e-mail is about as secure as sending out a postcard, it may not be the best choice for discussing confidential issues, such as psychiatric disorders, or for addressing health issues that must be resolved right away.

If You Have a Fear of Needles...

To make it less painful when your blood is drawn, ask the doctor or nurse to use the smallest gauge needle available or a butterfly needle with a silicone tip (a fine needle typically used on children).

Helpful: Numb the needle site by placing an ice pack on it up to 15 minutes before having blood drawn.

Also helpful: Do not watch the needle as it is going in. Instead, take your mind off what is happening by closing your eyes and imagining that you're in a place you love.

James G. Hamilton, MD, a family practitioner in private practice, Durham, NC. His review of needle phobia was published in *The Journal of Family Practice*.

 # Are You Taking Medications Properly?

The term *with food* means during a meal, not with a glass of milk or juice. *Before meals* means at least one hour before eating. *After meals* means at least two hours afterward. *On an empty stomach* means one hour before or two hours after eating. The type of food also matters.

Examples: Grapefruit juice will intensify some drugs, and calcium-fortified juice can prevent proper absorption.

Ask your doctor and pharmacist for the best way to take each medicine.

Joe Graedon, a pharmacologist in Durham, NC, and coauthor, with Theresa Graedon, PhD, of *The People's Pharmacy* (St. Martin's).

Timing Your Medications For Maximum Benefit

Michael Smolensky, PhD, professor of environmental physiology, and cofounder and former director of the Hermann Hospital Clinical Chronobiology Center, both at The University of Texas at Houston. He is editor of the medical journal *Chronobiology International* and coauthor of *Body Clock Guide to Better Health* (Henry Holt).

Most medical students are taught that the body is *homeostatic*—that is, having a "steady state" of biological functions. However, scientists now know that the body functions rhythmically.

The symptoms of chronic medical conditions, such as high blood pressure, arthritis and hay fever, vary greatly according to so-called *circadian* (24-hour) *rhythms*. By timing medications to your body's biological rhythms—a treatment approach known as *chronotherapy*—you can recover faster from a health problem or live better with a chronic illness. *Here are the latest findings in chronotherapy...*

HIGH BLOOD PRESSURE

One in every four American adults have high blood pressure. Most physicians agree that normal blood pressure should be 120/80 or below. (The top number is *systolic* pressure, when the heart beats...the bottom number is *diastolic,* when the heart relaxes between beats.)

Using a technique called *ambulatory blood pressure monitoring,* which measures pressure automatically 24 hours a day, doctors now know blood pressure exhibits a circadian rhythm.

In most people, blood pressure is highest after awakening, rising by at least 25 systolic points. Blood pressure remains elevated during the day and declines in the evening, reaching its lowest level during nighttime sleep. It is important that prescription blood pressure medications control daytime highs without overcorrecting nighttime lows.

New advances: In the US, there are four medications specifically designed to keep drug levels in the body in sync with the circadian rhythms of blood pressure. These medications, called chronotherapies, are the calcium channel blockers *verapamil* (Verelan PM and Covera-HS) and graded-release *diltiazem* (Cardizem LA)...and the beta-blocker *propranolol* (Inno-Pran XL).

Intended to be taken at bedtime, their drug-delivery technology ensures that no medication is released until four hours after ingestion. Medication is then released so that peak levels of the drug are circulated during the day when blood pressure rises and the lowest levels of the drug are circulated at night when blood pressure is lowest.

Clinical studies indicate that these medications optimize the control of the morning blood pressure rise, which has been linked to stroke in at-risk patients. These drugs may also minimize risk for morning heart attack.

Caution: If you are taking a nonchronotherapy drug, do not change your dosing schedule. Studies show that taking certain medications at the wrong times can cause extreme lowering of blood pressure during nighttime sleep and may not control hypertension throughout the day.

New finding: Low-dose aspirin, when taken at the correct time of day, may have a blood pressure–lowering effect. A study published in 2003 in the journal *Hypertension* found that taking low-dose aspirin before going to bed reduced systolic blood pressure by an average of five points but had no effect when taken first thing in the morning.

More research is needed, but the new finding suggests the importance of the body's circadian rhythm, even when taking a nonprescription medication, such as aspirin.

ARTHRITIS

Osteoarthritis (OA) is an age-related disease of painful, stiff and swollen joints. Rheumatoid arthritis (RA) is an autoimmune disease that causes joint inflammation. These two conditions are typically treated with the nonsteroidal anti-inflammatory drugs (NSAIDs), like *ibuprofen* (Advil), *ketoprofen* (Orudis) and *indomethacin* (Indocin).

New finding: Large clinical studies show that NSAIDs are more effective against symptoms of RA when taken at bedtime.

Moreover, NSAIDS produce fewer gastrointestinal (GI) complications, such as indigestion and stomach discomfort, when taken at bedtime than when taken in the morning.

Additional studies have found that patients with OA who experience their most severe symptoms in the afternoon and evening get the most relief from NSAIDs when they are taken at breakfast (even though there may be an increase in the risk for GI side effects at this time) or at midday with lunch.

If NSAIDs do not relieve arthritis symptoms, your doctor may prescribe anti-inflammatory corticosteroid medications, such as *prednisone* (Deltasone). These medications can cause side effects, such as insomnia, mood changes and appetite enhancement, especially when taken in high doses. Studies show that these medications are the most effective, and the least likely to cause side effects, when taken once a day, either in the morning or early afternoon.

HAY FEVER

Allergens, such as pollens, mold spores, dust mites or animal dander, cause this respiratory problem, also known as *allergic rhinitis*. Symptoms will include sneezing, an itchy, stuffed or runny nose and swollen, puffy eyes.

One in 10 sufferers experience symptoms seasonally, while the remainder suffer year-round. As all hay fever sufferers know, symptoms typically are worst in the early morning, after waking up, although many sufferers complain that sleep is disrupted at night due to severe nasal congestion.

The circadian rhythm of hay fever symptoms is thought to be due to fluctuations in adrenaline and cortisol. That's because these hormones, which counter allergen-caused inflammation and swelling, are at their lowest during the night.

To better control morning symptoms, such as sneezing and/or a stuffy, runny nose, take an antihistamine in the evening or at bedtime.

Drug Patches: Healing With Fewer Side Effects

Richard D. Hurt, MD, professor of medicine at Mayo Medical School and director of the Mayo Clinic Nicotine Dependence Center, Rochester, MN. He is a leading researcher in the use of patches for smoking cessation.

Many drugs are available in patch form, and more are awaiting FDA approval. Drug patches—or transdermal drug-delivery systems—offer important advantages and, in some cases, cause fewer side effects.

HOW PATCHES WORK

The medication's active ingredient is integrated into the adhesive gel on the "active" side of the patch. When you peel off the plastic cover and apply the patch, drug molecules pass through the skin into the bloodstream.

Several kinds of drugs are available in patch form, including…

●**Testosterone** for men with low levels of this hormone.

●**Estrogen and progesterone** for women as birth control or hormone replacement therapy.

●**Narcotic analgesics** (painkillers).

●**Antinausea drugs** for motion sickness and chemotherapy-related nausea.

●**Nitroglycerine** for angina.

●**Nicotine** to help people quit smoking.

Patches stay in place even when you swim or shower and can be removed with little or no discomfort. Some testosterone patches need to be placed on scrotal tissue, but most drug patches can go anywhere. Follow the manufacturer's instructions.

Do not put patches on elbows, hands or the bottoms of feet. The tough skin in these areas inhibits absorption.

You can wear more than one patch at a time —for example, a nicotine patch along with a patch for pain relief. Drug interactions can occur with patches just as they can with pills. If you're using one or more patches and/or taking oral medication and experience side effects, tell your doctor right away.

ADVANTAGES

Oral drugs need to be given in relatively high doses. That's because up to 90% of some active ingredients may be inactivated when they pass through the digestive tract and the liver. Patches bypass the liver and the intestines and deliver drugs directly into the bloodstream. This allows the use of lower doses and reduces the risk of dangerous side effects, including liver damage.

Other advantages...

Patches deliver steady doses of medication over hours or days, without the surges that occur with oral drugs.

Applying a patch just once a day—or once a week or every few weeks—is more convenient and easier to remember than taking oral drugs several times a day. With oral drugs, noncompliance—forgetting to take the drugs or skipping doses—is a huge problem, especially for people with chronic conditions.

Patients who have difficulty swallowing pills can use the patch form.

DRAWBACKS

Some people get hives where the patch is applied. This generally can be prevented just by applying patches to different areas of the skin on different days. Other patients may experience a generalized allergic reaction, such as an allover rash—but this is rare.

Be sure to remove old patches before applying new ones. Accidentally wearing multiple patches of the same medication could cause an overdose.

WHAT'S AHEAD?

Researchers are now developing patches that deliver drugs for asthma, depression, diabetes, Parkinson's disease and other conditions. These may be available within five years.

They're also working on patches that incorporate tiny electronic circuits and use ultrasound, heat or electric current to facilitate the passage of drugs—especially those with large molecules, such as insulin—through the skin. These high-tech patches also may be used to deliver painkillers more rapidly than conventional patches.

Drug Side Effects And Women

Women experience drug side effects more often and differently than men. Women's systems may absorb drugs at different rates or are just more sensitive to them.

Examples: The heartburn drug *cisapride* (Propulsid) and the antibiotic *erythromycin* are more likely to cause dangerous heart arrhythmias in women...asthma and epilepsy medications may not work as well during menstruation.

Women need to tell their doctors if they take more than one of these drugs, use alcohol or take any dietary supplements.

Raymond I. Woosley, MD, professor of medicine and vice president for health sciences at The University of Arizona, Tucson.

Are You Taking The Wrong Pain Pill?

George E. Ehrlich, MD, a pain specialist and adjunct professor of medicine at the University of Pennsylvania School of Medicine in Philadelphia and the New York University School of Medicine in New York City. He is co-author of *Conquering Chronic Pain After Injury* (Avery).

Far too many people fail to get adequate pain relief. This frequently occurs because pain sufferers are overly concerned about potential side effects of pain relievers. Or pain sufferers prefer to "tough" it out without using any medication.

This is unfortunate because pain is a leading cause of depression and stress. Pain can also escalate when it's not treated early.

Example: Suppose you hurt your knee while working in the backyard. A pain-causing chemical, *substance P,* released at the time of the injury irritates nearby tissues. To compensate for the pain, you'll put more weight on the other leg. Over time, this can cause chronic *secondary* pain in the back, leg or hip.

Pain that persists longer than 10 days should be evaluated by a doctor. He/she should examine you and perhaps order tests to rule out any underlying problem that will worsen without treatment. It's also important to ensure that you're taking the right analgesic.*

NONPRESCRIPTION ANALGESICS

In most cases, over-the-counter (OTC) analgesics work well. They often contain the same active ingredients as prescription drugs, though in lower doses.

The best choices...

•**Aspirin.** Also known as *acetylsalicylic acid,* aspirin reduces inflammation, blocks the transmission of pain signals through nerves and may lower levels of pain-causing chemicals called *prostaglandins.* The usual dosage is two 325-milligram (mg) tablets, four times every day—although your doctor may recommend larger doses for serious pain.

Use it: For arthritis, sports injuries, etc. The least-expensive analgesic, it has been used for pain relief for more than 100 years. However, since it can cause heartburn and other side effects, especially when taken for long periods, many people now choose newer painkillers that are better tolerated. Although most people can tolerate extended use of low-dose aspirin to prevent clogged arteries, painkilling doses should typically not be taken for more than 12 days without a physician's approval.

Avoid it: If you experience stomach pain, nausea, rectal bleeding or other gastrointestinal side effects. Aspirin inhibits the action of chemicals that are protective to the lining of the digestive tract.

Important: Do *not* use aspirin if you're taking an anticoagulant, such as *warfarin* (Coumadin), or an herbal product, such as ginkgo biloba, which also has blood-thinning effects. Never give aspirin to children, except in rare instances when it may be recommended by a physician. The salicylates in aspirin may trigger Reye's syndrome, a potentially fatal disorder that causes severe brain inflammation. Aspirin can also aggravate asthma.

*Pregnant women should consult their doctor before taking any painkiller.

•**Acetaminophen.** *Acetaminophen* is as effective as aspirin for short-term and chronic pain. It is also less likely to cause stomach upset or the other side effects associated with aspirin use. Children can take acetaminophen because it doesn't trigger Reye's syndrome.

Use it: For pain that isn't accompanied by swelling or inflammation, such as aches due to overexertion or headaches. Unlike aspirin, acetaminophen works only as a painkiller—it has no effect on inflammation. The recommended adult dosage is two 325-mg tablets, taken three to four times daily.

Avoid it: If you drink heavily. When combined with heavy alcohol consumption, acetaminophen can cause liver damage. In elderly people, liver damage can occur even without excessive alcohol consumption.

Caution: Extra-strength acetaminophen is generally no more effective for pain than regular acetaminophen, and the higher dosage is more likely to cause liver damage.

•**Nonsteroidal anti-inflammatory drugs.** Aspirin is an NSAID, but the term usually refers to other drugs that are less likely than aspirin to cause side effects.

Examples: Ibuprofen (Advil, Nuprin, Motrin)...and *naproxen* (Aleve).

Many people will choose an NSAID when aspirin or acetaminophen doesn't give them adequate relief or causes side effects.

Use it: For all types of pain, especially pain accompanied by inflammation, such as arthritis, sprains and other injuries. The recommended dosage varies for each NSAID. Check the label for instructions. The drugs are similar, but not interchangeable. You might get relief from one NSAID but not another. Count on trying several before finding the one that works best for you.

Avoid it: If you experience the same side effects as aspirin—stomach upset, bleeding, ulcers, etc. NSAIDs may also inhibit kidney function and shouldn't be taken by people with kidney disease without a doctor's supervision.

PRESCRIPTION ANALGESICS

Most patients will self-medicate with an OTC product, then consult a physician and progress to prescription-strength drugs if they don't get adequate relief. *I often prescribe...*

•**Cox-2 inhibitors.** *Celecoxib* (Celebrex), *rofecoxib* (Vioxx) and *valdecoxib* (Bextra) reduce pain and inflammation. They are less likely than aspirin to cause ulcers and other gastric side effects because they suppress only inflammation-causing Cox-2 enzymes—*not* the Cox-1 enzymes that protect the stomach lining.

Use it: For long-term pain that is accompanied by inflammation—injuries, arthritis, etc. Cox-2 inhibitors are expensive, so they are generally prescribed when the older NSAIDs don't work or cause too many side effects.

Avoid it: When you need fast-acting relief. Cox-2 inhibitors may take at least five days to be effective.

•**Narcotics.** These are the most effective of the analgesics. Codeine, acetaminophen with codeine, *oxycodone* (OxyContin) and others are taken orally, by injection or in slow-release patch forms.

Use it: For relief from acute pain.

Example: After surgery or to ease any type of severe pain. Narcotics are usually prescribed only for one to two days because of risk for abuse or addiction. They do not control inflammation.

Avoid it: When side effects—mainly drowsiness, mental confusion or constipation—are severe, or if you have a history of drug or alcohol abuse.

Peanut Alert

If you are allergic to peanuts, be sure to remind your physician whenever he/she prescribes a new medication.

Reason: Common drugs can trigger potentially fatal allergic reactions in people who are sensitive to peanuts, soybeans or soya lecithin.

Examples: Ipratropium (Atrovent) for asthma and *ipratropium with albuterol* (Combivent) for chronic obstructive pulmonary disease. Some

forms of these drugs contain some of the same proteins as the foods.

Important: Food allergies do not always appear in patients' medical charts.

Amy M. Karch, RN, assistant professor of clinical nursing, University of Rochester, NY.

Antibiotics and Calcium Don't Mix

Taking *fluoroquinolone* antibiotics, such as Cipro, Levaquin or Tequin, with calcium-rich or -fortified foods, such as milk, orange juice and breakfast cereals, can reduce antibiotic absorption. This makes treatment less effective and may lead to the development of antibiotic-resistant bacteria.

Self-defense: Whenever possible, take these antibiotics with water—and either two hours before or after meals. Ask your doctor how to take other antibiotics, which also may need to be taken separately from meals.

Guy Amsden, PharmD, Bassett Healthcare, Cooperstown, NY, and leader of a study of antibiotic absorption, reported in *The Journal of Clinical Pharmacology.*

 # Don't Take Antidepressants With Aspirin

Taking painkillers and antidepressants can cause dangerous stomach bleeding. Long-term use of aspirin, *ibuprofen* or other types of nonsteroidal anti-inflammatory drugs (NSAIDs) increases the risk of gastrointestinal bleeding. Prozac, Zoloft and other selective serotonin reuptake inhibitor (SSRI) antidepressants also can cause bleeding. Taking both types of drugs further increases risk.

Self-defense: People using SSRI antidepressants should ask their physicians about taking painkillers that don't cause bleeding—such as *acetaminophen* (Tylenol).

Important: To minimize side effects, talk to your doctor about taking the lowest effective dose of any drug.

Jay S. Cohen, MD, associate professor of family and preventive medicine, University of California, San Diego, School of Medicine, and the author of *Overdose: The Case Against the Drug Companies* (Tarcher/Putnam). His Web site is *www.medicationsense.com.*

Beware of Accidental Acetaminophen Overdose

Many over-the-counter medications contain *acetaminophen,* including some varieties of Alka-Seltzer, Benadryl, Contac, Dimetapp, Drixoral, Excedrin, Midol, Robitussin, Tavist, Theraflu and Vicks. If you take one of these products *and* the recommended dose of acetaminophen, as found in Tylenol, you risk liver damage. Risk for liver damage is also greater if you take acetaminophen and drink more than a moderate amount of alcohol.

Self-defense: Read labels carefully or ask your doctor or pharmacist. The maximum daily acetaminophen dosage from all sources is 4,000 milligrams (mg).

Peter Draganov, MD, assistant professor of medicine, division of gastroenterology, hepatology and nutrition, University of Florida College of Medicine, Gainesville.

Don't Become a Victim Of Medical Error

Charles B. Inlander, health-care consultant and president of the nonprofit People's Medical Society, a consumer health advocacy group in Allentown, PA. He is the author of more than 20 books on consumer health issues, including *Take This Book to the Hospital with You: A Consumer Guide to Surviving Your Hospital Stay* (St. Martin's).

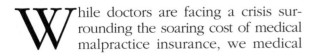

While doctors are facing a crisis surrounding the soaring cost of medical malpractice insurance, we medical consumers are facing a crisis of our own. The number of medical errors is on the rise, and despite a great deal of talk among medical experts, little progress has been made in reversing that trend.

Although most people think of medical errors as occurring in hospitals, they're just as common *outside* this setting. About four out of every 250 prescriptions filled at local pharmacies contain a mistake. That comes to 52 million erroneously filled prescriptions per year! Nonhospital-affiliated surgical centers are also a hotbed of errors and are rarely inspected by state governments or accrediting organizations.

I've always advised of the importance of getting second opinions and carefully checking out your doctor and hospital. *Additional advice to help you...*

●**Check your medications.** About 20% of all hospitalizations are related to pharmacy errors or reactions to medication. When your doctor prescribes a pill, ask him/her to give you a sample or show you a picture from a book, such as the *Physicians' Desk Reference.* Check out markings, size and color. If you get a sample, take it with you to the pharmacy and compare it with the drug that you are dispensed. Anytime you fill or refill a prescription, ask the pharmacist (not the pharmacy tech) to review the product and usage with you. Ask him to check the medication again and to explain the best way to use it and any warnings. He is required by law to do so if you ask.

●**Make sure your doctor communicates.** Studies show the number-one reason malpractice suits are filed is that the physician fails to communicate the risks and options associated with a treatment and his experience performing it. Several years ago, I assisted a woman whose surgeon had recommended a specific treatment for cancer. When she started to ask questions, he said, "I'm an expert at this. I'm telling you what you need." She acquiesced and did not question him further. The procedure was not only unsuccessful, but also caused her serious internal injury. She later found out the doctor had never performed the surgery before but had not told her. Afterward, she sued him and won. If your doctor dodges your questions or seems in a hurry to get out of the examining room, beat him to the door.

●**Use hospital-affiliated outpatient surgical centers.** While there is still a chance for error, the physicians at such surgical centers must have privileges at the hospital with which the center is affiliated, and personnel are usually hospital employees. Hospitals typically enforce stricter standards for their staffs than nonaffiliated centers. These centers are also accredited by the same agency that accredits hospitals.

By doing your homework and asking the right questions, you can greatly reduce your chances of being affected by a medical error.

More from Charles Inlander...

How to Pick a Hospital

Some on-line hospital rating sites have limited coverage...rely on unofficial information...or don't adjust ratings for the severity of cases treated at each hospital. Choosing a hospital requires research. Call and ask how many times a year the hospital has performed the procedure that you need. Compare three or four hospitals within 100 miles of your home. Both your doctor and the hospital should have performed the procedure often—higher volume tends to improve outcomes.

Charles Inlander knows about hospitals...

More Tips on Choosing A Hospital

To choose a hospital for a nonemergency treatment, find out the ratio of registered nurses (RNs) to patients—ideally, there should be at least one RN for every four patients. In intensive care units, there should be at least one RN for every two patients. Some hospital quality reports covering certain procedures can be found at the Centers for Medicare & Medicaid Services Web site, *www.cms.gov*. Check the National Voluntary Hospital Reporting Initiative, which lists hospital success rates for treating heart attack, congestive heart failure and pneumonia.

Why Hospital Computer Keyboards Could Be Making You Sick

In a recent study, 95% of cultures taken from computer keyboards at a teaching hospital had one or more microorganisms growing on them. Five percent were positive for germs known to be commonly transmitted at hospitals.

Theory: Since most keyboards aren't cleaned regularly, a health-care worker who uses the computer between patient visits can transmit germs from patient to patient.

Computer keyboards should be cleaned with hospital-approved moistened cleanup wipes.

Self-defense: Be sure that your health-care worker washes his/her hands before examining you.

Maureen Schultz, RN, infection control coordinator for the Veterans Affairs Medical Center, Washington, DC. Her study was published in *Infection Control and Hospital Epidemiology.*

Self-Defense Against ER Misdiagnosis

Hospital emergency rooms (ERs) misdiagnose about one in five patients with heart failure as having either asthma or chronic obstructive pulmonary disease (COPD).

Reason: Often these patients come in with shortness of breath and wheezing, symptoms that mimic lung disease. As a result, ER doctors are less likely to order tests that screen for heart failure. And, the treatment for COPD may even worsen heart failure.

If you go to the ER with shortness of breath: Ask your doctor to measure your level of B-type natriuretic peptide (BNP). A BNP of less than 100 can rule out heart disease. If your

BNP exceeds 100, and especially if it is over 500, you probably have heart failure.

Peter A. McCullough, MD, MPH, consultant cardiologist and chief, division of nutrition and preventive medicine, William Beaumont Hospital, Royal Oak, MI.

Take Aspirin in The Hospital

Aspirin may reduce infection risk in hospital patients. The *salicylic acid* that's in aspirin seems to inhibit reproduction of the *Staphylococcus aureus* bacterium, one of the most common causes of hospital-related infections, a new animal study has found.

Self-defense: Ask your doctor about taking one or two regular-strength (325-milligram) aspirin tablets two times a day while in the hospital. This may cut your risk of contracting a staph infection in half.

Ambrose Cheung, MD, professor of microbiology at Dartmouth Medical School, Hanover, NH.

Safer Surgery

Dale W. Bratzler, DO, MPH, principal clinical coordinator, Oklahoma Foundation for Medical Quality, a group that coordinates the national Surgical Infection Prevention Project, sponsored in part by the Centers for Disease Control and Prevention.

You probably already know that infection is among the biggest surgical risks. Doctors know it, too—but don't always do enough to prevent it. Overall, 2% to 5% of surgical incisions get infected.

Danger: Mortality rates for patients with an infection are two to three times higher than for those who recover without an infection.

Every major surgical society recommends giving antibiotics as a preventive (prophylactic) *before* making the first incision.

Unfortunately, surgeons often prescribe them at the wrong time.

Ideally, antibiotics should be given within the hour before the first incision is made. Adequate antibiotic levels should be maintained throughout the operation, then stopped at the end of surgery.

In a study, 20% of patients were given antibiotics too early…others got the drugs hours after surgery began. Giving an antibiotic late is no better than giving a placebo. If it's given too early, wound infection rates also are higher. *To protect yourself…*

● **Discuss the use of prophylactic antibiotics** with your surgeon ahead of time.

● **Insist on antibiotics if you're having a high-risk procedure,** such as cardiac, vascular or colon surgery, hysterectomy or hip or knee replacement.

These simple steps will go a long way toward ensuring your safety.

How to Reduce the Hidden Risk of Any Surgery—Anesthesia

Frank Sweeny, MD, anesthesiologist and the former medical director of St. Joseph's and Children's Hospital, Orange County, CA. A fellow of the American Board of Anesthesiology, he is also author of *The Anesthesia Fact Book* (Perseus).

Every year, about 40 million Americans undergo surgery or other procedures that require anesthesia. Some 2,000 or more will die or suffer serious complications, such as organ failure, brain damage or heart attack—not from the procedures themselves, but from factors related to the anesthesia. *To reduce risks…*

● **Ask who will administer the anesthesia.** Ideally, it should be either an MD anesthesiologist or a certified registered nurse anesthetist (CRNA). Both have extensive specialized training in anesthesia. An anesthesia *team* with a CRNA under the supervision of an MD anesthesiologist has the best safety record.

If you are scheduled to have anesthesia given by anyone other than an anesthesia specialist, inquire about his/her training in administering anesthesia and treating the complications associated with it. If you are having heart surgery, or if a young child requires anesthesia, ask for an anesthesiologist who regularly anesthetizes high-risk patients.

●**Meet with your anesthesiologist or CRNA.** Most anesthesiologists spend less than five minutes with their patients—even though a study showed that more than half the deaths caused by anesthesia were due in part to inadequate evaluations of patients prior to surgery. It is even more important to meet with your anesthesiologist if you have medical problems or if you or a family member has had trouble associated with anesthesia in the past. Ask your surgeon to help you set up a meeting with the anesthesiologist or CRNA who is scheduled to be in the operating room when you are having your procedure.

The anesthesiologist or CRNA who will administer your anesthesia should review your medical history, including whether anyone in your family has had problems with anesthesia. He should also perform a physical exam.

Be sure to tell him what medications you're taking, including herbs or supplements. Many herbs may interact with anesthesia to increase bleeding tendency (ginkgo, ginseng), cause cardiac stimulation (ginseng) or prolong the effects of anesthesia (kava, valerian). Discontinue all herbs and supplements at least two weeks prior to surgery.

●**Control medical problems.** One study indicated that almost half of anesthesia-related deaths occurred in patients who had underlying conditions, such as diabetes, high blood pressure, angina, etc., that weren't adequately controlled prior to anesthesia and surgery. If you have medical problems, visit your doctor well in advance of surgery to be sure you're in the best possible health. It usually is better to postpone surgery than to go forward when you aren't in the best shape.

●**Make sure the facility is JCAHO accredited.** That means that the Joint Commission on Accreditation of Healthcare Organizations surveys the facility at least every three years to make sure that operating standards, including the use of anesthesia, follow the latest guidelines and safety procedures.

If you're having complex surgery—heart, prostate, total joint replacement, etc.—find out how many of these operations are performed at the facility each year. Studies show that results are better in those facilities performing more of these procedures.

Be wary of in-office procedures. There have been increasing reports of problems associated with anesthesia and surgery in doctor's offices.

How to Recover From Surgery Faster

Stanley Fisher, PhD, an associate research scientist at Columbia University and a clinical psychologist in private practice, both in New York City. Dr. Fisher is the author of *Discovering the Power of Self-Hypnosis: The Simple, Natural Mind-Body Approach to Change and Healing* (Newmarket).

Whether you are undergoing a coronary bypass operation or an emergency appendectomy, surgery is the rational decision to preserve or restore your health. You know this. *But your body doesn't.*

From the body's point of view, surgery is a knife attack, pure and simple. Because your body can't distinguish between a surgeon and a mugger, it responds with primitive mechanisms designed to protect itself from harm. Stress hormones pour out, tensing muscles and pumping blood so your muscles are fueled and ready to fight. This is the opposite of how you want your body to respond to surgery. You need to be relaxed.

Even when you're unconscious on the operating table, your body is far from shut down. Surgeons maintain that no matter how well-anesthetized a patient may be, his/her body will perceptibly tense the moment the scalpel breaks the skin.

What you need is a way to communicate with your body to help it cooperate with the surgical process. Self-hypnosis allows just that. Recent research indicates that 89% of patients who use this method recover faster than those who do not.

WHAT IS HYPNOSIS?

The word "hypnosis" may smack of mysticism or quackery. In fact, it's a legitimate way to tap the mind's own powers.

Normally, your mind is constantly aware of the outside world. In the trance state induced by self-hypnosis, your awareness of the outside world slowly drifts away, and your attention is concentrated inward. This inward focus allows you to use your imagination to create changes in the way your mind and body behave during surgery.

Hypnosis makes it possible to induce the trance state at will. Functions that are normally automatic—such as pulse rate and muscle tension—come under conscious control. Although it may be easier to achieve a trance state with the help of an expert, it is more convenient to learn to do it yourself.

PRACTICING SELF-HYPNOSIS

Self-hypnosis consists of two stages—entering the trance state...and, once you are there, delivering well-chosen messages to your mind and body.

People differ tremendously in the depth of the trance that they enter. A person who is very susceptible to hypnotism may feel completely removed from the outside world and virtually unaware of his surroundings. Others feel nothing special beyond a heightened sense of relaxation, comfort and ease.

Fortunately, people who aren't very hypnotizable can achieve the same benefits as those who are. This is possible because the depth of the trance is less important than the repetition of the message.

During the week before surgery, all patients should practice self-hypnosis every couple of waking hours—that's about eight times a day. The day before surgery, patients should do it every waking hour.

After the operation, be sure to keep up the same hourly schedule but concentrate entirely on helping your body heal. It is impossible to overdose on this treatment.

Although there are many ways to induce a trance—and you can use any technique that works for you—many people get good results with this simple four-step process...

1. While sitting or lying comfortably, look up—with your eyes open—as if you're trying to see your eyebrows. Close your eyes, but keep looking up.

2. Take a deep breath. Hold it for the count of one...two...three.

3. Release your breath and allow your eyes to relax.

4. Imagine yourself floating down, as if on a soft, feathery couch or cloud, entering a safe, comfortable place, completely relaxed.

The entire process usually takes approximately 90 seconds.

After learning to induce the trance, you are ready to suggest to your body how you would like it to behave during and after surgery. Instruct your body to be limp, loose and very relaxed during surgery. Imagine how this will feel when you lie on the operating table.

Depending on the specific procedure, you may focus on relaxing the particular part of the body that will be operated on. Remind your body that the surgeon is there to help, not hurt. Imagine that you are working with the surgical team to bring health back to your body.

It's only natural to feel anxious before an operation. You can't make the fear disappear, but you can *put it aside*. Imagine how the fear looks and what it feels like. See yourself putting it in a big box. The fear is still there, but it won't bother you as much.

Other messages are related to recovery. Tell your body to keep the wound dry, clean and free from infection. You might imagine your immune system as an army of soldiers fighting bacteria, or a cleanup squad removing debris. Choose an image that feels right for you.

Motivation is a key to success. Remind yourself *why* you're having the surgery. Imagine yourself getting out of bed, feeling hungry, becoming more active and returning to your normal activities.

Use all of your senses. Think of how your muscles feel during a vigorous walk...savor the satisfaction of a gourmet meal...and the warm glow of a healthy and pain-free evening spent with those you love.

Surgery Patients Beware

Potentially fatal lung clots called *pulmonary emboli* can occur for up to eight weeks after an operation. Most of these emboli come from clots that develop in the legs or pelvis—a condition known as *deep vein thrombosis* (DVT)—and then travel to the lungs.

Self-defense: Ask your physician what measures are being taken to prevent DVT—blood-thinning drugs and compression stockings may be prescribed. Be sure to comply with instructions for medications, exercise and follow-up appointments. Be alert to leg pain or redness, breathing difficulties or unusual bleeding.

Samuel Z. Goldhaber, MD, associate professor of medicine at Harvard Medical School and director of the Venous Thromboembolism Research Group, Brigham and Women's Hospital, both in Boston. His study of clot prevention in 5,451 patients was published in *The American Journal of Cardiology*.

Plan Ahead for A Trip to the Emergency Room

Before you *must* go to an emergency room, ask your doctor which hospital in the area has the best trauma unit. Make sure you or someone with you tells the ambulance to go there. Carry your doctor's card, a list of medicines you take and—if you have a heart condition or are over age 50—a wallet-sized copy of your latest electrocardiogram. Be sure your doctor has your past medical records.

Joel Cohen, MD, urgent-care physician at Velda Rose Medical Center, Mesa, AZ, and author of *ER: Enter at Your Own Risk* (New Horizon).

Better Nursing Home Care

To get better nursing home care for someone you love…

●**Help staff interpret his/her actions**—you may recognize things the staff will not.

●**Give information about his earlier life,** habits, patterns and interests.

●**Ask questions**—find out why the staff does things a certain way.

●**Explain your relative's needs** to the social worker and director of nursing.

●**Consider joining the National Citizens' Coalition for Nursing Home Reform** (202-332-2275, *www.nccnhr.org*).

Sarah Greene Burger, RN-C, MPH, FAAN, private consultant and former executive director, National Citizens' Coalition for Nursing Home Reform in Washington, DC, and coauthor of *Nursing Homes: Getting Good Care There* (Impact).

3

Simple Solutions To Common Health Problems

Proven Home Remedies For Common Aches And Pains

You don't need a doctor for headaches and heartburn and other minor health problems. Most ailments can be treated easily with remedies made from common household items or naturopathic products available at pharmacies and health food stores.

Caution: Any symptoms that seem unusual …come on suddenly…or don't go away within one week always should be checked by a physician. Also, if you are taking any medications, check with your doctor before taking any additional remedies.

Conditions you can treat yourself…

TENSION HEADACHE

A tension headache usually is triggered by physical or emotional stress. Aspirin and other nonsteroidal anti-inflammatory drugs may help,

but they frequently cause stomach upset and, if overused, may trigger rebound headaches.

Remedies: Put a few drops of lavender oil on your index fingers, and rub it on your temples and the muscles at the back of your neck. Lavender penetrates the skin to slow activity in the limbic system, the part of the brain connected with emotions.

You also can try a combination supplement that contains *bromelain* (a pineapple enzyme) and *curcumin* (found in the spice turmeric). This combination suppresses the production of *prostaglandins,* pain-causing chemicals. Follow label directions.

HEARTBURN

This occurs when stomach acids surge into the esophagus.

Remedies: Add one-half teaspoon of baking soda to one cup of warm water and drink

---

Thomas Rogers, ND, naturopathic physician in private practice at Whidbey Island Naturopathic, Oak Harbor, WA, *www.whidbeynaturopathic.com,* and adjunct faculty member who teaches medical procedures and orthopedics at Bastyr University, Kenmore, WA.

it. This mixture neutralizes acid. Or take capsules that contain *deglycyrrhizinated licorice* (DGL). Follow label directions. Licorice creates a gel-like barrier that protects the esophagus from stomach acid. Another option is a supplement called *Robert's Formula,* which contains such soothing herbs as marshmallow and slippery elm (do not use this remedy during pregnancy and lactation).

FLATULENCE

Gas is produced when bacteria in the colon ferment carbohydrates that aren't digested. The resulting buildup of hydrogen, methane and other gases causes discomfort and sometimes embarrassment.

Remedy: Have a cup of fennel tea, available in tea-bag form. Or pour eight ounces of boiling water over one-half teaspoon of crushed fennel seeds. Cover the cup, and let steep for 15 minutes. Drink the tea as often as needed.

SINUSITIS

Sinusitis is an infection of the sinus cavities behind the facial bones around the nose and eyes. It can cause difficulty breathing as well as facial tenderness and headaches.

Remedy: Add one-half teaspoon of salt to eight ounces of warm water. Cup some of the solution in your palm (wash your hands first), and sniff it deeply into each nostril. Or you can use a commercially prepared saline spray. Do this up to three times a day to reduce swelling of the sinus lining, promote better drainage and inhibit growth of harmful organisms.

Avoid milk, cheese and other dairy foods during sinusitis flare-ups. Dairy triggers the production of excess mucus.

COUGH

A cough results when nerves in the respiratory tract are irritated by a cold, flu or other type of illness.

Remedies: For a wet cough (one that produces phlegm)—boil water in a pot. Turn off the heat, and add three drops of eucalyptus oil. Lean over the pot with a towel draped over your head, and inhale the steam. This helps open nasal and bronchial passages and expel phlegm. Do this twice a day.

For a dry cough—make up a tea from wild cherry bark. Just measure one teaspoon of dried chopped cherry bark into an eight-ounce cup, and pour boiling water over the bark. Cover up the cup, and let the bark steep for 15 minutes. Drink one cup three times a day.

PULLED MUSCLE

Soreness usually means that you have over-exerted a muscle, causing microscopic tears.

Remedies: Right after the injury occurs, wrap ice in a towel or T-shirt and apply to the area for up to 20 minutes. Repeat every few hours. If possible, elevate the area above the level of your heart.

In addition, you can place three 30C pellets of homeopathic *Arnica* under your tongue every 15 minutes for one to two hours to reduce pain and inflammation.

Also take 500 to 750 milligrams (mg) of magnesium citrate daily until the pain subsides. To prevent diarrhea from the magnesium, divide the dose into several smaller ones and take them throughout the day.

SWIMMER'S EAR

This infection of the outer part of the ear usually is caused by fungi that thrive in moist environments.

Remedies: Warm one-half of an onion in a microwave for about 10 to 20 seconds and hold it very close to, but not touching, the affected ear for a minute or two. Warm onion releases sulfur-based gases that inhibit fungi, bacteria and viruses and ease pain. You can reheat and reuse the onion several times. Or moisten a cotton swab with citrus-seed extract, and apply it to the outer part of the ear and ear canal. Citrus kills fungi and bacteria.

To prevent the infection from recurring, just swab the outer part of the ear with rubbing alcohol after swimming or bathing. This makes it harder for fungi to survive.

INGROWN NAIL

This irritation where the nail enters the skin is painful and slow to heal but rarely serious.

Remedy: To ease pain and inflammation, mix one-half teaspoon of bentonite clay with one-half teaspoon of goldenseal powder and enough witch hazel to make a paste. Apply it to the nail bed, and cover with a warm wash-cloth for 15 minutes. Do this twice a day until the area heals.

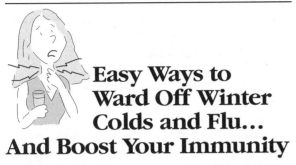

Easy Ways to Ward Off Winter Colds and Flu... And Boost Your Immunity

Robert Rountree, MD, director of Boulder Wellcare, a family practice in Colorado. He is also a member of the adjunct faculty at the Institute for Functional Medicine, Gig Harbor, WA. He has been researching immunity for more than 20 years and is a coauthor of *Immunotics: A Revolutionary Way to Fight Infection, Beat Chronic Illness, and Stay Well* (Putnam).

Some people are laid low by every ailment making the rounds, while others will sail through the winter with nary a sniffle. The strength of your immune system is the critical factor. This army of cells and chemicals guards your intestinal tract and mucous membranes and patrols your bloodstream.

Overwork, stress and insufficient sleep can sap the vitality of these disease fighters. Regular exercise is known to improve immune function. But above all, your defending troops must be well fed to stay strong.

FEEDING YOUR IMMUNE SYSTEM

The number-one cause of immune weakness is *micronutrient starvation,* a shortage of vitamins, minerals and protective plant-based substances called *phytochemicals.*

These micronutrients are abundant in fruits and vegetables, but only about 25% of Americans consume the five daily servings recommended by the National Institutes of Health.

To maximize your intake of the key micronutrients, eat for color. Choose deep-colored fruits and vegetables whenever you can. These are filled with natural disease-fighting phytochemicals, such as carotenoids and flavonoids.

Best fruits in order: Blueberries, blackberries, strawberries, raspberries, plums, oranges, red grapes, cherries, kiwis, pink grapefruit.

Best vegetables in order: Kale, spinach, brussels sprouts, alfalfa sprouts, broccoli florets, beets, red bell peppers, onions, corn, eggplant.

Choose organically grown fruits and vegetables. Preliminary research suggests that organic produce may have more phytochemicals than conventionally grown plant foods.

If you choose to use nonorganic fruits and vegetables, scrub them all thoroughly with a cleanser, such as Fit Fruit & Vegetable Wash, to help remove pesticide residues that can poison the immune system.

In addition to upping your intake of fruits and vegetables, eat fish at least twice a week. Fish contains omega-3 fatty acids, a type of polyunsaturated fat that boosts health and protects against some cancers.

I recommend wild salmon because it has very little mercury. Avoid large fish that are high in mercury, such as swordfish, shark, king mackerel and tilefish. Canned tuna is better than fresh because it comes from smaller fish.

If you don't like fish, you can take fish oil or flaxseed oil supplements. Be sure to follow instructions on the label.

Foods to avoid: Sugar-filled candies, cakes, cookies, jams and refined carbohydrates, such as white bread and pasta. These elevate blood sugar and interfere with the enzymes and cells of the immune system.

Foods that are heavy in saturated fat (such as red meat and whole-milk products) and trans fats (margarine and many commercially prepared desserts) weaken cell membranes and sabotage immune function.

SUPERCHARGERS

Everyone should take a daily multivitamin/mineral supplement that includes vitamin C, 2,000 milligrams (mg)...vitamin E in the form of tocopherol complex, 200 to 400 international units (IU)...magnesium, 200 to 300 mg...and selenium, 100 to 200 micrograms (mcg). If you're still getting sick, you may need to boost your immune system with additional supplements. This is particularly important if you are under stress, work in a school or hospital or travel extensively—all of which put you at high risk of infection. *You can take all of the following every day if you wish...*

●**NAC,** short for *N-acetyl-cysteine,* a type of amino acid. It boosts levels of *glutathione,* a keystone of the body's armor against the toxic free radicals. It thins mucus, making the respiratory system less prone to infection. NAC is particularly protective against colds, flu and sore throats.

Dose: 500 to 600 mg/day.

●**Grape seed extract,** which is rich in concentrated *proanthrocyanidins,* highly potent forms of the health-boosting bioflavonoids that are found in berries, citrus fruits and onions. These fortify the body against infection, help soothe inflammation, stimulate germ-fighting natural killer cells and increase the production of *interleukin-2,* a messenger chemical that activates other immune cells.

Dose: 150 to 300 mg/day.

●**Astragalus.** For thousands of years, traditional Chinese medicine has used this herb to strengthen the body's *we'i ch'i* ("defensive energy"). It is a general immune-system tonic that also can help fight a cold or flu if you're already sick. It stimulates the activity of *macrophages,* which swallow bacteria and viruses whole, and other disease-fighting cells.

Dose: 1,000 to 2,000 mg/day.

●**Probiotics.** The lower intestinal tract is host to colonies of bacteria, mostly friendly species that keep destructive germs in check by crowding them out, stimulating production and activity of white blood cells and producing natural germicidal substances. Poor diet and exposure to antibiotics (including those that have entered the food chain in chicken and beef) can deplete the body of its micro helpers.

Dose: 10 to 20 billion organisms of *L. acidophilus* daily in capsule or powder form. Follow package labels.

●**Green tea.** It is particularly helpful in the digestive tract, where it kills harmful bacteria. The antioxidants in green tea are more powerful immune boosters than vitamin C or E.

Dose: Two cups daily, or 1,000 mg of extract.

AN IMMUNE-FRIENDLY LIFESTYLE

Other ways to boost immunity…

●**Sufficient rest.** Sleep deprivation robs your body of the downtime it needs for self-repair. A single sleepless night markedly lowers immune activity. If you have trouble sleeping, try taking at bedtime L-theanine (100 to 400 mg)…or valerian (200 to 800 mg)…or melatonin (1 to 5 mg). If you are pregnant or taking medication, check with your physician.

●**Moderate exercise.** Physical activity invigorates your immune system, but exercising to exhaustion creates damaging stress. Don't try to make up for a whole week of inactivity on the weekend.

●**Home hygiene.** Drink only filtered water, and use unbleached paper goods and nontoxic cleaning supplies.

●**Workplace protection.** Run an ionizer/air purifier next to your desk. Don't use the pens, keyboards or phones of coworkers who are often sick. Be wary of bathroom doorknobs— push the door open with your arm or grasp the knob with a paper towel.

Hum to Help Your Sinuses

Humming can help relieve sinus infections. In a recent study, nitric oxide, a gas that is lethal to bacteria, increased 15-fold in the nose during humming. An increase in nitric oxide indicates improved sinus air exchange, whereby fresh air enters the sinuses and replaces "old air." Poor ventilation of the sinuses is a risk factor for sinus infections.

Self-defense: To ventilate sinuses, hum for one minute every one to two hours.

Jon O. Lundberg, MD, PhD, associate professor of physiology and pharmacology at the Karolinska Institute, Stockholm, Sweden.

Faster-Acting Sinus Infection Treatment

When taken with antibiotics, the supplement *bromelain,* made from pineapple enzymes, breaks down mucus and helps clear up a sinus infection faster than using antibiotics alone. Take 500 milligrams (mg) three times a day in addition to a doctor-prescribed antibiotic. Available in health food stores.

Benjamin Asher, MD, chairman, alternative medicine committee, American Academy of Otolaryngology, Alexandria, VA, and an instructor in surgery/otolaryngology, Dartmouth Medical School, Hanover, NH.

Allergy Relief for the Eyes

Much better relief is now available for seasonally watery and itchy eyes. Commonly used over-the-counter eyedrops are often ineffective for allergic conjunctivitis.

New treatment: Prescription eyedrops that contain antihistamines.

If you suffer from allergic conjunctivitis: Ask your doctor about prescribing *olopatadine* (Patanol), *lodoxamide* (Alomide) or the recently FDA-approved *ketotifen* (Zaditor).

Frank M. Graziano, MD, PhD, professor of medicine, University of Wisconsin Hospital and Clinics, Madison.

Foods That Trigger Hay Fever

Some foods and herbs contain proteins similar to those found in ragweed pollen and can cause allergy symptoms ranging from mild (itching, sneezing) to severe (asthma, sudden blood pressure drop).

Foods and herbs to avoid: Bananas, cantaloupes, cucumbers, honeydew, watermelon, zucchini, chamomile and echinacea.

Helpful: Avoid these items if they make your mouth tingle or itch when you eat them.

If you're allergic, these foods and herbs also may trigger hives, watery eyes, a metallic taste or itchy palate (roof of the mouth).

Leonard J. Bielory, MD, director, Asthma and Allergy Research Center, University of Medicine and Dentistry of New Jersey, New Jersey Medical School, Newark.

Number-One Cause of Headaches

Digestive trouble is the number-one trigger of headaches. Some food compounds are *vasospastic*—they cause the arteries to constrict, diminishing blood flow. This affects blood vessels in the head and can cause headaches.

If you're susceptible to headaches, avoid the vasospastic foods, which include dairy products, chocolate, wheat gluten and high-fructose corn syrup. These ingredients can bring on general, cluster and even migraine headaches.

Andrew L. Rubman, ND, adjunct professor of medicine, Lane College of Integrative Medicine in Orlando, FL, and medical director, Southbury Clinic for Traditional Medicines in Southbury, CT, *www.naturopath.org.*

Best Way to Treat Dandruff

Here is some helpful advice for various types of dandruff…

•**Periodic flaking.** You don't need special shampoo.

•**Mild flaking with red, itchy scalp.** Shampoos with *zinc pyrithione* (Head & Shoulders), *selenium sulfide* (Selsun Blue) or *ketoconazole* (Nizoral A-D).

•**Large flakes and scales on scalp.** Shampoos that contain *salicylic acid* (Neutrogena T/Sal), or try coal-tar treatments (Tegrin).

Caution: People who have blond or graying hair should avoid all coal-tar treatments, which may stain.

See a dermatologist if over-the-counter treatments don't help after one month. He/she may prescribe shampoos with corticosteroids.

Amy McMichael, MD, associate professor of dermatology, Wake Forest University School of Medicine, Winston-Salem, NC.

Amazing Nail Remedy

Howard Garrett, known as "The Dirt Doctor," *www. dirtdoctor.com*. He has devoted his career to educating the public about organic gardening. Mr. Garrett hosts the Texas radio show *The Natural Way* on WBAP. He is also author of *The Dirt Doctor's Guide to Organic Gardening* (University of Texas).

Ed Dillard was listening to my regional radio talk show on gardening and heard a caller ask how to get rid of fungus on roses. I answered, "Use cornmeal."

For 27 years, Dillard had been plagued by toenail fungus. He had thick, ugly yellow nails and wondered if cornmeal would work.

Dillard soaked his feet for one hour in cornmeal and warm water. There was no change in his nails. But about a month later, he noticed healthy pink nail tissue at the base of his big toenail, though he had only soaked one time. He repeated the cornmeal soak weekly and about a year later, he was fungus free.

He called me and told of his success on the air. Since then, I have heard from thousands of people who have used cornmeal to treat nail fungus, athlete's foot, ringworm and other fungal problems. Some physicians speculate that the microorganisms in cornmeal, activated by warm water, literally eat the microscopic fungi.

Cornmeal Rx: Put one inch of cornmeal, yellow or white, in a pan, and add just enough warm, not hot, water to cover it. Let this sit for 30 minutes. Then add enough warm water to cover up your feet. Soak for at least one hour once per week until the fungus is gone. For other fungal problems that require soaking in a bath, add two cups of cornmeal to the water.

Cleaner Dentures

Microwaving dentures kills 70% more microorganisms than soaking them in denture-cleansing solutions alone.

What to do: Ask your dentist if your dentures are safe to microwave. They should not contain any metal, porcelain or soft liners. Once you have received your dentist's consent, place dentures in a microwave-safe container at least twice as tall as the dentures. Fill the container with enough water to completely cover up the dentures and to allow two inches between the water and the top of the container. Add one denture-cleansing tablet and let it dissolve. Place a paper towel over the container. Microwave on high for two minutes. Let dentures cool. Rinse and wear. Microwaving three times weekly is enough for most healthy people.

R. Thomas Glass, DDS, PhD, professor of pathology and dental medicine, Oklahoma State University Center for Health Sciences, Tulsa.

Fight Cavities While You Sleep

To fight cavities while you're sleeping, use your finger or toothbrush to rub a dab of fluoride toothpaste along the gumline before bed. Overnight, teeth will absorb the enamel-strengthening fluoride.

Luke Matranga, DDS, associate professor of general dentistry, Creighton University School of Dentistry, Omaha.

Better Varicose Vein Treatment

A new varicose vein treatment has a 93% success rate—better than surgery. In Endovenous Laser Treatment, a doctor makes a small cut in the skin around the knee and inserts a thin laser catheter. Laser energy heats, shrinks and seals the diseased vein. The procedure is done under local anesthesia and does not cause the scars, clots or nerve damage that can result from surgery.

Cost: From $2,000 to $4,000 per treatment.

Robert J. Min, MD, director, Cornell Vascular, and vice chairman of radiology, Weill Medical College of Cornell University, New York City.

How to Prevent Heartburn When Eating Out

To avoid heartburn when eating out, choose meals carefully. Salads are usually safe—but ask for the dressing on the side so you use less.

Reason: Most dressings contain fat, which makes heartburn more likely in people prone to it.

More options: Pasta in a simple sauce, such as pesto or lemon sauce, but avoid spicy Italian food, especially in tomato-based sauces. Meat should be very lean. Mexican food usually is OK if you avoid the extra cheese and use mild salsa—but black beans sometimes cause heartburn. Avoid fried or sautéed foods—instead order grilled or broiled.

David Peura, MD, professor of medicine, University of Virginia, Charlottesville.

Natural Treatment for Indigestion

More than 60% of people who drank a glass of carbonated water daily experienced a reduction in bloating, nausea, belching, pain and other symptoms of indigestion and constipation, according to a recent two-week study.

Theory: Carbonated water will stimulate the proximal (or upper part) of the stomach, which promotes more efficient digestion. Carbonated water may also increase the efficiency of gallbladder emptying.

If you suffer from indigestion and constipation: Ask your doctor if adding carbonated water to other treatment strategies, such as a high-fiber diet, may be beneficial.

Rosario Cuomo, MD, assistant professor of clinical and experimental medicine, University of Naples "Federico II," Naples, Italy.

Folk Remedies That Really Work

Earl Mindell, PhD, RPh, professor of nutrition at Pacific Western University in Los Angeles, and an authority on nutrition, drugs, vitamins and herbal remedies. He is also the author of *Natural Remedies for 101 Ailments* (Basic Health) and *Earl Mindell's Vitamin Bible for the 21st Century* (Warner).

Physicians often dismiss folk remedies as quaint, not effective or potentially unsafe. That's a mistake.

Research has now found that some traditional remedies work as well—or even better—than drugs. What's more, most of these traditional treatments are safer than drugs because they rarely cause side effects or interact with other medical treatments.

Best folk cures*...

COLDS

There is good reason that mothers have long advocated chicken soup as an effective cold remedy. Studies have confirmed that chicken soup increases the activity of antiviral immune cells and at the same time reduces throat and sinus inflammation.

What to do: Eat a bowl of chicken soup twice daily at the first sign of a cold.

Helpful: Add a pinch of cayenne to chicken soup. *Capsaicin,* the chemical that makes cayenne and other peppers taste hot, reduces congestion as effectively as over-the-counter (OTC) medications.

HEADACHES

Most headaches are caused by muscle tension and/or emotional stress. Millions of Americans cannot take aspirin or other painkillers because of drug interactions or side effects, such as stomach irritation.

What to do: Using your thumb and forefinger, squeeze the area between your upper lip and nose for five seconds. Repeat as needed. This technique helps to block the nerve signals and will significantly decrease headache pain in many sufferers.

*Check with your doctor before trying these remedies. Herbs can be dangerous for some people, including pregnant or breast-feeding women.

45

INSOMNIA

Sleeping pills can be addictive and are notorious for side effects, such as dizziness, depression and headaches.

What to do: Drink a cup of valerian tea at bedtime. Valerian root, available in tea bags at health food stores, contains *valepotriates* and other sleep-inducing compounds. A traditional remedy for anxiety as well as sleeplessness, it's now recommended by Commission E, the European equivalent of the FDA.

Chamomile, hops and lavender teas will also help you rest, but they are not as potent.

NAUSEA

Ginger is the best treatment for all forms of nausea, including motion and morning sickness. The active ingredients, *gingerols,* are more effective than OTC antinausea drugs.

What to do: Each day you have nausea, drink two to three cups of ginger ale that contains natural ginger. This variety is available at health food stores. The ginger-flavored ingredients in commercial brands of ginger ale won't have the same effect.

As an alternative, make ginger tea. To prepare, chop about one tablespoon of fresh gingerroot and steep it in hot water for about 10 minutes. Drink one to three cups daily.

SORE THROAT

Most people have heard that gargling with warm saltwater reduces sore throat pain. However, few prepare and use the mixture properly.

What to do: Add three teaspoons of table salt to one cup of warm water and stir. Gargle with a full one-cup mixture at least two to three times daily. Viruses, which cause colds, cannot survive in a high-salt environment.

TOOTHACHE

Conventional treatments for toothache range from OTC products, such as Orajel, to powerful prescription painkillers. But one of the best treatments is a generations-old folk remedy.

What to do: Dip a toothpick in oil of clove, available at health food stores and some pharmacies, and apply it to the sore area. The pain will disappear almost instantly. Reapply as necessary. If pain persists for more than a few days, see your dentist.

Scents to Boost Energy, Mood, Memory and More

Alan Hirsch, MD, founder and neurological director of the Smell & Taste Treatment and Research Foundation in Chicago. He is a neurologist and psychiatrist, and author of *Life's a Smelling Success* (Authors of Unity) and *What Flavor Is Your Personality?* (Sourcebooks).

Scents stimulate important mental and physical functions. They trigger the release of neurotransmitters, chemicals that send signals to the brain. *What scents can do for you...*

CONTROL APPETITE

In a study of 105 people, we found that those who inhaled a chocolate-like aroma whenever they felt like eating lost nearly three pounds in two weeks. One study of 3,193 volunteers found that sniffing banana, green apple or peppermint scents resulted in an average weight loss of 30 pounds in six months.

Sniff the above scents often, and remember to smell every food before you eat it. Your brain will perceive that you're eating more, thus suppressing your appetite.

INCREASE ENERGY

These odors stimulate the part of the brain that promotes wakefulness...

● **Jasmine** causes an increase in beta waves in the brain, a sign of alertness. Jasmine tea is a great pick-me-up.

● **Strawberries and buttered popcorn** will cause exercisers to burn more calories.

● **Peppermint** works on sensory nerves and increases alertness. Try a peppermint candy or chewing gum.

● **Freshly brewed coffee** is very stimulating, probably because we associate the aroma with the energizing effects of caffeine.

BOOST ROMANCE

Both men and women are sexually stimulated by scents, but the odors that arouse them aren't the same.

For men: The smell of lavender or pumpkin pie increases blood flow to the penis by about 40%. The smell of doughnuts, black licorice, vanilla or women's perfume (any scent) also is sexually stimulating to men.

For women: The odors of cucumber and licorice are stimulating. Women are turned off by the smells of cherries, barbecued meat and men's cologne.

REDUCE ANXIETY

Fresh, natural scents, in general, induce calm. In one study we conducted, volunteers became extremely anxious when they were confined in coffin-like tubes, but then calmed down when the tubes were infused with the smells of green apple and cucumber. These odors seem to have an impact on the limbic system, the emotional center of the brain.

If you anticipate a situation in which you will feel anxious, wash your hair that morning with a green-apple–scented shampoo and/or put a dab of the shampoo in a cloth to take with you.

IMPROVE MEMORY

People who sniff floral scents increase retention of new material by 17%.

Sniff a floral odor when learning new material, then smell it again when you want to recall it. This is known as *state-dependent learning*. The material you learn in one state—while smelling roses—will be more accessible when you replicate that state in the future.

Next, stretch your arms above your head, palms up and fingers interlaced.

Drop your hands to your sides, then raise your right shoulder to your right ear, keeping your head vertical. Repeat this stretch with the left shoulder.

Finally, bend back the fingers of each hand. This is especially important if you use a computer for long periods.

- **Take 10 long, deep breaths.** Your belly should expand as you inhale and contract as you exhale.

- **Massage your eyes and ears.** Place your palms over your eyes. Slowly spiral your palms while applying gentle pressure. Do the same for your ears.

Blocking out all sights and sounds, even for just a few seconds, is a psychologically refreshing experience.

- **Try aromatherapy.** Put a drop of lemon-lime or orange essential oil in a saucer. These gentle scents relax you without making your home or office smell like an incense store.

Great resource: *www.aromaweb.com.*

Lower Stress in Five Minutes or Less

Dawn Groves, Bellingham, WA–based author of *Stress Reduction for Busy People, Massage for Busy People* and *Yoga for Busy People* (all from New World Library).

No time to relax? Don't be so sure. *It can take only five minutes to unwind and refresh your mind…*

- **Move around.** Take a quick trip through the halls of your workplace—or around the block. Walk up and down a flight of stairs. Do 15 jumping jacks.

- **Stretch while seated.** Lace your fingers under your knee, and draw it to your chest. Repeat with the other knee. This stretches the leg and lower back.

A Better Night's Sleep

The new medication *eszopiclone* (Estorra) improved insomniacs' ability to fall asleep, stay asleep and function during the day. Like other nonbenzodiazepine drugs, such as *zolpidem* (Ambien) and *zaleplon* (Sonata), Estorra has minimal side effects, including occasional dizziness and nausea. And, the drug is likely to be available soon.

Estorra's edge: It gives patients more hours of sleep.

Andrew Krystal, MD, associate professor of psychiatry and behavioral sciences at Duke University Medical Center in Durham, NC. His study of 788 patients was published in *Sleep.*

The Best Sleep

Early morning sleep is really the most restful sleep you can get.

Recent study: Men sent to bed at 2:15 am and awakened at 6:15 am slept more soundly than ones sent to bed at 10:30 pm and awakened at 2:30 am.

So, if you can get only four hours of sleep, stay up as late as possible to get the most benefit from your limited sleep.

Caution: This does not replace a full night's sleep. Resume a normal sleep pattern as quickly as possible.

Christian Guilleminault, MD, professor of psychiatry and behavioral sciences, Sleep Disorders Center, Stanford University, Stanford, CA.

When to Use Antibiotics On Cuts

Do not apply antibiotic ointments to every minor burn, cut and scrape. In clean minor wounds, there may actually be a larger risk for allergic reaction to the antibiotic than for infection. Also, use of antibiotics contributes to the development of antibiotic-resistant bacteria. So use antibiotics only when really necessary, on wounds contaminated with dirt.

Consumer Reports on Health, 101 Truman Ave., Yonkers, NY 10703.

Better Cut Care

Common wound cleaners can do more harm than good. *Mercurochrome* and *merthiolate* contain mercury, which is toxic. Rubbing alcohol damages and dries out skin. And, hydrogen peroxide and iodine damage the skin and slow

healing. Betadine in a concentration of 1% or less is safe for cleaning wounds, but it could cause iodine poisoning if used on large open wounds. Antibiotic ointments may help prevent infection in minor wounds, but they can cause skin irritation and allergic reactions.

What to do: Clean the wound under cool running water, or swab it with a clean, wet cloth. Use soap on the surrounding skin—not on the wound itself. Apply an adhesive bandage to keep the wound clean and moist to reduce scarring. Don't pick at scabs—these are the body's natural bandages.

UC Berkeley Wellness Letter, 632 Broadway, New York City 10012.

Injuries: When to Use Hot…When To Use Cold

First aid rules for injuries can be a bit confusing. *Here is the lowdown…*

● **Cold reduces inflammation.** Apply cold to acute injuries, such as a newly sprained ankle or a pulled muscle.

● **Heat improves circulation.** It's best for chronic pain, such as from tight muscles or a sore back.

● **Alternate heat and cold** if you have soft-tissue damage and/or stretched ligaments, such as an ankle sprain. Heat aids in restoring range of motion. Apply cold for 20 minutes per hour as desired for the first 24 hours. The next day, use warmth for 20 minutes per hour as desired.

Caution: Don't apply cold for more than 24 hours or warmth for more than 72 hours. If inflammation continues beyond 72 hours, see a doctor.

Richard O'Brien, MD, spokesperson for the American College of Emergency Physicians and an emergency physician at Moses Taylor Hospital, Scranton, PA.

4

Fitness Success

The Calcium Diet: Lose Weight Faster with This Vital Mineral

Why now are two out of every three Americans so overweight? Certainly we are eating more and exercising less. But there is another cause—a lack of the mineral calcium in our diets.

If you are among the Americans getting the lowest average level of calcium—which is 255 milligrams (mg) per day—you are 84% more likely to be overweight than if you are among those people getting the highest average level of calcium—1,346 mg per day—according to a recent examination of statistics from the federal government's Health and Nutrition Examination Survey.

Simply by getting adequate calcium in our diets, as many as four out of five of us could lose the extra weight.

CALCIUM AND YOUR FAT CELLS

Calcium does far more than just keep your skeleton strong. Without enough calcium circulating in your bloodstream, your heart wouldn't beat, your blood wouldn't clot, your hormones wouldn't regulate your metabolism and your nerves wouldn't transmit signals.

If calcium levels fall—if you eat a diet low in calcium, for example—the body releases more of the hormone *calcitriol*. Calcitriol increases absorption of calcium in the intestines, so you get the most calcium possible from food.

In addition, it increases reabsorption through the kidneys, so that you lose as little calcium as possible through excretion.

Calcitriol also controls how fat cells work. When you get too little calcium and more calcitriol is released, your fat cells make and store more fat, causing weight gain.

Michael Zemel, PhD, professor of nutrition and medicine and director of the Nutrition Institute, University of Tennessee, Knoxville. He is coauthor of *The Calcium Key: The Revolutionary Diet Discovery That Will Help You Lose Weight Faster* (Wiley).

MORE PROOF

In a study we conducted at the University of Tennessee, overweight people were put on one of three eating plans for six months.

●**Group 1** ate a diet that was 500 calories below maintenance level—the level at which you neither gain nor lose weight—and had no more than one serving of dairy a day for a total of 400 to 500 mg of dietary calcium.

●**Group 2** ate the same calorie-restricted diet but took an 800-mg calcium supplement for a total of 1,200 to 1,300 mg of calcium.

●**Group 3** also ate the calorie-restricted diet but included three servings of low-fat dairy a day, bringing their total calcium intake to 1,200 to 1,300 mg.

Results: Group 1 lost 6% of total weight… Group 2 lost 7.5%…and Group 3—the low-fat dairy group—lost 11%. Group 3 also lost more body fat than the other groups, particularly around the waist area. This is an important finding because a slimmer waist is associated with a lower risk of heart disease, stroke, diabetes and cancer.

This means that adding three servings of low-fat dairy to your diet can…

●**Increase the amount of weight you lose by 70%.**

●**Increase the amount of body fat you lose by 64%.**

●**Help you lose 47% more fat** from around your belly.

Other studies have replicated these findings as well. In a 10-year study of 3,000 people ages 18 to 30, researchers at Harvard University discovered that people who ate three servings of dairy a day had a 60% lower risk of being overweight than those who consumed less calcium.

FOOD VERSUS SUPPLEMENTS

Studies show that calcium from dairy foods is more effective for weight loss than supplements. Why? Food is a complex mixture of known and unknown components. There is a cooperation among the components that can't be reproduced in a nutritional supplement.

Dairy contains calcium and a host of other biologically active components, including the amino acid *leucine*. Recent research reveals that leucine may increase the ability of muscle to use fat.

WHAT TO DO

To lose an average of one pound per week, you need to cut calorie intake and increase calorie burning by about 500 calories per day, or 3,500 calories per week. To boost the loss to 1.5 to two pounds, you need three or four servings of dairy a day, for a total of 1,200 to 1,600 mg of calcium. The easiest way to get that is with three servings of no-fat (skim) or low-fat milk (eight ounces per serving), yogurt (eight ounces) or cheese (1.5 ounces or two ounces processed).

Strategy: Have milk before a meal. Studies show that getting a liquid form of dairy before eating helps you feel full sooner at that meal and eat less at the next meal.

If lactose intolerant, try yogurt with live cultures or cheese (it has very little lactose) or take a lactose supplement when consuming dairy.

To cut 3,500 calories a week: One brisk, hour-long walk will burn about 250 calories. If you do that four times a week, you still need to cut 2,500 calories per week, or about 350 calories a day. Look for one or even two high-calorie items that you can eliminate from your daily diet.

Examples: A 12-ounce cola has 150 calories…two tablespoons of full-fat salad dressing, 150…a glazed doughnut, 250…a four-ounce bagel, 300.

Just eliminating these items will help you to lose weight, but boosting calcium will help you lose more.

More from Michael Zemel…

Weight-Loss Secret

Yogurt helps you lose weight while protecting muscle.

Recent study: Overweight people who ate three servings of yogurt daily for 12 weeks lost 22% more weight, 61% more body fat and 81% more abdominal fat than people who ate a similar number of calories but no dairy products.

Spicy Foods Curb The Appetite

In one recent study, people who ate a sauce containing *capsaicin*—the compound that makes hot peppers spicy—consumed an average of 200 fewer calories over the next three hours than those who didn't eat the sauce.

Theory: Spicy foods are more satisfying, so there's less desire to eat more.

If you are trying to lose weight: In addition to cutting back on calories and fat and getting regular exercise, consider eating more spicy foods. For recipes containing hot peppers, go to Pepper Fool at *www.pepperfool.com.*

Angelo Tremblay, PhD, director, Institute of Nutraceuticals and Functional Foods, Laval University, Ste-Foy, Canada.

Raisins Before a Workout

Although exercise offers many health benefits, a strenuous workout can trigger the formation of free radicals. The damage caused by these harmful molecules can contribute to cancer or heart disease.

Helpful: Eating a handful of raisins (approximately one ounce) 15 minutes before a workout can significantly lower levels of free radicals—and the damage they cause. Raisins are rich in antioxidants, powerful compounds that protect the body.

Gene A. Spiller, PhD, director, Health Research and Studies Center, Los Altos, CA.

Almonds for Weight Loss

In one finding, people who ate a moderate amount of almonds, three ounces a day, lost more weight than those on high-carbohydrate diets who ate the same number of calories.

Theory: The fat in almonds may not be completely absorbed by the body.

Try a handful of almonds between meals to satisfy hunger and stop unhealthy snacking.

Michelle Wien, DrPH, RD, department of diabetes, endocrinology and metabolism at the City of Hope National Medical Center in Duarte, CA, and leader of a study of 65 overweight and obese adults, published in the *International Journal of Obesity.*

Herbal Weight-Loss Aid

Mice injected with ginseng berry extract consumed 15% less food and burned 35% more calories than animals that didn't get the herb. This extract is expected to be sold as a weight-loss aid in health food stores soon.

The Medical Post at One Mt. Pleasant Rd., Toronto, Ontario.

When It's OK to Use Diet Drugs

Prescription diet drugs are safe and effective when taken under a doctor's supervision. Many people are unaware that they are available and so have turned to potentially dangerous alternatives.

Effective diet medications: *Phentermine* is an appetite suppressant. *Xenical* blocks fat absorption. *Wellbutrin* is an antidepressant that has some weight-loss effects.

All these drugs can have side effects and require medical supervision. Your doctor will determine how long you can take them.

Louis J. Aronne, MD, director, weight-control program, New York–Presbyterian Hospital, New York City.

Lose Belly Fat and Save Your Life

Arthur Agatston, MD, associate professor of medicine, University of Miami School of Medicine, FL, and consultant, National Institutes of Health Clinical Trials Committee, Bethesda, MD. He is author of *The South Beach Diet* (Rodale), and his Web site is *www.southbeachdiet.com.*

The size of your waist is a better indicator of health dangers than your weight. Men who have waists that measure more than 40 inches and women whose waists measure more than 35 inches generally have excess visceral fat. Large amounts of visceral fat—which wraps around the internal organs, such as the heart—greatly increase your risk of diabetes, heart disease, stroke and cancer.

CARBOHYDRATE CONNECTION

Diet is fundamental to reducing visceral fat—specifically, a diet that contains little or no refined carbohydrates.

The carbohydrates that dominate the typical American diet—white bread, pasta, cereal, snack foods, cakes, cookies, candies, etc.—are stripped of fiber during processing. All these foods are quickly digested and absorbed as glucose, the form that sugar takes in the bloodstream.

The body needs to produce ever-increasing amounts of insulin to remove excess glucose and fat from the blood. Elevated levels of insulin promote fat storage in the abdomen.

Higher insulin levels will end up removing too much glucose from the blood. The resulting low blood sugar, called *reactive hypoglycemia,* triggers food cravings. The more you give in to the cravings, the more weight you gain.

I have developed a three-phase strategy that reduces insulin resistance and food cravings without the dramatic calorie reductions. People typically lose eight to 13 pounds during the first two weeks and then one to two pounds per week thereafter.

PHASE 1

For 14 days, eat all the lean meat, chicken, turkey and seafood that you want. Eliminate the refined carbohydrates—bread, pasta, rice, baked goods, candy and alcohol. All of these foods exhibit high glycemic indexes. The glycemic index measures the amount by which a specific food raises blood glucose levels.

Eliminating these foods for 14 days reduces cravings for carbohydrates and helps normalize glucose levels. Eventually, you will be able to add some high-glycemic foods back into your daily diet.

Fruits and root vegetables such as carrots and potatoes also have high glycemic indexes and should be avoided in this phase. You can have as much as you want of other vegetables. To find the glycemic index of various foods, go to *www.telusplanet.net/public/dgarneau/health3b.htm.*

You also can have mono- and polyunsaturated fats, such as olive and canola oils. These satisfy appetite, reduce food cravings and help lower levels of harmful triglycerides and LDL cholesterol—main risk factors in people with large stores of visceral fat.

Nuts also are allowed. They are filling and contain mainly monounsaturated fats. Nuts are high in calories, so limit yourself to about 15 almonds or cashews, 30 pistachios or 12 peanuts (technically a legume) daily.

Don't worry about eating too much. Eat until you're satisfied—you'll still lose weight. Most of the weight loss that occurs during this phase will come from your midsection.

PHASE 2

During the third week, you can reintroduce refined carbohydrates into your diet. Your body will respond more normally to insulin's effects. You can allow yourself a small serving of bread, pasta, potatoes or rice twice a day. Cookies, cakes, candy, alcohol and snack foods, such as potato chips, still should be avoided.

Continue to focus on foods that have low glycemic indexes. Foods that are rich in fiber, such as brown rice, whole-grain breads, etc., have the lowest glycemic numbers because they are digested slowly and release glucose into the bloodstream gradually.

Helpful: Prepare foods whole, or chop them as coarsely as possible. The more work your stomach has to do to digest the food, the more slowly glucose enters the bloodstream. Finely chopped foods—shredded potatoes in hash browns, for example—allow glucose to enter the bloodstream more quickly. Whole fruit is better than juice for the same reason.

Other Phase 2 strategies…

●**Eat fish at least twice a week.** The omega-3 fatty acids in fish have been shown to reduce heart attack and stroke risk. Salmon, mackerel and herring are particularly rich in omega-3s.

●**Eat a high-protein breakfast.** Morning protein suppresses food cravings and promotes weight loss. People who skip breakfast experience morning drops in blood glucose that trigger cravings. They also tend to eat more calories during the day. A study of teenagers found that those who ate sugary breakfast cereals consumed 80% more calories over the following five hours than those who ate omelettes.

Try an omelette with cheese or vegetables, such as asparagus or broccoli, or have Canadian bacon, turkey bacon, farmer cheese or low-fat cottage cheese.

●**Snack when you're hungry.** Always try to keep some food in your stomach. It's the best way to prevent sudden food cravings.

Rather than grabbing fast foods that are high in the glucose-raising carbohydrates, try cheese sticks or a serving of sugar-free yogurt. These foods are ideal because they provide appetite-suppressing protein with very little sugar.

PHASE 3

This is the maintenance phase of the diet. Once you have reached your desired weight, continue to limit refined carbohydrates to keep food cravings under control, minimize insulin resistance and maintain low levels of visceral fat.

Hidden Causes of Weight Gain

David E. Cummings, MD, endocrinologist and associate professor of medicine at the University of Washington and Seattle Veterans Administration Medical Center, both in Seattle.

Most people put on pounds as they get older. However, if there's been a sudden change in your weight, you could have a hidden health problem. *Medical conditions that can lead to obesity…*

HYPOTHYROIDISM

The thyroid gland helps regulate your body's metabolism. Hypothyroidism means that this gland is underactive, producing low levels of thyroid hormone. This causes the body to slow down and to burn fewer calories, leading to weight gain.

Other symptoms: Fatigue…a slow heart rate …dry skin…brittle hair…constipation…depression…reduced blood flow to arms and legs, which can make you feel cold all the time.

About 7 million Americans suffer from hypothyroidism. Most gain a total of 10 to 20 pounds with this condition.

Hypothyroidism can be diagnosed with two blood tests. One measures levels of the thyroid-stimulating hormone (TSH), produced by the pituitary gland. The other measures levels of the thyroid hormone *thyroxine.*

Treatment: The standard drug is the synthetic hormone *levothyroxine* (Levothroid, Synthroid). Taken every day for life, it will restore the body's normal metabolism with virtually no side effects.

CUSHING'S SYNDROME

This rare syndrome is caused by excess levels of *cortisol,* a stress hormone produced by the adrenal glands. People with this condition slowly gain a total of 10 to 25 pounds, usually in the upper body, face and neck.

Other symptoms: Elevated blood pressure …high blood sugar…purplish stretchmark-like patterns, or "stria," on the abdomen.

The most common cause of Cushing's syndrome is the long-term use of corticosteroids. These drugs are used to treat the inflammatory diseases such as rheumatoid arthritis, asthma, lupus and inflammatory bowel disease, and to prevent the rejection of a transplanted organ.

This condition also could be due to other causes, such as a benign tumor on the pituitary gland. In this case, it is called Cushing's disease, instead of syndrome.

Treatments: If the cause is corticosteroid use, your physician may be able to treat the syndrome by decreasing the drug dosage or by discontinuing the drug. If the cause is a tumor, surgery usually is recommended.

POLYCYSTIC OVARY SYNDROME

Women who have polycystic ovary syndrome (PCOS) can gain 50 pounds in two years. It is caused by excess production of *androgens*—the male hormones that promote weight gain. PCOS also has been linked to insulin resistance, a decline in insulin's ability to transport glucose into cells.

Other symptoms: Irregular or absent periods…infertility…acne…facial hair.

Up to 10% of women suffer from PCOS. It usually begins in puberty but often goes undetected for decades because the symptoms are subtle. PCOS is easily diagnosed with blood tests that measure hormone levels.

Treatment: Your doctor may prescribe one or more medications to manage the symptoms and risks of PCOS. He/she may prescribe *metformin* (Glucophage), which improves sensitivity to insulin. Taken daily for life, it reduces androgen levels, regulates the menstrual cycle and lowers risk of diabetes and heart disease.

For excessive hair growth, your doctor may add a drug such as *spironolactone* (Aldactone), which blocks the effects of androgens and lowers their production.

PRESCRIPTION DRUGS

Dozens of medications cause weight gain as a side effect, including steroids, antipsychotics and antidepressants, such as tricyclic antidepressants (TCAs) and monoamine oxidase inhibitors (MAOIs). Ask your physician or pharmacist to review all of your prescriptions. If one or more have weight gain as a side effect, ask if other drugs can provide the same benefits without adding pounds.

Medications That Cause Weight Gain

Medications can trigger weight gain by increasing appetite, slowing down metabolism or causing fluid retention.

Common culprits: Newer antipsychotics, such as Risperdal, Seroquel and Zyprexa…mood stabilizers, such as *lithium* and the anticonvulsants Depakote and Tegretol…steroids…tricyclic antidepressants, such as Aventyl, Elavil and Remeron…drugs to treat diabetes, such as Actos and Avandia.

Weight gain may be experienced fairly early in the course of therapy. If you gain weight after starting any medicine, consult your doctor. Prescription diuretics can help take off water weight. Increased exercise may be needed if a drug slows your metabolism.

Stephanie DeGraw, PharmD candidate and researcher at the Institute for Safe Medication Practices, Huntingdon Valley, PA, which publishes the consumer newsletter *Safe Medicine*. Their Web site is *www.ismp.org*.

Eating Out with America's Top Food Cop

Michael F. Jacobson, PhD, executive director, Center for Science in the Public Interest, a nonprofit group that has led a nationwide campaign to improve America's nutrition and health, Washington, DC. He is coauthor of *Restaurant Confidential* (Workman).

The average American eats at a restaurant more than four times a week. This practice may be very convenient—but it's not always healthful. Restaurant food has more fat, salt and cholesterol than home-cooked meals.

LUNCHTIME TRAPS

Is a veggie sandwich the ideal lunch? Not necessarily. The two ounces of cheese typically added to these popular lunchtime meals contain three-quarters of a day's allowance for saturated fat. Tuna salad, thanks to the mayonnaise usually used as a base, is packed with 720 calories. Chicken salad has 550 calories.

Best choices: Opt for a turkey, roast beef, chicken breast or veggie sandwich *without* cheese. Ask for extra veggies, light mayo, mustard, ketchup or light salad dressing.

Don't assume that a salad is diet food, either. A taco salad is served in a fried taco shell filled with ground beef, cheese, sour cream and guacamole. It contains 1,100 calories and a day's quota of saturated fat.

Greek salads are weighted down with feta cheese, which is high in saturated fat. An Oriental chicken salad contains 750 calories, due to the dressing, nuts and fried noodles.

Helpful: If you're ordering salad, ask for light dressing on the side. Use no more than a few teaspoons. Also order cheese, nuts and noodles on the side—and use them sparingly.

For the best lower-calorie fast-food lunch, consider the following...

•**Burger King's BK Veggie Burger**—with reduced-fat mayonnaise—contains 340 calories and 2 grams (g) of saturated fat. It's better than just about any burger at any other chain.

•**McDonald's Fruit and Yogurt Parfait**—low-fat vanilla yogurt layered with berries and topped with granola—is a nutrient-rich bargain at only 380 calories.

•**Subway's "7 subs with 6 g of fat or less."** These include ham, roast beef, chicken and turkey—ranging from 200 to 300 calories for a six-inch sub.

•**Wendy's Mandarin Chicken Garden Sensation Salad.** This creative salad of mixed greens, chicken and mandarin orange sections, roasted almonds and half a packet of Oriental sesame dressing is hard to beat at 470 calories.

Here's how to make the most healthful dinner choices when you're eating the following cuisines...

AMERICAN

The worst thing you can eat at a steak house isn't the steak—it's the appetizers. A fried onion served with dipping sauce has more than 2,000 calories. An order of cheese fries with dressing contains about 3,000 calories. Have a salad and bread instead.

The wrong choice of entrée can also send your calorie intake soaring. One trimmed, 16-ounce prime rib has about 1,000 calories and two days' worth of saturated fat. One trimmed, 20-ounce porterhouse steak isn't much better with a day-and-a-half's limit of saturated fat. A trimmed, 16-ounce T-bone steak has 700 calories and a day's quota of saturated fat.

As for side dishes, french fries or a loaded baked potato (sour cream, butter, cheese and bacon) add 600 calories.

Best choices: Sirloin steak or filet mignon are by far the leanest choices, with about 400 calories each and less than half a day's saturated fat per serving. A baked potato with sour cream or a vegetable of the day is the best side dish.

CHINESE

Many people assume that all Chinese food is low in fat and calories. Not so. A breaded and fried chicken main dish, such as General Tso's Chicken, contains 1,600 calories. And, one order of orange (crispy) beef or sweet-and-sour pork also contains 1,600 calories each.

Best choices: You can cut calories by ordering steamed rice instead of fried...braised or stir-fried foods instead of deep-fried ones... vegetable-rich dishes, such as Szechuan shrimp, chicken chow mein, shrimp with garlic sauce or beef with broccoli.

Helpful: Use chopsticks or a fork to lift the food out of the fat-laden sauce in the serving plate and transfer it into your rice bowl.

ITALIAN

Most people know that a cream-and-cheese-based dish, such as fettuccine Alfredo, is an "artery-clogger." But they may not realize that a single order has 1,500 calories.

There are other less obvious danger zones when eating Italian food. Most spaghetti (with meatballs or sausage) and parmigiana dishes (eggplant, chicken or veal) contain more than 1,000 calories each. And the typical order of lasagna, one of the most popular Italian dishes, packs as much saturated fat as two McDonald's Big Macs, not to mention about 1,000 calories.

Best choices: Pasta topped with marinara or meat (Bolognese) sauce (skip the meatballs) ...red or white clam sauce...or chicken Marsala.

A serving (a quarter of a large pie) of Pizza Hut's Stuffed Crust Pepperoni Lover's Pizza is about the same as eating two McDonald's Quarter Pounders. A typical serving of Pizza Hut's Hand-Tossed Veggie Lover's Pizza, on the other hand, has half the calories (550) and one-fourth the saturated fat (6 g).

Best choices: When ordering pizza, ask for half the usual amount of cheese. Vegetable toppings are lowest in calories. Chicken and ham are second best. Sausage and beef are the worst choices.

MEXICAN

At Mexican restaurants, the trouble starts with the appetizers. A complimentary basket of tortilla chips runs 650 calories. An order of cheese nachos or cheese quesadillas hits 900 calories. If you opt for the beef and cheese nachos, calories climb to 1,400.

Most platters at Mexican restaurants weigh in at more than 1,500 calories and a day's limit of saturated fat. This is due to the hefty side dishes (refried beans and rice) and rich condiments (sour cream and guacamole) that typically accompany the meat- and cheese-filled entrées (chimichanga, enchilada, burrito)—all of which contain high saturated fat levels.

Best choices: Stick with shrimp, chicken or vegetable fajitas…nonfried ("charro") beans instead of refried beans…soft tortillas with salsa instead of chips…or a couple of chicken tacos. Substitute salsa for sour cream and cheese.

Beware of "Light" Salad Dressings

Light salad dressings are loaded with sugar and salt. Read labels carefully.

Usually a better choice: Oil-and-vinegar dressing, which has no added sugar or salt and no saturated fat. It contains heart-healthy monounsaturated fatty acids. If you are concerned about the higher calorie count, have dressing served on the side.

Suzanne Havala Hobbs, DrPH, RD, adjunct assistant professor, School of Public Health, University of North Carolina at Chapel Hill. Her Web site is *www.onthetable.net.*

Helpful Weight-Management Web Sites

Anne M. Fletcher, RD, weight-loss expert in southern Minnesota and author of *Thin for Life* (Houghton Mifflin).

There are now numerous Web sites on the Internet for dieters and those concerned about good nutrition. *Here are some of the ones I recommend…*

• **www.navigator.tufts.edu,** from Tufts University, reviews other nutrition sites.

• **www.thedietchannel.com** has more than 600 links to sites with dietary and nutritional information.

• **www.healthyeating.net** has links to articles on healthful eating, weight and fat-intake calculators and fitness quizzes.

• **www.dietitian.com** is a question-and-answer site on dozens of topics, such as diets and vitamins.

• **www.foodfit.com** has weight calculators, menu planners and e-mail newsletters.

• **www.nutricise.com** offers a free healthy restaurant locator and other services, both free and fee-based.

How to Exercise Anytime, Anywhere

Joan Price, a Sebastopol, CA–based dance and fitness instructor who specializes in helping beginning exercisers. She is author of *The Anytime, Anywhere Exercise Book—300+ Quick and Easy Exercises You Can Do Whenever You Want!* (Adams Media).

We all know we should exercise on a regular basis—but only about one in every five Americans actually gets a 30- to 60-minute workout most days of the week. Even these committed exercisers often run into trouble when their schedule is disrupted by work, travel or family responsibilities.

The solution? Stop thinking of fitness as a separate undertaking and instead, start taking advantage of all the exercise opportunities that crop up during the course of your day-to-day activities.

In addition to keeping up with your regular schedule of cardiovascular exercise, here are eight strengthening and stretching exercises you can perform without missing a beat in your daily routine...

ABDOMINAL ALERT

This simple movement will give you an abdominal workout *and* improve your posture.

What to do: From a sitting position, sit up tall and pull your abdominal muscles in, lifting your chest and rib cage as you exhale. Hold for four to six seconds, then release slowly as you inhale. Repeat eight to 12 times.

Perform this: While driving, watching television or sitting at your desk.

Helpful: If you perform this exercise while driving, adjust your rearview mirror so you can see out of it only when you're in the "sitting tall" position. This will remind you to maintain this posture.

BACK STRETCH

If you spend long hours sitting in a chair, a back stretch provides welcome relief.

What to do: Stand about arm's length behind a chair, with your hands resting on the top of the backrest. Keeping your head upright, bend forward from the hips, lowering your upper body and pushing your buttocks away from the chair until you feel a stretch in your mid and upper back. Hold for 10 to 60 seconds. If your chair has rollers, increase the stretch by pushing it forward slightly as you lower yourself.

Perform this: While standing at your desk or watching TV.

CALF STRENGTHENER

Here's a good way to strengthen your lower legs, back and abdomen.

What to do: Stand on a telephone book (the bigger the better) with your toes facing the book's spine and your heels hanging over the edge opposite the spine. For better stability, this exercise can also be done standing on a step while holding a railing or on a curb while holding a signpost for balance.

Keeping your back straight, push up onto the balls of your feet while counting for two seconds, hold for another two seconds, then count for four seconds as you lower yourself back down. To help stay balanced, tighten up your abdominals and buttocks.

Keep doing for two minutes or until your calves tire, whichever comes first.

Perform this: While waiting for a bus or watching TV.

OUTER THIGH LIFT

This exercise strengthens and tones up your outer thighs while standing.

What to do: While standing on a step or on a curb, bend your left leg just slightly at the knee and slowly lift your right leg out to the side, keeping your knee facing forward and your foot flexed. Do this eight to 12 times, then switch legs and repeat.

BUN SQUEEZE

Here is an efficient way to tone up your buttocks whenever you're standing.

What to do: Squeeze the buttock muscles in both cheeks as tightly as you can, then hold the contraction for two seconds. Release for two seconds. Repeat eight to 12 times.

Perform this: While in line at the store.

NECK ROLL

A good neck stretch helps relieve neck and shoulder tension.

What to do: Let your head fall gently to the left side, until your ear is close to your left shoulder. Return to the upright position. Repeat the same movement on the right side. Continue alternating left and right four to six times.

Next, slowly roll your head from one shoulder down toward your chest, then back up to the opposite shoulder. Repeat in the opposite direction. Perform the full movement four times.

Do *not* tilt your head back. This can compress the neck and spine and may cause dizziness by impinging blood flow.

Perform this: While sitting at a desk, talking on the phone or taking a shower. In the shower, stand with your back facing the showerhead so the water hits your neck and shoulders.

JUNK-MAIL CRUMPLE

Believe it or not, crumpling up junk mail is a great way to strengthen your forearms and relieve wrist tension from typing or writing.

What to do: Open an envelope, pull out the letter and hold it in one hand. Starting at one corner, crumple the letter into your palm, bit by bit, until it forms a tight ball. Squeeze the ball a few times, then throw away.

Perform this: While opening your mail.

Exercise illustrations by Shawn Banner.

The Stretch Cure

Michelle LeMay, a Marina del Rey, CA–based fitness and dance instructor. She is the author of *Essential Stretch— Gentle Movements for Stress Relief, Flexibility and Overall Well-Being* (Perigee).

Everyone knows just how great a morning stretch feels upon awakening. But so few people realize that stretching can actually help alleviate stress-related ailments, such as headaches, anxiety, insomnia and overeating. Many people even report feeling more focused and energetic after several weeks of stretching.

Stretching will also increase your range of motion by lengthening tight muscles and increasing the movement of synovial fluid into joint cartilage, which lubricates and cushions your joints. Once your mobility begins to return with daily stretching, you'll find all physical activity—including sex—much easier and more enjoyable.

FULL-BODY STRETCHING

You can perform the following six stretches at least three times weekly. The entire workout takes less than 10 minutes to perform.

During all these exercises, visualize yourself breathing into the area that you are stretching. Exhale fully—then push a little more air out. This will automatically induce a deep, relaxing inhalation. Stretching is easiest to perform in a quiet, carpeted space.

● **Overhead reach.** Stand straight, with feet shoulder-width apart. Inhale deeply as you open your arms and reach toward the sky. Then interlace your fingers as you extend your torso. Release fingers and return your arms slowly to your sides. Repeat the overhead reach four times. This exercise will stretch muscles in the torso and increase range of motion.

● **Calf stretch.** Get on your hands and knees, with your shoulders directly over your wrists and the hips directly over your knees. Extend your right leg straight behind, with the ball of your right foot touching the ground. Press your right heel down toward the ground, feeling the stretch in the upper part of your calf.

While continuing to press your heel down, bend your right knee slightly, until you feel a stretch in your lower calf. Repeat four times with each calf.

This exercise will extend the muscles of the upper and lower calves and feet.

● **Butterfly contraction.** Sitting down on the floor, with your head up, knees apart and the soles of your feet pressed together, grasp your ankles with your hands. Exhale and round your upper back as you bring your chin to your chest. You'll feel the stretch in your neck and back. Inhale and return to the starting position. Repeat these steps eight times. The butterfly will loosen the muscles in your neck, back, hips and inner thighs.

● **Clam.** Lie on your back and pull your knees into your chest. Then wrap your hands around your lower legs and allow your back to sink into the ground. Hold for 30 to 60 seconds. This exercise relaxes and loosens your lower back and buttocks.

● **Seated forward bend.** Sit on the floor with your legs straight out in front of you. Gently lean forward, while dropping your head toward your knees. Place your hands on the floor to the side of each leg, and gently rock side to side for 20 seconds. Do not move so much that you experience discomfort. Roll up and return to the seated position. This exercise relaxes and loosens the neck, back, buttocks and hamstrings.

• **Child's pose.** Rest on both your knees, with your shins flat against the floor. Relax and bend 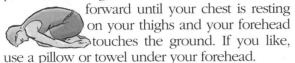 forward until your chest is resting on your thighs and your forehead touches the ground. If you like, use a pillow or towel under your forehead.

Breathe deeply and slowly, and allow your lower back to expand with each breath. Hold pose for two minutes.

This exercise expands lower back muscles and provides deep relaxation.

TENSION RELIEF

For quick tension relief, I recommend performing the following three stretches at least twice daily. Ideal times are midmorning and at the end of the day, before you go to sleep. The tension-relief workout takes about three minutes to perform.

• **Spinal roll.** Stand up straight, with feet shoulder-width apart. Relax your neck and gently drop your chin onto your chest. Allow your shoulders to slowly collapse forward, feeling the stretch in your upper back. This is a half-spinal roll. To do the full spinal roll, continue to roll down until both of your hands touch the floor, allowing your knees to bend gradually. Keep your arms, neck and back relaxed, feeling the stretch along the length of your spine.

When you've rolled down as far as you can, slowly roll back up to the starting position. Repeat four times.

The spinal roll helps to relax muscles in the neck and upper, middle and lower back.

• **Seated forward bend and clam.** These exercises are described on the previous page.

Stretching illustrations by Shawn Banner.

Health Benefits of Milder Exercise

Steven Blair, PED, president and CEO, Cooper Institute for Aerobics Research, Dallas.

H ealth experts no longer believe that you have to "break a sweat" to improve your health through exercise.

Numerous studies now indicate that people who merely walk, rather than jog or run, significantly reduce risk of heart attack, diabetes and other chronic illnesses.

Key: The primary determinant of the health benefit obtained from exercise is the total dose of the exercise, not its intensity. For instance, burning 1,000 calories per week through exercise will produce about the same health benefit whether you do it through 20 minutes of intense exercise three days a week or 30 minutes of moderate exercise five-to-seven days a week. The 30 minutes don't have to be in one session—they can be incurred, say, 10 minutes at a time at different times during the day.

More good news: When you start exercising after being sedentary, the largest health benefits occur right away. And, moving from moderate to strenuous exercise will further improve your health by only a lesser amount.

How to Exercise So That You'll Burn More Fat

D o the toughest exercise first. Then ease into more moderate effort. You'll burn up to 3% more fat.

Bonus: Exercising this way feels less difficult than starting moderately and building up.

Caution: Give yourself extra warm-up time to get muscles ready for high-intensity activity.

Jie Kang, PhD, assistant professor, department of health and exercise science, The College of New Jersey, Ewing.

The TV Workout

Exercising while watching TV can help keep you healthy. Whenever a commercial comes on, sit up in your chair with abdominal muscles tight and chest high (avoid arching your back). Keeping your feet shoulder-width apart, lean forward slightly and exhale while pushing up through your heels to a standing position. Then inhale as you slowly sit back down—using your leg muscles for control. Repeat this "sofa squat" throughout the commercial.

Linda Buch, American Council on Exercise certified fitness trainer based in Denver, and coauthor of *The Commercial Break Workout: Trim and Tone Two Minutes at a Time* (Crown/Random House).

Lose the Love Handles

The best way to get rid of love handles is to exercise less frequently—but longer. Longer workouts cause the body to burn more fat.

If you have love handles: Do at least two 90-minute cardiovascular workouts per week instead of six 30-minute sessions. Keep your heart rate at between 60% and 80% of its maximum during most aerobic exercise. To estimate your maximum heart rate, just subtract your age from 220. See your doctor before starting.

Eric Harr, professional triathlete in Marin County, CA, *www.ericharr.com* and the author of *Triathlon Training in Four Hours a Week* (Rodale).

Exercise at Any Age

In one study, sedentary women age 65 and older who started exercising had a 48% lower death rate over the next 12 years than those who remained sedentary. The best exercises for older women are the low-intensity ones, such as walking.

Edward W. Gregg, PhD, epidemiologist, Centers for Disease Control and Prevention, Atlanta.

A Stronger Body in Only 30 Minutes a Week

Fredrick Hahn, president and cofounder of the National Council for Exercise Standards, an organization of exercise, medical and scientific professionals. He is owner of Serious Strength Inc., a Slow Burn strength-training studio in New York City, and coauthor of *The Slow Burn Fitness Revolution* (Broadway). His Web site is *www.seriousstrength.com.*

We know the benefits of strength training. It will restore muscle…increase bone density…improve balance, decreasing the likelihood of falls…and promote weight loss and cardiovascular fitness. But the conventional strength training requires several hours a week and frequently causes injury.

New, better way: Slow Burn, in which the weights are lifted and lowered with incredible slowness—about 10 seconds up and 10 seconds down. *The benefits…*

●**It's safer.** Slow lifting reduces injury-causing stress on ligaments, tendons and joints. This means that even the elderly can do it safely.

●**It's more effective.** Without the aid of momentum, more muscle fibers are exercised.

●**It's more efficient.** You can get a complete workout in about 30 minutes each week —compared with at least three hours for conventional lifting.

HOW TO DO IT

In a Slow Burn workout, you complete a set of three to six repetitions of each exercise in 60 to 90 seconds. If you perform 10 exercises, you can complete your workout in approximately 10 to 15 minutes. Two workouts a week are all you need for total fitness.

To obtain the best results, raise and lower weights at the rate of about one inch per second. Allow a total of about 100 seconds for all repetitions of each exercise—push-ups, leg curls, etc. Breathe normally.

Helpful: Use a metronome to maintain the one-inch-per-second rhythm.

Repeat each exercise until the muscles are fatigued and you can't do another repetition in perfect form. If you pass the 90-second point and feel as though you could keep going, the weights are too light. If you cannot complete three repetitions in 90 seconds, the weights are too heavy. Experiment to find the right weight.

The following program stimulates all muscle groups. Do three to six repetitions of each exercise. For exercises that require switching arms or legs, do three to six repetitions with each arm or leg. You will need adjustable hand and ankle weights. Look for sets that adjust from one to 20 pounds.

●**Push-ups.** Kneel on a towel with both your hands flat on the floor in front of you, shoulder-width apart. Keep your back straight—don't let it sway or arch.

Take three seconds to lower yourself the first inch and at least seven seconds to lower yourself all the way, until your forehead almost touches the floor. Without resting at the bottom, reverse direction. Don't lock your elbows at the top. Just as soon as your arms are almost straight, reverse and go back down. If kneeling push-ups are too easy, do regular push-ups, with your toes on the floor.

●**Doorknob squats.** Open a door halfway so that you can grip both knobs. Place a stool or chair about two feet from the edge of the door. Stand arms' length away from the door. Then, lightly grasp the knobs for balance, and slowly bend your knees and lower your body as though you were sitting down. Take three seconds to lower yourself the first inch and seven seconds to go all the way down, until your bottom just touches the stool. Then reverse and rise back up. Be careful not to pull yourself up with your arms—use the muscles of your buttocks and thighs.

●**Side-lying leg lifts.** Try this exercise without ankle weights at first. If it's too easy, start with five-pound weights. Lie on your left side with your head propped on your left hand. Bend your left leg slightly so that your right leg rests on top of the calf. Slowly raise your right leg up toward the ceiling, moving from the hip. Take three seconds to move it the first inch and seven seconds to raise it all the way. Pause at the top, tightly squeeze the hip and buttock muscles for a few seconds,

then slowly lower the leg back down. Repeat with the other leg.

●**Single-leg curls.** Attach one five-pound weight to your right ankle. The weight may be too light, but it's a good place to start. Lean forward and put both hands on a stool or chair…keeping your right knee slightly bent and spine straight.

Curl your right leg so that the heel nears your bottom. Take three seconds to curl the leg the first inch and seven seconds to curl it the rest of the way. Pause at the top, squeeze the muscles in the back of your thigh, then slowly reverse direction. Repeat with the other leg.

●**Side shoulder raise and overhead press.** This movement combines two exercises. Start with five-pound dumbbells. With a dumbbell in each hand, sit on a chair with your back straight and your feet flat on the floor. Slowly raise the weights away from both of your sides, taking three seconds to move them the first inch and seven seconds to raise them until they're parallel to the floor. Pause at the top for a few seconds, then slowly lower the weights.

Without resting, move to the second phase of the exercise. Elbows bent, hold the weights at shoulder height, then slowly raise them overhead, taking three seconds to move them the first inch and seven seconds to go all the way up. Pause for a second, then gradually lower the weights until they're back at shoulder height. Do not lock your elbows at the top. Let your muscles support the weights.

●**Single-arm back pull-ups.** You need a stool or chair and a six- to eight-pound dumbbell. Hold the dumbbell in your right hand…then face the stool with your left leg forward…and support yourself with your left hand on the stool. Let your right arm hang beside the stool.

Slowly pull the dumbbell back and upward, taking three seconds to move it the first inch and seven seconds to raise it all the way. Your right elbow will be facing up and behind you.

Pause at the top, squeeze the arm and back muscles for a few seconds, then lower the weight back down. Don't let your arm hang down at the end of the movement. Keep tension on the muscles all the time. Repeat with the other arm.

● **Biceps curls.** Sit on a stool or straight-back chair with a five-pound dumbbell in each hand. Tuck your elbows into your sides, and keep them there throughout the exercise. The only thing that should move is your lower arm.

Curl the dumbbells toward your shoulders, taking just three seconds to move them the first inch and seven seconds to curl them all the way. Squeeze the muscles in the forearms and upper arms for a few seconds at the top of the movement, then slowly lower the weights back down.

● **Shoulder shrugs.** Sit on a stool or straight-back chair with a 10-pound dumbbell in each hand. Let your arms hang down away from your hips, with the elbows slightly bent.

Then, raise up the tops of your shoulders as though you're trying to touch them to your earlobes. Sit up straight. Don't slouch forward or backward. Take three seconds to move your shoulders the first inch and seven seconds to raise them as far as they'll go. Pause at the top to squeeze the muscles in your shoulders, then lower them back down.

● **Abdominal crunches.** Lie on your back with your feet flat on the floor and your knees bent at a 90° angle. Tuck a rolled towel under your lower back...hold your arms straight in front of you...and keep your chin tucked into your chest. Curl your torso upward and forward, taking three seconds to move the first inch and seven seconds to move forward. Do not try to sit all the way up. Keep your lower back in contact with the towel. Pause and squeeze abdominal muscles at the top of the movement, then slowly lower your torso

down. Don't rest your shoulders on the floor at the end. As soon as they brush the floor, repeat the exercise.

Slow Burn illustrations by Shawn Banner.

The 10-Minute Workout

Ten minutes of jumping rope equals 30 minutes of running at a pace of more than five miles an hour.

To be sure the rope is the right length: Stand on its center with feet together. Hold the rope against your sides—the handles should come within a few inches of your armpits.

Before jumping, warm up with 20 arm circles. While exercising, jump high enough for the rope to clear your feet.

Dan Robey, marketing and communications consultant, Miami, and author of *The Power of Positive Habits* (Abritt).

Avoid Germs At the Gym

With many people using the same equipment day after day, you'll want to protect yourself from germs at the gym. Wipe down machines before and after use. Use disinfectant spray if the gym supplies it or carry moist towelettes in your gym bag. Also, wash hands thoroughly before going home, especially if you have been using dumbbells and holding bike handlebars.

Shirley Archer, MA, health and wellness educator and fitness expert, Stanford University School of Medicine, Palo Alto, CA. She is the author of *The Everything Weight Training Book* (Adams Media).

5

Natural Solutions

Uncommon Cures for Asthma, Depression, Headaches and Other Common Ailments

Even though numerous major medical centers have begun combining alternative healing techniques with conventional medical therapies, most medical doctors in private practice still don't recommend these approaches to their patients. That's because most MDs aren't familiar enough with alternative medicine to know what works and what doesn't.

Here are four underused alternative therapies you may want to try*...

ACUPUNCTURE

In the US, acupuncture is used primarily to treat chronic pain and various addictions. The

*Before trying any of these treatments, consult your physician to ensure that they do not interfere with any other therapy you are receiving.

procedure is believed to stimulate the different types of nerves that activate parts of the brain involved in healing and in the transmission and perception of pain.

Each acupuncture session typically requires the insertion of eight to 12 needles, which usually penetrate the skin one to one-and-a-half inches. The procedure causes little to no pain. And, symptoms generally diminish within just six sessions.

Conditions that often improve with acupuncture treatments...

●**Asthma.** Prescription inhalers and medication are the first-line treatment for asthma—but adding acupuncture treatments usually helps to reduce the severity and the frequency of future attacks. In some instances, the use of acupuncture enables patients to decrease their asthma medication.

Larry Altshuler, MD, a former preceptor of the University of Oklahoma College of Medicine. He also is founder and medical director of the Balanced Healing Medical Center in Oklahoma City, and author of *Balanced Healing —Combining Modern Medicine with Safe & Effective Alternative Therapies* (Harbor).

●**Depression.** Acupuncture is believed to re-balance the brain neurotransmitters involved in depression.

In our clinic, we usually begin by prescribing acupuncture along with ongoing psychotherapy and natural antidepressants, such as St. John's wort—300 milligrams (mg) daily…ginkgo biloba—160 to 240 mg daily…and/or fish oil—4 grams (g) daily.

If there's still no improvement in the patient's depression, we then prescribe antidepressant medication.

●**Hay fever.** Acupuncture is the fastest and most effective way I have found to reduce or eliminate respiratory allergies. Most people can discontinue their medications following acupuncture treatment.

●**Migraines.** Acupuncture is one of the best treatments for an acute migraine attack, typically relieving pain within 30 minutes.

Each subsequent session also decreases the frequency and severity of attacks and may even cure them completely.

Most people can discontinue their medication, although some will still take it for occasional headaches or if they can't get in to see an acupuncturist.

●**Smoking.** Almost 80% of people can stop smoking with the help of acupuncture, according to studies.

If you try acupuncture, consult a practitioner trained in traditional Chinese acupuncture and certified by the National Certification Commission for Acupuncture and Oriental Medicine (703-548-9004, *www.nccaom.org*).

CRANIAL-SACRAL MANIPULATION

This technique, which is administered by a doctor of osteopathy (DO), involves manipulating the bones in the face and skull. It helps correct misalignments caused by obstructions, overloaded muscles and joints, and other structural problems in various parts of the spine.

Symptoms typically diminish with three to six treatments.

Conditions that often improve with cranial-sacral manipulation…

●**Sinus problems.** Sinusitis brought on by a structural obstruction responds well to this type of treatment.

●**Temporalmandibular joint (TMJ) syndrome.** Manipulation can be useful to ease the headaches associated with this misalignment of the TMJ, which connects the jawbone to the skull—especially when the misalignment results from an accident.

●**Tinnitus (ringing in the ears).** Manipulation helps to correct structural abnormalities in the bones surrounding the ear, which can lead to tinnitus.

If you want to try cranial-sacral manipulation, consult an osteopathic physician certified by the American Osteopathic Association (800-621-1773, *www.osteopathic.org*).

HYPNOSIS

In this mind-body technique, the hypnotist places you in a deeply relaxed state and makes positive suggestions regarding your emotions, habits and bodily functions. Symptoms typically diminish with two to three sessions.

Conditions that often improve with hypnosis treatments…

●**Anxiety and phobias.** In the cases where psychotherapy brings no improvement, hypnosis is often effective.

●**Chronic pain.** Hypnosis can decrease ongoing pain by addressing emotional and psychological triggers.

●**Irritable bowel syndrome (IBS).** Persistent IBS frequently has underlying psychological causes, which quite often can be alleviated through hypnosis. One recent study discovered that hypnosis therapy alleviated the symptoms in 90% of IBS sufferers.

●**Overeating.** Hypnotic suggestion can help curb the urge to eat between meals and reduce the desire to eat unhealthy foods.

If you try hypnosis, consult with a hypnotist belonging to the American Society of Clinical Hypnosis (630-980-4740, *www.asch.net*) or to the National Guild of Hypnotists (603-429-9438, *www.ngh.net*).

MASSAGE

Massage boosts levels of the feel-good neurotransmitter known as *serotonin* while lowering levels of stress hormones.

Two commonly used types of massage are Swedish massage (which uses gentle pressure and broad stroking movements to help relax the muscles) or shiatsu massage (in which finger pressure is placed on key healing points along the body).

Symptoms typically begin to diminish after the first massage.

Conditions that frequently improve with massage therapy…

•**Anxiety.** Massage is an excellent treatment for reducing mild anxiety states. It has been shown to reduce or block the effects of *cortisol* and *epinephrine,* hormones that can damage body tissue when they are produced at excessive levels during anxiety-provoking or stressful conditions.

•**Back problems.** Massage will provide the most relief when it's used in conjunction with over-the-counter nonsteroidal anti-inflammatory drugs (NSAIDs), hot/cold compresses and/or ultrasound treatment, which incorporates high-frequency sound (20,000 Hz) and heat.

•**Tension headaches.** Pressure applied to trigger points in the neck, forehead and temples relieves most tension headaches.

Thirty-three states now license massage therapists. To find one, contact the American Massage Therapy Association at 888-843-2682 or on the Web, *www.amtamassage.org.*

You also can ask your doctor for a referral.

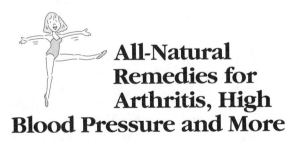

All-Natural Remedies for Arthritis, High Blood Pressure and More

Mark A. Stengler, ND, a naturopathic physician in private practice, La Jolla, CA. He is also associate clinical professor at both Bastyr University in Kenmore, WA, and the National College of Naturopathic Medicine in Portland, OR. He is the author of 15 books on natural healing, including *The Natural Physician's Healing Therapies* (Bottom Line Books) available at *www.bottomlinesecrets.com.*

The big advantages of most conventional drugs are that they work quickly and are standardized for predictable effects.

However, herbs, vitamins, minerals and other supplements can offer a safer approach because they are less likely to trigger side effects. Be patient—they may take as long as six to eight weeks to work.

Important: Never start a new treatment before consulting your doctor, especially if you currently are taking medication.

Here are six common health problems and the best natural treatments for each…

HYPERTENSION

About 50 million Americans have high blood pressure, the leading cause of stroke and cardiovascular disease. Conventional drugs work, but they often cause side effects such as fatigue, dizziness and anxiety.

Patients who have mild to moderate hypertension—a systolic (top) number of 140 to 179 and a diastolic (bottom) number of 90 to 109—often can achieve normal blood pressure with a low-sodium diet, exercise and weight loss. *These natural treatments also help…*

•**Hawthorn.** *300 milligrams (mg) three times daily.** This herb dilates arteries and improves coronary blood flow, reducing blood pressure. It also is a mild diuretic that reduces blood volume. Most patients who take hawthorn have a drop in blood pressure of 10 to 15 points over eight weeks. Once blood pressure is down, you may be able to reduce the dosage or stop taking the herb altogether. Ask your doctor.

•**Magnesium.** *250 mg twice daily.* You can take this with hawthorn to relax artery walls and increase blood flow.

INSOMNIA

The side effects of over-the-counter (OTC) and prescription insomnia drugs include daytime drowsiness and a high risk of addiction. Try out these natural treatments. Take each separately for two nights before making a decision about which works best for you.

•**Valerian.** *300 to 500 mg (or 60 drops of tincture) taken 30 to 60 minutes before bedtime and/or if you awaken during the night.* This herb appears to increase brain levels of *serotonin,* a neurotransmitter that's relaxing. It's also

*Recommended dosages are for people who weigh 150 to 200 pounds. Adjust the dosage up or down according to your weight. Consult your doctor for more details.

thought to increase the amount of the neuro-transmitter *gamma-aminobutyric acid* (GABA), which has a calming effect on the brain. Valerian is just as effective as the sleep drug *oxazepam* (Serax) but does not cause the "hangover" effect.

- **5-hydroxytryptophan (5-HTP).** *100 to 200 mg taken 30 to 60 minutes before bedtime and/or if you awaken during the night.* Levels of this amino acid, which helps elevate brain levels of serotonin, often are lower in people with insomnia.

- **Melatonin.** *0.3 mg taken 30 to 60 minutes before bedtime.* Levels of this sleep hormone rise during the hours of darkness—but many adults, especially those age 65 and older, have insufficient levels to achieve restful sleep.

SEASONAL ALLERGIES

It is best to avoid pollen as much as possible—by keeping windows closed and running an air purifier in the bedroom...staying inside during peak pollen times (usually mornings and evenings)...and washing bedding regularly. *The following natural treatments can be taken together and can prevent allergies...*

- **Nettle leaf.** *600 mg three times daily.* This herbal antihistamine is effective for mild to moderate allergies and causes none of the drowsiness of some antihistamines.

Helpful: After using nettle leaf for up to two weeks, cut the dose in half. The lower dose will be effective once the initial loads of histamine are reduced.

- **Quercetin.** *1,000 mg three times daily.* It belongs to a class of water-soluble plant pigments called *flavonoids.* Quercetin strengthens the immune system and inhibits the release of histamine in people with allergies.

PROSTATE ENLARGEMENT

About half of men age 50 and older suffer from benign prostatic hypertrophy, an enlargement of the prostate gland that can interfere with urination. The prescription drug *finasteride* (Proscar) will shrink this gland but may cause impotence. The following natural treatments don't bring on this side effect. *I often advise my patients to take all three for maximum effectiveness...*

- **Saw palmetto.** *320 mg daily.* This herb inhibits an enzyme that converts *testosterone* to *dihydrotestosterone,* the form of the hormone that fuels prostate growth.

- **Nettle root (not leaf).** *240 mg daily.* It reduces the hormonal stimulation of the prostate in a different way than saw palmetto and often is used in conjunction with saw palmetto.

- **Zinc.** *90 mg daily for two months, then 50 mg daily as a maintenance dose.* Also, take 3 to 5 mg of copper daily. Long-term supplementation with zinc depletes copper from the body.

OSTEOARTHRITIS

This is the leading cause of joint pain and stiffness. Conventional treatments (aspirin, *ibuprofen,* etc.) reduce symptoms but often cause stomach bleeding. The following natural treatments don't have this side effect. *They can be taken together...*

- **Glucosamine.** *1,500 to 2,500 mg daily.* Found naturally in the body, glucosamine promotes new cartilage growth and reduces inflammation. A four-week German study of patients with osteoarthritis of the knee reported that ibuprofen resulted in faster pain relief—but glucosamine supplements brought comparable pain relief after two weeks and were much less likely to cause side effects.

After a few months, you may be able to cut back to 500 mg daily. If you discontinue glucosamine completely, benefits wear off after a few months.

- **SAMe.** *400 to 800 mg daily.* Pronounced "Sammy," this chemical compound (*S-adenosylmethionine*) is found in all living cells. It promotes flexibility of joint cartilage and cartilage repair. One German study of 20,641 patients found that 71% of those who took SAMe supplements for eight weeks reported good or very good results.

MENOPAUSAL DISCOMFORT

Hot flashes and night sweats are caused by declines in progesterone and estrogen. Conventional hormone replacement therapy reduces discomfort but may increase risk of heart disease, cancer and other ailments. *Natural treatments without these risks (use one or both)...*

●**Black cohosh.** *80 mg daily for mild to moderate discomfort…160 mg daily for severe symptoms.* This herb inhibits the release of *lutenizing hormone* (LH) by the pituitary gland. Elevated levels of LH after menopause is the primary cause of hot flashes, night sweats and other symptoms.

●**Natural progesterone.** *20 mg of cream (about one-quarter teaspoon) twice daily.* Natural progesterone, derived from wild yams, is as effective as synthetic forms but less likely to cause side effects, such as water retention and weight gain. Apply the cream to breasts, forearms or cheeks for maximum absorption.

Important: Only use natural progesterone under a doctor's care. Blood levels have to be monitored very carefully, generally every six to 12 months.

What You Must Know About Inflammation

William Joel Meggs, MD, PhD, professor and chief of toxicology, and vice chair for clinical affairs, department of emergency medicine at the Brody School of Medicine at East Carolina University, Greenville, NC. He is author of *The Inflammation Cure: How to Combat the Hidden Factor Behind Heart Disease, Arthritis, Asthma, Diabetes, Alzheimer's Disease, Osteoporosis and Other Diseases of Aging* (McGraw-Hill).

Every time you fight a cold, sprain your ankle or cut your finger, your body reacts to protect or heal itself through a complex process called inflammation.

Marked by redness, swelling, heat and pain, inflammation involves the release of a cascade of chemical messengers in the body called *cytokines*. Depending on the type and severity of inflammation, the cytokines can trigger the immune system to attack and destroy foreign invaders, such as viruses or bacteria, or to heal a wound.

But too much inflammation, due to an infection, irritation, allergies or other reasons, can cause serious damage.

Examples: Inflammation of the joints contributes to arthritis, inflammation of the skin leads to dermatitis…inflammation of the gums leads to periodontitis.* In fact, most of life's most serious diseases—including heart disease, Alzheimer's disease and even some cancers—are fueled by inflammation.

INFLAMMATION CONNECTION

Scientists have known for generations that inflammation causes disease. Now, researchers are finding that many inflammation-related diseases are connected. This discovery could lead to more effective prevention and treatment of these types of diseases.

Imagine placing one drop of blue dye in a glass of water. The dye starts out concentrated in one spot, but eventually all the water turns blue. Similarly, when there is inflammation in one part of the body, repercussions develop in other—often distant and otherwise unrelated—parts of the body.

Example: Cytokines released in response to inflammation associated with atherosclerosis circulate throughout the body and seem to be associated with gum disease, type 2 diabetes and other inflammatory conditions.

Inflammation-related diseases include…

●**Atherosclerosis and cardiovascular disease.** High blood pressure or other irritation causes damage to artery walls. This will trigger inflammation that attempts to "repair" the damage with plaque—the same way that we use spackle to patch holes in walls. Exposure to cigarette smoke and air pollution, high cholesterol and other factors can cause this process to go awry. Then, instead of a nice, smooth patch of plaque, thick layers accumulate until the arteries become blocked.

But heart attacks also occur in people with small quantities of plaque in their arteries. In these cases, inflammation can make even tiny plaques fragile. If there is additional irritation, these plaques can burst, causing clots that block the arteries and result in heart attacks or stroke.

What you can do: Have your C-reactive protein (CRP) levels tested. This protein, which can be measured with a $20 blood test, is a powerful predictor of future heart disease. Even mildly elevated CRP *doubles* the risk for a future

*In medical terminology, the suffix *–itis* indicates inflammation.

heart attack. In addition, elevated CRP can increase risk for stroke.

●**Diabetes.** Recent studies have suggested that chronic and low-grade inflammation may increase the risk of developing type 2 diabetes, a condition in which the body's cells become resistant to insulin, a hormone that controls the amount of sugar in the blood.

It's well known that people with diabetes are at greater risk for heart disease...and now some scientists believe that the chronic inflammation associated with early atherosclerosis may actually contribute to the onset of diabetes.

What you can do: Decrease your overall inflammation load by losing weight. Body fat alone raises the levels of some pro-inflammatory body chemicals. Also, visit your dentist. Studies have shown that treating gum disease helps people with diabetes control their blood sugar better.

●**Fatigue.** Whenever you have unexplained fatigue, you have inflammation somewhere in the body. The cytokines released during inflammation affect the brain to cause fatigue.

The reason we feel so exhausted whenever we have the flu is because of the inflammatory processes that gear up in the infected tissues to fight the virus.

What you can do: If you experience debilitating fatigue that interferes with work and daily activities for more than two weeks, see your doctor for a checkup to make sure you aren't suffering from an underlying disease, such as a virus, allergy or cancer.

MORE WAYS TO FIGHT OFF INFLAMMATION

Reducing inflammation in the body is the best way to curb your risk for inflammation-related diseases, as well as age-related debilities, such as muscle weakness, an unsteady or slow gait and unintentional weight loss.

Because tobacco smoke is the single largest contributor to inflammation, anyone who still smokes must stop now. Avoiding secondhand smoke and other forms of air pollution, including furnace fumes and vehicle exhaust, is also important.

Other strategies...

●**Start exercising.** Exercise—of any kind—is one of the most effective inflammation reducers. Studies have shown that walking 30 minutes every day cuts CRP levels in half—and reduces the risk for heart attack by 20%.

Recommended: Take music with you. People who have difficulty exercising are able to walk farther when they listen to music they like.

●**Change cleaning habits.** Chemicals found in many cleaning products are irritants that can bring on inflammation of the mucous membranes of the eyes, nose, throat and lungs when inhaled. People with chronic asthma and sinus problems are most susceptible. Symptoms, such as headache, fatigue and wheezing, can result from irritant exposure.

Avoid breathing bleach and ammonia fumes, which are irritants that can lead to inflammation.

Never combine cleaning products. Combining bleach and ammonia can release highly toxic chloramine gas. When combined with other cleaning chemicals, toilet bowl cleaners containing hydrochloric acid can release chlorine gas, which was utilized as a chemical warfare agent during World War I.

Best approach: Use nontoxic cleaning products, such as those by Citra-Solv or Seventh Generation. They can be found at most health food stores and some supermarkets.

●**Use unscented products whenever possible.** Many of the chemicals often used in air fresheners, fragrances, perfumes, fabric softeners, detergents and scented household products can cause inflammation of the mucous membranes and skin.

To limit your exposure to potentially harmful artificial ingredients, personal hygiene products, such as deodorants, soaps, shampoo and anything else you use on your body, should also be unscented, whenever possible.

●**Limit meat consumption to two to three servings a week.** Animal products (with the exception of fish) are among the top inflammation triggers. Studies show that populations that eat more red meat have a higher risk for heart disease and some forms of cancer.

Dairy products rich in saturated fat, such as butter, should be used in moderation.

●**Eat fish three times a week.** Salmon, tuna, bluefish, sturgeon, herring and sardines are among the richest sources of omega-3 fatty acids, which have an anti-inflammatory effect in the body. Avoid fish with a high mercury content. This includes shark, swordfish, tilefish and king mackerel.

As an alternative, take a 1,000-milligram (mg) fish oil supplement or one tablespoon of flax-seed oil daily.

Caution: If you take blood-thinning medications, such as *warfarin* (Coumadin), check with your doctor before using these supplements.

●**Limit alcohol consumption to one to two drinks each day.** Moderate alcohol use increases life expectancy and reduces risk for coronary artery disease. Wine and grape juice contain chemicals, such as *tyrosol* and *caffeic acid,* which have additional benefits in modulating pro-inflammatory compounds.

Caution: Heavy alcohol consumption may lead to addiction, liver damage and some types of cancer.

Supercharge Your Immunity with Herbs

James A. Duke, PhD, a leading authority on medicinal plants and former chief of the US Department of Agriculture Plant Laboratory. He now teaches at the Tai Sophia Institute, center for patient care and graduate education in complementary medicine, Laurel, MD. He is the author of *Dr. Duke's Essential Herbs: 13 Vital Herbs You Need to Disease-Proof Your Body, Boost Your Energy, and Lengthen Your Life* (Rodale).

Medicinal herbs are rich in antioxidants that maintain health and slow the aging process. They also can prevent or alleviate age-related problems, such as arthritis, high blood pressure and failing vision.

World-renowned botanist James A. Duke, PhD, knows which herbs are most essential to healthy aging. Dr. Duke, age 74, has a half-acre medicinal herb garden at his homestead in Fulton, MD. Here he tells us about eight potent herbs that he uses himself.

While these herbs have no significant side effects and are far safer than most synthetic drugs, it is always wise to consult your doctor before treating a medical problem yourself.

Some herbs can interact with the prescription and nonprescription drugs, either magnifying or weakening their effects. In addition, some people may be allergic to herbs. Be alert to symptoms, such as a rash, when taking any herb.

With your doctor's approval, you can take these herbs all at the same time, along with vitamins, if you wish. Follow the dosages suggested on the labels.

BILBERRY: VISION DISORDERS

Bilberry is rich in *anthocyanins,* chemicals that keep the capillary walls strong and flexible. It also is loaded with antioxidants that defend delicate tissue against free radical damage.

In particular, bilberry protects the retina and its blood supply, preventing and improving vision disorders, such as macular degeneration.

Bilberry can ward off other eye problems, too, including cataracts, glaucoma and poor night vision.

CELERY SEED: GOUT AND ARTHRITIS

I have a special fondness for this herb, which has protected me from agonizing attacks of gout for the last seven years. It lowers blood levels of uric acid as effectively as *allopurinol,* the drug commonly prescribed for gout.

Celery seed, available in capsule form, also contains 25 anti-inflammatory compounds that can reduce the pain and swelling of arthritis. It has chemicals that make blood vessels relax and open, helping to alleviate high blood pressure and angina (chest pain caused by deficient blood flow to the heart).

In folk medicine, celery seed is reputed to be a digestive aid. It is used to relieve gas and heartburn, though its effectiveness has yet to be clinically proven.

ECHINACEA: COLDS AND FLU

This popular herbal medicine is a powerful ally against colds and flu. The purple coneflower from which it comes has been used medicinally by Native Americans for centuries. At least three of the chemicals it contains— *caffeic acid, echinacoside* and *cichoric acid*— have known antiviral properties. In addition, echinacea also helps to boost the body's own infection-fighting powers.

Take echinacea at the first sign of an upper-respiratory infection or flu. I also take it when I know I'll be in crowds or around other sources of infection.

This is not an herb for everyday use—the immune system eventually could stop responding to it. I do not take it for more than eight weeks in a row.

GARLIC: BLOOD PRESSURE AND CHOLESTEROL

This pungent bulb was prescribed by Hippocrates, the fifth-century BC Greek physician, and cited as a cure-all in an ancient Sanskrit manuscript. Today, we attribute its medicinal effectiveness to a high concentration of sulfur compounds.

Garlic lowers blood pressure and cholesterol. There also is evidence that it can reduce the risk of cancer, particularly in the gastrointestinal tract.

Garlic contains at least 25 germ-killing compounds and fights off bacterial, viral and fungal infections.

Eat at least one raw clove or four cooked cloves daily…or take garlic capsules.

HAWTHORN: POTENT HEART DRUG

An extract made from this flowering shrub can be useful against irregular heart rhythm, angina and shortness of breath. Hawthorn contains seven compounds known to prevent dangerous clotting and three that lower blood pressure. One study at the University of Madras in India suggests that hawthorn also may help reduce cholesterol.

MILK THISTLE: LIVER PROTECTION

The liver, the organ vital to detoxifying the blood, is under constant assault by pollution. Alcohol, also, is bad for the liver. Milk thistle, a relative of the artichoke, appears to protect the liver. It contains *silymarin,* which strengthens cell membranes and boosts the organ's ability to repair itself. Milk thistle even has been used to treat hepatitis A and C.

I take milk thistle capsules when I'm traveling and will be exposed to smog. If I lived in a major city with pollution problems, I would take it every day.

I also take it before a celebration, when I may be drinking a bit more alcohol than usual.

You can take silymarin capsules or eat milk thistle seeds, available in health food stores, as you would sunflower seeds.

SAW PALMETTO: PROSTATE PROBLEMS

At least half of men over age 50 have some trouble when urinating because benign prostate enlargement chokes off the flow. An extract of saw palmetto, a tropical shrub, has been used for years to treat this problem. A 1998 review in *The Journal of the American Medical Association* concluded that saw palmetto facilitates urination in men with prostate problems about as well as medication. Natural chemicals in the herb appear to block a testosterone-type hormone that promotes prostate growth. Men without prostate problems may choose to take it as a preventive measure.

Saw palmetto also may slow down male pattern baldness.

TURMERIC: HEART PROBLEMS AND ARTHRITIS

This spice, made from the root of the tropical plant *Curcuma longa,* is a common ingredient in mustard and Indian food—it's what makes curry bright yellow. Turmeric is packed with antioxidants and contains powerful anti-inflammatory compounds called COX-2 inhibitors—the power behind such arthritis drugs as Celebrex and Vioxx.

Some research suggests that turmeric can stop inflammation about half as effectively as steroids such as cortisone—but without all the troubling side effects. This makes it a valuable ally against arthritis. In addition, turmeric protects the heart. It makes blood platelets less likely to clump and form dangerous clots. It also fights cholesterol buildup in the arteries.

Turmeric is available as an herbal preparation. You also can add turmeric to your diet when cooking. I like to use it to make a curried celery soup.

WHICH BRANDS TO BUY

Herbal products are sold by many manufacturers, but there is no federal regulation to ensure quality control.

To be safe, select the major brands, such as Nature's Herb, Nature's Way and Solgar. These are available at most supermarkets, drugstores and health food stores. Buy preparations that clearly indicate on the labels the exact amounts of active ingredients.

Black Tea Boosts Immunity

People who consumed five cups of black tea a day for one week had five times more germ-fighting proteins in their blood than they did before they started to drink tea.

Theory: The immune-boosting capacity of black tea is derived from *L-theanine,* an amino acid that is found in black tea as well as other nonherbal teas.

Good news: Regularly drinking just two cups a day may confer many of the same benefits.

Because tea can reduce absorption of iron, people with iron-deficiency anemia should be sure to limit their intake of tea.

Jack Bukowski, MD, PhD, assistant clinical professor of medicine, Harvard Medical School and Brigham and Women's Hospital, both in Boston.

Secrets to Living Longer: Miraculous Supplements

Ronald Klatz, MD, president of the American Academy of Anti-Aging Medicine, Chicago, *www.worldhealth.net,* and cofounder and vice president of the National Academy of Sports Medicine, Calabasas, CA. He is author of 30 books, including *The New Anti-Aging Revolution* (Basic Health).

Aging damages the cells in our bodies—in our eyes, ears, brain, heart, lungs, skin, etc. The cells are assaulted by free radicals (by-products of the cells' normal metabolism) as well as by sunlight and pollutants. The accumulation of toxins hinders cell growth and repair. If we can prevent or reverse this cell damage, we can slow aging and live longer.

An important way to combat cell damage is with antiaging supplements. Below are seven of the most effective. You can take one, several or all of them.

Important: Don't take supplements without the approval of a qualified physician. To find one in your area, contact the American Academy of Anti-Aging Medicine at 773-528-4333 or go to the organization's Web site, *www.world health.net,* and click on "Physician Directories."

ALPHA-GPC

This nutrient, derived from soy, provides high levels of *choline,* which protects brain cells. It also increases levels of the neurotransmitter *acetylcholine,* which triggers an increased release of the human growth hormone (HGH)—a hormone that is naturally present in the human body when we are young but that decreases steadily as we age.

Studies show that increased HGH can reduce body fat, boost energy levels and restore youthful immune function.

In animal studies, alpha-GPC corrected age-related brain decline. And, in human studies, it helped stroke victims retain cognitive functioning and improved the mental functioning and mood of people with dementia.

Dose: 600 to 1,200 milligrams (mg) per day.*

ASHWAGANDHA ROOT

This herb is used extensively in Ayurveda, the traditional medicine of India. It stimulates immunity and, as an antioxidant, reduces cell-damaging free radicals, particularly within the brain cells. The herb's anti-inflammatory properties have been shown to be helpful for such inflammatory conditions as arthritis.

In one study, it increased oxygen-carrying hemoglobin, which rejuvenates cells. In addition, 70% of the men in the study said that their sexual performance improved—some men even reported fewer gray hairs.

Dose: 3 to 6 grams (g) of the dried root in capsule form per day.

BETA-GLUCAN

This nutrient is derived from baker's yeast, young rye plants and medicinal mushrooms. It

*Dosages vary by body weight. Consult your doctor for more details.

activates *macrophages,* key immune cells that fight bacteria, viruses and other organisms that cause disease. Beta-glucan enhances the effectiveness of conventional antibiotic therapy. It acts as a free radical scavenger, removing cells damaged by exposure to radiation, chemotherapy and environmental pollutants. It also decreases total and LDL (bad) cholesterol while increasing HDL (good) cholesterol. In addition, it reduces risk of infection by stimulating white blood cell activity.

Dose: 300 to 1,000 mg per day.

LEMON BALM

Lemon balm is an important antioxidant. It contains a high concentration of *phenols,* chemicals that fight cell-damaging toxins. This herb can improve sleep…decrease pain caused by inflammatory conditions including arthritis…boost mental functioning…and combat viruses and bacteria.

Dose: 1,000 to 1,500 mg per day.

Caution: Avoid lemon balm if you have glaucoma. Some animal studies have shown that it may raise pressure in the eye, which can worsen the condition.

OMEGA-3 FATTY ACIDS

Also known as essential fatty acids (EFAs), omega-3 fatty acids aren't manufactured by the human body and must be supplied by diet or supplements. They are found primarily in fish but also are present in smaller amounts in green, leafy vegetables…soybeans…nuts…and flaxseed and canola oils.

Omega-3s decrease blood levels of triglycerides (bad fats) and homocysteine (an artery-damaging amino acid) and decrease blood pressure. They help thin the blood, preventing blood clots. These effects lower the risk of heart disease and stroke, the number-one and number-three killers of Americans (cancer is number two).

Omega-3s also act like anti-inflammatories, helpful in the treatment of such autoimmune diseases as rheumatoid arthritis, chronic inflammatory bowel disease and psoriasis. They are a building block of the outer layer of brain cells and may help treat depression.

Dose: 3 to 10 g a day of fish oil capsules. Follow instructions on label.

Caution: If you have heart disease or diabetes, consult your doctor before taking these high doses, which may raise cholesterol and blood sugar levels.

To get omega-3 fatty acids from your diet, eat oily fish three to four times a week. These include mackerel, salmon, sea bass, trout, herring, sardines, sablefish (black cod), anchovies and tuna. Use omega-3–rich canola oil in cooking and salad dressings.

EVENING PRIMROSE OIL

Evening primrose oil is derived from the seeds of the evening primrose plant. The active ingredient is *gamma linolenic acid* (GLA), an omega-6 fatty acid.

As the body ages, it loses its ability to convert dietary fats into GLA. Supplementing with evening primrose oil is important in combating the general effects of aging. It also may help in treating rheumatoid arthritis, diabetes, nerve damage (neuropathy), multiple sclerosis and Alzheimer's-related memory problems.

Dose: 3,000 to 6,000 mg daily, which contains about 270 to 540 mg of GLA.

Caution: Evening primrose oil may worsen temporal-lobe epilepsy. It should be avoided by epileptics and schizophrenics who are prescribed phenothiazine epileptogenic drugs.

RESVERATROL

This is a naturally occurring antioxidant that's found in many plants—including the skins of grapes. Red wine is the main dietary source. Resveratrol decreases the "stickiness" of blood platelets, reducing the risk of blood clots. It also may help prevent the development and progression of various cancers.

Dose: 200 to 650 micrograms (mcg) daily. One eight-ounce glass of red wine contains roughly 640 mcg.

Get the Most from Vitamin and Mineral Supplements

Take your vitamins and minerals at the right times and in the right combinations to maximize effectiveness.

Examples: Take vitamin C by itself—it interferes with the absorption of some vitamins—and not with meals. Taking vitamins A and E and zinc together makes them work better. Take calcium and magnesium by themselves for maximum absorption—but with food. Take selenium by itself, between meals.

Information: National Institutes of Health Office of Dietary Supplements (301-435-2920, *http://dietary-supplements.info.nih.gov*).

Andrew L. Rubman, ND, adjunct professor of medicine, Lane College of Integrative Medicine in Orlando, FL, and medical director, Southbury Clinic for Traditional Medicines in Southbury, CT, *www.naturopath.org.*

More from Andrew Rubman...

Glucomannan: A Wonder Supplement

Most people would benefit a lot from taking the powdered root of the Japanese konjac plant (*glucomannan*) every day. By improving the liver's ability to excrete fat-soluble waste, it will lower cholesterol...promote weight loss... alleviate menopausal symptoms...and relieve headaches and premenstrual syndrome. Take one capsule before your largest meal. Consult your doctor before starting any supplement.

Cost: About $12 for 60 capsules, available in health food stores.

Fish Oil Supplements Are Harmful for Some

Fish oil supplements can be dangerous for some people. They can increase the risk of hemorrhagic stroke in people who have bleeding disorders or uncontrolled hypertension and those taking anticoagulants. Large doses—more than 3 grams (g) every day—can suppress the immune system, increase glucose levels in people with diabetes and cause nausea, diarrhea and other side effects.

Bottom line: Consult your physician before taking any supplement, and take only the recommended dose.

UC Berkeley Wellness Letter, 632 Broadway, New York City 10012.

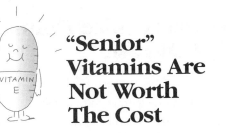

"Senior" Vitamins Are Not Worth The Cost

Special "senior" formula vitamins offer little more than regular multivitamin/mineral supplements—even for those age 65 or older. Formulas, including Centrum Silver and Geritol Extend, may provide more of the B vitamins but hardly any additional amounts of other important vitamins and minerals, such as vitamin E and calcium. Seniors require more nutritional supplementation because of their decreased ability to absorb nutrients and their generally less nutritious diets. However, basic all-purpose multivitamins should be sufficient. They're less expensive, too.

Michael Hirt, MD, founder and medical director, Center for Integrative Medicine, Tarzana, CA.

Protect Your Stomach From Daily Aspirin Therapy

Commonly taken as a blood thinner or pain reliever, aspirin can irritate or damage the stomach lining.

Recent finding: Taking vitamin C along with aspirin can mitigate this damage.

Theory: Vitamin C decreases levels of free radicals, unstable molecules that damage the stomach lining.

If you take daily aspirin therapy: Ask your doctor about taking 250 milligrams (mg) of vitamin C along with the aspirin.

Thorsten Pohle, MD, internal medicine specialist, Medicinal Clinic and Polyclinic B, University of Muenster, Germany.

Cranberry Juice Fights Heart Disease

Cranberry juice has long been used to help prevent urinary-tract infections.

New finding: Drinking three eight-ounce glasses of cranberry juice daily for one month raises HDL ("good") cholesterol levels by 10%. This theoretically would reduce heart disease risk by about 40%.

Theory: The juice's antioxidant activity confers the heart-protecting benefit.

Helpful: Only drink unsweetened varieties, which contain half the calories of regular cranberry juice.

Joe Vinson, PhD, professor of chemistry, University of Scranton, PA.

Split Peas for Heart Health

Better than soybeans for heart protection are kudzu and yellow split peas. These legumes are richer in *genistein* and *dadzein*—isoflavones thought to protect against heart disease—than soybeans. Kudzu seedlings contain at least 10 times more than soybeans…yellow split peas, almost twice as much as soybeans.

Important: To get the most protection from any of these legumes, wash and consume the seedling shoots as well as their roots, which

contain the greatest concentration of genistein and dadzein.

Peter B. Kaufman, PhD, professor emeritus of plant physiology and plant biotechnology, University of Michigan, Ann Arbor.

Drink Your Cocoa

Hot cocoa fights disease better than wine or tea. One cup of hot cocoa contains about 611 milligrams (mg) of *phenols* and 564 mg of *flavonoids,* two powerful antioxidants that protect against cancer and heart disease. By comparison, a glass of red wine has 340 mg and 163 mg, respectively, of these compounds, while green tea has 165 mg and 47 mg…and black tea has only 124 mg and 34 mg.

Bonus: Although chocolate also is very rich in antioxidants, it is high in saturated fat. The equivalent amount of cocoa contains less than 1 gram (g) of saturated fat.

Chang Y. Lee, PhD, professor and chairman, food science and technology, Cornell University, Geneva, NY.

Beer Combats Blood Clots

In a recent finding, men who consumed 12 ounces of beer a day for one month had 10% less of the clot-promoting protein *fibrinogen* in their blood than those who drank only mineral water. Blood clots increase risk for heart attack and stroke.

Theory: Compounds known as *polyphenols* found in beer—as well as in wine and fruit juice—act as antioxidants and may trigger this beneficial effect.

Self-defense: Ask your doctor whether moderate consumption of beer, wine or fruit juice is appropriate for you.

Shela Gorinstein, PhD, chief researcher and head of the international research group, department of medicinal chemistry and natural products, The Hebrew University of Jerusalem, Israel.

Sweet Treat Lengthens Life

Honey may help prevent heart disease and cancer. It is as rich in antioxidants as some fruits and vegetables. The darker the color, the higher the antioxidant level. Buckwheat honey has the highest levels. Clover honey—the most commonly available type—has two to three times less but still is a good antioxidant source. Use honey instead of sugar in cereal, tea, etc.

Nicki Engeseth, PhD, associate professor of food chemistry at the University of Illinois in Urbana, and leader of a study of honey's effect on human blood, published in the *Journal of Agricultural and Food Chemistry.*

Apples Really Do Keep The Doctor Away

In a recent finding, incidence of lung cancer was reduced by 60%...asthma by 20%...and death from heart disease by 20% in people who ate one apple a day.

Theory: Apples are rich in the bioflavonoid *quercetin,* which helps block the accumulation of free radicals in the body. The cell damage caused by free radicals contributes to the development of these diseases.

Self-defense: Eat one small apple a day for this benefit.

Other quercetin-rich foods: Onions, cabbage, blackberries and cranberries.

Paul Knekt, PhD, epidemiologist for the National Public Health Institute in Helsinki, Finland. His study was published in *The American Journal of Clinical Nutrition.*

Mighty Matcha

The type of green tea used in Japanese tea ceremonies provides 200 times more *epigallocatechin gallate*, a potent anticancer chemical, than the green tea served in the US. Known as matcha, the Japanese tea is powdered before steeping—a technique that is believed to release more of the active compound than crumpled leaves. Matcha is available in some health food stores and on the Web at *www.stashtea.com.*

Science News, 1719 N St. NW, Washington, DC 20036.

Vinegar May Help Fight Diabetes

In a recent study, healthy patients and patients with a prediabetic condition known as insulin resistance drank a vinegar drink (⅛ cup of vinegar, diluted with ¼ cup of water and sweetened with saccharine) or a placebo drink before a high-carbohydrate meal. The vinegar treatment improved insulin sensitivity by up to 40% in both groups.

Theory: Vinegar inhibits the breakdown of carbohydrates, thereby decreasing the blood glucose spikes that occur in people who have diabetes.

If you are diabetic or insulin resistant: Talk to your doctor about drinking diluted vinegar before meals.

Carol S. Johnston, PhD, professor of nutrition, Arizona State University East, Mesa.

Cinnamon for Diabetes

One-half teaspoon of cinnamon a day can reduce blood sugar levels in diabetics by 20%. Sprinkle ground cinnamon on toast and cereal, and stir it into juice or coffee.

Richard Anderson, PhD, research chemist, US Department of Agriculture's Beltsville Human Nutrition Research Center, MD, and leader of a study of type 2 diabetics, published in *Diabetes Care.*

Natural Help for Parkinson's

Parkinson's symptoms may be decreased by eliminating red meat and taking large doses of vitamin B-2 (riboflavin).

Background: Researchers hypothesized that excessive red-meat consumption may bring on Parkinson's in patients who absorb riboflavin poorly. Riboflavin deficiency may be linked to the brain degeneration found in Parkinson's.

New finding: Nineteen advanced Parkinson's patients were put on a no-red-meat diet and given 30 milligrams (mg) of B-2 every eight hours in addition to their usual medications. Their riboflavin levels, which were low despite adequate dietary intake, normalized after one month. After six months on this regimen, the average motor capacity increased from 44% to 71%, improving the clinical condition of the patients in the study.

Cicero Galli Coimbra, MD, PhD, associate professor of neurology and neurosurgery, Federal University of São Paulo, Brazil.

An Amazing Anti-Inflammatory

Serafina Corsello, MD, executive director, Wellness Medical Center, New York City. She is author of *The Ageless Woman* (Corsello Communications).

Wobenzym tablets contain numerous enzymes that help to fight inflammatory and autoimmune conditions, such as rheumatoid arthritis, lupus, Sjögren's disease, inflammatory bowel disease and mild osteoarthritis. Wobenzym, derived from pineapple stems, is available from health food stores and over the Internet.

Cost: About $25 for 100 tablets.

Caution: Consult a knowledgeable physician or naturopathic physician before using.

Dosage: Most people start with two tablets twice a day. Work up to five to eight tablets twice daily for mild conditions...10 to 15 three times daily for more severe conditions. As you increase your intake of Wobenzym, ask your doctor if you can taper prescription medications. People sensitive to pineapple may experience nausea, headaches or other discomfort. If so, stop taking it and try again a week later.

Breakthrough Treatments for Arthritis

Harris H. McIlwain, MD, a specialist in pain-related diseases at the Tampa Medical Group in Florida. He is board-certified in rheumatology and geriatric medicine, and is the coauthor of *Pain-Free Arthritis: A 7-Step Program for Feeling Better Again* (Henry Holt).

If you have arthritis, chances are you have a well-worn heating pad and a medicine cabinet full of painkillers. Unfortunately, these approaches provide only temporary relief for both osteoarthritis (an age-related disease that causes joint pain and stiffness) and rheumatoid arthritis (an autoimmune disease that triggers joint inflammation).

Even though there is no cure now for arthritis, several underutilized treatments can dramatically curb your symptoms...

EXERCISE

Arthritis patients often avoid exercise, fearing it will exacerbate muscle and joint pain. Yet research consistently shows that exercise alleviates arthritis symptoms and improves strength and flexibility. Exercise also helps to prevent weight gain, which has been shown to worsen arthritis pain.

Scientific evidence: Researchers at Wake Forest University School of Medicine discovered that aerobic or resistance exercise reduces the incidence of disability for key daily activities (eating, dressing, bathing, etc.) in arthritis patients by about 50%.

What to do: Stretch for at least 10 minutes daily. Perform an aerobic activity, such as biking or walking, very slowly working up to 30 minutes, five days per week. Do strengthening exercises—resistance machines or weight lifting—gradually working up to 15 minutes, three times a week.*

To minimize pain and prevent injury, apply warm, moist heat to arthritic joints or sore muscles for 15 minutes before and after exercise.

BOOST YOUR C AND D

Vitamin C seems to slow down the cartilage loss that comes from osteoarthritis, while a diet low in vitamin D may speed up the progression of osteoarthritis.

Scientific evidence: In research conducted as part of the ongoing Framingham Heart Study, doctors discovered that patients who ate a diet high in vitamin D, or who took D supplements, decreased their risk for worsening arthritis by 75%. And, a 2003 study of 25,000 people by the Arthritis Research Campaign in England found that a low intake of vitamin C may increase the risk of developing arthritis.

What to do: Take daily supplements that provide 500 to 1,000 milligrams (mg) of vitamin C and 400 international units (IU) of vitamin D.

DRINK TEA

Tea may help reduce arthritis inflammation and bone deterioration.

Scientific evidence: Researchers recently discovered that green tea contains a *polyphenol,* or chemical compound, that suppresses the expression of a key gene associated with arthritis inflammation. Black tea is made of the same leaves and may be as beneficial, even though it is processed differently.

What to do: Drink one to two cups of hot or cold tea daily.

EAT GRAPES

Grape skins contain *resveratrol,* the only natural compound known to perform like COX-2 inhibitors. Like the widely prescribed pharmaceutical COX-2 inhibitors *celecoxib* (Celebrex) and *rofecoxib* (Vioxx), resveratrol both suppresses the COX-2 gene and deactivates the COX-2 enzyme, which produces inflammation at the site of injury or pain.

*A physician or physical therapist can help you to devise a safe movement program that combines stretching, aerobic and strengthening exercises.

Scientific evidence: A study published in the *Journal of Biological Chemistry* confirmed that resveratrol acts as an antioxidant and a COX-2 inhibitor.

What to do: Eat one cup of white or red grapes daily.

Good news: Imbibing your grapes may be as healthful as munching them. All wines have some resveratrol, with red wine packing the biggest punch.

TRY SUPPLEMENTS

Dietary supplements can be a valuable adjunct to traditional drug treatments, allowing patients to reduce or, in some cases, eliminate expensive medications altogether.** *The most effective are…*

●**Glucosamine.** Derived from the shells of shellfish, this supplement appears to aid in the lubrication of joints and reduce arthritis pain and stiffness.

Scientific evidence: In a 2001 *British Medical Journal* report, 1,500 mg of glucosamine daily was found to slow cartilage deterioration in patients with osteoarthritis.

What to do: Ask your doctor about taking 1,500 mg of glucosamine daily. Glucosamine is often packaged with chondroitin, but there is less evidence to support the effectiveness of chondroitin.

Warning: People who have shellfish allergies should *not* take glucosamine.

●**SAMe.** Doctors in Europe commonly prescribe this natural supplement for depression and arthritis.

Scientific evidence: Studies indicate that it relieves pain and inflammation about as well as *naproxen* (Aleve), but without the stomach upset and other side effects. It has the added benefit of boosting mood, possibly by increasing production of the brain chemical *dopamine.*

What to do: If your arthritis does not get better with glucosamine, ask your physician about taking 400 to 1,200 mg of SAMe every day.

**Always consult your doctor before taking supplements. Some may interfere with the action or efficacy of certain drugs.

GET A MASSAGE

Manual manipulation by physical or massage therapists is among the most effective of treatments for relieving neck and back pain.

Scientific evidence: In a 2001 study recounted in the *Archives of Internal Medicine,* back pain patients who underwent 10 weeks of therapeutic massage took fewer medications the following year than did patients who were not massaged.

What to do: Consider getting regular massages, as needed, for pain.

Whenever possible, choose a state licensed massage therapist. To locate one, contact the American Massage Therapy Association at 888-843-2682 or *www.amtamassage.org.*

CONSIDER THERAPEUTIC TAPING

Therapeutic taping—wrapping a rigid tape around a joint to realign, support and take pressure from it—may have significant pain relief benefits for some osteoarthritis patients.

Scientific evidence: In one 2003 Australian study, 73% of patients with osteoarthritis of the knee experienced substantially reduced symptoms after three weeks of therapeutic taping. The benefits were comparable to those achieved with standard drug treatments and lasted three weeks after taping was stopped. Though the study looked only at knees, taping may work as well for elbows, wrists and ankles.

What to do: Ask your doctor if therapeutic taping is right for you.

Important: Taping must be done properly to be effective. If you try taping, you should have your sore joint wrapped by a physician or physical therapist who is familiar with the procedure. He/she can show you or a family member the proper technique.

If taping proves too difficult or cumbersome, a fitted neoprene sleeve (an elastic sleeve used by athletes) may provide similar benefits. It is available at most drugstores.

More from Harris McIlwain...

Arthritis Pain Relief Strategies

To minimize arthritis pain and protect your joints follow this helpful advice...

- **When grocery shopping, request plastic bags that can be looped over your arms,** between the wrist and elbow. This shifts the weight to your shoulders and upper body, instead of the more delicate wrist and hand joints.

- **Put foam "grips" around pens and pencils** (you'll find them in office-supply stores). You can use these same covers around crochet hooks and knitting needles, too.

- **Use pump toothpastes** rather than the squeeze tubes.

- **Choose clothing with Velcro closures** instead of zippers and buttons.

- **Women should wear bras that open in the front.**

Arthritis Food Cures

Isadore Rosenfeld, MD, Rossi Distinguished Professor of Clinical Medicine at Weill Medical College of Cornell University in New York City. He is also the author of nine books, including *Doctor, What Should I Eat?* (Warner) and *Dr. Isadore Rosenfeld's Breakthrough Health* (Rodale).

Both osteoarthritis and rheumatoid arthritis cause painful inflammation that usually becomes worse with age. But the proper food choices can help reduce this pain—without the side effects caused by some painkillers.

Best food: Fatty fish (salmon, mackerel, sardines, etc.). The omega-3 fatty acids in fish counter the effects of *prostaglandins,* chemicals that promote inflammation. Eat three or more fish meals weekly. If you are pregnant, ask your doctor whether you should eat fish.

Also helpful: Brazil nuts. They contain selenium, a trace mineral that may reduce arthritis symptoms. One Brazil nut supplies the recommended daily intake of 70 micrograms (mcg).

Approximately 20% of all osteoarthritis and rheumatoid arthritis cases are linked to food allergies. Common offenders include soy, coffee, eggs, milk, corn, wheat, potatoes, beef, pork and shellfish (especially shrimp).

I advise patients with severe arthritis to stop eating these problem foods, one at a time, to see if symptoms improve.

Surprising Secret to Stopping Back Pain

Arthur H. White, MD, a former president of the North American Spine Society and retired orthopedic spine surgeon in Walnut Creek, CA. He is coauthor of The Posture Prescription *(Three Rivers).*

The word "posture" has negative connotations for many people who were bullied into standing up straight as children. But good posture can help you to avoid, reduce—or even eliminate—most types of back pain. An exercise program that focuses on posture can help you forgo powerful painkilling drugs or surgery—the standard treatments recommended by most doctors.

Fortunately, the type of posture I recommend is *not* the straight-as-an-arrow position most of our parents nagged us about.

MECHANICS OF THE SPINE

When we stand, sit and move properly, the bones and disks maintain their optimum alignment and healthy function. If we add physical stress, such as repeated bending, lifting and sitting, to any part of the back, then the disks can tear, bulge and press on a nerve—or even rupture. When disks are damaged, large muscles of the back go into spasm to protect the spine, and body tissue may become inflamed and painful.

PROPER SPINE ALIGNMENT

Three separate exercises will help you attain proper posture. Repeat these exercises 10 times each, twice a day.

Important: Be patient. Although proper posture will feel awkward at first, these positions will seem comfortable and natural after about three weeks of practice.

•**Dorsal glide.** Sit in a chair with your back supported. Thrust your head forward without moving your back or shoulders. Feel the strain in your neck. Pull your head back, centered between your shoulders. Squeeze your shoulder blades to bring your shoulders upright.

Most people carry their heads forward, a position that contributes to neck pain and headaches. Your head should always be centered over the body with your chin parallel to the floor.

•**Shoulder squeeze.** Stand with your feet shoulder-width apart and your knees slightly bent. Clasp your hands together behind your back at about the level of your hips.

Without moving your lower back, lift your hands and arms to straighten your shoulders and squeeze your shoulder blades together.

•**Straight stick.** Grasp a yardstick or a three-foot dowel, pole or broom handle with both hands and hold it behind you at the level of your waist. Straighten your back so that your head, upper back and lower back are all touching the stick.

To straighten your lower back, tilt your pelvis forward by "tucking in" your buttocks. Then hold that position for about 30 seconds.

Better: Walk around for a few minutes while holding the stick behind your back to feel what it is like to move with a straight back.

PUTTING IT TOGETHER

•**Standing straight.** Stand with your feet a few inches apart, toes forward. Bend your knees slightly. Balance your weight evenly on both feet, without too much weight on either the toes or the heels. Don't shift your weight from one leg to the other. Make your lower back straight by tilting your pelvis forward. Relax your shoulders, then squeeze your shoulder blades together.

Finally, center your head over your body. Ideally, you should maintain this position whenever you are standing.

When you sit, the position of your lower back, upper back and head needs to be straight. Do not lean against the back of the chair. If you do, support your lower back with a cushion.

Smart idea: Watch yourself as you walk by mirrors, store windows or any other reflective surface to "catch" yourself if you start to slump. If you regularly sit for long periods, make sure the front of the chair seat is tilted upward so your knees are above your hips. As an alternative, rest your feet on a phone book or footstool. When standing for long periods, place one foot on a footstool.

MOVING PROPERLY

Your back compensates for weaknesses elsewhere. For example, if you lift a box that is too heavy for your arms, you are likely to lift with your back. Although back muscles are large and strong, using them improperly can cause strains, sprains and disk injury.

The following exercises will help you to develop the strength and flexibility you need to get through the day without injuring your back.

As these movements become more comfortable, integrate them into your daily life.

Example: Squat while pulling weeds in the garden or do the leg stretch while talking on the telephone.

●**The squat.** The best overall exercise is the squat because it allows a total stretch of your ankles, knees and hips, as well as your Achilles tendon and calf muscles. Just getting up from a squat will strengthen and firm up your thighs. This allows you to stand for extended periods without putting stress on your back.

With your feet apart, squat all the way down. Keep your feet flat on the floor, and bring your buttocks as close to your heels as you can.

Once you are in this position, straighten your back. Use the straight stick, if necessary.

If you cannot get all the way down, hold on to a flat, stationary surface, such as a desk or kitchen counter, and lower yourself as far as you can go. Hold this squat for at least 30 seconds, then raise yourself up using just your thigh muscles.

Perform the half squat 20 to 30 times a day. When you can do 30, switch to full squats. Then do one to two full squats five to 10 times a day. You can incorporate these into your daily

activities, such as getting something out of a low cabinet.

Caution: Do *not* perform the full squat if you have arthritis or total knee or hip replacement. Also, do not perform this exercise with dumbbells or barbells. The additional weight can damage the knees.

●**Leg stretch.** While in proper standing posture, position yourself in front of a table or other flat, stationary surface. Put your leg out straight and rest your left heel on the table. Hold on to the wall or other object for balance, if necessary. Hold for at least 30 seconds, then repeat with the other leg.

If this exercise is too difficult, start with a lower surface, such as a chair or a stair step. If this exercise feels too easy, you can gain an extra stretch by leaning your upper body toward your raised leg.

Perform the leg stretch 10 to 20 times a day. You can do it while reading or even talking on the phone.

Back exercise illustrations by Shawn Banner.

Avoid Sinus Infections... Naturally

Murray Grossan, MD, otolaryngologist, Tower Ear, Nose and Throat Clinic, Cedars-Sinai Medical Center, Los Angeles. He is a coauthor of *The Sinus Cure—7 Simple Steps to Relieve Sinusitis and Other Ear, Nose and Throat Conditions* (Ballantine).

Believe it or not, sinus infection, which affects 37 million Americans each year, is more prevalent today than it was in the preantibiotic age!

That's not to say that antibiotics aren't effective. When sinusitis (the technical name for a sinus infection) occurs, treatment with antibiotics is often essential to kill off the infectious bacteria.

Decongestants can help to relieve sinusitis symptoms. So can oral or topical steroids (to combat sinus inflammation) and antihistamines, if underlying allergies are involved.

Increasingly, doctors are realizing that to successfully fight off sinus infection and prevent it from recurring, *medication alone isn't enough.* You also have to ensure that the mucous membranes lining your nasal and sinus passages are healthy and functioning properly.

SYMPTOMS

Sinusitis occurs whenever the mucous membranes in your nose and sinuses become irritated by a cold, allergy, pollutants or exposure to dry or cold air. This irritation causes the membranes to become inflamed. When this happens, the motion of the cilia (the tiny hairs that coat all the mucous membranes and are responsible for moving mucus over their surfaces) slows down. At the same time, the irritation stimulates your mucous glands to secrete more mucus than usual to dilute the bacteria.

Result: Mucus gets trapped in the sinuses, where it can easily become infected because the swelling meant to dilute the bacteria now blocks the sinus openings, and prevents the body from washing away the bacteria. *Symptoms of sinus infection include...*

• **Facial pressure around the eyes,** cheeks and forehead.

• **Cold symptoms** lasting more than 10 days.

• **Thick, green/yellow mucus.**

• **Postnasal drip,** which occurs when excess mucus drips down the back of the throat.

• **Pain in the upper molars.**

• **Fatigue and a flu-like achiness.**

TREATMENT

The following natural treatments will help to keep your cilia healthy and functioning and prevent mucus from building in your sinuses. When a sinus infection does occur, these same treatments will help to increase the effectiveness of antibiotics and other medications—speeding healing and making a recurrence less likely.

1. Drink hot liquids. One of the best ways to unclog sinuses is to drink hot tea—black, green, herbal or decaffeinated, it doesn't matter—or hot chicken soup throughout the day. Drink enough so that your urine turns light in color. These hot liquids help moisturize your mucous membranes, speeding up the movement of your cilia and thus washing mucus out of your sinuses more quickly. Sorry, coffee lovers, but hot coffee isn't nearly as effective.

Note to travelers: The dry air on jet liners is particularly rough on the sinuses—so when flying, carry tea bags with you and ask your flight attendant for hot water to make tea.

2. Apply warm compresses to your face. Do this three times a day for five minutes. A small towel soaked in warm water, then placed over your face below and between the eyes, will help increase the circulation in your sinuses, which will also help speed up the movement of your cilia.

3. Irrigate your sinuses. For over 3,000 years, the yoga practitioners have kept their sinuses healthy through the practice of sniffing a saltwater solution rapidly in and out of their nose at low pressure.

Caution: Don't try this unless you have been taught how to do it.

Fortunately, for those of us who aren't yogis, a device called the Hydro Pulse Nasal and Sinus Irrigator will do this for you. The pulsating flow from the Hydro Pulse is so gentle that even five-year-olds use it.

An even simpler alternative is a Lavage irrigation bottle. Ideally, irrigation should be done using Ringer's solution, the solution used in hospitals for intravenous treatment, and sold over the counter in drugstores. Or you can use an isotonic saline solution (not too salty, just right) that does not contain any *benzalkonium.* Benzalkonium is a preservative that can impair nasal function and kids complain that it burns. To make up your own preservative-free saline solution, add one teaspoon of table salt to one pint of water.

If you're prone to sinus infections, I recommend irrigating your sinuses twice a day, especially during the cold winter months.

Ringer's solution, designed for irrigation use, is sold under the name Breathe-ease XL (it's also available as a nasal spray). To order the Hydro Pulse Nasal and Sinus Irrigator, a Lavage irrigation bottle or Breathe-ease products, visit the Web site *www.sinus-allergies.com.*

4. Clear your sinuses with aromatherapy. To help open up congested nasal passages and sinuses, drop some eucalyptus or menthol oil into a bowl of hot water, then breathe in the vapors—or simply open up a jar of either and inhale the fumes directly.

Vick's VapoRub is also effective. Simply dab a bit on the skin underneath your nose.

Other aromatherapy decongestants include horseradish (grate it and put it on a sandwich) and, if you're really brave, Japanese wasabi mustard. All of these therapies work best if used a couple of times a day, especially during the winter months.

5. Take breakfast in bed. When you sleep at night, your body temperature drops and your cilia movement slows down. By taking breakfast in bed along with a cup of hot tea, you'll give your cilia a chance to warm up and clear out the night's accumulated mucus before you start placing demands on your respiratory system.

6. Elevate your head when sleeping. Elevating your head with one or two pillows will help your sinuses and nasal passages stay open while you sleep. The more your head is elevated, the better the effect.

7. Dustproof your bedroom. Dust and dust mites can wreak havoc on your mucous membranes, especially when you're asleep and your cilia are at rest.

In your bedroom, avoid all heavy draperies and wall-to-wall carpeting (which is a notorious dust-collector). Use throw rugs instead, and toss them in the washing machine at least every six weeks. Overall, make your bedroom as bare as possible, and dust all surfaces and behind furniture weekly. To further reduce dust in your bedroom, I recommend using a HEPA air purifier, and running it throughout the day. (Most people find the filter too noisy for nighttime use.)

8. Get plenty of rest. If your sinuses are acting up, you will be amazed at how much improvement you'll see after taking the weekend off and spending it in bed. Be sure to get some mental rest at the same time. Turn off the phone and avoid the news. Instead, rent some funny videos, find a good book, lie back and enjoy. Relaxation can help the body heal.

Eating Fish May Lower Risk of Blindness

Age-related macular degeneration (AMD) is a leading cause of blindness. The *neovascular*—or wet—form represents 10% of AMD cases but causes 90% of AMD-related severe vision loss. Elderly people who eat more than one serving a week of broiled or baked fish are 36% less likely to have neovascular AMD as people who don't…people who eat more than two servings per week are half as likely to have neovascular AMD.

Likely reason: Long-chain omega-3 fatty acids—fish is the only significant food source.

John Paul SanGiovanni, ScD, researcher at the National Eye Institute, National Institutes of Health, Bethesda, MD, and leader of a study of 4,513 people, ages 60 to 80, presented at a conference of the Association for Research in Vision and Ophthalmology.

Natural Sun Protection

Get additional sun protection by eating all the right foods. Five daily servings of carrots, sweet potatoes, mangos, tomatoes and other carotenoid-rich foods can make your skin twice as resistant to the sun's rays. Beta-carotene and lycopene, the carotenoids that give these foods their deep, rich color, will build up in your skin over time and help protect you from sunburn and wrinkles. Protection against skin cancer hasn't been proven yet.

Important: You should continue to wear sunscreen while outdoors.

Wilhelm Stahl, PhD, professor of chemistry, Heinrich-Heine-University, Dusseldorf, Germany.

A Natural Treatment For Tinnitus

Ginkgo biloba may quiet chronic tinnitus. In four of five studies reviewed, a daily dose of 120 to 160 milligrams (mg), taken as tablets or in liquid form, had significant benefit for those with ringing in the ears.

Theory: Ginkgo biloba increases blood supply to the inner ear, which may help to relieve tinnitus.

If you suffer from tinnitus: Ask your doctor if ginkgo biloba would be a helpful treatment for you.

Caution: It can cause excessive bleeding if you take a blood-thinning drug, such as *warfarin* (Coumadin).

Edzard Ernst, MD, PhD, director, Complementary Medicine Unit, Universities of Exeter and Plymouth, England.

SAMe Fights Serious Depression

An over-the-counter (OTC) dietary supplement called *S-adenosylmethionine* (SAMe) is as effective as the prescription antidepressant *imipramine* for people diagnosed as clinically depressed.

Recommended: Severely depressed people can take up to 1,600 milligrams (mg) daily.

Side effects: Heartburn and indigestion at the start of use.

Check with your doctor before using.

Roberto Delle Chiaie, professor of stress medicine at the University of Siena, Italy, and leader of a study of 293 severely depressed people, reported in *The American Journal of Clinical Nutrition.*

My Favorite Natural Sleep Remedies

Jamison Starbuck, ND, a naturopathic physician in family practice and a lecturer at the University of Montana, both in Missoula. She is a past president of the American Association of Naturopathic Physicians and a contributing editor to *The Alternative Advisor: The Complete Guide to Natural Therapies and Alternative Treatments* (Time Life).

A good night's sleep is one of life's blessings. But, unfortunately, one out of three adults suffers from insomnia, which impacts their emotional well-being, immune health and vulnerability to infectious disease.

Medical doctors use prescription sedatives, such as *zolpidem* (Ambien), or antidepressants, such as *trazodone* (Desyrel), to treat insomnia. These drugs will generally work for short-term treatment, but their safety may diminish if they are used for more than 30 consecutive days. Both types of drugs cause side effects, such as constipation and drowsiness.

Unlike the prescription drugs, which simply knock you out, natural medicine treats the cause of your insomnia. *Here's my natural approach...*

The chief triggers of insomnia are emotional stress, pain and hormone irregularity. Determine which of these fits your situation and select one or more of the remedies listed below.*

If your sleeplessness is caused by emotional anxiety, my favorite homeopathic treatment is Calms Forté (Hylands). This formula has all the key ingredients, such as passionflower, oat and chamomile, and is found at health food stores. Two pellets, dissolved under the tongue at bedtime, quell both mild anxiety and the tendency to overthink. If you awaken frequently, you can repeat this dose up to three times throughout the night. I also recommend the herbs valerian and hops for stress-related insomnia. Take 60 drops of each herb together, in tincture form, in four ounces of hot water at bedtime. Both herbs are mildly sedating, generally safe and can be combined with Calms Forté.

Insomniacs who suffer from joint and back pain can improve their sleep by relaxing their

*Some of these remedies may be inappropriate for pregnant women or some people with chronic health conditions. Consult your doctor.

muscles at bedtime. Start with a warm Epsom salts bath just before bed (use at least two cups Epsom salts per tub). For even greater relaxation, also take 300 milligrams (mg) of magnesium along with a homeopathic preparation of magnesium known as Mag. Phos 6X (four pellets under the tongue). Take both at bedtime immediately after the Epsom bath.

Menopause, premenstrual syndrome, thyroid hyperactivity or a surge in stress hormones precipitated by life changes or excessive exercise can all cause insomnia. Hormone-related insomnia should be evaluated and treated by your medical doctor or naturopathic physician.

One hormone-related insomnia which most people can treat themselves is connected to seasonal affective disorder (SAD), a condition that causes mild to moderate depression from autumn to spring. One dose of 0.5 to 2 mg of the hormone melatonin, taken at bedtime, may well correct the insomnia linked to SAD. Melatonin is available at health food stores and pharmacies. Start with the 0.5 mg dose and increase after five days, if needed. I recommend discontinuing melatonin for SAD-related insomnia by the end of March.

Foods That Help Chronic Fatigue

Chronic fatigue syndrome, a condition characterized by fatigue and musculoskeletal pain, is linked to an imbalance of *phospholipids,* a type of fat, in the brain. *Eicosapentaenoic acid* (EPA), a fat found in fish, restores that balance by inhibiting the breakdown of phospholipids, and helping form new ones. Eating more salmon, white albacore tuna and other fatty fish rich in EPA may ease the fatigue and depression often associated with this condition. Consult your doctor about the best way to incorporate this dietary strategy into your treatment plan.

Basant K. Puri, MD, PhD, consultant and senior lecturer, Imperial College, University of London. His research was published in *Acta Psychiatrica Scandinavica.*

What You Can Do Now To Stay Healthy And Keep Out of A Nursing Home

Robert N. Butler, MD, president of the International Longevity Center in New York City. He is former chairman of the department of geriatrics and adult development at Mount Sinai Medical Center, New York City, the first geriatrics department in an American medical school. He won the Pulitzer Prize for his book *Why Survive? Being Old in America* (Johns Hopkins University) and is author of *The New Love and Sex After 60* (Ballantine).

People of a certain age get lots of sales pitches for nursing home insurance. Insurance companies assume that nearly everyone will spend time in such a facility. It is a distressing thought. But, fortunately, it's a fate you can avoid.

Key: Don't wait. The sooner you start a nonursing home plan, the better your chances of having it succeed.

GOOD NEWS ABOUT DEMENTIA

Dementia is common among nursing home residents. Not too long ago, we assumed that cognitive decline was simply a part of getting older. However, new research shows this isn't the case. *There are three specific factors that help maintain cognitive health...*

●**Daily physical activity.** This often surprises people, but the research is clear—we can actually measure that people who are active physically are stronger cognitively. When the Roman poet and satirist Juvenal said, "A healthy mind in a healthy body," he knew what he was talking about.

We advocate that most people walk 10,000 steps a day to be sure they are getting enough exercise. The average person walks just 4,000 steps, so you'll probably need to establish new habits (and buy a pedometer) to make 10,000 steps part of your everyday life.

●**Social interaction.** Being socially engaged doesn't mean that you have to maintain a full social calendar. What it does mean is that you remain involved with other people, whether through work or volunteering. For those who are retired, there are many volunteer opportunities, from your local community to the Peace Corps. And don't forget the importance of being active as a grandparent. That benefits all three generations.

•**Intellectual stimulation.** This directly impacts the brain. Many older people enjoy studying academic subjects, from history to astronomy, but we have found that learning another language is particularly good for strong cognitive skills. The work that goes into mastering foreign words and any unfamiliar language structure keeps the brain's neurons firing and busy.

FITNESS FACTS

The next crucial part of a no-nursing home plan is to create and maintain very good health habits. *To start, you must practice all forms of fitness, such as…*

•**Aerobic exercise.** Aerobic exercise—the kind that gets your heart rate up and keeps it there—is a must. To maintain heart and lung stamina, perform aerobic exercise for at least 20 minutes three or more times a week.

Examples: Fast walking, jogging, swimming laps.

•**Strength training.** This form of fitness is often overlooked by many older people and it's incredibly important as you age.

Being strong allows you to more easily perform what are called ADLs, activities of daily living. Without strong quads—the muscles in front of the thigh—you lose the ability to get up out of a chair, go to the bathroom, sit down easily. Without strong arm muscles you have trouble lifting bags or opening and closing windows. Strength training is crucial and you must keep it up throughout your life.

Examples: Squats, getting out of a chair without using your arms, chest presses.

•**Balance exercises.** Among older people, there are some 250,000 fractures a year and many of these fractures land the elderly in nursing homes. This is especially sad because many of the falls that cause broken bones can be prevented by improving balance. The sense of balance is like a muscle—you must exercise it regularly or it will weaken and lose its usefulness to you. The easiest way to practice balance

is to stand on one leg and move the other, bent at the knee, through space. Do this several times a day. Or try standing on one leg while you brush your teeth.

Safety reminder: Be sure to have something sturdy nearby to grab hold of in case you need additional support.

•**Stretching exercises.** Finally, you must practice flexibility, which refers to the range of motion of your joints.

Range of motion becomes increasingly important as you age. If it is compromised, it, too, intrudes on your ability to function in your everyday life. Your shoulders need range of motion to enable you to reach for things…your hips and knees need range of motion to bend properly. Keep your joints flexible through regular stretching exercises. Try stretching your arms across your chest. Or stretch the backs of your legs by standing with the palms of your hands braced against a wall while you stretch one leg at a time behind you.

OTHER HEALTH POINTERS

•**Eat a nutritious diet.** In addition to plenty of fruits and vegetables, your diet should be low in fats and have no trans fatty acids at all. Processed baked foods virtually always contain unhealthy trans fatty acids, but you're more likely to see "partially hydrogenated fat" on the label. They are the same thing and you should not eat them. Trans fats are created during the chemical process of hydrogenating oils and they increase "bad" LDL cholesterol, increasing your risk of stroke and heart disease.

•**Maintain a healthy weight.** This will help you avoid many diseases that frequently bring patients into a nursing home, such as type 2 diabetes and some cardiovascular disease, especially high blood pressure that leads to stroke.

•**Quit smoking.** I wish I had no need to say quit smoking, but there are still people who haven't kicked the habit even though statistics show it cuts seven years off the normal life span.

MAKE FRIENDS WITH YOUR DOCTOR

While it is important to remain as disease-free as possible, there is now some controversy about the benefit of having an annual physical examination. Statistics don't back them up as resulting in longer lives, but you should still find a way to get to know your doctor so that he/she is familiar with your medical history if something does happen.

We suggest having abbreviated checkups. Get routine testing for the problems that older people are prone to, such as glaucoma, high blood pressure and gender-specific ailments. And if you do have any kind of medical condition, chronic or otherwise, be sure to take your medication as the doctor has prescribed. Always call the doctor to discuss any concern you might have about a drug rather than make decisions about medicine on your own.

Life expectancy is higher than ever—an average of about 78 years compared with about 48 years in 1900. By adhering to these few simple measures, you'll greatly increase your chances of enjoying all the years ahead.

Protect Yourself From Dementia

Jeff Victoroff, MD, associate professor of clinical neurology and psychiatry at the Keck School of Medicine, University of Southern California in Los Angeles. He is also the author of *Saving Your Brain: The Revolutionary Plan to Boost Brain Power, Improve Memory, and Protect Yourself Against Aging and Alzheimer's* (Bantam).

O f all the illnesses that threaten us as we grow older, very few are more frightening than dementia.

Science hasn't yet devised a foolproof shield against the ravages of dementia, but you can take steps to put the odds in your favor.

AGING AND THE BRAIN

New evidence suggests that the brain damage of dementia is largely an exaggerated form of what happens to normal brains over time.

For example...

●**Neurodegeneration.** Brain cells are damaged by unstable molecules called free radicals. During aging, brain cells are less able to repair their own DNA. In addition, deposits of a protein known as *amyloid* form plaques that

impede the workings of neurons. Increasing numbers of brain cells die. This process can lead to dementia and Alzheimer's disease.

●**Vascular factors.** A narrowing and stiffening of small arteries may decrease the delivery of blood to certain areas of the brain, resulting in ministrokes—blockages that kill small pockets of cells in the brain. This process may impair brain function.

What will determine how fast these changes occur? Some brains are genetically programmed to degenerate more rapidly than others. But up to 50% of the changes can be attributed to environmental factors, which include a person's lifestyle choices.

FORTIFY WITH FISH

In one recent study involving 5,500 men and women, eating fish at least once a week led to a 70% reduction in Alzheimer's risk.

Why? Omega-3s, fatty acids found in certain fish, facilitate the transmission of messages between brain cells—the foundation of all mental activity. These same fats help maintain cardiovascular health and slow the circulation decline that plays a significant role in brain damage.

What's new: Recent findings from a study conducted in the Netherlands indicate that something in the fish other than the omega-3 content may play a role in its benefits. This means that fish oil supplements might *not* be as effective as the whole fish.

Helpful: Eat four ounces of fish at least four times a week, particularly fatty fish, such as salmon, sardines, herring, trout and mackerel. Canned tuna is also good. To avoid potentially dangerous levels of mercury, pregnant women should talk to their doctor before eating fish.

GET YOUR ANTIOXIDANT ARMOR

The body produces its own antioxidants to neutralize brain-damaging free radicals. They work much more effectively with the help of antioxidant nutrients—vitamins C and E and beta-carotene.

What's new: Two recent studies conducted by Martha C. Morris, ScD, at Rush-Presbyterian–St. Luke's Medical Center in Chicago, suggest that vitamin E—either from food or supplements—may reduce the risk for Alzheimer's disease.

Helpful: Ask your doctor about taking 400 international units (IU) of *natural* vitamin E (d-alpha-tocopherol) every day. The natural form crosses into the brain more readily than the synthetic vitamin. Also be sure to include vitamin E–rich foods, such as vegetable oils, wheat germ, almonds and other nuts and seeds, in your diet.

DRINK FOR BRAIN HEALTH

Moderate drinking—one or two glasses of wine, beer or liquor a day, for example—has been shown to protect the heart. This includes reducing the risk for brain-destroying strokes.

What's new: Alcohol consumption appears to be beneficial for brain function as well. Researchers at the University of Bordeaux in France followed 3,777 people age 65 or older and found that those who drank one or two glasses of wine per day were 45% less likely to develop Alzheimer's than were nondrinkers.

Helpful: Drink one glass of white wine a day. Other forms of alcohol may work too, but they are more likely to cause headaches, weight gain and other unpleasant effects. Beyond two drinks daily, the damaging effects of alcohol on brain cells may outweigh the benefits. Women should not exceed one alcoholic drink per day, because it may increase their risk for developing breast cancer, according to recent studies.

Important: If you have had trouble controlling your alcohol intake in the past, do *not* start drinking to protect your brain.

EXERCISE FOR BRAIN HEALTH

Aerobic exercise helps to maintain healthy circulation and protects the brain from slow deterioration.

What's new: A Canadian study of 4,615 men and women age 65 or older found that brisk walking at least *three times* weekly cut the incidence of Alzheimer's by one-third. Jogging reduced the risk by 52%.

Helpful: Exercise enough to get your heart rate up and break a sweat—jogging, biking, walking faster than three miles per hour—for 30 minutes at least five times weekly.

MENTAL FITNESS

Studies have indicated that higher education and mentally challenging work can reduce Alzheimer's risk and slow memory loss.

What's new: Research conducted at Columbia University suggests that even people with low-level educations will have a reduced risk for Alzheimer's if they take up mentally challenging jobs.

Examples: Writer, teacher, researcher, designer or any job that requires creativity and learning new skills.

Helpful: Make learning a lifelong pursuit. Take up chess…learn new languages…develop computer skills.

How to Help a Loved One Heal

Bernie Siegel, MD, founder of the Exceptional Cancer Patients (ECaP) therapy group, based in Woodbridge, CT, *www.ecap-online.org.* A retired general and pediatric surgeon, he is also the author of five books. His most recent is *Help Me to Heal—A Practical Guidebook for Patients, Visitors and Caregivers* (Hay House).

When a loved one is in the hospital or at home recovering from an illness, the way you interact with him or her can actually help speed—or slow—the healing process. *Here's how to be a healing presence…*

BE A GOOD VISITOR

● **Don't drop in.** Call ahead to the patient—or a family member—and ask what's the best time for you to visit. If you plan on visiting often, talk to other regular visitors and coordinate your schedules. That way, you will avoid overwhelming the patient—and give relief to his family members as well.

● **Be present.** Many people feel very anxious about spending time with someone who is ill. You may be scared about the patient's condition or uncertain about his frame of mind. Remember, you're not there to cure the patient, but to witness and be present for his journey.

● **Practice positive visualization.** Try this technique just before a visit.

What to do: In your mind's eye, picture your loved one as already healed, whole and vibrant. If you only see the patient as sick, you'll make him more fearful of the illness.

● **Knock before entering.** People will often mistake an open door as an invitation to walk in unannounced. Knock first, then wait for a response. By asking for permission to enter, you're empowering your loved one.

● **Sit down.** After entering the patient's room, sit down as soon as possible. If your loved one is lying in bed or sitting in a chair, this places you at eye level.

● **Ask open-ended questions.** When visiting someone who is ill, people frequently blurt out seemingly innocuous statements, such as "My, isn't it a lovely day?"…"You look wonderful"…or "Everything's fine—you have nothing to worry about!" These statements are really saying, "I can't deal with anything you want to talk about—so I'm going to talk for you."

Instead, ask open-ended questions, such as "How are you?"…"How are you feeling?"…or "How are things going?" This lets the patient choose how to respond. What your loved one may want most is simply to talk about what he is feeling and thinking. If so, listen very carefully. Do not feel pressured to make "constructive" comments.

● **Don't feel you have to speak.** The most important gift you can give is simply to be there, physically and emotionally. When people have their loved ones nearby, it can actually change their physiology for the better. Immune function improves, and levels of the stress hormone cortisol drop. If the patient doesn't feel like talking, that's fine. Simply sit and read silently by the bedside.

Even better: Offer some physical contact, such as a hand massage.

● **Ask how you can help.** While simply being there is the most important thing, your visit also is a chance to perform simple comforting tasks. Are there any problems with the nursing care? Do the pillows need to be fluffed? Are personal items within easy reach?

Helping with these tasks is about more than comfort—it also helps your loved one feel more self-sufficient and in control. Studies have shown that people who feel a greater sense of control over their immediate environment have stronger immune systems.

● **Bring gifts.** Even if your loved one doesn't ask for anything, bring along a gift, such as a book, tape or CD you think he might enjoy. You also can bring photographs of family and friends, wall hangings and personal items, such as a favorite blanket, to make the room more comfortable and familiar. If someone is convalescing at home, bring a home-cooked meal. Even if the patient does not eat or use what you've brought, the gesture shows that you care.

GIVING CARE AT HOME

The advice listed so far also applies when you're living with someone who is convalescing. *Additional points to consider when you're caring for someone at home…*

● **Eliminate unwanted noise.** Soft music may be soothing, but you may want to relocate your household phones and televisions to make sure the sound doesn't intrude on your loved one's healing space. Control the flow of visitors and other callers so that your loved one has company only when he wants it. By saying "no" to people he does not want to see, the patient will feel empowered.

● **Make it easy to communicate.** If your loved one feels like talking with people, consider installing a second phone line so that he can make calls without inconveniencing others in your home.

● **Be honest about your feelings.** You shouldn't hide your emotions behind a false front. If you're worried or upset, share these feelings openly with your loved one—but do not say things like, "How can I live without you?" Share your grief with a counselor, not the patient.

● **Say "no," when necessary.** Families can usually sense when a patient could be caring for himself but continues to ask for help with simple things, such as picking up a glass of water that is right next to him. Usually, the patient wants attention, particularly if he has never had it before. Even though you're there to help the other person heal, you also have a right to care for yourself. That means occasionally saying "no." If you don't, you may become angry or resentful. That is not good for you—or your loved one.

The Incredible Healing Power of Prayer

Dale A. Matthews, MD, an internist who practices in Washington, DC. He is also coauthor, with Connie Clark, of The Faith Factor: Proof of the Healing Power of Prayer *(Penguin).*

Many doctors and patients have learned from personal experience that religious faith is good medicine. In recent years, hundreds of clinical studies have demonstrated that this statement is not just a matter of faith, but rather of science.

THE FAITH FACTOR

People who regularly attend worship services enjoy better health than their counterparts with fewer religious ties. *Peer-reviewed studies have found that their advantages include...*

●**Lower rates of cancer,** heart disease and other serious conditions.

●**Speedier recovery from serious illness,** with fewer complications.

●**Longer life expectancy.**

●**Lower rates of depression,** anxiety and other mental illnesses.

●**Enhanced ability to cope with life-threatening and terminal illnesses** with greater tranquillity and less pain.

●**Decreased risk of addiction to alcohol,** drugs or tobacco.

●**Happier marriage and family life.**

These findings can be partly explained by the generally healthier lifestyle of religiously involved people.

Example: They are generally less likely to smoke, drink or take drugs, all of which have negative health effects.

But that is not the whole story. Even after the statistics are adjusted to take account of these factors, religious involvement is associated with better health.

RELIGION AND SPIRITUALITY

Many people dislike religious institutions and create their own personal forms of belief, often a smorgasbord of religious elements from different traditions. You might say that spirituality poses questions. Religion composes answers.

Religion focuses more on establishing communities, while spirituality focuses more on individual growth.

Religion is more objective and measurable to outside observers. Spirituality is more subjective.

Religion is based more on behavior and outward practices. But, spirituality is based more on emotion and inner experience.

Religion prescribes certain kinds of behavior and proscribes others. Spirituality has few prescriptions and proscriptions.

Religion is particular, as it distinguishes one group from another. Spirituality, however emphasizes commonality.

Studies suggest that health benefits are associated with specific forms of religious behavior—in particular, more frequent attendance at organized religious services. The effects of spirituality without religious practice have not been well-studied.

Among members of religious groups, those who have stronger internal religious and spiritual beliefs enjoy greater benefits than those who are motivated primarily by peer pressure.

BENEFITS OF ORGANIZED PRAYER

Worship services provide congregants with a break from their stressful day-to-day schedules. If congregants permit time for silent prayer or meditation, they also encourage the Relaxation Response. That's the health-boosting phenomenon first described by Harvard's Herbert Benson, MD.

Worship is performed in an atmosphere of beauty, encompassing the building, furnishings, prayers and music—all of which produce a sense of peace and meaning.

People sing and pray with their whole being, moving their bodies and enlisting their souls, producing a deep sense of harmony.

During worship, people confess to their sins and request forgiveness, unburdening themselves of guilt and refreshing themselves.

Participating in communal worship and familiar rituals and gaining strength through shared beliefs makes connections between worshippers and builds a community of people who will help each other and give emotional support in dealing with health problems and other challenges of life. Attendance at worship reinforces the belief that life has a meaning, which makes a positive contribution to health.

PRAYING FOR HEALTH

No one suggests that prayers for health—or anything else—will always be answered, but some studies have shown that they often help.

Here are a few suggestions based on my experience of ways to use prayer positively…

●**If you are sick, ask others to pray for you.** Family members and friends will probably be happy to help you, and many churches and synagogues maintain lists of people for whom they pray regularly.

●**Pray for your own healing.** Do not feel this is presumptuous. The Bible tells people to "ask, seek and knock…," i.e., to pray for their own needs.

●**Pray consistently.** Continuing to pray regardless of immediate results is an expression of faith and hope. This is good both for our souls and our morale.

●**Pray for others who are suffering.** No matter how busy you are, you can find time to say brief prayers that express your good wishes for the comfort and healing of others. It will bring comfort and healing to you as well.

Produce with High and Low Pesticide Levels

Apples, cherries, grapes, celery, lettuce and winter squash retain high levels of pesticide residue. Bananas, blueberries, mangoes, watermelon, broccoli, cauliflower and eggplant are likely to have little residue.

Self-defense: Buy organic produce, which has less residue…wash all produce well before you serve it (see article below).

Caroline Smith DeWaal, JD, food safety director, Center for Science in the Public Interest, Washington, DC, and author of *Is Our Food Safe?* (Three Rivers).

Does Washing Produce With Water Remove All Bacteria?

Washing fruits and vegetables with water doesn't completely clean away bacteria, such as *E. coli* and *Listeria,* which can cause food poisoning.

Better: Fill one spray bottle with white or apple cider vinegar, another with 3% hydrogen peroxide, the same strength commonly available in drugstores. Spray all produce with the vinegar first. Its acidity kills the majority of organisms. Then spray with peroxide, which is a strong oxidizer that helps eliminate Listeria. Rinse well with water.

These precautions are recommended for all produce, including organic products.

Susan Sumner, PhD, professor and head, department of food science and technology, Virginia Polytechnic Institute and State University, Blacksburg, VA.

6

Very Personal

Why We Love: The Science Of Sexual Attraction

If you have ever been a "fool for love," blame it on evolution. The phenomena of love, lust and the desire for attachment aren't just emotions. They are basic drives as powerful as hunger and crucial to our survival as a species.

Helen Fisher, PhD, one of the country's top experts on love, administered a series of experiments to look into the brains of people who are deeply in love and those who were just recently rejected. *Below, she answers some questions on what she discovered…*

●**Does the brain actually change when we fall in love?** There is a complex interplay of chemicals involved. My colleagues and I performed brain scans (functional magnetic resonance imaging) on 20 men and women in love. The people in our research had increased activity in the *caudate nucleus,* part of the brain's

reward system that produces the focus and motivation to achieve your goals. The subjects also showed activity in the *ventral tegmental* area, which is responsible for the intense energy and concentration that people in love experience. Increased blood flow in these areas explains the all-night talk sessions and endless letters and e-mails between lovers, as well as the outpouring of love-related poetry and art.

●**How does lust differ from love?** Humans have three basic mating drives—lust, romantic love and attachment. They happen in different regions of the brain and involve different hormones and neurochemicals—but they work in harmony to ensure reproduction and survival of the species.

●Lust is associated primarily with *testosterone,* the hormone that motivates men and

Helen Fisher, PhD, research professor of anthropology at Rutgers University in New Brunswick, NJ, and former research associate at the American Museum of Natural History in New York City. She is author of four books on human sexual and social behavior, most recently *Why We Love* (Holt). Her Web site is *www.helenfisher.com.*

women to have sex. People with higher levels of testosterone tend to have sex more often than those with lower levels.

●Romantic love is linked to *dopamine* and also most likely to *serotonin* and *norepinephrine,* brain chemicals that can produce feelings of ecstasy. In specific combinations, these chemicals motivate a person to focus his/her attention on a preferred individual and think obsessively about that person.

●Attachment, the desire of couples to stay together, is linked to elevated activities of *vaso-pressin* and *oxytocin,* neurohormones that promote the urge to bond and cuddle as well as to care for offspring.

Romantic love is metabolically expensive because people will lavish so much energy and attention on their beloved. It pays off in evolutionary terms because it leads to attachment and the desire to nurture and raise a family.

●**Can lust lead to love?** Love is far more likely to lead to lust than lust is to love. We find our new partners sexually attractive in part because increases in dopamine enhance the activity of testosterone.

●**Is "love at first sight" possible?** I think that love at first sight comes out of nature. With animals, brain circuitry must be triggered rapidly because they don't have much time to mate. We inherited this ability to prefer certain partners almost instantly.

●**Do men and women experience love differently?** Both exhibit similar elation and obsessive behavior—but men show more activity in a brain region associated with the integration of visual stimuli. Women have more activity in brain areas associated with memory recall.

Why this difference? Men are more visual than women, probably because for millions of years they sized up women by looking for signs of youth and fertility, such as clear skin, bright eyes, a big smile, etc. These and other visual cues caused men to become aroused and initiate the mating process.

On the other hand, a woman can't tell just from looking at a man if he would protect and provide for her and her future offspring. As we evolved, women probably depended more on memory—remembering if a man kept promises, was truthful, etc.

●**Why is rejection so difficult?** *There are two stages, each associated with different chemical changes...*

●The protest stage is very painful. You love even more deeply after you've been dumped. This is the time when you call constantly, write pleading e-mails, show up unannounced and generally make a fool of yourself.

Dopamine activity most likely spikes during the protest stage because the brain's reward system keeps churning it out in an attempt to recapture the beloved.

The behavior of jilted lovers often alienates the ones they love. This seems counterproductive from an evolutionary point of view, but it might be a way of conserving energy in the long run. The rejected one behaves in ways that sever the ties and allow both partners to move on and find new mates.

●The resignation stage is accompanied by a drop in dopamine. People experience lethargy, depression and a lack of motivation. The resignation stage may allow the body to rest and recover. It also sends out signals to others in the community that you need support, which can attract potential mates.

●**How can we diminish the pain?** It can take several months, or even years, to recover from rejection. Treat it as you would an addiction. Remove cards, letters and photos of the beloved. Don't call or write. Stay busy and get more exercise—physical activity increases dopamine activity. Sunlight also improves mood.

Seriously depressed people usually benefit from psychotherapy and/or antidepressants.

●**Is falling in love just a matter of brain chemistry?** Chemical factors clearly are involved, but many environmental elements also are at work. For example, you must be interested in meeting someone in the first place. If the timing is not right, you won't trigger the brain chemistry for romantic love.

●**How can long-married couples keep their love alive?** Novelty drives up the activity of dopamine. Couples who are spontaneous and try new things are aroused mentally as well as physically. Just going on vacation can spark your sex life and rejuvenate a relationship.

When Was the Last Time You Had Sex?

Michele Weiner Davis, MSW, who is an internationally renowned seminar leader and marriage therapist in Woodstock, IL. She is the author of six books on relationships, including *The Sex-Starved Marriage: A Couple's Guide to Boosting Their Marriage Libido* (Simon & Schuster). Her Web site is *www.sexstarvedmarriage.com.*

One in five couples has sex fewer than 10 times a year. A lack of frequent sex isn't a problem if both spouses are content with their sexual relationship. Conflicts develop when marital partners have significantly different sexual appetites. One in three married couples struggles with a gap in sexual desire. In fact, mismatched sexual desire is the number-one problem discussed in sex therapists' offices.

When couples have mismatched desire, one spouse yearns for more touching and physical closeness while the other doesn't understand why sex is such a big deal.

To the more sexual spouse, sex is important because it is about feeling wanted, attractive, loved and emotionally connected. Frequent rejection leads to resentment and hurt feelings, causing a rift in the marriage. That could result in infidelity and divorce.

CAUSES

The reasons why a spouse might lose interest in sex vary greatly. There might be a medical explanation, such as a hormone imbalance …a problem with the liver, kidneys or pituitary gland…undiagnosed diabetes…or a side effect of medication.

Stress, fatigue, depression, grief, a negative body image or unresolved issues from childhood, such as sexual abuse, also can sap your sexual desire. Other major libido busters are continuing arguments and feelings of anger between spouses.

IF YOU'RE THE SPOUSE WITH LOWER SEX DRIVE

In most marriages, low-desire spouses control the sexual relationship. They determine the frequency of sex. Too often, the low-desire spouse has the unspoken expectation, *I don't have to satisfy your sexual needs, but I expect you to remain faithful to our marriage.* This is an unfair arrangement. *Instead…*

●**Just do it.** Countless people in my practice have told me that they often weren't in the mood before they started making love, but once they got into it, they really started to enjoy themselves.

New research suggests that for more than half the population, sexual desire doesn't just happen. Most people have to be physically stimulated to feel desire for their partner. Ironically, this means that people who think they need to be in the mood to have sex might in fact need to have sex to get in the mood.

Example: A low-sex-drive wife conceded that while she frequently resisted her husband's advances, she usually enjoyed sex when she let her husband talk her into it. Her husband joked that she should write *I like sex* on her hand, so that she would remember it the next time he approached her.

●**Dispense with the checklist.** Some low-desire spouses convince themselves that they can't enjoy sex unless a long list of conditions is met.

Example: A man feels he can't make love unless the bills are paid, after-hours business calls are completed and the next day's appointments are reviewed.

Unless attending to an obligation is absolutely essential, make your marriage the priority.

●**Give your spouse a gift.** Although sex might not be important to you, it is to your spouse. In good marriages, people give their spouses what they want, even if they don't always want the same thing.

●**Find solutions to unresolved problems.** If relationship issues, such as anger or hurt feelings, or personal issues, such as depression or poor body image, are interfering with your desire for sexual intimacy, you may need professional help.

If you're a man whose interest in sex has dwindled, you may be a bit ashamed to ask for help. Don't be. Low desire in men is America's best-kept secret. Millions of men just aren't in the mood.

●**Schedule a complete physical** to rule out any underlying medical conditions.

IF YOU'RE THE SPOUSE WITH HIGHER DESIRE

The spouse with the greater sex drive often responds to sexual rejection by withdrawing emotionally or developing a short fuse. Both reactions tend to push the lower-desire spouse away further. *Instead…*

● **Search for the nonsexual triggers that will arouse your spouse.** Many highly sexed spouses try to boost a partner's libido with sex toys, X-rated videos or lingerie. People with low desire frequently feel more turned on by gestures of love outside the bedroom.

Example: A woman with low desire told me her biggest turn-on was when her husband went out on cold days to warm up her car for her. A low-desire man felt more passion for his wife when she acknowledged his hard work and financial contribution to the family.

Ask yourself, *What has my spouse been asking me for or complaining about?* Make a concerted effort to satisfy that request. Being responsive to your spouse's emotional needs is great foreplay.

● **Talk about your feelings.** Sharing feelings can be difficult, especially for men. It helps to discuss feelings of rejection openly and honestly. When you truly allow yourself to be vulnerable, your spouse is then more likely to feel sympathetic.

Example: A husband told his wife of 15 years that when she consistently said "no" to sex, he felt incredibly hurt and lonely in their marriage. He wondered why she didn't want him. For the very first time, she understood that her refusals had been hurting her husband emotionally, not merely denying him physical pleasure. She promised she would be more sensitive to his needs.

● **Steer clear of common turnoffs.** Blaming your spouse for the problems between you is one surefire way to keep him/her at arm's length. Mismatched sexual desire is the *couple's* problem, not just one spouse's problem.

Another turnoff to a low-desire spouse is when every touch, hug or kiss turns sexual. Make time for intimate touching without sex. It is also off-putting when a spouse is brusque all day and suddenly becomes loving in the bedroom at night.

● **Don't confuse denial of sex with intent to punish.** When a spouse continually refuses a mate's sexual advances, it is easy to perceive it as a punishment or personal rejection. That's unlikely to be the case.

● **Understand the ebb and flow of testosterone.** Both men and women are more turned on when their testosterone levels are high. Your sexual advances are more likely to be well received at those times.

Male testosterone levels typically peak early in the morning. Female testosterone is more likely to peak in the evening and mid to late in the menstrual cycle. Levels in postmenopausal women tend to be relatively constant throughout the day.

● **Spend more time together.** Schedule a relaxing day as a couple. Take time away from work. Turn off your cell phones. Hire a babysitter. Nonsexual time together without the kids can turn on a low-drive spouse.

● **Watch out for the sex substitutes that deepen the problem.** High-desire spouses will sometimes try to satisfy their unfulfilled sexual needs with behaviors that make their partners even less interested in making love, such as flirting, drinking or visiting pornographic Web sites.

The good news: A loving, pleasurable sexual relationship can be a tie that binds a marriage.

There is no reason why anyone wanting a more robust love life can't have one.

Nutrients That Boost Libido

There are some vitamins that can increase your sex drive…

● **Vitamin A** is important for estrogen and testosterone production. Get it from dairy, eggs, leafy green vegetables and meat.

● **Vitamin B complex** produces energy, sexual and otherwise. Good sources of this vitamin are whole grains, meat, fish, dairy, fruits, nuts and vegetables.

• **Vitamin C** can boost drive and strengthen sex organs. Berries, citrus fruits, potatoes, green peppers and broccoli contain it.

• **Vitamin E** is needed for the manufacture of sex hormones, which boost sex drive. Find it in wheat germ, liver and eggs.

Ian Marber and Vicki Edgson, both clinical nutritionists in London, *www.thefooddoctor.com,* and authors of *In Bed with the Food Doctor* (Collins & Brown).

Sexual Problems of Older People and How to Solve Them

Robert N. Butler, MD, president of the International Longevity Center in New York City. He is former chairman of the department of geriatrics and adult development at Mount Sinai Medical Center, New York City, the first geriatrics department in an American medical school. He won the Pulitzer Prize for his book *Why Survive? Being Old in America* (Johns Hopkins University) and is author of *The New Love and Sex After 60* (Ballantine).

Even healthy people who are in good relationships can do many things to improve their sex lives.

First step: Learn to ignore the signals sent by our society—that sex is only for the young. There's no reason that men and women can't have active, fulfilling sex lives into their 90s. In fact, some women become *more* orgasmic during their later years. While men typically take longer to get erections as they get older, their erections also tend to last longer, which can increase enjoyment for both partners.

Of course, getting older does bring certain physical changes, which can cause problems. Fortunately, these problems can almost always be treated.

CHANGES WOMEN CAN EXPECT

When women enter menopause, one of the most prevalent complaints is vaginal dryness during sex, which can make intercourse feel scratchy or even painful. Hormone replacement therapy (HRT) with an estrogen-progestin drug is often effective in restoring lubrication.

In light of recent warnings about long-term use of HRT, you may want to talk with your doctor about other treatments. Vaginal estrogen cream, applied directly to the vagina an hour before intercourse...a vaginal ring (inserted every three months)...and Vagifem (available by prescription only), an estrogen tablet that is inserted into the vagina twice a week, are all effective at counteracting vaginal dryness, while exposing the user to much lower doses of estrogen than HRT.

Another effective solution, already practiced by one out of three women in the US, is simply to apply a lubricant before sex. Make sure to use a non-oil-based lubricant such as K-Y Jelly, Astroglide, Slip or HR Lubricating Jelly. The oil-based lubricants, like petroleum jelly, mineral oil or baby oil, may cause vaginal infection.

Another option is a moisturizing gel in tampon form, such as Replens or Lubrin. Unlike the lubricants, these gels are simply inserted three times a week, and, therefore, do not interfere with sexual spontaneity.

CHANGES MEN CAN EXPECT

As I mentioned earlier, men take longer to get an erection as they grow older. They also usually require physical stimulation to become erect. It's important for their partners to realize that because a man may need to be *touched* to have an erection doesn't mean he's not attracted to his partner. It's just a natural part of aging.

But if a man has a consistent problem getting or maintaining an erection during intercourse, he may need to seek out treatment for erectile dysfunction (ED). The vast majority of ED cases have a physiological cause. If you're experiencing ED, have a physical, because ED may be symptomatic of an underlying medical problem.

The preferred treatments for ED include *sildenafil* (Viagra), *tadalafil* (Cialis) and *vardenafil* (Levitra). Cialis and Levitra are the newer drugs, but they have been used in Europe for years. Tens of millions of prescriptions have been written for Viagra in the US, and the data show that it is a very safe drug.

Viagra works by dilating blood vessels in the penis. It is not an aphrodisiac—but if you are stimulated erotically, Viagra will let you achieve an erection for several hours after it takes effect.

Viagra is safe and effective for men with diabetes, heart disease, hypertension, anxiety and depression, and men who have been treated for prostate cancer.

But someone who is taking nitroglycerin or any other nitrate heart medicine should not use Viagra under any circumstances.

Take Viagra about an hour before you plan to have sex. Viagra works best on a relatively empty stomach, and you should avoid smoking or heavy alcohol use while taking it. Once you've used it successfully for several months, try sex *without* Viagra—you may find you no longer need it.

Problem: Viagra can occasionally cause headaches or give a bluish tinge to your vision.

TESTOSTERONE SUPPLEMENTS

Testosterone is the hormone responsible for physical desire in men and women. In Europe, it has been widely used to treat low libido, and there has also been a surge in sales of testosterone in the US in the past few years. But the long-term benefits and risks of testosterone supplements still aren't clear.

If a man (or woman, for that matter) is deficient in testosterone, a testosterone patch or cream may be helpful in restoring sexual drive and function. But less than 4% of ED cases are related to testosterone deficiency. If you have either prostate cancer or benign prostate enlargement, testosterone supplements can exacerbate your condition.

What we really need is a long-term study of testosterone therapy to establish exactly what the pros and cons are.

More from Robert Butler...

Can Testosterone Make You Younger?

Everybody wants to be young and sexy—but as men age and their bodies produce less testosterone, they often start to feel weak, have trouble with memory and become less interested in sex. Wouldn't it be great if they could reverse the aging process?

Millions of American men are trying to do just that by replacing the testosterone that their bodies no longer supply. In 2002, nearly 2 million prescriptions for testosterone were written —a 30% increase from the number written in 2001. Sales were boosted by the availability of AndroGel, a prescription topical testosterone that is absorbed by the skin. Previously, testosterone could be delivered only by an injection.

DANGEROUS EXPERIMENT

Those men taking testosterone replacement therapy on their own are essentially participating in an uncontrolled and possibly life-threatening experiment. In the first place, nobody really is certain if male hormone replacement therapy works. Just because testosterone levels aren't as high as they were at age 30 doesn't mean that bringing them back to those levels restores virility.

Several studies have reported that older men (average age 52) who took testosterone developed big muscles but didn't get the muscle strength that usually goes along with muscle buildup. These men may have looked stronger, but they weren't any more robust than before they started taking the hormone—and nobody knows why.

More troubling is that doctors don't know how a person's biochemical system responds to artificially introducing hormones that the body has stopped producing naturally. They don't know if testosterone replacement promotes prostate cancer or has other negative effects on the body.

Red flags were raised when the Women's Health Initiative study released its disturbing findings. Women who had received hormone replacement therapy had a higher incidence of breast cancer, heart attacks and strokes. Another study reported that women who began hormone replacement therapy at age 65 or older were twice as likely to develop dementia, including Alzheimer's disease.

WHAT TO DO

Long-term studies are required to examine what happens over time to men who take testosterone replacement therapy.

Until we have answers, the best advice I can give a man who believes that he is suffering from low testosterone is to go see an endocrinologist—a physician who specializes in treating hormone imbalance. He/she can measure testosterone levels. If a man has total testosterone levels that are very low (200 nanograms per deciliter or lower), a trial of testosterone replacement may be considered.

The physician also will ask what medications the man is taking. Some drugs, including the blood pressure drug *spironolactone* (Aldactone) and the heartburn drug *cimetidine* (Tagamet), may cause testosterone levels to decline.

In many cases, lifestyle changes will be recommended. Men experiencing sexual dysfunction usually are advised to restrict their alcohol consumption since even small amounts of alcohol have been linked to a diminished capacity for achieving or maintaining an erection.

Men who are concerned about their mental function often are told to exercise more. Exercising three times a week for 30 minutes at a time fosters mental alertness. A study reported in *The New England Journal of Medicine* showed that social dancing four to five days a week is good for older brains as well as bodies. Similar benefits come from a variety of activities, including jogging, hiking, racquet sports, swimming, bicycling and use of exercise machines.

To fight off weakness, eat a well-balanced diet. Choose from the various food groups—include protein-rich plants (beans, nuts) and animal foods (lean meat, poultry, fish and eggs)…whole-grain foods…vegetables…fruits…and dairy products.

Although we can fantasize about a magic pill, sensible lifestyle changes are the answer right now—and they can be remarkably effective.

Top Doctor Answers Tough Questions On Viagra

Irwin Goldstein, MD, professor of urology and gynecology and director of the Institute for Sexual Medicine at Boston University School of Medicine. He has been involved with sexual dysfunction research since the late 1970s. He is also editor of the *International Journal of Impotence Research: The Journal of Sexual Medicine.*

Viagra has helped millions of men improve their sex lives. Now there are two other new drugs, Levitra and Cialis, that can help, too. *Here, straight answers to the most commonly asked questions about these drugs…*

●**I've heard that Viagra gives you an erection that lasts for hours. Is that true?** No. Viagra doesn't cause an erection, it *facilitates* one. It enhances the physiological processes that allow the penis to fill with blood and stay rigid in response to a signal from the brain. That signal is sparked by desire. Without the desire, nothing is likely to happen. After orgasm, you lose the erection, as you would if you weren't taking the drug.

Viagra doesn't kick in for at least an hour. It can facilitate an erection for up to 12 hours.

●**Does that mean that I can make love several times in one night?** Yes—though surveys indicate that only 10% of men choose to have a second interaction.

●**I have seen ads for Viagra on the Internet. Do I really need to see a doctor first?** Most emphatically yes. Erectile dysfunction is a medical problem and deserves a medical—and psychological—evaluation. It could be a symptom of a life-threatening illness, such as prostate cancer, heart disease or diabetes.

●**I tried Viagra once, but it didn't work. Would a stronger dose help?** I suggest trying Viagra at least five different times. If it still doesn't work, you may need a higher dose, or you can try one of the new drugs—Levitra or Cialis. Ask your doctor. If testosterone levels are low, normalizing them might make the Viagra more effective. Bringing down high cholesterol levels through diet and/or medication also might help.

●**I take an antidepressant that causes erection problems. Can Viagra help that?** Viagra is extremely effective when the problem is a side effect of medication, as can be the case with certain antidepressants, antihypertensives, diabetes and heart medications, etc. In fact, Viagra is very effective for a wide range of physical and psychological causes of erectile dysfunction. When erection problems are the consequence of radical prostatectomy, nerve damage or severe scarring to the penis, however, Viagra may not work well or at all.

●**I heard that some men died after taking Viagra. Is it dangerous?** Actually, Viagra is an amazingly safe drug—but the sex itself can be rather strenuous. As you near orgasm, blood pressure and heart rate rise. Some hearts cannot take this. It is not unusual to find men in the coronary care unit who have had heart attacks during sexual intercourse.

Important: Although Viagra is safe to take with most drugs, you shouldn't use it if you are taking nitrate medication, like *nitroglycerin,* for heart disease. This combination can cause fatal drops in blood pressure.

●**Does Viagra have side effects?** Viagra can cause headaches, stomach pain and/or intense facial flushing. A small percentage of men —maybe 2%—stops using it for these reasons.

●**My wife and I like to share a bottle of wine before we make love. Is that OK if I'm taking Viagra?** Alcohol may loosen up inhibitions, but it sabotages the ability to achieve an erection, whether or not you take Viagra. Consume alcohol only modestly.

●**My doctor told me not to take Viagra right after dinner. Why not?** Food interferes with absorption of Viagra, so take it at least 30 minutes before eating. I advise patients to take it in the late afternoon if they plan to have sex in the evening.

●**Can taking Viagra help women who have sexual problems?** It does benefit women with sexual problems caused by insufficient blood flow to their genitals. However, most of female sexual problems are related to diminished libido or diminished or absent orgasm unrelated to blood flow.

●**Will Viagra help my relationship?** Not necessarily. Some women believe that it makes men excessively goal-oriented—they think more about their erections and less about emotional intimacy. Some couples discover that even when sexual problems are resolved, relationship problems persist. They may need counseling as well.

●**I don't have erection problems, but I worry that I might in the future. Can taking Viagra now prevent trouble down the line?** Possibly. Nothing is better for the health of the penis than an erection. A German study of 100 men found that those who took Viagra nightly for one year had better erections than those who took it occasionally.

If you are at risk for erection problems—perhaps you have diabetes or high blood pressure or you smoke—ask your doctor about taking low-dose Viagra every night to prevent difficulties later on, just as you might take low-dose aspirin to prevent heart attack.

●**Are the new drugs, Levitra and Cialis, better?** Levitra is stronger—it works faster, lasts longer and the dose is smaller, so it may be of more benefit to some men. Cialis is effective for three days.

●**Should I be wary of Levitra and Cialis because they are new?** No. They have been used in Europe for years. Plus, they have gone through rigorous testing by the FDA.

Double Your Pleasure

The Wrigley Company has acquired a patent to manufacture a chewing gum that contains *sildenafil,* the active ingredient in the popular erectile dysfunction drug Viagra. The gum might appeal to men who can't take the pills or experience stomach upset from Viagra.

However: The gum will not be available before the year 2011. That is when Pfizer's patent for Viagra expires.

Internal Medicine News, 12230 Wilkins Ave., Rockville, MD 20852.

Help for Premature Ejaculation

Premature—or rapid—ejaculation (ejaculation that occurs after less than one minute of intercourse) isn't usually a psychological disorder, but a biological one. Recent research indicates it may be genetic and caused by a hyperactivity of the sympathetic nervous system, which controls the involuntary activities of the glands, organs and other parts of the body. Treatment with the selective serotonin reuptake inhibitor (SSRI) antidepressants, such as *paroxetine* (Paxil), may help to alleviate the problem by increasing serotonin levels in the brain. This neurotransmitter is believed to prolong ejaculation time. Talk to your doctor.

Pierre Assalian, MD, director, human sexuality unit at McGill University Health Centre, Montreal.

If Your Antidepressant Causes Impotence...

In a recent study, about 37% of men taking antidepressants reported some type of sexual dysfunction. However, when the pill was taken in the early morning, a significant number of men suffered no signs of erectile dysfunction during sex in the evening. If this doesn't help, *bupropion* (Wellbutrin) and *nefazodone* (Serzone) are two antidepressants that generally cause few sexual side effects. If you're unable to switch antidepressants, other drugs can help counteract the side effects. These include *buspirone* (BuSpar), an antianxiety drug, and the impotence drugs *sildenafil* (Viagra), *tadalafil* (Cialis) and *vardenafil* (Levitra).

Eric Hollander, MD, professor of psychiatry, director of clinical psychopharmacology, Mount Sinai School of Medicine, New York City.

Eat More Fish for Prostate Health

About 30% of American men have undiagnosed prostate cancer by age 60—but the incidence is only about 1% among Arctic Inuit men of that age group.

Theory: The fish and marine mammals, particularly whale products, in the Inuit diet are rich sources of prostate-protecting selenium and omega-3 fatty acids.

Science News, 1719 N St. NW, Washington, DC 20036.

Zinc Alert

Prostate cancer risk is linked to high zinc intake. Zinc, popular as a cold preventive, also is in many vitamin/mineral combinations.

New study: Men who took more than 100 milligrams (mg) of zinc daily over 10 or more years were more than twice as likely to develop advanced prostate cancer as men who took no supplementary zinc.

Self-defense: Avoid any supplements that contain many times the recommended dietary allowance—11 milligrams (mg) a day for men.

Michael Leitzmann, MD, DrPH, nutritional epidemiologist at the National Cancer Institute in Rockville, MD. His study of 46,974 men was published in the *Journal of the National Cancer Institute.*

To Lower Prostate Cancer Risk...

Frequent ejaculations can decrease prostate cancer risk.

Recent study: Men who ejaculate at least once a day during their 20s are one-third less likely to develop prostate cancer later in life.

Possible reason: Semen may have a carcinogenic effect if not expelled regularly from the prostatic ducts.

Graham Giles, PhD, director of the Cancer Epidemiology Centre, Cancer Council Victoria in Carlton, Australia, and the leader of a survey of 2,338 men, published in the *British Journal of Urology International.*

When a High PSA Reading Is Not a Problem

The blood levels of prostate-specific antigen (PSA) may increase temporarily because of inflammation in the prostate or because of recent ejaculation.

New study: Nearly 50% of men with high PSA readings—above 4.0—on one test had normal levels on subsequent tests.

If your PSA level is elevated: Wait at least six weeks before being retested. If the second reading is normal, you will have been spared an unnecessary biopsy. If not, the slight delay in further testing should not matter because prostate cancer typically progresses at a very slow rate.

James A. Eastham, MD, a urologic surgeon at Memorial Sloan-Kettering Cancer Center in New York City. His study of PSA levels in 972 men was published in *The Journal of the American Medical Association*.

Pumpkin for Your Prostate

Pumpkin seeds curb the symptoms of *benign prostatic hyperplasia* (BPH), the most common noncancerous enlargement of the prostate gland. In a six-month study of 2,245 men, German researchers found that prostate symptoms, like frequent urination and weak urinary stream, decreased by 41.8% in men who took pumpkin seed extract.

Theory: Pumpkin seeds are high in phytosterols, a compound that helps to shrink the prostate gland.

If you have an enlarged prostate: Take one 1,000-milligram (mg) capsule of pumpkin seed extract daily…or eat about one ounce of the seeds three times a week.

Andrew L. Rubman, ND, adjunct professor of medicine, Lane College of Integrative Medicine in Orlando, FL, and medical director, Southbury Clinic for Traditional Medicines in Southbury, CT, *www.naturopath.org*.

More from Andrew Rubman…

Best Herb for Male Urinary Tract Problems

Whole saw palmetto extract might work even better than standard saw palmetto

extract for male urinary tract problems. But, be sure to see a doctor formally trained in botanical medicine before trying any of the herbal medications.

Recommended: The Eclectic Institute's fresh freeze-dried berry extract, Serenoa serrulata (800-332-4372, *www.eclecticherb.com*).

Cost: About $18 for 120 600-milligram (mg) capsules.

Easy Ways to Overcome PMS

There are some easy things you can do to alleviate PMS symptoms…

• **Calcium**—1,200 milligrams (mg) daily significantly reduce PMS symptoms, including irritability and mood swings. Take supplements if you're not getting enough from dairy products and leafy green vegetables.

• **Chocolate**—just one-half ounce is enough to increase mood-boosting brain chemicals. PMS attacks are more likely when levels are low.

• **Small, frequent meals** throughout the day boost energy, balance moods, improve sleep and prevent water retention.

Sample menu: Breakfast—cereal and fruit… midmorning snack—yogurt and crackers… lunch—one-half sandwich and carrots…afternoon snack—one-half sandwich and milk… dinner—sushi.

Debra Waterhouse, MPH, RD, nutritionist, Orinda, CA, and author of *Outsmarting the Female Fat Cell After Pregnancy* (Hyperion).

Why Hugging Is Better Than Kissing

Women who hug their spouses often have better cardiovascular function and a lower stress response than those who do not. Frequent kissing does not show the same results.

Karen Grewen, PhD, assistant professor, department of psychiatry, University of North Carolina at Chapel Hill.

is needed, it sometimes can be done laparoscopically instead of via traditional methods.

Steven R. Goldstein, MD, professor of obstetrics and gynecology, New York University, New York City.

New Treatment for Hot Flashes

Recently approved by the FDA, the Femring is a flexible, self-inserted vaginal ring that releases a controlled dose of *estradiol,* the predominant form of estrogen circulating throughout a woman's body, three months at a time. After three months, you discard the ring and insert a new one. Estradiol alleviates hot flashes and other symptoms of menopause, which can include vaginal dryness, irritation and pain during intercourse.

Benefits: The ring will eliminate the need for medication every day and does not produce the dosage fluctuations of estrogen pills and patches, providing rapid, consistent relief. Once inserted, it's rarely felt by the wearer or her partner.

As with all other hormone products, the ring should be used at the lowest dose possible for the least amount of time to minimize estrogen absorption, which has been linked to increased risk for breast cancer.

Susan Ballagh, MD, assistant professor of obstetrics and gynecology, Eastern Virginia Medical School, Norfolk.

Most Uterine Fibroids Can Be Left Alone

Nothing can be done to prevent fibroids, but since they are not linked to cancer, it rarely is necessary to remove them. The location is important—a small fibroid in the central uterine cavity can cause bleeding and require surgery, while a larger one elsewhere may produce no symptoms and be left alone to shrink after menopause. If surgery, known as *myomectomy,*

How to Make Sure Your Mammogram Is Read Accurately

Alexander J. Swistel, MD, director of the Weill Cornell Breast Center and associate professor of surgery at New York Hospital–Cornell Medical Center, both in New York City. Dr. Swistel is widely recognized as a pioneer in the improvement of breast cancer care. He is also president of the Metropolitan Breast Cancer Group, the oldest and largest group of breast cancer specialists in the US.

Here are some of the questions you need to ask to find the right facility for your mammogram…

•**Has the office been accredited by the American College of Radiology?** If the facility is accredited, then the doctors must maintain accurate files on you, especially if cancer is suspected. The staff also is more likely to be well trained.

•**How many mammograms are performed there yearly?** Volume makes a difference. A facility that performs 50 mammograms a year is not going to be as competent as one that does 500.

•**Is the mammogram read at the facility?** Some places will send mammograms out to be read. The outside reader may not have pertinent clinical information or old films for comparison. If that's the case, the facility probably is not the best choice.

•**Is the mammogram read more than once?** A recent practice has developed called double-reading. One physician reads the mammogram, and then a second doctor reads it as well to guard against human error.

•**How old is the equipment?** The newer machines produce better images.

•**Can the facility perform biopsies and sonograms on-site?** This is an indication of a top facility. If there is any question regarding a reading, get a second opinion. Areas that might look cancerous can be benign—and vice versa. A second screening at a different facility may give the answer.

New Breast Cancer Test

A new breast cancer test helps women avoid unnecessary repeated biopsies that will follow a difficult-to-read mammogram and/or ultrasound. A radioactive material is injected into a vein in the foot and concentrates in any tumor cells. The breasts then are photographed with a gamma camera, which highlights abnormal tissue. This new test, called Miraluma, can be performed in a radiological facility at any major teaching hospital. Only some insurers cover it.

Typical cost: About $550.

Hemalatha Rao, MD, head of nuclear medicine, Coney Island Hospital, Brooklyn, NY.

Ibuprofen May Protect Against Breast Cancer

In a recent study, women who took two or more *ibuprofen* tablets a week for more than 10 years decreased breast cancer risk by 49%, compared with a 28% reduction for women who took aspirin.

Caution: The long-term use of ibuprofen or aspirin may cause stomach trouble—be sure to consult your doctor.

Randall E. Harris, MD, PhD, professor of preventive medicine and public health at The Ohio State University College of Medicine and Public Health, Columbus, and lead researcher in the National Cancer Center's Women's Health Initiative Observational Study of 80,741 women, reported in *Cancer Research*.

All About Virtual Colonoscopy

Virtual colonoscopy works as well as the conventional kind. A three-dimensional CT scan of the abdominal area detects precancerous polyps. No viewing device is inserted, so no anesthesia is required. Patients still prepare the night before by drinking a laxative.

Those who have a personal history of major polyps or symptoms such as rectal bleeding are better off with the conventional test, so any polyp can be removed immediately. With virtual colonoscopy, polyps often can be removed later that day or the next without re-prepping.

Perry Pickhardt, MD, associate professor of radiology, University of Wisconsin Medical School in Madison. His study of 1,233 adults was published in *The New England Journal of Medicine*.

Much Less Painful Hemorrhoid Surgery

The procedure for prolapse and hemorrhoids (PPH), or stapled *hemorrhoidectomy* is now widely used in Europe. It removes tissue and blood vessels that supply hemorrhoids so that they shrink within a few weeks. The procedure is done on an outpatient basis under local anesthesia. A patient can be back to normal activities after two days. Traditional hemorrhoidectomy requires up to six weeks of recuperation.

To find a doctor who performs PPH hemorrhoidectomy: Go to *www.pphinfo.com*. Look for a doctor who has done at least 25 of these procedures.

Check with your insurance company to find out if the procedure is covered.

Gary H. Hoffman, MD, a colorectal surgeon who performs PPH hemorrhoidectomy at Cedars-Sinai Medical Center in Los Angeles.

Don't Sweat It

If antiperspirants do not work for excessive sweating, try *Drysol,* a liquid form of concentrated aluminum that sticks in hair follicles and absorbs sweat. It is available only by prescription, so insurance may cover the cost. Another approach is a battery-powered product called *Drionic,* which uses electric current to reduce sweat production for six-week periods. Simply apply the device for 20 minutes to parts of the body that perspire heavily, such as underarms and feet.

Cost: $139.95.*

It's available from the manufacturer, General Medical Co. (800-432-5362, *www.drionic.com*).

Odor is caused by the bacterial breakdown of body oils. If over-the-counter (OTC) deodorants don't work, try applying an OTC antibacterial cream, such as Neosporin, instead of your usual deodorant.

Harold J. Brody, MD, clinical professor of dermatology, Emory University Medical School, Atlanta, and a dermatologist in private practice, *www.atlantadermatology.com.*

*All prices subject to change.

Embarrassing Problems That Just Won't Go Away

Dean Edell, MD, host of the nationally syndicated radio talk program "The Dr. Dean Edell Show." A former assistant clinical professor of surgery at the University of California, San Diego, he is the author of *Eat, Drink & Be Merry* (Quill).

Millions of Americans suffer needlessly from various niggling health problems that they assume are too minor to warrant professional help.

At the very least, these problems are just an annoyance. At worst, minor ailments are a sign of more serious, underlying conditions, such as infection. *The most common health problems that go untreated…*

ANAL ITCHING

The skin around the anus is always moist—a perfect breeding ground for fungi. Spicy foods or irritating chemicals in toilet paper also can cause anal itching. So can hemorrhoids or persistent diarrhea caused by some antibiotics.

What you may not know: Anal itching is *not* caused by poor hygiene. It's usually quite the opposite—vigorous scrubbing increases tissue damage and irritation.

What to do: Try daily applications of over-the-counter (OTC) 0.5% hydrocortisone cream. If the itching persists for more than a few days, ask your physician to test you for pinworms, fungal growth or other types of infections that may cause itching.

Also helpful…

•**Check your diet.** Some people are sensitive to acidic foods, such as tomatoes and citrus fruits. Avoiding these foods may reduce itching.

•**Wash very gently after having a bowel movement.** Moistening toilet paper with water will reduce irritation. Do not scrub the area, just pat gently. Dry the area thoroughly when you're done. OTC wipes, such as Tucks or disposable baby wipes, also can be used. Make sure that they don't contain alcohol, which can be irritating to the skin.

•**Avoid toilet paper with scents or dyes.**

•**Wear cotton underwear.** It "breathes" and reduces excess moisture.

•**Don't scratch.** It just irritates the skin and makes itching worse.

DANDRUFF

It's natural for dead skin cells to flake off and fall away—but people with dandruff can shed skin cells up to three times more quickly than normal.

Dandruff is linked to *Pityrosporum ovale,* a tiny fungus that lives on the skin. It's not clear if the fungus promotes rapid skin turnover or if it happens to thrive on people with an abundance of flaky skin.

What you may not know: Daily use of ordinary shampoo dries the skin and makes flaking worse.

What to do: Use a dandruff shampoo that contains *selenium sulfide,* such as Selsun Blue, or *ketoconazole,* such as Nizoral, every day for about a week. Then use it every few days, alternating with your regular shampoo, to keep dandruff under control. When shampooing, let the lather stand for about five minutes before rinsing it off.

EARWAX

The sticky, wax-like substance (cerumen) is produced by glands in the ear canal. It traps dust and other foreign particles and prevents them from damaging structures deeper in the ear. Earwax is unsightly and can potentially block the opening to the ear canal.

What you may not know: The amount and type of earwax (dry or oily) that you generate is genetic.

What to do: Use a wax-removal product that contains *carbamide peroxide* every few months.

Recommended brands: Murine Ear Drops and Debrox. Put a few drops in the ear, wait a few minutes, then flush out with a bulb syringe containing warm water.

Earwax that's interfering with normal hearing should always be treated by an ear, nose and throat (ENT) specialist, who will use a curved instrument called a curette to remove it. The procedure is painless and quick.

SMELLY FEET

Exposure to air quickly dries perspiration on other parts of your body, but shoes and socks trap moisture. Bacteria that thrive in the moist environment produce very strong odors.

What you may not know: Wearing the same shoes every day can cause feet to smell more.

What to do: Wash your feet several times daily with soap and water to remove bacteria. Some people apply rubbing alcohol to their feet to kill off germs. It works temporarily but dries the skin.

Go barefoot for a few hours daily to help keep the feet dry and odor-free. Wear only cotton socks. They absorb moisture and make feet less hospitable to odor-causing germs.

URINARY LEAKAGE

About 13 million Americans suffer from accidental leakage of urine from the bladder.

In women, the most common cause of urinary leakage is a weakening of the urinary sphincter or pelvic floor muscles as a result of pregnancy. And, urinary leakage in men is most often the result of a surgery to treat prostate enlargement or cancer. Obesity may also cause incontinence because it puts constant pressure on the bladder and surrounding muscles.

What you may not know: The majority of men and women who suffer from urinary leakage are too embarrassed to tell their doctors about the problem.

What to do: Both women and men often can regain bladder control with Kegel exercises that strengthen the pelvic floor muscles. These are the same muscles you tighten when you stop the flow of urine.

Several times every day, squeeze the muscles, hold for a few seconds, then relax. Repeat the sequence at least 10 times.

Also helpful for women and men...

●**For several weeks, go to the bathroom by the clock**—every half hour, for example, whether or not you need to go. Then slowly lengthen the time between bathroom visits as you achieve more control. With practice, you should be able to urinate every three to four hours, without "accidents" in between.

●**Antispasmodic drugs,** such as *tolterodine* (Detrol) and *dicyclomine* (Bentyl), calm an overactive bladder.

New Treatment for Incontinence

Urinary urge incontinence, a condition that results in urine loss before being able to get to the toilet, can be greatly eased by Milk of Magnesia.

Recent finding: Women who took one teaspoon of magnesium hydroxide—the active ingredient in Milk of Magnesia, Mylanta and Maalox—twice a day had significantly fewer episodes than those taking a placebo.

Theory: Magnesium hydroxide minimizes contractions of the bladder muscle that is responsible for an overactive bladder.

Farnaz Alams Ganj, MD, assistant professor, obstetrics and gynecology, Akbarabadi Hospital, Iran University of Medical Sciences, Tehran.

7

Money Confidential

More Than Two Dozen Ways to Save Money

Regardless of the state of the economy, you do not want to pass up any opportunity to save money. Of the hundreds of ways to save, here are some of the best. Stop procrastinating. Put them to work for you now.

PERSONAL FINANCE

●**Banking.** Credit unions are a thrifty alternative to banks—they usually charge less for consumer loans and pay more interest on savings. Call local credit unions to inquire about membership or contact the Credit Union National Association (*www.creditunion.coop*, 800-358-5710) to find the address of your state association. Ask about the credit unions you may be eligible to join.

Important: Only join a credit union that has deposits which are insured by the National Credit Union Administration (NCUA), since this organization provides federal protection identical to the protection that the Federal Deposit Insurance Corporation (FDIC) provides banks.

Check moneysaver: Order checks directly from a printer (such as *www.123checksonline. com, www.checkworks.com, www.checksinthe mail.com* or *www.checksunlimited.com*) rather than purchasing them from your bank. These checks can be used at any bank.

Savings: About 50%.

●**Debt.** Reduce your debt to save money.

One way: Use money from savings accounts that pay low interest to pay off high-interest credit card debt.

Example: If you have a money market account paying 0.75% and credit card debt costing 14%, you're losing 13.25% in interest each year.

Lucy H. Hedrick, an expert on time and money management and the founder and president of Hedrick Communications, a publishing consulting firm located in Old Greenwich, CT. She is author of *365 Ways to Save Money* (Hearst).

● **Credit cards.** Select the right type of card for your needs. Call around or visit *www.bank rate.com* to explore your choices. *What type of card you should look for…*

● If you carry a balance, opt for a low-rate credit card.

● If you pay off your balance each month, choose a no-fee card.

● If you spend a lot monthly, opt for special-offer cards. You can earn airline mileage, cash back or points toward merchandise.

Examples: Discover (800-347-2683, *www. discovercard.com*) gives up to 2% back in cash, and Shell MasterCard (866-438-7435, *www.866 getshell.com*) lets you earn 5% on purchases of Shell gasoline and 1% on any other purchases toward future gasoline purchases.

● **Insurance.** Comparison shop for your insurance needs to find the lowest prices. Check other insurers or go to *www.insure.com* to get quotes from more than 200 leading insurers. *More cost-cutting ideas…*

● Cut car insurance 30% by increasing your deductible from $250 to $500.

● Cancel collision coverage on cars that are older than five years.

● Do not take the insurance coverage when renting a car—your own policy, and even major credit card companies to which the rental is charged, will cover any liability.

YOUR HOME

● **Mortgages.** You can save thousands of dollars in interest costs by accelerating your mortgage. *Options…*

● Pay additional principal with each payment.

● Pay one-half of the monthly amount due every two weeks. That adds up to one extra payment each year.

● If there are more than 15 years remaining on your mortgage, refinance using a 15-year loan. You'll pay more in the short run but save thousands overall.

● **Utilities.** Check to see if your utility company offers two-tier pricing. If so, run major appliances (washer, dryer, dishwasher) at off-peak times—weekends, holidays and weekdays between 10 pm and 10 am.

Purchase only energy-efficient appliances. They may cost you more up-front, but you'll save in operating costs over the life of the appliances. To check out energy ratings, look at the Energy Guide label on the appliance or go to the Web site *www.energyguide.com.*

● **Selling your home.** Market it yourself to save the usual 6% real estate commission. Make sure you have the time and ability to advertise and show your home to its best advantage.

If you can't, consider using a discount Realtor. Foxtons (800-545-2001, *www.foxtons.com*), which operates in Connecticut, New Jersey and New York, charges 2%. Help-U-Sell (800-366-1177, *www.helpusell.com*) charges a flat fee that is payable at closing, the amount of which varies across the nation.

Savings: On a $200,000 home, you could pay as little as $4,000 (2%), rather than $12,000.

● **Moving.** *Save on the cost of a move by…*

● Moving on a weekday. Costs are 50% lower than on a weekend.

● Packing everything yourself, which saves at least 10%.

● Getting a binding estimate in writing before contracting with a mover. In about 25% of nonbinding estimates, the actual cost of the move exceeds the estimate. With a binding estimate, the price is guaranteed.

INVESTMENTS

● **Fixed income.** Buy the government instruments to save on purchase expenses and taxes. Savings bonds (Series EE and I) can be purchased from your bank or the US Treasury on-line at *www.savingsbonds.gov.* Interest is state tax free, while federal tax on interest can be deferred and may even be exempt if used to pay for higher education costs.

Treasury bonds and notes can be purchased directly from the Treasury on-line (*www.public debt.treas.gov/sec/sectrdir.htm*) or at a Federal Reserve bank. Here, too, there's no purchasing fee and interest is state tax free.

● **Equities.** Save on investment costs by buying no-load mutual funds—the annual management fee is usually less than 1% and there are no sales fees to buy or to sell.

Buy stock through dividend reinvestment plans (DRIPs), which enable you to purchase stock directly from the company and reinvest dividends for more stock. There's usually only a small administrative charge for purchases. See *www.moneypaper.com.*

THE LAW

●**Power of attorney (POA).** Giving a POA to a spouse, adult child or friend can save you money should you become incapacitated. Your family can avoid the expense (court costs and attorneys' fees) of going to court to have someone appointed to manage your financial affairs.

●**Divorce.** Mediated divorces cost about 50% of what contested divorces cost.

Caution: Don't use mediation if you have questions about your spouse's honesty, if he/she is involved in criminal activity, is mentally incompetent or there is current physical abuse.

CARS

●**Pump your own gas.** Also, add oil and windshield fluid yourself. Buy oil and fluid by the case at an auto discount store.

●**Think twice before buying an extended-service contract.** It may merely duplicate the manufacturer's warranty. Check out the facts on auto-service contracts at the Federal Trade Commission Web site at *www.ftc.gov.* Click on "For Consumers," then "Automobiles."

COMPUTERS

Purchase a used computer (if it has a vendor warranty) or a refurbished one (which usually comes with a vendor warranty, although it may be a limited one). The best is a manufacturer-refurbished computer, one which has been restored to exact manufacturer specifications and comes with a manufacturer's warranty. Look for these at *www.gateway.com, www.dell.com* and *www.ubid.com.* Prices usually run about 25% below a comparable new computer.

TRAVEL

●**Travelers as young as 50 qualify for discounted rates** on hotels, cruises, airlines and car rentals if they are members of AARP (formerly called the American Association of Retired Persons). You do not have to be retired to join. Membership is $12.50* per year.

●**When booking a hotel room, ask for a discount** through AARP, military, business or any other discount plan available to you.

*All prices subject to change.

●**If you have the time, volunteer to get off an overbooked flight**—in exchange for cash or free round-trip tickets.

How to Slash Outrageous Bank Fees

Edward F. Mrkvicka, Jr., president of Reliance Enterprises, Inc., 22115 O'Connell Rd., Marengo, IL 60152. He is author of *Your Bank Is Ripping You Off* (St. Martin's).

The key to bringing down many banking costs—and even boosting interest rates on savings—is developing a relationship with your local banker. No small bank will risk losing a large account because of a quibble over one-half of a percentage point in interest or a $25 monthly service fee. While Internet banks might charge less for checking, resolving problems can be a nightmare because you can't find out who is in charge or where records are kept.

Compare costs for services you need by calling at least three local banks.

Shortcut: Go to *www.bankrate.com* and click on "Checking & ATM."

To slash annoying banking costs…

OVERDRAFTS

The average fee for a bounced check is $26.* Even if you have overdraft protection, you will be charged a fee plus interest.

Solutions…

●**Ask the bank to refund the overdraft charge.** Many banks will oblige if you only make a mistake occasionally.

●**Avoid triggering overdraft.** Many charges result from debit cards as husbands and wives make purchases without telling each other. Use credit cards instead. Pay them off promptly to avoid interest charges.

●**Ask for "free" overdraft protection.** If you overdraw from your account, the bank will phone and give you a day—or more—to cover the shortfall at no charge.

*According to a 2003 survey of bank checking account fees by Bankrate.com.

Caution: Customers who frequently trigger overdrafts may lose this consideration.

CHECK COPYING

In the past, banks mailed canceled checks to customers for free. Now, many banks charge an $8 copy fee per check.

Solution: Use check registers that include carbon copies. Keep these copies for your records. If you need a copy from the bank, ask to have the fee waived.

MINIMUM BALANCE

This fee averages $6 to $11 per month if your account falls below the minimum for even one day. The average minimum required to avoid this fee is about $3,000 at traditional banks.

Solution: Choose an account with little or no minimum. Many banks offer truly free checking with no minimums for seniors and students.

INTEREST ON INSTALLMENT LOANS

If you take a three-year installment loan to buy a car, don't think that the interest costs will decline over time, as with a mortgage. In many cases, you will continue to pay interest on the initial amount throughout the loan's term.

Solution: Insist on a simple interest single-payment loan that will allow for monthly payments or a simple interest installment loan. Most banks make simple interest loans but don't necessarily volunteer this information.

Example: If you had a 48-month car loan for $10,000 at 10.25%, you would save $138.87 over the life of the loan with simple instead of traditional interest.

UNNECESSARY INSURANCE

When you take out a loan, bank officers will often try to sell you expensive *credit life and disability insurance,* which pays off the loan should you die or makes monthly payments should you become disabled. Some automatically write insurance into loan documents and don't discuss it with customers. Customers are afraid of disrupting the closing, so they don't question the extra charges.

Solution: Don't buy loan insurance from the bank. In the event of your death, it pays off only your loan balance. If you choose to protect a $10,000 four-year car loan, earmark $10,000 of your term life insurance policy for this purpose.

To compare term insurance rates, ask an independent agent or go to *www.insure.com* or to *www.term4sale.com*.

If unauthorized insurance is included in your loan documents, ask that it be removed before proceeding with the closing.

CASHIER'S CHECKS

Many banks charge $3 for cashier's checks.

Solution: Get a money order from the post office for about $1.

DELAYS IN CREDITING YOUR ACCOUNT

Many banks say they will not clear an out-of-state check for three business days. And, some checks take even longer. Since some banks are closed one weekday, if you deposit a check on the "wrong" day, your check might not clear for longer still.

Your bank receives payment for most checks from anywhere in the US within just 24 hours. Banks impose a waiting period and only count business days, not calendar days, so they can get free use of your money.

Solution: Ask for a brochure describing your bank's check-clearing policy. Direct deposits should clear immediately. If you need immediate access to cash, even from out of state, ask your banker to arrange it.

ATM FEES

Choose a bank that has no ATM fees. Locate other banks that don't charge ATM fees in case you are away from your branch's ATM. To find banks with no ATM fees, go to *www.bankrate. com* and click "Checking & ATM."

Credit Card Know-How

To get the most that you can from reward credit cards…

● **Use only one.** You will generate bigger rewards by funneling spending to one card.

● **Don't carry a balance.** Rebate-card interest rates are 1% higher on average than rates on other types of credit cards.

- **Shop for the best deal.** In the past, rebate cards offered frequent-flier miles or cash. Today, rebates can be used for store discounts, gasoline, gift certificates, cars, even college savings.

- **Heavy card users** should consider one that offers a greater rebate when you reach a certain spending level.

Greg McBride, CFA, senior financial analyst at Bankrate. com, North Palm Beach, FL.

directors and request it. Or join more than one credit union.

- **Location.** If you prefer dealing with a teller, you'll need a credit union that has a nearby branch. If you do your banking using automated teller machines (ATMs) and the Internet, the location might not matter. For easy access, make sure that the credit union you choose is part of a bank ATM network.

Credit Unions for Everyone (Almost)

Patrick Keefe, vice president at the Credit Union National Association, Washington, DC, *www.cuna.org*.

Credit unions offer comprehensive banking services—credit cards, on-line bill paying and home-equity loans. Some even have securities brokerage subsidiaries.

Important: Credit unions pay higher rates on CDs and savings accounts than banks, and they charge less for mortgages and auto loans because of their not-for-profit status. Average rates are listed at *www.bankrate.com*.

CHOOSING THE RIGHT ONE

With more than 10,000 credit unions, practically anyone can find one that meets his/her needs. To compare, check with my organization, the Credit Union National Association (800-358-5710 or *www.creditunion.coop*, click on "Locate a Credit Union.") *Features to consider...*

- **Membership criteria.** Some credit unions are only open to residents of a particular city... employees of a corporation or government entity...members of a union, professional organization or fraternal association, including the Elks and Knights of Columbus. They also are open to members' relatives.

- **Array of services.** Credit unions provide everything from insurance to small-business loans of $80,000 or less—an amount too small for most banks to spend their time on. Others will only provide basic savings and checking accounts. If your credit union doesn't offer a service you need, call a member of the board of

Monitor Your Credit Reports to Get Better Rates

Steve Rhode, president and cofounder, Myvesta.org, a nonprofit financial-management organization in Rockville, MD, *www.myvesta.org*. Mr. Rhode is coauthor of *The Ultimate Spending Plan Program Yearly Tracking Book* (Debt Counselors of America).

Actively monitoring your credit report will ensure that you get the best possible rates and let you catch identity thieves in the act. But it's not so simple.

The major credit agencies may not all have the same information about you. If you have just one report, you won't get the whole picture.

GET YOUR CREDIT REPORTS

Check your credit reports for accuracy at least once every year. If they are incorrect, you might pay unnecessarily high rates or even be turned down for loans altogether.

Cost: $9* per report...about $15 if you also want your credit score. But, under the *Fair and Accurate Credit Transactions Act of 2003* (FACT), annual reports should be free of charge starting in late 2004.

The three agencies: Equifax (800-685-1111, *www.equifax.com*)...Experian (888-397-3742, *www.experian.com*)...TransUnion (800-888-4213, *www.transunion.com*).

Easier: Obtain a consolidated report, which includes a credit score and data from all three of the agencies, for $34.95 from my organization,

*All prices subject to change.

www.myvesta.org (this report is only available on the Internet).

ANALYZE YOUR CREDIT REPORT

Review your report, and immediately tell the credit provider and credit agency about any inaccuracies. It takes about two months for closed accounts to disappear from your credit history. You can get expedited service for a fee. *Look for...*

●**Active accounts you do not recognize,** such as credit cards or store charge accounts in places that you don't shop. Someone may have stolen your identity, or another person's charge accounts may have been included accidentally on your report. This frequently happens to people who have common surnames, such as Jones and Smith.

●**Inaccuracies,** such as debts listed as unpaid that were settled and payments listed as late that were made on time. These entries will remain on your record for seven years unless you correct them. Make sure late payments are not listed as uncollected debts.

Fixing mistakes: Ask the credit agency for a dispute form. The agency generally must investigate your concerns and then report back to you within 30 days.

If the agency cannot verify the information that you questioned, it must delete it from your file and notify anyone who has requested your credit report within the past six months.

●**Old or unused charge accounts.** Too much credit can harm your rating even if most of the accounts are dormant.

What to do: Keep two or three of the oldest accounts open, and use them once in a while. Close the others.

Some Ways to Borrow Money Are Much Better Than Others

William G. Brennan, CPA/PFS, CFP, Capital Management Group, LLC, 1730 Rhode Island Ave. NW, Washington, DC 20036.

With interest rates near historic lows, now is a great time to borrow money if you need the cash to fix up your home, pay for college, or pay down credit card debt. In taking loans, keep tax rules in mind so that you maximize your interest deductions.

BEST SOURCE OF BORROWING

The tax law favors borrowing on your home. *Interest is fully deductible on loans...*

●**Up to $1 million to buy, build or substantially rehabilitate your main home** or a second home, plus...

●**Up to $100,000 of home-equity debt,** no matter what you use the proceeds for.

The proceeds from home-equity loans can be used to pay off your credit card debt or for any other purpose without affecting the deductibility of interest.

Remember that home-mortgage borrowing is secured by your home—if you have difficulties keeping up with monthly payments, you risk losing your home.

Points: If you pay points (a type of additional interest charged by the lender when granting a loan), you can deduct them in the year of payment provided they are for the purchase of a principal residence. If points relate to any other type of borrowing—for the purchase of a vacation home or to refinance an outstanding mortgage—the points must be deducted over the term of the loan.

You are not required to deduct points paid to acquire a mortgage to buy a principal residence—you can deduct them over the term of the loan. This may be advisable if you do not have sufficient deductions in the year of purchase to itemize deductions and use the entire write-off. In subsequent years, when your deductions are high enough for itemizing, you will then receive a tax benefit from your points deductions.

Refinancing: If you *refinance* your home mortgage, you can deduct in full the remaining points from a previous refinancing in the year of the second refinancing.

Pitfall: Interest on a home-mortgage loan—whether a first mortgage or home-equity loan—used for any purpose other than to buy, build or substantially rehabilitate your main or second home, or in connection with your unincorporated trade or business, is not deductible for alternative minimum tax (AMT) purposes. This means that sizable interest payments on mortgages used for other purposes can trigger or increase AMT liability.

FOLLOW THE MONEY

With the exception of home-mortgage borrowing, the tax treatment of interest on other debt depends on what you use the loan proceeds for. *If you use the money...*

● **To buy a business or equipment to contribute to your business**—interest is fully deductible business interest. There are no limitations on this deduction.

● **To buy new investments (other than tax-exempt securities)**—the interest is investment interest. This is deductible to the extent of your net investment interest income for the year. But unused interest expense in excess of the limit can be carried forward to future years.

● **To pay for higher education**—interest is deductible as an adjustment to gross income (no itemizing is necessary). The limit on this interest is up to $2,500 annually if your modified adjusted gross income (MAGI) is no more than $50,000 and $100,000 on a joint return. (MAGI is AGI plus certain income and minus certain deductions that are normally excluded or deducted.)

The deduction limit phases out for MAGI between $50,000 and $65,000 ($100,000 and $130,000 on a joint return). No deduction can be claimed if MAGI exceeds $65,000 ($130,000 on a joint return).

● **To pay for vacations, credit card debt, or other personal expenses**—interest is not deductible.

MORE SOURCES OF BORROWING

Where you borrow the money does not affect the tax treatment of your interest (other than interest on home-equity loans). But there are borrowing sources that provide more favorable interest rates and repayment terms than others. *Consider borrowing from...*

● **Your retirement plan.** If you participate in a retirement plan that permits loans, you can borrow up to 50% of your account balance or $50,000, whichever is less. This borrowing option now applies to self-employed individuals and other business owners. Prior to 2002, they had been banned from such borrowing.

Catch: The plan must be amended to allow for borrowing.

The good news: These loans are very easy to arrange. Simply request a loan from the plan administrator. Interest on the loan will probably be modest because the plan is not required to charge more than a "reasonable" rate. If the plan relies on the applicable federal rate (AFR), for example, the rate for a loan that's granted in August 2004 would only be 3.93% per year on monthly payments.

The bad news: You must repay the loan in level payments over a period of no more than five years. Any reasonable time is allowed if the proceeds are used to buy your home. If you are a "key employee" (highly paid executive or more-than-5% owner), you cannot deduct your interest payments, even if the funds are used for an otherwise deductible purpose, such as to buy investments. And if you leave the company, you must repay any outstanding loan balance at that time. Any amounts that are not repaid are treated as taxable distributions from the plan.

● **Family, friends or your business.** People you're close to might be willing to lend you money at little or no interest. If interest is less than the AFR for the term of the loan, the lender generally must report the forgone interest as income (it's called "imputed interest" or "phantom interest"). The borrower may be able to deduct imputed interest according to the rules above.

To arrange a loan: *Keep the following below-market loan rules in mind...*

●If the loan is no more than $10,000, there are no consequences if there is little or no interest charged. This is viewed as a "gift loan" and the imputed interest rules do not apply.

Be aware that the $11,000 annual gift tax exclusion for 2004 does not affect the $10,000 limit on gift loans. The $10,000 limit on gift loans is not adjusted annually for inflation.

●If the loan is no more than $100,000 and the borrower's net investment income is $1,000 or less, there is no imputed interest. If net investment income is more than $1,000, imputed interest applies but only to the extent of the excess investment income.

Important: In arranging intrafamily loans, be sure to put the terms (for example, the interest rate, the repayment schedule) in writing. Should the borrower be unable to repay the loan, the lender will be able to claim a bad debt deduction and will have the necessary proof on hand if the IRS questions the deduction.

●**Your brokerage account.** You can arrange for a margin account loan against your securities held with a brokerage firm. Generally, you can borrow up to 50% of the value of your securities (90% for Treasuries). Interest charged by the firm is usually tied to the prime rate so it can vary from month to month. But you have control over when and the extent to which you repay the funds. You can do so at any time.

Caution: If you borrow to the full extent of your loan limit and the value of your account drops because stock or bond prices decline, you still have to keep your loan within the limits. You may be forced to sell some securities at distressed prices or borrow elsewhere to pay off debt.

●**Your life insurance policy.** If you have a policy other than a term policy, you can borrow against its cash surrender value. Again, this borrowing is easy to arrange and interest rates are usually low. Older policies may carry very low interest rates under the terms of the contract. And, like margin account loans, repayment is within your discretion.

Caution 1: Any outstanding loan balance remaining at the death of the insured is subtracted from the proceeds payable to the beneficiary, which can leave the beneficiary short of funds.

Caution 2: If there is an outstanding loan on the policy and it is transferred, the new owner does not receive all of the proceeds tax free at death. A gift of a policy with an outstanding loan is treated as a "transfer for consideration" (because the original policyholder is relieved of repaying the loan). And, the new policyholder cannot exclude more than his/her financial obligation, plus any premiums paid after the transfer.

Example: A father has a $1 million life insurance policy with a cash surrender value of $250,000. He borrows this amount and gifts the policy to his son, who continues to pay the premiums. Five years later, when the father dies (assume no loan repayment has been made), the son receives $750,000 in proceeds ($1 million minus $250,000), but can exclude from income only $250,000, plus the premiums paid during the five years. Almost $500,000 is taxable to the son (it would all have been tax free if the father had not made the gift).

How to Make Debt Work For You

David Bach, CEO and founder of FinishRich Inc., financial experts and educators in New York City, *www.finish rich.com*. He is the author of *Smart Couples Finish Rich, Smart Women Finish Rich* and *The Finish Rich Workbook* (all from Broadway).

Few people seem to be aware that there is a science to borrowing that will actually *build* wealth. Debt interest drains potential savings, but some purchases can yield big future returns. How does your debt load stack up? *Debt in the average US household...*

Mortgage balance: $69,277.

Mortgage payment: $669/month.

Car loan: $23,065.

Car payment: $412/month.

Credit card balance: $8,367.

This is an enormous debt load. The average American now spends a little more than 14% of his/her after-tax income to pay credit card bills and other debts. Some people pay far more, with mortgages alone taking up to 30% of their after-tax income.

MAXIMIZE "GOOD" DEBT

Good debt is money borrowed to buy an asset that appreciates in value. It allows you to build wealth over the long term. *Examples...*

●**Home mortgages.** Most homes appreciate in value, mortgage interest usually is tax deductible, *and* you get a place to live. The average net worth of a renter is $4,200...of a home owner, $132,000.

●**Education loans.** An advanced degree can help to increase your earning ability by as much as 80%. Up to $2,500 per year in interest on student loans is tax deductible if you earn less than $50,000, or $100,000 if married.

●**Business-improvement loans.** These are some of the best investments. They usually directly increase revenue.

●**Home-improvement loans.** These also are good debt just as long as you don't *overimprove* your house to the degree that your investment remains unrecoverable when you sell. Recoverable improvements are those that make your house more desirable, such as a new kitchen or bathroom. However, the cost of marble floors in a modest home might be hard to recover when you sell.

MINIMIZE "BAD" DEBT

Bad debt is money borrowed for items that don't contribute to your financial future. *Some examples...*

●**Auto loans.** Even if you get 0% financing, you still are taking on $20,000 or more in debt that could be used for an appreciating asset. In addition, just as soon as you drive off the car dealer's lot, your investment value declines by about 30%.

Better: If you drive less than 10,000 miles a year as part of your job, consider leasing a car and deducting the expense. Otherwise, buy a used car at a fraction of the cost of a new car. You still can deduct the cost of mileage accumulated for work.

●**Loans for vacations,** clothing, furnishings, appliances and entertainment.

●**Loans for weddings,** anniversary parties and other big celebrations. The average wedding now costs about $20,000 and can take 10 years to pay off.

CONTROL ALL DEBT

●**Record every cent you spend for one week.** I call it finding your "latte factor." If you spend $3.50 per day on a caffe latte, that same amount invested over 30 years at a 10% return would be a fortune—$242,916.

Helpful: A free worksheet on spending is available at *www.finishrich.com.* Just click on "Worksheets."

●**Keep debt payments under 15% of net income.** Anything higher almost always indicates future debt problems. It also makes lenders reluctant to give you loans.

To calculate your percentage of debt to income: Total all your monthly expenses. Subtract your mortgage payments or rent. Include credit card bills, personal loans, student loans, medical bills for services already rendered and car loans. Divide this figure by your monthly after-tax income—including salary, investment income, alimony and child support.

Example: If you have monthly after-tax income of $4,000 and debt payments of $580, your percentage of debt to income is $580 divided by $4,000, or 14.5%.

MANAGING WEALTH

●**Determine the real cost of a purchase before buying.** Real cost includes the interest you will pay. People get into big debt trouble because they fool themselves about real costs.

Example: A new computer is attractive at $499—but if you charge it and take two years to pay off the balance, it really costs closer to $600. Is the computer still worth the money?

Use the calculator in the "Credit Cards" section of *www.bankrate.com* to figure out the real cost of purchases.

●**Think of spending as a series of "either/ or" choices.** Before you make any purchase, think about the trade-off—*If I buy this stereo, I can't go out to dinner for the next three months. Is the stereo worth it to me?*

●**Postpone buying anything that costs more than $100** until you think about it for

24 hours. This cuts down on impulse spending that you might regret later.

● **Automate your bill paying as much as possible.** Have your credit card payments and other debts automatically deducted from your checking account. Knowing that you'll have to pay off the balance in full each month might make you less likely to spend.

This practice also avoids interest penalties and puts an end to late fees, which now average about $30 per month.

Automatic payments can be made through most banks or through *www.paytrust.com* and *www.statusfactory.com.*

● **Fund your dreams.** Set aside a portion of your after-tax income for vacations and treats. You are less likely to binge if you have something to look forward to.

BEWARE OF DEBT TRAPS

The average American's credit card debt is more than three times what it was in the early 1990s—and the average interest rate is 14%.

● **Avoid store credit cards.** It's easy to be lured by aggressive promotions. Many retailers give you 10% off your first purchase when you open a credit card account and offer special discount incentives to retain cardholders.

Best: Turn down these offers, no matter how much money you save. The only advantage is if you pay off your balance. Virtually all of my clients have good intentions, but sooner or later they slip. That's why store credit cards, which typically charge more than 20% interest, are such a lucrative business. Also, lenders look negatively at your credit report if you have a dozen cards with tens of thousands of dollars in available credit—even if you don't use it.

● **Be wary of "one year interest free" deals on furniture and electronics.** The fine print on some contracts stipulates that if you don't pay off your entire bill within a year, you're liable for 15% to 22% interest on the entire amount for the year.

Shrewd Ways to Protect Your Assets from Creditors

Gideon Rothschild, Esq., CPA, partner in the law firm Moses & Singer LLP, 1301 Avenue of the Americas, New York City 10019, *www.mosessinger.com.*

You do have a legal right to set up your affairs in a way that protects your property from unexpected claims—as long as you're not defrauding existing creditors.

New asset protection opportunities have recently arisen but there are also several unanswered questions to keep in mind.

DOMESTIC SELF-SETTLED TRUSTS

In a handful of states, you can put your own money in a trust for yourself and have those assets protected from creditors. In those states, you can set up a trust for yourself—known as a "self-settled trust"—manage the money, receive the income, have access to principal and block your creditors from laying claim to the assets in the trust.

Rhode Island and Utah have recently joined with three other states—Alaska, Delaware and Nevada—in permitting residents to set up these asset-protection trusts.

Caution: There are no court decisions that indicate whether *nonresidents* can set up a self-settled trust in one of these states to gain asset protection. It may require US Supreme Court review to ultimately settle the issue.

Bottom line: There's no downside to a nonresident seeking asset protection in one of these states—other than the expense of setting up the trust. If a court permits creditors access to funds in the trust, the nonresident is no worse off than if the trust had not been set up in the first place. Also, there is the possibility that a court may uphold asset protection for nonresidents. Setting up such a trust creates a significant obstacle for any creditor, giving you negotiating leverage when settling a claim.

FOREIGN TRUSTS

Off-shore trusts (set up in another country) are also an effective way to protect assets from creditors. Foreign courts do not have to honor US court judgments.

Caution: Several US courts have just recently imposed civil contempt orders against debtors whose foreign trusts were set up after claims were made against the debtors. In such cases, the debtor is ordered to pay the US judgment with funds in the foreign trust or face an undetermined amount of jail time. Whether or not this trend will continue remains to be seen.

WILLS AND LIVING TRUSTS

You have an opportunity to create asset protection for your family when making your estate plans. Parents will often set up trusts for their children to run until the children attain a certain age. However, it may be advisable to let assets remain in the trust indefinitely to protect against your children's future creditors or divorce claims.

Suggestion: Draft the terms of the trust to give an adult child maximum control over the funds without losing asset protection. This can be done by permitting the child to replace a trustee with someone who will cooperate with his/her wishes. The trustee can be permitted to purchase assets, such as a vacation house, which the child can then use and enjoy without exposure to creditor or divorce claims. In order to avoid potential tax problems, as well as a perception that the child controls his own trust, make sure the replacement trustee is not related to or under the direct control of the child.

FLPs AND FLLCs

Family limited partnerships (FLPs) and family limited liability companies (FLLCs) can be used to provide a measure of asset protection. A creditor of a limited partner cannot obtain assets from the FLP. The creditor can only get a "charging order"—a right to any distributions made to the limited partner.

Result: Assets can then remain within the family, a creditor can only receive the distributions when and to the extent they are made.

Note: Where assets have been transferred to FLPs in an attempt to hinder or delay the claims of creditors, family limited partnerships do not protect assets from attachment by creditors.

529 TUITION PLANS

All states now allow college savings through tax-advantaged accounts known as 529 plans. Contribution limits and other rules for these plans vary by state. However, 529 plans may be the newest and best way to shelter funds from your creditors.

About a dozen states have legislated that 529 plan funds are protected from claims against *both* the person contributing the funds as well as the beneficiary. Other states protect those assets for either the contributor or the beneficiary. This protection exists even though a contributor retains control over the funds and can recoup them (albeit by paying a 10% penalty).

The limits of asset protection are high…

●**Contribution limits are substantial—** most plans have total (rather than annual) contribution limits, usually exceeding $100,000. Visit *www.savingforcollege.com* to find out about the contribution limits for each state. Or you could call the state education department for any state in which you are interested.

●**Contributors who set up plans for a beneficiary can avoid gift tax on contributions** up to $55,000 ($110,000 if a contributor's spouse joins in the contribution) by averaging the gift over five years to take advantage of the $11,000 annual gift tax exclusion.

●**Contributors are not subject to any income limitations—**wealthy individuals can make contributions. And, they can even set up accounts for their own benefit (sometimes referred to as "solo 529 plans").

Assets enjoy deferral of tax on income until withdrawal *and* no tax on earnings if distributions are used for qualified education costs.

Bonus: With few exceptions, there is no bar to a nonresident setting up a 529 plan in another state, so factor in asset protection when selecting which 529 plan to use. As is the situation with domestic self-settled trusts, it is not yet known whether the state law where the plan is adopted will determine whether the account is protected.

Caution: It is not clear whether funds in 529 plans would be protected if the contributor or beneficiary seeks bankruptcy protection. Federal bankruptcy legislation that has yet to be enacted may create an exemption for 529 plans.

QUALIFIED RETIREMENT PLANS AND IRAs

Qualified retirement plans, including 401(k) accounts, are protected from the claims of creditors under federal law.

Exception: A state court can issue a qualified domestic relations order (QDRO), directing that payments from a plan be made to a former spouse, dependent or other person as "alternate payee."

IRAs do *not* enjoy federal protection from creditor claims. However, many states extend asset protection to IRAs.

Important: Check whether the state protection applies to Roth IRAs as well. Go to *http://66.33.199.251/articles/files/protecting.htm.*

How to Find a Good Credit Counselor

Nancy Dunnan, a financial adviser and author in New York City. Ms. Dunnan's latest book is titled *How to Invest $50–$5,000* (HarperCollins).

The credit counseling agencies can be extremely helpful, but be careful—the number of unscrupulous ones is on the rise. Before signing up, you should spend as much time researching the agencies as you would a new car.

Most agencies contact all of one's creditors to arrange a more comfortable repayment schedule. They also attempt to negotiate lower interest rates on your outstanding credit card balances. In turn, you make one monthly payment to the agency, which then parcels out the payments to your creditors.

Three steps you should take before signing on with an agency…

●**Find out about the fees.** Members of the National Foundation for Credit Counseling, or NFCC (an umbrella organization for counseling agencies) charge anywhere from nothing up to $75* for setting up a plan for debt management. Maintenance fees are an additional $10 to $25 per month. Members of the Association of Independent Consumer Credit Counseling Agencies charge maximums of $75 to set up a program and $50 per month for maintenance. Avoid any agencies that charge more.

*All prices subject to change.

Recommended: Get a quote for the setup and management fees in writing. If the agency says it can't do this, walk out the door.

●**Go to the agency in person.** Schedule an appointment with at least two agencies. You want to meet the credit counselor in person and see his/her credentials. Work only with a certified counselor. The NFCC (*www.nfcc.org,* 800-388-2227) will help you find ones in your area.

Useful: Many people find a support group that meets on a regular basis helpful. Contact Debtors Anonymous (*www.debtorsanonymous.org,* 781-453-2743), to find out if there is a support group near you.

●**Run a check.** See if any complaints have been filed regarding an individual agency at *www.bbb.org.*

Balancing act: Using a credit counseling service may have a negative impact on your credit rating. However, it's less damaging than when a bankruptcy shows up on your credit report.

More from Nancy Dunnan…

Free Legal Help for Seniors

If you're age 60-plus, you should know about the not-for-profit Senior Legal Hotlines. Most of these are funded through the *Older Americans Act,* while several are supported by Legal Services Corporations or state bar funds.

The hotlines are staffed with attorneys who provide telephone advice and referrals for additional help.

The hotlines are now available in California, Florida, Georgia, Hawaii, Iowa, Kansas, Kentucky, Maine, Maryland, Michigan, Mississippi, New Hampshire, New Mexico, Ohio, Pennsylvania, Puerto Rico, Tennessee, Texas, Washington State, Washington, DC, and West Virginia.

The legal advice is free except in Florida and Pennsylvania. For a list of hotline phone numbers, visit *www.seniorlaw.com/hotlines.htm.*

Financial Help for The Military

Financial assistance for the military—including National Guard members and reservists called up for active duty—is available through the *Soldiers' and Sailors' Civil Relief Act of 1940.* The act entitles US service members to reduced interest rates on mortgages and credit card debt ...protection from eviction if monthly rent is $1,200 or less...and delay of civil actions, such as bankruptcy and foreclosure. Service members must contact their unit or installation legal assistance office for this benefit.

More information: See your financial adviser, or visit the Web site *www.defenselink.mil/ specials/relief_act_revision.*

Zynda Sellers, in-house counsel for AmeriDebt, a credit counseling service, Germantown, MD.

Check Out Your Financial Planner's Record

The Web site of the Certified Financial Planner Board of Standards, *www.cfp.net,* lists disciplinary actions against CFP professionals since 1994. Infractions include failure to disclose investment risks, recommending unsuitable investments and other rule violations of the board's Code of Ethics and Professional Responsibility. On the home page, just click on "Search for a Certified Financial Planner," then fill in the name and location of the planner. You'll see if he/she really is a CFP and whether he has been disciplined.

How to Get a Cool Deal in A Hot Real Estate Market

Robert Irwin, author of more than 50 books about real estate, including *Power Tips for Buying a House for Less, Tips and Traps When Negotiating Real Estate* and *How to Buy a Home When You Can't Afford It* (all from McGraw-Hill). He is a real estate broker who has worked in the Los Angeles area for more than 25 years.

Many home prices have at least doubled in the last five years, and properties often sell for *more* than their asking prices within days of being listed. Despite the weaker economy, lower interest rates are keeping the housing market red-hot.

If you want to buy a reasonably priced house in today's market, be creative. *My strategies...*

● **Do your own canvassing.** Find properties before the real estate agents do. It takes a lot of effort but can yield terrific results. *What to do...*

●Choose neighborhoods in which you want to live.

●Print small cards explaining to potential sellers that you are a "principal" (a buyer looking for a home, not an agent looking for a listing). The card should say, "I'm interested in buying a home like yours in this lovely neighborhood. I have the financial means to do so. If you are interested in selling in the near future, please give me a call."

●Distribute the cards yourself. It will give you a chance to meet home owners. Dress nicely. I find most owners are flattered and curious when I stop by. Even if they aren't selling, they are likely to know who is.

● **Be ready to buy fast.** You might lose your dream house if it takes more than one day to get your down payment together. *Before you visit properties...*

●Obtain a preapproval letter from a mortgage lender.

●Find out how long houses in your area usually stay on the market. Then you will know how quickly you need to make an offer. You can obtain this information through your local real estate board and member brokers.

●Have money ready to be transferred to an escrow account. You will need it for your down payment and closing costs.

●Use a mortgage calculator, such as the one at *www.eloan.com,* to see how various purchase prices and down payments would change your monthly mortgage payment.

●Familiarize yourself with purchase agreements. This will allow you to fill them out quickly —without having to ask any questions or consult with your attorney.

●**Look around for a fixer-upper.** A house that doesn't look good—heavily worn carpeting …broken windows…dirty walls…broken appliances…ugly wallpaper—is surprisingly difficult to sell. Even if the flaws are only cosmetic, buyers do have a psychological resistance to paying hundreds of thousands of dollars. I often buy these ugly ducklings for as much as 15% below prevailing prices. *What to do...*

●Watch for ads with phrases like "handyman's special"…"earn your down payment"…or "needs TLC."

●Ask real estate agents about fixer-uppers. Most have one or two that they don't like to show.

●Avoid anything that has significant shortcomings, such as a sinking foundation or serious termite infestation. An impractical layout also is a significant shortcoming. Cosmetic improvements alone are rarely enough to increase their value. *Example:* I once considered buying a rundown home with the bedrooms located right off the kitchen. Repainting and recarpeting the bedrooms wasn't going to quiet kitchen clatter or make the bedrooms any more appealing.

●Establish your offer price. Check out comparable properties in better shape to get a sense of "finished" market value. Offer to pay the comparable price less the cost of repairing the property and another 15% for the sweat equity you would put in.

To determine the cost of fixing any existing problems, hire a good inspector. You can find one through the American Society of Home Inspectors' Web site, *www.ashi.com.*

●**Consider a "For Sale by Owner" (FSBO).** Hot markets will spur a lot of FSBOs because home owners figure they can save the average 6% commission. Most buyers just don't want the hassle of dealing with a seller directly, so there is less interest in these properties.

Put in a low bid, especially if the home has languished on the market for two months or

more. The seller may be exhausted and accept all of your terms. After you agree on price and terms, hire a fee-for-service broker to handle the legal issues, documents and completion of the deal. They advertise locally.

Cost: $1,000 to $1,500. Brokers are best at sales negotiations, but you will want your lawyer to check the paperwork, too.

●**Take a hard line when making an offer.**

●Give the seller only 24 hours to accept your bid. In fact, I usually push to get an answer by midnight of the same day. It forces the seller to take action or risk losing you as a buyer. Even a rejection is better than no response at all. Should the seller counteroffer, you can then start serious negotiations. If he/she does not, you can either increase your bid and sweeten up the purchasing terms or begin looking elsewhere. *Important tip:* Never accept the excuse that the seller has gone away for a long weekend and will make a decision when he returns. This often is just a tactic to buy time and use your offer as leverage against other prospective buyers.

●**Use a buyer's agent.** More buyers are now using agents who work specifically for them. Any real estate agent can do the job, but make sure that you have a written declaration that the agent will work exclusively on your behalf.

Advantages: You will see a broader range of houses, including bank-repossessed properties and FSBO homes. A seller's agent gets no commission for these houses, so he has no incentive to show them. A buyer's agent provides untainted advice, such as how much to offer and how to negotiate for the best deal.

On some properties, buyers' agents cost you nothing—they get paid part of a co-brokering deal with the seller's agent. On others, buyers' agents charge from 1% to 3% of the home's purchase price. This may be worthwhile if the agent can help you buy a property at a significant discount.

Obtain recommendations for buyers' agents through your local real estate board.

Consider Buying a Home at an Auction

On average, houses at auctions will sell for 90% to 110% of what they would bring through traditional methods, but bargains can be found. The best deals are at *absolute* auctions, where the opening price is set by the bidders, and the seller must accept the high bid. To learn more about auctions, search the National Association of Realtors' Web site at *www.realtor. org,* using the keyword "auction." Inspect the house and the neighborhood before bidding. Also, set a maximum bid.

Dorothy Nicklus, broker and auctioneer and owner of 24/7 Auctioneer, Guttenberg, NJ, www.247auctioneer.com.

Better Refinancing

Refinance almost for free with a home-equity line of credit (HELOC). The average 15-year conventional fixed rate is 5.10%.* HELOCs are at or near the prime rate of 4.25%. They have no closing costs—only a nominal processing fee and, in some cases, a penalty of $250 if you retire the loan within three years. There is no cap on the annual rate increases as there is with adjustable-rate mortgages—but if you plan on staying in your home for four years or less, a HELOC makes sense.

Keith Gumbinger, vice president of HSH Associates, financial publishers of mortgage information, Pompton Plains, NJ, www.hsh.com.

*All rates subject to change.

It Really Pays to Negotiate Real Estate Commissions

If your local real estate market is hot, you can save one to two percentage points just by asking for a discount or mentioning that other brokers offer them—if that is the case.

Typically not negotiable: Commissions on low-priced homes or the high-end listings that require heavy advertising.

To improve your odds of a discount: List your home with the same broker who finds you a new home…or look for a broker who advertises discounted commissions.

Caution: Deep-discount brokers, charging 2%, might spend little on advertising…or might not list your property on the Multiple Listing Service (MLS) or conduct an open house. This may prevent you from selling quickly—and at the highest price.

Kenneth Harney, a nationally syndicated real estate columnist and managing director of the National Real Estate Development Center, which sponsors educational conferences for real estate professionals, Chevy Chase, MD.

Get a Cheap Mortgage Through Your Employer

Businesses can provide discounted mortgage services as an extra benefit to employees. Some banks and mortgage companies, including Wells Fargo and First Union/Wachovia, provide corporate discounts on closing costs, not to mention appraisal and credit report charges. Employees still must qualify based on personal credit history and pay the going mortgage rates.

Barbara Weltman, attorney in Millwood, NY. Her Web site is www.barbaraweltman.com.

Deductible Mortgage Points

Undeducted mortgage points from the early 1990s may be deductible now under certain circumstances if you refinance or sell your home. Until 1993, the IRS did not allow home owners to deduct seller-paid points and points that were paid as VA/FHA origination fees. But, the IRS changed those rules in 1993 and 1994, retroactive to as far back as January 1990. If you have paid these types of points before the IRS change and you sell or refinance your house now, you may be able to get a tax benefit after the sale. Discuss the issue with a knowledgeable tax professional.

Daniel H. Borinsky, JD, CPA, counsel, and Lisa A. Scarazzo, CPA, Esquire Settlement Services, Lake Ridge, VA, which was involved in obtaining the IRS Private Letter Ruling in 1999.

Reverse Mortgages

Reverse mortgages, which allow older people to borrow against their home's value without making any repayments until they die or move away, will surely become more popular as baby boomers retire with much of their net worth tied up in their homes. But it's an expensive solution because closing costs and interest rates can be high. For details, check the Web site of the National Reverse Mortgage Lenders Association at *www.reversemortgage.org*.

Smarter alternative: Downsize your home before retirement and you'll save on taxes, utilities, maintenance and insurance costs as well as free up home equity for spending.

Jonathan Clements, personal-finance columnist for *The Wall Street Journal*.

Cash In on Your Home

Gary Eldred, PhD, real estate investor and consultant, Gainesville, FL. He has taught real estate at Stanford University and the Universities of Illinois and Virginia. He is author of *The Complete Guide to Second Homes for Vacation, Retirement, and Investment* and *Investing in Real Estate* (both from Wiley).

If you own a large home and your kids are out of the house, reap your profit fast, before large homes lose their value. Baby boomers have already begun retiring and trading down to smaller homes. Over time, this could leave a surplus of large homes on the market. What's more, the rebounding economy has pushed 30-year mortgage rates up to around 5.7%.* If rates rise to 7% or 8%, large-home prices could drop.

Bonus: By buying a less-expensive home, you can invest a portion of your profit to ensure a comfortable retirement.

Give yourself at least one year to determine where to move and what kind of home to purchase. *Key questions to consider...*

HOW SOON SHOULD I SELL?

By selling soon, you may avoid capital gains taxes. The federal tax law permits you to shelter the profits from the sale of your home—up to $250,000 for a single person and $500,000 for couples. The house must have been your primary residence for at least two of the previous five years. If you hold on to your home a few years too long, even a modest increase in home prices may cause you to exceed those limits. You then will pay up to 15% tax on capital gains above $250,000 or $500,000.

SHOULD I GET A NEW MORTGAGE?

Plan to take a mortgage on your new home —even if you can afford to pay cash. While it may be appealing to be rid of monthly mortgage payments, it is wiser to invest some of the profit. Use it to bulk up your nest egg or your rainy day emergency fund.

If you plan to continue working after you trade down, deducting mortgage interest will shelter some income from taxes.

Note: Most retirees qualify for a mortgage as long as they show sufficient income from pensions or savings accounts.

WHAT ABOUT TAXES AND INSURANCE?

Don't assume that you will save on taxes by moving. In many areas of the country, property taxes are low because of outdated assessments. Your new house or condominium, however, will be taxed on its current assessed value.

Also check school taxes. As an empty nester, it no longer pays for you to live in a top school district, which typically has the highest tax. If you are a senior, ask about tax rebates.

*All rates subject to change.

Check on insurance premiums before you buy. If you want to move to a coastal community where flooding and hurricanes are common, you could wind up with higher annual costs for homeowner's insurance.

WHEN SHOULD I SELL?

It is best to sell your current home before you purchase a new one. You don't want to risk carrying two mortgages if your home doesn't sell quickly.

If you do buy a new home first—say you have your eye on a condominium in a hot market and are afraid it will be snatched up if you don't act fast—take steps to protect yourself.

Strategy: Use a contingency agreement. A motivated seller will oblige you. For instance, if you buy a condo as your new home but don't want to move in until you sell your old home, make the new deal contingent upon the condominium seller renting the condo from you for three months. And, the monthly rent should be equal to your new mortgage payment. This way if you are stuck with two mortgage payments you have one covered for at least three months. The contingency agreement is added to the sale contract and signed at the closing.

HOW BIG A HOME WILL I NEED?

Subtract from your current home's square footage the size of rooms you no longer need —kids' bedrooms, the pantry, extra bathrooms. Keep space for luxuries—a whirlpool bathtub or a den large enough for a wide-screen TV—as well as a guest room. It is disruptive to have guests sleep in the living room.

SHOULD I PURCHASE A SMALLER HOUSE OR AN APARTMENT?

There are pros and cons to both.

● **Smaller house…**

Advantages: Privacy—perhaps it would have a backyard and a garage.

Disadvantages: You would be responsible for property maintenance and repairs.

If you opt for a smaller house, stick to your guns. Real estate agents tend to nudge buyers toward houses that are bigger than they really need or want.

● **Apartment…**

Advantages: The condo/co-op association is responsible for maintaining the building and the grounds as well as for certain repairs. Many buildings have extensive security.

Disadvantages: Shared entryways and parking…association rules restricting certain lifestyle decisions, such as how long visitors may stay over and whether pets are allowed.

If you opt for an apartment…

● Check out the renter-to-owner ratio. If less than 80% of the units are owner-occupied, look elsewhere. *Reason:* Renters have little stake in caring for the property. They also have less interest in building community with neighbors.

● Inspect a condo just as you would a house. Many developers make only cosmetic improvements when they convert rental buildings to condos, leaving outdated roofs, plumbing, heating and electrical systems.

● Attend a home-owners' association meeting as a guest of the seller. See who lives in the complex and how well the residents get along. If the board meets infrequently, chat with the residents about the spirit of the community. Look for an area where people are friendly.

● Request an up-to-date "resale package" from the seller. It should include legal documents, notification of any litigation and details of the repairs for which the association is responsible. In most associations, residents are responsible for fixing problems within the space of their own walls. Mechanicals of the building—wiring, heating, etc. —are covered by the association.

Make sure the board has adequate financial reserves. Otherwise, you may be hit with special assessments. Confirm that there's enough to fund major capital items (replacing the roof, maintaining recreational facilities). Check the association's history of special assessments to see if past reserves were adequate. Ask a professional condo management firm how the reserves compare with those of similar buildings.

SHOULD I MOVE FAR AWAY?

Ask yourself if you are willing to move away from your community and possibly your family.

It's easier and cheaper than ever to stay in touch via e-mail and long-distance calls. Airfares also are affordable. Yet only 21% of people over age 55 who relocate move to another state, according to the most recent US census.

Before you rule out moving far away, consider the potential savings on all major living expenses, including groceries, utilities, transportation and health care.

Example: The cost of living in San Francisco is much steeper than that of St. Petersburg, FL. Housing costs also are about 300% higher in San Francisco.

Resource: *http://cgi.money.cnn.com/tools,* click on "Cost of Living."

Affordable locations for empty nesters who want to downsize…

●**Sarasota, FL.** Located on the western coast of Florida, this city is affluent yet has avoided the inflated home prices of Naples, FL. Vibrant cultural scene. Thirty-five miles of beaches. No state income tax.

Median home price: About $176,100.

●**Bellingham, WA.** On the Pacific Northwest coast between Seattle and Vancouver, British Columbia. Restored Victorian- and Craftsman-style homes. Year-round outdoor recreation.

Median home price: About $147,000.

Other resources: *Where to Retire: America's Best and Most Affordable Places,* by John Howells (Globe Pequot)…*America's 100 Best Places to Retire,* by Elizabeth Armstrong (Vacation Publications).

What to Do With an Inherited House

David Schechner, real estate attorney at Schechner & Targan, West Orange, NJ.

In many cases, it is a mistake to rent out an inherited house unless you want to own investment property. Typically, the income doesn't compensate for the cost and aggravation. It's best to sell it and find other investments.

Exceptions: You plan to live in the house in the near future or you can get a hefty rent.

To decide whether to rent or sell, determine…

●**The extent to which taxes and other costs offset rental income.**

●**Cost of cosmetic improvements and repairs** to comply with building codes.

●**Cost and hassle of complying with various laws**—health, safety and tenants' rights.

Also check in your state to see if you can remove a tenant without cause at the end of his/her lease. In many states, you can't unless you sell the property.

Important: See a lawyer about lease terms …make sure your insurance liability coverage is adequate.

Should You Sue?

Cora Jordan, attorney and mediator in private practice, Oxford, MS, and author of *Neighbor Law: Trees, Fences, Boundaries & Noise* (Nolo).

To determine if a lawsuit is really worth your time and money, ask yourself these important questions…

●**What's the damage?** Identify the damage, and confirm that it was caused by the party you want to sue.

●**Is the damage significant enough?**

●**What are the alternatives?**

Example: Mediation costs less and takes less time than litigation. Plus, you don't have to accept the mediator's recommendations.

●**Am I willing to put several years of time,** effort and money into a lawsuit—even though I might lose?

●**Do I have a very strong case?**

●**What are the consequences if I win?** If you successfully sue a neighbor, how will you feel about continuing to live near him/her?

IF YOU THINK YOU WANT TO SUE

Ask a lawyer…

●**Is my case as strong as I think it is?**

●**Is there anything I'm missing?**

●**Even if I feel I am right, is the law on my side?**

●**How will a jury see the case?**

●**Will the settlement exceed the cost** of bringing the lawsuit?

8

Insurance Checkup

How to Survive Big Health Insurance Traps

New health insurance plan changes are cutting benefits and raising premiums for participants in each age bracket and income level. Many people are being left with limited or no coverage at all.

Any major life event—retirement, job change, divorce, the death of a spouse—puts you at risk of losing your insurance. It's not simply a problem for low-income families. Half of all Americans with health insurance fear that they won't be able to afford increases or that their benefits will be cut.

Top patient advocate Terre McFillen Hall tells how to avoid the traps. *Here are the most common crises and what you can do...*

PREEXISTING CONDITIONS

A 60-year-old Dallas woman had the opportunity to leave a company after 15 years to take a better job. She suffered from Parkinson's disease and was afraid that her new company's insurer would not provide coverage for her preexisting condition.

If the woman accepted the new position, she would have to honestly answer medical questions from her new insurer. Under the *Health Insurance Portability and Accountability Act of 1996* (HIPAA), however, she can't be denied the same insurance offered to all other employees because of her Parkinson's, nor can her new insurer charge her a higher premium.

Important: HIPAA doesn't guarantee that she will receive the same benefits as her old plan—her current doctor might not participate in the new insurer's plan, for example. Deductibles and claim limits can vary. She should examine the new policy before switching jobs. She also should look into getting a supplemental insurance policy.

Terre McFillen Hall, executive director of The Center for Patient Advocacy, a nonprofit organization that lobbies members of Congress on patients' concerns and promotes fairness in the US health-care system, McLean, VA, *www.patientadvocacy.org.*

JOB CHANGE

A 48-year-old man from Alexandria, VA, quit his job in June and contracted to start a new one in September. He planned to spend the summer traveling but worried about the three-month gap in coverage. *There were two alternatives available to him...*

● **Consolidated Omnibus Budget Reconciliation Act (COBRA).** Under federal law, his old employer is required to extend coverage for him (and his family) for up to 18 months after he leaves.

Caution: He has up to 60 days after leaving his job to elect COBRA coverage, which then becomes retroactive for those 60 days. He will have to pay the premiums in full without any company contribution, plus a 2% administrative fee. COBRA applies only to businesses that have 20 or more employees.

Bonus: COBRA is particularly valuable for those who have a preexisting condition. They cannot be dropped, nor can the insurance company single them out for a rate increase should their care become increasingly expensive.

More information: Read *Health Benefits Under the Consolidated Omnibus Budget Reconciliation Act: COBRA,* free from the US Department of Labor. Call 866-444-3272 or visit *www.dol.gov/ebsa/pdf/cobra99.pdf.*

● **Short-term medical insurance might be cheaper if he is healthy.** This usually provides coverage for two to six months and only for the major medical services—hospitalization, intensive care and services such as X rays and laboratory tests.

Example: Less than $100 per month, with a $250 out-of-pocket maximum and a 20% co-payment up to $5,000. It doesn't cover preexisting conditions or pregnancies.

The cost/benefit of a plan depends on individual circumstances. COBRA, while more expensive, might be a better choice, depending on his family's needs, any preexisting conditions and anticipated medical treatments.

Companies to try: Fortis Health (800-800-1212, *www.fortishealth.com*)...Golden Rule (800-444-8990, *www.goldenrule.com*).

UNINSURED ADULT CHILDREN

In San Francisco, the parents of a 22-year-old college graduate were worried. Their daughter worked as a temp and couldn't afford an individual health-care policy. Since she never got sick, she decided to go without insurance.

About one in three people between the ages of 18 and 24 has no health insurance, the highest proportion of any age group. A serious accident could wipe out this woman's savings, put her in debt for years and compel her parents to authorize her care if she should need hospitalization. This could then put them on the hook for her unpaid medical bills and wipe out their retirement savings. *Strategies...*

● **The parents should check their own policies first.** Some of the employer-sponsored plans allow dependent children of employees to be covered until age 23.

● **The daughter should get catastrophic major medical coverage at the very least.** If necessary, her parents can pay for the policy. Plans differ from state to state. Ask your doctor for recommendations.

Example: In California, for only $41 per month, a healthy person in his/her 20s can purchase a Blue Shield plan with a $2,400 deductible and a $6 million lifetime cap.*

SELF-EMPLOYED

A 50-year-old man from Philadelphia planned to start up his own business, but comprehensive coverage was beyond his reach without an employer sharing the cost. *Options...*

● **Managed-care policies,** such as HMOs, that require clients to use in-network physicians are the most affordable for individuals. More-expensive plans let you pick an out-of-network doctor. He can keep premiums down by electing high deductibles ($500 or more) but he should not skimp on prescription-drug coverage ($30 to $50 extra per month).

Reason: If he develops a condition that requires medication later on, he might not be able to get the coverage.

Example: The cholesterol-lowering drug *atorvastatin* (Lipitor) might cost $700 a year for an uninsured person, versus $100 a year in co-payments for an insured person.

*Subject to change.

●**Use a health insurance broker to help find the best individual policy.** The National Association of Health Underwriters at 703-276-0220 or *www.nahu.org* can suggest member agents in your area. He should obtain quotes from several companies, including Digital Insurance at 888-470-2121 or *www.digitalinsurance.com*...eHealth Insurance Services at 800-977-8860 or *www.ehealthinsurance.com*).

●**Form his own small insurance group.** By forming a small company, he can get premiums that are 20% to 50% lower than individual policies.

Example: In New Jersey, just two people can qualify as a group as long as each works a minimum of 25 hours per week in his/her company and pays Social Security taxes.

●**Join a professional or trade association** or an alumni group that offers group coverage.

Examples: AARP (888-687-2277, *www.aarp.org*)...National Association for the Self-Employed (800-232-6273, *www.nase.org*)...United Service Association for Health Care (800-872-1187, *www.usahc.com*)...for US military members and their families, USAA (800-365-8722, *www.usaa.com*).

Devastating Health Plan Scams and How You Can Avoid Them

Hal Morris, veteran Las Vegas–based consumer affairs journalist who writes widely about scams, schemes and other rip-offs.

Con artists have latched on to health care as an easy way for them to make some quick money.

TOO GOOD TO BE TRUE

The scam: Unlicensed "health insurers" are promising lofty benefits, with premiums as much as 50% below prevailing rates.

Easy marks: Small-business owners as well as individuals seeking to bypass skyrocketing insurance coverage.

Those who fall for this scam discover that their premiums have disappeared and are left holding hefty unpaid medical bills. People seeking supplemental insurance to pay medical expenses not covered by Medicare are also victims of these scams.

Promoters of health insurance rip-offs often sway local insurance agents to market the plans. Those selling the coverage call themselves labor consultants or business agents.

While claims may be paid initially, the scammers then delay payments through a variety of excuses, leaving consumers and employers responsible for paying mounting bills.

MAIL-ORDER SCAM

Unscrupulous companies also pitch inappropriate coverage through the mail. The US Postal Inspection Service cites the case of a 93-year-old woman who, thinking she was purchasing a valuable health insurance policy, wound up with *maternity* insurance.

Postal officials urge recipients of deceptive or unsuitable health insurance promotions to bring them to the attention of the local postmaster or nearest postal inspector.

10 WARNING SIGNS

Red flags that mark a questionable health insurance plan...

1. Coverage is offered at rock-bottom rates. Be suspicious of a policy pitched as costing "only pennies a day."

2. References to "benefits" rather than insurance..."contributions" instead of premiums..."consultant fees" in place of commissions...sales and marketing materials that generally avoid use of the word "insurance."

3. Coverage typically is offered regardless of the state of an applicant's health—no medical examinations or even medical questionnaires are required.

4. Joining a "union" or "association" may be stipulated to obtain health coverage. Or payment of "dues" may be necessary prior to obtaining a policy.

5. With small employers, the agent pitches a deal tied into the *Employee Retirement Income Security Act* or to a union. Legitimate ERISA or union plans are established by unions for their members or by employers for employees and are *not* sold by insurance agents.

Also appearing in the mix are plans that are offered exclusively through associations, guilds, trusts, unions or MEWA (Multiple Employer Welfare Arrangements). True MEWAs are designed to give the small employers access to low-cost health coverage on par with terms available to large firms.

6. Agent appears far too eager to sign you up for coverage.

7. Agent appears ill-informed on specifics, avoids sharing information and does not have precise responses to your questions.

8. Agent has no commission schedule and bases rates on ability to pay.

9. Agent doesn't have the name of the carrier underwriting the product—even as he/she markets the product as "fully insured," "fully funded" or "reinsured."

10. Name of so-called "insurer" may have a familiar ring to it—often it closely resembles the name of a legitimate organization. Also be on guard for names that suggest a connection with the federal government or Medicare.

HOW TO PROTECT YOURSELF

To establish that a health insurance plan is legitimate…

●**Carefully read all materials and Web sites of health insurance plans.** Verify that a genuine insurance company is involved and not one with a similar name. Also, call your state insurance department and check that the agent and product are state licensed.

Caution: Insurance scammers wrongly say federal law exempts state licensing. It doesn't.

●**Don't be influenced by glossy and well-illustrated marketing literature** or the high-pressure sales pitches, including mention of "it is your last chance" or "apply immediately." Verify information, and read the fine print.

●**Compare various insurance policies and costs.**

●**For small businesses, seek references of employers enrolled with the provider.** Ask the references about benefit payment history and claim turnaround time.

●**If you're suspicious of a plan, contact your state insurance department** about a firm's proposed coverage. Some states' Web sites make this task easy—type a name in a box on the screen.

●**Deal only with reputable agents.** Confirm via your state insurance department that the person offering the product is a licensed insurance agent with a proven reliability record. Insurance fleecers often use unlicensed agents to market their wares.

●**Be leery of a request to pay premiums in cash** or a year in advance.

●**Contact your state insurance department with any questions.** It is the very best resource for company/agent licensing requirements and available products. Also, if needed, consult with an accountant, attorney or other trusted adviser.

Suggestion: For the best route to state health insurance departments, visit the National Association of Insurance Commissioners' Web site at *www.naic.org/state_contacts/sid_websites.htm,* or call 816-842-3600.

The New Medicare Drug Benefit: What It Means for You

Jim Miller, editor of *Savvy Senior,* a syndicated newspaper question-and-answer column for senior citizens, Norman, OK, *www.savvysenior.org.* He is author of *The Savvy Senior: The Ultimate Guide to Health, Family and Fitness for Senior Citizens* (Hyperion).

Controversial? Definitely. Political? Absolutely. Beneficial? Maybe. The new prescription benefit is the biggest change to Medicare since it began covering health care for elderly and disabled Americans in 1965.

Bad news: When the drug benefit program begins in 2006, most seniors will save only a modest amount.

Good news: Effective immediately, the legislation also enables people age 64 and younger to put away some money tax free for healthcare expenses using special new health savings accounts. Until 2006, Medicare participants will be able to save 15% or more on prescriptions.

Here is a look at what you can expect from the new Medicare legislation…

EFFECTIVE IMMEDIATELY

●**Health savings accounts.** Many people reduce health insurance costs by buying policies that have high deductibles. The law permits tax-sheltered savings accounts to finance these deductibles—at least $1,000 a year for individuals, $2,000 for couples. You can receive a tax deduction for these contributions, invest the money and pay no taxes on the earnings upon withdrawal, provided the money is utilized for health expenses, including long-term-care services. Otherwise, a 10% penalty applies.

●**Drug-discount cards.** Until the drug program begins, Medicare recipients can obtain a discount card for up to $30 per person that will reduce prescription costs by 10% to 25%.

●**Low-income subsidy.** In 2004 and 2005, recipients whose income is below federal poverty guidelines will receive annual subsidies of $600 credited to the drug-discount cards to help defray drug costs.

Both the discount card and low-income subsidy end in 2006, when the new drug plan goes into effect.

NEW DRUG PLAN

More than 10 million of the 40 million Americans covered by Medicare currently have drug coverage, mostly through a former employer. The new drug benefit, called Medicare Part D, will increase those numbers. However, this plan doesn't make sense for everyone.

Medicare beneficiaries can sign up for the new drug plan beginning in 2006. It gives the biggest savings to those with low incomes who don't receive Medicaid and those who spend heavily on prescriptions. If you enroll in the plan, you cannot buy supplemental Medicare (Medigap) to help defray drug costs.

DRUG COST

Amt Spent/Yr.	You Pay…*	You Save…
$1,000	$857.50	$142.50 (14%)
$1,500	$982.50	$517.50 (35%)
$2,000	$1,107.50	$892.50 (45%)
$2,500	$1,420.00	$1,080.00 (43%)
$3,000	$1,920.00	$1,080.00 (36%)
$5,000	$3,920.00	$1,080.00 (22%)
$10,000	$4,265.00	$5,735.00 (57%)

WHAT TO DO

Add up your annual drug costs. If you spend less than $810 a year on drugs, it doesn't pay to participate. You will spend more on the premium ($420), the deductible ($250) and out-of-pocket medication costs than you will get back. *Cost breakdown…*

Premiums: Anticipated to be $35 monthly ($420 per person per year), but they could be higher in certain parts of the US.

Deductibles: $250 deductible for prescription drugs per year.

Out-of-pocket charges: After the deductible, Medicare covers 75% of drug costs up to $2,250.

Coverage gap: For any amount above $2,250 ($750 out-of-pocket**), Medicare pays nothing until you reach $5,100 ($3,600 out-of-pocket).

Catastrophic coverage: When costs exceed $5,100 ($3,600 out-of-pocket) not including the $420 yearly premium, Medicare will pay for 95% of each prescription. Members will be responsible for the remaining 5%.

Low-income subsidy: People eligible for Medicaid will pay no premium or deductible and have no gap in coverage. They will pay $1 per prescription for generics and $3 for brand names. Co-payments are waived for those living in nursing homes, regardless of income. Other benefits are available on a sliding scale to families with incomes below the federal poverty line, depending on assets.

*Total out-of-pocket expenses, including $420 annual premium, $250 deductible and 25% of additional costs based on a complex formula.

**($2,250 - 250) x 25% plus $250 deductible.

For more information on the drug plan, contact Medicare at 800-MEDICARE. Or go to their Web site at *www.medicare.gov.*

OTHER CHANGES

●**Medicare Part B.** While Part A covers hospital care, Part B insurance helps pay for physicians' services as well as outpatient hospital and emergency room services.

Premiums: Premiums for doctors' services and outpatient care will be higher for people who have annual incomes over $80,000. The premium would increase with income, roughly tripling for people with incomes of more than $200,000.

Deductibles: They will rise from $100 per year to $110 in 2005 and increase by a small percentage each year thereafter.

Expanded medical coverage: Medicare will cover an initial physical examination for new beneficiaries and the screenings for diabetes and cardiovascular disease. It will provide coordinated care for people with chronic illnesses and increase payments for doctors administering mammograms to encourage preventive care.

●**Private health plans.** The government is offering $12 billion in subsidies to entice private insurers to offer basic health insurance through the Medicare system. *These plans will include...*

●Preferred provider organizations (PPOs), which encourage use of in-network doctors but allow patients to go outside the network if they pay extra.

●Private fee-for-service plans, which allow patients to see any doctor.

●**Employer incentives.** Tax breaks worth more than $70 billion over 10 years will be provided to employers who maintain drug coverage for retirees once the Medicare drug benefit begins in 2006. If you already have retiree medical coverage, ask your former employer if it will continue to offer this benefit. Some might reduce it or drop it.

●**Drugs from Canada.** The current law permits drugs to be imported from Canada if the Department of Health and Human Services certifies their safety. So far, the department has refused to do so.

Prescription drugs sold in Canada are 10% to 50% cheaper than comparable drugs sold in the US.

New Options in Long-Term Care

Charles B. Inlander, health-care consultant and president of the nonprofit People's Medical Society, a consumer health advocacy group in Allentown, PA. He is the author of more than 20 books on consumer health issues, including *Take This Book to the Hospital with You: A Consumer Guide to Surviving Your Hospital Stay* (St. Martin's).

About one in four people age 70 or older will rely on some form of long-term care during his/her lifetime. Unfortunately, most people assume that this means nursing home care. But nursing homes are actually the least commonly used form of long-term care. *Here's what you must know about the four main categories of long-term care, ranked in descending order of usage...*

●**In-home services** are the most commonly used type of long-term care. They are specifically designed to keep you in your home and out of more expensive health-care settings. In most areas, a variety of home services now are available, including those for individuals who are just out of the hospital and need assistance with medications, monitoring of vital signs, etc. Depending on your medical needs, some of these costs may be covered by either Medicare (if you are eligible), Medicaid (if you meet the income requirement) or private insurance. To learn about the services available in your community, check with your local Area Agency on Aging (listed in your phone directory).

●**Assisted-living facilities** have been popping up across the country in the past decade. And, they now serve about 2 million people in 20,000 facilities. Assisted-living facilities typically are private residential facilities (although some counties and municipalities operate their own) that provide assistance to people who need help with physical tasks, such as dressing, bathing, eating and daily chores. No government insurance programs pay for assisted living, although some long-term-care insurance policies may cover part of the cost. States vary in how they regulate assisted-living facilities.

• **Skilled-care nursing homes** offer care by registered and licensed practical nurses on the orders of an attending physician. Most people in such facilities are quite sick or very fragile, and need extensive care. Skilled-care nursing homes serve approximately 1.7 million people in 17,000 facilities. This is the *only* type of nursing home that Medicare will reimburse for—and then only up to a maximum of 100 days a year, after having been in the hospital for at least three days and meeting a number of other stringent conditions. To understand requirements for Medicare coverage, consult the official Medicare Web site at *www.medicare.gov.*

• **Intermediate-care nursing homes** provide less intensive care than skilled nursing care and generally cost less. Normally, residents are not confined to a bed but still are treated by registered nurses and licensed practical nurses. However, these facilities usually provide more rehabilitation and other therapeutic services for the handicapped, including the developmentally disabled and stroke victims, as well as physical and occupational therapies. Medicare provides no benefits for this category of nursing home, but your state may have programs available to help cover the cost. Check with your state's department of welfare.

Best Ways to Pay for Long-Term Care

Charles Mondin, director of the United Seniors Health Council, an educational program of the National Council on the Aging aimed at helping seniors shop intelligently for health care, Washington, DC, *www.ncoa.org*. He is a contributor to *Planning for Long-Term Care* (McGraw-Hill).

Nursing home stays cost an average of $55,000 a year. In-home care is as much as $50 an hour. None of us knows what our needs will be, but we all face potentially tremendous costs.

Shop for a nursing home or nursing care now so that you won't be shocked if and when you must find a facility quickly. Facilities, level of care and prices vary widely.

There are several ways to come up with the money you will need. The sooner you address your future, the more options you will have to self-insure or buy long-term-care (LTC) insurance. Consult your financial adviser about the best choice for financial security.

YOUR NEST EGG

If you can pay nursing home costs out of your retirement savings, you probably do not need LTC insurance.

The main problem with self-insuring is that you don't know when—or even if—you actually will need the coverage, and there is no way to know how long you might need it.

The average stay in a nursing home is about one year. To be safe, assume that you might have to spend two years in a home.

General rule: If you can afford to cover at least two years for both you and your spouse, you should be adequately prepared.

If there is a family history of illness that might require a nursing home, LTC insurance probably is a good investment. But if you now have a chronic condition, you may not qualify.

The further ahead you think about LTC, the greater the possibilities you will have. If you're in your 40s or 50s, find out from an agent what LTC insurance would cost at your present age. Then see whether you can essentially self-insure less expensively by investing those premiums in an annuity to cover the cost of your care.

Annuities are available with a range of features, some providing guaranteed fixed income for life. Any financial planner should be able to do the comparisons for you.

YOUR HOME

Your home just may be your best financial resource to help pay for your care. Selling it would boost your nest egg and increase future income from investments. Consult several qualified real estate agents to learn its value.

Renting out your home is another alternative. You need a regular stream of income to pay for a nursing home—not a lump sum of cash.

A reverse mortgage allows you to tap your home's value while you continue to live in it. It provides you with income—in a lump sum or in regular payments over numerous years. The reverse mortgage loan is paid off upon your death—usually by selling the home.

Caution: It is possible to outlive the term of a reverse mortgage.

LTC INSURANCE

LTC is one of the most complicated types of insurance. Buy a policy at age 55, and you will probably pay less than $1,000 a year—but for 20 or 30 years.

Wait until age 75 to buy, and you'll pay up to $5,000 per year for a restrictive policy that might cover a nursing home stay but not home care and might not kick in until you've been in a nursing home for more than 90 days. A comprehensive policy for someone age 75 might run $7,000 a year. Wait even longer than age 75, and it becomes prohibitively expensive.

Ask your state's senior health insurance office for guidance. LTC terminology can be very confusing even to experienced insurance agents.

Example: Most companies provide "level premium" coverage. This doesn't mean that the premium is guaranteed to remain the same. It means that if you bought at age 60, your premium always will be what the company currently charges to insure any new 60-year-old policyholder—and that price can go up.

What to look for when you shop for LTC insurance…

Benefit period: Purchase coverage that lasts your lifetime, not a time period.

Benefit amount: Buy a policy that pays at least $100 a day and covers nursing home and in-home care. The benefit amount you need depends on the cost of nursing homes in the area in which you plan to live. The average nursing home now charges around $150 a day. However, more-expensive facilities can cost $200-plus a day. Be financially prepared to pay the difference.

Deductible/elimination period: The longer the elimination period—meaning the more of the nursing home stay you pay for before insurance kicks in—the less coverage will cost you. For most people, an elimination period of 60 to 90 days is the best value. You might save 10% on the premium that has a longer elimination period, but your expenses could eat up the savings. Also consider a rider that adjusts the benefit for inflation.

When you qualify for care: Be careful about how the insurer determines whether it will pay benefits. Policies that require a prior hospital stay or a physician to find you "ill" or "injured" can be too restrictive.

Less-restrictive policies require only that you need care because of a mental or physical impairment. You become eligible for the benefits if mental deterioration makes you a danger to yourself or to others, or if physical problems make it impossible for you to perform two or more activities of daily living (ADL)—such as eating, dressing, bathing, moving from bed to chair and using the toilet.

Since ADL definitions vary by insurance company, make sure you know how a company's policy defines them.

GOVERNMENT CARE

When your retirement income and assets are below levels set by your state, you may qualify for Medicaid to pay nursing home bills.

It is administered by each state, and the rules for coverage vary.

Life Insurance vs. Long-Term-Care Insurance

Think about switching from life insurance to long-term-care insurance. In a two-income family with children out of college and a paid-for home, life insurance—which replaces the income of one spouse—may not be necessary. But, long-term-care insurance may be increasingly important—just one year in a semiprivate room in a nursing home now costs between $30,000 and $100,000, depending on the location. This strategy requires careful planning, so consult your financial adviser.

David Hennings, financial planner and syndicated columnist, Oak Park, IL.

How to Slash Life Insurance Costs Big Time

Seymour Goldberg, Esq., CPA, Goldberg & Goldberg, PC, One Huntington Quadrangle, Melville, NY 11747, *www.goldbergira.com*. One of the country's foremost authorities on IRA distributions, Mr. Goldberg is the author of *Practical Application of the Retirement Distribution Rules* (IRG Publications) available at *www.goldbergreports.com*.

You can dramatically cut the after-tax cost of life insurance by owning it through a tax-favored qualified retirement plan—so that the premiums are paid with mostly tax-deductible rather than after-tax dollars...

TAX FACTS

Almost everybody needs life insurance during his/her working years—and people who own their own small businesses are likely to need it more than most.

Keys: The death benefit paid by a life insurance policy is tax free to the policy beneficiary—however premiums paid for insurance are not tax deductible. So one must earn more than the premium amount to obtain enough after-tax dollars to pay it.

Example: If you're in the 35% tax bracket, you must earn $1,538 of income to obtain the after-tax dollars needed to pay every $1,000 of premium cost.

But many people don't realize that the Tax Code permits qualified retirement plans (generally company plans) to invest in life insurance. By purchasing insurance through a retirement plan, you get in effect a tax deduction for insurance premiums—because you deduct the plan contributions that are used to pay them.

If you are in a high tax bracket, this could reduce the after-tax premium cost by one-third or more after state and local taxes are considered. And the insurance death benefit remains tax free.

IRA LOOPHOLE

While the law allows qualified retirement plans to invest in life insurance, the terms of the plan itself must also allow it...

- **If you are an employee,** check the terms of your employer's retirement plan to see if it allows insurance purchases.

- **If you own your own business** and it doesn't have a qualified retirement plan that provides a life insurance investment option, you can either set up a new plan that has such an option or amend a current plan to give it one.

Legal note: The option to invest in life insurance must be available to all plan participants in a nondiscriminatory manner. And, life insurance should be among investments in the summary plan description distributed to employees. Do not amend a plan to become able to buy insurance for yourself while failing to tell employees about the option.

IRAs, unlike qualified retirement plans, cannot invest in life insurance. However, it is possible to use your IRA funds to buy insurance by transferring the funds to a business's qualified retirement plan.

IRA-to-qualified-plan rollovers have become much easier to make since the 2001 tax act. The use of IRA funds makes it possible to buy life insurance through a qualified plan that otherwise would lack the funds to do so.

Example: After 20 years as an employee at a big company, you then quit to start your own business and roll over your balance in the company's 401(k) retirement account to your own IRA.

You want to buy a million-dollar life insurance policy to protect your family. But the qualified retirement plan that you set up for the new business lacks the money to buy the insurance.

Provide it with the necessary money by rolling over your IRA into the new company's plan if permitted by the plan, and having the plan use that money to buy the insurance.

If you already own life insurance outside your retirement plan, paying after-tax dollars for it, it may be possible to transfer the policy to the retirement plan through tax-free exchange. The insurance would then be paid for with pretax dollars. This can be a much better option than canceling your existing insurance and buying a new policy through your plan.

For a Department of Labor opinion approving the sale of life insurance to a retirement plan for the policy's cash value, see Department of Labor Advisory Opinion 2002-12A, *www.dol. gov/ebsa/regs/aos/ao2002-12a.html.*

INCLUSION AMOUNT

The amount of an insurance policy's death benefit in excess of the policy's cash value remains tax free to the policy beneficiary of the retirement plan.

However, owning insurance through a retirement plan does not make the policy completely tax free.

Each year, a small amount is included in the policyholder's income that is attributable to the value of the policy, as determined by IRS Table 2001, published in IRS Notice 2001-10. However, the cost is much less than the savings obtained from holding the policy through the plan.

Example: For a 45-year-old person, each $1,000 of coverage will result in $1.53 being included in income. So $100,000 of coverage would create an annual maximum tax liability of $53.55—based on the top tax rate of 35%.

This small cost will be much less than the savings attained from the arrangement. Moreover, if you have a "rated" policy—so that you have to pay higher than average premiums—the amount included in income, "the inclusion amount," is a bargain because it is based on a "standard" IRS table.

In addition, the inclusion amount is recovered income tax free when the policy pays off, increasing the amount of the policy proceeds that are tax free.

This is because while the portion of the policy proceeds that are attributable to the policy's cash value are taxable, the amount that has already been taxed through the annual inclusion amount is tax free.

Example: An insurance policy offers a $100,000 benefit. When the insured dies, the policy's cash value is $6,000, and $4,000 was previously taxed to the insured through the annual inclusion amount. The amount that the beneficiary will receive tax free is $98,000—consisting of the $94,000 by which the benefit exceeds the policy's cash value plus the previously taxed amount of $4,000.

ESTATE TAX

The only drawback to owning life insurance through a retirement account is that the policy proceeds will be subject to estate tax. But that is only a problem if your estate is large enough to be subject to tax (currently more than $1.5 million)—and even so, estate tax probably can be prevented through a well-drafted overall estate plan.

However, you can avoid that problem. After you retire, you can transfer ownership of the insurance policy from the retirement plan to a life insurance trust or other individual, and if you live three years after doing so, the policy proceeds will escape estate tax as well.

Note: There are some income tax liabilities when you take the policy out of the plan.

Bottom line: Owning life insurance through a retirement plan can be a big cost saver.

Best: Talk to your insurance and retirement plan advisers.

Life Insurance Rates Are Likely to Come Down

New tables reflecting longer life expectancies will be adopted by many states in 2004 and 2005. This will lead to cost savings that many insurers will pass along to consumers on new life insurance policies. Expect a decrease of as much as 15% for a 30-year level-term policy.

Strategy: If you need insurance now, purchase 10-year term, which often is a better value than annual renewable term. Postpone buying longer-term insurance for at least a year. Shop for a new policy at Compulife's Web site, *www. term4sale.com.*

Warning: You will need to take a new physical examination.

Glenn Daily, a fee-only insurance consultant based in New York City, *www.glenndaily.com.*

Save Hundreds On Car Insurance

Most insurance companies will lower your premium by 5% when you drive less than 8,500 miles a year.

Other factors that can reduce your rates by 5% to 10%: Moving from an urban location to a rural area…reaching age 50…insuring your home and auto with the same company. Savings will vary, depending on your insurance company and home state.

Important: Notify your insurance company as soon as there are any changes involving your vehicle. This information affects your premium as well as your ability to collect on a claim.

Alejandra Soto, communications manager, Insurance Information Institute, New York City, *www.iii.org.*

More from Alejandra Soto…

If You Have a Teen Driver…

Giving your teen an older car and having him/her take out insurance on it may cost less than placing him on the family's policy as a driver of the family's other autos. Ask your insurer if your teen then can have access to other family cars as well. Insurers view older, less-expensive cars as lower-risk, so rates tend to be low. You may need less collision and comprehensive coverage on an old car than on a newer one.

Caution: Older cars may lack safety features found on newer cars.

When to Change Car Insurance

Consider switching car insurers if you are hit with a double-digit hike in price. Rates are rising significantly whether or not you have had

accidents—but not all companies charge similar amounts to insure the same car.

To shop around: Use an independent agent —find one through the Independent Insurance Agents and Brokers of America (800-221-7917, *www.iiaa.org*)…go on-line to InsWeb.com for price quotes…contact one company that sells directly, such as Geico (800-861-8380, *www. geico.com*)…and try State Farm (800-782-8332, *www.statefarm.com*), which sells only through its own agents.

Jeanne Salvatore, vice president, consumer affairs, Insurance Information Institute, New York City, *www.iii.org.*

More from Jeanne Salvatore…

Home Insurance Savings

Check out the following list for possible ways to save on your homeowner's policy…

●**If you are retired and age 55 or older, ask for a discount**—some companies give them, believing that retirees spend more time at home and are therefore more likely to catch problems early.

●**If your house is made of fire-resistant brick or concrete,** you may qualify for a discount. A fire-resistant roof may get you lower rates in fire-prone areas, such as California.

●**Keep your credit score high**—insurers frequently charge higher rates to people with low credit scores.

●**Increase your deductible.**

●**Avoid small claims**—they will cause your rates to rise and may result in your policy not being renewed.

Getting a Fair Settlement From Your Home Insurer?

David W. Barrack, executive director, National Association of Public Insurance Adjusters, Potomac Falls, VA.

Consult a public insurance adjuster to find out if you're getting what's due to you from your home insurance plan. Insurers

—smarting from stock market losses—are pressuring their claims adjusters to keep damage claim payouts at or below the industry average. A public insurance adjuster safeguards the interests of the consumer. He/she will evaluate the damage and then recommend whether a loss is large enough to warrant filing a claim. He also reviews your insurance policy to advise you of the extent of your coverage—and helps you recover a fair and equitable settlement.

Cost: Typically an initial evaluation is free. If you decide to use the adjuster, the fee usually ranges from 10% to 15% of the payout. On a large loss claim, the fee could be reduced.

To find a public insurance adjuster: Check the Web site of the National Association of Public Insurance Adjusters at *www.napia.com* or look in the *Yellow Pages* under "Adjusters."

to $120 per year. *Extended- or long-term-care insurance* helps pay for nursing expenses after you leave the hospital. With shorter hospital stays and people living longer, odds are that you'll need it. The cost is about $1,400 a year for a 60-year-old. The younger you are when you purchase this insurance, the lower your premiums will be.

Plans to avoid: Commuter insurance, which pays your beneficiaries if you are killed or seriously maimed—but only while commuting. *Disaster mortgage insurance,* which covers your mortgage payments for up to two years and pays your homeowner's policy deductible (up to $500) if your home is destroyed in a natural disaster. For most people, a homeowner's policy is sufficient.

Which Types of Insurance Are a Good Idea, Which Are Not

Lee Rosenberg, CFP, founding partner, ARS Financial Services, Inc., Jericho, NY.

Some types of insurance plans are really worth the cost, while others are not. *Take a look below...*

Insurance plans almost everyone should have: Credit-monitoring insurance prevents would-be thieves from stealing your identity. Your credit card issuer notifies you within 24 hours of suspicious credit activity and helps with credit cleanup, if necessary. The cost is $50

When Looking for an Insurance Company...

To find a consumer-friendly insurance company, check the Web site of the National Association of Insurance Commissioners, *www. naic.org.* Just click on "Consumer Information Source." You can find out how many complaints have been filed against an insurer and get a ratio of complaints to policies written—an indicator of the insurer's record.

Also: Contact your state insurance department, found in the blue pages of the phone book or through links at the NAIC site.

Joseph Annotti, vice president of public affairs, Property and Casualty Insurers Association of America in Des Plaines, IL.

9

Tax Answers

How to Shelter Your Income from the IRS

When doing your tax planning for the year, even just a few dollars put in the wrong place could cost you thousands of dollars (see below).

Example: This year, you can deduct up to $4,000 for college tuition for yourself or any family member if your adjusted gross income (AGI) is $130,000 or less on a joint return and $65,000 on a single return. If AGI is $130,001, your deduction drops to $2,000. If your AGI is more than $160,000 ($80,000 single), you will get no deduction.

How to preserve tax breaks, including those made more generous by recent tax legislation...

SHELTER PERSONAL INCOME

Ways to reduce AGI if you don't own your own business...

●**Defined-contribution plans.** If your employer sponsors a 401(k) or similar salary-deferral plan, contribute the maximum—$13,000 in 2004...$16,000 if you're age 50 or older.

Even if your employer does not match your contributions, putting the maximum allowable amount in a 401(k) reduces your AGI and expands your eligibility for other tax benefits.

●**Deductible IRAs.** If your employer does not sponsor a retirement plan, you can deduct a contribution of $3,000 to a traditional IRA in 2004—$3,500 if you're age 50 or older.

If you participate in your employer's retirement plan, you can make a fully deductible IRA contribution if your 2004 AGI is $65,000 or less on a joint return ($45,000 single). Smaller deductible contributions are allowed for AGIs of up to $75,000 ($55,000 single).

Sidney Kess, attorney and CPA, 10 Rockefeller Plaza, New York City 10020. Mr. Kess is coauthor/consulting editor of *Financial and Estate Planning* and coauthor of *1040 Preparation, 2004 Edition* (both from CCH). Over the years, he has taught tax law to more than 710,000 tax professionals.

●**Capital losses.** Up to $3,000 of net capital losses can be deducted each year. Additional losses can be carried forward indefinitely.

Example: Near year-end, you tally your investment trades for the year and discover a $2,700 gain. Sell enough holdings to generate $5,700 worth of losses for a deductible $3,000 net loss.

●**Tax-free income.** If you are in a high tax bracket, choose municipal bonds, tax-managed mutual funds and growth stocks—which don't pay dividends—instead of investments that raise your AGI with large amounts of interest and dividends.

Helpful: Keep only your emergency funds in bank accounts and money market funds to reduce your taxable income and monthly interest payments. Use any surplus to pay down credit card balances.

SHELTER SOCIAL SECURITY INCOME

Even moderate-income seniors may find that some or all of their Social Security is subject to income tax—but there are ways to reduce it.

Whether benefits are taxable depends on your "provisional income." *To calculate provisional income, total…*

●**Your AGI.**

●**Tax-exempt interest income** from municipal bonds and bond funds.

●**One-half of your annual Social Security benefits.**

Example: With an AGI of $20,000, tax-exempt income of $5,000 and annual Social Security benefits of $12,000, provisional income is $31,000 ($20,000 + $5,000 + $6,000).

Some facts to be aware of…

●No Social Security benefits are counted as taxable income if provisional income is up to $32,000 when married and filing jointly ($25,000 for single filers).

●Up to 50% of benefits are included if provisional income is more than $32,000 ($25,000 for single filers).

●Up to 85% of benefits are included if provisional income is greater than $44,000 ($34,000 for single filers).

Use these tools to safeguard Social Security benefits from Uncle Sam…

●**Tax-deferred annuities.** Even with the recent tax-law change, these provide a shelter that is not subject to income limits. They make sense for people who have maxed out retirement plan contributions and want to build more savings for retirement.

Two types of annuities…

●Fixed. An insurance company provides a guaranteed rate of return for a certain period. You might invest $50,000 and get a 5% guarantee for one year. After a year, your account balance will be at $52,500 and a new—usually lower—interest rate will be set.

●Variable. These don't offer a guaranteed return. Instead, they allow you to invest in mutual fund–like accounts with higher potential returns and risks. Look for low commissions and no surrender fees (payments to the annuity issuer if you sell before a certain period).

●**Loans.** Borrowing allows you to generate cash flow without boosting your taxable income. *Consider these options…*

●Tap a home-equity line of credit or a margin account.

●Take out a reverse mortgage.

●Refinance your home or your investment property.

●Borrow against your home or cash-value life insurance, such as whole life or variable universal life. Make sure tax savings offset your interest payments.

SHELTER BUSINESS INCOME (EVEN A SIDELINE BUSINESS!)

Opportunities to trim your AGI are greatest when you or your spouse is a business owner. *Deductions…*

●**Health insurance.** All premiums paid by self-employed individuals (as well as by owners of S corporations and limited liability companies) are now deductible.

●**Retirement plans.** Many plans offer rich write-offs for those with business income.

●Simplified employee pension (SEP) IRA plans. You can deposit up to $41,000 in 2004, pretax, with these small-business IRAs. To set one up, fill out a simple form at a mutual fund firm or other institution.

●Defined-benefit pension plans. These types of plans can provide even higher deductions than a SEP if you're in your late 40s or older. Rules are complex. Consult a professional adviser.

●**Children on the payroll.** You can deduct the salaries of your children and grandchildren on your Schedule C, and they'll owe no tax on up to $4,850 in earned income in 2004.

●**Equipment.** Under the recent tax legislation, up to $102,000 worth of expenses for business equipment may be written off in the year it is purchased, subject to income limitations. Previously, the limit was $24,000.

TAX BREAKS FOR EVERYONE

These strategies provide generous tax breaks regardless of income...

●**Tax-deferred annuities.** Again, you are taxed when you withdraw the money—but at that point, you are likely to be retired and in a lower income tax bracket. There is a 10% penalty on withdrawals made before age 59½.

●**Permanent life insurance.** These policies have high premiums, so they make sense only if you need life insurance for many years—for instance, if you are the sole breadwinner in a family with a disabled child. Cash value grows tax free. After a buildup period, you or your beneficiaries can tap it via tax-free withdrawals and loans against the cash value of your policy.

●**College savings plans.** *Consider the following options...*

●Section 529 college savings plans. In most states, you can set up plans for yourself, your child, grandchild, other relatives and even friends. Some states, including New York and Missouri, permit you to deduct contributions from state taxes. There's no federal income tax deduction for contributions, but investment income is tax free if used for education expenses.

If the money is withdrawn to pay higher-education expenses, no tax will be due. *More information:* Visit *www.savingforcollege.com,* or check with your state's department of education.

●Coverdell education savings accounts or ESAs. Officially, married couples with AGIs of more than $190,000 ($95,000 single) can't make a full contribution. *Loophole:* If you're over the limit, give money to relatives in a lower bracket or even to your children, who then can use it to contribute up to $2,000 per year to Coverdell ESAs. There are no deductions, but the investment grows tax free.

Shrewd Tax-Saving Moves for Year-End

Do not miss out on these very smart tax-planning moves for the last few months of the year...

●**Review capital gains and losses.** Managing long-term and short-term gains is now even more important with the top tax rate on long-term gains reduced to only 15%, while short-term gains are still taxed at as much as 35%.

At year-end, you want to be able to offset any short-term losses against the highly taxed short-term gains—not against long-term gains that otherwise would be tax favored.

If it's close to year-end, and your investments for the year to date have produced net short-term losses and net long-term gains, you might want to realize some extra short-term gains before year-end to offset the short-term losses.

Short-term gains that otherwise would be taxed at high rates can be taken tax free when offset by the short-term losses, while preserving your tax-favored net long-term gains.

Best: Review your entire investment portfolio well before year-end, so you can make last-minute moves to net out gains and losses in the optimum manner.

If you have gains on investments that you've held for almost a year, don't forget the tax savings that will come from holding them for more than a full year. Don't sell them too soon.

●**Make gifts to family members.** The tax rate for both dividends and capital gains is only 5% for persons in the 10% or 15% tax bracket—which now covers income up to $58,100 on a joint return or $29,050 on a single return.

This makes the opportunity to save taxes by shifting investment income to family members in these low tax brackets greater than ever before. *Examples...*

●A child faces college tuition costs that you intend to cover by selling appreciated stocks. If you instead make a gift of the stocks to the child and have the child sell them for his/her own account, the tax rate due on their appreciation may be only 5%!

•A family business run as a regular "C" corporation holds accumulated earnings. If you make gifts of stock in it to low-bracket family members, you can then distribute its accumulated earnings to them through dividends taxed at only 5%.

Gifting money can also serve to reduce your taxable estate.

Opportunity: The annual gift tax exclusion lets you make as many gifts as you wish of up to $11,000 per recipient, free of gift tax. The limit is $22,000 when gifts are made jointly with a spouse. But gifts must be completed by December 31 to use the exclusion for 2004.

Example: If you don't make gifts by the end of 2004, then the chance that you and your spouse have to make a $22,000 tax-free gift to each of your children, or other recipients, will be lost for the year.

•**Hire children before year-end.** If you have your own business, even if it is only a sideline, you can hire your young children or grandchildren to give them tax-free or low-tax income for the year. Your business can deduct the salaries at its higher tax rate.

Children can receive up to $4,850 of earned income tax free, and up to $29,050 owing no more than a 15% tax on a single tax return.

Bonus: The earned income can enable the child to make a Roth IRA contribution of up to $3,000 for the year. Investment returns on these funds can compound for many years and then be withdrawn by the child tax free—which gives the child a great head start on financial security.

In addition, once a child has the qualifying earned income, you can make a gift to the child of the funds used to make the Roth contribution.

Strategy: If your children don't have earned income yet this year, try to get them some by year-end—from someone else if not you. Even a small amount contributed to a child's Roth IRA can compound into big benefits in future years.

•**Time marriage and divorce around year-end.** The new tax law significantly reduces the "marriage penalty" by giving married couples a standard deduction equal to the standard deduction for two single taxpayers combined, and by increasing to $58,100 the amount of income on a joint return that is covered by the 15% tax bracket.

Planning: Being married now is more likely to save taxes for a couple when one spouse has little or no income. Because marital status at the end of the year determines tax treatment for the full year, people who are planning to marry or divorce around the turn of the year may want to marry before year-end and divorce after year-end.

•**Use increased retirement plan contribution limits.** The maximum contributions to tax-favored retirement plans generally increased in 2004. And, persons over age 50 now can make "catch-up" contributions to 401(k)s, IRAs and other kinds of retirement accounts.

Make the most of the higher contribution limits in 2004. Check that you've maximized contributions for 2004, and plan to make contributions for 2005 early in the year whenever possible. The sooner funds are put into a tax-favored account, the more time they will have to earn returns.

•**Beware of state taxes and the alternative minimum tax (AMT).** Be alert to the fact that many states have not adjusted their tax laws to conform with the new changes in the federal law. Therefore, steps that take advantage of the federal law changes could very well result in an increased state tax bill.

Plus, the federal AMT may pose increased risk to those who take advantage of the federal law changes in ways that increase state taxes.

Example: A large federal tax deduction for state and local taxes is one of the common triggers of the AMT, which you pay if it is higher than your regular tax. So persons who take advantage of the new lower federal tax rate on long-term capital gains by taking a lot of them, and who incur increased state taxes on the gains they take, may find themselves facing the federal AMT as a result.

Safety: Be sure to consider state taxes and the AMT when you plan your best tax strategies for the rest of the year.

Also from Sidney Kess...

Faster Tax Refunds

The quickest way to get a refund is to file your return electronically requesting direct deposit of your refund into your bank account. This way, you'll get it weeks faster than if you file by mail and get a refund by check.

Last-Minute Actions to Take

Be sure to take advantage of these last-minute tax-saving strategies before the year comes to a close…

●**Charge deductible expenses on your credit card before year-end.** You can deduct the expense this year, even if you don't pay the charge off until a later year.

Examples: Medical bills, charitable contributions, business supplies.

Note: This rule applies only with general-use charge cards (Visa, MasterCard, etc.), not store cards.

●**Make charitable contributions**—and get acknowledgments of them. Last-minute donations can reap charity deductions—but remember, you need an acknowledgment from the charity for any gift over $250.

●**Exhaust flexible spending accounts (FSAs).** If you have a medical or dependent-care FSA at work, spend all your contributions to it by year-end. If not spent by December 31, the remaining money is forfeited.

Some possibilities: See your physician, purchase prescription drugs, eyeglasses or other medical items.

●**Adjust paycheck withholding.** If you've underpaid or overpaid your taxes so far, you can balance your payments for the year by changing withholding on your last paycheck. *If you've…*

●Overpaid, reduce withholding to get your refund in advance through an increased paycheck.

●Underpaid, increase withholding to avoid an underpayment penalty.

Save Big on Taxes

Larry Torella, CPA, tax partner at Eisner LLP, 750 Third Ave., New York City 10017. He is author of Eisner's annual year-end tax-planning guide.

You can save tens of thousands of dollars on taxes with these year-end strategies. But watch out—the new tax rules also increase the chance that you will be hit hard with alternative minimum tax (AMT).* *Seven dos and don'ts…*

●**Don't prepay property taxes or state and local income tax**—at least not until you check with your tax adviser. Many Americans who pay estimated income tax make their January tax payments before December 31 in order to deduct the payment one year sooner.

Trap: Tax law changes in the past few years are likely to reduce your regular tax more than what you would owe under AMT. If you prepay taxes, you will further reduce your regular tax relative to AMT. Prepaying could result in your owing AMT because state tax payments can't be deducted from AMT.

●**Don't accelerate deductions**—for the same reason as above. Again, check with your tax adviser. Unreimbursed medical expenses, such as eyeglasses and certain medical procedures, can be deducted if the total exceeds 7.5% of your adjusted gross income (AGI) for the year. Don't make next year's expenditures early to meet that threshold until you check with your adviser about your AMT exposure.

The same goes for miscellaneous deductions —for tax preparation, unreimbursed employee business expenses and investment expenses, such as publications and software. These can be deducted for regular tax purposes if the total exceeds 2% of your AGI.

●**Sock away more for retirement.** Contribution limits for 401(k) plans now are $13,000 —$16,000 for those age 50 or older.

*AMT is a tax that an increasing number of Americans must pay instead of regular tax. You must calculate your tax both ways and then pay whichever amount is higher. *Especially vulnerable:* People with many dependents, high state income tax or high miscellaneous deductions.

Caution: 401(k) contributions are deductible for purposes of regular tax and AMT. Nevertheless, consult a tax adviser to make sure contributions don't make you subject to AMT.

● **Make gifts.** You can save even more by giving appreciated stocks or fund shares instead of cash. Recipients who qualify for the new 5% capital gains tax rate—single taxpayers age 14 or older with taxable income of up to $29,050 in 2004…or married taxpayers with taxable income of up to $58,100—would benefit most from gifts of appreciated property that they can then sell.

Opportunity: You can remove thousands of dollars from your taxable estate. In 2004, you and your spouse can give $22,000 a year as a couple to each recipient, including charities, without owing gift tax.

● **Buy a sport-utility vehicle (SUV) or a truck** if you need a sizable car for your business—even if it is a sideline business.

You can deduct up to $102,000 for any business that purchases no more than $410,000 of equipment this year. Business cars don't qualify for the full expensing deduction, but SUVs that weigh more than 6,000 pounds qualify because they are considered trucks.

Example: Purchase an SUV or truck for $50,000, and use it for business 80% of the time. You'll be entitled to a $40,000 deduction (80% of $50,000).

Act fast to take advantage of this opportunity. Congress might curtail this loophole.

For any expensing deduction, equipment must be in use by December 31. It does not matter if you make the payments this year or the next.

● **Use losses to offset capital gains.** Losses that exceed your gains can be deducted against income—up to $3,000 a year.

Example: In early December, you determine that you have net long-term capital gains of $10,000. You owe $1,500 to the IRS (15% capital gains tax). The tax is higher for any short-term gains.

Take $13,000 worth of losses by December 31. Now you will have a $3,000 net capital loss ($13,000 − $10,000) for the year, which you are allowed to deduct.

In the 35% tax bracket, you'll save $1,050 (35% of $3,000) instead of *owing* $1,500.

Losses in excess of $3,000 can be carried forward to future years indefinitely to offset capital gains. That amount is in addition to the $3,000 annual net loss deduction.

Reminder: Under the wash-sale rule, when selling at a loss, wait at least 31 days to buy back the stock or fund. Before 31 days, the capital loss won't count. To avoid being out of the market, immediately buy a similar stock or fund to replace the one that you sold.

Example: When you sell one large-cap growth stock fund, purchase another one run by a different manager.

● **Don't invest in a fund before its annual distribution.** Most distributions occur at year-end. Call to check the distribution date. Invest after that date.

Opportunity: You'll get shares at a lower price, and you will not owe tax on gains that you didn't receive.

Deductible Home Improvements

Connie Lorz, EA, president of the California Society of Enrolled Agents, Sacramento.

A hurdle to deducting medical expenses is that only those in excess of 7.5% of your adjusted gross income (AGI) are deductible.

But costly home improvements made for medical purposes may get you over the hurdle.

Examples: Modified bathrooms, widened doors and stairways, elevators, wheelchair ramps, air-conditioning and even swimming pools all may qualify as deductible medical expenses.

Rules: The improvements must be primarily for a medical purpose and are deductible up to the extent their cost exceeds any increase in the home's value.

But if a home improvement gets you over the 7.5%-of-AGI threshold, all your other medical costs in addition to it—such as for prescription drugs—become deductible, too.

Easy Ways to Reduce Your Property Tax Bill

Nancy Dunnan, a financial adviser and author in New York City. Ms. Dunnan's latest book is titled *How to Invest $50–$5,000* (HarperCollins).

You have the right to protest a property tax bill. But do the footwork, or hire a specialist—a property tax consultant or attorney (most charge on a contingency basis). *If you do it yourself...*

● **Call your local tax assessor's office to find out about the appeals deadline.** It is typically 30 to 120 days after property tax bills are mailed out.

● **Check your written assessment for any errors**—look at square footage and number of bedrooms and bathrooms, etc.

● **At the tax assessor's office, compare your assessment** against at least five comparable homes of the same age and size in your neighborhood that have lower tax bills.

● **Take photographs of comparable houses** as backup.

● **Attend someone else's hearing** in order to familiarize yourself with the procedure and officials involved.

● **Ask for an informal meeting** with the tax assessor.

If your request for a meeting is denied, then be sure to follow your town's procedures for a formal hearing.

Also: Check out *How to Fight Property Taxes,* available from the National Taxpayers Union at *www.ntu.org* or 703-683-5700.

Cost: $6.95 (price subject to change).

How to Write Off The Cost of Supporting An Elderly Relative

Benjamin Bohlmann, CPA, shareholder, Mallah, Furman & Company PA, Brickell Bay Office Tower, 1001 Brickell Bay Dr., Miami, FL 33131. The past chair of the South Florida–based US Taxation of Multinationals Discussion Group, he is now treasurer of the Greater Miami Tax Institute.

As America ages, middle-aged sons and daughters are increasingly called upon to help provide for their ailing parents and other elderly loved ones. If you're in that category, tax benefits may help defray your costs.

DEPENDENCY EXEMPTIONS

In some situations, you may be able to claim a parent as your dependent. In addition, you might claim that a nonparent who lives in your home is a dependent.

Benefit: In 2004, a dependency exemption provides a $3,100 deduction.

Required: Your parent, friend or other relative must be a US citizen or a resident of North America. He/she cannot file a joint tax return, unless the return is filed only to receive a refund for taxes paid.

Two other criteria must be met...

● **Gross income.** The dependent's gross income must be below $3,100 in 2004.

● **Support.** You must provide over half of what it costs for that person to live throughout the year.

DRILLING DOWN

● **The gross income test** may be easier to pass than you think.

Loophole: If someone's Social Security benefits are not taxed, then they're not included in gross income for this purpose. That usually is the case for an elderly person who might be a dependent.

Gifts, insurance proceeds and tax-exempt interest also are excluded from the gross income calculation. However, such items may have an impact on the support test, explained on the next page.

141

Strategy: If your parent's gross income is just over $3,100, try to get below that amount. Bank CDs or bonds paying taxable interest might be switched to tax-exempt bonds or funds.

● **The support test** is easier to pass if the would-be dependent lives in your house.

Strategy: Count the fair rental of the housing you provide.

Example: Your elderly mother lives with you this year. The cost of her food, clothing, transportation, recreation, health care and similar necessities totals $5,000.

You also provide her with a room that you could rent to a third party for $400 a month, or $4,800 a year. Thus, the total cost of her support is $9,800 in 2004—$5,000 plus $4,800.

You must provide more than half, or at least $4,901. Because you have provided $4,800 worth of lodging, another $101 in support puts you over this threshold.

Key: Keep track of your parent's expenses and see that you're over the 50% mark. If it's a close call, ask your parent not to spend personal funds on major expenses such as travel.

MULTIPLE SUPPORT AGREEMENTS

If you can't meet the support test, you still may qualify for the dependency exemption.

Key: You and one or more siblings provide more than 50% support.

Strategy: Use a multiple support agreement to claim your parent as a dependent. Participating siblings can decide who will claim the exemption each year.

Required: The taxpayer taking the exemption must contribute to more than 10% of the parent's support. That taxpayer can claim the tax exemption by filing Form 2120, *Multiple Support Declaration,* with his federal income tax return. The form must be signed by *all* the eligible parties.

Problem: High-income taxpayers lose most or all of the value of dependency exemptions, which phase out as the adjusted gross income (AGI) reaches certain thresholds ($214,050 on a joint return, in 2004, for instance).

Strategy: In a multiple support agreement, the dependency exemption should be taken by someone whose AGI is less than $214,050

on a joint return this year, or under $142,700 as a single filer. Such taxpayers can get the maximum benefit.

DEPENDENT CARE CREDIT

In addition to the dependency exemption, you might get a dependent care credit for a parent. Despite its name, the dependent care credit is not just for dependents. You can claim the credit for someone if you meet all the dependency tests except for gross income.

How it works: To get this credit, you must hire someone to take care of a parent so that you can go to work.

Payoff: You generally can take a 20% credit for up to $3,000 worth of expenses. That's $600 in annual tax savings. If you hire someone to care for two people, that 20% credit could be applied to $6,000 in expenses.

MEDICAL EXPENSES

You also may be able to add the money you spend for a parent's medical expenses to your own itemized medical deductions. Such expenses might include the payment of a parent's long-term-care insurance premiums, up to Tax Code limitations.

Caution: For these expenses to qualify, you must pay the bills directly. Don't give money to a parent so that he can pay.

Required: The same standard applies here as it does for the dependent care credit. The person whose bills you pay must meet all the dependency tests, but not necessarily the one for gross income.

Loophole: If your parent lives in your home, some capital expenses may be deductible.

Required: The outlays must be made to treat a specific condition at a doctor's written recommendation.

Example: Say your mother's doctor prescribes swimming to treat severe arthritis, so you spend $20,000 on a home pool.

Before-and-after appraisals state that the pool increased your home's value by $15,000. The $5,000 difference may be taken as a medical deduction.

Other examples of capital improvements that might lead to medical deductions include the installation of central air-conditioning for breathing disorders and providing wheelchair access.

Benefit: Health-care bills you pay for a qualified person can be added to your other medical costs. In turn, those amounts might put you over the 7.5%-of-AGI threshold for deducting medical costs.

Example: Your AGI this year is $100,000, so you would need to go over $7,500 in medical expenses in order to get the deduction. Total medical bills are only $6,000, so no deduction is allowed.

However, this year you contribute $5,000 to your mother's medical bills, and your mother qualifies under all the dependency rules that are mentioned in this article.

Therefore, your total medical expenses are now $11,000. You're over the $7,500 threshold, so $3,500 worth of medical expenses are tax deductible.

Limitation: Money that you spend on dependent care also may qualify as a medical expense. But, you can't take the credit and the deduction for the same outlays. Do the math to see which provides the greater tax benefit.

HEAD-OF-HOUSEHOLD STATUS

If you're not married and you help to support a parent, you may claim head-of-household filing status.

Benefit: You'll owe less than you would as a single filer.

Required: To qualify, you need to provide more than half of your parent's housing costs or nursing home bills. Alternatively, your parent can live with you for more than half the year.

Various other tax rules are much more favorable for head-of-household filers than for singles, so this can be a valuable tax break for those who qualify.

OTCs Can Now Be Paid for Through FSAs

Over-the-counter (OTC) medications now can be paid for through health-care flexible spending accounts (FSAs).

FSAs are provided by many employers to let employees pay medical costs with pretax dollars—giving the equivalent of a tax deduction. Employees contribute a portion of pay to their FSA each year. The contributed money escapes tax and is used to pay costs not covered by a medical plan.

Key: Many former prescription drugs now are sold OTC. This has increased health costs for many because OTC drugs are not covered by most medical plans and are not deductible. The new rule is meant to give relief for this cost.

Consider OTC drug purchases when deciding how much to contribute to an FSA.

Joanne Mitchell-George, Esq., author of the American Payroll Association Basic Guide to Payroll *(Aspen).*

Cell Phone Write-Off

Donate your old cell phone to charity, and receive a tax write-off.

What to do: Drop off your phone, charger and accessories at a participating wireless carrier's store. The wireless industry's charitable programs are now listed at *www.recyclewireless phones.com,* or contact your wireless provider.

When possible, the phones are restored and money from the sale is earmarked for charities. Even if your cell phone is not in good enough condition to restore, you still will receive the write-off. Consult your tax adviser to determine the value of your phone for tax purposes.

David Diggs, executive director, Wireless Foundation, which initiates and oversees philanthropic programs using wireless technology, Washington, DC. The organization's Web site is www.wirelessfoundation.org.

Summertime Tax Breaks

Michael E. Mares, Esq., CPA/ABV, tax member, Witt, Mares & Company, PLC, 701 Town Center Dr., Newport News, VA 23606. He is coauthor of the *Guide to Limited Liability Companies* (Practitioners).

New opportunities for tax write-offs surface as the temperatures rise. *Some of the ways you can enjoy tax benefits from your summer activities...*

TRAVEL EXPENSES

●**Combine business with pleasure.** Even if you take personal side trips while traveling on business, you can still write off your full airfare.

Required: You must be able to prove that the trip was primarily for business purposes. Each case is different depending on the facts and circumstances.

Lodging and meal costs (subject to the 50% deduction limit) can be written off only for the business portion of the trip.

Loophole: If you stay for a weekend to take advantage of the lower airfare you get with a Saturday night stay, your lodging and meals for those additional days are considered business expenses even when you have spent the whole weekend sightseeing.

Caution: There are different rules that apply to foreign travel.

●**Perform charitable work.** If the purpose of your trip is to do work for a charity, you can deduct your travel costs as an unreimbursed volunteer expense. You claim this as a charitable contribution deduction.

●**Continue your education.** Whenever you take courses to keep up your job skills, you can write off both your travel expenses and the cost of the courses. If you are an employee, these costs are deductible as a miscellaneous itemized deduction to the extent such costs exceed 2% of your adjusted gross income (AGI). When you're self-employed, these costs are treated as fully deductible business expenses on Schedule C.

●**Lose weight.** If you suffer from obesity or any other medical condition that requires you to lose weight, a stay at a health spa may be a deductible medical expense. Remember, though, that medical expenses are deductible only to the extent that they exceed 7.5% of your AGI.

●**Take your spouse (or a companion) along.** When your spouse accompanies you on any of the travel activities mentioned above, his/her travel expenses are considered nondeductible. However, as a practical matter, if you travel by car, there's no added expense for his travel. And in many cases, the cost of a second person's hotel stay is free, so the only nondeductible costs are your spouse's meals.

VACATION HOMES

By renting out your vacation home, you can cover some—or all—of the home's expenses. If you rent the place for fewer than 15 days, you do not have to pay tax on the rental income— no matter how much it adds up to. However, you can't deduct any operating expenses, such as maintenance. Your deductions are limited to those of any home owner—mortgage interest as well as real estate taxes.

If you rent the home for 15 days or more, your write-offs are governed by a complex set of rules.

Boats and RVs: If you finance the purchase of a boat or recreational vehicle, your interest payments can be fully deductible home-mortgage interest if you designate the purchase as a second home. To qualify as a home, the boat or RV must include eating, sleeping and bathroom facilities.

KIDS ON THE PAYROLL

Benefits for you: You can deduct salary paid to your child. This lowers your self-employment income and saves on income taxes *and* self-employment taxes. If your child is younger than age 18, you do not have to pay Social Security and Medicare (FICA) taxes on his wages.

Paying your child a wage for working for you will not cost you a dependency exemption no matter how much he earns as long as he is either younger than age 19 or younger than age 24 and a full-time student.

Caution: Make sure that the wages are reasonable for the work performed. Keep records of the time and nature of your child's work.

Benefits for your child: In 2004, your child can earn up to $4,850 without owing any income tax. This means your child can earn $12 an hour for 10 weeks (40 hours per week) and owe no tax. The child can use the money to pay for school, personal expenses, or to fund a Roth IRA that will produce tax-free income in his retirement years.

Added benefit: In this tough job market, working for you may be the only job opportunity available…and your child will gain valuable work experience that will help in finding a future job.

SUMMER CAMP

If your preteen child attends day camp so that you can work, the cost of the camp can be used to figure the dependent care credit. Expenses up to $3,000 per year can be taken into account for one child, $6,000 for two or more children. Depending on your adjusted gross income, up to 35% of these costs becomes a tax credit, reducing your taxes dollar for dollar.

Caution: The dependent care credit may not be claimed for sleepaway camp, even if you send your child there so that you can work.

Deduct Fun from Your Taxes

Sandy Botkin, Esq., CPA, president of the Tax Reduction Institute, 13200 Executive Park Terrace, Germantown, MD 20874, *www.taxreductioninstitute.com*. He is a former IRS attorney as well as a senior tax law specialist and author of the best-selling *Lower Your Taxes Big Time!* (McGraw-Hill).

What's even better than spending lots of wonderful weekends and evenings out on the town? Legitimately deducting the expenses from your business taxes. You can do this if you have your own business— even if it is only a sideline…and it should not increase your risk of an audit.

MEALS AND ENTERTAINMENT

You can deduct *half* the cost of meals and other entertainment that has a business purpose. There is no limit on the amount that can be deducted, and receipts are not necessary for expenses of $75 or less.

IRS requirements…

●**A business purpose.** It could be as simple as soliciting business from a prospect. Depending on your particular industry, *anybody* could be a prospect.

●**Surroundings conducive to discussing business.** The IRS will not believe you talked business at the theater or while playing golf. You must set aside some time to talk undisturbed within 24 hours of incurring your expense. Even a telephone conversation will do.

Example: You take business prospects out for dinner, then to a play and for drinks afterward. You don't have to mention business during the fun, just as long as you discuss it at some other point within 24 hours.

●**Adequate records.** These need to include who was entertained…when…where…the specific business purpose of the entertainment…its cost…and a receipt (if the cost was more than $75). Record the amount in a business diary or ledger on the same day.

Caution: All five items must be recorded in a "timely" manner—near the date on which the entertainment occurs—in order for the deduction to be allowed.

HOME ENTERTAINMENT

Expenses incurred when entertaining at your home are among the most overlooked deductions. The IRS considers your home conducive to business…and costs often are less than the $75 minimum for receipts.

Regulations don't require you to spend a specific amount of time discussing business, so it is easy to qualify everyone attending an event as a business guest.

Example: You invite a guest and his/her spouse to your home for a dinner party, during which you have a one-minute discussion with the guest about obtaining referrals for your business. This lets you deduct half the cost of entertaining both the guest and his spouse. You can repeat the process with other guests.

Larger parties can make it difficult to discuss business with every guest and record each conversation in your diary.

Better: Demonstrate a business purpose for the party by announcing it in the invitation and having some form of display showing a business intent or discussion.

Example: Celebrate your business's anniversary, and put up a business-related display. For proof, take pictures of it with all the guests milling around. Also save the invitation.

FOLLOW THE RULES

●**Spouses and guests.** If your business guest brings his spouse or another guest, you also can bring a spouse or guest and then deduct half the costs for all four people.

●**Season tickets.** When you purchase season tickets to sporting or cultural events, you must deduct each event separately.

Example: You have season tickets to eight football games per year. If you invite business guests six times, you can deduct half the cost of the tickets to those six games only.

●**"Dutch treat" meals and those you buy for yourself.** If you split the cost of a business meal with another person or pay for your own meal, you can deduct half your expense to the extent that it exceeds your average meal cost.

Useful: My experience is that IRS auditors typically determine average meal costs by using a "50%/30%/20% rule." Total your food receipts for one month, and the IRS will deem 50% of the total to be for dinner…30% for lunch…and 20% for breakfast.

Example: If your food bills average $140 per week, $70 would be for dinner. The average cost over seven days would be $10 per dinner. Under the "Dutch treat" rule, your business dinners would be deductible to the extent that their costs exceed $10. Thus, if you and a business associate spend $200 on a fancy business dinner and split the cost, you could deduct half of $90.

SPECIAL 100% DEDUCTIONS

You can deduct the full cost of some business expenses…

●**Entertaining employees.** If you host an event to entertain your employees, you must invite an entire group or department—not just your friends.

Example: You own a small business. You invite all of your employees and their spouses for a night on the town as a business celebration. You can then deduct 100% of these costs for everyone.

●**Sales promotions.** You can deduct the cost of food and beverages provided *during* a presentation at your home, office or an off-site location—not afterward.

GIFTS

●**Business gifts of up to $25 per recipient annually.** There is no limit to the size of a gift and no dollar limit to the deduction if you give your gift to a company or department without naming a specific person.

THE PIG RULE

All of these deductions are subject to what CPAs call the *pig rule*—the deduction amounts must be reasonable.

Example: A doctor who deducted $35,000 for meals said that he "ate only for business reasons." He lost all of those deductions.

Tax Breaks for The Military

The *Military Family Tax Relief Act of 2003* became law on November 11, providing lots of new tax breaks for military personnel and their family members.

It retroactively liberalizes rules for tax-free home sales for personnel stationed away from home—even sales made before 2001. It also liberalizes tax rules for dependent-care assistance, overnight travel expenses for National Guard and Reserve members, combat zone pay, etc. File an amended return to claim a refund if you failed to claim these tax breaks on an original tax return.

More information: Visit *www.irs.gov* and click on "The Newsroom" and then on "Armed Forces," or consult your tax adviser.

Laurence I. Foster, CPA/PFS, consultant and former partner at Eisner LLP, 750 Third Ave., New York City 10017.

How to Save Big on Taxes If You're Divorced Or Separated

Julian Block, Larchmont, NY–based attorney, syndicated columnist and author of *Marriage and Divorce Tax Guide*, available from the author at *julianblock@yahoo.com.*

The new tax law makes marital breakups a lot easier on the pocketbook. *To save on taxes if you are divorced or legally separated, check out the following advice…*

• **File as head of your household.** In many cases, your tax bill will be lower than if you file as a single person or married filing separately.

The 15% bracket now covers up to $29,050 in taxable income for single filers and married people filing separately in 2004. For heads of household, the 15% bracket covers income up to $38,900. Beyond those thresholds, the tax rate jumps to 25% for all categories.

You can file as head of household when you meet four tests…

• Your home was the principal residence of a dependent child for more than half the year.

• You file a tax return separately from your spouse.

• Your spouse did not live with you during the last six months of the year.

• You paid more than half of your household's costs during the year.

Tax rates on joint returns are the most favorable, but you might not want to file jointly if your marriage is in trouble. If the IRS audits a joint return and finds a shortfall, it usually can dun either spouse for the entire amount of additional taxes, interest and penalties.

You can actually be a head of household even though you can't claim the child as a dependent because you signed IRS Form 8332, *Release of Claim to Exemption for Child of Divorced or Separated Parents.*

Loophole: Even if you are not divorced or legally separated, you can qualify for favorable head-of-household tax rates if you meet the four tests.

• **Use previous years' tax returns to help locate hidden assets.** In property settlement negotiations, a spouse might try to hide assets. *Look at these forms to get your fair share…*

• Schedule B, *Interest and Ordinary Dividends,* requires the names of mutual funds, brokerage firms, banks and other sources of dividends and interest if the amounts involved are substantial —more than $1,500.

• Schedule D, *Capital Gains and Losses,* enables you to more easily track sales of securities and investment property.

• Schedule E, *Supplemental Income and Loss,* discloses income or loss from rental real estate, royalties, trusts, partnerships and S corporations.

Strategy: If this information is on a joint return that you signed, ask your tax preparer for copies. You are entitled to see copies, even if your spouse provided all the income. If you filed a joint return without a preparer, submit IRS Form 4506, *Request for Copy or Transcript of Tax Form,* to get copies. This form doesn't have to be signed by your spouse. The IRS generally keeps copies of returns for five years, so you'll have access to information as you negotiate a property settlement.

• **Value all assets on an after-tax basis.** Divorce and separation agreements typically involve horse trading—you get the house, I keep the stocks, etc. But an asset might not be worth its face value to you after taxes.

Example: An asset with a current face value of $100,000 was purchased for $40,000, its cost basis for tax purposes. A $60,000 unrealized gain will carry over after the property distribution. At a 15% capital gains rate on a sale, you will pay $9,000 in tax. This asset will be worth $91,000 to you, not $100,000.

AMT trap: If you liquidate assets that have gone up in value, you may have to pay state and local income taxes on the sale, which could make you subject to the alternative minimum tax (AMT).

• **Use the home exclusion.** You owe no tax on gains of up to $250,000 on the sale of your principal residence. For married couples, the exclusion is as much as $500,000. Formerly, a spouse who moved out after a divorce or legal separation lost this break because the home was no longer his/her "principal residence."

Thanks to a change in tax law, the ex-occupant now can retain the $250,000 exclusion.

To qualify: The ex-occupant must remain an owner…a divorce or separation agreement must grant him use of the home…the ex-spouse must have lived in the home for at least two years at any time before the sale. The ex-occupant can claim the $250,000 exclusion even if the sale occurs years after the divorce.

When one ex-spouse ceases to be a joint owner: In most cases, the spouse who receives the home will be able to sell immediately and claim a $250,000 exclusion. A two-year wait will not be necessary.

However, if the owner-spouse remarries, the new husband or wife has to live in the home for at least two years for this couple to qualify for the full $500,000 exclusion.

●**Factor in dependency exemptions.** In 2004, you can deduct $3,100 for each dependent that you claim. In a divorce or separation, dependency exemptions will go to the custodial parent specified in the divorce or separation agreement. Without such an agreement, the parent with physical custody for most of the year gets the tax break.

Strategy: A lower-income custodial parent can sign over all the dependency exemptions to the higher-income parent on IRS Form 8332. These exemptions may result in greater tax savings for the higher-income parent.

Example: For those in the 33% bracket, each $3,100 exemption saves more than $1,000 in federal income tax. For anyone in the 15% bracket, each $3,100 exemption saves $465.

In return for signing Form 8332, the custodial spouse should receive concessions in the separation or divorce negotiations.

Best: Sign away exemptions on a yearly basis rather than granting an indefinite waiver. It will help to assure compliance with child support and alimony obligations.

The noncustodial spouse should make concessions only when his adjusted gross income (AGI) is well below six figures and he is not subject to the AMT. In 2004, exemptions are reduced at an AGI of $142,700 for single filers. Once a single filer's AGI tops $265,200, dependency exemptions provide no tax benefits.

●**Factor in child tax credits.** The child tax credit is now $1,000 per child under age 17. This credit makes dependency exemptions more valuable, so negotiating for these exemptions is more important.

Caution: Again, income limits will restrict taxpayers' ability to claim the child tax credit. And, the credit starts to phase out when AGI exceeds $110,000 for any married couples filing jointly… $75,000 for single individuals or heads of household…and $55,000 for married couples who are filing separately.

Make Charity Sweeter with Innovative Donation Techniques

David Scott Sloan, Esq., deputy chair of Private Wealth Services, Holland & Knight LLP, 10 St. James Ave., Boston 02116, and a member of the firm's board of directors where he chairs the strategic planning committee. He has served as chairman of both the Tax Legislation Committee of the Massachusetts Bar Association and the Estate Planning Committee of the Boston Bar Association.

When you make a substantial gift to charity—let's say more than $10,000—there are better ways than simply writing out your check. Sophisticated "planned giving" strategies can provide you with lifetime income or the use of valued property, as well as tax savings.

In the planned giving area, there are many vehicles from which you can choose.

CHARITABLE GIFT ANNUITIES

How they work: You make a gift to a charity and then receive an annuity, a guaranteed stream of income at a fixed rate that can go on for your lifetime or for a specific term.

Some charities stipulate a minimum amount for gift annuities, such as $10,000.

The older you are when you make the donation to the charity, the greater the periodic income you can receive.

Examples: With Charity A, a 60-year-old donor might receive 5.7%, or $5,700 per year on a $100,000 gift. An 80-year-old making that same $100,000 gift might receive 8%, or $8,000 per year.

A couple will receive lower payments than a single recipient because of their longer joint life expectancy. If that 80-year-old donor has a 75-year-old spouse, and payments are to continue until they both die, the annuity rate might drop from 8% to 6.6% per year.

Tax treatment: In all these situations, part of the income stream will be taxable and part will be a tax-free return of capital.

Loophole: When the gift annuity is funded with appreciated assets, the capital gains obligation is tax deferred—the taxable gain is spread across the annuity payments. With any gift annuity, donors get partial tax deductions as well.

Example: A 75-year-old might be entitled to a deduction equal to 40%—the difference between the value of what was given away and the value of what is expected to be paid back.

Key: Gift annuities offer fixed income as well as security because the obligation to pay the annuity is a claim on all the assets of the issuer.

Payments from charitable gift annuities may be deferred.

Example: You make a gift at age 55 but stipulate that annuity payments not begin until you reach age 65. The payment stream will be greater, to take into account 10 years of growth in the interim.

Loophole: With this strategy, you may obtain a charitable deduction now, while you're in a high tax bracket, yet defer the income until you're retired and your tax rate is lower.

CHARITABLE REMAINDER ANNUITY TRUSTS

A charitable remainder annuity trust is similar to a charitable gift annuity.

How they work: You make a donation and then your "income beneficiaries" (often, you and your spouse) receive fixed payments for life or for a specific term. After the income interest terminates, the remainder (what's left in the trust) goes to charity. Again, by giving away appreciated assets you can defer capital gains tax.

How does a charitable remainder annuity trust differ from a gift annuity?

● **Expenses.** If a trust must be created, some legal expenses will be involved. Gift annuities tend to be simpler and cheaper.

● **Control.** You have more control with an annuity trust. You set the income you wish to receive, but it must be at least 5% of the initial trust principal.

Example: If you donate $100,000 to a charitable remainder annuity trust, you must receive at least $5,000 per year.

Trade-off: The more income you decide to receive, the less will be left to charity and the smaller your up-front charitable deduction.

CHARITABLE REMAINDER UNITRUSTS

How they work: A unitrust resembles an annuity trust but with one key difference. You receive a payout that's based on a percentage of the value of the trust assets rather than a fixed amount. Again, the minimum is 5% a year.

Key: Your income will grow if the trust fund earns more than the payout percentage you set. A unitrust provides inflation protection if the income stream grows in time.

Variation: A net-income-makeup charitable remainder unitrust allows donors to give now and receive income after waiting a period of years, often after retirement.

Drawback: For all types of remainder trusts, donating appreciated assets has been a popular strategy. This approach is less popular now that the tax on capital gains has been reduced.

Moreover, lower interest rates decrease the appeal of unitrusts because they put upper limits on payout percentages.

Comparison: The unitrusts are more flexible than annuity trusts because, with the former, additional contributions can be made after the trust is created.

On the other hand, annuity trusts are easier to administer and provide a dependable income stream.

When you set up a charitable remainder trust, you can serve as trustee, which gives you some ongoing control over the trust funds. In addition, you can decide to change the charitable beneficiaries.

Caution: Serving as a trustee can involve a great deal of work. There are records to keep, tax returns to file and fiduciary rules to follow. Trustees fees can vary, depending on what the circumstances are.

CHARITABLE LEAD TRUSTS

This type of trust is the opposite of a remainder trust.

How they work: The charity gets a stream of income first and the trust assets eventually are distributed to someone you designate.

Advantage: Lead trusts can be useful if you want to fulfill annual charitable obligations yet you want to transfer assets to your children or grandchildren while minimizing gift taxes.

Example: Suppose you have pledged to contribute $10,000 per year to a favorite charity for the next 15 years. You might set up a 15-year lead trust with $250,000 worth of securities. After 15 years, any of the remaining assets will go to your children or grandchildren.

Loophole: Depending on interest rates at the time you establish the trust, the value of the taxable gift might be zero, or near zero. That's true even if the securities appreciate and turn out to be worth $300,000, $400,000 or more by the time the trust expires and the beneficiaries receive the assets in the trust fund.

Key: Low interest rates boost the appeal of charitable lead trusts. The lower the interest rate, the lower the value of the taxable gift to the trust beneficiaries.

POOLED INCOME FUNDS

How they work: These funds are essentially mutual funds run by a charity. Net earnings are paid out to participants on a pro rata basis.

Result: A donor's income depends upon the investment success of the fund's manager.

Benefits: Pooled income funds may appeal to those making gifts too small for a unitrust but who do not want to lock themselves into a fixed income stream. You can increase your contribution to a pooled income fund over time, and increase your income.

BARGAIN SALES

Suppose you bought real estate several years ago for $75,000 and it has appreciated in value to $250,000. You would like to give it to charity, avoiding the capital gains tax, but you are not eager to make a $250,000 gift.

Strategy: Sell the property to the charity at a bargain price, perhaps $125,000. Thus, the charity would gain $125,000, while you put $125,000 in your pocket.

Result: Half of the appreciation ($87,500) would be a taxable gain for you while you are entitled to a $125,000 tax deduction. This deduction may wipe out your tax obligation from disposing of the property and give you an additional write-off.

RETAINED INTEREST GIFTS OF REAL ESTATE

You can give property (including your home) to a charity now but retain the right to use the property for your lifetime, and perhaps your spouse's lifetime as well.

Loophole: You'll get a partial tax deduction now for a future gift. The deduction depends on your life expectancy and the interest rates in effect at the time.

Bottom line: It doesn't matter which type of planned gift you choose, you can expect recognition once the gift becomes irrevocable, even though the assets may not go to the charity for many years.

Valuation Guide for Charitable Donations of Small, Used Items

When used goods are donated to charity, you can deduct their value—but you may not know how to determine that number.

Helpful: Check The Salvation Army's on-line donation valuation guide. Go to *www.salvation armyusa.org,* then in the search box enter "valuation guide." This will produce a link to a valuation guide that covers men's, women's and children's products, appliances, dry goods and furniture.

Loopholes in Tax Return Preparation

Edward Mendlowitz, CPA, partner, Mendlowitz Weitsen, LLP, CPAs, which is one of only 800 CPA firms nationwide approved to audit public companies, K2 Brier Hill Ct., East Brunswick, NJ 08816. He is also author of *Introducing Tax Clients to Additional Services* (American Institute of CPAs).

To save money and reduce the odds of an audit, use these strategies to prepare and file your return.

***Loophole:* Report incorrect or missing 1099 information on your return.** Banks, brokerages and other payers of income will file directly with the IRS, which crosschecks the information with the Forms 1099 that individuals report on their returns. Discrepancies automatically trigger written inquiries from the IRS …and can lead to an audit.

Example: Your bank sent you a 1099 reporting an incorrect amount of interest earned on your account in 2004.

You need to enter on your tax return the actual amount of taxable interest income you received or were credited with. On another line, indicate the amount reported on the 1099. Beneath that, show the 1099 amount as a negative number and then write the following explanation beside that figure—*The interest amount reported by my bank is incorrect. A corrected 1099 was requested but not yet issued. The correct amount is reflected on my tax return.*

***Loophole:* Reconstruct missing W-2s.** If a company you worked for went out of business or your employer hasn't yet given you a Form W-2, *Wage and Tax Statement,* you can reconstruct your salary and withholding records on Form 4852, *Substitute for Form W-2, Wage and Tax Statement,* or Form 1099-R, *Distributions From Pensions, Annuities, Retirement or Profit-Sharing Plans, IRAs, Insurance Contracts, etc.*

On the form, estimate your salary and withholding, explaining how you arrived at the figures, and send it in with your tax return.

***Loophole:* If one spouse owes back taxes and the other expects a refund, file separate returns.** While this may increase the overall tax rate for the couple, filing separate returns protects the refund. Otherwise, the IRS may apply the refund to the other spouse's tax bill.

If the back tax bill is paid within three years, you can file an amended return claiming the joint filing status for that year. This lowers the tax rate, and you can file for another refund. However, if you filed a joint return originally, you cannot later refile separate returns.

***Loophole:* Carefully consider the business code number you enter on the company's tax return.** The IRS targets certain types of businesses for audit, such as cash businesses (small retail stores, restaurants, auto repair shops). Refer to the audit guides at *www.irs. gov.* When your business could fit into more than one category, choose the business code number that's not on the IRS's hit list.

***Loophole:* File all the required supporting documents.** You'll reduce your audit risk and secure your deductions. *Examples…*

●When claiming a home-office deduction, be sure to file Form 8829, *Expenses for Business Use of Your Home.*

●For charitable gifts of property valued at more than $500, you must file Form 8283, *Noncash Charitable Contributions.* You also need a professional appraisal for any donated property worth more than $5,000.

***Loophole:* Disagreeing with the IRS.** When you take a position contrary to an IRS rule, you are required to disclose your position. You can file Form 8275, *Disclosure Statement,* which explains the reasoning supporting the position you took or attach a sheet to your tax return with the same information.

Best: Attach a written explanation to your return instead of filing the official IRS form.

Reason: All the Forms 8275 are automatically reviewed, raising your chances of being selected for an audit.

***Loophole:* Ask for an automatic extension to file your return.** Returns for 2004 are due on April 15, 2005, but you can extend the due date for filing to October 17 by getting two extensions from the IRS.

The first extension gives you four months and is granted automatically.

The second is given at the discretion of the IRS when you provide adequate reasons.

Example: You may not have all of your information and need the additional time to collect it.

Bonus: An extension will also extend the amount of time that you can contribute funds to a self-employed income Keogh or SEP plan.

***Loophole:* Estimated taxes.** If you are required to pay estimated taxes and are requesting an extension, include the first quarter 2005 installments as part of the tax due for year 2004 with the extension.

This covers any shortfall in your projection of the amount that you will owe when you file your 2004 tax return. The cushion is important because the penalties and interest for failure to pay taxes owed are higher than the penalty for underestimating year 2005 taxes.

When It Pays to File Separate Tax Returns

Marc A. Aaronson, Esq., CPA, partner, Eisner LLP, 750 Third Ave., New York City 10017.

D o not assume that filing a joint return is always the best thing for a married couple to do. Recent tax law changes should prompt some to think again about filing separate returns.

NEW TAX BREAKS

As a general rule, the tax law discourages separate filing for married couples—separate filers are usually not treated as well as single individuals. But the new law contains key tax breaks that equate the benefits for joint filers to twice the amount for singles. Separate filers have also been given some breaks—equating them to single filers.

●**Tax brackets.** The 10% tax bracket for the joint filers has been increased by $2,000. The tax bracket for both unmarried persons as well as married persons filing separate returns has

been increased by $1,000. Similarly, the 15% tax bracket for married persons filing jointly is one-half that for joint filers (the same as for single taxpayers).

Impact: More married persons will not be penalized for filing separately.

●**Standard deduction.** The standard deduction amount for joint filers has been doubled to twice that of unmarried persons filing separate returns. Again, married persons filing separately now have the same standard deduction as single individuals.

Example: Each spouse earns income of $25,000 and claims the standard deduction. It will make no difference to the couple's federal income tax bill if they file jointly or separately. They would each pay $2,200 on separate returns or $4,400 on a joint return.

The tax law changes effectively have made filing for married couples with income up to a certain level tax neutral—the tax bill comes out the same way for the couple whether they file jointly or separately. With this tax neutrality as a base, there are now key instances when filing separately can produce an overall tax savings for the couple.

TESTING THE WATERS

There is no magic formula to use in determining whether filing separate returns makes sense. Filing jointly usually saves taxes, especially where one spouse has little or no income. *But there are some situations where it may pay to file separately…*

●**Capital gains and dividends.** Suppose one spouse with capital gains and/or dividends is in the 10% or 15% tax bracket. This means that this income will be taxed at only 5%, compared with a 15% rate that would apply on a joint return if combined income pushes the couple into a tax bracket above 15%.

Example: A married person filing a separate return can have taxable income of up to $28,400 while still falling within the 15% tax bracket. Assume that a spouse has $5,000 from a part-time job, dividends of $10,000 and interest of $10,000. Since this spouse is in the 15% tax bracket, the dividends are taxed at only 5%. If the couple had filed jointly and were in a tax bracket of 25% or higher, the couple would pay

15% on the same dividends, or an additional $1,000 in taxes.

●**Medical expenses.** If the spouse with the smaller income has the greater share of medical expenses, separate filing may save taxes. This is because it may be easier for expenses to exceed the 7.5%-of-adjusted-gross-income (AGI) threshold for deducting medical expenses.

Example: A spouse who has $20,000 of income has $10,000 of unreimbursed medical expenses. Filing taxes separately would mean that only the initial $1,500 in medical expenses is nondeductible ($10,000 − [$20,000 x 7.5%]). Thus, $8,500 of medical expenses is deductible. If the couple's combined AGI is $100,000, and the other spouse has no medical expenses, the deductible portion drops to just $2,500.

Separate filing should be considered to maximize deductions for casualty and theft losses and miscellaneous itemized expenses. Also, if one spouse itemizes his/her deductions, the other spouse must do so as well and cannot use the standard deduction.

●**Child tax credit.** The adjusted gross income threshold for claiming the $1,000 child tax credit is $110,000 on a joint return and $55,000 for married filing separately. When the couple's combined AGI exceeds the $110,000 limit, one of the spouses may be able to claim the credit by falling under the $55,000 limit. That spouse must meet the other requirements for claiming the credit (i.e., the child must be the spouse's dependent).

Important: Run the numbers both ways—filing jointly and separately—to determine which alternative is better. Tax preparation software allows for these "what if" calculations. *Some things to be aware of...*

●Even if the numbers show joint filing to be better, separate filing should still be used by a spouse who is concerned about liability for the tax related to the joint return. Separate filing is really the only way to guarantee freedom from the other spouse's tax debt.

●Once you file jointly, you cannot change your filing status for that year. But if you file separately, you generally have three years to change your status and file a joint return.

SPECIAL ISSUES

There are two traps to avoid in separate filing. Even though separate filing may save regular federal income taxes, it could end up costing more in overall taxes by increasing alternative minimum tax (AMT) or state income taxes.

●**AMT.** Regular income taxes are not the only factor to consider in choosing filing status. An increasing number of taxpayers are falling subject to the AMT by reducing their regular taxes.

For the purposes of AMT, married persons filing separately have half the exemption amount of the joint filers ($29,000 versus $58,000). The smaller exemption for married persons filing separately may subject them to AMT, reducing or eliminating any savings that resulted for regular tax purposes from choosing this filing status.

●**State income taxes.** In many states, filing status for federal income tax determines your state filing status—if you file separately on your federal return, you must also file separately for state tax purposes. And state taxes may not necessarily provide any benefit for this filing status—it may even impose an added tax cost that can wipe out federal income tax savings.

WHEN TO AVOID SEPARATE FILING

Don't opt to file separate returns if you want to take advantage of certain tax benefits that require joint filing. *These tax benefits include...*

●**$25,000 rental loss allowance.**

●**Credit for the elderly.**

●**Education credits.**

●**Dependent care credit.**

●**Earned income credit.**

●**IRA deduction for a contribution** on behalf of a nonworking spouse.

●**Converting a traditional IRA to a Roth IRA.**

●**Savings bond interest exclusion.**

●**Opportunity to exclude all or half of Social Security benefits** (if income permits).

Note: Some of these benefits may be claimed on a separate return if spouses live apart for the last six months of the year, or the entire year (depending on the benefit).

Bottom line: The decision on filing status is a complex one. If you have questions, consult a tax adviser.

When to File an Amended Return...and When Not To

Marvin Michelman, CPA, director of tax controversy, Deloitte & Touche, LLP, Two World Financial Center, New York City 10281. He worked for the IRS for 19 years, beginning as a revenue agent and becoming the senior regional analyst in charge of field audits.

Even after you file your federal income tax return, you have three years to file an amended return using IRS Form 1040X, *Amended US Individual Income Tax Return* to obtain a refund. If you received an extension, you have three years from the extension date your return was filed. For bad debts or worthless securities, you have up to seven years to file an amended return.

Filing an amended return may make sense —but not always.

UNDERPAID/OVERPAID TAXES

File an amended return as soon as possible if you discover that you have *underpaid* your federal income tax.

Example: You overlooked income you should have reported or took an iffy deduction.

Advantages: You stop the interest on your underpayment from accruing. And you reduce the chance of having to pay penalties if the IRS discovers the underpayment.

What if you can't pay the tax you owe? File an amended return anyway. This won't stop interest from building up, but you may eventually be able to negotiate a payment schedule with the IRS.

If you've overpaid: You are entitled to a refund of those overpaid taxes plus interest. However, if the refund amount is insignificant, you may want to forgo the refund, and not increase your audit exposure.

To receive a tax refund, you must attach an explanation to Form 1040X. An IRS employee will read that explanation and decide whether more questions need to be asked.

The IRS insists that filing an amended return does not increase your audit risk. Indeed, the IRS can't possibly audit the millions of amended returns that are filed each year. Nevertheless, filing Form 1040X does mean coming to the attention of the IRS one more time.

Bottom line: When substantial amounts are involved, don't hesitate to submit an amended tax return.

REDUCE YOUR AUDIT RISK

There are ways to decrease the chances that an amended tax return will be subject to additional examination...

● **Be neat and complete.** Make sure your 1040X is filled out properly and legibly.

● **Be thorough.** Attach a full explanation for a refund claim and all necessary documentation. Use exact, rather than estimated, numbers to indicate precision on your part.

Payoff: If the IRS employee processing your return is convinced that you can sustain your refund claim, he/she likely will move on to the next taxpayer.

Red flags: Be extra careful if your amended return claims a refund for items that the IRS treats with skepticism.

Examples: Travel and entertainment, unreimbursed employee business expenses, casualty losses, home-office deductions, donations of property to charitable organizations and transactions involving family members.

NEW CLAIMS

Less controversial are the refund claims supported by favorable new laws, IRS rulings or court decisions. Some new laws are retroactive.

Examples: Much of the 2003 tax act was retroactive to January 1, 2003. A tax law passed in March 2002 increased depreciation deductions on many types of assets. Under this law, assets purchased after September 11, 2001, qualified for bonus depreciation.

Taxpayers who had made qualifying purchases in late 2001 and had already filed their 2001 returns could file an amended return and claim a refund.

Strategy: If you filed your return in early 2002, you have until early 2005 to claim your tax refund.

New opportunity? Retroactive tax savings are likely under the new tax law, so be ready to file amended returns, if indicated.

In other situations, an IRS ruling or court decision will illustrate tax benefits you could have taken on a prior return.

Example: In 2002, the Tax Court ruled that the maintenance outlays for a home swimming pool were deductible as a medical expense. A doctor had prescribed swimming as therapy for two members in a household. [*Robert Emanuel,* TC Summary Opinion 2002-127.]

File Forms 1040X for any tax returns that you have submitted within the past three years if such deductions would result in refunds.

ROTH IRA CONVERSION

Fallen investment value may be cause for an amended return.

Example: You converted a $200,000 IRA to a Roth IRA in 2004 and pay $80,000 in income tax when you file your 2004 tax return. Later the Roth IRA falls in value to $160,000.

You can file an amended return any time up to October 17, 2005. Just attach Form 8606 to report the recharacterization of your Roth IRA to a regular IRA and claim an $80,000 refund.

Strategy: Wait for at least 30 days after the recharacterization, then reconvert your now-regular IRA back to a Roth. (This assumes your 2005 income isn't more than $100,000.)

Benefit: Even if your IRA has rebounded to, say, $175,000 by then, you'll still have saved taxes while you have the Roth IRA you wanted.

DISASTER LOSS

If you suffer a casualty loss in a presidentially declared disaster, you may then deduct the loss on your tax return for the year of the disaster, or you may amend the prior year's return and deduct the loss in that year. The best strategy depends on several factors, including your tax brackets for both years.

LAST CHANCE

One savvy tax-planning practice is to examine each tax return just before the three-year statute of limitations expires. If you discover that you overpaid tax on your old return, file an amended return before the deadline and request a refund.

Although the amended items have to withstand three years of scrutiny, no additional tax can be assessed by the IRS once you pass the three-year mark.

What to look for: A few years ago, you might have filed as married filing separately for some reason. You and your spouse (or now ex-spouse) may earn a refund by refiling jointly, which can result in a lower tax bill.

Pay attention to any partnership returns, too. Often, the K-1 forms submitted by investment partnerships arrive too late for the April 15 filing deadline. There may be a loss from a past year's K-1 that you never claimed.

Don't Be Led Astray by IRS Error

The fact that you relied on an erroneous IRS form or publication when making a mistake with your taxes won't save you from the resulting tax bill.

Useful: The IRS Web site maintains a list of errors on forms and publications. Check the list to avoid being led astray by an IRS error.

How: At *www.irs.gov* go to "Forms and Publications" and then to "What's Hot in Tax Forms, Pubs and Other Tax Products."

It's Still Risky to Ask the IRS for Advice

During the April 2004 tax season, auditors from the Treasury posing as taxpayers went to IRS Taxpayer Assistance Centers to ask questions about the tax law.

Result: IRS personnel answered only 74% of the questions correctly and suggested that the taxpayers do research on their own or referred them to someone else in the rest of the cases.

Warning: The fact that you relied upon bad advice received from the IRS will not relieve you of any resulting tax liability.

Treasury Inspector General for Tax Administration audit report #2004-40-029.

On-Line Tax Help

The Internet can be a great resource for tax help. *Check out the Web sites below...*

IRS: Tax forms, publications, the same audit guides that IRS auditors use, IRS rules and regulations and much more. *www.irs.gov.*

State taxes: Directory of official sites for state and local tax agencies in all 50 states and the District of Columbia, plus state tax-preparation resources. *www.taxsites.com/state.html.*

Locate a tax professional: The National Association of Tax Practitioners can help you to find a tax professional near you. *www.natptax.com.* The American Institute of Certified Public Accountants site provides a listing of member CPAs and personal financial planning specialists. *www.aicpa.org.*

Tax information: Directory of tax information from government and private-sector resources. *http://govspot.com.* Click on "Taxes."

Tax-Preparer Fraud

IRS Fact Sheet FS-2004-10.

The IRS warns taxpayers to beware of tax return preparers who earn their fees by obtaining improper tax refunds that are based on fraudulently increased deductions or omitted income.

Trap: Even if you don't know that your preparer is doing anything wrong, you are held responsible for the return you file.

Warning signs...

● **A preparer claims to be able to obtain larger refunds** than other preparers.

● **The preparer's fee is a percentage** of your total refund.

● **The preparer won't sign your return** or provide you with a copy to keep for your own tax records.

● **The preparer asks you to sign a blank tax return.**

Safety steps...

● **Consider whether the preparer or the preparer's firm will still be around** years from now to answer questions that may arise on an audit.

● **Ask others who have used the preparer** whether they are happy with his/her services.

● **Review your return** and ask the preparer questions to be sure you understand it.

If for any reason you suspect preparer fraud, report it to your local IRS office or call the IRS's Tax Fraud Hotline at 800-829-0433.

Inside the IRS

In the following articles, Ms. X, Esq., a former IRS agent who is still well connected, reveals inside secrets from the IRS...

WHAT NEVER TO TELL YOUR ACCOUNTANT

Never confide to your accountant that you failed to report all of your income. One of the first people the IRS will contact when they suspect that you have committed a tax crime is your accountant. It will ask the accountant to cooperate by telling it everything that you told him/her about your tax-evasion scheme. Trust me, I've heard it too many times. The accountant will spill his guts at the first interview.

Better strategy: If you have evaded tax and now want to remedy the situation, speak to an experienced criminal tax attorney. He will generally arrange for a newly hired accountant to prepare your amended tax returns. The new accountant will be under the umbrella of the attorney-client privilege.

HOW TO DEDUCT HOBBY LOSSES

IRS agents still love to disallow losses they believe come from a hobby and not a bona fide business. Any activity that is seen as "fun" will generally be attacked as a hobby—car racing, collecting, horse breeding, travel writing. Even Amway distributorships have been classified as nondeductible fun on the grounds that the participants can socialize while purchasing products at reduced rates.

Strategies: Keep good business records and change the manner of conducting your business if a profit has not materialized after a reasonable period of time—say two years. Develop a business plan and be prepared to demonstrate why it made sense to continue to lose money while you attempted to convert the business into a profitable success.

DONATE YOUR CAR WITHOUT COLLIDING WITH THE IRS

The IRS is very sensitive about taxpayers who claim charitable contributions for old vehicles and overstate their value.

Recent Treasury proposal: There is an effort underway to require that taxpayers obtain their appraisal from a "qualified" professional appraiser before being allowed a deduction. Another approach being considered is to allow a deduction without an appraisal but limit it to a portion of the blue book value of the vehicle.

Caution: There is now pending legislation to require an appraisal if the claimed value is more than $500.

WHAT IF THE IRS WANTS TO SEIZE YOUR HOME?

The *IRS Restructuring and Reform Act of 1998* (RRA) made it much harder for the IRS to seize any residential property. To begin with, residential property is exempt if the levy is $5,000 or less. Additionally, the 1998 law stipulates that judicial approval by a federal district court judge be obtained before the IRS can seize a residential property. The IRS must produce evidence in court to establish that all administrative procedures were followed properly, the taxpayer still owes the liability and no collection alternative exists. For amounts under $5,000, the IRS can still collect when the house is sold.

WHEN THE IRS WILL NOT PAY A REFUND

Those taxpayers who don't file their personal income tax returns on time may find the IRS will not pay them the refund reflected on the tax return. The tax law [Internal Revenue Code Section 6513 (b)] treats withholding and estimated taxes as having been paid on the date the tax return is due, without regard to any extensions. This means that if you file more than two years after the due date, you will lose your ability to be paid a refund if the refund is a result of withholding or estimated tax.

Caution: Complex fact patterns may extend the ability to be paid a refund for up to three years—speak to your tax adviser.

There Are Legal Ways to Escape A Tax Bill You Can't Pay

Donald W. MacPherson, head attorney, The MacPherson Group, PC, 3404 West Cheryl Dr., Phoenix 85051, specialists in criminal, tax and bankruptcy law.

If you owe a big tax debt to the IRS, there may be ways to avoid it and protect more of your wealth than you would expect to in the process.

Many tax professionals don't know about the "bad boy loophole," which enables even nonfilers and perpetrators of tax fraud to escape their tax debts. They also don't realize how a homestead exemption can put $100,000 or more beyond the reach of the IRS.

There are two ways to reduce or escape a big tax debt legally—through an offer in compromise (OIC) or a bankruptcy filing. These methods can also be combined to further preserve wealth.

Trap: Most tax professionals know about OICs but few understand bankruptcy, so they often fail to realize when bankruptcy can save more wealth than an OIC.

It is vital to know the rules for OICs *and* bankruptcy when you are planning to escape

157

a tax debt—not only to choose between them but to coordinate the use of both. *Basics...*

OFFER IN COMPROMISE

An offer in compromise is an agreement that is reached with the IRS to settle a debt for less than the full amount. It requires extensive financial disclosures that the IRS will use to assure it receives the maximum you can afford to pay.

For rules for OICs as well as the IRS's "collection standards," which indicate the settlement amount the IRS may be willing to accept on a given set of circumstances, visit the IRS Web site at *www.irs.gov.* Click on "Businesses," "Small Bus/Self-Employed," "More Topics" and "Offer In Compromise"—or call 800-829-3676.

If the IRS accepts your offer, this is the most straightforward way to escape the full tax bill.

Bonus: While the IRS is considering your OIC, it is barred from taking any enforcement actions against you, such as issuing liens against or seizing property.

Trap: The IRS's collection standards could be a lot tougher than those of bankruptcy court, providing you with even less than that court would. Also, the IRS will expect, at a minimum, your net worth. So, if you owe them $100,000 and have $40,000 in home equity, they expect at least the $40,000.

Worse, the IRS may reject your OIC. Since it will then know all about your finances, it will be better able to take effective collection action against you. With the current backlog of OICs, this could take as long as two years, with interest accruing during the entire time.

BANKRUPTCY

There are two forms of bankruptcy that can be considered...

●**Chapter 7.** This is when your property is liquidated to pay off debts to the fullest extent possible. The remaining debts are discharged (wiped out) to give the debtor a fresh start. *For income taxes to be discharged, several conditions must be met...*

●Tax debt cannot be the result of fraud.

●Timely tax returns for the tax years at issue must have been due at least three years before the bankruptcy filing...or late returns filed at least two years before.

●Taxes must have been assessed at least 240 days before the bankruptcy filing (giving the IRS time to file tax liens to secure the tax bill).

●Taxes cannot be assessed after the bankruptcy petition. If there is no tax lien prior to the bankruptcy, you keep your homestead exemption as provided by state law.

●**Chapter 13.** Here, you can keep assets that would be lost under Chapter 7 in exchange for paying off some of your debts out of income over the next three to five years. The payments may be small. Typically only 2% to 5% of taxes owed must be paid.

The "bad boy loophole": Taxes can be discharged under Chapter 13 even if tax returns were not filed, were filed late or the tax debt resulted from fraud. In fact, people convicted of tax fraud have had their tax debts discharged under Chapter 13.

Being a "bad boy" actually benefits the tax debtor because the IRS doesn't learn about the tax that is owed until *after* the bankruptcy filing is made. Thus, it doesn't have the chance to file tax liens to secure the debt until it is too late. The bankruptcy filing automatically stays all IRS collection action, such as issuing liens.

Common error: Many tax professionals do not know about the "bad boy loophole." The IRS doesn't discuss it in its publications for obvious reasons, so even many tax experts believe Chapter 7 rules apply to tax debts in *all* bankruptcy cases—and thus that taxes can't be discharged in bankruptcy if returns weren't filed years earlier or if fraud was involved. But this is not so!

Major requirements for Chapter 13...

●If the tax assessment predates the bankruptcy petition, the petition must be filed after 240 days from assessment.

●Good faith.

●Unlike Chapter 7, there is no two-year rule.

●Unlike Chapter 7, the post-bankruptcy petition assessment rule does not apply if you are a "bad boy"—you are a nonfiler, a late filer and haven't met the two-year rule, or committed fraud.

●The tax return must have been due at least three years ago.

●The individual's total liabilities (tax and nontax) cannot include more than about $290,000 of unsecured debts or approximately $870,000 of secured debts and they can change every year, but not by much.

HOMESTEAD PROTECTION

Another advantage of using bankruptcy to escape a tax debt is that a state's "homestead exemption" from bankruptcy can then be used to place wealth beyond the reach of the IRS. The homestead exemption covers your home and other specified assets that are placed beyond the reach of a bankrupt's creditors by state law. Rules vary by state, but amounts can be large.

Examples: Homestead exemptions can total up to $100,000 in California and Arizona …$200,000 in Massachusetts…$500,000 in Minnesota…and unlimited amounts in both Florida and Texas.

So the myth that bankruptcy means "losing everything" is false as well. In a state with an unlimited homestead exemption, millions of dollars of wealth can survive bankruptcy.

Important: Prior to a bankruptcy filing, the IRS can place liens on assets that would be protected by a homestead exemption and the liens will survive later bankruptcy proceedings. So it is vital to file for bankruptcy before the IRS files such liens. A "race to the courthouse" against the IRS to file first may determine who gets that wealth.

So if you learn that the IRS may be about to file a lien against you, don't delay. Get expert help immediately.

COMBINING STRATEGIES

Whether an OIC or bankruptcy filing is better to escape a tax debt depends on the specific case.

Use bankruptcy when…

●**The only asset of an individual who owes a large tax bill** is the equity in his/her home in a state with a homestead exemption. The IRS will want that value and will put a lien on the home sooner or later. Declaring bankruptcy first may save the home by using the homestead exemption.

●**A person who hasn't filed returns** or who has committed tax fraud that hasn't yet been discovered by the IRS. As soon as the IRS does find out, it will issue big tax liens. Using

the "bad boy loophole" may head off the liens and discharge his tax debt.

●**Comparing the collection standards of the IRS and the bankruptcy court** shows that the court will leave the individual with more assets and income.

●**The individual also has many other nontax debts** he can't afford to pay.

Use an offer in compromise when…

●**Terms available from the IRS are acceptable** and the individual wishes to prevent the credit-rating consequences of bankruptcy.

Combination use: A person can't file Chapter 7 because the return due date isn't three years old. But you can file an OIC—and possibly stop the IRS from issuing any liens while it considers the OIC. That may take as long as two years, during which time the three-year limit may pass. If the IRS then rejects the OIC, you can quickly file under Chapter 7, avert liens again and obtain a tax discharge. If returns are filed late, the delay also cures the two-year rule. However, the 240-day rule must be met before or after the OIC because the running of the rule is tolled (suspended) during the course of the OIC. Make sure that all discharge rules are met for each tax assessment.

Important: The way in which bankruptcy, tax and state laws interact is complex, so be sure to consult with an expert.

Bankruptcy And the IRS

William Holmes owned $200 million of Worldcom stock when its value crashed. Margin calls forced him to sell shares at a gain as their value fell—and incur a $10 million tax bill. He declared bankruptcy and offered to settle the tax bill with the IRS for $600,000 as part of his reorganization plan. But the IRS said it does not consider any offers from taxpayers in bankruptcy.

Court: The Tax Code specifically says that the IRS "may compromise any tax obligation."

Its automatic rejection of offers from those in bankruptcy violates the Tax Code and defeats the purpose of the bankruptcy law. So it must consider such offers.

William K. Holmes, Bankr, MD Ga., No. 02-52793 RFH.

What the IRS Is Focusing On Now…and How to Stay Out of Its Way

Frederick W. Daily, Esq., tax attorney, Incline Village, NV, and the author of *Tax Savvy for Small Business* and *Stand Up to the IRS* (both from Nolo.com).

The IRS is entering a new era under its current Commissioner, Mark W. Everson, with tax enforcement making a return to center stage.

It is hiring more auditors and criminal investigators, improving the ability of its computers to scan returns to detect tax underreporting, and starting special enforcement programs in targeted areas—so know that your next tax return may receive more scrutiny than returns have in years past.

WHAT'S HAPPENING

The IRS audit rate has plummeted in recent years as the IRS focused on reorganizing, modernizing and improving the quality of its "customer service."

The previous IRS Commissioner, Charles O. Rossotti, notably wasn't a tax expert but a business manager. During his tenure, IRS enforcement resources diminished as large numbers of personnel changed jobs and spent time training for these positions.

Result: IRS audit rates fell to historic lows— recently, only about 0.6% of all personal returns have been audited. The numbers of liens and levies issued by the IRS fell sharply, too.

But the big IRS reorganization now is largely complete. Commissioner Everson has a more traditional view of enforcement and has made increasing it a top priority. The IRS is currently adding new personnel to its enforcement functions. *Some examples…*

●**The IRS Criminal Investigation Division is adding 150 new agents** in 2004 and is planning to add 576 more in 2005.

●**The IRS plans to add more than 1,000 personnel to general audit functions in 2004**—and wants to add on another 5,000 in 2005, mostly working on enforcement.

While these numbers aren't final yet, they show that the IRS is serious about increasing its audit coverage in the near future.

KEY AUDIT AREAS

Not every return will face the same increase in audit risk. *Top targets…*

●**Self-employeds/small businesses.** Almost half of the IRS's planned increase in audit resources during 2004 is scheduled to be applied to this one area.

Self-employed individuals and small businesses may receive income that has not been reported to the IRS on information returns, such as 1099s and W-2s. This gives them a greater opportunity to underreport income—as well as greater opportunity than most individuals to exaggerate or abuse deductions.

Specially targeted: Those with high "total positive income" (TPI) before taxes but low net taxable income after claiming deductions and other tax breaks.

Self-defense: The ratio of TPI to net taxable income that is considered "high" by the IRS varies by type of business. Taxpayers can learn what this ratio is—and learn of other specific audit "red flags"—for various particular kinds of businesses from *Audit Technique Guides* published by the IRS.

These audit guides are the same ones used by the IRS tax examiners when conducting an audit. The IRS has published more than 60, on businesses ranging from Alaskan commercial fishing to veterinary medicine. They are available free on the IRS Web site, *www.irs.gov.* Click on "Businesses" and then "Market Segment Specialization Program."

●**Pass-through entities.** These are a new major examination target in the IRS business plan for 2004. Pass-through entities are partnerships, S corporations and trusts that have their income taxed on the personal tax returns of their owners. *Key issues to the IRS...*

• These entities report the income paid to their owners on IRS Schedule K-1—however, the IRS has recently admitted that its computers do not match K-1s to individual tax returns the way that W-2s and 1099s are matched up. Very large amounts of money are reported on K-1s, so this has been a big gap in the IRS's "computer matching" program.

In response, the IRS has developed a computer matching program for K-1s which matches them to individual returns. So, if you suspected that your K-1s weren't being matched in the past, you were right—but that won't be the case from now on.

• Complicated tax calculations frequently are made when a pass-through entity computes its own income, which it then passes through to its owners. Therefore, calculations don't appear on the personal tax returns of the owners—and are not visible to an IRS examiner who may look at an owner's personal return.

This creates the opportunity for abusive calculations at the entity level in order to reduce personal taxes.

In response, the IRS plans to assign more than 250 new agents during 2004 to examine the filings of pass-through entities.

MORE AUDIT TARGETS

• **Foreign credit card users.** Persons who have bank or investment accounts in foreign countries may fail to report income earned in them, thinking the IRS will never find out. However the IRS has started identifying these people through their credit card records. That's possible because people with foreign accounts often tap the money in them by using credit cards that are issued by their foreign financial institutions.

The IRS is now examining the records of major credit card companies and of businesses that accept credit card charges to identify US users of foreign-issued credit cards.

And while it is perfectly legal to have a foreign credit card, if you do have one, the IRS will want to see that you have been reporting the income that's earned in your foreign financial account.

• **Unreported income.** IRS computers flag tax returns for audit utilizing a "discriminate index function" (DIF) that identifies when a return's deductions and other items are out of line from the norm. But when income was left entirely off a return and not reported to the IRS on a 1099 or W-2, the IRS often would have no idea that the income existed at all. So, unreported income has become more costly to the IRS than improper deductions.

New: The IRS has now developed an "Unreported Income DIF" to enable its computers to flag tax returns that are most likely to have omitted income.

• **High-income nonfilers.** IRS computers have long done a good job of matching W-2 and 1099 information returns to filed tax returns and catching discrepancies between them. But surprisingly, if the IRS found no return filed reporting income shown on a W-2 or 1099, IRS systems often would do nothing about it.

Now the IRS's systems have been upgraded. If information returns are found without a corresponding tax return, the system will then flag a likely nonfiler for further examination.

• **Abusive schemes and false tax shelter promotions.** These have multiplied in recent years, often using bogus trust arrangements to purportedly make wages or income tax free or to make personal living expenses deductible. There has also been a spread of false claims, such as that employment taxes need not be paid, that income tax is voluntary, that tax reparations are available to the descendants of slaves and so on.

The IRS has begun a program of criminally prosecuting those who profit by marketing these scams, as well as identifying and sending tax bills to those who use them.

More information: Click on "Phony Tax Arguments" at *www.irs.gov* or call 800-829-0433.

Another IRS Audit Target

Individual retirement accounts (IRAs) are yet another IRS audit target.

Special caution: If you're taking required minimum distributions from your IRA, be sure that you calculate the proper amount to avoid any penalties.

The IRS also is checking that people who inherit IRAs—Roth and regular—make required withdrawals. Some who inherit Roth IRAs, in particular, mistakenly believe that they don't have to make withdrawals.

Ed Slott, CPA, a nationally recognized IRA expert, 100 Merrick Rd., Rockville Centre, NY 11570. He is editor of *Ed Slott's IRA Advisor.* His Web site is *www.irahelp.com.*

Where to Find Missing Tax Records

Randy Bruce Blaustein, Esq., senior tax partner at R.B. Blaustein & Co., 155 E. 31 St., New York City 10016.

It is not so difficult to dig up the tax documents you might need when preparing your tax return...

•**Canceled checks.** Request copies of these from your financial institution.

•**Records of purchases.** Credit card companies can provide summaries of past charges. For cash expenses, compile your own records.

Example: If you bought *The Wall Street Journal* every weekday to check on your investments, then reconstruct what it would have cost you for the year (five days a week x $1 x 52 weeks = $260).

•**Tax returns or transcripts** showing line-item entries from original returns. These are available from the IRS for the past six years.

Cost: $39* per return...transcripts are free. Use IRS Form 4506, *Request for Copy or Transcript of Tax Form,* which you can download from *www.irs.gov* or request by calling 800-TAX-FORM.

•**Schedule K-1s.** Every partnership and S corporation issues these to owners. If you have sold your stake but haven't been able to get your K-1 from the entity or its accounting firm, ask the IRS for a copy.

*All prices subject to change.

More from Randy Bruce Blaustein...

The New Assault on Tax Shelters

The IRS is starting what it calls an unprecedented assault on tax shelters. *Key elements of the plan...*

•**New IRS regulations require tax shelter promoters** to disclose potentially abusive transactions to it, and to maintain customer lists the IRS may examine during an investigation.

•**The IRS has authorized 112 new examinations of tax shelter promoters**—more than five times as many as two years ago—including accounting and law firms and investment banks.

•**The IRS is coordinating its activities** with the states, Justice Department, and other law enforcement agencies.

Self-defense: Before investing in a tax shelter, click on "Phony Tax Arguments" and "IRS & States to Share Data" at *www.irs.gov.*

10

Investing Tips and Traps

Six Surprisingly Accurate Stock Market Indicators

Stock market gyrations are not entirely random. Over 37 years, the *Stock Trader's Almanac* has offered amazingly reliable indicators of market performance. Consult a financial adviser if you have questions or trends seem contradictory. You still need to analyze individual stocks before investing.

THE JANUARY BAROMETER

The stock market usually sets its direction for the whole year in January. The S&P 500 Index has reflected this tendency 92.3% of the time since 1950. Eleven bear markets out of 17 —including the most recent one—began with a poor January.

PREPRESIDENTIAL ELECTION YEAR

Prepresidential election years are a time of stock gains. Presidents intentionally juice up the economy—with tax cuts, increased spending, etc.—in preelection years.

We haven't had a down market in the third year of a presidential term since 1939—when the outbreak of World War II pushed down the Dow by 2.9%. Since 1914, the average gain for the Dow from the market low (during the second year of a presidential term) to the high in the preelection year is an astounding 50.2%.

BEST SIX MONTHS FOR INVESTING

Since 1950, the stock market has performed best from November through April and worst from May through October. Only twice since 1950 has the Dow posted a double-digit loss during the November-through-April period—in 1970, during the invasion of Cambodia, and in 1973, during the OPEC oil embargo.

DECEMBER'S FREE LUNCH AND THE SANTA CLAUS RALLY

Investors will typically dump losing stocks in December in order to realize tax losses. By late

Jeffrey Hirsch, president of The Hirsch Organization, an investment research firm, 184 Central Ave., Old Tappan, NJ 07675. He and his father, Yale Hirsch, edit *Stock Trader's Almanac* (Wiley) and publish *Almanac Investor Newsletter*. Their Web site is *www.stocktradersalmanac.com*.

December, many stocks have been hammered down to bargain prices. The New York Stock Exchange stocks selling at their 52-week lows near the end of December usually outperform the market by February. Over 29 years, these stocks have averaged a 13.9% increase in that short span, compared with the NYSE Composite, which gained 4.2% over the same period.

A short but robust rally during the last five days of December and the first two days of January—the Santa Claus rally—will come to Wall Street most years. Since 1969, the gain from this rally has averaged 1.7% over just those few days. In 2003, it was 1.2%. There have been 25 Santa Claus rallies in the last 33 years.

Beware of Santa's claws: When there's no Santa Claus rally, trouble often is ahead. Hence the couplet—*If Santa Claus should fail to call, bears may come to Broad and Wall* (where the New York Stock Exchange is located). There was no Santa Claus rally in 1999. The bear market began on January 14, 2000.

PRE–ST. PATRICK'S DAY RALLY

Experienced traders know that the market often rallies before major legal holidays. People are about to get time off, so they feel upbeat. Most traders don't realize how strong the market is the day before St. Patrick's Day—which isn't a legal holiday but is celebrated. Going back to 1953, the S&P 500 has gained an average of 0.33% on that day—equal to a 30-point advance for the Dow at today's levels. I think of this indicator as just for fun, but people have made money following it.

DOWN FRIDAY AND MONDAY

Trouble often looms when stock prices are down sharply on both a Friday and the following Monday—six times out of seven, the market will go lower within five days. In 1987, the Dow lost 108 points on Friday, October 16, and 508 points the following Monday.

How to Find Great Stocks

To find great stocks, start by looking at companies that have headquarters or significant

operations near you. Also, look into companies for which friends and family members work. Check out job fairs and classified ads for names of companies that are hiring, and try to find out if the hiring is because of expansion or due to turnover. Read the local newspapers to find out which companies are growing, moving into the area or building new facilities. Attend a firm's annual meeting if it is open to the public. Once you have identified good companies, consider their stocks as potential investments.

Margaret Kelly, president of the Chicago West chapter, National Association of Investors Corporation.

A Stock Market Rally Could Be a Bear Market Blip

Maggie Mahar, PhD, journalist and market historian based in New York City. She is author of *Bull! A History of the Boom, 1982 to 1999: What Drove the Breakneck Market—and What Every Investor Needs to Know About Financial Cycles* (HarperBusiness).

Are we experiencing a new bull market or a sucker's rally? *Here's what history can teach you about bull and bear markets and which investments you should make now...*

●**Bull markets end badly.** Long, strong bull markets beget long bear markets. Stock market history indicates a pattern of alternating strong and weak cycles. Each of these cycles last an average of nearly 15 years.

Going back as far as 1882 (the first year for which inflation-adjusted data on the S&P 500 are available), history shows that during a strong cycle, investors who put money into the S&P 500 and plowed dividend income back into their portfolios reaped returns averaging 18% a year.

During dry spells, average "real" (inflation-adjusted) returns decreased to below 2%. Investors who didn't reinvest dividends *lost* nearly 3% a year.

Recent cycles fit the pattern with ruthless precision. From January 1967 through December 1982, when investors reinvested their dividends, their returns averaged 0.2% annually. While the investors who became discouraged and pocketed their dividends lost an average of nearly 4% a year for those 16 years.

In 1982, the cycle turned. From January 1983 through December 1999, real returns averaged 12.1%. Investors who reinvested dividends were rewarded with average annual returns of 15.7%.

●**Long bear markets are treacherous.** Investors are lured back in by impressive but short-lived rallies. *Examples...*

●1929/1930s. Following Black Monday, which was October 28, 1929, the market rebounded. By the spring of 1930, it had recovered 48% of what it had lost, and many investors began to move their money back in. Then came the second leg down. From April 1930 through July 1932, stocks lost 86% of their value. It would be nearly two decades before a new bull market would begin.

●1970s. After flirting with 1,000 in the late 1960s, the Dow crashed in 1970, falling to 631. Then it rallied. By January 1973, the benchmark index had climbed to a high of 1,060.

Investors thought that a new bull market had begun, but, in fact, the bear was playing possum. What followed was the bloody crash of 1973–1974. When it was all over, the Dow came to rest at 577—seven points below its value in 1958, some 16 years earlier. A new bull market wouldn't begin until 1982.

●**Long cycles often are punctuated by "minicycles"**—brief bull and bear markets. For example, during the bull market of 1982 to 1999, the bull paused in 1987, 1990 and 1994. These down years were merely corrections in a bull-market cycle.

Similarly, there will be rallies during a long bear market that can last a year or more, but it is very difficult to take advantage of them. An investor has to know how to move in and out at just the right times. That is why, in most cases, these cyclical bull and bear markets are best ignored.

●**Markets always revert to the mean.** No matter how high the markets climb, the pendulum always swings back to the center. Even if people say, "It's different this time," it isn't. History has shown that this is true of all bubbles, whether it's in the US, Japan or Germany...in stocks, junk bonds or gold. In order to revert to the mean, the market must, by definition, spend some time *below* the mean.

What is the mean for the US stock market? Historically, the S&P 500 has traded at an average of 16 to 17 times earnings, while dividends have averaged 4%. In July 2004 the S&P traded at roughly 28 times earnings—still far *above* the mean—and offered dividends of less than 2%.

●**Investors get carried away.** In both bull and bear markets, investors will go to extremes. During bull markets, they overinvest in stocks. And, during bear markets they underinvest.

Examples: In 1999, investors poured $176 billion into stock mutual funds. They kept buying on dips long after the bear market began on January 14, 2000—the day the Dow hit its peak. A record $260 billion flowed into stock funds in 2001, and $54 billion more in 2002—long after the bear market was under way.

By contrast, during the bear market of the 1970s, very few investors purchased stocks—even though they were cheap. In 1979, *Business Week* sounded the death knell for stocks with a cover story headlined "The Death of Equities."

BEAR-PROOFING YOUR PORTFOLIO

In a bear market especially, investors should look beyond US stocks. Bonds are the obvious alternative, but US bonds also have enjoyed a long bull market and are poised to have a drop in price.

Alternative opportunities: Funds that are investing in commodities/natural resources, precious metals, emerging-markets securities and foreign currencies, all of which now show potential for growth.

You can research these alternatives and find funds by consulting an investment Web site such as *www.morningstar.com*. Search under the keywords "alternative investments."

Commodities/natural resources: Traditionally, natural resource funds have invested primarily in natural gas and oil. Newer funds are investing in a range of commodities, such as timber.

Gold, copper, silver and other metals: Look for diversification. Some gold funds own bullion as well as gold-mining shares. Others funds buy many precious metals—copper, silver and gold.

Emerging-markets stocks and bonds:
Funds investing in these markets—Asia, Latin America, Africa and Eastern Europe—offer investors excellent long-term opportunities. They have done very well recently. Wait for a correction before buying.

Alternative: The foreign closed-end equity funds trade like stocks and offer opportunities to invest in specific countries as well as entire continents.

Best: Funds trading at a discount to their net asset values.

Information: Closed-End Fund Association at *www.closed-endfunds.com.*

Foreign currencies: In the face of a declining dollar, investors may want to choose foreign stock and bond *funds* that don't hedge away foreign currency risk. They stand to profit if currencies rise further against the dollar. Check the funds' prospectuses, or ask the representatives if their funds tend to hedge currencies.

Alternative: Take a direct stake in foreign currencies by purchasing foreign certificates of deposit (CDs) through Everbank at 888-882-3837 or *www.everbank.com.* Although these CDs are FDIC insured, they still may lose value if the foreign currency falls versus the dollar.

Don't Make These Investing Mistakes

Just as investors throughout the '90s erred in thinking the bull market would last forever, blindly believing corporate financial statements and opinions of analysts, and taking excessive risks in unproven technology stocks, there are new ways to go wrong now.

Today's misguided wisdom: Avoiding stocks altogether…sticking with only "ultrasafe" investments, such as the money market funds… overweighting gold…buying bond funds with long maturities—the ones that will lose the most if interest rates rise.

Sheldon Jacobs, editor, *The No-Load Fund Investor,* 410 Saw Mill River Rd., Ardsley, NY 10502.

How to Buy Great Stocks At a Discount

Arne Alsin, CPA, founder of Alsin Capital Management, Inc., an investment firm with $45 million under management, including The Turnaround Fund, a no-load mutual fund, Eugene, OR. For more information, call 800-525-7222 or visit *www.alsincapital.com.* Mr. Alsin is also a columnist for TheStreet.com and editor of *The Turnaround Report.*

Many investors still believe that the richest rewards are reaped only with high risk tech, biotech and high-price-to-earnings-ratio (P/E) stocks—despite the fortunes lost when the tech bubble collapsed.

I buy cheap, solid companies in old-fashioned industries that are undervalued because of short-term problems. As soon as these problems are fixed, share prices rise sharply—no matter what is happening in the market.

Turnaround investing means lower risk. Bad news is already public and has been factored into the stock price.

If any more problems come to light, the stock already is so low that I risk a smaller drop in price. If the company fails to turn around, my loss per share is much less than it might be for a high-priced stock.

WHAT TO LOOK FOR

●**Small- to mid-cap stocks.** These tend to be underfollowed by the analysts. That means individual investors are more likely to discover them before the pros do.

●**Steady, unglamorous companies**—those with stock prices that are much lower than the value of the business. I choose companies with clean balance sheets, strong franchises and a history of profits.

●**Catalysts that will help turn around the company.** Many times, cheap stocks remain cheap. You need to be confident in the company's management and its ability to unlock value. This may entail a top-to-bottom restructuring and aggressive cost trimming or a new marketing plan that will take away sales from competitors.

Case study: I compared two stocks during the tech downturn. One tech heavyweight that designs business software was enjoying peak net profit margins and strong sales but had a high P/E. An office-supply company, crippled by slow sales, was selling at about book value. The tech heavyweight appeared to be a more interesting company with a sexier future. However, the unexciting office-supply company had a strong balance sheet, enthusiastic insider buying and was number one in its industry category, so I bought it. In 2001, the tech stock lost 52.5%, while the stock that I bought gained a huge 160.2%.

WHAT TO AVOID

●**Listening to Wall Street hype,** such as analysts' upgrades, market guru chatter and forecasts about interest rates.

●**Excessive debt,** which slows turnarounds. It is easier to take cost-cutting steps than it is to pay off a huge debt.

●**Industrywide problems.** Obstacles specific to one company can be surmounted faster than problems plaguing an entire industry. Be sure a company's problems are fixable, openly disclosed and quantifiable.

Case study: One large toy company overpaid for royalty contracts to produce items associated with a movie series. Revenues peaked in 1999 but became more volatile and dependent on the movie industry. The company renegotiated the contract in 2002 to get more favorable terms and invested future capital in its core toy and game business.

Its balance sheet improved, with debt falling from $1.17 billion to $857 million. The stock has more than doubled from its low of $9 in 2000 to almost $19 in July 2004.

To understand a stock, get comfortable with the company's financial statements and governmental filings, including 10-Qs and 10-Ks. If you lack confidence in your valuation skills, take a course at a local business college.

Recommended reading: Value Investing: A Balanced Approach (Wiley) by Martin J. Whitman...How to Think Like Benjamin Graham and Invest Like Warren Buffett (McGraw-Hill) by Lawrence A. Cunningham.

How You Can Benefit From Wall Street Analyst Layoffs

With the ranks of analysts thinned, fewer stocks—especially of small and midsized companies—are being followed by brokerage firms, so more bargains may go undiscovered.

Downside: You'll need to do some detective work to find these gems.

Scan publications—like *BusinessWeek, Forbes* and *The Wall Street Journal*—for stocks whose names you do not recognize. Research companies at such sites as Zacks (*http://my.zacks.com*) and Reuters (*www.reuters.com*) as well as the companies' Web sites.

Brian Wenzinger, CFA, associate at Aronson + Johnson + Ortiz LP, an institutional investment management firm in Philadelphia that manages $10.5 billion and specializes in finding undervalued stocks.

How to Profit From Tomorrow's Technology Today

Glenn Fishbine, chairman of the board, Exact Identification Inc., a biometrics company in Sacramento, CA, and a scout for a consortium of European venture capital firms. He has 25 years of experience in technology management and is the author of *The Investor's Guide to Nanotechnology and Micromachines* (Wiley). His Web site is at *www.glenn fishbine.com.*

Nanotechnology will represent a $1 trillion industry over the coming decade.* Many people have never even heard the term —but it's worth everyone's time to keep abreast of this field, which could change the world.

Broadly explained, this new technology involves materials that are less than 100 nanometers in size—roughly one-millionth the width of a pinhead. It can take mechanical, chemical or biological form.

Within this decade, nanotechnology will enable us to produce thread that is stronger than

*National Science Foundation estimate.

steel…fabrics that won't stain…high-strength, lightweight auto parts…as well as hundreds of other products.

Around the world, governments are pouring more than $2 billion annually into nanotech research. Japan has been particularly aggressive. Venture capitalist interest also is increasing rapidly. But, only a few of the 450-plus companies in this new sector are publicly traded.

Prospective investors should research each company thoroughly and understand that this technology is in its infancy. Assume that many of these early companies will not be successful in this field.

Some of nanotechnology's most promising potential applications…

CORROSION RESISTANCE

By the end of the decade, nanotech research will significantly reduce corrosion and wear in everything from drill bits to automotive parts. This should help drive down costs of industrial manufacturing.

Example: Scientists based in Japan have found that when "buckyballs"—molecules that contain 60 carbon atoms arranged into a spherical shape—are combined with paint, the paint becomes highly resistant to corrosion and wear. To make the technology commercially viable, someone must find a way to produce buckyballs in large quantities at a reasonable price.

Among publicly traded companies, Japanese conglomerate Kobe Steel, Ltd., is a leader in buckyball research. It's working on developing paint that could protect ships from salt spray. Such technology could eventually be applied to auto bodies.

STAIN-FREE FABRICS

Nanotechnology can be utilized to create a stain-resistant coating of "nanowhiskers" on standard fabrics. These whiskers are too small to be seen by the naked eye, and they don't significantly affect the feel of the fabric. Yet they cause fluids to bead and roll off without reaching the cloth itself.

Levi Strauss already has brought this technology to market in its Dockers brand. Expect other manufacturers to follow. Nano-Tex, LLC, a private company, is the leader in this new technology.

BULLETPROOF CLOTH

Nanofibers—extremely narrow threads typically made from strings of carbon atoms—could be used to manufacture fabrics that are 60 times stronger than steel. The US military is pumping about $100 million into this research on the theory that nanofibers can be woven into lightweight, bulletproof clothing.

We can expect military applications within four years…and consumer applications, such as blue jeans that won't wear out and ultrastrong, but lightweight automotive components, shortly thereafter.

Within 20 years, ultrastrong nanofibers could be used to dramatically reduce the cost and risk of sending people and equipment into space. It currently costs about $10,000 per pound to launch something into orbit. If one end of a nanofiber was attached to a satellite and the other anchored to the ground, an elevator could lift payloads into orbit for as little as $2 per pound. Gravity wouldn't pull the satellite back down to Earth because the gravitational pull would be offset by the centripetal acceleration of the satellite pulling away from Earth.

Most research on nanotech materials is conducted by government and university laboratories, not private companies. But Dow Chemical Co. could benefit when technology reaches the production phase because of its experience in fabricating polyesters in bulk.

BIOCHIP MEDICAL TECHNOLOGY

A biochip is a microchip that contains thousands of tiny sensors. Together, these sensors serve as minuscule testing centers where thousands of biological tests can be performed at the same time.

Example: A current Affymetrix biochip, about the size of a postage stamp, has been used in gene research to determine which of perhaps 100,000 genes has been "turned on" in a specific type of cell—for example, hair color in a hair follicle cell. In principle, this biochip could be designed for the early detection of genetic diseases, such as certain forms of breast cancer. This would provide doctors and patients with early information concerning future risk.

This type of technology will save lives and money because results will be comprehensive and almost instantaneous. Biochips will identify a virus or bacterium in blood, food or air. Virtually *any* disease could be detected in the early stages with a mere drop of blood.

Affymetrix, Inc., has long been the leader, but the company faces a growing field of competitors, including ACLARA BioSciences, Inc., Caliper Technologies Corp., Ciphergen Biosystems Inc., Nanogen, Inc., and SurModics, Inc.

The large firms, such as Dow Corning Corp., IBM Corp., Motorola, Inc., and NEC Corp., also are researching biochips. But in companies of such size, these chips won't have much impact on the bottom line over the short term.

DRUG DELIVERY

Healing may be revolutionized by nanotech. In principle, it is possible to design microscopic devices that can enter any type of cell in the body and repair it.

It is already possible to fill extremely small capsules with a drug and then coat them with a layer of antibodies designed to cause the capsules to cluster around virtually any type of cancer. By doing this, specific targets can be treated rather than the entire body. This reduces side effects. Human trials of this technology could begin soon.

A significant number of small biotech firms are pursuing this research, including C Sixty Inc. and NanoBio Corp, both private.

QUANTUM COMPUTING

Modern computers encode information as a series of ones and zeros. The computers of the future might encode data in the spin direction of electrons.

For example, an electron spinning up could be read as one and an electron spinning down could be read as zero. In theory, this would allow computers to do calculations thousands of times faster than today's microprocessors. The physics are extremely complicated, and development still is in the early stages.

Quantum computers might not reach consumers for 20 years—but expect to see major advances in this technology shortly.

The most advanced quantum research is being done at IBM Corp. and Delft University of Technology in the Netherlands.

FASTER SEMICONDUCTORS

Circuitry in the next generation of semiconductors (minuscule electronic switching devices) will slip below 100 nanometers. But that *doesn't* mean the sector will become a great place in which to invest.

Semiconductor manufacturing is very competitive and has huge capital expenses. Modern chip plants can cost $10 billion. Expect semiconductor stocks to continue their cyclical pattern even if nanotech spurs new growth—they are not yet worth investing in.

The Magic of Concentrated Investing

John W. Rogers, Jr., founder of Ariel Capital Management, Inc., Chicago, which has $13.5 billion under management. Mr. Rogers is portfolio manager of the Ariel Fund (ARGFX). For more information, call 800-292-7435 or visit www.arielmutualfunds.com.

A recent study by Standard & Poor's has found that you have a better chance of outperforming the market if you place bets on a few top investment ideas. In the previous decade, concentrated funds—which hold fewer than 40 stocks and have at least 30% of assets in only 10 stocks—outperformed more diversified funds.

John W. Rogers, Jr., who has had double-digit gains over the past 10 years, discusses concentrated investing below…

WHAT TO LOOK FOR

Start with stable industries that have high barriers to entry—businesses that are not easily imitated and that have strong brand names. I generally find these characteristics in financial services, consumer goods, consumer services and media. *I buy if the stock is undervalued based on one or both of these calculations…*

Method #1: Purchase a stock when it trades at 40% below the company's intrinsic value—the price per share that a knowledgeable buyer would pay for the entire company today.

Example: I was attracted to one global advertising giant. The stock had declined significantly because the company's accounting practices had been called into question in the wake of the Enron scandal. Our private market value estimate was in the mid-$80s, but the stock was trading at $50 per share—a 40% discount to this measure of intrinsic value—so I bought it.

Method #2: I see if the stock is undervalued based on potential earnings and initiate a position when the stock is selling below 13 times my earnings estimate.

Example: Based on this calculation, the advertising company also qualified for purchase.

Helpful: A discounted cash-flow measure of intrinsic value is now available at *www.quicken. com,* or you can read up on the topic in *Investment Valuation* by Aswath Damodaran (Wiley).

HOW TO CONTROL RISK

Even if you err in valuing a company, when you buy at a discount, your price will be low enough so that you are less likely to do much harm to your portfolio.

Example: In the 1990s, a large eye-care company expanded into lasers for eye surgery. But, by mid-2000, the laser-surgery division was struggling. The company fell short of analysts' earnings estimates. The stock decreased from $80/share to the low $30s—almost 50% *below* my intrinsic value estimate—so I bought it.

WHEN TO SELL

Sell a winning stock when it reaches your intrinsic value estimate, or reduce your position if the stock grows to more than 6% of your portfolio. Equally important, sell a stock when its long-term business fundamentals deteriorate.

Example: By late 2002, I realized I had made a mistake with the eye-care company. The new management showed little interest in developing the brand name overseas. I sold it in the mid-$30s, the price at which I began buying shares.

Important: Investors who can't devote the time to focused investing should invest a small percentage of their portfolios in a few favorite stocks. The rest should be in professionally managed mutual funds.

ETFs: Alternative to Mutual Funds

William G. Brennan, CPA/PFS, CFP, Capital Management Group, LLC, 1730 Rhode Island Ave. NW, Washington, DC 20036.

To invest tax efficiently at low cost, consider purchasing exchange traded funds (ETFs) instead of mutual funds.

Rather than owning shares in a mutual fund company that owns a portfolio of stocks, ETF shares represent direct ownership of a portion of the stock in a large diversified portfolio. *Advantages of ETFs...*

● **Tax efficiency.** Unlike mutual funds, ETFs don't make taxable internal trades that can result in gains that are passed on to investors.

● **Low cost.** ETFs don't have annual management fees, which could take 2% or more from an investment each year.

Purchases of ETFs are subject to brokerage commissions, but buy-and-hold investors still come out ahead paying them.

Test: Whenever your financial planner offers you a mutual fund, ask for an explanation of the difference between it and an ETF. Make sure you get a clear answer why one is better than the other for your situation.

Why an S&P Index Fund May Not Be the Way to Go

For true exposure to the entire US stock market, an S&P 500 Index fund might *not* be your best choice. This index—and the funds that follow it—focuses on large stocks. Instead, consider a fund that tracks the Wilshire 5000 Index. These frequently are called *total market funds*. If you already hold an S&P 500 Index fund, you can supplement it with a fund that tracks the Wilshire 4500 Index—US stocks that are not included in the S&P 500 Index. These frequently are called *extended market funds.* Among the fund companies offering both total market and extended market funds are Fidelity Investments (800-343-3548), T. Rowe Price (800-638-5660) and Vanguard (800-523-7731).

Jonathan Clements, personal-finance columnist for *The Wall Street Journal.*

Bigger Investment Deductions for Active Investors

Janice M. Johnson, CPA, JD, consultant, financial services, 301 E. 52 St., New York City 10022.

I f you are an active investor, you may be entitled to tax refunds for bigger investment expense deductions than you had claimed in recent years. Even better, unrealized losses you are holding due to the recent stock market slump may be 100% deductible against ordinary income. *Here's how to make this happen…*

SMART INVESTING

Obtaining these larger deductions involves…

•**Electing "trader" status** for all or some of your stock-picking activities.

•**Then making a Section 475(f) election** to have your trading activity follow the "mark-to-market" rules each year, so that losses are deducted against ordinary income.

How it works: While no formal definition of "trader" is given in the Tax Code or regulations, to be a trader you should typically…

•Hold most of your investment positions for the short term (less than one year), intending to gain from short-term price changes rather than from long-term appreciation.

•Make stock trades frequently.

•Spend a significant amount of time and effort actively managing your trading. But no required minimum number of trades or average holding period has been specified by the IRS.

A trader's gains and losses normally are taxed under regular capital gains rules, with the difference that traders can fully deduct their trading expenses as business expenses.

Contrast: The deduction for investment expenses under normal rules is likely to be much smaller. That is so because they are included among miscellaneous deductions, the total of which is deductible only to the extent it exceeds 2% of adjusted gross income. Furthermore, the miscellaneous deductions are not deductible in computing the alternative minimum tax.

In addition, a trader can elect to have trading securities marked-to-market every year. *This means that instead of investments being taxed under normal rules when sold…*

•Gain or loss on the value of investments is taxed every year at year-end—even if investments are not sold.

•All gains are taxed as ordinary income.

•Losses are fully deductible against ordinary income.

Contrast: Under the ordinary rules, capital losses are deductible only against capital gains, with no more than $3,000 of a net loss deductible against ordinary income, and unused losses carried forward to future years.

Payoff: By making the mark-to-market election when you have large unrealized losses in your portfolio, you can obtain a full deduction right away for losses that otherwise would not be fully deductible for many years.

When you act as a trader by seldom holding securities positions for more than one year, making the mark-to-market election is virtually a no-lose proposition—your short-term trading gains are taxable at ordinary income rates anyhow, so no cost is incurred there, while a larger deduction is obtained for losses. However, you may lose if you have capital losses from other sources with no capital gains to offset them.

Important: You do not have to elect trader status for all your investments. You can still take tax-favored long-term capital gains for other investments that are separate from your trading activity—such as real estate and even stock market investments that are segregated from your trading account.

TO BECOME A TRADER

●**Elect trader status.** You do so simply by filing your tax return—or amended return—and reporting your investment activity under trader rules.

Refund opportunity: If you are sure that you acted as a trader during the stock market boom but filed your taxes using the rules for normal investors, you can file amended returns now, for up to three prior years, to get larger deductions for your past investment expenses.

●**Make the mark-to-market election.** *This requires you to do two things...*

●Notify the IRS by sending a statement that you intend to make the mark-to-market election under Section 475(f) of the Tax Code for this and future years.

Attach the statement to your tax return or extension request due this April 15. The statement is for 2005 and later years even though you attach it to your tax return for 2004. *And...*

●File IRS Form 3115, *Application for Change in Accounting Method.* This can be filed with your 2004 return for a 2004 change.

Loss deduction opportunity: If you have big unrealized losses in your trading portfolio due to the recent stock market slump, by making the mark-to-market election you may get a 100% deduction against ordinary income for them this year. This would be a much larger and faster deduction than you could ever have expected.

PROTECTING CAPITAL GAINS

To save tax-favored long-term capital gains treatment for your appreciated investments after filing the mark-to-market election, you will need to keep your trader investments strictly segregated from them. At the least, this means conducting your trading activity through a separate account and never commingling trading funds with other funds. If you do commingle, an IRS auditor could try to extend your mark-to-market election to all your long-term stock market investments as well.

Safest: The best way to segregate trading activity is by setting up a separate legal entity to conduct it, such as a limited liability company or a partnership that you form with an associate or family member. These are known as "pass-through entities," so their gains and losses pass through directly to their owners.

By having such a separate legal entity conduct the trading, make the mark-to-market election and report trading results on its own return, you safely separate the trading activity from all of your own normal long-term investments for which you wish to preserve tax-favored capital gains treatment.

Important: There are rules applying to the trader and mark-to-market elections, and state law may affect the choice of pass-through entity that you use to segregate trading activity, so be sure to consult an expert.

More from Janice Johnson...

Bond Swaps Pay Off

Use bond swaps to create tax losses that save taxes on stock gains or other capital gains.

Interest rates have risen from long-term lows, and can be expected to rise more in the future.

Key: As interest rates rise, the value of bonds goes down—but the stock market has risen at the same time.

Strategy: Sell any bonds that have fallen in value and repurchase similar but not identical bonds—such as bonds paying the same rate from another issuer. There's no economic cost since you end up in the same investment position you were in before. But the sale creates a capital loss you can use to shelter capital gains. This is a fine way to shelter short-term stock gains that otherwise could be taxed at up to 35%. However, try to avoid offsetting any long-term capital gains that would be taxed at 15%.

Get the Best Financial Advice From the Internet

Ryan M. Fleming, vice president and managing director, Investment Analysis, Armstrong, MacIntyre & Severns, Inc., a financial planning firm in Washington, DC.

Eric Jacobson, senior analyst and fixed-income editor, Morningstar, Inc., Chicago.

Layne Aurand, statistician for the *No-Load Fund Investor,* Ardsley, NY.

Gary Schatsky, Esq., president of The ObjectiveAdvice Group, a financial advisory firm based in New York City and Florida, *www.objectiveadvice.com.*

Sam Stovall, chief investment strategist for Standard & Poor's Corp., New York City.

There's a wealth of financial information on the Internet. But how do you find the best Web sites? We asked five top financial experts to point us to the sites they find most useful and tell us why. All the sites listed below are free, although many have a charge for extra features.

RYAN M. FLEMING LIKES...

● **www.fool.com.** This site is well-known for teaching people how to be their own personal financial managers. It encourages and empowers them to do the necessary research. The site has links to every financial Web site imaginable and some wonderful guides for improving your financial well-being.

The additional charge for a one-year subscription to *The Motley Fool Money Advisor* is $199.* With this you can get personalized objective advice and a financial helpline.

Best feature: "60-Second Guides" on topics such as opening an IRA and choosing a broker.

● **www.morningstar.com.** The fund-rating service Morningstar is a great place to start your research on investments—stocks, mutual funds, closed-end funds and annuities. It has an excellent "College Savings Center" with special reports, including information about 529 plans.

Additional charge for premium membership that includes analysts' reports on 1,000 stocks and 2,000 funds, plus exclusive alert services, is $115/year.

*All prices subject to change.

Best feature: Ratings for more than 2,000 funds to help you compare one fund against another.

● **www.kiplinger.com.** The Kiplinger site is particularly rich with information on financial-planning topics related to its newsletters, such as *Tax Letter, Retirement Report* and *Agriculture Letter.* It contains a number of financial calculators and other helpful tools.

Best feature: "KiplingerForecasts.com," which is updated several times per day. News about gross domestic product, interest rates, unemployment, housing and retail sales. The cost is $84*/year.

ERIC JACOBSON RECOMMENDS...

● **www.smartmoney.com.** This is a useful site with lots of good information and tools.

Highlights: Breaking financial updates and analysis and commentary on the trendsetting stocks and tax matters as well as articles covering mutual funds and personal finance.

An additional charge for the service "Smart Money Select" is $109 per year. You receive real-time price quotes, market analysis and "Fund Map 1000," where you can see which fund categories, fund families and individual funds are ahead of the pack, based on 18 different criteria.

Best feature: "This Week From Barron's," which comes out the same time as Barron's.

● **www.sec.gov.** At this site, you'll be able to look up a variety of reports and filings from companies. For stocks, you can get access to 10K (annual) and 10Q (quarterly) reports. For mutual funds, you can do prospectus research, obtain annual and semiannual reports, and 13D reports that show who owns more than 5% of a fund.

Best feature: Company filings and forms.

● **www.investinginbonds.com.** Sponsored by The Bond Market Association, this site covers Treasuries and municipal, corporate and mortgage-backed securities. There are investors' guides and a bond glossary, plus links to more than 400 sites with market and price information for all segments of the bond market.

Best feature: Seven simple steps to learn about investing in bonds.

*All prices subject to change.

● **www.economist.com.** Learn more about the role of the world in the marketplace. Special sections on science and technology, finance and economics, and business, together with data on world markets.

The charge for premium content is $89*/year to get full access to the content of *The Economist* before it hits the newsstands.

Best feature: Financial news from Asia, Europe, the Middle East and Africa.

LAYNE AURAND SINGLES OUT...

● **http://finance.yahoo.com.** On this site you'll get more than basic information about the vast majority of funds. You'll also receive many analytical tools allowing you to compare and contrast performance, cost, etc.—without any annoying registration.

The charge for "MarketTracker," which provides streaming real-time quotes and market coverage including upgrades and downgrades, is $9.95/month.

Best feature: "Investing Ideas" from TradingMarkets.com, Morningstar.com and others.

● **www.schwab.com.** You don't need an account to access much of the information targeted for customers of this discount brokerage. Its mutual fund screener lets you search for specific funds based on criteria such as performance, expense ratio and investment category. (However, the "Schwab Equity Ratings," which give you an objective way to evaluate more than 3,000 stocks, is restricted to customers.)

Best feature: "Market Insight" button connecting you to "Workshops," which features investing workshops and self-paced courses.

GARY SCHATSKY, ESQ., FAVORS...

● **www.cbsmarketwatch.com.** This site offers real-time financial news, personal portfolio tracking (including allocation analysis, company financials, charting and relevant news to help you track your portfolio), stock quotes, expert commentary and personal financial features on topics such as mutual funds, life and money, retirement, real estate and taxes.

Best feature: Commentary from the daily-featured columnists.

*All prices subject to change.

● **http://moneycentral.msn.com/home. asp.** The features of this comprehensive investment site include "My Money," a customized snapshot of your finances, stocks and related news. Another section called "Investing" includes a portfolio manager that tracks investments, market reports, breaking news, stock quotes and ratings and a mutual fund screener and directory.

Best feature: A link to CNBC TV providing market news and stock picks.

● **www.money.cnn.com.** This site, from CNN and *Money* magazine, covers markets and stocks, company news, the economy, world business, technology, mutual funds, personal finances and more. "Money 101" is an interactive course in managing your finances and "Calculators" has a mortgage refinance calculator.

Best feature: Commentary from Lou Dobbs.

SAM STOVALL DIRECTS INVESTORS TO...

● **www.fidelity.com.** This site, which is *not* restricted to Fidelity mutual fund shareholders, has stocks and mutual fund recommendations from Standard & Poor's and Lehman Brothers, an archive of articles, portfolio tracking and asset allocation.

Best feature: Under "Research" find links to "Market News," "Mutual Funds" and interactive tools that enable you to compare stocks, track the Dow and more.

● **www.bloomberg.com.** This provides a quick stop to get world, financial and earnings news as well as news archives and stocks on the move. At Bloomberg University, you can register for their free on-line investing classes.

Best feature: News and commentary.

● **www.businessweek.com.** This extremely comprehensive site has S&P investment outlooks (picks and pans), and a free S&P stock report every day. The site has market outlooks, sector outlooks and economic analysis. "Special Reports" and "Video Views" give timely investment advice. There is an archive of articles and the BW 50 (which are the S&P's 500 best performers).

Best feature: "Today's Market," which links to a free S&P stock report, market movers, market snapshot and "S&P Stock Picks & Pans."

To Find Better Brokers...

Be sure to check out a brokerage's financial security and legal history before opening an account, and periodically monitor the company's condition.

Free resources to check on a brokerage's legal past: Call the National Association of Securities Dealers at 800-289-9999 or use the BrokerCheck program at its Web site, *www.nasd. com,* which provides information about criminal regulatory actions, complaints, etc. You can download Weiss Ratings' Crisis of Confidence on Wall Street at *www.weissratings.com/crisis_of_ confidence.asp,* which ranks the 18 largest retail brokerage firms from worst to best in terms of financial history.

Note: The Securities Protection Investors Corporation insures brokerage accounts for up to $500,000 and up to $100,000 for cash claims in the event that a brokerage fails. Most firms carry additional private insurance to cover any losses beyond that.

Martin D. Weiss, PhD, chairman, Weiss Ratings, Inc., a financial-services ratings firm, Jupiter, FL.

financial planning, asset-allocation advice and tax strategies.

●**Pitching unsuitable products.** Your broker should be attuned to your financial goals, strategy and appetite for risk. Beware the broker who pushes funds or stocks that do not match your risk tolerance.

●**Making promises.** If a broker promises a rate of return on any stock, take your business elsewhere. Promises simply can't be made in the investment game. Using the word *guarantee*—as in "this mutual fund is guaranteed to return 15% a year"—is also a big no-no. Every investment involves risk.

●**Inflexibility.** One of the greatest obstacles that a brokerage client faces is an adviser who refuses to adapt to his changing financial needs.

Example: You need to sell a large block of stock to buy a new home. Your broker stalls or offers myriad excuses as to why it is a bad time to act.

Brokers are obligated to inform clients of the ramifications of their decisions, but they ultimately must do what their clients want, whether or not they agree with it.

Inflexibility may indicate a hidden agenda, such as a broker who is desperate not to lose assets that would affect his compensation.

Is It Time to Trade in Your Broker?

John Markese, PhD, president, American Association of Individual Investors, a nonprofit investor education organization at 625 N. Michigan Ave., Chicago 60611. Their Web site is www.aaii.com.

Here are five telling signs that you really need to start looking around for a new financial adviser...

●**Unauthorized trading.** Any trade made without your knowledge or authority is a violation of trust. Worse, it is illegal.

●**Selling...selling...selling.** Beware if your broker calls you only when he/she has stocks to sell to you. The best financial advisers provide a full range of services—research reports,

Have You Been Overcharged by Your Broker-Dealer?

Some mutual fund investors may have been overcharged on commissions—an average of $364 per transaction. A recent report found that broker-dealers selling front-end-load funds (A shares) often failed to deliver sales load discounts based on the amount invested. Typically, discounts are applicable at investment levels of $50,000, $100,000, $250,000, $500,000 and $1 million. Failure to provide discounts rarely was intentional. Ask your broker if you are entitled to discounts. If you do not get satisfaction, file your complaint with the SEC at *www.sec.gov/ complaint.shtml.*

Mary Schapiro, vice chairman of the National Association of Securities Dealers (NASD), Washington, DC, *www.nasd.com.*

Deduct Losses From Fraud

If you lost money in an investment due to fraud by top executives, analysts or a stockbroker, you may be eligible to deduct 100% of the loss (subject to certain limits). Unlike capital losses, which are limited to $3,000 a year in excess of capital gains, losses from fraud—perhaps your broker placed you in securities that the brokerage's analysts were fraudulently promoting—may be ordinary theft losses. You can get a refund for theft losses going back three years if you file an amended return. Consult an attorney or tax professional. Definitions of theft vary by state.

Dan Brecher, attorney in New York City specializing in claims against stockbrokers.

The Mutual Fund Scandal

Prominent shareholder activist Mercer E. Bullard, president and founder of Fund Democracy, the nonprofit advocacy group for all mutual fund investors at *www.funddemo cracy.com.* He is a securities law professor at the University of Mississippi, Oxford, and former assistant chief counsel at the Securities and Exchange Commission (SEC).

For decades, mutual funds enjoyed a sterling reputation. But not anymore. Scandal is now tarnishing the industry, triggering a demand for reform and prompting investors to pull billions of dollars out of their funds.

The crisis is escalating, with more and more funds being implicated. What does it mean to each of us? Which funds are still reliable? *Law professor and former securities regulator Mercer E. Bullard gives his insights...*

•**What is the scandal all about?** The scandal involves trading corruption by mutual fund companies and wrongdoing by a large number of their employees, including top fund executives. Some of those trading abuses have been going on for years.

•**How do these abuses hurt funds?** They drive up trading costs, which are borne by *all* fund shareholders. Higher trading costs reduce returns. Returns also suffer if a fund manager is forced to sell securities so that a big investor can cash out.

In their prospectuses, many funds state that they prohibit market timing or impose redemption fees on investors to discourage the practice. Yet some funds have disregarded their own rules. *Two types of abusive trading are taking place...*

•Late trading. To boost their own profits, mutual fund companies secretly give special trading privileges to favored shareholders, such as multimillion-dollar hedge funds. After the 4 pm close of trading, such hedge funds are allowed to buy and sell shares at the closing price. If there is news that seems likely to boost the fund price, the hedge fund buys more shares and sells them the next day for a quick profit. If the news is bad and the price seems likely to fall, the hedge fund sells shares immediately to avoid losses.

Late trading is illegal and likely will result in criminal charges for many firms and individuals.

•Trading based on stale prices. This type of trading is not limited to big institutions. Any savvy person can take advantage. *Common ploy:* There is positive news affecting a major foreign stock market. An investor buys shares of a particular international mutual fund. The fund share price, which isn't updated in a timely manner, doesn't yet reflect the news. The investor sells the shares for a quick profit in a day or two, after the stale price has been updated. Again, such market timing likely is prohibited in the fund's prospectus.

Some international stock funds value their shares in a more timely fashion, which discourages speculators. Failing to update fund prices is illegal. Unfortunately, the Securities and Exchange Commission (SEC) has done little to address this problem.

•**How common is the problem?** Half of fund firms have some relationship with market timers, and one-quarter of brokerage firms do permit customers to trade fund shares illegally after the daily purchase deadline, an SEC survey found.

•How much does this frenetic trading cost? Academic studies suggest that stale pricing costs fund shareholders billions of dollars and late trading practices cost hundreds of millions each year.

In 2000, I published two articles describing the stale-pricing problem. I estimated that stale prices could cost a fund in excess of 2% of assets in a single day. I suspect that shareholders in some international funds have lost 5% to 10% of their assets over a number of years. That is the worst-case scenario. Many investors have lost little or nothing—but in every instance, their trust has been betrayed.

•Are 401(k) plans affected by this scandal? Yes. Many of the funds targeted by regulators are in 401(k)s. In addition, some employees who invest in 401(k) plans tried to make quick profits by trading based on stale prices. In one case, 28 members of a New York boilermakers union each executed from 150 to 500 short-term trades in Putnam funds in their 401(k)s over a three-year period. Profits ranging from $100,000 to $1 million came directly out of the pockets of all the fund shareholders, including their fellow union members.

•With new mutual fund families being implicated all the time, how do I know which funds I can trust? Several mutual fund firms still enjoy excellent reputations—Fidelity, TIAA-CREF, T. Rowe Price and Vanguard, all of which provide no-load funds. American Funds, which charges commissions, is a good option for those who prefer using a broker. A solid alternative is Dimensional Fund Advisors, but individual investors must purchase their funds through fee-only investment advisers.

•What kind of restitution can shareholders expect? Individual investors are unlikely to get big payouts. Whatever they do get won't come for at least a year or two, even though a few cases already have been settled.

•How do I know if I'm eligible to receive money? If you own shares of a fund involved in the scandal, look for updates on the fund company's Web site or call its customer service department. If your mutual fund was involved

in a settlement, details are available at the SEC's Web site, *www.sec.gov.*

•If my fund is involved, should I hang on in case shareholders receive compensation? If you were invested at the time the scandal first broke in September 2003—even if you since have cashed out—you are still entitled to compensation. It is unlikely that shareholders who left a fund years ago will be compensated.

No one wants to invest with a fund company they can't trust or that has broken the law, but don't act hastily. You could shift money into a fund that is just as disreputable as the one you are leaving.

Before making a move, beware of commissions (if you have a load fund) and examine the tax consequences. If the money is in a taxable account, selling might trigger capital gains. If the money is in a retirement account, such as an IRA or a 401(k) plan, you can move to different funds without owing taxes.

Mutual Fund Monkey Business

Many mutual funds continue to charge marketing (12b-1) fees even after they close to new investors.

Average fee: A hefty 0.65% of fund assets—higher even than the total expenses of some mutual funds.

Self-defense: If your fund is closed to new investors, make sure that it stops charging a 12b-1 fee.

Caution: 12b-1 fees are charged by 63% of US funds—both load and no-load.

Phil Edwards, managing director, funds research, Standard & Poor's Corp., New York City.

More from Phil Edwards...

Mutual Fund Know-How

Funds that follow the same indexes are not created equal. Examine a fund's tracking error—the amount by which it diverges from its benchmark. Tracking error will reflect fund expenses. The greater the expenses, the higher the tracking error.

Cut Mutual Fund Fees And Expenses

As a result of big bear-market losses, many mutual funds have fewer assets under management and so collect less in management fees. To make up this loss, many funds are raising the fees and expenses they charge to investors.

When returns from stocks are in the long-term "normal" range of about 6% to 10% annually, even a 2% annual fee can greatly decrease compound returns over time.

What to do: Examine all fees and expenses charged by the mutual funds you invest in and compare them with other alternatives. Consider investing only in index funds, which charge the lowest fees. Look around for funds that charge less than 0.4%.

Example: The Vanguard 500 fund's annual expense is only 0.18% (at press time).

Russel Kinnel, director of mutual fund research, Morningstar Inc., writing in *Morningstar FundInvestor,* 225 W. Wacker Dr., Chicago 60606.

More from Russel Kinnel...

Invest Like the Big Guys

Institutional mutual funds typically have low expenses, but they also have high minimums of $1 million or more.

You can buy into institutional funds through a discount brokerage fund supermarket, such as TD Waterhouse. You might pay a transaction fee —TD Waterhouse will charge $30* on amounts of up to $10,000, to a maximum of $75 for each transaction—but account minimums usually are about $1,000.

Make sure that the amount you save in expenses each year exceeds the transaction costs. Check the expense ratio in the mutual fund's prospectus.

*All prices subject to change.

Alternative: Purchase a retail fund that has a low minimum run by the same manager.

Do Well While Doing Good: Best Socially Responsible Mutual Funds

Alisa Gravitz, vice president of the Social Investment Forum, a nonprofit organization that provides research and education on socially responsible investing, Washington, DC, www.socialinvest.org. She also is the executive editor of Co-Op America's Real Money newsletter on environmental shopping and investing, www.realmoney.org.

You can invest in those companies that have the highest environmental, labor and product-safety standards and fatten your wallet, too.

Nearly three-quarters of mutual funds that use "socially responsible investing" (SRI) guidelines currently receive above-average ratings from one or both of the major mutual fund analysis firms—Lipper at *www.lipperweb.com* and Morningstar at *www.morningstar.com.*

SRI funds have become so popular over the last 25 years that they now hold over $2.1 trillion—or more than $1 out of every $9 that is invested in the US.

While most mutual funds lost investors in 2002 as they withdrew from the markets, SRI funds grew by $1.5 billion in new investments.

HOW THEY WORK

SRI funds invest in stocks and bonds that their managers consider promising investments while also meeting a specific set of ethical standards. They generally won't invest in firms that have poor environmental records or questionable labor practices, or those that manufacture unsafe products, such as alcohol or tobacco.

WHY THEY WORK

SRI funds have been successful primarily because they avoid any corporations that engage in practices that will lower shareholder value. The Domini 400 Social Index of large, socially responsible companies gained more during the past 10 years than the S&P 500 Index—11.86% annually, versus 11.07%. *Reasons...*

●**SRI funds avoid expensive disasters,** such as the massive legal judgments against tobacco companies and the expensive 1989 *Exxon Valdez* oil spill.

●**Socially responsible companies tend to have friendlier labor relations.** This helps them retain the best employees and avoid lawsuits and strikes.

●**Consumers will often use a company's good environmental or labor reputation** as the tiebreaker when choosing between closely matched products.

●**Environmentally careful companies tend to be more efficient** with such resources as fuel. This keeps costs down.

The extra research required for SRI need not add a lot to fund expenses. Our analysis of SRI fund expense ratios indicates that the average SRI fund costs about the same as similar unscreened mutual funds, and some have very low expense ratios.

BEST SRI FUNDS

There are 200 SRI mutual funds available to American investors. The links to most of these funds can be found at *www.socialinvest.org* and *www.socialfunds.com.*

SRI funds occasionally differ on which companies pass muster. They do agree most of the time, however, about key business issues, such as the environment, labor and civil rights. Investors should base their choices on a fund's investment performance and not get bogged down in particular social policies.

For more information: *Responsible Investing: Making a Difference and Making Money* (Dearborn).

The following socially responsible funds have received high rankings, but be sure to research their latest performance figures before investing. Please note that these funds have a load unless otherwise indicated.

LARGE-CAP FUNDS

●**Calvert Social Investment Equity Enhanced Fund (CMIFX).** This index fund starts with the Russell 1000 Index of large-cap stocks, removes companies that do not meet its social criteria, then makes some minor adjustments. 800-368-2748, *www.calvertgroup.com.*

●**Calvert Social Investment Equity Fund (CSIEX).** 800-368-2748, *www.calvertgroup.com.*

●**Women's Equity Fund (FEMMX).** Primarily invests in companies that have women-friendly policies, such as women in upper management or day care facilities for employees' children. No load. 888-552-9363, *www.womens-equity.com.*

MID-CAP FUNDS

●**Ariel Appreciation Fund (CAAPX).** This fund invests primarily in the steady, predictable companies between $1 billion and $10 billion in size. No load. 800-292-7435, *www.arielmutual funds.com.*

●**Calvert Capital Accumulation Fund (CCAFX).** Looks for long-term capital appreciation by investing in mid-cap stocks. 800-368-2748, *www.calvertgroup.com.*

●**Pax World Growth Fund (PXWGX).** Pursues long-term capital growth through the fast-growing companies that reinvest their earnings into expansion, acquisitions, research and development. Up to 25% of assets may be invested in foreign companies. No load. 800-767-1729, *www.paxfund.com.*

SMALL-CAP FUNDS

●**Ariel Fund (ARGFX).** A value-oriented small-cap fund. No load. 800-292-7435, *www.arielmutualfunds.com.*

●**Calvert New Vision Small Cap Fund (CNVAX).** Seeks long-term capital appreciation through innovative companies. 800-368-2748, *www.calvertgroup.com.*

●**Citizens Small Cap Core Growth Fund (CSCSX).** Tracks the Citizens Small Cap Index—300 small companies that pass social and environmental screens. No load. 800-223-7010, *www.citizensfunds.com.*

EQUITY INCOME AND BALANCED FUNDS

●**MMA Praxis Value Index Fund (MVIAX).** Seeks capital appreciation by trying to mirror the S&P 500/BARRA Value Index while screening companies to ensure that they meet socially responsible specifications. 800-348-7468, *www.mmapraxis.com.*

● **Pax World Balanced Fund (PAXWX).** Its objective is primarily income and capital pre-servation…capital growth is second. Invests no more than 75% of assets in stocks. No load. 800-767-1729, *www.paxfund.com.*

● **Walden Social Balanced Fund (WSBFX).** Seeks capital growth and income from stocks, bonds and money market instruments. *Minimum:* $100,000. No load. 800-282-8782, *www. waldenassetmgmt.com.*

BOND FUNDS

Bonds are appropriate for those in search of income, not growth.

● **Calvert Social Investment Fund Bond (CSIBX).** Invests in bonds and other securities to provide as high a level of income as prudent while preserving capital. 800-368-2748, *www. calvertgroup.com.*

● **Domini Social Bond Fund (DSBFX).** Seeks high income by investing at least 85% of assets in intermediate-term fixed-income instruments. No load. 800-762-6814, *www.domini.com.*

● **Pax World High Yield Fund (PAXHX).** Primarily invests in high-risk, high-yield bonds. No load. 800-767-1729, *www.paxfund.com.*

Hedge Funds Are Not For Novices

Lewis J. Altfest, PhD, CPA/PFS, CFA, CFP, president, L.J. Altfest & Co., Inc., a fee-only financial planning firm, 116 John St., New York City 10038. He is also professor of finance at Pace University, in New York City as well.

Hedge funds, which have the ability to be "long" on stocks (own stocks) or "short" on stocks (sell borrowed shares in hopes of buying them back later for less), can effectively neutralize market swings. They also arbitrage (meaning play one side against another) in proposed mergers to get the best deal for their shareholders.

Their diversification potential, including performance that is less sensitive to market forces, makes selected hedge funds interesting for a tricky market. But they were primarily intended for highly sophisticated large investors. Regulators are concerned about recent moves to make hedge funds available to investors for as little as $25,000, and are trying to make their dealings more transparent. Don't go into them without expert advice from a fee-only financial planner. There are many different types of hedge funds and some are much riskier than others.

For Tax-Free Gains… Buy Mutual Funds with Built-In Losses

Sue Stevens, CPA, CFP, CFA, founder, Stevens Portfolio Design, 861 Fountain View Dr., Deerfield, IL 60015. She is also director of financial planning for Morningstar Inc., a financial information provider.

Stock market investors have been trying to make something of their losses for three years by selling stocks that have plunged in value and writing off whatever losses the law allows.

Mutual fund investors, though, have an even better opportunity. If they buy the right funds, they can benefit from other investors' losses.

Whether or not the three-year bear market is over, there are plenty of funds available with large built-in tax losses.

Those losses can set the stage for huge tax-free gains.

REVERSAL OF FORTUNE

For years, it seems, mutual fund investors worried about paying tax on phantom gains.

Example: You owned 1,000 shares of ABC Fund in 1999. During that year, ABC sold a number of stocks at a profit. As a result, it made $2 per share in capital gains distributions. As a result, you had to recognize $2,000 in taxable income, even if you reinvested all of those distributions and never received a penny in cash.

The worst tax results were suffered by investors who bought right after a fund had a large string of gains. Such investors were buying fund shares with a built-in tax obligation.

Example: You invested in ABC Fund in early 2000, at the peak of the bull market, when the fund had $1 billion in assets. However, ABC had paid only $600 million for those shares.

You had bought into a fund with $400 million in unrealized gains. At a 20% tax rate, the rate then in effect for long-term gains, you were buying a piece of an $80 million (8% of assets) tax obligation. In effect, you were paying $1 for assets that were worth only 92 cents, after tax.

Current events: After the extended bear market, the situation has changed. Most stock funds now have unrealized losses, not gains.

Loophole: You can buy funds at a discount to their after-tax value and avoid paying tax on capital gains distributions, perhaps for many years to come.

GAINS FROM LOSSES

There are two kinds of net losses that mutual funds may have…

●**Realized losses.** In any given year, most funds engage in multiple trades, most of which will result in a gain or a loss. In recent years, many funds have realized more losses than gains on their trades.

●**Unrealized losses.** Funds also might be holding on to stocks that have fallen in value since their purchase by the fund. These holdings may be converted into realized losses at any time.

Significant redemptions from a fund make it more likely for unrealized losses to become realized. The fund manager may have to sell to get the cash for redemptions.

Unlike realized gains, funds cannot pass realized losses through to their shareholders. However, they can "bank" realized losses and carry them forward for up to eight years. During this time, realized gains may be sheltered from tax.

Example: In 2001 and 2002, DEF Fund had realized losses totaling $5 per share. In 2003 and 2004, as the market recovered, DEF realized $3 per share in gains.

DEF does not have to make any capital gains distributions. Its carried-forward loss offsets the $3-per-share realized gains, and the fund still has $2 per share in banked losses to offset future realized gains.

Note: Stock *dividends* will still be passed through to you and taxed. However, most stock funds pay meager dividends these days and the federal income tax on those dividends will be no higher than 15%.

STOCKS ON SALE

When you buy into a fund with unrealized capital losses, you're buying at a discount—after tax.

Example: GHI Fund now holds $1 billion in assets. Those assets, stocks bought in prior years at higher prices, have a basis of $2.5 billion. Therefore, you're buying into $1.5 billion of unrealized tax losses—150% of the fund's assets. At the 15% tax rate on capital gains, that's a 22.5% bonus. Therefore, you're buying $122.50 worth of assets for every dollar you invest in GHI Fund.

Funds with unrealized tax losses may enjoy increased flexibility. They can take gains on selected issues—even short-term gains—without worrying that shareholders will be unhappy.

Such realized gains will have no impact on shareholders if the fund can cover them with realized losses.

Caution: Such tax-free gains will apply only within a fund. If you sell your fund shares at a profit, you'll owe tax.

Loophole: Gains on fund shares held more than one year are taxed at only 15%—or 5% if you're in one of the two lowest tax brackets (10% and 15%).

To enjoy all of these tax benefits (untaxed internal gains, low-taxed dividends and long-term gains), you must hold a fund in a taxable account. Funds held in a tax-deferred retirement plan will generate fully taxed income as money is withdrawn from the plan.

DOUBLE YOUR BENEFIT

Mutual fund investors now can implement a two-pronged strategy…

●**Offload funds selling below the prices you paid.** Such sales will bring about capital losses that capital gains can offset. These net capital losses can be deducted (up to $3,000 per year) and carried forward indefinitely to offset future gains.

●**After you sell, reinvest the proceeds in similar funds with large built-in losses,** realized and unrealized. Going forward, your new fund is unlikely to distribute capital gains, perhaps for many years.

Such a maneuver won't violate the wash-sale rules, so you'll get to take the capital losses.

Example: You sell Fidelity Growth Company, taking tax losses, and reinvest the proceeds in Fidelity Aggressive Growth Fund. The latter fund had built-in losses equal to 290% of its portfolio value at the end of the first half of 2003, according to Morningstar, so any trading gains will be tax free for several years.

Your portfolio will be about the same, however you will be in a position to enjoy twin tax benefits.

MORE INFORMATION

How do you find out about a fund's tax-loss position? If you're interested in a fund, check into its annual financial statements.

For more current information, go to Web sites such as *www.morningstar.com* and look for "potential capital gains exposure."

When that number is negative, the fund has built-in tax losses available to new investors. Many growth-stock funds now have built-in losses, especially those invested heavily in technology stocks.

Caution: Do not invest in a fund solely to obtain large losses. Look for a loss-carrying fund that seems likely to produce sheltered gains in the future, based on past performance and the stature of current management.

Beware of Bond-Fund Yield Claims

Bond-fund yields may be lower than some funds claim.

Reason: Some funds will quote two yield figures—the standard one mandated by the Securities and Exchange Commission (SEC)…and a second one, called *annualized dividend* or *distribution rate,* which might be one full percentage point higher. This number annualizes the amount the fund paid in income distributions during the most recent month. In reality, distributions vary from month to month. While this number might be higher or lower than the SEC yield, it has been higher in the current interest rate environment.

Self-defense: Compare funds based on their SEC yields, not on their distribution rates.

Gene Gohlke, associate director, SEC Office of Compliance Inspections and Examinations, Washington, DC.

For the Highest Tax-Free Yields…Leveraged Closed-End Muni Funds

Donald L. Cassidy, senior research analyst, Lipper Inc., a unit of Reuters Group PLC, 1380 Lawrence St., Denver 80204. He is author of five books on investing, including *Trading on Volume* (McGraw-Hill).

Closed-end funds provide the same advantages as open-ended mutual funds. You benefit from diversification, professional selection of securities as well as low minimum investments.

If the fund holds municipal bonds, the tax-exempt interest from those bonds is passed to shareholders. Single-state funds often provide interest that is completely tax exempt.

Difference: Closed-end funds do not redeem their shares every day. Instead, most closed-end funds trade on a stock exchange and their share prices usually vary from actual net asset value (NAV) per share.

Some closed-end funds also use leverage to boost current yields.

Example: The closed-end fund ABC raises $100 million from investors in an initial public offering of its *common* shares. That $100 million is invested in municipal bonds yielding 5%.

Then, in a subsequent issue, ABC sells off $50 million worth of its floating-rate *preferred* shares to institutions and high-net-worth individuals. These are designed to be alternatives to tax-exempt money market funds so the current yield (at press time) is around 1%.

The payoff is that ABC is paying 1% annual interest to holders of its floating-rate preferred shares. The $50 million it raised from them is invested in long-term munis paying 5%.

This is a 4% spread, generating profits of $2 million per year (4% of $50 million) if that spread is maintained. That $2 million can be distributed to all the common shareholders, increasing their yield, perhaps to 7%.

Alternative: Instead of getting leverage by selling their short-term preferred shares, some closed-end funds borrow money. The result is the same—a spread between short-term borrowing costs and the yields on long-term securities purchased with the borrowed funds.

How to profit from the yield curve: The greater the difference between the (low) short-term interest rates and (higher) long-term rates, the more profit you can earn by using this type of leverage.

DEALING IN DISCOUNTS

Closed-end funds differ from mutual funds in one other vital area—they can trade at a discount or at a premium to their net asset value. When you buy a fund at a discount, your yield increases.

Example: Closed-end fund XYZ has 10 million common shares outstanding. The value of the securities it owns is $120 million. The NAV per share is $12 ($120 million divided by 10 million shares).

The trading price of XYZ is set by supply and demand for its shares. If investors are willing to pay only $11.50, that's a 4.2% discount from its $12 NAV.

Currently, the municipal bond market is depressed by several factors, including concerns about state and local budgets, lower tax rates and the AMT. Most closed-end muni funds trade at discounts. And, these discounts can nudge a fund's effective yield up slightly.

WEIGHING THE RISKS

If you are collecting 7% tax-exempt yields in a 4% world, you must be taking some significant risks. That's certainly the case with leveraged closed-end muni funds. *The major risks...*

●**Market risk.** The demand for municipal bonds might fall even lower. Municipal credit concerns could heighten or the other types of bonds could gain popularity. Reduced demand could drop the trading price of your closed-end muni fund.

●**Discount risk.** A muni fund discount can widen, or a premium can diminish. Even if you buy a fund at, say, a 5% discount to NAV, reduced demand might expand that discount to 10% and hammer down the trading price.

●**Interest-rate risk.** If the interest rates rise from their current levels, the prices of all bonds (and bond funds) will fall. An economic recovery could lead to higher rates.

●**Leverage risk.** Just as leverage can help to increase your returns, it also can work against you in adverse market conditions.

SQUEEZING THE SPREAD

A steep yield curve will increase the spread between the short- and long-term rates, so that investors profit. If the yield curve flattens, a smaller spread may cut the other way.

Example: ABC fund sells its *floating-rate* preferred shares at 1% and uses the proceeds to buy 5% bonds, for a 4% spread.

Suppose short-term rates rise from current historic lows. Fund ABC is locked into a 5% yield on the long-term bonds it owns so the spread might shrink to 3%, 2%, etc.

A smaller spread means lower profits to distribute to the common shareholders. Lower distributions, in turn, almost surely will mean a lower trading price for ABC shares.

Insult to injury: If a narrowing spread is accompanied by generally rising interest rates, bond-market losses could be exacerbated by closed-end funds' use of leverage.

Example: From 1993 to 1994, the entire bond market headed south as interest rates rose. The average leveraged closed-end muni fund that existed at the start of 1992 saw its NAV decline by 18% in 44 weeks while its market (trading) price fell by 22.5%.

PROCEED WITH CAUTION

Don't ignore the risks presented by leveraged closed-end muni funds. Do not buy just because a broker calls and pitches "7% yields, tax free."

However, leveraged closed-end muni funds might deserve a place in your portfolio, especially if your investment goals include substantial tax-free income.

Leveraged closed-end muni funds really work best as long-term commitments rather than as trading vehicles.

Before investing, be sure to do your homework. Learn what bonds a fund owns, how it obtains leverage, and how the managers have performed throughout the previous interest-rate cycles.

For best results, don't pay a premium for a closed-end fund. Whenever you buy assets, it's best to buy them at a discount.

Best Way to Buy Treasury Bonds

With interest rates still low, bond investors are now buying at high prices and risk losing principal if rates rise with the recovery. Instead of bond funds, which have no fixed maturity date on which you are guaranteed to recoup face value, it's smarter to purchase individual bonds directly (no commission) from the government at *www.treasurydirect.gov.*

More information: Visit *www.investingin bonds.org.*

Mike Holland, chairman, Holland & Co., 375 Park Ave., New York City 10152.

Benefits of Tax-Exempt Bonds

Tax-exempt bonds are attractive to investors in the highest tax brackets in spite of the dividend tax cut.

Advantages: (1) Tax-exempt bonds are completely tax free while dividends are taxed at up to 15% and other interest-paying investments produce income taxed at up to 35%. (2) Tax-exempt bonds can be safer investments than dividend-paying stocks.

Result: For the unique combination of after-tax income and safety, tax-exempt bonds are still the investment to beat for income-oriented investors.

However, keep in mind that stocks have the potential for capital appreciation.

Christine Benz, editor, *Morningstar FundInvestor,* 225 W. Wacker Dr., Chicago 60606.

How to Make Money in Any Economy— Invest in Rental Property

Gary Eldred, real estate adviser in Gainesville, FL, *www. stoprentingnow.com.* He is the author of nine real estate–related books, including *Investing in Real Estate* (Wiley).

Most rental-property owners continued to profit handsomely, even when stock investors took a bear-market beating.

When you factor in rental income and the tax advantages, rental-property owners can receive healthy—and steady—returns year after year. *How it's done...*

RENTAL INVESTING

Let's say you purchase a four-unit apartment building for $400,000. You invest $100,000 as the down payment and take out a $300,000 mortgage at 6% interest.

An appropriate rent might be set at $1,000 a month per apartment. Allowing a loss of 6% a year for vacancies, your rental income would total $45,120 a year.

Cash being spent for the building comes to $37,600. This includes about $21,600 a year in mortgage payments...$8,000 in property taxes ...$4,000 for insurance...and another $4,000 for maintenance.

The remaining $7,520 in net annual rental income comes out to a 7.52% annual return on your $100,000 investment. Do not forget that your rents probably will increase annually and improve the rate of return.

In addition, as you pay down the mortgage, your equity in the property increases. You also gain through property appreciation. This allows you to increase your investment by refinancing and borrowing more cash. That will allow you to buy additional property or sell the first property and buy an even bigger building.

TAX INCENTIVES

Tax laws favor property owners…

•**Property owners can deduct expenses** that are directly related to the maintenance of rental property. *These include…*

  •Advertising, legal and accountant fees.

  •Cost of travel to an out-of-town property.

  •Caretaker's salary.

•**Depreciation rules give property owners a tax break.** They allow owners to deduct the value of the building itself over a 27.5-year period (the building is worth about 80% of the total value of a property, assuming that the land value is 20%).

Example: That four-unit, $400,000 apartment building could be depreciated by up to $320,000 (80%) over 27.5 years, resulting in an annual tax deduction of $11,636.

Important: When you sell, all your profit is then subject to capital gains tax. However, the portion of the gain reflecting depreciation is taxed at 25%, not the more favorable 15% rate on the balance of the gain.

WHAT YOU NEED TO DO

•**Plan to spend three hours a month on each rental property of up to 12 units**—on paperwork and showing apartments to prospective tenants. The time adds up when you own several buildings.

Individual investors should start with houses, town houses or small apartment buildings of no more than four units, which are more easily rented and maintained.

•**Select tenants carefully.** This prevents problems, including the need to chase down tenants who are late with rent. Don't approve a tenant based on a recommendation from anyone who has known him/her for less than several years.

Important: Have prospective tenants obtain and present you with their credit reports from *www.myfico.com.*

Cost: $12.95.*

For additional safety, order a criminal record check from an investigative agency.

Cost: $30 and up.

Or get a local credit firm to provide a public record check on the prospective tenant, which will show any evictions.

•**Hire a handyman who lives nearby.** He should be on call 24 hours a day, seven days a week. Retired people are excellent for the job, and they can be hired for $10 to $40 an hour, depending on the area. Smaller buildings usually do not require more than a few hours of maintenance a month, and payment for maintenance is deductible from gross revenue.

BUYING PROPERTY

Look for areas in which…

•**The job base is growing.**

•**Young couples are purchasing** because they've been priced out of more fashionable neighborhoods.

•**Houses are well-maintained.**

•**New home owners are making capital improvements.**

Avoid buying cheap property in depressed areas with the hope of making a huge profit when the neighborhood turns around. That is speculation, not investment.

Consider real estate investment trusts (REITs) if you don't want to spend any time managing rental property. REITs are stocks, but they function like mutual funds that invest in real estate. REITs offer high income. However, don't expect profits as high as when you own the property.

FAVORITE CITIES

There are thousands of small and midsized communities with great rental investment potential. *Some of my favorites…*

•**Bloomington, IN…Ithaca, NY…Oxford, MS,** where major universities have helped to attract upscale home buyers.

•**Bend and Ashland, OR,** which are close to both the coast and the mountains.

*All prices subject to change.

- **Florida**—Panama City and areas in the Panhandle still are relatively underdeveloped, unlike most of Florida's coastline. Vero Beach, where zoning restrictions have largely spared the city from high-rise apartment buildings, has increasing competition for rentals.

- **Vancouver, Canada,** where rental-property owners also stand to gain if the Canadian dollar continues to appreciate against the US dollar.

Smarter Investing in Gemstones

Antoinette Matlins, a gemologist consultant and consumer advocate based in Woodstock, VT, and author of *Colored Gemstones: The Antoinette Matlins Buying Guide* (GemStone Press, *www.gemstonepress.com*).

Before investing in gemstones, be aware that more than 90% of rubies, emeralds and sapphires are treated to improve their color and clarity.

Untreated stones command the most value—and are likely to be the best investment in the future. The fourth quarter of 2003 saw significant growth in sales for extra-fine rubies, sapphires and emeralds. High demand drove prices up by 20% over the previous year, and prices are expected to climb another 30% over the next year.

Valuation: A "natural" untreated emerald or ruby might be worth double the value of an otherwise comparable treated stone. Untreated sapphires also are more valuable than treated ones, often by 30% to 50%—and rising.

Investing key: Even the most sophisticated gem purchasers are not aware that most gems have been treated to enhance color. As their awareness grows, they are likely to increasingly seek out untreated stones for purchase, and drive their value up.

Smart buying: *If you decide that investing in gemstones is for you, then...*

- **Educate yourself about the stone and about color treatments,** using information from sources such as the Gemological Institute of America, *www.gia.org.*

- **Inquire with reputable sellers** regarding their policies and standards for dealing with color-treated stones.

- **Obtain an independent laboratory report** on a stone before you decide to make a major purchase.

11

Getting Your Money's Worth

Super Penny-Pincher Shows You How to Slash Monthly Bills

People tell me that they cannot save enough money even when they cut back on luxuries. My solution? Cut recurring *base* costs. Most people can decrease so-called fixed costs by 10% and still live well. That means a family of four living on $90,000 a year should be able to save $9,000 —or $750 a month. *Here's what you can do...*

SAVE ON CELL PHONE CHARGES

●**Contain cell phone costs with a pre-paid phone.**

My favorite: Virgin Mobile (888-322-1122, *www.virginmobileusa.com*), which is popular in Europe. The phone can cost as little as $59* after discounts and rebates at selected retail stores, such as Best Buy. You pay for minutes in advance and talk until your time runs out.

*All prices subject to change.

Calls cost 25 cents per minute for the first 10 minutes a day, then decrease to 10 cents per minute. If you use this phone infrequently or only for emergencies, you can pay $20 every 90 days for a minimum of 80 minutes.

●**Lower your monthly rates.** Almost 40% of my listeners are unhappy with their cell phone service, mostly because it's too expensive.

To find the most economical plans in your area, compare prices at sites such as *www.get connected.com...www.letstalk.com...www.my rateplan.com...*and *www.point.com.*

Important: Before signing a new contract, request a 30-day trial period for new phone service. Then rigorously test the service from key locations at peak use times.

SAVE ON ELECTRICITY

●**Ask your utility company about "time of day" energy programs.** You will be charged less for energy use during off-peak hours.

Clark Howard, a self-made millionaire and host of *The Clark Howard Show,* an Atlanta-based consumer-advice radio show syndicated on 140 radio stations around the country. He is author of *Get Clark Smart* (Longstreet).

Example: Washington State residents pay 31 cents* per kilowatt-hour (kWh) between the hours of 7 am and 7 pm, but just four cents per kWh at all other times.

●**Inquire about any "power credit" programs.** These plans let the utility company control the amount of power used by your home's air-conditioning system. In return, you get a sign-up credit (typically $20) and save as much as $40 per month.

Example: In Georgia, the power company installs a switch on the outside of your home that connects to your central air-conditioning unit. At peak times (weekdays between noon and 7 pm), the power company controls your air conditioner and reduces the length of time it runs. You get a rebate of $2 each time it activates the switch. The change to your home's temperature is only a few degrees.

●**Ask your power company if it offers senior discounts** if you're age 50 or older and if it allows you to budget your payments with a preset monthly amount.

HALVE YOUR INTERNET SERVICE BILL

Get rid of your mainstream Internet service provider (ISP). At $20 or more per month, ISPs like AOL, Earthlink and MSN are up to four times as expensive as other ISPs.

Better: The discount long-distance provider *www.bigzoo.com* offers 150 hours of Internet service per month for $5.95 if you pay for six months up-front. And, for $9.94 a month, *www. walmart.com* offers unlimited Internet access, plus a 700-hour free trial...*www.netzero.com* provides unlimited access for $9.95 per month.

REFINANCE YOUR MORTGAGE

It is not too late. Over the past several years, mortgage companies made a killing as so many Americans refinanced. Now the pool of people refinancing is smaller, so lenders have had to knock down their prices. The spread between the interest rates that mortgage lenders get and what they charge customers has decreased by one-half point. *It might pay to refinance if...*

●**You can shave at least one-half point off your current interest rate.**

*All prices subject to change.

●**You have an adjustable-rate mortgage.** Refinance to a fixed rate if you plan to be in the home for more than 18 months. Otherwise, the closing costs (generally $2,000 to $2,500) may outweigh savings. Check the rates at *www.bank rate.com* and *www.monstermoving.com.*

Secret: Most airlines have formed marketing alliances with mortgage lenders. So, the higher your closing costs, the more miles you will get. Alliances generally aren't advertised—be sure to ask your credit card or mortgage company.

SAVE ON LONG-DISTANCE CALLS

Use your computer and/or calling cards. *My favorite computer-call offer now...*

●**www.net2phone.com** charges two cents per minute for calls from your PC to any phone in the US. Special software routes calls over the Internet and onto standard phone lines.

The minimum requirements: Sound card, speakers, computer microphone as well as *Windows 95.*

Other good calling-card offers...

●**Costco/MCI card gives you 670 minutes for $19.99.** That is 3.3 cents per minute. The offer does not appear on Costco's Web site. Call your local club for information.

●**Sam's Club/AT&T card offers a 1,500-minute card for $52.04...**or a seven-pack of 120-minute cards for $29.14. Each charges 3.47 cents per minute for domestic calls. Go to *www. samsclub.com.* Click on "Prepaid Phone Cards."

●**www.callwave.com** is Internet answering-machine software that records incoming calls. It lets you use one phone line to surf the Internet and receive calls.

Cost: $3.95 per month with a 30-day free trial.

Resource: Go to *www.callingbooth.com* for the latest rates on discount long-distance, PC-to-phone and PC-to-PC calls.

FREE DIRECTORY ASSISTANCE

The phone company will typically charge $1 per request. Besides the phone book, the very same information is also free at *www.411.com* ...*www.anywho.com*...*http://people.yahoo.com* ...and *www.whitepages.com.* You can often get e-mail addresses and maps with driving directions at these sites.

*All prices subject to change.

How One Woman Saved $65 In Minutes

Marjory Abrams, editor of *Bottom Line/Personal,* Boardroom Inc., 281 Tresser Blvd., Stamford, CT 06901.

If you think reviewing your bills is a thankless chore—think again. *Recent errors a colleague caught on her phone bills...*

●**Charges from her old long-distance provider** after she had switched ($42.88).

●**A $20 switching fee** that she wasn't supposed to pay.

●**A $2 charge for an international call option** that she didn't elect.

●**And...a federal excise surcharge tax** ($0.42) was charged twice.

Gary Schatsky, Esq., president of a financial advisory firm in New York City and Florida says not reviewing your bills is a missed opportunity. *Examples...*

Cell phones: People who consistently exceed the free-minute allotment on their wireless phone plans should ask their service providers if another plan would save them money. You may be able to change your plan retroactively —rescinding charges from the previous month. This once saved me $500.

Tax bills: If the IRS sends a notice that you underpaid taxes, penalties may be waived even if the assessment is valid. Ask your accountant.

Hospital bills: These are particularly error-ridden. Patients pay an estimated average of $1,300 in overcharges per year, so always ask for an itemized statement.

Health insurance: If a claim is rejected by your health insurer, find out why. It may be a simple error. Fight any "no." If you expect a battle, consider consulting a professional.

Resource: Patient Advocate Foundation at 800-532-5274 or *www.patientadvocate.org.*

Credit card bills: Occasionally a vendor puts through a charge twice—and not necessarily in the same billing cycle. I once had a $704 charge posted in December and reposted in February. Compare receipts to monthly statements.

Magnificent Moneysavers For People Over 50

Linda Bowman, Tucson, AZ–based professional bargain hunter. She is frequently a guest on television talk shows and syndicated radio shows and is author of *Free Stuff and Good Deals for Folks Over 50* (Santa Monica Press). Her other books in the series describe "free stuff and good deals" for kids and pets and on the Internet.

Do the words "senior discount" conjure an image of old folks lining up for the early bird special? Things have changed! Mature adults' opportunities to save are now so abundant that I wrote an entire book describing thousands of them—and had to update it only two years later.

Just look around. *You'll find freebies and discounts available almost everywhere...*

●**Museums.** By proclaiming your senior status, you'll save 50 cents* (off $3 admission) at the Paul Revere House in Boston (*www.paulreverehouse.org*)...$4 (off $6) at the Museum of Contemporary Art, San Diego, in La Jolla, CA (*www.mcasd.org*)...and $5 (off $15) at the Solomon R. Guggenheim Museum in New York City (*www.guggenheim.org*).

●**Sports.** Ask the public relations department of a local stadium, auditorium or arena (or the office of teams that play there) about individual or group senior discounts, year-round discount cards, special membership opportunities or senior citizen days.

Caveats: Many offers have restrictions.

Always carry your driver's license, passport, resident alien card, Medicare card or membership card in an over-50 group, such as AARP (formerly called the American Association of Retired Persons), as proof that you deserve a break despite your youthful appearance.

You must speak up. No one will say, "You look old enough." Would you want them to?

WHO'S A SENIOR?

"Senior citizen" once meant "Medicare recipient." Now, the lower limit of "senior" may be as young as age 50.

Some folks just passing 50 or 55 say they're embarrassed to request a discount. I ask them,

*All prices subject to change.

"Do you want to save money or do you want to save face?"

I'm 56. My husband is 57. Thrift is a way of life for us. We seldom pay retail for anything. Although we're new to senior discounts, we try to remember to ask for them. And we celebrate our victories.

If you quail at the word "senior," consider this—AARP is the largest organization for seniors in the country. (*Membership cost:* $12.50*/year.) When I make a reservation for anything—plane, train, car, bus or hotel—I ask, "Do you have an AARP discount?" (I got a reduced price that way for a bed-and-breakfast in Sedona, AZ.) State your eligibility to join and you may not even have to be a member.

Failing that, I ask about discounts for automobile club members (i.e., AAA, *www.aaa.com*).

Note: AARP also lists best Web sites for people age 50 and older at *www.aarp.org/internet resources*.

LOOK FOR HIDDEN DISCOUNTS

Ferret out discounts everywhere. At a mall, visit the customer service kiosk and ask which of the stores are offering coupons or senior discounts. When you visit your hair salon, shoe repair shop, hardware store or dry cleaner, say, "I'm a senior. May I get 10% off my bill?"

If your request is declined, ask to speak to the owner and suggest creating such discounts. Mature adults reward providers of dependable service by returning again and again.

Resort and retirement areas in places such as Tucson, where I live, are swarming with age-50-plus visitors and residents. Attracting our business is good business.

Occasionally, I hear a radio spot advertising 5% off purchases by seniors at a chain of local grocery stores. Yet I've never seen such a sign in the store.

Some local taxi companies sell senior citizen discount coupons. Even your local gas station may have senior days.

Ask your state Office on Aging (listed in the blue pages of your phone book) for a membership card which will give you discounts at participating establishments.

*All prices subject to change.

In some areas of the country, companies that offer senior discounts display a special symbol on their display ads in the *Yellow Pages*.

TRAVEL

Cruises, walking tours and other trips often have senior discounts…

●**Airlines.** Carriers offering senior fares—America West Airlines (age 62 and up), 800-235-9292 or *www.americawest.com*, and Southwest Airlines (age 65 and up), 800-435-9792 or *www. southwest.com*.

●**Trains.** On some Amtrak trains (800-872-7245, *www.amtrak.com*), you'll get a 15% discount after you turn 62.

●**National Parks.** At 62, you can purchase a Golden Age Passport for $10* at any National Park Service facility that charges an entrance fee. This lifetime pass to national parks, monuments, historic sites, recreation areas and wildlife refuges also admits anyone in your car, as long as it is a private vehicle—and on foot, your accompanying spouse, children and parents.

Note: You must be a citizen or permanent resident of the US.

●**Hotels.** Hotel chains want your business. Many offer senior rates.

Caution! Ask about other rates. Sometimes a promotion that's available to the general public costs less than the senior discount.

●**International travel.** ElderTreks (800-741-7956, *www.eldertreks.com*), based in Toronto, will take small groups of people ages 50 and up on safaris to Antarctica, Europe and more. Your Man Tours in Inglewood, CA (800-922-9000, *www.ymtvacations.com*), is among the least expensive of the travel companies specializing in senior travel.

Interhostel (800-733-9753, *www.learn.unh. edu/interhostel*), sponsored by the University of New Hampshire, arranges moderately priced two-week educational experiences for people over 50 at colleges and universities in Europe, China and Australia. Through the related Familyhostel, you can take your kids and school-aged grandkids.

EDUCATION

For 30 years, the not-for-profit, Boston-based Elderhostel (877-426-8056, *www.elderhostel.org*)
*All prices subject to change.

has offered low-cost, high-quality learning experiences. Last year, 250,000 people age 55 and over took part in programs throughout the US and in more than 90 other countries. Scholarships are available.

The North Carolina Center for Creative Retirement (828-251-6140, *www.unca.edu/ncccr*), established in 1988 by the University of North Carolina at Asheville, sponsors a College for Seniors (50-plus), Creative Retirement Exploration Weekends and the Un-Retirement Option for those who are still working but are ready to plan their retirement.

Many colleges and universities will let seniors audit classes for nominal fees, sometimes with a meal plan. Campus housing is usually available only in the summer.

Age requirements vary: For example, a "senior" at the University of Vermont (800-639-3210, *www.learn.uvm.edu*) is 65-plus (and must also be a Vermont resident).

At some state schools, participants must be state residents. Schools allowing seniors from anywhere to audit courses free or at minimal cost include the Universities of Connecticut, Illinois and Massachusetts.

Living the Good Life For Lots Less

Shel Horowitz, Northampton, MA–based author of the electronic book *The Penny Pinching Hedonist,* available at the Frugal Fun Web site, *www.frugalfun.com.*

My wife and I travel, eat well and attend shows for a fraction of what others pay. *Our secrets...*

FRUGAL TRAVEL

•**Rent an apartment instead of staying in a hotel.** Furnished apartments can cost half as much. Since they have kitchens, you also save on meals. Type "furnished apartments" or "vacation rental apartments" and the name of your destination into an Internet search engine, such as *www.google.com.* Also check the "furnished apartments for rent" classified ads in the area's

newspapers or through *www.onlinenewspapers. com.* Many large rental agencies will rent apartments for periods as short as one week.

•**Try Smarterliving.com.** It provides a free e-newsletter detailing last-minute bargains on hotels and airfare. It has listed great deals, such as $158 round-trip airfare from Chicago to Los Angeles and $119/night at The New York Helmsley Hotel.

•**Reserve a rental car far in advance for peak-season travel.** At some firms, you can lock in prices that are 25% to 50% below peak rates by calling at least one month before peak travel periods.

•**Visit US museums on free days.** Unlike most attractions, museums will typically waive admission fees one day a week. Inquire about free museum days at the local visitors bureau as soon as you arrive.

Example: Washington, DC's major museums are almost all free. In Chicago, at least one museum is free every weekday.

FRUGAL FUN AT HOME

•**Volunteer as an usher at concerts and plays.** Ushers will seat the audience before the show and after intermission, then help sweep up. You must arrive a little early and stay a bit late, but you are pretty much free to enjoy yourself during the performance. There often is an open seat. Promoters' names and phone numbers generally are listed on advertising posters. Call as far in advance as possible to ask if volunteer ushers are needed.

•**Take advantage of radio giveaways.** Put the station's number in your phone's memory so you can call quickly when a giveaway is announced. College stations provide the best odds since they have fewer listeners than commercial stations. I win tickets to at least five shows a year when I call stations regularly.

•**Go to the best restaurants in town**—for dessert and coffee. Even at high-end eateries, this shouldn't cost more than $10 or $15 per person. True, you won't experience everything the restaurant has to offer, but you'll get to linger and enjoy the ambiance at very little cost.

Helpful: This is best done on weeknights and after 9 pm. Restaurants don't appreciate guests who arrive during peak hours and then spend little money.

•**Attend real estate showings at mansions.** You'll tour beautiful homes in the ritzy neighborhoods. Keep an eye out for high-end listings in local papers.

Fine Dining for Less

On-line discounts are available for 1,100 upscale restaurants in the US. Most are in California, Florida, Illinois and New York. Book an off-peak table through *www.dinnerbroker. com* and save up to 30%—applied before your bill is handed to you. At *www.restaurant.com,* you can buy gift certificates at half price. And, if you dine out often, you can earn points toward dining "cheques" for every reservation you book at *www.opentable.com.*

Kiplinger's Personal Finance, 1729 H St. NW, Washington, DC 20006.

Discounts Just for The Military

The Veterans Advantage program offers veterans and those in the military, National Guard and Reserves—and their families—up to 70% off hotel rooms, 25% off car rentals, 25% off Airborne Express, 10% off Dell computers and 65% off prescription drugs. The program also offers 15% Everyday Savings on Amtrak plus discounts at theme parks, sporting events and more. Visit *www.veteransadvantage.com* or call 866-838-2774.

How to Cancel Your Cell Phone Plan or Internet Service

Some companies can make it difficult for customers to discontinue their cellular phone or Internet service.

To make sure your cancellation request is not ignored: Write down the date, time, name and ID number of the representative handling your call. Use the words "cancel" and "disconnect" in your request. If your bill is paid automatically from your bank account, direct your bank in writing to no longer allow withdrawals earmarked for the company. If you continue to receive bills, write to the company. If service still is not discontinued, write to your state attorney general and public utility commission, and send a copy to the company.

Also: If you paid by credit card, dispute the charge with your credit card company.

Michael Ostheimer, attorney at the Federal Trade Commission, Bureau of Consumer Protection, Washington, DC, *www.ftc.gov.*

Your Very Own 800 Number

An 800 number is not just for business. Personal 800 numbers are offered by many long-distance companies. Encourage kids away at college or other family to call you by letting them call toll-free on your personal 800 phone number. You can save money, too, with rates as low as 2.9 cents* per minute for interstate long-distance calls.

Bill Hardekopf, CEO, SaveOnPhone.com, a phone service comparison Web site, Birmingham, AL.

*All prices subject to change.

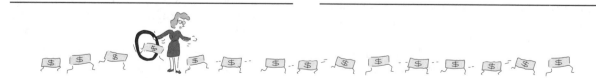

Save 75% on Home Energy Bills

William Browning, founder of the Rocky Mountain Institute's Green Development Services, a consulting group that helps to engineer energy efficiency. The White House and the Sydney Olympic Village are among its clients. He has coauthored two books, including *A Primer on Sustainable Building* (Rocky Mountain Institute).

Americans could be saving a full three-quarters of the $150 billion they spend on energy each year.

Best ways to save money without spending a fortune...

●**Upgrade to modern super windows.** Super windows, filled with argon or krypton gas and covered with a special film, are up to 12 times more efficient than regular windows. Yet they still look like normal glass.

These windows, which are widely available, buffer noise and prevent ultraviolet light from fading carpets, upholstery, drapes and artwork. They also cut down on drafts caused by ordinary windows.

Example: A window rated R-7 or better—meaning that the window has seven times the insulating value of a single pane of glass—will gain more heat in the winter than it loses, even when it faces north in Buffalo.

Specialists can suggest windows with properties that are appropriate for your climate. Look in your *Yellow Pages* under "Windows."

Cost: 15% to 50% more than the standard double-pane windows. However, they can pay for themselves in less than a decade, and some utility companies offer rebates.

Average price for a standard-sized super window: $150.

●**Install heat barriers.** In hotter climates, a radiant barrier placed above the attic insulation can decrease cooling costs by up to 15%. This plastic film has an aluminum coating on one side that reflects heat from the sun and can save up to $30 a year.

Cost: 10 cents to 45 cents per square foot installed. A heat barrier pays for itself in as little as 10 years in average Sun Belt homes, but it is rarely cost-effective in the north.

●**Repair the heating/cooling systems.** Air escaping from ducts can reduce heating, ventilation and air-conditioning (HVAC) efficiency by up to 20%. Sealing the seams can save $260 of a typical household's annual $1,300 energy bill.

Hire an HVAC contractor to seal your ducts for $500 to $900. Or do it yourself if the ducts are accessible in the attic or crawl space. Check your ducts every 10 years. Use mastic, a high-strength adhesive that is applied with a trowel or brush.

Cost: $10 to $15 per gallon. A typical house might require five gallons. Mastic is available at home-improvement stores and heating-supply wholesalers.

Beware: Duct tape, despite its name, does not effectively seal ducts. Over time, it dries out and loses its seal.

Helpful: Replacing your HVAC system's filter every six months can increase efficiency—saving up to $20 a year.

●**Repair caulking and weather stripping.** Every year, about $13 billion worth of energy escapes through holes and cracks in heated and air-conditioned US homes. A one-eighth-inch gap under a door is the equivalent of a two-inch-square hole in a wall.

Plugging the air leaks around windows and doors reduces heating/cooling bills by as much as 30%—or up to $400 a year on the average home. The job should take less than 10 minutes per door or window. Check for new leaks every five years.

Cost: Less than $5 per window and $10 per door in materials.

●**Block conduits.** As part of your weatherization project, install rubber gaskets behind electrical outlets to prevent hot and cold air from escaping.

Cost: Less than $1 per gasket, available in home-improvement and hardware stores.

●**Fill insulation gaps.** As homes age, insulation settles and sags, creating gaps behind walls and in attics. You can locate these gaps with infrared cameras, often loaned out by utility companies. Some utilities also will perform a free energy audit for you.

Cans of expanding foam insulation are available for about $5 each and pay for themselves in just a few months. If you can't reach the problem area easily, call a professional. Sometimes he/she has to inject insulating foam inside your walls.

●**Insulate your water heater.** This saves about $40 a year if you have an electric water heater…$15 a year for a gas one.

Cost: About $20 for a tank wrap. Call your energy provider for details.

BUILDING IN ENERGY EFFICIENCY

More energy-saving opportunities are cost effective when you build or buy a house…

●**Select a smart design.** The shape and orientation of your house can cut heating/cooling costs by 30%.

In the cold regions, the longest sides of the home should run east-west to increase exposure to the sun in the south. Buildings in hot climates should be long and run perpendicular to the prevailing winds to increase ventilation.

●**Build with generous insulation.** I suggest twice the insulation factor that is required by code. One way to do this is by using structural insulated panels (SIPs). The panels consist of a layer of insulation that's sandwiched between two layers of strand board. They can save 40% to 60% in heating/cooling costs.

Homes built with SIP walls are sturdier than most timber-frame houses. The energy savings can pay for the additional 10% in construction costs within 10 years—less in extreme climates. In addition, the initial cost can be offset because you will need a much smaller furnace.

●**Don't be impressed by the phrase "built to code."** Code is only the minimum standard allowed by law. If a builder says a home's insulation "meets code," he/she is saying that if it was any worse, it would be illegal.

Instead, ask how the house compares with federal Energy Star guidelines or if there is a state energy rating system. Click on "Improve the Efficiency of Your Home" at *www.energy star.gov* to compare your house with the Energy Star criteria.

●**Look for Energy Star–certified homes to save 30% on energy.** This government energy program evaluates the energy efficiency of appliances and will certify houses when builders or developers request the service. Such homes use about 30% less energy, a savings of about $400 a year in an average house. They don't cost any more than typical houses, but they use insulation, insulated windows, architectural layout and other techniques to achieve the savings.

Bonus: Reduced mortgage rates and fees are available from some lenders for these homes. For more information, click on the "Find Local Home Builders" section of Energy Star's Web site, *www.energystar.gov.*

●**Consider your commute.** Even the most energy-efficient home won't reduce your total energy bill if it's miles from your work, favorite stores and entertainment. Money saved on electricity and heating will be spent on gasoline.

Example: If a couple adds 25 miles each way to both of their daily commutes, they add approximately $1,800 to their yearly gasoline bill, assuming their vehicles get 25 miles per gallon and gasoline costs $1.75 per gallon. That is more than the average family spends on home energy in a year.

Best: Live near your job and in a town that is conducive to walking.

Save Money on Heating Your Water

When water sits in hot-water lines, it turns cold. Then, to get hot water, you need to first run the cold water out of the faucet. This wastes energy and water.

New saver: The Autocirc pump senses when water in the hot-water line cools to "warm" and recirculates it to the water heater, pulling new hot water into the hot-water line.

Results: Hot water is available at all times… water heating costs are cut because the heater heats warm rather than cold water…water is not wasted.

Savings: For the average family, the savings will be approximately 15,000 gallons of water and up to $400 off utility bills annually.

Cost: About $350.

More information: Visit *www.autocirc.com*. *The Family Handyman*, 2915 Commers Dr., Eagan, MN 55121, *www.familyhandyman.com*.

How to Be a Savvy Medical Consumer

Charles B. Inlander, health-care consultant and president of the nonprofit People's Medical Society, a consumer health advocacy group in Allentown, PA. He is the author of more than 20 books on consumer health issues, including *Take This Book to the Hospital with You: A Consumer Guide to Surviving Your Hospital Stay* (St. Martin's).

For more than 30 years, I have been helping consumers to help themselves when dealing with the maze that is the American health-care system. If there is one thing I have learned, it is that the savviest medical consumer generally gets the best care.

But being savvy is not always so easy. Although many medical providers work hard to keep their patients informed, others fall short. For example, very few doctors advise men who are scheduled to have a prostate-specific antigen (PSA) test that they should not ejaculate during the four days prior to the test. It has been standard medical knowledge for more than a decade that this can lead to a false positive PSA test result. Studies also show that up to half the time, pharmacies are not distributing literature about the drug being dispensed, even though this is required by law. And most patients report getting little or no information about how to care for their condition when they are discharged from a hospital, even though they should be receiving it.

Here's some advice...

•**Speak up.** Whether you are dealing with a doctor, hospital or pharmacy, ask questions. Remember, you are the customer. You need to make the decisions. And you have the right to an answer. If it's not your style to ask questions —or you're too sick—then bring along a family member or a friend who can speak for you. Courts throughout the country have upheld your right to have someone of your choice with you in an examining room or at the hospital.

•**Be your own medical researcher.** Several years ago, a prestigious medical center told a Midwestern couple that their son had an inoperable growth on his brain and had just a few months to live. When the family called me to find out what they could do, I advised them to get on the phone, the Internet and into the library to learn as much as possible about their son's condition. Within a few days, they discovered a surgeon in New York City who routinely operated on children with this condition. They took the boy to see him and within a week the growth had been removed. That young man has been healthy ever since. Web sites, such as *www.webmd.com* or *www.healthcentral.com*, are good resources. Reference books published by the American Medical Association, Harvard Medical School or the Mayo Clinic are also helpful to own.

•**Take nothing for granted.** As intelligent as your physician may be, he/she cannot know everything. That's why it's so important to obtain second or even third opinions for a serious diagnosis or invasive treatment. Studies show that up to 20% of all diagnostic second opinions do not confirm the first opinion.

Serving as your own health-care advocate requires effort, but it always pays.

More from Charles Inlander...

Avoid Being Taken by Medical Billing Errors

In 1982, when our daughter was just born, I discovered that our $3,000 hospital bill contained $1,000 worth of errors. After weeks of making calls and threats, my insurer received a refund. But, sadly, not much has changed when it comes to medical billing. Several studies have found that more than 90% of all hospital bills have errors in them, as do a large percentage of physicians' bills.

Many people who discover errors let them go because insurance companies, Medicare or Medicaid pay most medical bills. That's a costly mistake. If you pay a copayment or deductible, your out-of-pocket costs are higher if there is an error. Plus, unfixed billing errors contribute to higher insurance premiums the next year.

Here is how to make sure your medical bills are accurate...

●**Insist on itemized bills.** Many hospitals, clinics and medical practices send out bills that lump services into broad categories, such as "pharmacy" or "medical equipment." That's not good enough. You should receive an itemized bill, listing each specific charge. Look for questionable items, such as the same medication given more than two or three times a day or charges for doctors you neither saw nor authorized. Don't be afraid to challenge anything that looks wrong. Ask the billing office to show you a written order from the doctor or the nurse's record of the service or care.

●**Keep a log.** It's often hard to remember exactly what happened at a doctor's visit or a hospital stay. That's why it is a good idea to keep a written log of the services you received. Jot down who treated you and what service was administered. A woman once showed me a bill that claimed blood was drawn from her six times on each of the eight days she was hospitalized. She knew blood was only taken once a day because she wrote everything down. She knocked more than $1,800 off her bill!

●**Use your doctor as an ally.** If you see something fishy on the bill, call your doctor. A friend of mine did this when he was charged for a series of outpatient lab tests that he didn't remember receiving. His doctor looked into it and found that his lab tests had been mixed up with another patient's at the lab's billing office.

●**Take action.** If you discover a questionable charge, call the hospital or the office where the error occurred. If you are not satisfied with their response or they are taking too long, call your insurance company and ask for the "fraud division." You'll get faster service and attention. If they do not act, contact your state's attorney general's office and ask them to intervene. If you are covered under Medicare, call 1-800-MEDICARE (633-4227) to report the problem. The federal government has become extremely aggressive in recent years about billing errors.

With more than $1.3 trillion being spent on medical care each year, billing errors are bound to occur. But the numbers can be drastically reduced if we all carefully review and report the errors we find.

Better Drugstores

Independent drugstores are more likely than big drugstore chains to have fast service and helpful pharmacists. Supermarket pharmacies and ones at mass merchants, like Target and Wal-Mart, also may be better.

Surprising: Drugstore chains' prices were found to be the highest. The on-line pharmacies cost least, followed by mass merchants, supermarkets and independent pharmacies.

Reader survey conducted by *Consumer Reports* at 101 Truman Ave., Yonkers, NY 10703.

Sorting Through The Medicare Drug-Discount Cards

Jim Miller, editor of *Savvy Senior,* a syndicated newspaper question-and-answer column for senior citizens, Norman, OK, *www.savvysenior.org.* He is author of *The Savvy Senior: The Ultimate Guide to Health, Family and Fitness for Senior Citizens* (Hyperion).

More than 100 companies are now selling some version of Medicare's new drug-discount card. Pharmacies currently are accepting these cards, which offer savings of 10% to 25% (depending on the drug). They are available until 2006, at which time Medicare's Part D prescription drug benefit will take effect and the cards will no longer be necessary.

Here's what you need to know...

●**You can get only one Medicare-endorsed drug-discount card.** There is no enrollment deadline for 2004, but you pay the full fee no matter when you sign up.

Cost: Up to $30*/year.

●**Different companies' cards cover a different array of prescription drugs.**

●**Discounts can change each week**—but once you sign up, you can't switch cards until next year's enrollment (November 15 through December 31, 2004).

●**Your pharmacy might not accept all cards.** Check before you choose.

Helpful: Medicare's Web site at *www.medicare.gov* offers a drug-discount card comparison tool. And, the State Health Insurance Counseling Program offers free counseling on selecting your card. To sign up for a card, contact Medicare at 800-633-4227 or visit your local office. Links are at *www.medicare.gov/contacts/related/ships.asp.*

OTHER PRESCRIPTION OPTIONS

You might save as much or more by buying from mail-order pharmacies and using existing drug-manufacturer discount cards. See the following article.

*Free for seniors with annual gross incomes of $12,569 or less and couples with combined incomes of $16,862 or less.

Best Ways to Slash Prescription Drug Costs

Gary Nave, director, Cost Containment Research Institute, a consumer advocate organization, 4200 Wisconsin Ave. NW, Washington, DC 20016.

Perhaps you know one of the 43 million Americans who have no health insurance. Or perhaps you know a couple who do have insurance but have little or no coverage for prescription drugs.

Seniors, among others, are stuck paying full price for the medicines they require. *There are, however, some ways to cut drug costs...*

GOVERNMENT PLANS

You may qualify for a state drug-assistance program. More than half the states have prescription plans for the elderly, disabled and Medicare recipients. Review your state's plan at *www.rxassist.org/pdfs/state_programs.pdf.*

Example: New York's Elderly Pharmaceutical Insurance Coverage (EPIC) allows residents who are age 65 or older and have an annual income of $20,000 or less if single ($26,000 or less if married) to pay a modest fee quarterly for low-cost drug coverage. Higher-income seniors are required to meet a modest deductible and then pay a small copayment on their prescriptions. *Savings:* 50%.

Note: All honorably discharged veterans who use Veterans Administration medical facilities pay only $7* for most prescriptions. The savings vary according to the prescription. For information, contact the Department of Veterans Affairs at 800-827-1000 or *www.va.gov.*

MANUFACTURER AND PHARMACY PROGRAMS

●**Free drug programs.** More than 100 manufacturers offer programs covering more than 1,400 drugs. These rarely publicized programs give away an estimated $2 billion of medication annually.

Requirements vary by company. Generally, a person qualifies if he/she has no insurance providing prescription coverage, doesn't qualify for Medicaid and has an income of less than $50,000 per family a year.

A complete list of these programs is available from the Cost Containment Research Institute. The cost is $6 for a printed copy and $4.95 for an on-line copy.

To order: *www.institutedc.org* or Institute Fulfillment Center, Box 210, "Free and Low Cost Prescription Drugs," Dallas, PA 18612-0210.

For more information, visit *www.needymeds.com* and *www.themedicineprogram.com.*

●**Free drug-discount cards.** Advance PCS (800-238-2623) offers a free discount card covering all drugs dispensed at participating pharmacies. Anyone is eligible.

Savings: 13% to 25%.

For a complete list of drug discount card programs, contact the Medicare Rights Center at *www.medicarerights.org.*

Five pharmaceutical manufacturers have drug discount cards...

●GlaxoSmithKline/Orange Card (888-672-6436, *www.gsk.com*).

*All prices subject to change.

●Eli Lilly/LillyAnswers Card (877-795-4559, *www.lillyanswers.com*).

●Novartis/Together RX Card (800-865-7211, *www.together-rx.com*).

Information is available through Volunteers in Health Care at *www.rxassist.org*. The programs cover hundreds of medications, but savings vary according to medication. All programs require applicants to be Medicare recipients who have no other prescription coverage.

DOCTOR-PROVIDED ASSISTANCE

●**Ask your doctor for a generic drug.** By using a generic instead of its brand-name counterpart, you can save up to 93%. Most generics have the same active ingredients, are the same in strength and dosage and meet the same government quality-control standards.

Caution: Some generic drugs are not exactly the same as the brand-name drug. Check with your doctor.

●**Ask your doctor for an older medication.** He might automatically prescribe a new drug that is being heavily promoted (and is considerably more expensive). Ask if an older drug will work just as well—and obtain the generic, if possible.

●**Ask your doctor for free samples at every visit.** Always get samples of any new medication your doctor prescribes before filling a costly prescription. That way, you'll find out if you can tolerate it and whether it does what it's supposed to do—free.

YOUR OWN COST SAVINGS—
EIGHT PRACTICAL TIPS

●**Stop using drugs you no longer need.** Review all prescriptions with your doctor at each visit. You may be wasting your money on drugs you no longer need.

●**Use a pill splitter.** Several medications are priced the same for all strengths (for example, Lipitor). Ask your doctor to prescribe the medication in double dosages.

Example: If you usually take a 20 milligram (mg) pill, ask for a prescription for 40 mg pills. Use a pill splitter—available at drug stores—to cut the pill in half. *Savings:* 50%.

Caution: This method is inappropriate for certain medications. Check with your doctor.

●**Buy a 90-day supply.** If you have prescription drug coverage, you may be able to purchase a 90-day supply if you order through the mail. This cuts your copayment to one-third of what you would have paid for three of the usual 30-day supplies. Even if you do not have drug coverage, a larger supply may be less expensive than smaller monthly supplies.

●**Get only a seven-day supply of any new medication.** If your doctor doesn't have samples, ask for a prescription limited to a week so you can try it out. Federal law prohibits returning unused medications once dispensed.

●**Use over-the-counter drugs.** In some cases, they are just as effective as prescription drugs but they can be had for only a fraction of the cost. Ask your physician. One $2 over-the-counter cold medication contains the very same decongestant properties as a prescription medication that costs up to $60.

●**Comparison shop.** Ask about costs at different drugstores in your area. Have the name of your medication, pill count and dosage in milligrams with you.

Saving strategy: If you obtain a lower price at a pharmacy that is across town, give your local druggist a chance to match it. Both Wal-Mart and Kmart have said they'll match the lowest price in the area. And, RiteAid will match the lowest price for uninsured customers.

●**Get drugs by mail.** Some Internet pharmacies offer 60% off prescription drugs—though some charge an annual fee.

Caution: Look for Web sites with the VIPPS seal, which means it's a Verified Internet Pharmacy Practice Site that adheres to pharmacy standards. Avoid any site that offers to dispense prescription medication without requiring a prescription. Some good Web sites—*www.accurate pharmacy.com, www.clickpharmacy.com, www. drugstore.com.*

●**Cross the border.** If you live near Canada or Mexico, you can buy there and save 75% off US prices. It is also possible to order over the Internet. Cross Border Pharmacy.com at *www. crossborderpharmacy.com* and Affordable RX at *www.affordablerx.com/ccri.html* both let you compare prices.

Technically, purchasing drugs from another country violates federal law, but the FDA looks the other way as long as no more than a three-month supply is involved. The US Customs Service, however, has warned against the danger of buying any counterfeit drugs or those that are unapproved, unsafe or ineffective.

Best: If you plan to order outside the US, opt for Canada rather than Mexico. Canada's drug regulations and testing systems are comparable to those in the US.

Bad news: GlaxoSmithKline has stopped providing its drugs to Canadian Internet pharmacies and wholesalers unless they promise not to export to US citizens. Other drugmakers may follow this practice. If so, access to drugs from Canada would eventually stop.

Personalized Report Cuts Prescription Costs

If you're age 55 or older, you can now get a personalized report on programs you qualify for that can help you reduce your prescription drug costs. The National Council on the Aging has created a new Web site that will provide the report directly to you.

How it works: You just enter your personal information and more than 1,200 programs in all 50 states are searched through to find benefits that you qualify for. More than 1,450 brand-name and generic medications are included. Visit *www.benefitscheckup.org*.

Custom-Fitted Clothes at Off-the-Rack Prices

Custom-fitted clothing is available on-line for only a little more than off-the-rack clothes. Lands' End, at *www.landsend.com*, started the

service, which now makes up 30% of its sales of jeans and chinos. Check on-line for others.

Robert Holloway, CEO of Archetype Solutions, developer of the software used by on-line retailers for custom-made clothing, Emeryville, CA.

No Need to Spend a Lot on Running Shoes

A recent study of persons who buy running shoes found that while most people willingly pay high prices for them, the buyers of expensive shoes suffer just as many injuries as those of cheap shoes. More than 70% of buyers spent more than $80 for their running shoes—but there was no significant difference in the incidence of injury between those who paid $20 for shoes and those who paid $120.

Conclusion: Proper fit and comfort are what's important in a running shoe, not price.

Nancy Kadel, MD, assistant professor, Orthopaedics & Sports Medicine, University of Washington, Seattle.

Sofa Smarts

Jackie Hirschhaut, vice president, American Furniture Manufacturers Association, High Point, NC.

To test the quality and comfort of a sofa you are considering, follow this advice from the American Furniture Manufacturers Association...

●**Lift the frame**—it should feel heavy and sturdy.

●**Pull firmly on an arm**—it should not move or creak.

●**Sit at one end, then have someone else sit at the other end**—you should not sense any impact.

●**Sit or curl up as you would at home** to be sure you feel comfortable.

●**To test fabric**—vigorously rub the edge of your fingernail along the swatch—reject it if the pile begins to wear or color starts to fade.

- **Try to snag a thread with a fingernail,** if the fabric has raised weave or texture. If you can snag a thread, reject the sofa.

- **Avoid fabrics so thin that you can see through them** when you hold a swatch up to the light.

seal is not tight. Vacuums that use cyclone filtration instead of bags keep the suction constant and remove more dirt. Most cyclone vacuums have lifetime HEPA filters that can be rinsed and reused. Finally, look for a hose at least 12 feet long to make cleaning stairways easier.

Tom Gasko, owner, Vac Shac, Festus, MO.

Best Type of Mattress for A Bad Back

Although doctors usually recommend firm mattresses for their patients with bad backs, new research shows that back pain in people who slept on medium-firm mattresses was twice as likely to improve than in those who slept on firm mattresses.

However: Because there's no standard measurement in the US for determining a mattress' firmness, you should always test out a mattress before buying it to ensure that it is comfortable for you.

Self-defense: Shop for a mattress at a store with display models that you can try out. Some stores even offer a three-month trial period.

Francisco M. Kovacs, MD, PhD, director of the scientific department, Kovacs Foundation, a nonprofit institution dedicated to the clinical management of back pain, Palma de Mallorca, Spain.

Better Vacuum Cleaner Buying

When purchasing a vacuum cleaner, focus on airflow, not motor power. Airflow is measured in cubic feet per meter (CFM). Look for at least 100 CFM for heavy-duty cleaning. Also, choose a vacuum with a high-energy particulate air (HEPA) filter. These remove 99.9% of dust particles but work only if properly sealed. Test the seal by turning on the vacuum in a dark area and shining a flashlight onto it. If you see dust particles swirling out of the vacuum, the

How to Get the Best Prices for Tires

If you know what tires you want, go to the Web sites such as *www.tirerack.com* or *www. tires.com* to find a low price for tires delivered to a garage near you. But before placing your order, phone local garages and give them a chance to meet the on-line price. Even if they do not, they may give you free mounting and balancing or other services that could more than make up the price difference.

Jennifer Stockburger, auto and tire test engineer, Consumer Reports, 101 Truman Ave., Yonkers, NY 10703.

Best Time to Buy Electronics

Retailers clear out inventory to make room for newly upgraded electronics equipment in January and June. Prices of older models typically fall by 10% or more.

Caution: Before buying, find out what new features are about to come to market. If they are ones you care about, purchasing an older model may not be a bargain after all.

Money, Time-Life Bldg., Rockefeller Center, New York City 10020.

How to Save on Big-Ticket Items

Always ask for discounts on big-ticket items, including appliances, electronics and high-end clothing. Research an item on-line so you know the fair price, then go to a local store and negotiate for at least 10% to 15% off that price. Don't *demand* a lower price—ask nicely if one is possible. This works best at stores where you shop regularly and know the salespeople and managers. Also, offer to pay cash in return for a discount.

At the very least, find out when an item will be going on sale. Be prepared to leave if you don't get the price you want. The manager may make an offer as you head for the door.

Gerri Detweiler, credit specialist in Sarasota, FL, and author of Invest in Yourself: Six Secrets to a Rich Life *(Wiley).*

More from Gerri Detweiler...

Watch Out for Department Store Come-Ons

Beware of department store credit card offers that give you 20% off your first purchase. If you do not pay off your balance quickly, you'll end up spending far more than you save. Store credit cards carry an average interest rate of 19.8%—much higher than major credit cards, whose rates average 14%. If you make the minimum payment, the interest alone can cost you more than the original price of the item—even with your 20% savings.

Example: As a new cardholder, you save $500 on a $2,500 couch. By paying the minimum amount each month (around $40)—it will take you almost nine years to pay off your debt and cost you $2,260 in interest. Increase the monthly payment to $75, and you'll pay it off in three years but still fork over $657 in interest.

Best: Take advantage of the 20% savings, but pay off the entire amount immediately or transfer the balance to a low-interest major credit card before the introductory period expires.

Is Shipping Insurance Worth the Cost?

Don't buy shipping insurance when sending a small gift through the US Postal Service. Though insurance costs only a few dollars, the Post Office rarely loses or damages items, so insurance is unnecessary on packages that are worth less than $100.

Eric Tyson, MBA, Weston, CT–based financial counselor and syndicated columnist. He is the author of Investing for Dummies *(Wiley).*

Save Time At the Doctor, Stores, Restaurants, More

Barbara Myers, owner of The Time Manager, Newark, OH, which offers personal organizing assistance and workshops for several hundred clients in the Midwest. She has written 10 organizing guides, including "200 Ways to Save Time at the Office" (available at www.ineedmoretime.com*).*

Waiting for service eats up hours of our time every week. *Here is how you can save at least one hour a day...*

● **Have groceries brought to you** rather than going to get them. Some major supermarkets allow you to shop on-line and will deliver.

Examples: Stop & Shop, *www.peapod. com* (Chicago, East Coast)...Safeway, *www. safeway.com* (West Coast). Local markets may also offer delivery—ask your grocer.

● **Run errands when they're most convenient...**not when they become urgent. That way, you can avoid long lines.

● **Share errands with a close neighbor.** See if either of you can save the other a trip.

● **Buy in bulk to save time and money.** This works especially well for common items you often run out of, such as stamps, greeting cards, wrapping paper, soap, paper products, lightbulbs, etc.

DOCTOR/DENTIST APPOINTMENTS

•**Be the first appointment in the morning...**or the first one after lunch, when you are less likely to have to wait.

•**Make follow-up appointments before you leave**—even if your next visit isn't for six months. You'll have your pick of the schedule, and you won't waste any time calling for an appointment and negotiating the best opening.

•**Call before leaving for any appointment** to see if the doctor is running behind schedule.

SUPERMARKET

•**Shop on Tuesdays and Wednesdays.** Midmorning and late evening are best.

•**Turn the bar codes on items toward the cashier** as you are checking out.

RESTAURANTS

•**Make reservations.** It seems obvious, but those people standing in line didn't plan ahead.

•**Ask for the check at the same time you order your last item.** Pay the bill, and then sit as long as you want.

POST OFFICE

•**Order stamps, shipping containers and more from the US Postal Service's Web site,** *http://shop.usps.com.* Delivery is within three to five days for a $1* fee. Otherwise, midmorning or early afternoon in the middle of the week is when the post office is least crowded. Stamps also may be purchased at local drugstores, grocery stores and banks. To find locations nearest to you, log on to *www.usps.com/buy/waystobuy stamps/welcome.htm.*

DELIVERIES AND REPAIRMEN

•**Bunch appointments.** It's unlikely that everyone will show up on time. Even if they do, it usually is manageable.

•**Turn waiting time into found time.** Keep a list of small tasks around the house that need to be done.

My favorites: Go through the medicine cabinet to toss out expired drugs...straighten up a room and clear out items that I no longer want.

MAKE THE MOST OF WAITING

Sometimes you have no choice but to wait in line or for an appointment. I always carry a

*All prices subject to change.

small bundle of necessary tasks for those times. It includes bills to pay and my checkbook... thank-you cards to write...articles I never seem to get to read...as well as a mail-order catalog or two to browse through.

Best Times to Do Things

Shop for groceries early in the morning, or at night while most people are watching prime-time TV shows. And, try to purchase a house from mid-November through mid-January, when prices stabilize or drop in most areas. Go to the department of motor vehicles the day before a holiday, when most people are shopping. Paint your home in autumn, or whenever your area has mild weather and low rainfall. Finally, try to remodel your bathroom in winter, when contractors are less busy.

Lisa Goff, freelance writer, *Good Housekeeping*, 959 Eighth Ave., New York City 10019.

Get Free Government Newsletters by E-Mail

Government newsletters on a wide range of subjects are available on the Internet.

Examples: Health and medicine, business, travel, housing, safety and consumer protection, military affairs, Social Security and much more.

Requested newsletters will be sent directly to your e-mail address. For a complete list of what is available, log on to the government's Internet portal, FirstGov, at *www.firstgov.gov.* Just click on the site map, then scroll down to "Reference Center." "Free e-Mail Newsletters" is under the heading "Publications."

12

Retirement Guide

Stop Uncle Sam From Stealing Your Retirement Dollars

From the moment you make your first deposit in a traditional IRA or 401(k), you are building up a savings account —*for the IRS.*

Uncle Sam eventually gets a big chunk of your money. All withdrawals are taxable and at ordinary income tax rates of as high as 35%, not at the lower capital gains rate. If your retirement accounts and other assets grow to more than $1.5 million in 2004, your heirs will owe estate tax on traditional and Roth IRAs upon your death. *Five ways to protect your nest egg...*

USE ROTH IRAs

This is Uncle Sam's greatest gift to retirement savings. Yet six years after the Roth's debut, relatively few people have taken advantage of it. Roth IRAs give no up-front tax deduction, but your money grows tax free. And, Roth IRA

beneficiaries do not owe income tax on the distributions. A beneficiary can "stretch" the benefit, leaving the money to continue growing tax free over his/her life.

What to do...

• **If you're planning to open a new IRA, make it a Roth.** Your adjusted gross income (AGI) must be less than $110,000 (single) or $160,000 (married filing jointly).

• **Convert a traditional IRA to a Roth.** In this case, your AGI must not exceed $100,000, whether you are single or married filing jointly. You will have to pay tax on gains on the traditional IRA. Ask the financial institution that handles your IRA what your tax liability will be. If bear market losses have reduced the value of your IRA, you will owe less tax.

You can't roll over money from a 401(k) directly to a Roth. You must first roll it into a traditional IRA and then convert that to a Roth.

Ed Slott, CPA, a nationally recognized IRA expert, 100 Merrick Rd., Rockville Centre, NY 11570. He is editor of Ed Slott's IRA Advisor. *His Web site is www.irahelp.com.*

203

Ask your tax adviser for instructions on rollovers and conversions.

Loophole: Your AGI only has to fall below $100,000 for one year to qualify for conversion. If your income is a few thousand dollars more than $100,000, shift some income to the following year and/or sell stocks to take capital losses in taxable accounts. Losses also might put you in a lower bracket and reduce tax on the conversion.

Trap: Anyone who is married but files a separate return cannot convert a traditional IRA to a Roth regardless of income.

HELP FUTURE GENERATIONS DODGE TAXES

When your 401(k) or IRA assets pass to heirs, they in turn can stretch the tax shelter over their lives. *Examples...*

Example 1: A husband leaves an IRA to his wife. She names their children as her beneficiaries. After her death, her children can then get tax-free compounding on the amount that's remaining. In this manner, tax deferral could go on for generations.

Example 2: Your daughter is 40 when she inherits your traditional IRA. According to IRS tables, a 40-year-old has a life expectancy of another 43.6 years, but she must begin taking required minimum distributions (RMDs) in the year after the year of the IRA owner's death.

WATCH OUT FOR WITHDRAWAL PENALTIES

Uncle Sam's 10% early withdrawal penalty applies to both Roth and traditional IRA withdrawals made before age 59½.

There is a 50% penalty when you neglect to take RMDs on traditional IRAs. If your RMD is $20,000 and you miss the deadline, your penalty is $10,000. *What to do...*

●**Traditional IRAs.** Start taking RMDs by April 1 of the year after you turn 70½. The percentage you must withdraw each year is determined by the IRS from life expectancy tables. For more information, call 800-829-1040, or go to *www.irs.gov* or *www.irahelp.com.*

●**Roth IRAs.** There are no required distributions for Roth IRA owners.

Loophole: You can withdraw money without penalty from any IRA before age 59½ using one of three IRS formulas. But watch out—if you start spending your nest egg early, you might not have enough savings for retirement.

LET LIFE INSURANCE PAY YOUR TAXES

Employer-sponsored retirement plans, such as 401(k)s, and traditional and Roth IRAs count toward your estate, so purchase insurance to pay the estate tax. Estate tax in 2004 is as high as 48% for estates of more than $1.5 million. The income tax on distributions from traditional IRAs can be as high as 35%.

While the estate tax is supposed to vanish in 2010, it is scheduled to come back in 2011. Base your planning on the tax as it is today, affecting estates that are bigger than $1.5 million. If there is no estate tax, your heirs will get to keep the payout.

What to do: Assume that estate tax will be 50% of the value of assets—cars, homes, retirement plans, other investments, etc. Purchase enough life insurance to allow for this potential tax. At your death, insurance proceeds are free from income tax.

Important: Create a life insurance trust to own the policy so that the value is kept out of your estate. You can name beneficiaries—your spouse or children—as trustees. Make annual gifts to beneficiaries, which they should use to pay the insurance premiums. You will not owe any gift tax if the payments are no more than $11,000 per recipient per year ($22,000 if given by a couple). For information, consult with an experienced trust attorney.

PROVIDE FOR BENEFICIARIES NOW

Whether you have a traditional or Roth IRA, you must name your beneficiary on a retirement plan beneficiary form, which takes legal precedence over your will.

If you don't take the right steps, a lengthy and expensive probate court process will determine who inherits your IRA.

Update beneficiary forms whenever there is a marriage or divorce, new child or grandchild or other change that would affect your beneficiary choice. Keep beneficiary forms filed with other important papers as well as with your attorney and tax adviser. Then they can be located readily by family members and the executor of your will upon your death.

Your Pension Is in Peril

Michael Clowes, editorial director of *Pensions & Investments,* 711 Third Ave., New York City 10017. He is author of *The Money Flood: How Pension Funds Revolutionized Investing* (Wiley).

Millions of people are relying on company pensions to provide funds for retirement. Yet mergers and corporate failures have wiped out thousands of pensions. Also, the Bush administration is encouraging a new variety of pension—a cash-balance plan—which could result in lower benefits for many workers, especially those ages 45 to 55.

Michael Clowes, who has followed pensions since the early 1970s, answers some questions…

● **How serious is this crisis?** It is acute among traditional pensions, known as defined-benefit (DB) plans. Unlike 401(k)s, these plans guarantee a specific monthly benefit at retirement. Employers contribute all the money and make the investments.

The crisis was beginning before the bull market, but its severity was masked by abnormally high investment returns during that period. In the past three years, most funds *lost* money, making the crisis highly visible. We've gone from 165,000 DB plans in 1985 to 40,000 today. Most surviving plans have insufficient assets to cover benefits. If a plan can't pay, the federal government's Pension Benefit Guaranty Corporation (PBGC) takes over—but it pays a maximum of only $44,386 per individual per year.

● **Are the 401(k) plans in trouble, as well?** The defined-*contribution* plans, such as 401(k)s, have gone down in value due to the bear market, but I don't know any 401(k) plan in danger of collapse.

● **How can I tell if my pension is in trouble?** The summary plan description, which your employer must send to you each year, includes a brief statement of assets and liabilities (benefits). If it doesn't, check the pension footnote in your company's annual report. If assets are less than 80% of liabilities, the plan is at risk. If you work for a private company, ask for a copy of Form 5500, the plan's annual report, prepared for the US Department of Labor and the Internal Revenue Service (IRS).

● **Where can I find the plan's investment results?** Companies do not have to disclose them, and they seldom do. That said, you might be able to find the interest rate assumption—the long-term return that the company assumes it will earn on plan assets. Often, you'll find it in the pension footnote of the annual report.

The higher the expected return, the less the employer needs to contribute to the plan. In the 1990s, when the stock market was soaring and the largest plans had an average of 61.4% in stocks, interest rate assumptions were as high as 11%. Now employers must reduce assumptions because of the recent down market. A more reasonable rate, given today's market conditions, is around 7%.

● **What happens if the PBGC takes over my company pension?** You are likely to be hurt only if your pension normally would be above the $44,386 level the PBGC guarantees. Other limitations may apply.

● **What happens if a company terminates its pension plan?** The employer still would be responsible for all pension benefits. If necessary, the PBGC would put a lien on the company's assets to satisfy pension claims.

There is concern about the PBGC itself being in some financial danger. Even so, nobody believes the federal government would allow the PBGC to default on its obligations.

● **What if I'm drawing a pension and my former employer folds?** At most companies, a retiree's pension benefit is used to purchase an annuity from an insurance company. That annuity pays the pension.

Some companies offer employees the option to take a lump sum when they leave. Do not just automatically choose this alternative—even when you are worried about your employer's financial condition. Few people have the skills to manage a windfall. Besides, once your pension has been annuitized, it is the insurance company's obligation to pay it—not your employer's.

● **Can I pull my money from the plan and invest it somewhere else?** Not until you are vested—meaning that you have earned a legal right to at least part of your pension—

and you leave the employer or retire. Even in those cases, many employers don't permit you to take the money as a lump sum.

●**Can you explain vesting?** The company can vest you in stages, from your third through seventh year as an employee in the plan. Or it can choose to use "cliff vesting," in which all of your assets belong to you after five years. Either way, legally you must be fully vested no later than your seventh year.

If you were fully or partially vested in any pension on your retirement date—even from a job you left decades ago—be sure to notify the former employer so that it can arrange for benefit payments.

●**I hear scary things about cash-balance plans. What's the fuss?** While the traditional pensions base benefits on salary throughout an employee's last five or 10 years of employment, cash-balance plans will base the benefits on the employee's average salary during his/her tenure with the company. What most employees might lose in pension benefits would be offset by the fact that cash-balance plans are portable. That means employees can take the vested portions of cash-balance plans with them whenever they change jobs. As with a 401(k), the money could be rolled into the new employer's pension plan or an IRA.

The controversy involves how benefits are calculated.

While those within 10 years of retirement usually are grandfathered into the old plan, those employees ages 45 to 55 are at risk of losing out on substantial future income in the transition to cash-balance plans.

The question of whether cash-balance plans discriminate against middle-aged employees has prevented many companies from using them. Recently, the US Treasury and the IRS made a preliminary ruling that these plans don't discriminate. A final ruling is likely before year-end.

●**What can I do to protect myself if my employer chooses a cash-balance plan?** Encourage your human resources department to adopt a transition formula that allows you to keep all or most of your promised benefit. Since a prominent lawsuit over IBM's cash-balance plan, companies are more open to complaints.

Helpful: To calculate how your own pension would fare under a cash-balance plan, log on to the SmartMoney Web site at *http://university. smartmoney.com/departments/retirement401k/ cashbalanceplans.*

Four Ways to Rebuild Your Retirement Nest Egg

Jonathan Clements, personal-finance columnist for *The Wall Street Journal.* Based in Metuchen, NJ, he is author of *You've Lost It, Now What? How to Beat the Bear Market and Still Retire on Time* (Portfolio).

Low interest rates and the long bear market have left many retirees strapped for cash. *Here are four strategies that can help bolster your finances…*

●**Work part-time.** If you work just part-time during retirement and earn $10,000 a year, it's like having an extra $200,000 in your retirement nest egg. Why? For every $100,000 in savings, you can expect to receive $5,000 per year in income. You also are giving your nest egg extra time to grow.

True, those extra earnings may make 50% to 85% of your Social Security retirement benefits taxable. Even after taxes, however, you still will have more money in your pocket.

●**Move to a less expensive home,** perhaps in a more affordable part of the country. You will slash property tax, homeowner's insurance and home-maintenance expenses, thus freeing up money for everyday expenses. Looking to relocate? Be sure to check out *www.bestplaces. net* or *www.retirementliving.com.*

Caution: Buying and selling homes is expensive. Purchase a place that you expect to live in for the rest of your life.

●**Take out a reverse mortgage.** This allows people age 62 or older who own their homes outright to tap into the equity without actually selling. Provided you don't move or sell your home, the mortgage doesn't have to be repaid until after your death, at which time the amount owed can't exceed your home's value.

You can receive the money as monthly income, a lump sum or a line of credit.

Get a free guide to reverse mortgages from AARP (888-687-2277, *www.aarp.org/revmort*).

•**Cut taxes.** Time withdrawals from retirement accounts and sales of taxable investments strategically. Attempt to generate just enough income each year to get to the top of the 15% federal income tax bracket, but no higher. That means income of $36,200 this year if you are single and $72,400 if you are married and filing jointly. These figures, which assume you take the standard deduction, will be slightly higher if you are age 65 or older or if you itemize your deductions.

Generate surplus taxable income now—for example, by selling stocks—if you expect to be in a higher tax bracket in the future. Legally required retirement-plan withdrawals at age 70 could nudge you up into the 25% income tax bracket and possibly higher.

For Tax-Free Income... Variable Universal Life Insurance

Herbert Daroff, JD, CFP, director, estate and business planning, Baystate Financial Services, LLC, 699 Boylston St., One Exeter Plaza, Boston 02116. Mr. Daroff is also an adjunct assistant professor of finance at Bentley College in Waltham, MA, and has served on the CFP Board of Professional Review and the CFP Board of Practice Standards.

In early 2000, when the Dow Jones Industrial Average was more than 11,700, investors were stampeding into the stock market.

Four years later, with the Dow around 10,000, stocks are priced 15% or more lower than they were at their peak. And today, investor interest in stocks is again picking up.

Strategy: For long-term investors, equities are more attractive now than they were at the peak of the bull market. That's especially true if you take advantage of an opportunity for tax-free stock market gains.

Tax-free stock market gains? Yes, you can get them in a Roth IRA, if you meet certain income tests. However, the upper limit on contributions is $3,500 per year (for someone at least 50 years old).

Better: After contributing the maximum to a Roth IRA, consider allocating additional dollars to a variable universal life (VUL) policy. There are no income restrictions and few limits on the amount you can allocate.

Caution: To qualify for the tax benefits of a VUL, you must purchase sufficient life insurance coverage, as defined in the Tax Code. So use a VUL only if you have a financial need for the life insurance.

With a VUL policy, you direct your premium payments among several subaccounts, including those that function just like mutual funds. Many VUL policies offer a wide variety of stock and bond funds. You can alter your allocation periodically if you desire.

Loophole: No taxes will be due as long as the money stays in the policy, and the policy remains in force. Thus, you can invest in stock funds and move your money around when you want to. If your subaccounts grow, you can take long- or short-term gains tax free.

POLICY PAYOFF

You can access your VUL policy's cash value income tax free.

Strategy: When you want to tap your cash value, first make tax-free withdrawals until you reach the amount of the money you've contributed. Then, take tax-free policy loans.

Such loans will typically charge interest at an extremely low net rate. Generally, these loans (and the interest charged) reduce the policy's cash value and death benefit.

Caution: For full tax benefits, the policy should be paid for over a number of years, not with one up-front payment.

Example: You pay $80,000 in premiums over eight years. After another seven years, your cash value might have grown to $150,000. (Such an increase is not guaranteed but is possible, based on historic returns.)

Then you might withdraw $12,000 (8% of your cash value) per year.

For almost seven years, you are making withdrawals. Once you've withdrawn $80,000, you take policy loans.

Key: These loans and withdrawals need not be equal—they can vary from year to year.

Strategy: Keep policy loans to around 8% of the cash value each year so the rest of your cash-value balance can continue to grow. By monitoring your cash value closely, you can avoid a policy lapse that will trigger all the deferred income tax.

Death benefit: Keeping your policy in force provides that there will be a substantial payout to your beneficiary or beneficiaries subsequent to your death.

Loophole: Variable universal life provides a death benefit in excess of the cash value—and no income taxes will be due in most instances (unless the "transfer for value" happens during your lifetime).

Payoff: VUL can provide tax-free retirement income to you, as long as you tap the policy carefully, and an income tax–free death benefit to your loved ones.

CLEARING THE HURDLES

•**Avoid lapse.** As already mentioned, in order to avoid paying tax on investment income, you must not let your policy lapse. That means do only moderate withdrawing or borrowing from the policy.

•**Pare the paperwork.** Many insurers require you to make a separate request (by mail, phone or on-line) each time you want cash. Those requests can take time to move through all the channels.

To speed up the process, ask your insurer for the automated income option. Such a feature can deliver monthly payments into a designated bank account or money market account.

•**Monitor cash value.** Ask your insurer or insurance agent for regular statements in order to maximize tax-free withdrawals and loans.

Example: You ask for tax-free transfers of $1,000 per month from the cash value of your VUL policy. On an annual statement, your insurer calculates that you can receive six months' worth, while keeping the policy in force. Next year's statement might show a longer or shorter

projected time period. As a result, you might request an increase or decrease in monthly transfers from your VUL policy.

Alternatively, you can request a monthly payment that will increase by 3% every year, to offset inflation.

Key: By working closely with your insurer or your agent, you can receive tax-free income with a minimum of hassle—as long as you're careful not to trigger a policy lapse.

ADDED ATTRACTIONS

Investing through a VUL provides other benefits as well…

•**Flexibility.** Because these are universal life policies, you can increase or decrease your premium payments over the years to fit your circumstances. However, you may need to increase the amount of insurance coverage (subject to new insurability requirements) if the increase in your premium exceeds the Tax Code restrictions. Again, consult your insurance agent.

•**Lower costs.** During recent years, the expenses incurred by insureds in VUL policies have come down.

•**Family protection.** If you die while your family is still dependent on your income, the income tax–free proceeds can provide for your loved ones.

•**Creditor protection.** Many states prevent creditors from seizing life insurance policies.

•**Care packages.** Some VUL policies offer long-term-care (LTC) riders. If you should need care, such policies may pay tax-free benefits.

WORDS OF CAUTION

VUL policies offer advantages but there are downsides, too. To make the VUL's cash value work for you, expect to hold the policy at least 10 years (the longer the better). This may be needed to provide enough time for the cash value's tax-free compounding to outweigh the up-front costs.

Even if your subaccounts lose value, the promised payoff to your beneficiary won't fall below the agreed-upon level unless the policy lapses or if loans have reduced the original face amount.

Problem: While the strategy described here may shelter stock market gains from income taxes, estate taxes are another story. If you want access to a VUL policy's cash value, the death benefits probably will be included in your taxable estate.

To avoid estate inclusion yet still provide access to the cash value for a spouse or another loved one, sophisticated planning is needed.

In any event, you won't have access to all the cash value during your lifetime, tax free.

If you follow the strategy described here, a large portion of the payoff will go to your loved ones. Thus, a VUL policy makes sense only if you have someone you wish to provide for after your death.

All About Annuities

Rick Fingerman, CFP, president of Financial Planning Solutions, Inc. in Medford, MA, *www.fps2.com,* which specializes in retirement planning. He also is chairman of the Financial Planning Association of Massachusetts.

The recent upturn in stock prices has generated new interest in variable annuities, while low interest rates have left many people less than enthused about fixed annuities.

What should you do if you are now thinking about buying or selling an annuity? *Here are the new rules...*

HOW ANNUITIES WORK

An annuity is a contract between you and an insurance company. You either pay a lump sum or make a stream of payments. In return, you eventually receive regular payments for life or a set period and/or a lump sum. You can decide when to begin withdrawing your money from the annuity.

TAX ASPECTS

There is no up-front tax deduction on the money that you invest. This is why you should consider an annuity only after you have contributed the maximum to every tax-deferred retirement plan for which you are eligible—this includes a 401(k) plan, IRA, self-employed retirement plan, etc.

Once your money is in the annuity, it compounds tax-deferred until you begin making withdrawals. Unlike 401(k)s and IRAs, there is no limit on the amount you can invest. The higher your tax bracket, the greater your need for tax-sheltered growth, so the more an annuity makes sense.

You pay taxes on payments from an annuity whenever they begin. As with all tax-deferred retirement savings vehicles, taxes are assessed at ordinary income tax rates.

With an annuity, however, the portion of the payment representing a return of principal is not taxed. In most instances, you must pay a penalty if you begin receiving payments before age 59½.

FIXED VERSUS VARIABLE ANNUITIES

• **Fixed annuities are sold by insurance companies and banks.** Premiums are invested by the insurer or bank only in fixed-rate instruments, such as bonds or mortgages. And, your money earns a fixed return each year for a certain term, as spelled out in your annuity contract—usually with a floor, below which the rate won't drop. A fixed annuity will be worth more than your invested principal since your money is never at risk.

You want the highest rate guaranteed for the longest time. Today, the average rate, guaranteed for five years, is about 4.5%. At the end of the guarantee period, the insurer sets a rate—usually a minimum of 3%—for the next period, which lasts one year or longer.

• **Variable annuities are sold by insurance and mutual fund companies.** You decide how to invest premiums. You can transfer your money freely among the company's "subaccounts"—stock, bond and money market funds—without incurring taxes.

The value of your variable annuity is determined purely by how much your investment selections earn—or lose—over time. The death benefit will never be less than the total premiums paid, less any withdrawals.

Check that the range of subaccounts is wide enough to meet all of your investment needs. Investment returns of variable annuity subaccounts are listed in *Barron's.*

WHAT'S BEST FOR YOU

Even in a bear market, the best choice for most people is still a variable annuity. Since it can be invested in stocks, it has a better chance than a fixed annuity of outpacing inflation. Even at age 65, you are likely to live another 25 years and can benefit from the inflation-beating potential of a variable annuity.

●**Asset allocation.** How you invest within the annuity depends on your age, risk tolerance and other investments. *Here are my suggested allocations…*

At age 35: 80% stocks…20% bonds.

At age 55: 60% stocks…40% bonds.

At age 75: 40% stocks…60% bonds.

Fixed annuities are suitable only for investors who are past age 66 or who are very conservative and who otherwise might put the money into a taxable certificate of deposit.

The most important consideration for your annuity is safety of principal. Only buy from an insurance company with a top rating from such agencies as A.M. Best Company (908-439-2200, *www.ambest.com*) and Weiss Ratings (800-289-9222, *www.weissratings.com*). Of course, the company's creditworthiness won't protect you against the investment losses that are within a variable annuity.

●**Fees and costs.** Generally, there are no fees on fixed annuities, only early withdrawal "surrender" charges, described below. Fees on a variable annuity can swallow more than 3.5% of your money a year if you don't buy from a no-load or low-load firm.

Here's how a variable annuity's expenses will stack up…

Maintenance fee: About $25 to $50 per year.

Insurer/mortality expense (for providing guaranteed minimum benefit): Up to 1.5% of assets per year.

Investment expenses: They can exceed 2% of assets.

Surrender charge: Some firms charge stiff penalties if you bail out within a certain period, typically seven years. The charges can run from 5% to 8% of assets, depending on how quickly you sell.

Investors who don't need professional advice may save 1.5% or more with low-cost variable annuities offered by discount brokerages, such as Fidelity (800-544-4702, *www.fidelity.com*)… the Charles Schwab Corporation (888-311-4887, *www.schwab.com*)…and TD Waterhouse (800-622-3699, *www.tdwaterhouse.com*), whose subaccounts use multiple investment firms. Or save by obtaining an annuity from such mutual fund companies as Fidelity (800-544-4702, *www.fidelity.com*)…TIAA-CREF (800-223-1200, *www.tiaacref.org*)…T. Rowe Price (800-341-5516, *www.troweprice.com*)…Vanguard (800-523-1154, *www.vanguard.com*).

RESEARCHING ANNUITIES

These resources provide quotes and other information on insurance products, including annuities…

●**AccuTerm** at 800-752-2999 or *www.accuterm.com.*

●**Annuities Online** at 866-812-6800 or *www.annuity.com.*

●**Insure.com** at 800-556-9393 or *www.insure.com.*

ADVICE TO CURRENT OWNERS

If you are in a high-cost annuity and/or you have sustained a loss, it may be very tempting to sell or shift to a new annuity. Insurers are adding to the pressure by providing products that appear to make it advantageous to shift. "Bonus" annuities add 5% to 8% to your principal to offset part of your investment loss and/or surrender charge.

Example: If you invested $100,000 and the value of your annuity is down to $50,000, you will be credited with $52,500 if you buy a 5% bonus annuity. Most likely, you will pay a surrender fee to switch. If the fee is 5%, there goes the bonus.

Switching, however, will greatly reduce the death benefit.

Example: Say you invested $100,000 in an annuity from Company A. No matter how low the account's value falls, your beneficiaries still will receive a $100,000 death benefit, assuming that no money was withdrawn. If the value of your account has dropped to $50,000 and you switch to Company B, the most your heirs will get if you die that day is $50,000.

My advice: Stick with your original annuity, even if your principal is far less than you put in. Only switch if you have held the annuity long enough to avoid a surrender charge and you can get a more comprehensive and better-performing array of investment choices from another company. Also, make sure that the new annuity has no surrender charge or a surrender period of no more than three years.

Marriage May Increase Your Social Security Benefit

Each spouse earns as much Social Security as he/she qualifies for based on his/her employment history. Each individual also qualifies for Social Security based on his/her spouse's earnings. You get the higher of the two benefits.

John Clark, public affairs officer, Office of Communications, US Social Security Administration, New York City.

Try Flipping Properties To Beef Up Your Retirement Income

William Bronchick, attorney and CEO of Legalwiz Publications, 2620 S. Parker Rd., Aurora, CO 80014. He consults and lectures on real estate investing and is also cofounder and president of the Colorado Association of Real Estate Investors at www.carei.com. Mr. Bronchick is author of Flipping Properties (Dearborn Trade).

If you have free time, energy and initiative, you can turn quick profits by buying and then reselling real estate—a practice called "flipping." It's a great opportunity for seniors looking for income to supplement their retirement savings.

Traditional real estate investing requires both capital and time. If you purchase a property, you might have to wait 25 years to realize the full return.

Flipping real estate, on the other hand, seeks to turn properties over in just months or even weeks. It requires virtually no capital and the profits can be virtually instantaneous.

HOW TO FLIP

Depending on your skill level, experience and how much money you have to invest, you can wear one of three hats...

•**Scout.** Scouts don't actually buy property. They locate deals and pass the information to investors who do the actual buying. As a scout, you'll receive a fee from the investor.

•**Dealer.** Dealers not only find properties, but sign purchase contracts with sellers. The aim is to close on the contract and sell the property—or just the contract—to another investor. As a dealer, your profit will come from the spread between the purchase and sale price.

•**Retailer.** Retailers actually buy the property —frequently from a dealer. The goal is to renovate it so it can be sold at a profit to an owner-occupant.

I pay my scouts from $500 up to $1,500 for finding me deals. I am paid the same when I act as scout. As a dealer, I've made as much as $10,000 by flipping a property to a retailer.

Helpful: I work only with residential properties. Commercial real estate is much riskier—it takes more technical knowledge than dealing in single-family homes or condos.

LEARNING THE ROPES

When it comes to flipping, determination can count for more than experience, or even capital. Learn as much as you can about mortgages and deeds and how a real estate closing works. The practice of flipping can be learned from books, seminars and from actually going out and doing it. (My book, *Flipping Properties,* covers the entire topic in only 200 pages.)

You'll find other books at bookstores and libraries. Look at ads in personal finance magazines and elsewhere for workshops and seminars on real estate investing. Many community colleges offer courses on buying real estate.

Strategy: If you're short on capital and real estate experience, start as a scout, finding deals for other investors. Once you gain experience, contacts and capital, you might then become a dealer. If you have a skill that could be useful in rehabilitating a property—maybe you were a plumber or electrical contractor—you could buy run-down properties, fix them up and sell them. Then you would be a retailer.

GETTING STARTED

Once you've learned the basics, jump in and start scouting properties. Nothing beats on-the-job training. *Here's how to begin...*

● **Surround yourself with like-minded people.** Seek out real estate investors in your community. They know the ropes and will buy the deals you scout for them.

There's a local chapter of the National Association of Real Estate Investors (NAREI) in every major city. Visit *www.narei.com* to find a chapter near you.

Each chapter consists of 200 or so real estate investors who meet once every month and talk about the deals they are doing. You will meet rehabbers looking for properties to buy and dealers with properties to sell. If you want to flip real estate, this is the network you need to become part of.

Important: Do enough research before your first meeting so you don't come across as absolutely green. No seasoned investor will take the time and trouble to teach you the basics. The more knowledgeable and eager you seem, the more you'll be accepted as someone who might uncover promising deals.

● **Talk only to motivated sellers.** That's the key to flipping—finding properties going at below-market prices because the owner is in a financial bind. By the time a property is in foreclosure, everyone will know about it. You want to find properties *before* they go into foreclosure.

Where to look: Run newspaper ads looking for distressed properties. Concentrate on a single neighborhood—send out postcards, use flyers and rent ad space on bus-stop benches.

If you follow that strategy, you will need to spend some money on advertisements, business cards and the rest. Set your ad budget (about

$500, more in large cities), and consider it the cost of doing business.

If you would rather commit time than capital, look for deals by driving through your target neighborhood. Check out the *for sale by owner* signs. If the property looks run down and in need of repair, phone the owner. Better still, pick up the newspaper and call everyone in that neighborhood with a house for sale. You don't want to know about the house as much as you do about the seller's needs.

Ask each seller, "How quickly do you want to sell?" If the answer is, "When I get a good deal," they're not motivated. If the answer is, "As quickly as possible," you have a motivated seller. If you start Saturday morning, you will have a fistful of leads by Sunday night.

● **Be persistent.** Few deals are made on the first try. Most deals won't be made until you've talked to the seller four or five times.

When you start out, be prepared to get one useful lead for each 100 properties you scout. When you get good, at least one lead in 20 that comes your way will be worth money.

I've been investing in real estate for 12 years, and I'm at a point where people call me and e-mail me every day with deals. I don't advertise at all anymore. But it took a long time to finally reach that point.

HOW TO SELL

It's best to approach the sales process backward—locate the investor/buyer before trying to find the seller.

Strategy: Say you are working as a dealer, and you're looking for properties to flip to other investors. Line up your investors first. When you find what they're looking for, you already have the property flipped before you sign the contract to buy it. That is where your network among local real estate investors pays off, since they're the people who will buy the deals you turn up.

Of course, these investors could find dealers on their own. However, it saves a lot of time and legwork if you can deliver the deals directly to them.

You Can Buy Real Estate With Your IRA

Patrick W. Rice, licensed real estate broker and investment manager for more than 25 years. His company, IRA Resource Associates in Camas, WA, *www.iraresource.com,* purchases properties for its clients' IRAs. He is coauthor of *IRA Wealth: Revolutionary IRA Strategies for Real Estate Investment* (Square One).

Something your stockbroker won't tell you —you can purchase the retirement home of your dreams with your IRA.

Traditional and Roth IRAs can purchase all kinds of property, ranging from homes to apartment buildings.

By owning real estate, you diversify away from stocks and bonds and keep ahead of inflation. Returns for real estate average 14% a year, versus the 12% 30-year average for stocks.*

Although banks and brokerage firms typically don't offer this alternative—it is costly to administer and does not generate trading commissions—it's easy to add a real estate strategy to your retirement plan.

Reasonable allocation now: 25% or more of your retirement assets.

Beware: If you buy a home for retirement, you cannot live in it until you take its entire value as a distribution from your IRA after age 59½. Until then, rent it to a permissible third party. Profits are reinvested in your IRA.

CASE STUDIES

●**Residential property.** Harry dreamed of retiring to Galveston, TX, near his brother. He bought a house there using money in his IRA.

Purchase price: $120,000.

Expenses: $4,500/year for taxes, insurance, utilities, etc.

Net operating income: $7,500/year (annual rent of $12,000 less annual expenses of $4,500).

Annual income: 6.25% (net operating income divided by the purchase price). Assuming that the home appreciates in value by 6% per

*According to Ibbotson Associates, which used real estate investment trusts as a proxy for real estate.

year, Harry will then wind up with a 12.25% annual return.

Harry achieved his goal by renting out the house until retirement and then taking the house as a distribution from his IRA. His tenants moved out. He moved in and became the new owner instead of his IRA.

●**Commercial property.** Steve's IRA purchased a building that housed a Pizza Hut restaurant in Malta, MT. The tenant was three years into a 10-year lease with options to extend the lease for five years.

Purchase price: $325,000.

Expenses: Nominal. Utilities, taxes and insurance were paid by the tenant.

Net operating income: $30,000/year.

Annual income: 9.23%.

While Steve's income is at the low end of the average for commercial property (the range is 8% to 14% a year), Steve liked the security of the long-term lease. Costs also were contained because the tenant was responsible for most expenses. Steve got the building for less than the $350,000 asking price because he agreed to pay cash and was able to close quickly. He still owns this building.

SET UP YOUR PROGRAM

Transfer your existing IRA or roll over money from a qualified plan—a 401(k) or a pension— to a special account called a *self-directed IRA.* It should be overseen by a custodian, such as a bank, which receives an annual fee of 0.5% to 1.5% of assets. Fees decline as assets increase.

My favorite custodians: Lincoln Trust (800-825-2501, *www.lincolntrust.com*)...PENSCO Trust Co. (800-969-4472, *www.pensco.com*).

You also will need a property manager to maintain and rent out the property to tenants. You are not legally permitted to manage it yourself because the IRS considers you a "disqualified party."

FINANCE YOUR PURCHASES

Banks generally won't provide mortgages to IRAs because they can't seize IRA assets other than the property in the event of a default (if the value of the property falls below the mortgage amount there's a deficit and the bank loses out).

If you can't afford to buy a property outright, try these strategies…

● **Ask the seller to finance** the purchase.

● **Invest your money with others** in a limited liability company (LLC). The LLC invests in the property. There are no restrictions on eligible investors. For instance, the LLC can buy the property with your IRA and/or your spouse's IRA as well as with nonretirement accounts belonging to you and your spouse.

WATCH OUT FOR TAX TRAPS

If you want to rent to family members, consult a tax attorney. If you violate IRS rules, you will pay tax on the entire investment. *IRS rules are tricky…*

● **You cannot lease the property** to parties that have been disqualified by the IRS, such as yourself, parents, children, spouse, grandchildren or their spouses. The law *does* allow you to lease the property to your siblings, cousins, uncles and aunts. You also can name a sibling, etc., to manage the property. You pay that person a salary.

● **You cannot use IRA-owned property as collateral** for a home-equity loan or for a line of credit.

● **You cannot use non-IRA funds to pay for expenses,** such as insurance, taxes and repairs.

Exception: Legal fees. Make sure the property generates enough income to cover all these costs. If necessary, you could transfer money from other IRAs to your self-directed IRA in order to cover expenses.

To keep legal fees down, only use an attorney to draw up and review documents, not to negotiate deals. It is best to pay legal fees with non-IRA money so that you can deduct the cost from your taxes.

● **If you move into the property after age 59½, you must take it as a distribution** from your IRA and pay tax based on the current value of the property. Plan ahead for the tax—it could be sizable. If the property is in a Roth IRA, you pay no taxes.

CHOOSE YOUR INVESTMENTS

Base real estate decisions on the amount of time you're willing to commit, your risk tolerance and the size of your IRA.

● **Residential property.**

Who it is good for: Conservative investors who want to secure their dream home now or purchase a home for an investment.

How it works: Since you will have to hire a property manager to take care of the property anyway, there is no reason to limit your search to your own neighborhood. Homes around the US can be candidates.

● **Commercial property.**

Who it is good for: Those investors who are willing to take more risk for higher capital appreciation.

How it works: You will need a commercial broker to help you select the potential investments—such as stores, office buildings, hotels and land.

For referrals to real estate agents, contact the National Council of Exchangors, a nonprofit organization (800-324-1031, *www.infoville.com*).

Retain a firm that handles a well-maintained property in the area to manage your commercial property.

Cost: 4% to 10% of the annual rent collected.

There are good buys on commercial properties all over the US now. I recently purchased buildings in California, Kentucky, Missouri, New York and Washington.

Build Your Nest Egg with The Hot New Health Savings Accounts

James Shagawat, a fee-only financial planner at Baron Financial Group in Fair Lawn, NJ, *www.baron-financial. com*. He has done extensive research on HSAs because they might be useful to his clients, many of them corporate executives.

You can get big tax breaks for medical and long-term-care insurance costs with new health savings accounts (HSAs) created by recent Medicare drug legislation.

Bonus: These accounts also offer a new way to build wealth.

If you have an HSA, you still can contribute to an individual retirement account (IRA), a 401(k) and a flexible spending account (FSA).

LIKE AN IRA—ONLY BETTER

HSAs are so much like IRAs, they could be called "health-care IRAs." *Benefits...*

• **Money grows tax-deferred,** potentially for decades.

• **You can contribute up to $2,600 a year** ($5,150 for a family) and deduct the amount from your federal income tax. Taxpayers age 55 and older can contribute an additional $500.

• **Tax benefits are more generous** than those for traditional or Roth IRAs. Contributions are tax deductible, *and* withdrawals used to pay health-care expenses are not taxed. In comparison, traditional IRAs offer deductible contributions but withdrawals are taxed. Roth IRA withdrawals are tax free, but contributions are not deductible.

• **Money can be withdrawn for any purpose without penalty after age 65**—but you will have to pay income tax if expenses are not health-related. Before age 65, if cash is used for other purposes, you will be hit with income tax and a 10% penalty.

• **An HSA can be transferred to a spouse or another beneficiary** upon the account holder's death. If it's transferred to a spouse, the account remains an HSA, so no tax is owed. If transferred to another beneficiary, the account is no longer an HSA. The beneficiary must include the fair market value of the assets as of the date of the HSA owner's death in his/her gross income.

• **An HSA can be established at any financial institution,** just like an IRA, although many institutions don't yet offer them because they are so new. (Until HSAs are readily available, keep money in a traditional IRA.) An HSA can invest in stocks, bonds, mutual funds, etc.

Requirements: You must be under age 65 and have health insurance with an annual deductible of at least $1,000 ($2,000 for a family).

Numerous corporations are now expected to introduce high-deductible plans during the next benefits open-enrollment period this fall in order to trim insurance expenses. Some firms might use a portion of the money they save to contribute to employees' HSAs—as they do for 401(k) plans.

IS AN HSA FOR YOU?

You are a good candidate for an HSA if...

• **You have a high-deductible health plan** through your employer.

• **You are self-employed.** The HSA tax write-off can help ease the burden of paying your own medical costs.

• **You are in a high tax bracket.** Affluent people can use HSAs to generate tax-free savings. For maximum tax benefits, let money in an HSA grow for as long as possible and pay deductibles and other medical costs from taxable accounts. An HSA holder is never required to spend the money in the account.

HOW MUCH CAN YOU SAVE?

Here are two examples of health-care costs that can be saved using HSAs*...

Example 1: A single 60-year-old male makes a $2,500 contribution to an HSA for a $2,500 tax deduction.

Taxable income: $65,000

Federal tax rate: 28%

State tax rate: 3%

Gross health insurance policy expense: $1,795 per year ($2,500 deductible)

Annual tax savings: $775 [(28% + 3%) x $2,500]

Net health insurance cost: $1,020 ($1,795 – $775).

Example 2: A family of four—parents in their late 40s, two children in high school—makes a $4,500 contribution for a $4,500 tax deduction.

Taxable income: $125,000

Federal tax rate: 28%

State tax rate: 3%

Gross health insurance policy expense: $3,410 per year ($4,500 deductible)

Annual tax savings: $1,395 [(28% + 3%) x $4,500]

Net health insurance cost: $2,015 ($3,410 – $1,395).

*Source: eHealthInsurance.com.

HSAs VERSUS FSAs

Some experts now believe that HSAs eventually will replace FSAs because FSAs have the following drawbacks...

•**IRS regulations require that FSA holders forfeit any unused balance at year-end.** Participants must plan carefully. With an HSA, unspent dollars grow tax free.

•**FSA holders have to provide documentation of medical expenses** before being reimbursed for them. This is not necessary with an HSA. However, you should maintain evidence of medical expenses in case of a tax audit.

COMPARING HEALTH PLANS

With the health insurers gearing up to offer high-deductible plans to corporations and individuals, it really pays to shop around. To compare high-deductible health insurance policies, contact Insure.com (800-556-9393, *www.insure. com*). Also check *www.ehealthinsurance.com.*

Before signing up with an insurer, check out its consumer complaint history at the National Association of Insurance Commissioner's Web site, *www.naic.org.* Search under "Consumer Information Source."

Protect Retirement Accounts from Medicaid

Protect all retirement accounts from Medicaid claims if you lack long-term-care insurance.

Most Americans still don't have such insurance. The uninsured who cannot afford long-term care can obtain it through Medicaid—but Medicaid will take their "available assets," which may include IRAs, 401(k)s and other retirement accounts, to recover the cost.

Key: The state rules will have a big impact on your planning.

Example: In some states, once an IRA's required annual distributions begin at age 70½, the IRA balance is no longer an available asset, and only a portion of each distribution can be diverted to Medicaid. So converting a regular IRA to a Roth IRA—which has no required distributions—can be a costly mistake.

Consult with a local Medicaid expert to protect assets under your state's law.

Vincent Russo, Esq., Vincent J. Russo & Associates, PC, 1600 Stewart Ave., Westbury, NY 11590. His Web site is at *www.russoelderlaw.com.*

Free Legal Help for AARP Members

Lawyers in AARP's* Legal Services Network (LSN) offer a free initial consultation, during which many concerns of people over age 50 can be handled. For more extensive work, lawyers accept special rates negotiated by AARP.

Examples: $75** for a simple will...$35 for a financial power of attorney.

Information: 888-687-2277 for a free list of participating attorneys...search in the *Yellow Pages* under "Attorneys" or "Lawyers" and then under the heading "AARP-Legal Services Network"...or search on-line at *www.aarp.org/lsn.*

Jim Miller, editor of *Savvy Senior,* a syndicated newspaper question-and-answer column for senior citizens, Norman, OK, *www.savvysenior.org.* He is also author of the book *Savvy Senior* (Hyperion).

*Formerly known as the American Association of Retired Persons.

**All prices subject to change.

13

Estate Planning Wisdom

So You Thought the Estate Tax Was Dead?

Your children's inheritance is still in danger. While the federal government is now phasing out the estate tax, so-called death taxes in 18 states and the District of Columbia will no longer be deductible from federal tax.

This means that residents will be subject to both federal *and* state taxes until the federal estate tax disappears in 2010.

TAX UNDER THE OLD LAW

Previously, state death tax had no effect on an estate's total tax bill.

For example, if a person died in 2001, leaving a taxable estate, the state death tax became a federal tax credit. (A credit is a dollar-for-dollar reduction in tax liability.) Thus, the amount owed to the federal government was reduced by the amount paid to the state.

TAX UNDER THE NEW LAW

The federal government began phasing out its credit for state death tax for the estates of Americans who die after December 31, 2001. For the estates of those who die in 2004, the credit is reduced by 75%. In 2005, it will disappear altogether and be replaced by a deduction for the amount of actual state death taxes. (A deduction is an offset to income and less valuable than a tax credit.)

The amount that can be passed to future generations free of federal estate tax will increase until the federal estate tax disappears altogether in 2010. As this federal exemption increases, fewer estates will be subject to federal estate tax at all.

However, several states that previously tied their death taxes to the federal estate tax credit now require payment of state death tax in an amount equal to the federal credit that was in effect in 2001.

Mark Garten, CPA, chairman of Mahoney Cohen & Company, CPA, PC, New York City. He is director of the firm's personal financial planning department.

Result: Residents of some states, such as New York, will pay more tax than residents of other states, such as Florida, that limit state death tax to the federal state death tax credit.

Example: Paula dies in New York in 2004, leaving a taxable estate of $2 million to her daughter. The resulting gross federal estate tax is $225,000, less the reduced state death tax credit of $24,900, which produces a net federal tax of $200,100. However, her daughter also has to pay New York's death tax of $99,600 instead of $24,900* because New York no longer ties its estate tax to the federal state death tax credit. *The total tax to be paid:* $299,700.

Had Paula died in Florida, the estate would have paid the same $200,100 to the federal government, but the estate tax paid to the state of Florida would have been $24,900. *The total tax owed:* $225,000. Once the federal government's state death tax credit is completely phased out in 2005, Florida will be without an estate tax.

ASSET-PROTECTION STRATEGIES

Even though the federal estate tax is supposed to disappear in 2010, it is scheduled to return in 2011. *No matter where you live, if you expect to have a sizable estate, consult a qualified attorney for ways to protect your assets…*

●**Use disclaimers.** For 2004 and 2005, the federal estate tax exemption increases to $1.5 million and you can leave unlimited amounts free of estate tax to your spouse or a charity.

Strategy: Leave everything to your spouse in a tax-free bequest. She can disclaim (decline or renounce) a portion of the assets to minimize the family's ultimate tax burden yet still provide for her own comfort.

Example: Mark leaves his entire estate to his wife, Ellen. Upon Mark's death, Ellen can decide how much she wishes to disclaim. That money would be placed in a trust for the benefit of Ellen and the children. Upon her death, the assets would pass, tax free, to the children.

If Ellen chooses not to disclaim any assets, upon her death, those assets might end up in her estate and potentially be subject to tax.

●**If you live in a state that has death tax,** you may want to limit the "sheltered" amount

*This example is based on the $1 million exemption for New York in 2004.

to the state's exemption. Put the rest in a trust (as in the previous example).

States with death taxes: Illinois, Kansas, Maine, Maryland, Massachusetts, Minnesota, Nebraska, New Jersey, New York, North Carolina, Ohio, Oregon, Pennsylvania, Rhode Island, Vermont, Virginia, Washington and Wisconsin as well as the District of Columbia.

Tax legislation is pending in several states. For updates, check your state's tax authority.

●**Relocate from a high-death-tax state** to a tax haven. Don't forget to compare state income taxes as well.

Death tax havens: Arizona, Florida, Nevada and Texas.

You need to spend a greater portion of the year in your new state than in your old state or the move will be invalid for tax purposes. *Steps to take…*

●File a Declaration of Homestead and Declaration of Domicile where you live.

●Move all your bank accounts, auto registration, voter registration and driver's license to the new state.

●Establish relationships with a local doctor, lawyer, accountant, broker, etc.

●Join a house of worship.

●Pay your federal income tax from your new address.

●Change your address on legal documents, including your passport.

●Draft a new will.

Beware: There is no guarantee that your new state won't introduce its own death tax.

The Truth About Estate Tax Repeal

Don't count on the estate tax being repealed when making your estate plan. The much-publicized repeal does not occur until 2010—and then for only one year. So an estate won't be protected by it unless its owner dies within that year.

And currently, with budget deficits having returned and the rebuilding of Iraq to finance, it is less likely that even that brief repeal will take place. Even if this tax should die at the hands of Congress, it's more than likely that it will be reincarnated, as has happened three times in the past. Instead, you can expect more compromises and changes in the law.

Important: Uncertainty regarding the future of the estate tax makes estate planning more important because of the many possibilities that need to be covered. Be sure your estate plan is up to date and review it frequently.

Irving L. Blackman, CPA, founding partner, Blackman Kallick Bartelstein, LLP at 10 S. Riverside Plaza, Chicago 60606, *www.taxsecretsofthewealthy.com.*

Protect Your Money From Greedy Relatives

David S. Rhine, CPA, regional director, family wealth planning, Sagemark Consulting, a division of Lincoln Financial Advisors Corp., registered investment adviser, Rochelle Park, NJ.

Your savings represent a huge opportunity to greedy relatives, friends and even overeager investment advisers. The standard advice—just say "no"—is easier said than done. It's hard to protect your nest egg from the pleas of an adult child or a new spouse.

How to keep your money safe…

KNOW WHAT YOU CAN SPARE

As you near retirement, you must conserve principal so you can live off this income. The bear market probably has damaged your investments. In addition, many companies are reducing retirement health benefits. Account for these needs *now*. Meet with your financial planner to determine how much you'll need for retirement and how much you can give away.

MAKE A PLAN FOR GIVING

In order to protect your assets, you must set up rules for how and when to give away your money. You might want to set aside some for grandchildren's college tuitions and close family members' weddings. Effective giving and estate planning also can save as much as 50%—sometimes more—in estate taxes.

Keep expectations reasonable. Let children and grandchildren know that you can't afford to give them down payments on houses but that you will offer them $5,000 or even $10,000 toward them. Consider noncash gifts of appreciated stock, for example, to save on capital gains and estate taxes. When a beneficiary sells the stock, he/she might be left with more than if you had sold the stock and given him the proceeds. His capital gains tax rate easily might be lower than yours.

One client wasn't in a position to give much cash, but she had beautiful jewelry that she no longer wore. Since her children would eventually inherit the jewelry, I suggested she give it away now. The gifts were satisfying to her and cherished by her children.

PROTECTION THROUGH TRUSTS

Deep down, many people realize that they can't afford to give large gifts—but some can't say it.

Strategy: If you can't or do not like saying "no"—or fear that your spouse won't be able to turn down requests after your death—put your wealth into a trust.

Three kinds of trusts are most helpful…

●**In a grantor trust,** you are the grantor—putting your assets into trust. You keep earning income from the assets, but the trustee—not you—deals with requests for money.

Important: Grantor trust assets are taxed in your estate. Tax consequences are the same as they would be without a trust.

●**A credit shelter trust** uses the amount that can pass tax free to your heirs to prevent those assets from being taxed in the estate of your spouse. It also can shield money from your spouse, children or others. That amount is $1.5 million in 2004 and 2005. This trust can be funded either during your lifetime, if you are willing to part with the funds, or at death.

●**A qualified terminable interest property (QTIP) trust** can be used to prevent the assets of a first marriage from being carried away by beneficiaries of a second or third marriage.

The trust needs to provide lifetime income to a surviving second spouse. When the second spouse dies, all or part of the estate passes to whomever you designate, such as your children from a previous marriage. The trustee for a grantor or a QTIP trust (or any other kind of trust) can be a financial professional, a lawyer or even a family friend or sibling—but *you* must pick someone who is willing to say "no."

Big Tax Savings From Trusts: Best Loopholes Now

Edward Mendlowitz, CPA, partner, Mendlowitz Weitsen, LLP, CPAs, which is one of only 800 CPA firms nationwide approved to audit public companies, K2 Brier Hill Ct., East Brunswick, NJ 08816. He is also author of *Introducing Tax Clients to Additional Services* (American Institute of CPAs).

You do not have to be superrich to take advantage of the tax-saving opportunities created by trusts. *Consider the following possibilities…*

IRREVOCABLE LIFE INSURANCE TRUSTS

Loophole: **Use an irrevocable life insurance trust to avoid estate tax on insurance proceeds.** Set up a trust and have the trustee apply for a policy on your life. The proceeds payable to the trust at your death will be free of all estate tax just as long as you have no control over the policy.

Strategy 1: You can give the trust enough money each year to cover the premium payments on the policy. These gifts can qualify for the $11,000 ($22,000 with a consenting spouse) annual gift tax exclusion as long as the trustee notifies the trust beneficiaries of their right to withdraw the amounts you give.

Strategy 2: Transfer your existing policy to a newly created irrevocable life insurance trust.

Caution: The policy proceeds will be taxable in your estate if you die within three years after the trust transfer.

QTIP TRUSTS

Loophole: **Defer estate tax and retain control over property with a qualified terminable interest property (QTIP) trust.** Money left to a QTIP trust qualifies as a marital bequest, so no estate tax is payable until the death of your surviving spouse.

As the person who sets up the trust, you designate where the trust fund will go after your spouse dies. QTIP trusts are especially useful if you're remarried and have children from a previous marriage.

Trap: For a QTIP trust to work, all of the income must be paid to your surviving spouse, and your spouse must have the right to a reasonable return on assets. Otherwise, estate tax will be due at your death.

BYPASS TRUSTS

Loophole: **Reduce your estate taxes by creating a bypass trust.** Everyone can leave $1.5 million worth of assets totally free of estate tax in 2004 and 2005.

How to do it: When you draft your will, create a bypass trust (also called a credit shelter trust) that will be funded with up to $1.5 million. Typically, the surviving spouse receives the income from the bypass trust and the trust assets pass to other named beneficiaries—usually the couple's children—when the surviving spouse dies.

Key: Even if the trust fund increases from the original $1.5 million to $5 million or more by the time your surviving spouse dies, no estate tax will be due on the appreciated value of these assets.

QPRTs

Loophole: **Keep a house in the family with a qualified personal residence trust (QPRT).** You can transfer a personal residence or a vacation home into the trust during your lifetime. When the trust term is complete, the house passes to the trust beneficiaries.

Strategy: You can retain the right to use the house for the trust term. You can also arrange to keep using the house after the trust terminates, as long as you agree to pay a fair rent to the new owner.

Key: The deferred gift reduces the gift tax cost. The longer the term of the trust, the smaller the taxable gift. A typical term is 10 to 15 years.

Example: A 65-year-old might transfer a $400,000 house to a 10-year QPRT and incur a taxable gift of just slightly more than $230,000. (There may be no immediate tax because of the lifetime $1 million gift tax exemption.) *Trap:* The house will be included in your taxable estate if you die before the trust term ends. Therefore, you should choose a trust term you're likely to outlive given your health and life expectancy.

CRTs

Loophole: Enjoy a three-way tax break with a charitable remainder trust (CRT). Contributing to a CRT gives you an immediate income tax deduction, estate tax savings and, if you donate appreciated assets, relief from capital gains tax.

Extra advantages: You (and perhaps your spouse) can receive lifetime income. After your death (or the deaths of you and your spouse), the trust fund goes to a charity or charities of your choice.

Strategy: Donate appreciated securities to a CRT instead of selling them. You will receive an income stream based on the full value of the assets you contribute. Those assets will not be included in your taxable estate and no gift tax or capital gains tax will be owed.

Options: You can specify a certain amount of income each year to a charitable remainder *annuity* trust, or income based on a percentage of trust assets to a charitable remainder unitrust. Charitable remainder annuity trusts give stable income, *unitrusts* offer growth potential.

Limits: The minimum payouts are 5% of the trust contribution (annuity trust) or 5% of the trust fund (unitrust). And, the larger the income payments, the smaller your up-front tax deduction as a percentage of trust assets. There is a 50% maximum payout limitation.

GRATs

Loophole: Receive income along with tax advantages with a grantor retained annuity trust (GRAT). You can donate assets—securities, real estate, shares in a family business—to a trust and retain the right to receive a certain amount of income each year. After the trust term expires, the assets pass to the beneficiaries.

Example: You transfer $500,000 worth of assets to a 15-year GRAT and retain the right to receive $35,000 a year. Depending on the current level of interest rates, you might incur a taxable gift of only about $200,000.

Strategy: The higher the trust payout and the longer the trust term, the smaller the taxable gift.

Key: If the trust assets appreciate at a greater rate than the income you receive, more wealth can be passed to the younger family members tax free.

Again, you need to outlive the trust for tax benefits to be realized.

Helpful: Instead of one 15-year GRAT, use three GRATs with terms of five, 10 and 15 years. Place one-third of the assets into each trust. This may ensure that your family will receive some tax benefit even if you die within 15 years.

Wealth-Saving Way to Finance Tax-Free Life Insurance

IRS Letter Ruling 9809032.

If you purchase life insurance on your own life, the policy proceeds normally will be included in your taxable estate—so a portion may go to the IRS rather than to protecting your family or other intended purposes.

However, policy proceeds can be kept out of your estate if you transfer all ownership rights in the policy—such as the right to change beneficiaries—to an irrevocable life insurance trust.

Catch: A way must be provided for the trust to pay premiums on the policy. Frequently gifts are made to such a trust for this purpose, using the annual $11,000 gift tax exclusion or $1 million lifetime exclusion. But these gifts reduce one's own wealth.

Alternative: An individual funded such a trust by making loans to it that were required to be repaid to his estate out of the proceeds of the insurance policy upon his death.

When he did die, and the trust made the payment to his estate, a question arose as to whether the estate's right to repayment from the policy constituted an ownership interest in it sufficient to cause all the policy proceeds to be taxed back to the estate.

IRS ruling: For the estate. It receives the loan repayment from the insurance proceeds, while the rest of the proceeds are retained by the trust and removed from the estate.

Protect Assets Against Creditor Claims

Create an irrevocable trust to protect your assets against possible creditor claims in the future. Fund the trust before anyone does come after your assets so that creditors cannot claim it was set up fraudulently. Name an independent trustee, like a bank, attorney or accountant, not yourself or a close friend. State a reason for establishing the trust other than asset protection.

Examples: Estate planning...or to provide support for a family member.

Keep accurate records, and operate the trust in a businesslike way.

Christopher R. Jarvis and David B. Mandell, financial planners, Los Angeles, and authors of *Wealth Protection* (Wiley).

Don't Let Your Pension Die with You

Robert S. Keebler, CPA, MST, partner, Virchow, Krause & Co., LLP, 1400 Lombardi Ave., Green Bay, WI 54304. Mr. Keebler is the author of *A CPA's Guide to Making the Most of the New IRA* (American Institute of CPAs).

Most pension plans will offer the participants two payment alternatives when they retire—either a monthly check or a lump-sum payout. The choice that you make depends on your need for retirement income... and your concerns for your heirs.

DILEMMA FOR SINGLES

The law requires the pension plan to offer married employees a "joint and survivor option" so that some monthly benefit will go to a participant's spouse subsequent to his or her death. But, a spouse can waive this right, allowing the participant to receive a larger monthly benefit or take a lump sum.

Unmarried participants have the same choice, either a monthly benefit or lump sum. But the joint and survivor option does *not* apply to unmarried employees.

On the death of an unmarried participant who has opted for monthly benefits, no further payments will be made to any of the participant's beneficiaries. The pension dies with the participant. This is the case no matter how much he has accumulated in the plan.

LUMP-SUM SOLUTION

Unmarried participants—and in many cases married participants—should opt for the lump-sum payout.

Why? Because a lump-sum payment can be rolled into an IRA. *Impact...*

● **The participant can still collect monthly benefits**—from the IRA. Basing monthly benefits on life expectancy and the rate of return on investments will ensure that the funds in the IRA last as long as the IRA owner lives.

● **Whatever remains in the IRA goes to his beneficiaries,** when the participant dies.

LUMP-SUM LIMITATIONS

Before opting for a lump sum in lieu of the monthly payments, consider the following...

● **Pension plans are insured** by the federal Pension Benefit Guaranty Corporation. Monthly payments, if you choose them, are guaranteed.

In contrast, IRAs are only as safe as the investments they are in. Stocks and bonds can decline in value, reducing funds available for retirement income as well as for an inheritance for heirs.

● **Pensions are professionally managed.** With IRAs, you're responsible for making the investment decisions.

Helpful: If you're intimidated by the thought of managing investments for a sizable account, think about retaining a professional money manager to handle your IRA.

●**Pensions are fully protected against the claims of creditors.** IRAs may receive similar protection, but regulations will vary from state to state.

If there is any concern about creditor claims, be sure to check state law to find out if IRAs are protected.

Important: Check out the rules for both the state in which you live in now as well as the state to which you may retire.

Suppose that you decide against a lump sum because you have serious concerns about creditor protection. But you still want to provide for someone other than a spouse after your death. In this case, you should consider life insurance. The amount of coverage you take can be tied to the funds your beneficiary would have received from your retirement money had you rolled the pension into an IRA.

Beneficiaries' Pension Rights

What will happen in the event that your monthly pension payments are subject to IRS levy when you die? A recent court case, *Asbestos Workers Local 23 Pension Fund* (MD Pa., 1/12/04), holds good news for the beneficiary who is to receive the pension benefit after the death of the participant.

The court ruled that the person receiving the benefit only had an interest in designating who was to be his beneficiary. Amounts to be paid after his death did not constitute "property," which the IRS has a continued right to levy.

Bottom line: The participant's beneficiary receives the pension payments free and clear of the IRS levy.

Ms. X, Esq., a former agent with the IRS who is still well connected.

More from Ms. X…

When You Owe the IRS Money And Then Die…

The death of a taxpayer usually ends his/her responsibility to pay the IRS from certain assets. This is important to the beneficiaries. For instance, even though a federal tax lien attaches to a taxpayer's vested interest in his pension plan, the IRS cannot levy amounts payable to a beneficiary as a death benefit. Life insurance? A federal tax lien attaches to the cash surrender value of a life insurance policy but not to the proceeds otherwise payable at death.

Put Pets in Your Will

You can include pets in your will, living trust and other estate-planning documents. Pets are legally considered property that you can deal with as you wish. Specify how your pet should be cared for and by whom. Leave sufficient money for care during the pet's expected lifetime, or look into a pet retirement home, sanctuary or shelter. More than a dozen states have pet trust laws.

More information: Call the Purdue University Peace of Mind Program at 800-830-0104.

Michael Martindill, attorney specializing in estate planning with an emphasis on animal law, La Mesa, CA.

Pass on Your Values and Wisdom

Also known as a legacy statement, an ethical will passes on your values, beliefs and wisdom. Around for more than 3,000 years, they have become more popular since the terrorist attacks of September 11, 2001. An ethical will is a nonlegal, personal letter that expresses your innermost thoughts. It can be given to a child or grandchild anytime, on any occasion.

Barry K. Baines, MD, CEO, The Legacy Center, a group that helps to preserve individual's stories and wisdom, Minneapolis, *www.ethicalwill.com*, and author of *Ethical Wills: Putting Your Values on Paper* (Perseus).

Very Wise Ways To Revise Your Will

Martin Shenkman, CPA and attorney who specializes in estate and tax planning and asset protection, Teaneck, NJ, and the author of over 30 books, including *Inherit More: Protect Your Inheritance from Taxes, Creditors, Claimants, Medicaid and More* (Wiley). His Web site, at *www.laweasy. com,* offers free sample forms and documents.

Most everyone knows to change their will when they get married or divorced. *Below are three smart reasons to revise your will anytime…*

BETTER BEQUESTS TO HEIRS

***Common mistake:* You leave stock to one child and real estate to another.** If you make provisions for the changes in asset value, your executor will be instructed to make up the difference with "equalizing payments."

Catch: Many assets can be difficult to value. Heirs will have a motive to contest valuations in order to demand payments or prevent them from being made to others.

Better: While you can put in a clause disinheriting anyone who challenges the will, a better solution is to leave each heir a part of your estate, not a specific asset.

Leave specific assets to heirs only under special circumstances.

Example: You wish to leave control of a family business to the child who is managing it.

BETTER BEQUESTS TO CHARITY

***Common mistake:* You leave many small bequests—$500 or less—to many different organizations.**

Catch: Legal and administrative costs to the estate could exceed the value of the bequests.

Better: Write a letter to your heirs. Encourage them to give individual gifts to specific charities, in your memory, using the funds they receive from the estate. Tell them that they are likely to get personal income tax deductions for their own charitable gifts.

Bonus: You help instill a culture of giving.

BETTER WAY TO PROTECT YOUR SPOUSE

***Common mistake:* You try to minimize estate tax by using a simple bypass trust.** You leave the "maximum amount" excluded from estate tax, $1.5 million in 2004 and 2005, in a trust that will provide an income for your spouse for his/her lifetime. After your spouse's death, the money in the trust will be paid to your children.

Catch: The excluded amount could become a higher proportion of the estate, so that your spouse gets less than you intended. *Reasons…*

● **The excluded amount will increase under the new law,** in steps, to $3.5 million in the year 2009.

● **Your assets might decline in value.**

Better: Leave a specific dollar amount to the trust. If your estate is small when you die, more assets will pass outright to your spouse. If your estate is large, your spouse can disclaim part of the bequest. Those assets instead would go back into the trust to be protected from estate tax by your personal estate tax exclusion.

More from Martin Shenkman…

Give to Charity Even If You Don't Have a Lot of Cash

To make a large charitable donation without a lot of cash, consider naming a charity as the owner and beneficiary of a life insurance policy. You also can use life insurance to guarantee that regular contributions to a favorite charity will continue after your death.

Example: You donate $1,000 each year. The charity uses the donation to purchase a $40,000 insurance policy on you, naming the charity as the beneficiary. Upon your death, the charity will have $40,000 to invest. If the investment earns 2.5% per year, then the charity will effectively continue to receive the same $1,000 long after you're gone. *Key:* You get a tax deduction, which helps reduce your cost burden.

Intrafamily Loans: Keep Wealth in the Family Without Paying Tax

Gregory A. Hayes, Esq., partner in the law firm Day, Berry & Howard LLP, One Canterbury Green, Stamford, CT 06901.

Interest rates are still near their lowest levels in decades. And, that's good news for many types of borrowers, including your children and grandchildren.

Now it is possible to lend money to your loved ones and set very easy repayment terms. Done properly, this can help you to avoid gift taxes while allowing your family members to deduct any interest they pay.

GIFT TAX ISSUES

Financially successful parents and grandparents often lend money to younger relatives—to help them buy or renovate a home, start a business, etc. *But these types of loans may cause some problems...*

●**Payment obligations.** If large amounts are loaned at market rates of interest, young borrowers may have difficulty handling the interest payments.

●**Gift tax consequences.** If you charge little or no interest, the IRS may consider the loans gifts. You could be required to pay a gift tax, along with income tax on interest and possible tax penalties.

But today's low interest rates allow you to lend money to your children at minimal rates, avoiding gift taxes while minimizing interest payments. Moreover, the low interest rates may make it possible to forgive those payments, if you wish, while staying within the annual gift tax exclusion.

Current rates: In August 2004, the Applicable Federal Rates (AFRs) were...

●2.37% for loans of less than three years.
●4.00% for loans of three to nine years.
●5.21% for loans longer than nine years.

CUT-RATE LOANS

The AFRs change every month (check the Internal Revenue Bulletins at *www.irs.gov/taxpros/lists/0,,id=98042,00.html*). As long as you charge at least the current AFR on intrafamily loans, no taxable gift will be imposed.

Example: You lend $300,000 to your son and daughter-in-law so they can buy a home. Your loan is interest-only, with the principal due 30 years later. You can charge them as little as 5.21%, assuming that the long-term AFR is at that level when you make the loan. No gift tax will be charged as long as the interest rate is at least the AFR.

Result: Your son and daughter-in-law get to borrow at a rate that's below the standard mortgage rates—without all the paperwork hassles. At a 5.21% rate on a $300,000 loan, the interest is $15,630 per year, which they may be able to afford comfortably.

Strategy: If the loan is secured by the house, the borrowers will be able to treat the interest on their loan payments as completely deductible home mortgage interest.

FORGIVE OR TAKE

As the lender, you have two options regarding the loan interest...

●**Accept the payments.** At 5.21%, the interest is higher than you would receive from a money market fund or bank certificate of deposit (CD) these days. Moreover, you will have the satisfaction of helping your son.

●**Waive the interest due.** If you wish, you can forgive the interest payments in any given month or year. If you do, you will pay tax on $15,630 worth of interest income each year while your son and daughter-in-law receive a $15,630 tax deduction.

What about gift taxes? Waiving $15,630 worth of interest is equivalent to making a $15,630 gift.

Annual tax exclusion: The annual gift tax exclusion is currently $11,000 per recipient per year. Thus, you can give up to $22,000 worth of assets to your son and daughter-in-law this year, with no gift tax consequences.

In this example, you can waive all the interest and still give this couple another $6,370 this year, free of gift tax.

Trap: Waiving the interest *occasionally* is permissible. However, if there is an understanding (expressed or implied) that all the interest will be waived, year after year, the IRS is likely to claim that the original transfer was really a gift and not a loan.

As mentioned, this may result in gift taxes, interest and penalties.

Strategy: To avoid the risk of an IRS challenge, make an intrafamily loan look like a regular commercial transaction. The loan should be in writing, with a stated interest rate and repayment schedule. Also, the loan agreement should describe the actions you will take in case of default.

GIFT OR LOAN

Intrafamily gifts have traditionally been used as a means of reducing a senior generation's taxable estate. Today, though, some people are reluctant to make gifts because of uncertainty about the future of federal estate tax.

Also, the three-year stock market decline has made numerous people hesitant to make gifts to their own children or grandchildren. Parents and grandparents fear that they might need the money themselves one day.

Solution: Make intrafamily loans instead of estate-reducing gifts. Such loans might have call provisions. As mentioned, the low interest rates make such loans affordable to younger relatives while you collect needed income.

If you find that you need the money, you can call the loans. Hopefully, your children's careers will progress and they'll be able to repay you. Or, they might tap a home-equity line to raise the required cash.

If the stock market rebounds and your retirement funds are replenished, you may not need the money after all. You can forgive the interest and part of the principal, using your annual gift tax exclusion.

Strategy: If you're married, you and your spouse have a double exclusion, up to $22,000 per recipient per year in 2004.

You also can use your lifetime $1-million-per-donor gift tax exemption to cancel intrafamily debt without paying gift taxes.

DON'T SWEAT THE SMALL STUFF

When you make an intrafamily loan of less than $100,000, special tax breaks apply…

● **Loans of $10,000 or less** can be interest free with no income or gift tax consequences.

Required: The loan proceeds may not be used by the recipient to purchase an income-producing asset. Your son can't use an interest-free loan to invest in a bank CD, for instance.

● **Low-interest loans in the $10,000 to $100,000 range** qualify for income tax relief.

Example: You make a two-year, $100,000 interest-free loan to your daughter. Assuming the short-term AFR is 2.37%, the IRS deems that you have made a gift of $2,370 per year (2.37% of $100,000), for two years. You can use your annual gift-tax exclusion to cover the present value of this deemed gift.

As long as your daughter's net investment income is less than $1,000 per year, you won't have to recognize any income from this particular transaction.

However, when your daughter's annual net investment income exceeds $1,000, the excess will be attributed to you. If her net investment income is $2,000, for instance, the excess $1,000 is taxable income to you.

Why a Health-Care Proxy Is More Important Than Ever

Bernard A. Krooks, Esq., managing partner at Littman Krooks LLP, attorneys at 655 Third Ave., New York City 10017, *www.elderlawnewyork.com.*

The new federal law prohibits health-care providers from discussing a patient's status—even with close family members—unless proper written consent forms are signed.

For an adult patient, nobody—not even the spouse, parent or child—has a right to medical information if the patient has not specifically designated the individual *in writing* as their "personal representative."

Danger: Hospitals and other health-care providers that are afraid of breaking the law may keep even the closest family members in the dark about a patient's condition, making informed decisions impossible. *What you need to do now...*

●**Meet with a lawyer** to draw up health-care proxies for all family members that meet the confidentiality requirements of the *Health Insurance Portability and Accountability Act of 1996* (HIPAA).

●**If a problem arises with a health-care provider due to HIPAA,** call the toll-free hot-line set up by the federal government to assist families in dealing with it, 866-627-7748.

●**Learn more about the privacy rules** of HIPAA from the Web site developed to explain them by the Health & Human Services Administration, *www.hhs.gov/ocr/hipaa/.*

Legal Tools to Care for Aging Parents

Robert M. Freedman, Esq., elder law specialist and partner, Freedman and Fish LLP, New York City.

If your parent suffers a stroke or other life-threatening medical condition, making decisions can be especially difficult if you don't have the necessary legal tools.

MEDICAL DECISIONS

A *living will* is a statement of wishes regarding medical care. And, a *medical power of attorney* or *health-care proxy* designates someone to make medical decisions if a parent is incapacitated. It's best for your parent to have a living will *and* one of the other two documents.

If your parent has no advanced directives, you must follow your state's procedures for substituted decision making.

Sample forms: Partnership for Caring (800-989-9455, *www.partnershipforcaring.org*).

FINANCIAL CONSIDERATIONS

Ask for copies of all key documents. If your parent doesn't want you to have this information yet, it can be put in a sealed envelope and kept in an accessible place in case of emergency. *Documents to request...*

●**Doctors' names and phone numbers.**

●**Health insurance policies.**

●**Medicare ID number.**

●**Policy for medicare supplemental insurance.**

●**Long-term-care insurance policy.**

●**Catastrophic insurance** and any other health insurance policies.

●**All life insurance policies.**

●**List of assets and liabilities,** and people to contact with regard to them.

●**Power of attorney.**

Short-term medical emergencies, such as a fractured hip, which last only several months, should be covered by insurance. But you may need access to funds to pay your parent's bills.

Long-term conditions, such as Alzheimer's disease, require planning. Consult an attorney to determine how care will be paid for...and a geriatric care manager about how care will be provided. To find a geriatric care manager in your area, contact the National Association of Professional Geriatric Care Managers (520-881-8008, *www.caremanager.org*).

The Best Place to Keep Your Organ-Donor Card

Organ-donor agreements should be kept at home, where family members can locate them—not with your driver's license. When the donation agreement is on the license, someone who has never met you or your loved one may make the decision about when to harvest your organs. When death is very near, organs may be harvested before family members are ready—

perhaps when a person is brain dead and there is an urgent need for organs. This is less likely to occur if the family is involved in the decision.

Henry Abts III, chairman and founder, The Estate Plan, producer of living trust documents, Reno, NV, and author of The Living Trust *(McGraw-Hill).*

Is a Do-It-Yourself Will for You?

Do-it-yourself wills, using programs published by Nolo Press at *www.nolo.com* or some other software program, are recommended only if your situation is not complicated and you know exactly what you want to do. Have your attorney review whatever you put together. *I urge you to consult a lawyer if...*

• **Your will might be contested,** for instance, if there is family discord.

• **You have a child who is disabled** or other dependents.

• **You want to disinherit a spouse** or other close relative.

• **Your estate is in excess of $1.5 million** and therefore subject to federal estate tax.

• **You operate your own business.**

• **You gave up a child for adoption.**

• **You own many pieces of real estate** in more than one state.

• **Some of your income is derived from royalties.**

Nancy Dunnan, a financial adviser in New York City, and author of The Widow's Financial Survival Guide *(Putnam/Perigee).*

More from Nancy Dunnan...

When a Spouse Dies

Don't rush into any major financial decisions after a spouse dies. *Only a few things must be done in the weeks after a death...*

• **Find your spouse's will and other important documents,** such as tax returns.

• **Notify his/her employer,** the Social Security Administration and insurance companies.

• **Keep a record of estate-related expenses for tax purposes** and the names and phone numbers of the people with whom you speak about them.

• **Pay bills on which both you and your spouse are named**—but don't pay bills that are only in your spouse's name. Tell creditors the estate will be paying them.

If You Want to Disclaim an Inheritance...

Disclaiming an inheritance can let money or property pass to a secondary beneficiary.

Example: Your father's estate may pass to your children if you disclaim it.

You might want to disclaim it if your own estate already is large and an inheritance would subject you to more taxes. Discuss any decision to disclaim with a knowledgeable estate planner. It must be made in writing, in a specified form and within specific time limits of the individual's death.

Diane Pearson, CFP, Legend Financial Advisors, Inc., financial planners, Pittsburgh.

14

The Savvy Traveler

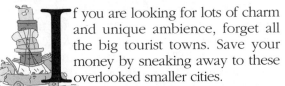

Great Vacation Opportunities in Overlooked US Cities

If you are looking for lots of charm and unique ambience, forget all the big tourist towns. Save your money by sneaking away to these overlooked smaller cities.

PROVIDENCE, RHODE ISLAND

The billion-dollar revitalization program has recently transformed Providence, RI from an old industrial backwater to one of the liveliest, most colorful Eastern cities. Although it has been thoroughly modernized, Providence retains the feel of colonial America because so much of its original architecture has been preserved and restored to its former glory.

The Performing Arts Center, renovated railroad station, State House, gigantic convention center, upscale Providence Place Mall and six major hotels are all clustered conveniently in or around downtown along the riverfront called Waterplace Park. A stunning gathering place and home to summer concerts, street performers, gondolas, restaurants and shops, it is famous for WaterFire, which is an installation of 100 bonfires lit in the river every night from May through November.

Cross the Venetian-style bridges spanning the rivers and walk to Benefit Street, where you'll find the largest single collection of restored colonial homes in America. The walking tour through the neighborhood is a must. Also not to be missed are the many museums, such as the Rhode Island School of Design Museum and the John Brown House, the home of the founder of Brown University. For a look at a traditional Ivy League campus, walk around the grounds of Brown University.

This city is easy to see by riverboat, walking or bus tour, or the hop-on-and-off trolley buses. And as you go, be sure to look at the outdoor

Joan Rattner Heilman, an award-winning travel writer based in New York State. She is the author of *Unbelievably Good Deals and Great Adventures That You Absolutely Can't Get Unless You're Over 50* (Contemporary).

sculptures decorating the downtown area, even on the light poles.

Information: Providence Warwick Convention and Visitors Bureau (800-233-1636, *www. goprovidence.com*).

INDEPENDENCE, MISSOURI

Independence, a charming Midwestern city laden with Victorian mansions on leafy tree-lined streets, is best known as the hometown of President Harry S. Truman. The biggest attractions in town are the Truman Historic Home and the Truman Presidential Museum and Library, open to the public year-round, and the new Truman Walking Trail, 44 sidewalk plaques that guide visitors along the same route the president strolled every day after his retirement.

The National Frontier Trails Museum (open year-round), also in the historic downtown area, explains the city's history from the Lewis and Clark expedition (1804–1806) to its role as the starting point for Western expansion in the mid-1800s. Among the original buildings are the 1827 Log Courthouse, once the only courthouse between the Missouri River and the Pacific Ocean, and the Pioneer Spring Cabin, a typical frontier home. Also open to the public are the limestone cells in the 1859 jail once occupied by Confederate Civil War guerrillas and famous outlaws, like Frank James and Cole Younger, who both rode with the Jesse James gang.

Not to be overlooked in Independence is the Mormon Visitors Center. The Center commemorates Joseph Smith, founder of the Mormon Church, who proclaimed Independence to be the City of Zion and the site of the second coming before he left for the West.

Information: Independence Tourism (800-748-7323, *www.visitindependence.com*).

PORTLAND, OREGON

Portland, a sophisticated city with a relaxed atmosphere, is loaded with cultural institutions and events. Its most popular gathering place is Pioneer Courthouse Square, an art-filled plaza in the heart of town with an amphitheater, a waterfall fountain and a 25-foot sculpture that forecasts the weather.

An eminently walkable city, Portland is the home to a handful of theatrical companies, a symphony orchestra and an opera company, as well as 239 parks and gardens. Two of the biggest and most popular parks are Forest Park, the largest urban wilderness in an American city, filled with forested walking trails, and Washington Park, where visitors flock to the many attractions, including the International Rose Test Garden with more than 500 varieties of roses, the Oregon Zoo and the Hoyt Arboretum. Across town is The Grotto, a 62-acre forested religious sanctuary that also includes the Botanical Gardens.

Making your way through the historic Old Town District, known for all its cast-iron buildings, take time to stop in at any of the many microbreweries and hip coffeehouses. Plan to see the Portland Saturday Market, the nation's largest open-air market, open during weekends from March through December 24. It's known for the crafts and jewelry made by local artisans, its food court and street performers.

To see Portland from the water, cruise the Willamette River on the *Portland Spirit,* a sleek, modern-looking yacht that runs year-round. Food is available on board.

Information: Portland Oregon Visitors Association (877-678-5263, *www.travelportland.com*).

CLEVELAND, OHIO

Cleveland is another former industrial town that has transformed itself into a major cultural center. It boasts of the largest performing arts center in the nation outside of New York, with five restored 1920s theaters that are home to the renowned Cleveland Opera, the Ohio Ballet, the Great Lakes Theater Festival and traveling Broadway shows.

Some of Cleveland's newest attractions can be found along the shores of Lake Erie—the Rock and Roll Hall of Fame, the Great Lakes Science Center and the Cleveland Browns Stadium. And stretching out along the banks of the Cuyahoga River, which meanders through town, is the Flats, the entertainment and warehouse district that's chock-full of restaurants and nightclubs.

About four miles east of downtown is University Circle, the country's largest concentration of cultural arts and medical and educational institutions (more than 50 of them) within one square mile. The sites include the Cleveland Botanical Garden, the Museum of Art, the HealthSpace Museum, Severance Hall, which is home to the world-renowned Cleveland Orchestra, and the Cleveland Botanical Garden, which re-creates a Costa Rican rain forest and a Madagascan desert under a glass roof.

Cleveland is also where you'll find Case Western Reserve University, with its flamboyant Peter B. Lewis Building designed by the architect Frank Gehry. His buildings—the Guggenheim Museum in Bilbao, Spain, concert hall at Bard College in New York State and the Walt Disney Concert Hall in Los Angeles—have thrilled people around the world.

Information: Convention & Visitors Bureau of Greater Cleveland (800-321-1004, *www.travel cleveland.com*).

ST. AUGUSTINE, FLORIDA

America's oldest city, St. Augustine, FL, was founded in 1565. It boasts Spanish colonial and revival architecture found nowhere else in the country, splendid gardens, beautiful beaches and good birding.

Walk along the narrow tree-lined streets of the historic district, with its early 18th-century houses and massive 19th-century Spanish revival hotels. Visit the Fountain of Youth Archaeological Park (Ponce de Leon may have found the legendary fountain here when he discovered Florida in 1513) and be sure to take a sip.

And, don't miss the Castillo de San Marcos, an imposing fortress which overlooks the Atlantic Ocean, the Spanish Quarter Museum, the St. Augustine Alligator Farm, the only place in the world with every species of crocodile on display, and the lighthouse and museum, with 219 steps to climb for a panoramic view of Matanzas Bay and the Atlantic Ocean.

Don't miss the free guided tour of the Ponce de Leon Hotel, a lavish Spanish revival structure built by the millionaire developer Henry Flagler at the end of the 19th century. The hotel, with its Tiffany stained glass, gold-leafed Maynard murals and electricity done by Thomas Edison, is now the home of Flagler College.

Information: St. Augustine, Ponte Vedra & the Beaches Visitors and Convention Bureau (800-653-2489, *www.visitoldcity.com*).

More from Joan Rattner Heilman...

Pet-Friendly Travel

An increasing number of lodgings—from low-cost motel chains to luxury hotels—now welcome pets in guest rooms. Some even offer amenities like special pillows, bowls and gourmet menus.

Facilities have opened up in many cities to provide daytime or overnight care for your pet while you are doing the town. There are even doggy country clubs, complete with swimming pools, gourmet biscuits and massages.

FINDING A HOTEL

At least one-third of all locations of the largest lodging chains, which include Super 8, Howard Johnson, Holiday Inn and Travelodge, give the nod to pets. All the La Quintas will welcome them if they are under a certain size. And so do many inns, bed-and-breakfast establishments and, surprisingly, even luxury hotels, like the Four Seasons in Atlanta and the Hotel Monaco in Chicago.

For listings of thousands of hotels, motels, bed-and-breakfasts and inns that accept pets, go on-line to such Web sites as *www.petsonthego. com, www.petswelcome.com* or *www.takeyour pet.com* and click on the area or city where you would like to stay. These sites also dispense other helpful information about leaving home with a pet and even include periodic e-letters.

Guidebooks are another route to finding a welcoming destination. *Pets on the Go!* (Dawbert) describes appropriate lodgings throughout the US along with information about the surrounding areas. The new edition of AAA's *Traveling With Your Pet—the AAA PetBook* also lists thousands of hotels that accommodate pets along with their owners. Both the publications include advice for making the trip more enjoyable for everyone.

If you prefer to stay at a specific hotel or lodging chain, call and ask about its pet policy or check its Web site. For example, Holiday Inn's Web site at *www.holiday-inn.com*, enables you to look up the pet policy at any of its locations worldwide.

RESTRICTIONS

Sometimes there are restrictions on the type of creatures that may share your room. Many motels or hotels allow only dogs and/or cats.

Often there is a limitation on the size of these guests. Some do specify, for example, that dogs and cats may weigh no more than 15 pounds. La Quinta takes them up to 50 pounds.

Some lodgings do insist that the animal be housebroken and that you take your dog with you on a leash when you leave your room. At least one specifies no barking. Cats are usually no problem when it comes to noise.

LUXURY HOTELS

There is an amazing number of upscale hotels around the country that are so eager for visits from you and your pet that they offer special amenities just for them. *Examples...*

●**Loews Hotels.** Its "Loews Loves Pets" program, available at 18 hotels in the US and Canada, offers a complimentary bag of pet treats and a toy, specialized bedding for dogs and cats, place mats with food and water bowls, a room service menu that includes a variety of dishes such as grilled chicken or lamb for dogs, liver or salmon for cats.

More information: Call 800-235-6397 or visit *www.loewshotels.com.*

●**Four Seasons.** Goodies offered at the Four Seasons Hotel in Atlanta include a ceramic pet bowl, a dog biscuit made by the pastry chef, room service featuring both chopped steak and grilled chicken breast, and a newsletter, *The Pampered Pooch,* that tells you such things as the best places in town to walk your dog.

More information: Call 800-332-3442 or visit *www.fourseasons.com.*

●**Fairmont.** Four-legged guests at the Fairmont Scottsdale Princess in Arizona can get the "Paws on Board" package—a welcome biscuit, special bowl, a pet room with soft beds, toys, gourmet food and more.

More information: Call 866-540-4495 or visit *www.fairmont.com.*

●**Kimpton.** Most of the Kimpton Boutique Hotels are well-known for pampering their pet guests. For example, the Hotel Monaco Chicago has its "Furry Friends Package" in which dogs get a special bed, a bowl and a doggy bone. Cats receive a disposable litter box and bowl and a special kitty treat. Both get a souvenir bandanna. Upon request, the hotel also provides a complimentary goldfish companion during your stay.

More information: Call 866-610-0081 or visit *www.monaco-chicago.com.*

IT'S A GREAT LIFE

●**Biscuits & Bath Doggy Village** in New York City provides day care for your pooch, a lap pool for refreshing swims, indoor grassy running fields, birthday parties and Sunday brunches for both of you.

More information: Call 212-419-2500 or visit *www.biscuitsandbath.com.*

●**America Dog and Cat Hotel** offers free time to hit the casinos for travelers who take pets to Las Vegas. Sign up for day care or overnight stays in private pet suites with color TVs, super-soft beds and an enclosed yard. Other amenities include bubble baths and limousine transfers.

More information: Call 702-795-3647.

●**Paradise Ranch** in La Tuna Canyon, California, is a bed-and-breakfast for canine guests only, with full-sized furnished bedrooms and real beds, play yards with waterfalls and wading pools. For dogs staying overnight accustomed to sleeping with their owners, a human "bed buddy" is provided for an extra fee.

More information: Call 818-768-8708 or visit *www.paradiseranch.net.*

ODDS AND ENDS

●**Take a pet to Britain.** Dogs and cats can now travel to the UK from the US without undergoing six months' quarantine. They must, however, meet certain criteria set up by the UK Pet Travel Scheme, such as vaccination against rabies, treatment for tapeworms and an ID microchip. Continental Airlines now operates services for pets from Newark, Houston and Cleveland to London.

More information: Call 212-745-0277 or visit *www.britainusa.com/pets.*

●**Finding a pet-sitter.** If you would rather leave your pet home when you travel, consider finding a professional and certified "in-home pet-sitter."

More information: Contact the National Association of Professional Pet Sitters at 800-296-7387 or visit *www.petsitters.org.*

Also from Joan Rattner Heilman...

Free (or Almost Free) Lodging Around the World

Why should you pay even the lowest rates for hotel rooms when you can find lodgings that are absolutely free, or almost free?

Join a "hospitality exchange," and you will be able to stay in other people's homes in the US and abroad. In return, you agree to host visitors in your home at your convenience.

Bonus: This is a great way to make new friends, and many hosts are happy to act as local guides.

Exchange clubs differ in purpose. Some clubs were formed to promote peace and friendship among peoples of the world, while others are strictly about cheap lodgings.

Some charge yearly membership fees. Most provide on-line directories of their members and leave the visit arrangements up to you. In many instances, it is recommended that you request lodgings for no more than a few nights.

HOSPITALITY EXCHANGE

This association of "friendly, travel-loving people" publishes two directories per year full of listings of members who want to stay in one another's homes. You make your own contacts and plan your visit at a time that is convenient for both parties.

Membership cost: $20* a year, $35 for two years.

Information: 406-538-8770, *www.hospex.net.*

AFFORDABLE TRAVEL CLUB

This exchange club is limited to travelers over age 40. You receive an annual directory from which you choose your hosts and others choose you. Visitors pay hosts $15 for a single room or $20 for a double per night and $10 for each additional person. The club also offers

*All prices subject to change.

house-sitting and pet-sitting services where club members move into your house while you are on vacation and enjoy a visit to your neighborhood in exchange for caring for your house or pets.

Membership cost: $60* a year.

Information: 253-858-2172, *www.affordable travelclub.net.*

GLOBAL FREELOADERS.COM

Everything is free in this cooperative network of people willing to accommodate travelers, from membership to your home stay. In return, you must host other travelers whenever convenient. Although most members are Australian, American, British or Canadian, there are about 12,000 members in more than 130 countries.

Cost: Free.

Information: *www.globalfreeloaders.com.*

EVERGREEN BED & BREAKFAST

This club is exclusively for travelers over age 50. You pay $10 for a single room or $15 for a double for each overnight stay, including breakfast. Choose host families from the club's directory, and arrange your visit directly with them. A quarterly newsletter keeps you up to date.

Membership cost: $60 a year single, $75 per couple.

Information: 800-962-2392, *www.evergreen club.com.*

ELDERTRAVELERS.ORG

Eldertravelers.org is a Web site for mature travelers that helps match guests with hosts in the US, Canada and several other foreign countries. Members post information about themselves, their homes and communities and may even include photographs.

Cost: Free.

Information: *www.eldertravelers.org.*

SERVAS

Servas, the world's oldest free hospitality exchange, was formed more than 50 years ago to promote friendship and peace among people throughout the world. Working through mutually arranged visits, it enables hosts and visitors "to share their lives, interests and concerns regarding social issues."

*All prices subject to change.

More than 14,000 hosts in 130 countries welcome other members in their homes for a night or two without charge. It is open to travelers of all ages, who must provide two letters of reference and be interviewed for acceptance.

Cost: $50* a year for travel within the US only, $85 for US plus international travel.

Information: 212-267-0252, *www.usservas. org.*

LESBIAN AND GAY HOSPITALITY EXCHANGE INTERNATIONAL

This network of approximately 500 people around the world offers hospitality to other members at no charge beyond the membership fee. Established as a way to make the world a friendlier place for its members, LGHEI issues an annual directory from which to choose potential hosts for two-night stays.

Membership cost: $30 per household.

Information: *www.lghei.org* or LGHEI, c/o J. Wiley, Schonleinstr. 20 D-10967, Berlin, Germany. 011-49-30-691-95-37.

WOMEN WELCOME WOMEN WORLD WIDE

This club was formed to foster international understanding and friendship among women from many cultures. Women Welcome Women World Wide (5W) now has approximately 3,000 members in 70 countries.

In addition to providing a listing of all members with descriptions of themselves and their homes, it also schedules conferences and gatherings that are announced in its three newsletters each year. Partners, family and friends are allowed to accompany members on visits, although they may not join the club.

Membership cost: $47 a year.

Information: 011-44-1494-465441, *www. womenwelcomewomen.org.uk.*

*All prices subject to change.

Inns, Cruises, Spas— For Adults Only

David West, a travel writer based in Grand Rapids, MI. He is coauthor of *Adults Only Travel* (Diamond), one of Amazon.com's top-selling travel guides.

It's no fun vacationing without kids if everyone else around the pool brought theirs. *Here are inns, spas, resorts and cruises for adults only…*

B&Bs/INNS

● **Berkeley Springs Spa & Inn,** Berkeley Springs, WV. Set on 30 acres of Appalachian countryside, two hours northwest of Washington, DC. The town's mineral springs have been attracting visitors since the 1700s. The package deal includes one massage and one other spa treatment per person and gourmet meals. Eight rooms. $350 per night per couple or from $550 to $630 for two-night packages.* 304-258-4536, *www.berkeleyspringsinn.com.*

● **China Clipper Inn,** Ouray, CO. Located in the "Switzerland of America," so-called because of its charming Alpine architecture. Skiing, hot springs, art galleries and good restaurants are all nearby. 12 rooms. $85 to $230. 800-315-0565, *www.chinaclipperinn.com.*

● **Cliff House Bed & Breakfast/The Cottage,** Freeland, WA, on Whidbey Island, 25 miles northwest of Seattle. Private woods, miles of Puget Sound waterfront and spectacular sunsets. You can do your own cooking. Continental breakfast is included. Cliff House sleeps four, $450. The Cottage sleeps two, $195. 800-450-7142, *www.cliffhouse.net.*

● **Evening Shade Inn,** Eureka Springs, AR. Located in the woods of the Ozarks. Eureka Springs' architecture and winding streets evoke 19th-century Europe. Breakfast included. Eight rooms. $120 to $180. 888-992-1224, *www. eveningshade.com.*

● **Felton Crest Inn,** Felton, CA. Located minutes from Big Basin Redwoods State Park and Monterey Bay. There are more than 40 local wineries in the area. Four luxury suites,

*Rates are per room per night unless otherwise noted. All prices subject to change.

each with private bath and Jacuzzi. Continental breakfast is included. $375 to $445.* 800-474-4011, *www.feltoncrest.com.*

CRUISES

●**Aqua Cat Cruises,** Miami, FL. A 102-foot, 11-cabin luxury catamaran offers snorkeling and scuba-diving cruises to the Bahamas and Exuma Islands. About 90% of cruises are adults only. $1,695 per person for an eight-day cruise. 305-888-3002, *www.aquacatcruises.com.*

●**Windstar Cruises,** Seattle. Four-masted sail-yachts cruise to the Caribbean, Mediterranean, Central America, New Zealand and the Greek isles from ports in foreign countries.

Example: A Caribbean cruise might depart from Barbados.

About 85% of the cruises have no children onboard. Seven- to 10-day cruises cost $1,395 to $5,000 per person. 800-258-7245, *www.windstarcruises.com.*

ISLAND RESORTS

●**Royal Plantation,** Ocho Rios, Jamaica. This beachfront resort offers a choice of gourmet restaurants, massages on the beach, scuba diving and golf. Required carts and caddy services are extra. All 80 suites have ocean views...many provide Jacuzzis. $320 to $1,430. 888-487-6925, *www.royalplantation.com.*

●**Harmony Club Resort,** Paget Parish, Bermuda. Provides 68 guest rooms in five charming buildings, each built in the island's traditional English style. Walk to nearby Stonington Beach. Includes all meals and afternoon tea. From $318 per night per person for three nights...$1,047 for five nights. Golf package available for an additional $120 per person per day. Rates based on double occupancy. 888-427-6664, *www.harmonyclub.com.*

●**Rendezvous Castries,** Castries, St. Lucia, West Indies. Each room has an ocean view. Scuba diving, waterskiing and tennis are available, with basic instruction at no extra cost. All-inclusive. 100 rooms. $170 to $300. 800-544-2883, *www.rendezvous.com.lc.*

SPAS

●**Canyon Ranch Health Resort,** Tucson, AZ. All-inclusive spa featuring classes on stress

*Rates are per room per night unless otherwise noted. All prices subject to change.

and weight management. Four-night packages start at $2,701 per person, double occupancy.* 800-742-9000, *www.canyonranch.com.*

●**Tennessee Fitness Spa,** Waynesboro. This spa, 95 miles southwest of Nashville, is set in 100 acres of forest, with miles of hiking trails. Meals included. $675 to $1,450 per person per week. 800-235-8365, *www.tfspa.com.*

*Rates are per room per night unless otherwise noted. All prices subject to change.

Another Side of Disney

The Nature Conservancy's Disney Wilderness Preserve is a 12,000-acre protected area only about 40 minutes from Disney World. A seven-mile trail system begins at the visitor center. Hikers may see eagles, blue herons, alligators and other wildlife.

Details: The Nature Conservancy (407-935-0002, *www.nature.org/florida*).

Backpacker, 33 E. Minor St., Emmaus, PA 18098.

Impartial Reviews of Hotels, Resorts and Vacation Spots Worldwide

At *www.tripadvisor.com* you'll find comprehensive travel information including unbiased reviews, travel guides and recommendations for hotels, resorts, inns and travel and vacation packages. There's also a search engine that lets you find the best deals at major travel-booking Web sites, such as Orbitz, Expedia and Travelocity. Plus, you can get maps and other information about potential destinations. And after a trip, you can post your own reviews and travel experiences for the benefit of others.

Family Fun, 114 Fifth Ave., New York City 10011.

How to Shop Smart For a Cruise

Susan Tanzman, who is frequently named one of the top 200 travel agents in the US by *Travel Agent* magazine. She is president of Martin's Travel & Tours, 3415 Sepulveda Blvd., Los Angeles 90034.

Today's growing number of cruise lines, ships, itineraries, onboard activities and pricing systems make it easier than ever to pick a cruise that's fun and affordable.

By knowing the ropes, you can spend as little as $80 a day per person for an inside cabin for two, $150 a day for a cabin with a sea view or $400 to $500 for a luxury cabin or suite.

You can cruise on a ship that has 3,000 other passengers or on a craft with only a few hundred. If you have already been on the familiar Caribbean routes, consider a cruise to Quebec City on Celebrity Cruises, the California wine country on American Safari Cruises or Monte Carlo on SeaDream Yacht Club.

Internet discounters and cruise lines themselves frequently offer cut-rate prices, but it's often wiser to book through a travel agent, unless you're already familiar with the cruise lines and their ports of call.

Reason: Knowledgeable travel agents can give you the information that cruise companies might be reluctant to share or that Internet sites don't have.

BOOKING SMART

Tell the travel agent exactly why you want to go on a cruise—to visit interesting ports, take part in onboard activities or just to lounge on deck and enjoy the ocean.

Once the agent suggests several cruises, ask…

●**How large is the vessel?** The number of passengers often determines the atmosphere of a cruise.

If you're one of 3,000 passengers, you'll have the opportunity to meet lots of people and participate in a wide variety of onboard activities.

But it's usually best to choose a much smaller vessel if you're looking for a romantic cruise where you can dine, dance and stroll the deck with someone you love.

Rule of thumb: Whenever there are more than 1,200 passengers, the multiple seatings will likely make meals less relaxed.

●**Who are the other passengers?** Cruise lines cater to different types of passengers. Crystal Cruises, for instance, attracts many passengers over the age of 50. Many cruises cater to parents traveling with their adult children. Others have activities for kids traveling with their parents or grandparents.

●**What activities does the cruise offer?** Activities usually include gambling, swimming, exercise classes, dancing, nightclub entertainment, non-gambling games and lectures on a wide range of subjects.

Examples: History, sea lore and wildlife.

●**What's the cabin size?** Ignore pictures of cabins in brochures and on the Web that make accommodations appear larger than they actually are.

Important: Ask for the actual dimensions and ask about portholes.

SAVING MONEY

Myth: To get a bargain price, you must book a cruise a few days before the ship sales.

Reality: Whenever a cruise isn't fully booked as quickly as the company anticipates, it routinely discounts the fare, even if the departure date is months away.

Here's how to get the best value for your money when looking for a cruise…

●**Don't book cruises when school is out.** Discounts are seldom available at these peak periods, and airfares to the port of departure are also higher.

Moreover, cruises at high seasons are rarely as much fun as they are at other times.

Example: Crowded ships and overworked staffs are the norm for most European cruises in July and August and for many Caribbean cruises in early January.

●**Book your own transportation to the port of departure.** All lines will provide air or transfer services to passengers of their cruise line. In many cases, allowing your travel agent to make these transportation reservations can provide you with tremendous savings in the cost of these services.

●**Ask about the price of shore excursions.** Some excursions are well worth the $40 to $200 that they typically cost, but others are a waste of money. In many port cities, for instance, you can walk or take an inexpensive taxi to the most interesting areas.

●**Ask about group rates.** Some lines have group rates for organizations or a certain number of people that are much lower than individual fares. Others offer discounts on the amount of money that group members spend on board.

●**Find out what's included in the price.** Some cruise lines include beverages, games and entertainment in their prices—others don't.

●**If you plan to drink alcoholic beverages on a cruise,** consider bringing some of your own or buying a bottle at your first port. Also pack some soft drink mixes, especially if you travel with children who might charge several sodas a day to your bill.

Bringing drinks of your own can mean a big savings because most cruise lines charge high prices for them.

Example: A couple who enjoys several soft drinks during the day and a cocktail or two in the evening can easily spend $300 to $400 on beverages on a week-long cruise.

STAYING HEALTHY

The cruise ships occasionally report incidents where a large number of passengers become ill, often with stomach problems. Though there are no complete statistics available, it's doubtful that you are more likely to become ill on a cruise ship than at any restaurant. *Recommended...*

●**Purchase travel insurance just in case.** It should cover medical expenses, including evacuation if needed. Most policies also cover travel delays and loss of luggage.

Typical price: $20 to $30 a day.

●**If you are concerned about tobacco smoke,** choose a cruise that limits smoking to certain areas of the ship.

SEASICKNESS

Don't necessarily give up on a cruise because you're vulnerable to seasickness. *To reduce the chance of becoming ill...*

●**Book cruises on large vessels,** which are less susceptible to the movements that cause seasickness.

●**Don't sail at a time of year when waters may be rough.**

Example: November in the Caribbean waters. The travel agents who book cruises are usually very knowledgeable on the subject.

●**Ask your doctor to prescribe a medication** for motion sickness.

●**Consider a cruise on the Mississippi River** (Delta Queen Steamboat Co., *www.delta queen.com,* 800-543-1949). These cruises are as stable as boat rides can be.

Cruise Line Rip-Off

Many cruise companies now automatically add a charge of $40 to $120 for trip insurance unless you specifically state that you do not want it.

Best: If you do want trip insurance, you can probably get it for a better price elsewhere. Ask your travel agent.

Arthur Frommer's Budget Travel, 350 Fifth Ave., New York City 10118.

The Best Cruise Lines

Top cruise lines, based on itineraries, crew, service, cabins, food and activities...

●**Small ships**—Seabourn Spirit (800-929-9391, *www.seabourn.com*)...Silversea Silver Shadow and Silver Wind (800-722-9955, *www. silversea.com*)...Radisson Seven Seas Paul Gauguin (800-477-7500, *www.rssc.com*)...Windstar Wind Spirit (800-258-7245, *www.windstar cruises.com*).

●**Large ships**—Celebrity Infinity, Mercury and Galaxy (800-722-5941, *www.celebrity.com*)

...Princess Sea Princess and Dawn Princess (800-774-6237, *www.princess.com*)...Royal Caribbean Enchantment of the Seas (800-398-9819, *www.rccl.com*).

View the entire survey at *www.concierge. com/cntraveler*. Click on "All Lists," then on "Cruise Poll."

Survey of almost 29,000 readers by *Condé Nast Traveler,* Four Times Square, New York City 10036.

On-Line Travel Auctions

On-line auctions for travel can get you very good deals—if you do some research first. Don't assume that the retail value listed at auction sites is accurate—it may reflect high-season or full-fare rates. Check sites with firm prices, such as *www.bestfares.com*...*www.travelocity. com*...and *www.expedia.com,* then set a bidding limit before visiting an auction site.

Caution: Auction-site packages often don't provide specific dates. You must make reservations after winning the auction—on a space-available basis. If you're not flexible about travel dates, you may be unable to use the trip.

Best travel auction sites: www.luxurylink. com...www.skyauction.com.

Tom Parsons, editor, Bestfares.com, 1301 S. Bowen Rd., Arlington, TX 76013.

When Your Airfare Drops Before the Flight...

If the airfare drops on a scheduled flight, you may be able to get a refund for the difference. But, it depends on the airline. Airlines usually will refund the difference if you find a lower fare for which you still qualify—on the same airline, for the same flight.

Example: If your current ticket requires 14-day advance purchase and the cost drops 15 days before your departure.

Some airlines charge fees of $50 to $100 to change your flight. Some will post a refund to your credit card...others only will give you a voucher for future air travel—usually good for one year.

Randy Petersen, publisher of *InsideFlyer,* 1930 Frequent Flyer Point, Colorado Springs 80915.

If You're Switching to a New Frequent-Flier Program...

When switching to a new carrier's frequent-flier program, you may be able to get elite status without accumulating the required miles. Show the airline your elite-level travel patterns on your current carrier and which of the new carrier's routes you expect to use.

Helpful: Contact the vice president or manager of the carrier's frequent-flier program, and explain how much you will be flying in the future. Request a specific level. Once enrolled, you must fly enough to maintain the status.

Bob Jones, consumer specialist for OneTravel.com, a value-oriented travel Web site, East Greenville, PA.

Better Overnight Parking At the Airport

Overnight parking at the airport is getting more and more expensive. As an alternative, several hotel chains have park/fly packages. If you spend the night before your flight at a hotel that offers this package, you can then leave your car in the hotel's well-lit, guarded parking lot—for free. Most include a shuttle to/from the terminal, coffee (sometimes breakfast) and a morning newspaper.

The typical package includes up to seven nights' parking. However, you may be able to negotiate a low (but not a free) parking rate for longer stays.

Among the chains providing this deal are Hampton Inn (800-426-7866, *www.hampton inn.com*)...Radisson (800-333-3333, *www.radis son.com*)...and Red Roof Inns (800-733-7663, *www.redroof.com*).

Nancy Dunnan, editor and publisher of *TravelSmart,* Dobbs Ferry, NY, *www.travelsmartnewsletter.com.*

More from Nancy Dunnan...

Travel Free by Becoming A Group Leader

Many travel companies and packagers will provide free travel to an individual who puts together a large enough group for a trip. Often the number is 12, but it may be lower and also may be negotiable in today's tough environment for the travel industry. Such deals are offered by hotels, cruise lines, airlines and packagers—but you have to call them and ask for the group planning department.

Alternative: Have a travel agent make the inquiries for you, and you'll still get a big break on price.

To Avoid Long Check-In Lines at the Airport...

Send your luggage ahead to avoid the long check-in lines at the airport and at baggage claim. Luggage Free charges $2* per pound of luggage with a minimum cost of $95, for shipping anywhere in the US, which includes Alaska, Hawaii and Puerto Rico. And, the cost is $4 per pound for Canada and $5 per pound for Western Europe. It supplies all shipping labels, wraps luggage in heavy plastic, picks up bags, tracks them and will let you know when they arrive. Bags are automatically insured for up to $1,000, and additional coverage is available.

Information: 800-361-6871, *www.luggage free.com.*

*All prices subject to change.

Your Rights In an Airport Search

Before you go through airport security, be sure you know your rights...

●**If selected to be patted down,** you may ask to have it done out of view of other passengers and by a screener of the same gender.

●**You may ask to be examined by hand** instead of by X-ray machine.

●**If you take injectable medicines,** you may carry syringes that have a professionally printed label.

●**If you have a pacemaker,** you may request a pat-down inspection instead of walking through a metal detector.

●**You may request a pat-down** if you do not want to go through the metal detector for religious or cultural reasons.

More information: On-line at *www.tsa.dot. gov,* click on "Travelers & Consumers."

Get the Best Seat On the Plane

To find the best airline seat check *www.seat guru.com.* Select the airline you're flying and the type of plane, and the site will tell you which seats are the roomiest and quietest. All seats are color coded for "bad," "beware" and "very good."

How to Minimize Jet Lag

To help minimize the effects of jet lag, adopt your destination's time schedule in advance —for example, research indicates that eating meals on the destination's time schedule for several days before you leave is helpful. Also, sleep on the airplane to be rested when you arrive—take a short-acting sleeping pill when needed—and avoid caffeine and alcohol on the flight. At your destination, exposure to sunlight will help you feel more alert.

Bradley Connor, MD, president, International Society of Travel Medicine, Stone Mountain, GA, *www.istm.org.*

Much Smarter Long-Distance Travel

On trips to distant locations, consider planning a several-hour layover en route. This can provide a low-cost vacation dividend.

Example: Whenever you are flying from the US to Europe or beyond, you can schedule your flights to create a long layover—as long as it is no more than 24 hours—in Paris or London. The airline may even provide food vouchers for meals during the layover. The result is a free day in Paris or London.

Arthur Frommer's Budget Travel, 350 Fifth Ave., New York City 10118.

Rent Cars Away From the Airport For Big Savings

One of the big national car-rental companies recently quoted a price of $68/day for a car rented at the San Diego airport...or $42 for the same car rented downtown.

More: Getting into town from the airport is easier and less costly than ever in many major cities—using public transportation, airport shuttles or even taxis at some in-city airports.

Family Fun, 114 Fifth Ave., New York City 10011.

More Rental-Car Savings

If you are picking up and returning a rental car to the same location, bid for car rentals at *www.priceline.com* and *www.hotwire.com.* They only cover same-city rentals and may get you much lower rates than rental companies offer by phone or on-line.

Strategy: Find the best rate companies offer. Then start with a much lower bid for a full-size car. If it is not accepted, go down one size and up slightly on the bid...or try again 72 hours later, when these bidding sites allow rebids.

Jens Jurgen, publisher and editor, *Travel Companions,* Amityville, NY 11701, *www.travelcompanions.com.*

More from Jens Jurgen...

Better On-Line Bidding For Hotel Deals

First research hotel room rates and deals at travel sites, such as *www.orbitz.com...www. travelocity.com...www.travelweb.com...www. hotwire.com...*and *www.hotels.com.* Also check with the hotel directly, then bid for a room at *www.priceline.com.* You often can get a room for 30% to 75% less than the lowest price at other sites, especially for late bookings.

Helpful: Access *www.biddingfortravel.com* before making a bid. Successful bidders post their results at this site—giving you guidelines for your bids.

Safer Hotel Stays Overseas

For safer hotel stays when abroad, look for a hotel with space between the entranceway and the building itself—for example, a courtyard—and a parking garage that is not located directly under the building for greater safety from car bombs. Also, look for a hotel with only a few entrances, which are always watched. And, book a room on the third or fourth floor—rooms on these floors are less vulnerable but still low enough for easy evacuation if necessary. Finally, spend as little time as possible in the lobby.

Condé Nast Traveler at Four Times Square, New York City 10036.

On-Line Travel-Health Resources

The following useful Web sites will help you stay healthy when you travel...

•**Centers for Disease Control and Prevention (CDC)** gives information on problems in specific regions. *www.cdc.gov/travel.*

•**Travel Health Online** has easy-to-read information. *www.tripprep.com.*

•**International Society of Travel Medicine** lists travel health clinics and physicians. *www.istm.org.*

•**International SOS** helps travelers obtain advice from Western-trained doctors. *www.sos-international.com.*

David Freedman, MD, professor of medicine and director, Travelers' Health Clinic, University of Alabama School of Medicine, Birmingham.

Stay Away from These Cities If You Have Health Problems

Avoid traveling to the three smoggiest cities —Mexico City, São Paulo and Cairo—if you have cardiac or pulmonary diseases, such as congestive heart failure, asthma, bronchitis or emphysema. The poor air quality may exacerbate symptoms.

Also avoid: Large cities in Southeast Asia and the major cities of China, even though most SARS-related travel restrictions have been lifted.

If you must spend time in any heavily polluted cities, minimize activities on the smoggiest

days—stay indoors in an air-conditioned room. Have your medical condition evaluated before travel, and bring enough medicine to last you through the trip.

Stuart R. Rose, MD, president of Travel Medicine, Inc., providers of information and products for safe travel, 369 Pleasant St., Northampton, MA 01060, *www.travmed.com.*

Safer Overseas Travel

For more secure travel abroad during these turbulent times...

•**Register with the US embassy at your destination before leaving the US**—go to *http://usembassy.state.gov* and click on the country you are planning to visit to download registration forms.

•**Read government travel warnings** from the US at *http://travel.state.gov* and from Britain at *www.fco.gov.uk/travel.*

•**Check global news** through the *International Herald Tribune's* Web site, *www.iht.com,* and look for English-language papers available at your destination at *www.onlinenewspapers.com* and *www.newsdirectory.com*

•**Stay in hotels that receive CNN or BBC** broadcasts so you can keep abreast of the news.

Condé Nast Traveler at Four Times Square, New York City 10036.

Safety Guidelines for Solo Travelers

Nadine Nardi Davidson, travel consultant, Travel Store, Inc., Los Angeles, and author of several books, including *Travel with Others Without Wishing They'd Stayed Home* (Prince).

Traveling alone can be adventurous and fun, but at the same time solo travelers need to take important safety precautions like the following...

●**Leave a copy of your itinerary with a friend** or relative back home, so you can be tracked down.

●**Read guidebooks and carry maps of the cities you plan to visit,** so you don't get completely lost.

●**Check in with the US consulate.** Ask about trouble spots.

●**Only stay in hotels or motels with interior hallways.** Take the same precautions in a foreign city that you take at home.

●**Don't walk down dark alleys** or in dimly lit streets at night.

●**Latch the chain-lock** when you're in your hotel room.

●**Don't wear expensive jewelry** or carry expensive luggage, particularly when in a Third World country.

●**Carry your money—and passport—in a money belt** or pouch that you wear under your clothes.

●**Take public transportation only in daylight,** so you can see where you're going and assess the area for safety.

When sightseeing, keep an eye on the time and make sure you have a safe way—a taxi, for instance—to get back to your hotel.

More from Nadine Nardi Davidson…

How to Make Solo Travel More Enjoyable

If you prefer to travel alone, but still would like to be with people, consider…

●**Escorted tours,** with a guide and group of 10 to 40 people.

●**Hosted packages,** in which you join the group when you wish and are on your own the rest of the time.

●**All-inclusive resorts,** where you can mingle as you like.

●**Participating in a language class** at your destination.

●**Joining a cooking class** in the region you are visiting.

Tipping Basics

Not sure how much to tip the bellman or housekeeping? *Take a look at these handy guidelines…*

●**Airport skycap and porter,** $1 per bag—more if luggage is heavy.

●**Taxi or limousine driver,** 10% to 15% of the total fare.

●**Shuttle-bus driver,** $2 per person.

●**Hotel bellman,** $1 to $2 per bag.

●**Doorman,** $1 for each taxi.

●**Hotel housekeeping,** $1 to $2 per day.

●**At restaurants,** 15%…or 20% for outstanding service…10% if you eat in the bar.

●**Coat check,** $1.

●**Restroom attendants,** 50 cents to $1.

Information: *www.tipping.org.*

What You Need to Do Before Going on Vacation

Before you go away on a vacation…remove first-floor window air conditioners, and lock windows before leaving…consider installing security bars (with interior quick release, in case of fire), especially on ground-level windows that are not easily seen from the street, such as those in the basement or the back of the house …and finally don't leave garage-door remotes in cars left at home in the driveway.

Jean O'Neil, director of research and evaluation for the National Crime Prevention Council, Washington, DC, *www. ncpc.org.*

15

Having Fun

Fun at the Races—Easy Rules to Boost Your Odds

A day at the races can provide the excitement and conviviality that are missing today in many other pastimes. And winning can make the experience even more fun.

Although only the experts who analyze races for hours a day can expect to win consistently, casual race goers can increase their chances by following a few simple rules...

SET LIMITS

Put a ceiling on how much you'll bet during any one day at the track. A useful rule is to risk what you would be prepared to spend on dinner for two at a fine, but affordable, restaurant. For many people, that would be about $100.

USE RELIABLE DATA

The vast majority of race fans rely on the *Daily Racing Form* for information on horses, tracks, jockeys, trainers and other factors that influence the outcome of races. The publication is on sale at most large newsstands for about $5.

Information: 800-306-3676, *www.drf.com*.

It takes a while to learn how to read and interpret the data, but casual race goers can benefit from these two statistics...

• **Beyer Speed Figures.** These are comparative numbers based on the performance of each horse in every race it has entered, as adjusted for the particular speed of the tracks on which it has run.

Examples: The Kentucky Derby winner might have a Beyer Speed Figure of 120, while a habitual also-ran at minor racetracks could have a figure of 30.

In general, horses with higher speed numbers will beat those with lower figures. Though a horse with a speed figure of 97 won't always beat one with a figure of 96, a horse that has a

Andrew Beyer, horse racing columnist for *The Washington Post,* creator of the *Daily Racing Form's* Beyer Speed Figures and author of several books on handicapping, including *Beyer on Speed* (Houghton Mifflin).

243

figure of 105 will nearly always finish ahead of a horse rated at 75.

● **The trainer's record.** Statistically, the record of a trainer is much more important than that of a jockey. The *Daily Racing Form* makes it easy to compare trainers' records.

Strategy: Bet only on horses whose trainers have a winning record above 20%. Avoid betting on horses with a trainer whose winning percentage is in single digits.

Note: Even experienced bettors occasionally ignore trainer records.

Example: In the 2002 Kentucky Derby, War Emblem had one of the country's top trainers as well as the highest Beyer Speed Figure, but when he won, he paid odds of 20 to 1.

Helpful: If you don't see a clear choice after looking at the speed number and other information, don't bet, or don't bet heavily.

AIM HIGH

Strive for one or two big wins for the day rather than trying to limit your losses with a series of small bets. You can do that either by betting a large portion of your $100 on one race or by playing the exacta or another type of combination bet where the payoff is big.

The logic: It's more fun to aim for a big payoff. In the long run, your chances of winning, say, $200 on one combination bet are just as good as the odds of winning that much by making small, "safe" bets on each race.

Typical combination bets…

● **Exacta.** Picking the winner as well as the second-place finisher in a single race.

● **Trifecta.** Picking the first three finishers in a single race.

● **Superfecta.** Picking the first four finishers in a single race.

● **Daily double.** Picking the winners of two designated races—usually the first two.

● **Pick three.** Picking the winners of three designated races.

● **Pick four.** Picking the winners of four designated races.

LEAVE EMOTIONS AT HOME

Basing bets on your emotions is a sure way to lose.

Example: If you lose a bet in an excruciating photo finish, you may feel the urge to bet the next race heavily in a desperate effort to recoup. Resist that temptation.

If you've won several races in a row, you might become overconfident and start to bet rashly. Resist that temptation, too.

Helpful: Whenever you're tempted to let emotions replace discipline, skip a couple of races. Go to the lounge and relax.

If you maintain betting discipline, racetracks can be a bargain. The general admission at most racetracks is about $3, clubhouse figures a little higher. Today's best tracks also have excellent restaurants and elegant lounges where you can watch simulcasts of the races.

Mr. Beyer's favorite tracks…

● **Belmont Park,** Elmont, NY, 516-488-6000, *www.nyra.com/belmont.*

● **Del Mar Thoroughbred Club,** Del Mar, CA, 858-755-1141, *www.delmarracing.com.*

● **Gulfstream Park,** Hallandale Beach, FL, 800-771-8873 or 954-454-7000, *www.gulfstream park.com.*

● **Santa Anita Park,** Arcadia, CA, 626-574-7223, *www.santaanita.com.* For information on special luncheons for seniors that are held several times a year, call 626-574-6400.

● **Saratoga Race Course,** Saratoga Springs, NY, 518-584-6200, *www.nyracing.com/saratoga.*

Better Las Vegas Sports Betting

Don't bet on teams that have a national following—handicappers know that fans favor these teams, so the odds aren't the best. Instead, become an expert on a small conference—since the small-school games generate limited interest, line makers give them much less attention, so a knowledgeable bettor can have an edge. Sports betting is legal only in Nevada.

Stanford Wong, a professional gambler in Las Vegas, and author of *Sharp Sports Betting* (Pi Yee).

Top Poker Player's Winning Strategies for All

George Epstein, columnist for *Poker Player,* a biweekly newspaper, available free at many casinos throughout the US. He is also the author of *The Greatest Book of Poker for Winners!* (T/C).

I t is now estimated that more than 50 million Americans play poker regularly, whether it's in card rooms, casinos or their own homes. For most, the primary goal isn't winning—it is enjoying an evening with friends. But even in casual low-stakes games, winning makes playing more fun. *A few simple strategies, described below, can improve your chances...*

READ YOUR OPPONENTS

Body language and betting patterns provide clues to the strength of your opponents' hands. When cards are dealt, don't look at your hand right away. Instead, check out your opponents. *Look for...*

• **Posture.** A player might sit up straighter after receiving a card that helps his/her hand. Conversely, a player might slouch or even lean back in his seat or cross his arms when a hand doesn't come together as he had hoped.

• **Reaching for or glancing at chips.** This often signals that a player has a good hand.

• **Feigning boredom, then betting.** A player who looks away from the table and appears disinterested, then bets, almost certainly has a good hand.

• **Covering the mouth.** If a player has a hand in front of his mouth when he makes a bet, there's a very good chance he is bluffing—unless he is trying to trap you.

• **Trembling hands.** When an opponent's hands are shaking as if he were cold or scared, it's a good sign that he has very strong cards.

• **Fidgeting.** If a player is drumming the table or otherwise fidgety after receiving his final card, wait for him to look at you, then slowly move your betting hand toward your chips. If the drumming stops, he's probably bluffing. If it continues, he likely has a strong hand.

FOLD MOST HANDS

The single biggest mistake that poker players make is playing mediocre hands. If there are seven players in the game, only one of the seven hands is the best at the table. Stay in significantly more often than that, and you're almost certainly playing at a disadvantage.

Fold if you start with a bad or marginal hand. In "Seven-Card Stud," a marginal hand is a small pair or three to a flush. In "Texas Hold 'Em," it is two to a medium-high flush. Folding early costs only your ante. Also fold if your hand isn't improving but betting is getting costly.

Helpful: Players who stay in too often typically do so because they get bored while waiting for the next hand. Don't think of time not playing as wasted time. Use the opportunity to study your opponents' tendencies and betting patterns. Try to determine what hands they stay in with.

PICK THE RIGHT SEAT

If you know your opponents, choose a seat just to the left of the most aggressive bettor. Since a player to your right generally has to act before you, you can see how much he bets and determine if you want to stay in the game.

PICK THE RIGHT GAME

Most home games are "dealer's choice," in which the player gets to select the variety of poker when it is his turn to deal.

If you're one of the stronger players at the table, select games that have no wild cards, such as "Seven-Card Stud" or "Texas Hold 'Em." If others in the game are stronger, pick games that have wild cards. Wild cards increase the role of luck and decrease the need for skill.

MAKE THE OCCASIONAL BLUFF

Bluffing is a good strategy for two reasons...

• **You'll win some pots,** even if you don't have a great hand, by driving out opponents.

• **Even if you lose the hand,** you'll give your opponents the impression that you sometimes stay in when you don't have great cards. This encourages them to call your bets later, when you may have a winning hand.

One of the best times to bluff in seven-card games is after you receive a sixth card that gives you four to a flush or four to an open-ended straight. A big bet might convince some opponents that your straight or flush already is made. Even if you don't make the straight or flush on the seventh card, follow it up with a big bet on the last round if you sense weakness in your remaining opponents. Timid players are easier to bluff out.

Caution: Bluffing when there are three or more opponents is tough.

Helpful: By the seventh card, there usually is enough money in the pot to make it worth calling one last bet, even if you think you have lost. Fold if an opponent can beat you with his face-up cards.

SHREWD PLAY FOR SEVEN-CARD STUD

One of the most common poker variations is "Seven-Card Stud." Each player is dealt two cards face down, followed by four face up, then a final face down, with a round of betting after each of the final five rounds of cards. Each player makes his best five-card hand out of the seven cards he has been dealt.

The most important decision of the game frequently is whether to stay in after the initial three cards…

●**Be cautious with low-pair hands.** If you possess a pair after receiving your first three cards, it might seem like you're doing well. But low-pair hands often turn into costly second-place finishes.

Example: Your first three cards are 5-5-2. You might have the best hand at this point, but odds are against your winning. With only two 5s left in the deck, the odds are less than 5% that you'll be dealt another 5 for three of a kind. Even if you receive another deuce later, your two low pairs still will lose more often than they win.

In general, stay in with a low pair only if your nonpaired card, or "kicker," is very high—say, 5-5-King—and other players aren't already in possession of the cards you need to improve the hand. Fold if either of the 5s you need for three of a kind or more than one of the kings you need to pair your high kicker are face up in other players' hands. These rules can be bent if betting remains very low.

●**Bet high or raise on a high pair,** a pair of 10s or better. A pair of aces or kings after three

cards is likely to win roughly 75% of the time if only two people stay in the hand. The odds drop to less than 60% with three players left in the game and to about 30% with five left. Bet high early to drive out some opponents before they get a chance to improve their hands.

Helpful tip: Three cards to an open-ended straight or three cards to a flush are both strong "drawing" hands worth playing—but don't bet heavily until after the fifth card has been dealt. If you make your straight or flush, you're likely to win even if everyone stays in—and you'll win a bigger pot.

How to Play the Slots and Win

Victor H. Royer, a gambling industry consultant in Las Vegas who has worked for some of the leading casinos and slot machine manufacturers. He is author of 18 books on casino gambling, including *Powerful Profits from Slots* (Kensington).

Until the mid-1980s, slot machines truly were one-armed bandits with the house having an advantage of 20% or more.

Since then, casinos have come to rely on slot machine players for most of their revenues. This has created competition among casinos and dramatically sweetened the odds for the players.

Here's how to maximize your chances of winning when playing the slots…

WHERE TO PLAY

●**Visit Vegas.** Slot machines in Las Vegas offer the best odds in the country, giving the house an advantage of just 2% to 4%. Only an expert blackjack player has better odds in a casino. But beware—slot machines in bars or other non-casino locations generally offer terrible odds.

Slots in Reno and in the tribal casinos of the East Coast are not quite as advantageous as those in Las Vegas, but they're still better than those in Atlantic City, where house advantages of 6% to 8% are common. Riverboat and tribal casinos of the Midwest generally offer the worst odds, with house advantages of as much as 10%.

•Look for high-profile "slot islands." Casinos want gamblers to see people winning. In most casinos, slot islands—clusters of four to six slot machines (sometimes on slightly raised platforms)—are placed where the aisles intersect. These machines often offer the best chance of a jackpot.

Also try slot machines located near the main casino cage, where winnings are collected.

•Avoid slot machines near table games. Casinos don't want the noise of slot machine payouts to disturb the people playing blackjack or craps.

Also skip slot machines located near buffet lines. Casinos know that people standing in line will play the slots out of boredom even without frequent payoffs.

PICK THE RIGHT MACHINE

•Choose $1 slots. Quarter slot machines typically have much lower payback rates than $1 machines. The $5 or $10 slots offer even better odds, but most recreational gamblers would go through their money too fast to make these machines enjoyable.

•Choose three-reel machines. These tend to have slightly better odds.

•Look for "double-up" or "triple-up" machines. These offer two or three times the usual payout as well as marginally better odds.

My favorite slots: All reel and video slots from IGT, including Double Diamond, Triple Diamond, Triple Lucky 7s and Triple Double Dollars.

•Don't invest too much in "progressive" slots. These machines—which offer a shot at huge jackpots that build up over time, sometimes into the millions of dollars—will typically have poor odds. They exist for the same reason that lotteries exist—people like to dream big.

MORE STRATEGIES

•Bet the most coins per pull that a machine allows. The majority of slot machines offer a better percentage of return when more coins are played.

Example: The highest jackpot on a $1 machine might be $800 if a single $1 coin is played. However, if two $1 coins are played simultaneously, the jackpot becomes $2,000—that is a 150% increase in return for a 100% increase in your investment.

•Play after the crowds. Most slot machine players visit the casinos between the hours of 5 pm and 11 pm. If you play just after all the crowds leave, the slot machines are likely to be full of their money. That's when you will have a better chance of finding a machine that will produce a winning jackpot.

•Switch machines if you have several "almost" jackpots. If a machine comes close to a jackpot several times—say, all three sevens are visible but not in the payout line—that does not mean it is about to pay off. My experience suggests it is less likely to hit the jackpot anytime soon.

Winning Scrabble Tricks

Joe Edley, the only three-time National Scrabble Champion. He is the director of clubs and tournaments for the National Scrabble Association in Greenport, NY, and coauthor of *Everything SCRABBLE* (Pocket).

Knowing just a few simple strategies can help you to win big the next time you play Scrabble…

•Learn two-letter words. The 96 accepted two-letter words provide you with opportunities to "play parallel."

Example: If the word "man" is on the board and you have the word "deluge" in your hand, you can add your word by placing your *u* under the *m*, your *g* under the *a* and your *e* under the *n*. *Mu, ag* and *ne* are accepted two-letter words. You'll score a total of 17 points for all four words you created—plus any premium letter or word square bonus.

Other strategic two-letter words: Aa, ae, ai, bm, mm, oe, xi, xu. For a complete list—along with all of the three-letter words—look in *The Official SCRABBLE Players Dictionary* (Merriam-Webster).

•Do not waste an *s*. *S* tiles are valuable because they can be added to the ends of many words to create openings on the board. Never use an *s* unless you can earn at least eight points over what you could collect otherwise.

● **Know the words that contain a *q* but no *u*.** *Faqir, qaid, qanat, qat, qindar, qindarka, qintar, qoph, qwerty, sheqel* and *tranq* can help you use the 10-point *q*. You can add an *s* to the end of any of the above except *qindarka* and *sheqel*.

● **Watch for common prefixes and suffixes,** such as *re-, un-, -ing, -ies, -ier, -ent, -ate, -sion* or *-tion*. They often can help you play all seven tiles, so you can earn an extra 50 points.

Example: Let's say you have the letters *a, i, n, o, o, r, t.* After you put *tion* together, it is easier to see that you have the seven-letter word *oration.*

● **Don't be afraid to trade in letters.** Average players rarely trade in letters because they must forfeit a turn to do so—but trading in can be a smart move. You don't have to dump all of your letters, just the ones you don't want. *Some strategies…*

● If you have all vowels, trade in five or more tiles. Keep an *e* and an *a* if you have them.

● If you are one vowel away from a great seven-letter word, trade in the odd letter. *Example:* If you have *e, l, n, r, s, t, v,* trading in the *v* might get you *rentals, relents* or *linters.*

● If the highest scoring word you can make is 10 points and you're using fewer than five tiles, strongly consider trading in a few tiles.

● **After three minutes, make your play.** There is a 90% chance that you'll have found the best play you could have within that time. Any longer, and you won't enjoy the game.

Sports News Anytime, Anywhere

John Skilton, president of SkilTech, Inc., which designs and maintains Web sites for more than 25 professional sports teams and leagues, Elkton, MD, *www.skiltech.com.*

Want to check a score and can't wait for tomorrow's paper? Want to confirm a rumor about a coach leaving your favorite team? Or maybe you are just curious about who holds the record for the most blocked shots in the NBA? (See below for the answer.) *Free, fascinating sports news and trivia await you on the Web…*

FOOTBALL

● **College news, scores and standings for every level,** from Division I-A through Division III. Includes a complete NCAA football rule book and record book. *www.ncaafootball.net.*

● **Division III college football.** You can follow teams that don't get much coverage in the media. Links to Internet audio broadcasts of many games. *www.d3football.com.*

● **The National Football League's official site offers statistics,** schedules and links to team sites. *www.nfl.com.*

● **NFL news, stats and schedules.** See what your team might look like next year with the mock draft at the Pro Football News Web site. *www.profootballnews.net.*

BASKETBALL

● **College and pro news for men's and women's teams,** plus a basketball record book that has *the answer* to the question asked above —Elmore Smith holds the record for the most blocked shots in an NBA game (17 on October 28, 1973). *www.basketball.com.*

● **College basketball coaches,** such as Oklahoma's Kelvin Sampson and Cincinnati's Bob Huggins, check in with their own sports columns. *www.collegeinsider.com.*

● **Division III basketball.** A great way to keep tabs on these college basketball teams. *www.d3hoops.com.*

● **Basketball news about every level,** from the high school level through the NBA and WNBA. *www.insidehoops.com.*

● **Business side of basketball.** Interesting articles and news. Check which teams owe others draft picks from past trades or own the rights to other teams' future picks. *www.realgm.com.*

HOCKEY

● **Historical hockey stats.** The Internet's largest repository of hockey data. *http://hockeydb.com.*

Example: Mark Messier passed Gordie Howe for the National Hockey League's (NHL) most-games-played record.

- **The NHL's official site has scores,** schedules and links to team sites. *www.nhl.com.*

BASEBALL

- **Official site of Major League Baseball.** Find season statistics and links to team sites. *www.mlb.com.*
- **On-line photos of hundreds of major- and minor-league ballparks.** A great way to select interesting parks to visit on vacation. *www.digitalballparks.com.*

GENERAL

- **CBS Sportsline.** Sports coverage from the CBS TV network. *www.sportsline.com.*
- **ESPN.** One of the largest sports sites. *www.espn.com.*
- **Our Sports Central.** Minor-league sports articles and links. *www.oursportscentral.com.*
- **Pro Sports Daily.** News and rumors about big-league baseball, football and basketball. *www.prosportsdaily.com.*

A Unique Book Program

Leave books for strangers and brighten the lives of others through reading. You can register books at *www.bookcrossing.com*—where more than 1 million books are currently registered. After registering, paste an ID label on the inside cover so future readers can report the book's location to the site. Then simply leave books where others are likely to find them, with a "Read Me" sticker on the front. Books have been left everywhere from restaurants to the hands of park statues.

Ron Hornbaker, cofounder of BookCrossing.com, and president and chief technical officer, Humankind Systems, Inc., a software and Internet development company, both in Kansas City, MO.

Starting an Art Collection

To build an art collection, choose a medium that you like, such as oils, watercolors or lithographs. Or buy a variety of media with a single subject, such as flowers or bridges. Purchase what appeals to you—not only at galleries, but also at street fairs, tag and estate sales, and on the Internet. Buy what you like—do not focus on whether it will go up in value.

Family Circle, 110 Fifth Ave., New York City 10011.

Family Reunion Basics

Start planning a family reunion at least a year in advance. Choose a chief planning coordinator and a child-friendly location. Look for a place with attractions for people of all income levels, and be sure there are plenty of ways to get there. Also, plan ahead for still photos and videos and consider giving out disposable cameras to everyone on arrival.

Helpful: Family Reunion by Jennifer Crichton (Workman), *Your Family Reunion: How to Plan It, Organize It, and Enjoy It* by George Morgan (Ancestry) and Web sites such as *www.myfamily.com* and *www.familyreunion.com.*

Ladies' Home Journal, 125 Park Ave., New York City 10017.

Anniversary Celebration Ideas

To celebrate a big anniversary, show wedding photos, invitations and mementos at the party. Also, have younger family members read a story or produce a skit about how the couple met. If celebrating outdoors, plant a tree or bush.

Before the celebration: Have family members and friends send favorite anecdotes about the couple along with photos. Arrange them in a memory album or make a collage for presentation at the party.

Robin A. Kring, author of *Happy Anniversary! A Guide to Fun and Romantic Anniversary Celebrations* (Meadowbrook). Ms. Kring is based in Denver.

Dinner Gift Myth

Wine or food brought by guests does not have to be served with dinner. The host has already planned his/her menu, including drinks to be served. Rather than put your host on the spot, when you present your gift, say that it is something that can be enjoyed on another occasion.

Good Housekeeping, 959 Eighth Ave., New York City 10019.

Smart Fund-Raisers For Your Club, Society Or Church

Andy Robinson, fund-raising consultant in Plainfield, VT, and author of *Selling Social Change (Without Selling Out)* (Jossey-Bass).

Scott Pansky, partner, Allison & Partners, Los Angeles–based marketing firm that works with nonprofits.

Valerie Reuther, Coupeville, WA–based trainer of professional fund-raisers.

Fund-raising has become very difficult in recent years. Here are four offbeat-but-effective techniques that may work for your next fund-raiser.

FROM ANDY ROBINSON

●**Send invitations to an event that isn't going to happen.** Explain that there will be no dull speeches, rubber chicken or blistering walks. If they just send in their $50 "entry fee," they can stay home with their families.

Example: The Community Food Bank in Tucson sponsors an annual "Full Sun, No Run" charity marathon. Participants receive T-shirts that read *I didn't run.*

●**Collect stuff, not money.** Ask members to donate items for a yard sale. Post flyers and place classified ads in papers—many will run ads for free. See if the town will donate a location, such as a park.

FROM SCOTT PANSKY

●**Trade publicity for goods and services.** Contact the PR department of a local company that can help you.

Examples: A nursery could provide supplies for your garden club in exchange for being the club's sponsor. Or a sporting-goods chain could let your runner's club distribute membership forms in its stores. Dole Foods donated food to a walkathon for the United Autism Alliance. Dole's name was on T-shirts and brochures.

FROM VALERIE REUTHER

●**Throw small parties, not huge events.** Ask group members to host dine-around dinners in their homes. Bring the parties to a central place for dessert and coffee. Attendance is better at intimate parties than at large, formal dinners—and there are no catering costs.

All of these ideas work well as annual programs—and the planning will become easier. Good luck!

16

Automotive Know-How

Your Car Could Be Making You Sick

 ealth dangers could be lurking in a place where you would least expect to find them, inside your automobile.

Your car can cause backaches, carpal tunnel syndrome, respiratory illness, even brain dysfunction. *The problem areas...*

INADEQUATE VENTILATION

Highway air contains ozone, carbon dioxide, carbon monoxide, methane, hydrocarbons, various dusts and pollens and many other pollutants. Exposure is dangerous for everyone, but especially individuals who suffer from anemia, heart disease or lung diseases, including asthma.

What's more, the air *inside* a moving car can be dirtier than the air outside, according to the International Center for Technology Assessment. The intake system sucks in pollutants emitted by the vehicle that's in front. When that vehicle

has a diesel engine, the level of pollutants inside the vehicle behind it is six to eight times greater than it would be if the front vehicle had a regular engine.

Before you buy a car: Ask to review the owner's manual. It contains information about the car's filter. Microfilters screen out varying degrees of particulate matter, including dust and pollen. Any microfilter that allows the passage of particles that are five microns or larger is worthless.

Three types of filters offer the best protection —activated charcoal, carbonite or, best of all, zeolite. These remove most harmful gases and other pollutants.

If you already own the car: You can place charcoal filters over the air-intake ducts under

Basil M. RuDusky, MD, physician in private practice in Wilkes Barre, PA, specializing in internal medicine, cardiology and forensic medicine. He also is a lifelong automobile enthusiast who has achieved an international reputation as an automotive consultant. Dr. RuDusky is author of *Your Car Can Be Hazardous to Your Health: The Book Automakers and Politicians Prefer You Not Read* (1stbooks Library).

the hood, just in front of the windshield cowl (which supports the rear of the hood and the windshield). The filters are available at most home-supply stores. Cut the filter to fit, and seal it in place with duct tape. Change the filter yearly. Also, when driving in traffic, close the car's air vents to the outside.

TOXIC NEW-CAR SMELL

Those new-car fumes can make you sick. A Japanese research group measured "outgassing" from test cars' interior leather, plastic, foam, vinyl and glues and discovered 114 harmful compounds, including formaldehyde gas. The group concluded that the interiors of new cars were 45 times worse than the World Health Organization's standards for indoor air quality. Even people who seem unaffected by the new-car smell can be at increased risk of health problems in the future. People with lung and heart problems are especially vulnerable.

Before you buy: Sit in the car with the doors closed for at least 10 minutes—longer if possible. Pay attention to any changes in your nose, eyes, throat and chest, such as tearing, burning or dryness. Be aware of strange tastes in your mouth, headache or feelings of dizziness or lightheadedness. These can be signs of trouble ahead.

If you already own the car: Driving with the windows open whenever possible may help somewhat. Leave the car windows open when it is in the garage. It can take anywhere from several weeks to several years for the new-car smell to dissipate.

POORLY DESIGNED SEATS

Poor seating can cause low back pain, sciatica (pain that travels from the small of the back down the sciatic nerve in the leg) and nerve damage to your back and thighs. Some of the most common seating problems in cars you'll encounter include insufficient padding...poor lumbar support...excessively hard bolsters... and inadequate adjustability.

Before you buy: Adjust the seat to be sure that it supports your lower, middle and upper back. Some car manufacturers offer seats with additional lumbar support as an option. Ask your dealer. Make sure the seat bottom has adequate downward and forward tilt to ease

pressure on your thighs. If you feel like you're sitting *on* the seat rather than *in* it, you'll never be comfortable. Take the car out for a 30-minute test drive—the bumpier the road, the better. Does the shock absorption seem satisfactory?

If you already own the car: You may be able to compensate for a poorly designed seat with a lumbar support (sold in many auto-supply stores) or a rolled up towel placed behind the small of your back.

ILL-FITTING HEADRESTS

These can wreak havoc on your neck, head and shoulders.

Before you buy: Measure how far you must tilt your head backward to reach the headrest. If it's more than two inches, then move on to another car. You never will be comfortable and surely will suffer a whiplash injury if you are involved in an accident.

Also beware of boxtop headrests, which are so hard that they increase the risk for injury. So-named because they resemble rectangular cubes, they occasionally crop up in some cars.

If you already own the car: You may be able to improve comfort and safety with inserts or covers for the headrests. Ask for these at an auto-supply store.

POOR POWER STEERING

A car that is difficult to steer can cause neck and/or arm strain. It also can cause or exacerbate bursitis, tendinitis, tennis elbow, cervical disk syndrome, osteoarthritis and carpal tunnel syndrome, among other ailments.

Before you buy: Steer the car using only your thumb and two fingers of one hand. If you can do this easily, then the power steering is adequate.

If you already own the car: Unfortunately, in this case, there is nothing you can do to improve the steering.

HEALTHIEST CARS

Cars from German and Swedish companies, which traditionally have emphasized health and safety, are among the best.

My favorites: Audi...BMW...Buick Century ...Mercedes-Benz...Saab...Saturn...Volkswagen ...Volvo.

GET YOUR MONEY BACK

If you own a car with problems that can't be corrected, appeal to the dealer or manufacturer. Many states give car dealers three chances to correct unresolved defects that the consumer has documented in writing to the dealership and the manufacturer.

After that, you have the right to request that the manufacturer send a technical-support specialist to the dealership to fix the problem.

If that's unsuccessful, you can contact your state's attorney general's office or hire an attorney. I know of several cases in which manufacturers took back a car and reimbursed the owner in full.

Protect Yourself From Air Bags

Tim Hurd, spokesperson for the National Highway Traffic Safety Administration, Washington, DC.

Car air bags can be dangerous. Air bags have saved 7,500 lives since being introduced in the 1980s—but also have killed more than 200 people who would have survived without them.

Key: Most of these deaths occurred when riders weren't properly belted into their seats, and then were thrown rapidly forward into an inflating air bag.

Safety: You must be at least 10 inches from the steering wheel or dashboard that contains an air bag to be safe from injury when it is released. The proper use of seat belts keeps riders in a vehicle from being thrown forward within this distance.

Note: If you move your car seat forward, be sure you maintain this distance from the steering wheel or dashboard by raising or lowering your seat if it is adjustable.

Do I Really Need to Turn Off the Engine When Fueling My Car?

David Solomon, a certified master auto technician and chairman, Nutz & Boltz, a consumer automotive membership organization, Box 123, Butler, MD 21023, *www.nutz andboltz.org.*

Your car won't explode if you keep the engine on when fueling, but there are other dangers associated with fueling your automobile.

Worries about explosions date back to the days when cars backfired frequently, producing sparks that could ignite fuel.

Today's dangers stem from doing something else while fueling, such as…

●**Getting back into the car to stay warm in winter.** The friction caused by getting in and out of the car when air is dry produces static electricity, which can spark a fire. Wait until you are done fueling to get back in the car.

●**Using a cell phone.** Your phone could create sparks that might cause an explosion.

The main danger of keeping the engine on while fueling is to your wallet. A car's emissions system constantly tests itself while the car is running. When the engine runs during fueling, the vapor containment system may report a problem. Then the "check engine" light will come on shortly after you leave the station. Diagnosing the problem could cost $150 or more.

More from David Solomon…

What You Need to Know Before a Tow

Before your car is towed, read the tow contract carefully. If it gives the towing company exclusive rights to repair your vehicle, cross out that clause before you sign. Then tell the tow driver that you want to retain the right to have the car fixed where you choose. Tell him/her where to drop off the vehicle. Walk around the car with him, and note on the contract any damage—or lack of damage—before towing starts.

Pothole Protection

To protect your car from potholes, follow this advice…

●**Don't use the brake if you are about to hit a pothole**—let the vehicle's springs and shock absorbers handle it.

●**Watch cars in front of you.** If a car suddenly swerves or bumps up and down, slow down and expect a pothole ahead.

●**Be cautious about driving cars with low ground clearance**—low cars are more likely to be damaged. Low-profile tires have narrower sidewalls, so their wheels are more likely to be damaged by potholes.

●**If you hit a pothole hard, pull off the road** and look for tire or wheel damage. Make sure that your hubcap is in place. Even if everything seems fine, have a mechanic check your wheel alignment as soon as possible.

Anthony Ricci, president, Advanced Driving & Security Inc., North Kingstown, RI, www.1adsi.com.

Do You Need to Tune-Up Your Car?

Auto tune-ups are less important now than they were in the past. They can cost as much as $300 and do little for today's models, which have onboard diagnostic systems, long-lasting spark plugs and few electromechanical components. If your car is not running properly, a tune-up won't find the problem. Instead, ask your mechanic to focus on the particular complaint, find its cause and correct it.

Donald Johnson, supervisor of the California Bureau of Automotive Repair's San Jose field office, which monitors repair garages for compliance with state consumer-protection laws.

Car Fact vs. Fiction: Take This Quiz

Eric Peters, Washington, DC–based veteran automotive columnist and author of Automotive Atrocities: Cars You Love to Hate *(Motorbooks International).*

Think you know the difference between car fact and fiction? Try this quiz, and see how you do. *True or false…*

●**Air-bag–equipped cars are always the safest vehicles you can buy.**

A. False. When it comes to safety, the size and the weight of a car are the most important considerations. A 4,000-pound, full-sized sedan provides better passenger protection in most crashes than a 2,500-pound compact. While air bags make compacts and subcompacts more crashworthy, they don't provide the protection of larger, heavier vehicles.

Bottom line: Buying an older "land yacht" can be a safer bet than a late-model compact. For the safest car, I recommend a large wagon, like the Volvo V70 or the Chrysler Pacifica.

●**Sport-utility vehicles (SUVs) are more dangerous than cars.**

A. False. In general, bigger, heavier SUVs are safer in most crashes. SUVs equipped with four- or all-wheel drive also are less likely to slide out of control. It is true that some high-riding SUVs have a greater risk of rolling over during abrupt maneuvering. On the rare occasion when an SUV does roll over, the roof might not hold up as well as a passenger car's. Why? Government regulations exempt most SUVs from both the bumper-impact and roof-strength standard imposed on passenger autos. Some of the safest 2004 SUVs rated by the Insurance Institute for Highway Safety include Volvo XC90, Lexus RX 330 and Ford Explorer.

●**Modern cars with antilock brake systems (ABS) are safer than older cars without them.**

A. True—if the driver knows how to use ABS. Many drivers with ABS-equipped cars are afraid to fully depress the brake pedal in a panic stop. They don't realize that ABS prevents the wheels from locking and possibly skidding.

Instead, they pump the brakes, so the vehicle may not stop in time to avoid a collision.

●**Minivans are safer than most cars.**

A. False. Minivans aren't required to comply with the same bumper-impact and roof-strength standards as passenger cars, and they lack the weight of SUVs. Even a minor impact can result in serious damage to the van and its passengers. Research each model.

Two of my favorites that meet regular passenger vehicle safety standards: Honda Odyssey and Toyota Sienna.

●**More people are saved by seat belts than become trapped by them in wrecks.**

A. True. The odds of being killed or seriously injured when not wearing a seat belt are significantly greater than the chances of being trapped inside by one. People not wearing seat belts are four times more likely to die or be seriously injured if ejected.

●**You should never buy a former rental automobile.**

A. False. There are some advantages to buying a rental car. Rental fleets usually are well maintained and serviced according to a strict "severe duty" schedule that includes more frequent oil changes. Documentation of all work performed also should be available.

Best: Family cars and sedans.

Worst: High-performance and sporty models, which may have been rented for joyriding or other abusive driving.

More from Eric Peters...

How to Fix a Scratch or Chip on Your Car

If you have scratches on your car, beware. Bare steel is susceptible to rust. Even a small area showing the primer coat will corrode quickly. This can result in a big repair bill.

Fixing a small scratch or chip is easy. All you need is a tube of touch-up paint in the correct factory pigment as well as several cardboard matches. The parts counter at your car dealer or an auto-parts store can sell you the right color for your model.

Cost: About $6. A body shop would charge you about $60 to do the job.

When the scratch is bigger than a pencil eraser or metal is dented, take your car to a body shop for professional attention.

To repair the smaller chips—one-quarter-inch or less...

●**Clean and dry the area** using regular car-wash soap and water.

●**Thoroughly mix the touch-up paint.**

●**Work a small drop of paint onto the spot** using the ragged edge of a paper match. (The applicator brush that comes with some paint is hard to control.)

●**Dab on just enough paint to cover the damaged area.** Don't paint outside the edge of the chip or scratch. Use paint sparingly.

●**Allow the first coat to dry for several hours,** then dab on a second coat. Two light coats are better than one thick coat.

●**Let the car sit overnight.**

●**Use polishing compound to blend the repaired area** with the surrounding paint. My favorite products for this are Turtle Wax and Meguiars Dual Action Cleaner Polish.

Cost: Less than $19.

●**Finish the job by waxing the entire car.** When this is done right, the repaired area should be very hard to distinguish.

Also from Eric Peters...

Get Top Dollar for Your Used Car

It takes some savvy planning to get the most for your old car and to get it quickly. Do it right, and you'll be several hundred dollars richer. *Eight steps to getting more for your car with the least hassle...*

●**Find out the fair market price.** Check out the Kelley Blue Book at *www.kbb.com* or the National Automobile Dealers Association at *www.nada.org.* Guides are available in libraries and bookstores.

You can save time by selling to a used-car dealer or a gas station. Expect to be offered as much as 10% below what you could get if you sold it on your own. If you want to keep that money or the offers are too low, then sell the car yourself.

●**Set your price.** Decide on the price you want, and pad it by 10% so you can negotiate with people who want to haggle.

●**Prepare the car.** Clean the vehicle inside and out. This can increase your selling price by up to 15%. Fix problems—especially those that affect safety. Most people won't buy cars with existing problems. Weigh the cost of a repair against your expected return. If the cost is high, disclose the problem and discount the price.

Caution: If you knowingly sell a car with a safety problem but don't disclose it, you can be sued.

Cars in poor mechanical shape and worth less than $1,000 are good candidates to sell for scrap or to give to charity for a tax deduction.

Get a new state inspection sticker to show that the car meets requirements. Some states insist on an updated emissions certificate before new tags/registration can be issued.

●**Advertise.** Put an ad in your local newspaper's auto section.

Include: The make, model, year, mileage, options (air conditioning, automatic transmission, sunroof, etc.), color, an honest description of condition, your telephone number and times to call. If the vehicle is in poor shape, has faded paint or needs work, mention it. People will find out when they visit, so don't waste your time or theirs.

●**Showing the car.** Talk up your car's best points, show repair records and cite the used-car guide valuations if a prospect makes you an offer that's too low.

Always accompany a prospective buyer on a test drive. Do not be hesitant about refusing this courtesy if you have any doubts about the individual—people have been carjacked during test drives. If you agree to a test drive, ask to see his/her driver's license and proof of insurance. If something were to happen, your insurance company might demand proof that you confirmed the test driver was trustworthy. Jot down the information, and leave it behind.

Caution: Don't permit anyone under age 18 to drive your car without a parent or guardian present. People under 18 rarely have their own insurance. If he has an accident, you could be held responsible for the damage and any injuries. Furthermore, as a minor, he cannot enter into contracts or sign any legal documents, such as a car title. A parent or guardian must sign on his behalf.

●**Preparing paperwork.** Draw up a bill of sale yourself listing the sale price, the car's year, make, model and vehicle identification number (VIN). The VIN is on the car's title and also on the left side of the dashboard near the windshield. Date the document and state that the vehicle is sold "as is" to ensure that an unforeseen problem does not come back to haunt you. Print your name and the buyer's name. Each of you sign the agreement and keep a copy.

Example: Sold one (YEAR, MAKE, MODEL), VIN (XYZPDQ), with (XX,XXX) miles, to (PRINT BUYER'S NAME) for the amount of $X,XXX. Vehicle is sold "as is." Signed, (SELLER) (BUYER) (DATE).

●**Transfer title.** On the car title, there is a box in which the owner must sign before the buyer can go to the department of motor vehicles and have a new title issued in his name. Don't sign the bill of sale or the title until you are paid in full. Accept only cash or a certified check or money order.

Beware: The new owner's plates must be on the vehicle when it leaves your home. You don't want to receive his parking or speeding tickets. Acquiring new tags is the responsibility of the buyer.

●**Notify the department of motor vehicles and your insurance company of the sale.** Most departments of motor vehicles have Web sites that explain how to do this. Go to a search engine, such as *www.google.com,* and search under the keywords "DMV" and your state. Call or write your insurance company after the vehicle has changed hands.

How to Be Sure a Used Car Hasn't Been In a Serious Accident

Many used cars are rebuilt after they have been "totaled." Your best bet is to have a qualified and trusted mechanic examine the car thoroughly and check out its history with Auto-Check at *www.autocheck.com* and/or CarFax at *www.carfax.com.*

Both services will charge $19.99* for a basic report. You'll need the car's vehicle identification number (located on the dashboard or door-post of the car). The report will indicate if the preowned car was in a flood, hailstorm, accident or fire…if it was stolen, salvaged, rebuilt or used as a rental car, taxi or police car…and if it's had an odometer rollback.

Moneysaver: As we go to press, both Car-Fax and AutoCheck are offering one free record report (a list of how many records there are on a specific vehicle).

Nancy Dunnan, a financial adviser and author in New York City. Ms. Dunnan's latest book is titled *How to Invest $50–$5,000* (HarperCollins).

*All prices subject to change.

More from Nancy Dunnan…

How to Get Out of a Car Lease

To get out of a car lease, try using one of the "early termination services." They will not only try to match you with someone interested in taking over your lease, they will also walk you through the procedure. Either you or the buyer will have to pay a fee, but that is something you can negotiate.

Two services: LeaseTrader (800-770-0207, *www.leasetrader.com*) and Swapalease (866-792-7669, *www.swapalease.com*).

Good Reasons to Buy a New Car Instead of Used

Here are three sound reasons to purchase a new vehicle instead of a used one…

●**The interest rate on a bank loan for a new car is lower than that for a used car.**

●**The average new-car buyer now spends approximately $23,200** and keeps the car for eight years, while the average used-car buyer spends $11,000 and keeps the car for three to four years. So over time, the cost for new and used cars is almost the same.

●**Used cars cost more to repair.**

Ashly Knapp, CEO, AutoAdvisor.com, a nationwide consumer auto-consulting service, Seattle.

More know-how from Ashly Knapp…

Better Negotiating for a New Car

When purchasing a new car, negotiate the price based on the dealer's invoice.

Example: Don't negotiate a specific dollar figure for the new car. Instead, offer "$200 less than the invoice price"—and avoid going higher than "$100 more than the invoice price."

Reason: If you offer a specific dollar figure, you then are subject to the standard contract clause that requires you to pay any retail price hike that may occur before your new automobile arrives.

If you negotiate based on invoice, however, the dealer's invoice will remain the basis of your cost.

Finally from Ashly Knapp…

How to Get a Great Deal on a New Car

To get the best deal on a new car, price the exact car you want at the manufacturer's Web site. Also price the car at *www.kbb.com*… *www.autoadvisor.com*…and *www.edmunds. com.* Check with three local dealers for availability and their best price. Then go to the manufacturer's Web site and enter the zip codes of areas within a 1,000-mile radius—a weekend of driving—to get dealer names and phone numbers. Make an offer to local dealers…car-buying services, which you can locate using any Internet search engine…and dealers in the other cities. Typically, local dealers will try to match your best price.

Car Loan Savings

Save hundreds to thousands of dollars by refinancing your car loan. These loans are available at rates as low as 4.95%.* The better your credit, the lower your rate. Your only cost is a recording fee, usually $15 or less, to register the name of the new lender. Car loans are available through most AAA Clubs at *www.aaa.com,* as well as credit unions, banks and the on-line lenders, such as Capital One Auto Finance at *www.capitaloneautofinance.com* and E-Loan, Inc. at *www.eloan.com.* Lenders typically will not refinance loans for less than $7,500.

Barbara Wilson, product manager for financial services, Automobile Club of Southern California in Los Angeles at *www.aaa-calif.com.*

*All rates subject to change.

Extended Warranty Warning

Extended car warranties may not deliver on their promises.

Example: National Warranty Risk Retention Group, which backed close to one million extended warranties, recently shut its doors.

Self-defense: Buy a service contract from an auto manufacturer or a nationally known repair chain. Before buying a warranty, ask the company selling it if it will honor the warranty's terms if the insurer fails.

Charlie Vogelheim, executive editor of *Kelley Blue Book,* a vehicle-pricing resource with information on factory original, extended and third-party warranties, Irvine, CA, *www.kbb.com.*

Prepare Now For an Auto Breakdown

GM Motor Club, Southfield, MI, *www.gmmotorclub.com.*

Be sure you keep the following essential items in your vehicle in case it happens to breakdown…

- **Jumper cables.**
- **Tire changing equipment**—an inflated spare tire, jack and lug wrench.
- **Flares and/or reflective devices** to warn other drivers.
- **Cell phone to use to call for help…**or a *call police* sign.
- **"Approved" empty gasoline container.**
- **Blanket.**
- **Bottled drinking water.**
- **Flashlight and extra batteries.**
- **Message pad and writing marker.**
- **First aid kit.**
- **Copy of your health insurance card.**
- **List of emergency contacts.**
- **Automobile registration.**
- **Proof of insurance.**
- **Motor club membership card.**

Before You Back Up…

Accidents when backing up are responsible for 30% of vehicle-related child fatalities. This type of accident happens because of blind spots behind vehicles—particularly SUVs, pickups and minivans.

Best: Before driving, walk behind the car to check for children.

For extra safety: Consider a rear-mounted camera, which works on any vehicle.

Cost: $400 or more, plus installation.

Consumer Reports at 101 Truman Ave., Yonkers, NY 10703.

17

Taking Care of Home and Family

How to Profit from Cleaning Up Your House

It pays—quite literally—to look through your house periodically and either sell or give away possessions that you no longer need or want.

Some of these items may be far more valuable than you might expect them to be. Postcards, fountain pens, photographs and everyday dishes are just some of the often-overlooked objects for which the collectors seem to have an endless fascination.

Before selling any of your possessions: Consider whether it is an heirloom that might best be kept in the family. If so, choose a family member who will cherish it and pass it on when the time comes.

When you give a valued possession to a relative, make sure that he/she understands its importance to your family history as well as its monetary value.

APPRAISALS COME FIRST

If you decide to sell the item, get an appraisal to establish the item's age, authenticity and monetary value. The first and most important rule of selling your possessions is never to sell anything before you know what it is worth.

Appraising 20 items will take a professional appraiser about two hours. The charge ($100 to $350 per hour) can almost always be recouped by being able to sell items for more than you might otherwise have thought they were worth.

To locate an appraiser: Ask for referrals from the trust department of your bank, your attorney or your homeowner's insurance agent. Ask the prospective appraisers to let you speak with several of their previous clients, and reject any who won't.

If an appraiser offers to buy any of the items he's pricing, thank him for his time, and then look for another appraiser. Tell the person you

Joe L. Rosson, an antique columnist and cohost, with Helaine Fendelman, of *Treasures in Your Attic* on PBS TV and a coauthor of *Price It Yourself!* (HarperResource). Mr. Rosson lives in Knoxville, TN.

choose that you want the items appraised for their "fair market value." That's the amount you may reasonably expect to receive.

It's never a good idea to take your possessions to an antique shop or mall to obtain an appraisal. Often, proprietors aren't appraisers, and their goal may be to buy your items rather than to give you useful information. Once your possessions have been appraised, consider the options for selling them at maximum profit.

AUCTIONS

If the fair market value of any of your possessions is more than $1,500, the international auction houses, such as Sotheby's (212-606-7000, *www.sothebys.com*) and Christie's (212-636-2400, *www.christies.com*), can provide you with a better chance of selling them for their estimated value—and sometimes much more.

Reason: International auction houses attract a large number of serious buyers who have serious money.

The drawback is that the auction house may believe your item isn't something it can sell, and its fees can be significant. You might also have to wait six months before your item actually comes up for sale.

Best strategy: Send the auction house a picture and description of an item, say that you're *considering consigning it for sale* and ask for an estimate of what it would bring. Estimates are free, and if they are in error, it's usually on the low side.

Caution: Don't ask an international auction house for an appraisal unless you have large quantities of fine things and are willing to pay big bucks.

Alternatives…

●**Local auction houses.** They can be an efficient route for selling a large number of objects that are not valuable enough for international auction houses.

Most local auction houses will pick up your goods (sometimes for a charge that may be a small percentage of sales), sell them and give you 65% to 75% of the proceeds.

Be aware that local auctioneers are seldom experts in art or antiques and need all the information you can provide. In addition, hometown auctions are not effective for selling items worth less than $25 because these are often lumped together in box lots.

Visit your local auction houses to find out which has the largest audience and most spirited bidding. Choose the one that is most businesslike and seems to be getting the best prices.

●**Internet sales.** If you are Internet-savvy, eBay and other on-line auction services can be an easy way to sell possessions because they reach millions of potential buyers. Fees average about 6% of the sales price, much lower than at traditional auction houses.

On the Internet, however, you will compete against a large number of sellers with similar objects. As a result, your items may be lost in the vast number of items being offered for sale and may not get a satisfactory bid.

OUTDOOR MARKETS

You can usually rent space at a flea market or an outdoor antique show for less than $100 a day. It can be a way of selling your possessions and also having fun.

Keep in mind that flea market shoppers are bargain hunters. Outdoor antique shows, on the other hand, will draw serious, knowledgeable collectors, often with deep pockets.

YARD SALES

If you are selling what some people might call junk, yard sales can be a quick way of disposing of it at a small profit.

The disadvantages are that no object is likely to bring more than $50 (and usually less) and that you could miss more profitable opportunities at local auction houses.

When having a yard sale, post a sign saying, "All merchandise sold as is. All sales final."

Also check local rules, which often restrict or even prohibit outdoor neighborhood sales.

CHARITIES

If you have any possessions that are difficult to sell, giving them to charity is a great way to help an organization and reduce your taxes at the same time.

Caution: To satisfy the IRS, keep a copy of the appraisal and a picture of any item given to charity. And, of course, consult your tax adviser.

Don't Run Out of Hot Water

Consider installing a second water heater if you often run out of hot water. If your current heater is ready for replacement, it may make sense to have two new ones installed. They may cost less than buying one larger-capacity heater and will supply more hot water to all faucets.

Cheaper but less efficient: Insulate hot-water pipes going to your bathrooms so that less heat is lost on the way.

Roger Peugeot and Tim Carter, both syndicated home-repair columnists in Cincinnati, *www.askthebuilder.com*, and authors of *The Home Ranger Helps You Figure It Out!* (Prometheus).

Upgrade to Wood Flooring

Wood floors cost more than carpet, but last longer. Plus, they cost much less than stone or tile and are easier on the feet. Wood also softens a room's acoustics and is easy to clean if protected with a polyurethane finish.

Home, 1633 Broadway, New York City 10019.

Information Please

Useful tips and tidbits on more than 2,000 subjects are available free at *www.tipking. com.* The site suggests olive oil to get paint off hands, vinegar to brighten laundry and much more. Search by topic—new ideas are posted daily. You can even add your own useful information and advice.

Katie Weeks, freelance writer, *Home,* 1633 Broadway, New York City 10019.

To Find an Owner's Manual...

Lost the owner's manual for an appliance? Go to *www.appliance411.com/service/owners manual.shtml* for links to most major manufacturers' Web sites—many of which have on-line manuals for their products.

Aspirin Keeps Plants Healthy

With regular doses of aspirin—every two months—indoor and outdoor plants will grow more, bloom better and have fewer fungus and pest problems. Aspirin prevents plants from producing a substance that hastens aging or wilting.

To make one gallon of aspirin solution: Dissolve a regular-strength, uncoated aspirin tablet in one cup of water...discard one-quarter cup of the solution...then add enough plain water to make a full gallon.

Marion Owen, master gardener and instructor, Kodiak College, Kodiak, AK, and coauthor of *Chicken Soup for the Gardener's Soul* (Health Communications). Her Web site is *www.plantea.com*.

Don't Let the Bugs Bite

While the chemical mosquito repellents are effective, they carry their own health risks. *If you prefer not to use chemical-based insect repellents, try these natural methods to keep the bugs away...*

●**Eat foods that are rich in vitamin B-1 (thiamine).** These include sunflower seeds, Brazil nuts and fish—or pop a 25- to 50-milligram (mg) B-1 supplement three times a day starting two weeks before your expected exposure to mosquitoes.

•**Plant marigolds wherever possible...**or line your yard with potted geranium plants to keep mosquitoes away from your porch, patio, yard or pool.

Joan Wilen and Lydia Wilen, New York City–based sisters and the authors of *Chicken Soup & Other Folk Remedies* (Ballantine) and *Folk Remedies That Work* (HarperCollins).

Is Your Home Making You Sick?: Mold May Be the Culprit

Jeffrey C. May, president of May Indoor Air Investigations, LLC, which conducts indoor environmental surveys of homes, schools and offices, Cambridge, MA, *www.may indoorair.com*. A nationally recognized expert on indoor air quality, Mr. May is coauthor of *The Mold Survival Guide: For Your Home and for Your Health* and *My House Is Killing Me!* (both from Johns Hopkins University Press).

A couple of years ago, television personality Ed McMahon filed a $20 million lawsuit because he believed that a botched repair of a broken water pipe caused mold to infest his Los Angeles home, making him and his family ill and killing his dog. He settled the suit for $7 million.

In 2002, US insurers paid out $3 billion for mold-related claims, more than double the $1.4 billion in 2001.

Although some doctors do question whether molds cause all the ills attributed to them, molds do produce allergens, substances that trigger allergic reactions. People who are very sensitive to molds may experience a stuffy nose, sneezing, headache or other allergy symptoms. Under certain conditions, some of the molds, particularly *aspergillus* and *stachybotrys,* may produce toxins that, in high concentrations, can trigger skin irritation or respiratory problems and even increase the risk of cancer.

Signs of dangerous mold: Musty smell... discolored walls...black spots in damp places.

MINIMIZING MOLD

Mold can grow anywhere there's moisture— in bathrooms and basements, under the carpets and on or in appliances. The key to minimizing mold is preventing leaks and controlling indoor relative humidity (RH). Keep RH below 65% upstairs and 50% in the basement, especially if your basement is finished. You can monitor RH with a hygrometer, available at hardware stores for less than $50. I suggest putting one near the bedrooms and one in the basement.

To keep humidity down, use a dehumidifier. In dry weather, open the windows and doors. Promptly repair any leaks in sinks, showers, toilets, air conditioners, etc. When renovating, let the plaster and concrete dry before applying paint or wallpaper or laying down carpet.

Warning: For some people, disturbing mold and breathing or touching the spores can trigger severe reactions. Wear goggles, gloves and a face mask rated N95 by the National Institute for Occupational Safety and Health (NIOSH). You can purchase these items at any hardware store. Make sure the mask has two straps. The single-strap models don't fit tightly enough to block airborne mold spores.

Below are common household trouble spots and what to do. In general, on nonporous surfaces (ceramic tile, vinyl, etc.) you can safely clean moldy areas with detergent or a bleach solution (three-quarters of a cup of bleach to one gallon of water). If the moldy area is large or on a porous surface, such as bare wood, you may need to call a contractor who has experience in mold removal.

CARPET

Molds can grow in dust, especially in carpets that are on concrete basement floors. Vacuum frequently, using a vacuum that has a high-efficiency particle arrestor (HEPA) filter. Pay special attention to areas where carpets meet exterior walls, a common site for mold growth. If a carpet is wet for more than 24 hours, depending on the temperature, it may have to be discarded. Look for signs of mold.

AIR CONDITIONERS AND HEATING SYSTEMS

To keep a central heating and cooling system clean, use a pleated media filter, not a fiberglass one. A moldy system should be cleaned by a professional.

If a window air conditioner gets moldy, it must be removed for a thorough cleaning.

Regularly vacuum up all the dust from baseboard heaters. Many people experience winter mold allergies when the heat comes on and disperses the spores.

BATHROOMS

Mold that grows on tiles or grout usually is harmless. Wipe it off with a mild bleach solution or a commercial tile cleaner. Periodically inspect grout for any cracks, and repair them immediately. Even a hairline crack can allow water to leak through the wall and encourage harmful mold growth where you can't see it. Remove moldy wallpaper.

REFRIGERATORS

The water line of an automatic icemaker may have a slow leak that sets the stage for mold growth. Move the refrigerator occasionally to check for dampness. Call a repairman if there's even a hint of moisture.

The drip tray underneath a frost-free refrigerator is another problem area because moisture, dust and bits of food collect there, creating a rich environment for mold. Clean the drip tray several times a year with bleach and water. Add a few tablespoons of salt to the tray to discourage mold growth.

Clean the refrigerator coils yearly to remove dust. Also clean the gaskets around the doors to remove food particles.

CLOTHES DRYERS

The accumulation of lint and moisture is a natural haven for mold. The dryer vent hose should be short enough to lead directly from the dryer to the wall. Long vent hoses that travel through cold attics or garages may allow air to cool, moisture to condense—and mold to grow.

Don't use devices that vent warm air from the dryer into the house. The heat can lower energy bills, but one load of laundry vents several pounds of moisture into the air. This moisture can condense in the attic and cause a mold problem.

SINKS

Occasionally move items stored under the sink to check for dampness. If you have a sink sprayer, check it for leaks. Water can run down the hose and into the cabinet beneath.

When cleaning a sink, scrub overflow holes as well as the rim around the drain with a mild bleach solution.

FURNITURE

Mold can be found on unfinished wood surfaces, such as the back of a dresser. If you do notice a musty smell or suffer from allergy-like symptoms, take furniture outside and wipe any unfinished surfaces with rubbing alcohol. Then apply a layer of shellac to seal in mold spores and prevent new mold from growing.

Upholstered furniture that is moldy must be reupholstered or discarded.

CARS

If your car has an earthy odor, consider taking it to an air-conditioner service shop to have the system cleaned and checked for leaks.

Also, inspect carpets or mats for dampness. Water could be getting in through defective window or trunk seals.

If there is mold on vinyl or leather upholstery, it usually can be washed away with a bleach solution. If fabric gets moldy, it might need to be replaced. Consult a mold specialist.

CLOTHING

Clothing that has a musty smell should be washed and aired in the sun until the smell is gone completely.

Closets have limited circulation, which is ideal for mold growth. Sweep or vacuum closet floors as part of your cleaning routine. Open doors periodically to allow air to circulate. If you have a walk-in closet that seems damp, get a dehumidifier just for that space.

GETTING HELP

If the mold keeps coming back, hire a mold investigator to find out why. If it covers a large area, hire a mold abatement specialist for the cleanup. You may be advised to move out until the cleanup is completed. Mold specialists are listed in the *Yellow Pages.* Call the firm's references, and check its complaint record with the Better Business Bureau (703-276-0100, *www.bbb.org*). Costs for professional help range from a few hundred dollars for an inspection to thousands to treat a large area.

Air Pollution May Be Worse Indoors

The Environmental Protection Agency says that air pollution levels sometimes are two to five times higher inside homes than outside.

Why: The two leading causes of indoor air pollution are the sealing of homes to increase energy efficiency while leaving inadequate ventilation, and increasing household use of chemically based products.

Safety: Eliminate sources of potential dangers, such as carbon monoxide, radon and gas from all appliances…adequately ventilate your entire home, and keep all chimneys and flues clear…use air filtering and air cleaning devices.

Michael Vogel, PhD, professor of housing and environmental quality at Montana State University in Bozeman, www.healthyindoorair.org.

Protect Yourself From Chlorinated Water …in Your Home

Showering with and drinking chlorinated water increases your exposure to carcinogens. Cancer-causing compounds known as *trihalomethanes* (THMs) develop when chlorine reacts with naturally occurring organic matter in water. When you take a shower, the shower spray distributes THMs in the air throughout the house, which is then inhaled.

Self-defense: Take shorter showers…install a chlorine-removing showerhead.

Cost: Less than $100.

Put a carbon filtration system (about $50) on faucets to remove chlorine from water that will be ingested…or let water sit in an open pitcher exposed to air for at least five hours to allow chlorine and THMs to evaporate.

Richard P. Maas, PhD, codirector, Environmental Quality Institute, University of North Carolina–Asheville.

Lead Is Risky for All— Young and Old

Ellen Silbergeld, PhD, professor, environmental health sciences at the Johns Hopkins University School of Public Health, Baltimore. Her study of the link between lead levels and mortality was published in the Archives of Internal Medicine.

Lead poisoning can cause elevated blood pressure, nerve disorders and other problems in adults…yet, unlike kids, they are not routinely tested for it.

Lead-poisoning symptoms: Fatigue, loss of appetite, stomach upset, forgetfulness, headaches, insomnia, weakness in arms and legs and anemia.

New: Elevated levels of lead are associated with increased mortality rates.

Despite the 1978 ban on lead-based residential paints and the elimination of leaded gasoline, there still are some sources of exposure…

●**Lead solder** in plumbing and jewelry and other crafts.

●**Paint residue** in old homes and surrounding soil.

●**Lead crystal** and some ceramic ware.

Also: People experiencing age-related bone loss are exposed when thinning bones release lead into the bloodstream. This is particularly a problem for women after menopause. Exercise and other interventions to protect bone health can reduce exposure.

SELF-DEFENSE

●**Get a risk assessment if your home was built or renovated before 1978.** Call your local health department to locate a well-qualified professional.

●**Be cautious when renovating an older home.** Contact the Environmental Protection Agency (800-424-5323, *www.epa.gov/lead*).

●**Don't remove lead paint on your own.** Contact your state department of health to find a licensed contractor.

●**Test water for lead.** Ask your local health agency to recommend kits.

Cost: About $65 for kit and analysis.

Increase the Value Of Your Home

David Gershon, CEO of Empowerment Institute, which works with local governments to form and promote active neighborhood improvement programs, Woodstock, NY, *www.empowermentinstitute.net*. Mr. Gershon is the author of *The Livable Neighborhood: About Making Life Better on the Street Where You Live* (Empowerment Institute).

How do you increase the value of your home, beautify your neighborhood and get to know your neighbors? Start a street association.

My own organization has helped thousands of community groups to deal with noise, traffic, crime and pollution—and have fun doing it.

ORGANIZE

The best way to get people involved is by going door to door. Chat about neighborhood issues, then invite neighbors to your first meeting. Once you get together, a frank discussion of the neighborhood's needs and the residents' abilities will help the group decide where the focus should be.

Inspiration is the key to success. Prepare for the meeting with lists of problems and possible solutions. Then let the group brainstorm its own creative ideas. Don't force your own agenda.

Common problems and possible solutions to bring up...

TRAFFIC

Speeding vehicles are a problem everywhere.

Actions: Have all the members of your neighborhood association display signs in their yards reading *30 Is Legal, but Neighbors Drive 25* or *Thanks for Not Speeding.*

Neighbors can take turns holding up these signs throughout rush hour. Remember to wave and smile at all the drivers as they pass by—especially since you will know some of them.

Ask the police to set up radar-activated electronic signs that display the speed of passing cars. Or request that they set up speed traps periodically.

Request speed bumps, stop signs or other remedies from your area's traffic department.

CRIME

Don't wait for police to improve security.

Actions: Ask police and political leaders to set up a block watch or a community-oriented policing services (COPS) program. These organize residents into a watchful presence that helps police prevent trouble. This can range from simply learning how to watch for suspicious activity throughout your neighborhood to actually walking the streets as part of a neighborhood patrol.

Example: In one Philadelphia community, the neighborhood watch met to discuss techniques for getting rid of the drug dealers. Some of those same drug dealers also attended to see what they were up against. When they realized the community was getting organized, the drug dealers left the area.

Meet regularly with a police liaison to discuss other problems and what can be done to solve them.

Important: Don't institute such efforts without the proper training—you could endanger yourself and your neighbors.

If your town has no such programs, contact the National Crime Prevention Council (202-466-6272, *www.ncpc.org*) for help.

BEAUTIFICATION

You don't have to let an eyesore go unchallenged. *Possible solutions...*

Actions: Planting trees on the public land along your street can increase property values by 15%. Designate a landscape committee, and have its members list the streets that could be improved by planting trees. Contact your local parks department about recommendations for trees to plant, and ask for permission to put them in. When no such program or department exists, ask for government permission to plant trees and get planting advice from a nursery.

Important: Be sure to appoint group members to care for newly planted trees during the first year.

Make the most of what your neighborhood has. Expose and landscape rock outcroppings. Paint old-fashioned streetlights and bridges. Such special touches can make your neighborhood *the* place to own a home. If you're lucky enough to have wetlands or a stream, schedule a clean-up day. Ask for help from your local government's department of parks, solid waste or environmental protection. The reward is a beautiful spot.

BETTER LIVING

Street and neighborhood associations make life much more fun, healthful and cheaper, too. *Additional ideas to discuss at your meeting...*

● **Walking and jogging clubs** motivate members to exercise together.

● **Baby-sitting and day-care collectives** let parents trade certificates, each of which represents one hour of babysitting/child care.

● **Food cooperatives** are organized by people who buy in bulk at lower prices. Some of these groups contract with local farmers to get fresh vegetables.

Information: National Agricultural Library at *www.nal.usda.gov/afsic/csa.*

14 Easy Ways To Sell Your Home Faster

Jim Fite, president of the Dallas-based Century 21 Judge Fite Company, one of the largest Century 21 affiliates in the world, with more than $800 million in annual sales and 600 associates, *www.century21judgefite.com.*

Don't ever underestimate the power of a good first impression. A home that is attractive from the road can sell in as little as half the time, making it less likely that you'll have to reduce the asking price.

LANDSCAPE

1. Edge lawns and flowerbeds. A sharp edge gives a well-maintained look. Conversely, grass or weeds sprouting up from cracks in paths and driveways implies neglect.

2. Add color. Plant flowers to make the front of a house come alive, particularly if the home itself is white or a dark color.

3. Patch cracks in walkways and sidewalks, even if the sidewalk is the town's responsibility. If tree roots have shattered a section, consider rerouting the sidewalk around the tree. Also, sweep all walks.

4. Trim overgrown trees and shrubs. Remove dead or dying plants.

HOUSE FACADE

5. Polish the doorknob. If the main entryway's doorknob or knocker is showing signs of age, it's worth spending $150 or so for the set to replace it.

6. Remove potted plants, statues and decorations from the front stoop. They make it look cluttered and smaller.

7. Use similar drapes in front windows. Most home owners select drapes and blinds for the way they look inside the home—but different colors and shapes in the front windows make a home look unbalanced.

8. Replace broken and missing shingles. Just a few bad shingles give the impression of roof problems—a major turnoff for potential buyers.

OTHER DETAILS

9. Remove weathered basketball hoops. Only keep them up if they look new and have nets.

10. Match your mailbox to your home. A cutesy mailbox is appropriate if you have a cutesy home. A $500,000 home shouldn't have a $10 mailbox.

11. Take down a dilapidated backyard fence, particularly if it can be seen from the street or driveway.

12. Remove any of your decorative items that could be considered clutter. Walkway lights and garden fountains are fine. Garden gnomes, out-of-season Christmas lights and other ornamentation should be packed away.

13. Keep garage doors closed. Even tidy garage interiors just do not look as neat as closed garage doors. Garbage cans, rakes, bikes, etc. should be stored inside.

14. Maintain the *For Sale* sign. A post that is leaning or in need of painting implies your home has been on the market for a long time. That suggests problems.

Getting Your Home Ready for Sale

Make your home more saleable by paying attention to small details…

●**Take out the trash before prospective buyers visit.** If odors remain, bake bread or boil cinnamon.

●**Use higher-wattage bulbs** to make the house look brighter.

●**Make closets seem roomier** by storing some of your clothes elsewhere temporarily.

●**If you have a cat,** be sure the litter box is clean and hidden.

Barbara Corcoran, chairman and founder, Corcoran Group, real estate brokerage firm, New York City.

Big Trouble Spots When You Buy an Older Home

Weldon Sikes, spokesperson, American Association of Home Inspectors Inc., Lubbock, TX, *www.aahi.com.*

Older homes often are better built than new homes, but they also are likely to have particular problems due to their advanced age.

Common problems in older homes, according to a survey by the American Association of Home Inspectors…

●**Inadequate surface drainage,** such as deficient grading, that can lead water to penetrate basements.

●**Inadequate wiring for today's needs** or that has been unsafely installed over the years —a real safety hazard.

●**Roof damage** caused by old or damaged shingles or inadequate drainage.

●**Heating systems with inadequate or malfunctioning controls** or with blocked or unsafe exhaust.

●**Inadequate overall maintenance** leading to crumbling masonry, makeshift wiring, broken fixtures, etc.—older homes need more maintenance than new ones.

●**Damage to structural components,** including the foundation walls, floor joists and door headers.

●**Plumbing problems** due to old or incompatible piping materials, and faulty fixtures and waste lines.

●**Inadequate caulking on windows,** doors and wall surfaces, which allows water and air to penetrate.

●**Poor ventilation** due to the "oversealing" of a home to save energy. Making a home excessively airtight can cause excessive interior moisture, which rots joists, beams and rafters.

Self-defense: When thinking about the purchase of an older home, have it professionally inspected to identify these and other potential costly problems.

Surviving Holiday Get-Togethers

Mariana Caplan, PhD, a family counselor in Berkeley, CA, *www.realspirituality.com,* and author of six books, including *When Holidays Are Hell: A Guide to Surviving Family Gatherings* (Hohm).

Aunt Susan and Uncle Ned are constantly fighting…most of your siblings are not even speaking to each other…and your cousin drinks too much. No wonder you dread family get-togethers.

Here's how to keep tension to a minimum this holiday season…

STRATEGIES FOR PEACEFUL DINNERS

Arguments often start at the dinner table. It is the one time the whole family is together with no option but to talk to one another.

●**Be ready to change the subject.** It might be obvious to everyone what you're doing, but that doesn't mean it won't preserve peace. Ask a family member about his/her favorite hobby or a recent vacation. Talk about sports or even the weather.

If changing the subject doesn't work, then acknowledge the point of contention and try to set it aside without placing blame.

Example: "When we talk about this, we always end up fighting. We're not going to resolve it now anyway, so is it OK with you if we talk about something else?"

●**Invite a nonfamily member.** Families are less likely to bicker when an outsider is around. Few want to make a scene in front of someone they don't know well.

Invite a friend or coworker who has no family or lives too far away to return home. This person even might help you see family members in a more positive light. Your guest might be delighted by the sister you find overbearing.

●**Be generous with praise.** When people feel good about themselves, they're less likely to argue. Tell family members that they look great …you're impressed by what they've accomplished this year…they have wonderful kids. This may elicit compliments in return.

●**Be considerate of less-affluent siblings.** Are you telling your brother about your new boat because you think he wants to hear about it…or because you want to show him how successful you are? If it's the latter, stop. You're raising the family tension level. If it's the former, the honesty of your excitement should keep any feelings of rivalry to a minimum. Still, change the subject if your sibling doesn't seem interested in your most recent acquisition.

If, on the other hand, your relative is bragging about his/her latest acquisition, change the subject or excuse yourself to use the bathroom or help the host in the kitchen.

●**Limit alcohol consumption.** Alcohol can escalate arguments. If you're hosting the gathering, be slow to offer drinks and refills. Consider buying only a limited amount of liquor. Family members might be peeved if you run out, but at least they'll be sober.

If there's a problem drinker in the family, you have a right to ask him to keep his drinking under control. Call him before the holidays. Let him know that you're really looking forward to seeing him but that it makes you and others uneasy when he drinks too much.

This is an especially important point if there will be children at the gathering.

OTHER TENSION REDUCERS

●**Bring something funny.** Nothing heads off problems like a good laugh. Bring a funny movie on DVD or videotape…photos of your family pet doing something stupid…or a humorous book from which you can read aloud.

●**Suggest a family outing.** Getting out of the house gives everyone a bit more space and an opportunity to have fun together. Take a hike in the woods…visit an historic site in the region.

●**Give children the gifts they want.** Children aren't always tactful when they receive gifts they don't like. Their disappointment can raise the tension level of the whole family. Ask them or their parents ahead of time what they want, or have them pick their own gifts.

Example: Give your grandchild a coupon that reads, *This entitles you to a shopping trip with me to pick out something you really want.* Include a dollar limit if appropriate.

●**Make a prearranged support call.** When you visit family, you may feel cut off from the friends on whom you depend. Even one short phone conversation with a good friend can remind you that you're a sane, successful adult.

●**Check into a hotel.** Staying with family can exacerbate tensions. If you decide to stay in a hotel, don't give your family the impression that you don't want to be with them or that their house isn't big enough.

Better: Call ahead and say, "I know it's extra work for you when we stay at your place. We thought we would try a hotel this time"…or "My kids are going through a rowdy phase right now. I think a hotel will make it easier for everyone."

●**Break the every-year expectation.** Skipping a year probably won't go over well with the family initially. In the long run, however, they may end up treating you better because they won't take your presence for granted. Be sure to give everyone as much notice as possible so they can get used to the idea.

Great excuses: "My kids need some time with just Jan and me"…"We need to spend the holiday with Jack's family"…"We all agreed to spend this Christmas working for a homeless shelter in our town."

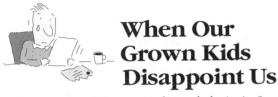

When Our Grown Kids Disappoint Us

Jane Adams, PhD, a research psychologist in Seattle who studies American families and social change. She is the author of *When Our Grown Kids Disappoint Us* (Free Press) and *I'm Still Your Mother* (iUniverse). Her Web site is *www.janeadams.com*.

The dreams that parents have for their grown children sometimes clash with reality. Children may still live at home… cannot get or keep a job…maybe even abuse drugs or alcohol. Or the disappointment may be more subtle—a son hasn't lived up to his potential or a daughter married someone you don't like. *How to best deal with grown children who disappoint us…*

●**Recognize that it's not your fault.** During the 18 years that it takes to raise a child, it is inevitable that parents will do things they regret. They may miss important school events…not listen when their kids try to tell them things… make poor decisions, etc.

However, these regrets have very little effect on the big picture. Children's lives are shaped by thousands of events. Only in extreme situations—for example, when parents abandon or abuse their children—are parents to blame for their children's problems.

If your child blames you, you might then say something like, "I regret I wasn't always able to give the proper guidance, but it didn't destroy your life. I won't let you use it as an excuse."

●**Let them find happiness.** Parents often feel that it is up to them to make their children happy. Children grow up expecting us to provide happiness and fulfillment rather than finding these things on their own.

Happiness needs to come from within. Adult children have to find it the same way everyone else does—in the satisfaction of work, achievement, relationships, etc.

●**Don't sugarcoat problems.** Parents often are the last to admit when their kids are in trouble with drugs or alcohol or have emotional or mental problems. I've heard parents whose children are abusing drugs say, "She's just experimenting" or "We did the same thing when we were young." It's hard to admit that children have serious problems because parents tend to view them as a reflection on their parenting skills. You have to confront what's really going on in order to make appropriate decisions.

Example: If your adult child is abusing drugs, you might offer to pay for therapy or drug rehab…provide transportation to a clinic …or even invite him/her to stay with you during recovery.

●**Help but don't rescue.** *Help* is giving grown kids an occasional hand—paying half of a semester's college tuition or letting them stay with you until they get a few paychecks. Rescue is taking over responsibilities that should be theirs.

Example: I talked with a woman who was always saving her 20-something son from his own bad decisions. When he got fired from his job, as had happened many times, she arranged job interviews. She gave him the money for rent whenever he spent his own funds carelessly. He never learned to take care of himself because he knew Mom always would bail him out.

●**Focus on your own needs.** When children are grown, it's time for parents to consider new careers or hobbies and to reconnect with each other as adults, not just parents. Couples who stay too intimately involved with adult children lose this valuable opportunity.

A recent trend is for adult children to move back home with their parents. This is a great deal for the kids, but it can make parents feel resentful. Mothers, in particular, may find themselves back in a caretaking role.

Welcoming grown kids back to the nest is fine—temporarily. Work together to establish boundaries and expectations—payment of rent, responsibility for chores, etc. And, determine in advance how long the situation will last. This usually depends on the goal of the arrangement —saving money for college tuition or to move out, for example.

Helping Elderly Parents

Watch an aging parent's home for signs he/she may be having trouble managing it.

Examples: Home is in disrepair...spoiled food...dim lighting...unwashed dishes or laundry. Also observe the neighborhood's safety.

If you see problems: Discuss types of home care. If cost is an issue, try to help pay if you can. Give gift certificates for food delivery or housecleaning. Offer to help with home safety.

Theresa Foy DiGeronimo, adjunct professor of English, William Patterson University of New Jersey in Hawthorne, and the author of *How to Talk to Your Senior Parents About Really Important Things* (Jossey-Bass).

Web Sites for Family Issues

Helpful Internet information on marriage, divorce and stepfamilies...

●**National Council on Family Relations** at *www.ncfr.org.*

●**Children's Rights Council** at *www.gocrc.com.*

●**Council on Contemporary Families** at *www.contemporaryfamilies.org.*

●**Stepfamily Association of America** at *www.saafamilies.org.*

●**Institute for Certified Divorce Planners** at *www.institutecdp.com.*

Margorie Engel, PhD, president and chief executive, Stepfamily Association of America, Lincoln, NB.

Support for Caregivers

Getting outside support can make it easier to handle the ongoing stress of taking care of an aging spouse, parent or relative. *For general support or referrals to caregiver support groups...*

●**Children of Aging Parents** (800-227-7294, *www.caps4caregivers.org*).

●**Family Caregiver Alliance** (800-445-8106, *www.caregiver.org*).

●**National Alliance for Caregiving** (301-718-8444, *www.caregiving.org*).

●**National Family Caregivers Association** (800-896-3650, *www.nfcacares.org*).

How to Keep an Aging Pet Happy

If you have an elderly pet, provide soft bedding and an elevated food dish to reduce arthritis pain. Also, switch to food designed for older pets for the best nutrition and to keep weight down—too much weight will strain the heart, lungs, muscles and skeleton. Finally, see your veterinarian if your pet's eyes become hazy—this could indicate cataracts, which can cause blindness.

Kristen Tiglias and Meghan Yudes, editorial associates and dog lovers at *Family Circle,* 110 Fifth Ave., New York City 10011.

18

Better Ways

If Life's Got You Down, Turn It Around

Are there parts of your life that are not working? Are you failing to achieve the joy and satisfaction you'd hoped for? *If your answer to either of these is yes, here are six questions to consider to add joy and balance to your life...*

●**Do you give away your power?** Anytime you make someone or something outside of you more important than what is inside you, you're giving away your personal power.

Example A: You let others make decisions for you, ranging from what concert to see to where you live.

How to change: Start making this type of decision for yourself, being sure that it represents your true desires, not your need to please.

Example B: You assume that your destiny depends on something beyond your control, such as the stars, politics or the workplace.

How to change: You can choose to fret and become miserable—or choose not to worry and be cheerful. Sculpt your life through your own attitudes and outlook.

●**Are your expectations too low?** All of us inherit a set of beliefs. The key question is, do you live your life bound by them or do you expand your beliefs to encompass all that life has to offer? By hanging on to self-defeating beliefs and low expectations, you will continue to operate at a low level instead of moving full throttle ahead. *Here are some ways to loosen the bonds of negative beliefs...*

●Forgive others. Don't waste your precious life stewing over someone else's bad behavior.

●Forgive yourself. Instead of revisiting past actions and feeling guilty, ask yourself how the experiences moved you to a new place and be thankful you arrived there.

Alan H. Cohen, author of 17 inspirational books, including *Why Your Life Sucks and What You Can Do About It* (Jodere Group). Mr. Cohen is also a faculty member of the Omega Institute in Rhinebeck, NY, conducts life mastery seminars in Hawaii and is a popular keynote speaker. His Web site is *www.alancohen.com.*

●Expect that good can—and does—come to you frequently. Your life will shrink or expand according to your expectations, so think big and accept more.

●**Are your thoughts sinking you?** Many people have been programmed to think of life as a sea of troubles. In fact, life is an ocean of possibilities, a wonderful adventure to really be enjoyed. Many people perceive themselves as *deprived*—of money, love, time, etc. The tricky thing about perceptions is that they can become self-fulfilling. Focus on abundance.

Some ways to do this: Make a gratitude list. As you are going to bed, think about the things you appreciated during the day. Avoid watching the dark side of the news. Quit complaining about what isn't working for you, and concentrate on what you can do to make your life work.

Choose to talk about what you enjoy—a visit to an art gallery, a great book, an afternoon at the beach. See how it lightens your life. Don't dwell on the negative.

●**Do you waste your time doing things that bring you down?** Write down your activities during the course of one week. Then rate each according to whether it enhances your life or diminishes it, with 10 being the best. This will tell you what erodes the quality of your life. Now write next to each item all the ways that you can maximize what lifts you up and minimize the downers.

●**Do you think *you* have to fix everything —including other people?** Control freaks don't have a power problem, they have a trust issue as in, "Nothing gets done right unless I do it myself."

The truth is, our expectations of others play a major role in how they behave. Expect the best and that's what you are likely to get. Trust people for a change, and invite others in to help. You'll give yourself the gift of more time to pursue the activities that renew you. Those around you will appreciate you more, not less, for your faith in them.

While you're at it, give up trying to fix others. No one can fix anyone else, and no one can make someone else happy or unhappy. Only the person himself/herself can do that—even though he might try to persuade you otherwise.

●**Are you enjoying the journey?** The happiest people evaluate life by the quality of their experiences, including those that have ended. Honor all your past shining moments as you embrace the present. A day is no less glorious because it gives way to night…a glowing career is no less satisfying because you retired…a relationship that once brought you happiness is no less wonderful because it finally came apart in the end.

Flattery Gets You Somewhere

Richard Stengel, author of *You're Too Kind: A Brief History of Flattery* (Touchstone).

Everyone "knows" that all brides are beautiful, all babies are adorable and the dinner our hostess prepares is always delicious. Thus it can be challenging to pay compliments that are truly meaningful.

There is an art to giving praise. *Some rules…*

●**Be specific.** Generic compliments don't mean much. Instead of telling an author "your book is the greatest," try "I loved your book, especially when you describe how it felt to be abducted by the tentacled alien."

●**Don't charge for praise.** A compliment won't seem genuine—and neither will you—if you ask for a favor immediately afterward.

●**Flatter behind the person's back.** If you tell someone that you think her idea is brilliant, she might suspect an ulterior motive. So, tell a mutual friend. When the friend passes on the compliment, she'll know you're sincere.

●**Agree, but not with everything.** Agreement on the big picture is more credible when you disagree on something trivial. "I think your marketing strategy is brilliant, but I think the design could be crisper…"

It seems counterintuitive, but it's easier to flatter people who have high self-esteem than those who are insecure. The mega-star expects adulation. Praising the clumsy assistant violates his/her sense of reality.

Best: Be moderate when you praise someone who is insecure.

Flattery can go both ways. Watch how others pay *you* compliments. If you spot a motive, you can avoid paying for the compliment.

If you think your boss is buttering you up just to dump another project on you, make a preemptive strike. Thank him for the compliment and say you're pleased you did so well, considering how much else you have to do.

It's Never Too Late to Overcome Shyness

Bernardo J. Carducci, PhD, professor of psychology and director of the Shyness Research Institute at Indiana University Southeast, New Albany. He is author of *Shyness: A Bold New Approach* (HarperCollins).

Shy people come in all sizes and shapes—rich and poor, old and young, male and female. But just about all have one thing in common—they often wish they weren't shy.

You can't change who you are. But you can learn to feel more comfortable in social situations and to quiet the butterflies that leave you tongue-tied when it's time to speak.

WHY SHY?

Although its exact cause is not really known, shyness no doubt mingles nature and nurture, temperament and life experience. Some people are shy most of the time, others feel ill at ease only in certain situations. For many it's a personality trait they've had since childhood, but it can surface at any time—even late in life.

Example: Retirement, divorce or death of a spouse can suddenly mean your familiar lifestyle and social contacts are no longer there to support you. You have to meet new people and deal with new situations. You don't know how to go about it.

If you're shy, you're not alone. Nearly half the population shares your difficulties, and virtually everyone has had firsthand experience of feeling shy on occasion.

SHY DYNAMICS

Years of scientific studies and thousands of interviews have clarified what happens when people are shy…

● **Approach/avoidance.** Shy people like, need and seek contact with others. But they're afraid of being judged. They feel socially inept, anxious and sure they'll be rejected. The stand-off between approach and avoidance makes it hard to initiate a conversation, even to think very clearly.

● **Warm-up period.** People don't just rush into new situations. We hold back at first, listening to our instincts and determining how to behave. Shy people require extra time for this process—they're slow to warm up.

● **Comfort zone.** We feel at ease in familiar environments (at home, our own desk at the office or at a favorite table in a restaurant) and among people who understand and appreciate us. We extend our comfort zone by incorporating new people and situations into it. However, for shy people, the comfort zone is small and inflexible.

● **Stress reaction.** Everyone is subject to the stress reactions—a fast pulse, perspiration, stuttering, racing thoughts—the body's response to danger. Shy people find them a major cause of discomfort and difficulty in social situations.

Shy people also think differently. They regard every conversation as an evaluation, think all eyes are on them and attribute unsatisfactory social interactions to their own missteps.

TAKING CONTROL

Being successfully shy means taking control of all these factors—tipping the balance from avoidance to approach…using your warm-up time effectively…extending your comfort zone …dealing more effectively with your shy mind and body.

Keep a "shy life journal," in which you record just how you feel, what thoughts you have, how you behave in situations where you're shy. Analyze your difficulties, and develop concrete strategies to overcome them.

Example: You find conversations awkward. Write down what makes them difficult, such as, *I feel I have nothing interesting to say.*

Solution: Read more newspapers and magazines, and have some topics ready for the next occasion.

SOCIAL GATHERINGS

Parties and other types of big gatherings are often intensely uncomfortable and some shy people avoid them altogether. *These strategies can help…*

●**Come early.** Many shy people think that if they arrive late, they'll blend in more easily. But this ignores the need for a longer warm-up period. Instead, come just when a party is getting under way. You will have more time to adjust, as well as to chat one on one with people as they arrive.

●**Don't drink too much.** Alcohol is a social lubricant, calms the nervous system and eases jitters. But it also can dampen the creativity and judgment you need for successful social interactions. Worst of all, you will give alcohol the credit if you enjoy yourself, and conclude you can't do it alone.

●**Learn how to join a conversation.** Following "the rules" of social behavior, ease in to your entrance. Hover at the edge of the group and listen. This gives you time to get used to being there, and gives them time to adjust to your presence. Wait for a lull and then ask a relevant question.

Helpful: Introduce yourself with a social grace, like asking, "Can I get anyone something to drink?"

SMALL TALK

Casual chitchat may seem trivial, but it's the cornerstone of civility. It's how people connect with one another, make new acquaintances and keep up everyday relationships. If you're not good at it (many shy people aren't), small talk may seem daunting, but this social skill can be learned. *How the socially adept do it…*

●**Setting talk.** Most conversations with strangers will begin with neutral remarks about the surroundings ("It's stuffy in here today") as a stepping-stone to other subjects.

●**Name exchange.** This seems natural and polite at the start of any conversation. It shows your interest in the other person and creates familiarity. The longer you wait, the more awkward it will feel.

●**Pretopical sequence.** Confident people fish around for something to talk about by asking questions like "What's your profession?" or "How do you know our host?"…or with general reflections on current events.

●**Taking turns.** Once the subject has been selected, alternate speaking. Read the other person's face and speech patterns (pauses, etc.) for cues and timing.

●**Self-disclosure.** Volunteer some personal information—like where you grew up or went to school—and anecdotes that match your partner's. It helps find common ground.

If a topic you suggest is rejected, don't take it personally. Look for shared areas of interest, try to put the other person at ease and when unsure of what to say, ask a question.

CHANGE YOUR MIND

Challenge the thoughts that take over when you're shy. Paralyzing self-consciousness feeds on the assumption that everyone is judging your every move. Just a little observation and introspection (how closely are you watching others?) will show this to be false. *Other common patterns…*

●**Negativity.** Feel like you're always making social faux pas? The reason they stand out in your mind, actually, is because they're so rare.

●**False attributions.** When you feel socially inept (a conversation languishes, for example), don't assume you're to blame. The other person may be tired, distracted or just rude. Check out the facts, or forget about it.

●**Unrealistic comparisons.** Many shy people look enviously at the life of the party and feel even worse about themselves. Instead, look to people more like yourself for role models.

More from Bernardo Carducci…

Expand Your World

Fight shyness by volunteering in a hospital, shelter or school. Becoming involved in the lives of others is an effective antidote to the self-preoccupation that feeds shyness.

New activities expand your comfort zone by bringing you into a new setting. Negative evaluation is not a threat, expectations are low and you needn't be perfect to be appreciated.

A shared activity gives you ample opportunity to practice your small talk skills and lets you warm up to other volunteers and add them to your social circle.

How to Defend Yourself Against Passive-Aggressives

Scott Wetzler, PhD, vice chairman and professor of psychiatry and behavioral sciences at the Montefiore Medical Center and Albert Einstein College of Medicine, both in New York City. He is the author of *Living with the Passive-Aggressive Man: Coping with Hidden Aggression—From the Bedroom to the Boardroom* (Fireside).

A colleague disagrees with you over his role in a new project. He says nothing but later bad-mouths you to a big client.

You make romantic overtures to your spouse before bed. She isn't interested. But, instead of responding nicely, she says, "Don't you have to get up very early tomorrow morning?"

Passive-aggressiveness is a destructive personality disorder. All of us have used this behavior when we were children to rebel against authority. However, some people just never outgrow it. They sabotage marriages and/or careers—preying on spouses, children and coworkers.

Most of us occasionally lapse into passive-aggressive behavior as adults. This is especially true in situations where we have little control or have to deal with large bureaucracies or a domineering boss or spouse. We do such things as ignore orders or skirt rules because it makes us feel powerful.

Passive-aggressiveness is the result of feeling powerless and fearful. As the name indicates, people with this disorder will strike out passively because they want to cause you pain and are afraid to show anger.

PASSIVE-AGGRESSIVE BEHAVIORS

• **Manipulators make uncertain commitments.** They create confusion and blame others for misinterpreting the mixed messages that they send.

• **Promise-makers rarely follow through.** They procrastinate, then artfully evade responsibility for their actions.

• **Reality-twisters turn situations around** so that they are the victims suffering your anger and discontent, no matter how wrong they are.

• **Sulkers regard you as overbearing** and controlling if you offer useful suggestions for them to help themselves.

MANAGING A PASSIVE-AGGRESSIVE

These strategies can help you to immunize yourself against all the frustrations that passive-aggressives can cause…

• **Set boundaries.** Be clear about what behavior is acceptable to you. Enforce the rules, or he/she won't take you seriously.

Example: Your spouse constantly writes checks without registering them in the checkbook. And, every time there is an overdraft, you have to straighten out the account at the bank. Tell him how his actions bother *you*. Say, "It is humiliating for me to fix these mistakes. I feel that you're being disrespectful to me."

Then explain the consequences. Say, "I can no longer keep our checkbook alone. You will have to help."

Avoid sweeping criticisms. They provoke defensive and unproductive responses. Stay specific. Keep your tone firm, but don't make him feel that you're being vindictive or authoritarian.

Beware: Passive-aggressive people have an unerring instinct for tapping the weak spot in your willpower, so stick to your standards of acceptable behavior.

• **Maintain self-control.** A passive-aggressive person needs an adversary to make him feel powerful. When you retaliate with threats and recriminations, you reinforce his behavior.

Example: You and your spouse are shopping for a new home. You want your spouse's input, but she keeps making sarcastic, evasive remarks. If you get upset and say, "Why am I wasting my time even looking with you?" then your spouse has sucked you into her behavior. She now can play the victim and say, "Can't you take a joke? Why are you jumping all over me? Buying a house is supposed to be a team effort. Why are you ruining it?"

Instead of focusing on her anger, listen for feelings of fear and powerlessness. Ask yourself, *Why is my spouse being so evasive? Is she worried about the money or the move?* Confront her in nonthreatening ways. Tell her just how her words make you feel. You can say, "Discussing the house is important to me. When you make jokes, it upsets me—I think you're not interested. It would be helpful to me if you would talk about your thoughts on moving."

Beware: Passive-aggressive people can cloud issues with petty arguments. Stay focused, and restate your point.

Helpful: If you can't talk without overreacting, write all your feelings in a letter that your spouse can read in a neutral setting later.

● **Make the passive-aggressive feel valued.** Remind him of his strengths and the opportunities available to him.

Example: Your colleague loses out on a promotion. He responds by skipping an important meeting. Instead of allowing him to sabotage his job and your department, point out the constructive choices he can make. He could use the situation as a catalyst to get a new job with a company that better appreciates his talents, or he could continue his good performance and perhaps get a shot at another promotion.

● **Get the passive-aggressive to express his anger appropriately.** When he learns how to express anger constructively, you both will benefit. If he does open up, avoid criticizing. This also might be a good time to suggest that he consider psychological counseling.

WHEN TO CUT YOUR LOSSES

Have you given deadlines for improvement that have passed? And, is this person harmful to your mental health or your ability to function? If so, consider firing him or breaking off the relationship.

Cutting ties gradually or remaining friends with a passive-aggressive doesn't work. He will reform just enough to draw you close again, then fall back into old patterns. Physical distance without contact is the only way to make an effective break.

If you are in an office situation where firing the passive-aggressive or quitting yourself isn't an option, then keep him at a distance. Don't

let him interfere with your productivity or environment at work. Be sure to protect yourself as well as your interests.

● **Stop fixing things for him** or getting caught up in all the details of his screwups. Allow him to fail. Perhaps he will be fired or transferred.

● **Use daily memos to document your accomplishments.** On joint projects with a passive-aggressive, describe in detail the allocation of responsibilities.

● **Never rely on him in a crisis.** He is the person most likely to freeze or withdraw when you need someone to act quickly and wisely.

Standing Up to Grown-Up Bullies

Jane Middelton-Moz, MS, a clinical psychologist and director of the Middelton-Moz Institute for Consultation, Intervention and Training, which provides advice to corporations, schools and organizations on anger management and harassment issues, Montpelier, VT, *www.ippi.org*. She is author of *Bullies: From the Playground to the Boardroom* (Health Communications).

Bullies aren't found just in schoolyards. Ninety percent of office workers suffer frequent and deliberate cruelty from a belligerent coworker or boss.

Sometimes, it's as public as being shouted at in front of others. Often, the tormentor is more subtle, such as sabotaging people by leaving them out of the information loop...starting or spreading destructive rumors...sending rude or threatening e-mails...or continually assigning someone to terrible tasks.

HOW ADULT BULLIES THINK

Research suggests that men and women are equally likely to be bullies. It often starts when, as children, they are punished at home, no matter what they do. The behavior is reinforced when they themselves start to bully and are defended or rewarded for their actions.

These young people struggle with social interaction and feel deeply vulnerable, terrified of losing control in their lives. To mask their inadequacies, they amass power by manipulating people, using aggression, arrogance and even charm.

As they age, bullies become more skilled at intimidation. In fact, companies often reward them because they take control of projects, departments—even the company itself.

HOW TO DEFUSE A BULLY

Your parents and teachers probably told you to handle a bully by either being tough and fighting back or letting him/her know just how much he was hurting you.

Neither of these strategies will be effective. In fact, these responses actually feed the bully's behavior because they show how much he can rattle you.

Remember: A bully is always trying to transfer his own feelings of powerlessness to you. This makes him feel more in control.

●**Take a firm, proactive stance**—but don't get dragged into a fight. A bully doesn't know how to back down. The more aggressive and emotional you become, the more he will attack. You remain in control as long as you keep your emotions in check.

If a bully makes a joke at your expense, do not take the bait.

Better: Name the behavior you don't like, and state what is expected. For teasing, say, "Lay off. I'll listen to you, but I'm not willing to let you put me down."

●**Keep rebuttals simple.** It does no good to analyze a bully's motivations, lecture him about mature behavior or get into an argument over facts. Instead, respond with brief, direct and behavior-oriented statements. Say, "I will be happy to listen to your comments, but not when you are yelling at me in front of others."

●**Don't use absolute expressions such as "always" and "never."** For instance, "You never give me any credit." A bully needs to be right and save face. Absolutes will only fuel his need to win.

Better: Focus on the matter at hand. Say, "I worked hard on this project, and you gave me far less credit than I deserved this afternoon."

●**Don't let a bully interrupt you.** It's a classic intimidation tactic. Respond by saying, "I want to hear your opinions, but I won't continue speaking with you if you do not let me voice my concerns." Repeat this every time he interrupts.

●**Use confident body language.** Bullies can sense fear in their victims and thrive on it. Speak in a calm voice, look him in the eye, avoid slumping your shoulders, touching your hair or clenching your teeth.

●**Address him at the same physical level.** It's easier for any bully to be aggressive when he's standing and you're seated. Get him to sit down. If he won't, stand up slowly. You don't want to appear to be taking a fighting stance.

●**Don't let a bully ignore you.** When you respond, say, "I do want to exchange points of view with you, but I can't if I don't have your full attention."

●**Seek support.** A bully's favorite tactic is to isolate his victim. If the bully is in a position of power or if the bullying has gone on for an extended period, it's more effective to confront him with others. It is difficult for him to manipulate or intimidate when he is faced by two or more people.

The goal isn't to gang up on him or shout him down—this will just make a bully more aggressive. Each person should speak one at a time and specifically about the bullying.

●**Make allies**—especially bosses and upper managers—who will listen to you. Don't be surprised if they want to give the bully the benefit of the doubt or characterize the problem as a personality conflict. Managers simply might not want to get involved. Part of your job is to educate them. Say, "Has this ever happened to you before? How did you feel?" This makes them recall their own pain and sympathize. Then say, "That is how it feels for me." Explain to them in specific and factual terms how you have tried to stop the bullying.

RESOURCES

Brutal Bosses and Their Prey, by Harvey Hornstein (Riverhead).

The Bully at Work: What You Can Do to Stop the Hurt and Reclaim Your Dignity on the Job, by Gary Namie, PhD, and Ruth Namie, PhD (Sourcebooks).

The Workplace Bullying & Trauma Institute at *www.bullyinginstitute.org* offers on-line educational resources and research on coping with adult bullying.

The National Employment Lawyers Association (415-296-7629, *www.nela.org*). Here you can find an attorney who specializes in workplace bullying issues.

The Best Kind of Friends

Emotional responses of spouses and close friends tend to become more similar over time. The less-dominant person in a relationship will usually move toward the emotional response pattern of the more-dominant one.

Helpful: Choose only happy, emotionally stable friends—this may help you to become more emotionally positive and upbeat over time.

Cameron Anderson, PhD, assistant professor, department of management, Leonard N. Stern School of Business, New York University, New York City.

How to Double Your Reading Speed

Rick Ostrov, speed-reading expert and author of *Power Reading: The Best, Fastest, Easiest, Most Effective Course on Speedreading and Comprehension Ever Developed!* (Education Press). He is the director of instruction for Education Press, San Juan, CA, *www.educationpress.com.*

Unless you are one of the very few extra-ordinary readers in the world, you will never have the ability to read thousands of words per minute and understand everything you read. The human brain just isn't built for reading that fast.

Good news: Most people can double their reading speed with a month or two of daily practice and understand just as much as they do at slower speeds.

The average reading speed in the US is 225 to 275 words a minute for everyday materials such as newspapers and magazines. Technical and legal texts take longer to read, typically a minute for every 75 to 100 words.

Doubling your reading speed to about 500 words per minute means that you'll be able to spend half the time reading the same amount. Or you'll be able to read twice as much in the same amount of time.

Result: If you decide to read more, you'll have twice as much data on which to base important decisions, including those on investments, health care, travel, taxes and family matters, which will result in more successful decision-making.

How to test your reading speed: Select the type of material you usually read, whether it is a novel, newspaper or technical journal.

Read for 10 minutes in the way that you normally do, without trying to rush. Then stop and count the number of words you read.

To make the computation easier, count the words in several lines to get an average of words per line. Then count the number of lines in what you read, and multiply the number of lines by the average number of words.

Finally, divide the total number of words you read by 10 to get your words-per-minute speed.

READING REALITIES

Reading myth: Slow readers aren't as intelligent as those who read at high speeds.

Reality: The inability to read fast usually results from less experience in reading and a lack of need for reading quickly.

Reading myth: Reading speed deteriorates with age.

Reality: Except where age is accompanied by declining visual or mental acuity, older people often read just as fast as others. In fact, comprehension often increases because of an accumulation of experience with all different types of reading material.

TO INCREASE YOUR READING SPEED

●**Build up vocabulary.** Even if your vocabulary is adequate, it pays to keep enlarging it throughout your life.

Reason: New words are constantly added to the English language, thanks largely to technology, world events and contemporary culture. At the same time, many old words change meaning, such as "icon" and "cool."

The traditional way to increase vocabulary is to memorize lists of new words and practice using them.

More effective: Look up all words whenever you doubt their meaning. And though you may be able to infer the meaning from the context, do not rely on this because words usually have more than one meaning.

Consider carrying a pocket dictionary or electronic dictionary, and buy a large, unabridged dictionary for your home, such as *The American Heritage Dictionary of the English Language.*

Incentive: Building up vocabulary will not only increase your comprehension and reading speed, it also builds self-confidence. You may find it easier to interact with people.

●**Envision improvement.** A technique used by professional athletes works to improve reading speed. A golfer, for instance, creates a mental picture of the perfect swing and a flawless drive toward the green.

In the same way, readers can envision themselves moving faster down the page and comprehending more of what they read.

Psychologists have different ideas about why the technique works, but few doubt that envisioning a successful performance actually contributes to one.

●**Preview the material.** When you read anything—except, perhaps, the chapters in a novel—take a few seconds to scan through the material so that you know what to expect, such as charts, lists, pictures or dialogue.

This way, you can choose the sections on which you would like to concentrate.

Example: If you live in Pennsylvania and are reading a magazine article on gardening, you probably wouldn't be interested in the section on palm trees. But unless you scan the article first, you might read halfway through the section on palm trees before realizing it does not apply to you.

Previewing material also helps you take control of what you read, a process that increases your power of concentration and makes it easier to envision yourself reading faster.

●**Push yourself.** Any time that you try to change your behavior—whether losing weight or reading faster—it pays to keep the pressure on. When it comes to reading, don't be satisfied with your reading speed until you feel slightly rushed.

It's beneficial to practice when you are actually pressed for time.

Example: Instead of leisurely reading the morning paper over breakfast, wait until your time is limited, such as on a short train ride or while waiting for an appointment.

If you don't foresee any rushed situations, try allowing yourself half the time that it would normally take you to, say, read the paper.

●**Review what you read.** When you finish reading, mentally review the subject matter. This not only helps you remember what you've read but also lets you know if you're sacrificing comprehension for speed.

After pushing yourself to read the morning paper, for example, you'll know you're trying too hard if it's difficult to remember much content of the first few articles you read.

CONSIDER TAKING LESSONS

Most people see an improvement in reading speed within just a few weeks of beginning the steps to improve it. And the new speed rarely decreases unless you go through a long period of not reading at all. When that occurs, start the regimen over again until you reach at least 500 words a minute.

Also consider formal speed-reading lessons. There are hundreds of programs throughout the country at virtually all price ranges. To find them, consult schools and colleges in your area, search the Internet for "Speed Reading" or, in large cities, search in the *Yellow Pages* under "Reading."

There are two main types of programs—those that seek to improve only speed and those that combine an increased speed with greater comprehension. I advocate the latter.

279

Some speed-reading programs are taught in classes with instructors, and others instruct you how to improve on your own, without the aid of an instructor.

Caution: Most people should avoid programs that seek to increase speed faster than 700 to 900 words per minute. Studies show that comprehension often deteriorates rapidly when people go beyond that rate.

Secrets of Writing Difficult Letters

Rosalie Maggio, an award-winning author of 18 books, including the best-selling *How to Say It: Choice Words, Phrases, Sentences, and Paragraphs for Every Occasion* (Prentice Hall/Perigee). She is based in Frazier Park, CA.

I've never seen such a proliferation of books on letter writing, anthologies of correspondence and books of letters by the famous—all at a time when fewer people than ever are writing letters.

We needn't abandon the graciousness and etiquette of previous generations just because we're "busy."

When you write a letter, you create good feelings and feel good about yourself. The fact of your writing is more important than what you write. The recipient will be glad to receive anything personal among the daily avalanche of bills and junk mail. If most people realized *how* glad, they would write more.

In addition, letter writing can be a fine outlet for communicating with (and by) people who are hard of hearing.

Example: For my elderly father, who has trouble hearing, talking on the phone is no longer the joy it once was. Instead, he sends letters and e-mail messages to family members and friends.

OVERDUE LETTERS

People often ask me which kind of letter is most difficult to write. I think it's the one that's been put off. The longer you let it sit, the more you dread thinking about it.

The letter you set aside looms larger and larger every day. It may not get written, or if it does—it may not be written well.

In his delightful book on manners for teens, *How Rude!,* Alex J. Packer exaggerates only a little when he writes, "Thank-you notes get exponentially more difficult to write with each day that passes. By the second day, they are four times harder to write. By the third day, they are nine times harder, and if you wait 12 days, they are 144 times harder to write!"

Surprisingly helpful: I divide my letters requiring a reply into three piles—those that can wait indefinitely…those that don't have to be answered this week…and those that *must* be answered this week. Thinking about the whole pile overwhelms me, but getting a couple of urgent letters in the mail always seems possible.

Don't feel you have to write three times as much or four times as charmingly just because you're late. The pressure will prevent you from writing. Write what you would have written if you had written sooner. Be honest—say you have no excuse and are sorry for the delay.

SYMPATHY CARDS

When my mother died recently, I was astonished at how much the notes comforted my family and me. No two of the 800-plus commercial sympathy cards that we received were alike, and none contained simply a signature. Everyone had written at least one line under the message.

People wrote promptly and to the point: *We were so sorry to hear of the loss of your mother* [or, to my father, *your wife*]. *She was a wonderful woman.* None of us—not Dad, not any of us eight siblings—stopped to analyze the writer's grammar or phrasing. What we cared about was that people had made the effort.

LETTERS YOU WANT TO WRITE

Writing letters you don't *have* to write can help to get you in the mood. Make a habit of sending notes of congratulation or appreciation. A note of appreciation is one of the most pleasant to receive because we do not expect it and one of the most satisfying to write because we are not obliged to send it.

Mary Kay Ash, founder of Mary Kay Cosmetics, said, "Everyone wants to be appreciated. If you appreciate someone, don't keep it a secret."

In the process, you will have established the habit of writing, complete with a supply of note cards and other stationery.

GETTING STARTED

●**Focus on the recipient.** You may be feeling inadequate in the face of death or serious illness, embarrassed about some faux pas for which you must apologize or irritated about having to thank someone for a useless gift. Set your negative feelings aside. Focus on what you want your recipient to hear: *I'm thinking about you. How good of you to think of me. I'm counting on you to forgive me.*

●**Think before you write.** When we are stumped, we aren't very clear in our own minds about what we want to write. Say your message aloud as though you're speaking to a friend. On scratch paper, jot down the message you want to get across. In a difficult letter, the message is usually simple: *I'm sorry. Thank you.* So, write exactly that, elaborate a bit and you will have your note.

●**Review your letter,** and let any potentially prickly letter sit for one day before mailing it. Show it to someone you trust, and ask for a frank opinion.

●**Send a card.** When the prospect of sending a letter is too overwhelming, rely on the incredible array of commercial greeting cards. It's far better to send a card than to send nothing. Choose your card with care and always, always add a line or two.

●**Send an e-mail.** I have received messages of sympathy and thanks by e-mail from those people with whom I communicate primarily by e-mail. But there is no substitute for "snail mail." A letter of congratulations elevates the situation. A handwritten note communicates respect and acknowledges an event's importance.

●**Admit your reluctance to yourself.** Sometimes it helps to say out loud: "I don't like writing letters. I'm not good at it. I don't want to write this letter." Take one moment to sigh. Then pull an envelope toward you, address it and get started.

Also helpful: Keep note paper, stamped picture postcards and a pen near the TV to write letters during commercials...near the phone, to jot down thoughts while "on hold"...in the kitchen, to use while dinner cooks.

More from Rosalie Maggio...

Helpful Phrases to Get You Started

Words that will help you compose hard-to-write letters and cards...

Belated letters: Please forgive my tardiness ...there is no excuse for...I have been asleep at the wheel.

Get-well letters: Be up and around soon... hope for an early recovery...felt so bad to hear ...wishing you healthier days ahead.

Neighbor problems: Ask your cooperation ...get together to discuss...wanted you to be aware that...would you consider.

Refusals: I'm sorry to tell you...I must say no to...I would like to help out, but...previous commitments...we find that we are unable to.

To Keep Your Creativity Flowing...

Bev Bachel, an artist and communications consultant located in Minneapolis. She is the founder of Idea Girls, *www.ideagirls.com,* a national network of women helping one another pursue their creative dreams, and author of *What Do You Really Want? How to Set a Goal and Go for It! A Guide for Teens* (Free Spirit).

To rekindle your creative spark at home or at the office, consider trying out the following helpful strategies...

●**Every day, do at least one thing that intimidates you**—write it down in the morning and do it that day.

Example: Call someone you just met and invite him/her for coffee.

●**Change your routine.**

Example: Drive a different route to your friend's house.

●**Try thinking about things from some-one else's perspective.**

●**Make connections between unfamiliar things,** just for fun.

Example: Think about what a soap bubble and a fresh tulip might have in common.

●**Do something silly.**

●**Write regularly** in a journal about your experiences, dreams and thoughts.

●**Randomly pick a word from the dictionary** or an object in your home or office and use it as a basis for ideas.

Keep Your Brain Healthy and Improve Your Memory

Gary Small, MD, director of the Memory Clinic and Center on Aging at the University of California, Los Angeles. He is author of *The Memory Bible: An Innovative Strategy for Keeping Your Brain Young* (Hyperion).

By middle age, most of us will occasionally forget names, and important dates slip our minds. We miss an appointment or misplace our keys from time to time. As the years pass, it gets worse.

Beyond the simple nuisance, the worry persists—are these the first signs of Alzheimer's? Can anything be done?

Actually, there's a good deal you can do to sharpen your memory *and* reduce the risk that you'll fall victim to dementia.

UNDERSTANDING BRAIN AGING

As the brain ages, the synapses (connections between brain cells) function less efficiently. Brain cells die, leaving behind bits of abnormal protein—plaques and tangles—that accumulate in damaged cells. The brain actually shrinks.

Loss of brain cell function is most marked in the areas responsible for memory—near the forehead (frontal lobe) and near and above the temples (temporal and parietal regions). But while some people have significant memory loss by age 60, other people remain sharp into their 90s.

What makes the difference? Some factors, such as our genes, we *cannot* control. But we *can* have an influence on the lifestyle factors, including exercise, diet and stress levels.

BRAIN-FRIENDLY LIFESTYLE

Memory loss can be triggered by heart disease, anemia, thyroid disorders and dehydration. High blood pressure and diabetes can also accelerate aging of the brain, but proper treatment of these conditions will help reverse much of your memory trouble.

Many medications can also impair memory. These include blood pressure drugs, sleeping pills, tranquilizers, stomach acid reducers and corticosteroids.

If your memory has worsened since you started taking a new medication, ask your doctor if it could be affecting your memory.

In addition to checking for medical conditions that may trigger memory loss, you should adopt a lifestyle that promotes cardiovascular health. This will improve blood circulation to the brain and reduce the risk for small strokes (transient ischemic attacks, or TIAs) that hasten its deterioration.

To promote brain health, pay attention to...

●**Exercise.** Regular aerobic exercise protects against heart attack and stroke. Some studies suggest that it even lowers the likelihood of Alzheimer's. Walking 30 minutes three times a week may be enough to gain this benefit.

Physical exertion also results in *immediate* brain gains. Immediately following any exercise, people are better at problem-solving and complex reasoning.

●**Diet.** Eat a low-calorie, low-fat diet that is rich in the omega-3 fats found in fish, flaxseed and olive oil. An Italian study found that a diet that includes three tablespoons of olive oil daily reduces memory loss.

Antioxidants, particularly vitamins E and C, protect the brain against damage by free radicals. Get these nutrients in your diet—almonds and leafy, green vegetables for vitamin E...citrus fruits for vitamin C. In addition, take daily supplements—400 international units (IU) of vitamin E...500 milligrams (mg) of vitamin C.

●**Stress.** Research has shown that the stress hormone *cortisol* reduces a person's ability to retrieve information and memory. Even worse, this same stress hormone is linked to progressive shrinking of the *hippocampus*—an important memory center in the temporal region. High levels of stress also promote depression, which severely impairs memory and increases the risk for dementia.

To reduce stress, try relaxation exercises. Sit quietly, and breathe deeply and slowly. Relax each part of your body, starting with the top of your head and finishing with your toes. Look for humor in tense situations…and talk about your feelings with family members, friends or a therapist, if necessary.

Memory Fitness: How to Keep Your Brain Strong

Cynthia R. Green, PhD, president of Memory Arts, LLC, in Upper Montclair, NJ, which provides memory fitness training to corporations and nonprofit organizations, and assistant clinical professor at Mt. Sinai School of Medicine in New York City. She is author of *Total Memory Workout: Eight Easy Steps to Maximum Memory Fitness* (Bantam).

It is undeniable that aging will bring with it some changes in memory. These include the "tip of the tongue" phenomenon, the word that is achingly familiar but won't pop into your consciousness. This might happen because a delay in the way the brain processes information may be associated with age, so that you cannot retrieve information as quickly as you could when you were younger.

But there is no reason to give up. While you cannot reverse any physiological changes in the brain, there are ways to work around them. By creating healthy memory habits—memory fitness—you'll be remembering names, even to-do lists, in no time. *Here's how…*

BASICS

Underlying all memory techniques is the A.M. principle. Putting this principle to work will help you sharpen your memory immediately.

● **"A" stands for attention.** Often the reason people can't pull a word or name out of their consciousness is that they just didn't pay enough attention to it in the first place. If you want to remember something, you must pay close attention so that you really absorb it. You will need to develop two basic habits to accomplish this. *They are…*

● Be aware. Rather than mindlessly parking your car at the mall or meeting a new neighbor, remind yourself that you need to pay attention.

● Make the effort. You've reminded yourself to pay attention, now focus and do it. Take in the information on the spot that you'll need to recall. *Everyday example:* You need to retrieve something from the other room. Instead of wandering in and forgetting what it was you wanted, say to yourself what it is as you get up to get it.

● **"M" stands for meaning.** Giving information meaning will help to make it memorable. Assigning meaning also helps your memory bank store the information, making it easier to find when you need it. *Three ways to help give information meaning…*

● Organize it. The best example of this is a way to learn a series of numbers. Rather than try to remember nine numbers in a row—intimidating for anyone—"chunk" them into groupings. Seem familiar? This is what you do anytime you learn someone's phone number with area code —you chunk it into three parts.

● See it. You can make many things memorable just by picturing them, be it visualizing the errands you must run, someone's e-mail address or even certain names. For some information, visual memory is stronger than verbal recall.

● Connect it. Think of this as cross-referencing in your brain—connect something you want to remember with something you already know. *Example:* If you meet someone named Eloise, think of the Plaza Hotel—and the precocious young girl of fiction who roamed its halls in search of adventure.

TECHNIQUES

Below, you'll find six techniques for encoding information to memory. What they all have in common is that they get you to pay attention and give meaning to what you want to learn. These aren't all meant to work for everyone— what some people find useful, others will view as cumbersome. Choose only the ones that appeal to you and put them to work.

●**The repetition technique.** This is exactly what it says—if you need to remember something, give it your complete focus and then repeat it to yourself several times.

●**The link technique.** This technique is perfect for remembering any list. Think of it as dominoes—one word links up the next to the next. Although most of us generally write out our grocery lists, it's a good way to practice the link technique. Start with, say, potatoes (for mashing)—that links to butter to milk to steaks to salad greens. Once you get the hang of it, this technique is useful for just about any list.

●**The storytelling technique.** Making up a story connects information and gives it meaning. Say you have just met someone named Rose Cinder. You might come up with a quick story about a rose growing from the ashes. Although this one is more involved than most of the other techniques, many people favor it, in part because it's fun.

●**The connection technique.** Attach what you need to learn to something you already know. Say that you meet someone with the unusual last name "Sertage." While there is virtually no visual prompt in that name, it links nicely with a word you know well—"certain," but with a soft "g" ending.

●**First-letter association technique.** You know this one already, the surefire trick of creating acronyms to remember a word grouping —"TGIF" says something to everyone. Use that same idea to remember the birth order of your niece's five kids. This approach doesn't work for everything, in particular if the words you need to remember all start with consonants. But for certain needs, it can be a great deal of fun as well as effective.

●**The snapshot technique.** While the visual memory is a powerful tool for remembering information, people tend to overlook it. For this technique, create a mental image of what you are trying to learn.

Example: To remember a recipe someone is giving you, get a picture of each item in your mind's eye as the person tells you. It's an easy technique to learn. And, as a bonus, it's a good way to boost your brainpower.

PRACTICE PERFECTS

Keep in mind that just as you need to work out regularly to keep your muscles strong, you'll need to practice memory techniques regularly. Take advantage of your spare minutes by practicing on whatever's handy—license plate numbers, telephone numbers, to-do lists and even e-mail addresses.

Proven Patience Boosters

M. J. Ryan, coauthor of the *Random Acts of Kindness* books and the founder of Conari Press. Her most recent book is *The Power of Patience: How to Slow the Rush and Enjoy More Happiness, Success, and Peace of Mind Every Day* (Broadway).

In this fast-paced world, patience has never been needed more. *Try these simple strategies to help you increase your patience quotient...*

●**Drop a pebble in your pocket.** When irritation rises, move the pebble to another pocket, which interrupts the anger cycle and creates a moment to think the situation through.

●**Reduce your caffeine intake.** Caffeine, a stimulant, can cause jitters and irritability.

●**Seek practical solutions** to frustrations with your mate.

Examples: Driven nuts when she hasn't replaced the toothpaste cap? Buy toothpaste in a pump. In a meltdown when he forgets to fill the ice cube trays? Your next refrigerator should have an automatic ice cube maker.

●**Take a walk.** When you reach your tolerance limit, go for a vigorous walk. You'll burn off accumulated stress hormones...and make it easier to reengage patience when you return.

●**Count to 10—or 20.** In a heated discussion, do this before responding. As you count, decide which matters more—finding an effective solution or blowing off steam.

●**Thank others for their patience.** Do this when you're the one holding things up, such as while fumbling for the right change. You'll defuse the tension while encouraging others to be patient as well.

19

Business and Career Smarts

How to Be a Hero at Work

The early stages of an economic recovery are the perfect time to introduce new moneymaking ideas. If your workplace is stuck in cost-cutting mode, you might miss the opportunity to boost profits and propel your career.

Winning firms and managers today are paying greater attention to how they hatch exciting concepts. *Ideas for jump-starting innovation…*

PLANT THE SEED

Four ways to inspire yourself and your team to think creatively…

●**Anticipate what your customers want.** Use information, such as warranty cards, to identify the customers who buy the latest versions of your products. What insights can customer feedback on the cards provide about where your industry may be headed and how you can position your organization?

●**Encourage smart borrowing.** Whenever a product or idea really impresses you or your colleagues, ask, "How can this be an opportunity for us?" What works well in one industry or region frequently can be applied successfully to another.

Case study: In 1987, managers in the poultry-processing division of Springdale, AR–based Tyson Foods noticed that the company was selling more chicken wings in Buffalo than anywhere in the country. Sports bars were buying the wings to serve as finger food during happy hours, creating lucrative demand for a chicken part that previously had been unmarketable.

Tyson's "aha"—borrow the idea of "Buffalo wings" and promote its own Tyson Flyers nationally—boosted sales in the retail and food-service markets.

●**Make your service or product more convenient.** Brainstorm ways to save customers time and reduce hassles.

Robert B. Tucker, president of The Innovation Resource Consulting Group in Santa Barbara, CA, whose clients include Fortune 500 companies, *www.innovationresource. com.* He is author of *Driving Growth Through Innovation* (Berrett-Koehler).

Case study: Managers at Fort Knox Federal Credit Union in Kentucky realized that customers were annoyed by long lines. The credit union had no space for additional tellers, so it mailed members suggestions on how to avoid long waits and installed TVs near lines to make customers feel that they were using their time productively.

Result: Complaints practically disappeared.

●**Add value to existing products and services.** Remind yourself about your customers' most pressing need and why they select you over competitors.

Example: For years, the housekeeping franchise Merry Maids, in Downers Grove, IL, competed based on how well it cleaned homes. Research revealed that customers were more concerned about allowing strangers into their homes. Merry Maids tightened its hiring practices and changed its advertising to tout peace of mind as well as a clean home, and between 1998 and 2003, revenues increased by 32%.

CREATE AN IDEA-GENERATING CULTURE

Ask everyone from support staff to senior executives for ways to reduce inefficiency, increase revenue and wow customers.

Case study: Appleton Papers in Appleton, WI, was the world leader in a product that had a shrinking market—carbonless paper used for filling out forms in triplicate. To survive, Appleton's managers began regularly soliciting ideas from the company's 2,500 employees, and they were pleasantly surprised by the response.

Each month, 50 ideas are fed to nine innovation teams, which present the most promising ones to Appleton's executive committee. Several new products have been launched as a result, including a coated paper that makes it difficult to change or counterfeit secure documents, such as birth certificates.

How to make generating ideas a big part of your business…

●**Set aside time at weekly meetings to hear new ideas.** Appoint an "idea" person to take written submissions.

Example: Citibank, with headquarters in New York City, has appointed some employees to act as "innovation catalysts" in each of the 102 countries where it operates.

●**Involve everyone in the search for ideas.** Three times a year, the Walt Disney Company holds its own *Gong Show,* an internal idea-pitching confab, at which any employee can pitch a concept or movie plot. A revolving group of executives wastes no time hitting a giant gong if it considers an idea a dud.

Important: If submissions seem off base, add a few words of encouragement to steer employees in the right direction.

●**Set idea goals.** Innovative companies don't wait for happy accidents to bring them breakthrough ideas.

Case study: At medical technology pioneer Medtronic, based in Minneapolis, the goal is for 70% of the current year's revenue to come from products that didn't exist two years ago.

●**Recognize and reward submissions.** *Some suggestions…*

●Emphasize team or company-wide recognition rather than individual achievements. At the beginning of staff meetings, acknowledge how associates came up with ideas and implemented them. Remember to recognize the behavior that you want more of.

●Create a special club for risk takers. This ensures that your culture will continue to welcome offbeat ideas. *Example:* In the late 1970s, Hewlett Packard engineer Chuck House defied cofounder David Packard by continuing to work on a computer graphics monitor. Ultimately, the product was a big moneymaker. The company created a Medal of Defiance to remind staffers that it is better to ask for forgiveness than for permission.

●**Rethink your meetings.** Require invitees to write down 10 questions before they can attend any meeting, and ask them to share at least one. This will cut down on unnecessary gatherings. With fewer meetings, workers will have more time to generate ideas, set goals and spend time with customers.

Case study: For two days each month, SC Johnson & Sons in Racine, WI, bans meetings for its 3,500 employees to give them a chance to think without any interruptions.

Big deal? You bet. Managers I survey informally say that lack of time is a major barrier to innovation.

More Effective Voice Mail Messages

The next time you leave a voice mail message, be sure to keep these tips in mind...

●**Begin the message with the name of the person** you are trying to reach.

●**State in a single sentence** what you want the call to accomplish.

●**Repeat important information**—such as your name and phone number—twice so that the recipient does not have to replay the whole message to catch it.

●**Tell the person you will call back** if you do not hear from him/her by a specified date or time.

Renee Grant-Williams, a voice coach in Nashville, www. myvoicecoach.com, and author of Voice Power (Amacom).

An Actor's Guide to Giving a Great Speech

David Booth, an actor who has appeared on such TV shows as The Practice, Providence and Judging Amy and in the film Scream. He and his partner Deborah Shames co-founded Eloqui, a presentation and communication training firm, Topanga, CA, www.eloqui.biz.

Businesspeople often find themselves in the spotlight, giving presentations as well as making speeches. Yet very few know the techniques that actors use to mesmerize an audience. *Here are great ways to make any presentation better...*

●**Get your opening down cold.** Most anxiety occurs at the beginning of a performance.

If you really know your opening lines, the rest will be easier.

The opening sets the tone, connects you with the audience and introduces your topic. The best openings reveal something about you, your values or your take on the subject. Starting with a personal anecdote or story is better than the old-fashioned technique of beginning with a joke.

●**Focus on your "super objective."** An actor doesn't fixate on every last detail when he/she performs. He concentrates on his character's main goal. For example, an actor playing Macbeth would think, *I want to be king.*

Speakers should focus on the goal they wish to achieve.

Examples: We will do business together ...I want you to be as excited about this topic as I am.

●**Ignore distractions.** A performer must be in the moment to deliver a message effectively. Direct your attention outward to engage your audience. Worrying about your performance or that person in the audience who isn't paying attention only detracts from your presentation. If a distraction creeps into your mind, refocus on your objective.

●**Depict images.** People in business often believe that their goal in a presentation is to deliver information. The reality is that information presented in a speech is seldom remembered. Images, metaphors and anecdotes are what stick in listeners' minds.

Example: A financial adviser was giving a presentation about retirement planning. Instead of focusing on tables, numbers and graphs, he used this anecdote—"Bruce and Irene thought they had enough to retire. They forgot about taxes, inflation and living past the average life expectancy. I recommended that they turn their hobbies into revenue streams. So, now Irene's quilts are sold in local galleries, and Bruce refinishes furniture that he sells for a profit on eBay."

●**Use your space.** Actors do not stand still during their performances—and neither should speakers. During your most important points, move away from the lectern and closer to the audience. This breaks the barrier between you and your listeners and captures the audience's attention. Change where you stand when you switch subjects to help differentiate topics for the audience.

●**Improvise.** When an actor forgets a line, he might repeat the prior line in a slightly different way.

Other strategies: Ask the audience a question…walk to the lectern to refer to your notes …look thoughtful and say, "How best to express this?"…or briefly summarize what you already have said. Try not to stammer or fill the empty air with "Um."

●**Add a voice.** To vary the presentation and keep it fresh, convey information via dialogue or quote someone influential.

Example: In the middle of your talk, you might say, "As the CEO of XXX Corporation said to me…"

What to Do with Unused Vacation Pay

An employer's vacation policy says unused vacation may not be carried forward into the following year. However, an employee may elect to have the employer contribute the value of unused vacation time to his/her account in the employer's profit-sharing retirement plan.

IRS ruling: Amounts contributed to the retirement plan under this arrangement are free from income tax and FICA employment taxes.

IRS Letter Ruling 200311043.

Correct Hiring Mistakes Quickly

Make it clear to prospective employees that dismissal within the first 90 days need not be for cause. If possible, have the prospective employee confirm his/her understanding of this with a signed and dated form. And, use this

provision if a person turns out to be a bad hire or not a good match for the job.

Problem: Most employers wait too long—six to eight months—to terminate new employees.

Daniel Abramson, president, StaffDynamics, St. James, NY, www.staffdynamics.biz.

Lost Your Job? Smart Strategies to Get More Severance Pay

Alan L. Sklover, Esq., partner with Sklover & Associates, LLC, a law firm in New York City that represents individual employees only, *www.executivelaw.com.* He is author of *Fired, Downsized, or Laid Off: What Your Employer Doesn't Want You to Know About How to Fight Back* (Owl).

Many laid-off workers leave thousands of dollars in cash, benefits and other concessions on the table. They do not realize that even in tough economic times, severance packages are negotiable…or they're too angry, ashamed or overwhelmed by the loss of their jobs to think straight.

Generally, companies offer secretarial-level workers severance pay of one week per year of service…low-level managers, two weeks per year…and senior managers, three weeks per year of service.

Do not immediately agree to the severance package you're offered. Explain that you need a few days to review the terms. Use that time to plan your negotiating strategy.

You're in the strongest negotiating position while the severance package is on the table. There is no downside, though, to making a respectful request even months later.

FIND LEVERAGE

The company might appear to hold all the cards, particularly if you don't have a formal employment contract, but you have more power than you think. Your employer may be worried about a potential lawsuit or just plain feel guilty. *You may be able to base negotiations on…*

●**Promises.** Has your boss ever said that you would be with the firm at least until the completion of a project? That your job was safe as long as you kept up your sales figures? Such verbal promises have legal weight and can be used for negotiating leverage.

Important: Whenever your boss makes a verbal promise related to your job security, e-mail him/her a thank-you note. Print out the note and any reply you receive to save in your files at *home*. If the company doesn't follow through on the promise, the e-mail will help you establish that the conversation occurred, strengthening your negotiating position.

●**Discrimination or unequal treatment.** Were all the older workers laid off first? Is there reason to suspect that race was a factor? Were you fired shortly after taking maternity or medical leave?

●**Defaming statements.** Corporations will sometimes try to justify firings by falsely claiming that laid-off employees were bad at their jobs or broke rules. Such "defaming statements" could form the basis of a lawsuit and can serve as ammunition in negotiating severance—even if you have no intention of hiring a lawyer.

●**Whistle-blowing.** Legally, whistle-blowers can't be fired for reporting unethical behavior by a supervisor or the company.

●**Need.** Are you caring for a loved one with a chronic illness? Did your spouse lose his/her job earlier in the year? Though it's not a legal argument, a legitimate need-based appeal can result in increased severance benefits.

●**Tough job market.** For every $10,000 of gross compensation, it takes at minimum one month to find a job that equals your current income—longer if you are over age 50.

●**Pipeline value.** Are you involved in an important project or a major deal that is not yet complete? Is there a chance that you could be called to testify at an important corporate trial? Tell the company representatives that if they help you with improved severance, you'll help them with their needs.

●**Ownership of intellectual property.** Could you make a case that you own the rights to work that you produced while with the company? If you had an idea for a new product or process on your own time, you might be able to argue that you own the rights to it. Even if

such a strategy is a long shot, your employer might increase your severance pay rather than risk a lawsuit.

●**Past successes.** Remind your employer of the time you instituted a moneysaving program...closed a big deal...brought about other changes that proved successful for the firm.

APPEAL TO POWER

Pick a senior executive who is very familiar with you and your work. Ideally, this executive should have a personal stake in you because he/she likes you...acted as your mentor...was responsible for hiring you...or, failing that, because he dislikes you enough to want you out the door quickly.

Write a polite letter that explains why your severance package should be improved. When your argument is based on legal reasons—for example, discrimination, defaming statements or ownership of intellectual property—don't threaten legal action. Instead, present improved severance as a way to *avoid* legal action.

Possible words to use: Please understand that I am not trying to sound adversarial. I don't want to seek legal representation—that's why I'm writing to you. I'm trying to reach a reasonable basis for leaving, what some would call an "honorable discharge."

Chances are, this executive will pass your letter to human resources with instructions to "deal with it." Though you're right back to the human resources department, your situation has improved substantially.

OTHER BENEFITS

If you cannot get additional severance pay, ask for...

●**Departure letter.** Many firms now are unwilling to provide references for fear of legal consequences. Ask instead for a "departure letter," which should explain that you were a great employee who was let go because of corporate restructuring.

●**Outplacement alternative.** If you don't want the outplacement assistance offered by the company, see if you can have cash instead. Outplacement services can cost the company $3,000 or more each month for one mid-level executive.

• **Tuition.** Perhaps the corporate training budget can pay for classes to upgrade your skills.

• **Relocation allowance.** If your firm has asked you to sign a noncompete contract that restricts your ability to seek work in the region, you could make a particularly strong case that relocation expenses are warranted.

Over 50 and Out Of Work?...Beat The Age Barrier

Jean Erickson Walker, EdD, professional effectiveness coach with Pathways/OI Partners, Inc., which specializes in coaching people at midlife, Portland, OR, *www.oipartners. net/pathways*. She is author of *The Age Advantage: Making the Most of Your Midlife Career Transition* (Penguin), *www. theageadvantage.com*.

Finding a new job isn't easy in this economy. It can be especially hard for people over age 50. They face age discrimination. Employers tend to believe younger candidates are more familiar with new technology, and they can pay younger employees less.

Age discrimination is usually subtle and not always deliberate, but the result is brutal. It takes people over age 50 nearly 40% longer to find new jobs as those under age 35.* The *Age Discrimination in Employment Act of 1967* is intended to protect most people over age 40 from discrimination in hiring, layoffs, salary, promotion, assignments and training.

Victims of age discrimination can sue employers or prospective employers—but these cases are hard to prove. The employer can say that the candidate simply wasn't the best person for the job.

The best strategy is to *outsmart* age discrimination. *Here's how...*

• **Confront technology-skills stereotypes head-on.** When a 25-year-old applies for a job, everyone just assumes he/she has computer skills. When a 55-year-old applies, most people assume he doesn't.

*Study by the human resources consulting firm Drake Beam Morin.

Self-defense: Mention technological expertise during interviews. On your résumé, list the computer programs you know or certifications you have earned.

Example: Ken, age 56, consented to take early retirement after 27 years at his position. For four years, he searched unsuccessfully for a similar management post. At my suggestion, he got his project management certification. Then he positioned himself as an up-to-date telecommunications manager with extensive experience. Now he has a great new job.

• **Select the appropriate companies and industries.** If possible, visit the company to get a sense of its culture. If it doesn't feel like a good fit, look elsewhere. If you have been laid off from a youth-focused industry, emphasize your transferable skills or, if necessary, leave the industry. The technology, telecommunications and advertising sectors, for example, tend to favor younger hires.

The banking, government and utility sectors frequently hire younger employees and promote from within. An older job applicant in these industries should angle for a consultant's role rather than a promotion-track position.

Every year, AARP (formerly known as the American Association of Retired Persons) compiles a list of the top companies for older workers. To check the most recent list, go to *www. aarp.org/bestemployers*. Industries with the best opportunities now include teaching, health care and retail.

• **Dress for success.** Match the culture you're hoping to join, but also look sharp. Clothes are only as good as the body wearing them. Get in shape. Managers want to hire people who look like they could run—and win—a race.

• **Show flexibility.** A common stereotype holds that an older worker thinks his way is the only way to do things and he won't consider new ideas.

Self-defense: Design a résumé that reflects a range of positions and changing responsibilities. This is especially important if you have worked for the same firm for many years.

Example: Mention occasions when you implemented cutting-edge strategies.

●**Play the role of "possibility thinker" in interviews.** Mention a possible scenario, and run through the company's options should it actually occur. When young people do this, they come off as loose cannons trying to fix things that aren't broken. When older, more experienced people do it, they seem adaptable and innovative.

●**Don't abbreviate your résumé**—contrary to standard advice. Some older applicants only include their most recent experience.

Let your résumé run two or three pages, so long as each description is succinct and demonstrates all your accomplishments. Do not try to hide your age by withholding any employment dates. Emphasize how your experience can help the firm deal with problems.

For information on your rights…

●AARP (888-687-2277 or *www.aarp.org/careers*).

●US Administration on Aging (202-619-0724 or *www.aoa.gov*).

●US Equal Employment Opportunity Commission (800-669-3362 or *www.eeoc.gov*).

Job Market for Seniors to Boom in Coming Years

As the baby boomers reach full retirement age, growth of the workforce will slow sharply or stop, while demand for workers will continue to grow.

The number of US born workers ages 25 to 54 grew 44% over the last 20 years—but no growth at all is expected during the next 20 years. By the year 2011, when the first baby boomers reach age 65, available jobs may outnumber workers by more than four million—rising to 35 million by 2031.

Implication: More opportunities in the future for seniors to have a second career and prolonged employment on better terms than ever before.

The Employment Policy Foundation, Washington, DC.

Millions of New Jobs: Where to Find Them

Sophia Koropeckyj, director of industry economics at Economy.com, an economic research firm in West Chester, PA. The firm's clients include some of the country's largest banks, insurance companies and financial-services firms.

The growing economic recovery should create 1.6 million new jobs this year—about 60% of the jobs lost during the recession and the bear market. Growth should add another 2 million jobs a year through the end of the decade, but not every economic sector will benefit.

Don't expect lost factory or information technology jobs to come back. They will continue to move overseas at a rate of about 300,000 per year. Many jobless people will need to switch careers. *What you need to know about the new job market…*

HOT INDUSTRIES

Data from the US Bureau of Labor Statistics show two trends—our aging population is demanding more health services and home-based care…and every business must upgrade its software and technology systems continually in order to stay competitive.

The fastest-growing sectors for jobs are health care (currently 14 million employees) and non-Internet technology industries (currently 5.8 million employees). Both of these hot sectors will nearly double in size by the end of the decade.

HOT PROFESSIONS

Top health-care jobs: Physicians' assistants …medical billing and health information technicians…occupational therapists…fitness trainers/aerobics instructors…veterinary assistants/laboratory animal caretakers…mental health/substance-abuse social workers…technicians in pharmacies…hospital managers.

Note: Most of the new health-care jobs created through year 2010 will not require medical degrees. For example, if you're an unemployed middle manager, consider switching to health-care administration. Hospitals will need 123,000 more managers by the end of the decade, an increase of about 30% from current levels.

Top technology jobs: Software engineers… network administrators…desktop publishers… database administrators.

WHERE THE JOBS ARE

Within the next three years, many new jobs will be in smaller cities. According to a Milken Institute survey, locations with the fastest job growth include Fayetteville, AR (near the headquarters of still-fast-growing Wal-Mart)…San Diego and San Luis Obispo, CA, and Fort Myers and West Palm Beach, FL (cities that have up-scale retirees and brisk tourism).

States with greatest job growth projections until 2010: Nevada anticipates a 50% increase in jobs…Colorado, 38%…Arizona, 34% …Idaho, 31%.

The Bureau of Labor Statistics projects growth by occupation and education level at *www.bls. gov/emp.*

INCOME OUTLOOK

Do not expect to make as much money at these new jobs. While individual salaries differ, the average wage of jobs created in 2004–2005 is predicted to be $35,855. That's almost 18% less than the $43,629 average wage of jobs lost between 2001 and 2003.

For a Better Job Search…

To find out which companies are downsizing or are going out of business—so you know where not to apply for a job—check out *www. bankruptcydata.com…www.thestreet.com…* and *http://finance.yahoo.com.*

Ron and Caryl Krannich, PhDs, career writers and consultants, Manassas, VA, and authors of *America's Top Internet Job Sites* (Impact).

Smarter Job Hunting

Specialty recruiters will often have high placement rates in certain fields.

Consulting: Raines International, New York City…Dise & Co., Cleveland.

Energy: Preng & Associates and Independent Power Consultants, both in Houston, TX.

Finance: Higdon Barrett LLC and Prince-Goldsmith LLC, both in New York City.

Hospitality: Hospitality Executive Search, Boston…Global Hospitality, Pasadena, CA.

Software: Rusher, Loscavio & LoPresto, San Francisco…Wyatt & Jaffe, Minneapolis.

Kennedy Information, Inc., recruitment industry experts, Peterborough, NH, *www.executiveagent.com.*

Make Your Résumé Stand Out

J. Michael Worthington, Jr., partner, ResumeDoctor.com, a nationwide résumé-consulting service for job seekers in all industries, Burlington, VT, *www.resumedoctor.com.*

In today's ultracompetitive job market, a single opening might draw more than 1,000 responses. Most résumés receive only a 10-second skim. That's why yours has to make a great impression.

We recently surveyed more than 2,500 recruiters and headhunters, asking them for their résumé pet peeves. Some of their responses, such as lies and typographical errors, come as no surprise. Others are not so obvious. *Don't be surprised if one or two of these mistakes are lurking in your résumé…*

CONTENT

●**Missing industry specifics.** Recruiters hate it when résumés don't mention the field in which prior employers are engaged. Unless a past employer is a household name, such as IBM or Wal-Mart, always include the industry, company size and whether the firm was public or privately held.

●**Meaningless objective statements.** Some résumés include objective statements that are so generic, they're worthless.

Example: *My objective is to find a challenging position in the advertising field.*

Instead, put a "headline" right under your contact information to focus the recruiter's attention. It should be customized to match the job description.

Example: *Senior-Level Health and Safety Manager with Extensive Experience Working with FDA Regulations in the Pharmaceutical Manufacturing Arena.*

● **Unnecessary personal information.** Recruiters don't care that your hobby is tennis—unless you're applying for a job at a company that makes tennis racquets.

● **Employment gaps.** It is better to address gaps in employment directly than to leave the recruiters wondering.

Examples: *August 2000–November 2000, took personal sabbatical to travel in Europe... October 2003–present, looking for suitable position in field.*

● **Too duty-oriented.** Many résumés focus on job titles and day-to-day responsibilities. But, employers really want to know what you have accomplished.

Example: If you write *project manager,* your résumé will be like hundreds of others. Instead, write *project manager who oversaw rollout of new product line generating $50 million in annual sales,* and then you'll get their attention.

● **Functional résumés.** Some applicants arrange their experience into skill categories. Recruiters strongly prefer a chronological résumé, which starts with the most recent position and works backward.

FORMAT

● **Résumés longer than two pages.** Shorten your résumé by summarizing jobs from more than ten years ago in one *Previous Employment* section that includes titles, companies and dates. Elaborate only if an earlier job seems relevant to the position for which you're applying.

● **Long paragraphs.** Write in a fast-paced, bullet-point style. Think of a résumé as an ad in the newspaper that's selling you.

Example: Don't say, *I spent three years as a marketing manager, where I oversaw a staff of*

12. Instead say, *Three years as senior marketing manager. Oversaw staff of 12. Developed marketing plan that increased sales by 25%.*

● **Résumés that look good on paper but not on a computer screen.** Even if you don't submit your résumé on-line, today's recruiters and employers are likely to scan it into their computers. The scanning process can make an attractive résumé look messy.

To avoid problems: Don't use tables, templates, boxes or graphs...don't expand margins beyond six inches in width...and don't use tab stops more than absolutely necessary.

For an approximation of how your résumé will look on a computer screen, highlight the text, copy it and paste it into your computer's "Notepad" program.

● **Odd fonts.** Unusual fonts, small font sizes or italicized text might be difficult or impossible for recruiters to read on computer screens.

Use 10-point Arial for text and 12-point bold Arial for headings. Also acceptable is 11- or 12-point Times New Roman, in conjunction with 14-point bold headings.

● **Résumés not sent as Microsoft Word files.** Recruiters generally will not even open non-Word files.

Helpful: Name your résumé file using your own name, such as *Smith, John Resume.* Approximately 90% of all on-line résumés are simply titled *Resume.*

● **No e-mail address.** On more than 27% of résumés, contact information does not include e-mail addresses. This only inconveniences the recruiter and raises concerns about the applicant's familiarity with technology.

Also: Do not use an e-mail address with an inappropriate nickname or one that's likely to change in the coming year. Even if you don't get this job, the employer might contact you at a later date.

Caution: Don't use your corporate e-mail account—your employer might be monitoring your e-mails. Create a free e-mail account at Yahoo! or Hotmail.

The Five Most Common Networking Mistakes

Andrea R. Nierenberg, president of The Nierenberg Group in New York City, which provides training in sales, customer service, presentation skills and networking to businesses worldwide. She is the author of *Nonstop Networking* (Capital).

You know that networking is the key to finding a great job—but there's a fine line between getting someone's respectful attention and turning someone off.

The five most common networking blunders and how to avoid them...

Mistake #1: **Asking instead of giving.** People who always ask for favors come off as selfish opportunists. Instead, find ways to help people before asking something of them. This can be as simple as passing along articles you think they might be interested in...writing letters of reference...or recommending them to headhunters.

People that you have helped will remember —and will be more likely to help you.

Mistake #2: **Hit-and-run networking.** People who move quickly from person to person at events, never having a real conversation, are not networking. They inadvertently are giving the message that other people don't matter.

Example: A woman at a party abruptly interrupted a conversation I was having, handed me her business card and said, "Call me. I'm a photographer." Then she walked away and did the same thing to someone else. She made a terrible impression because it was obvious that she was only interested in getting something for herself.

Give your complete attention to the person with whom you are speaking. And, get to know him/her. Inquire about hobbies or families. Discuss your common interests. Phone or e-mail on occasion. Networking means developing relationships, not merely "contacts."

Mistake #3: **Blatant selling.** Be subtle in your approach. Suppose you are interested in finding a marketing job and happen to meet the CEO of a local company at a party. Don't come right out and say that you're looking for a job. Ask questions to learn more about the company's marketing campaigns, philosophy, etc. Then say something like, "It sounds like a fascinating place to work. How did you get your start?"

You'll gain valuable information. The CEO will remember you more favorably than if you had moved in like a shark. Afterward, send the CEO a handwritten note on good stationery. Say, "I really enjoyed meeting you and learning about your company. Down the road, I hope we will have another opportunity to meet."

Mistake #4: **Ignoring people who don't "count."** You never can tell who might be able to help you in some way. The wider you cast your net, the greater the opportunities. And, yet many people will totally turn off their energy to people they think can't help them. They look around the room or give one-word answers.

Instead, view everyone as an important contact. Someone in the mail room might know about openings in other divisions of the company before you do—or eventually may work his way up to a high-level position and have the opportunity to recommend you for a job.

Mistake #5: **Not following up.** Neglecting to follow up when people meet with you or help in some way makes them feel used—and guarantees that they won't help you again in the future. Let people know that you value them and care enough to cultivate the relationship.

Example: Send a thank-you note or even a bouquet to a person who arranges a meeting for you with a company executive.

Ace That Job Interview: 18 Insider Tricks

Rob Medich, senior editor, *MBA Jungle* magazine at *www.mbajungle.com* and contributing editor, *JD Jungle* magazine at *www.jdjungle.com*, both in New York City.

With the high rate of unemployment, it is more important than ever to know how to ace a job interview. *Here are some shrewd strategies from top recruiters and career consultants...*

TACTICS FOR THE FIRST TWO MINUTES

1. Don't arrive early. Everyone knows not to be late. But recruiters say that arriving early is almost as bad. In fact, showing up even 10 minutes ahead of time may irritate the interviewer. You interrupt what he/she is doing, which can sow the seed of resentment. It also sends the message that you're overeager.

Arrive no more than five minutes early. Find a coffee shop or a bench outside, and wait until the appointed time.

2. Remain standing while waiting for the interviewer to greet you. You don't want the first thing the interviewer sees to be you arranging your things and adjusting your clothing.

3. Hold your briefcase in your left hand and let your right hand hang loosely at your hip, ready to shake hands. This creates open, positive body language. This is important because, as sociolinguists at Stanford University discovered, body language accounts for 55% of a first impression.

4. Use the assistant's name when speaking to him. Introduce yourself when you first meet. Later, when you're leaving, a simple, respectful, "Thanks, Denise," could mean a kind word later from Denise to her boss.

5. Choose the right seat. When an interview is held in a conference room, there can be a potentially awkward moment when you decide where to sit. If the interviewer hasn't taken a seat yet, rest your hand on one of the chairs and ask, "Is this a good place for me to sit?"

If the interviewer has already set up shop, choose a seat directly across from him. If the table is round, sit next to him, but push your chair away so you can look him in the eye. Or sit with one chair between you.

6. Sit like an executive. Sit up straight in the middle of the chair, with one arm on the armrest and the other on the table. You'll look and feel more confident.

7. Prepare a 60-second "commercial spot" that summarizes your responsibilities at your last job. Cap it with your reasons for pursuing this position. Use this when the interviewer opens with, "Tell me about yourself." Resist the urge to go on at length. You want to release information throughout the interview, not all at once.

RULES FOR BREAKING THE ICE

8. Ask about photos or memorabilia on the interviewer's desk. Family photographs can be a great conversation starter. But avoid assumptions—the woman in the photo who you think is his daughter actually might be his wife. Instead, ask where the picture was taken.

9. Stay away from all jokes. The interviewer might not find them funny, making both of you feel awkward.

10. Never talk about traffic, sports or the weather. You do not want to be the eleventh automaton that day to say, "Wow, it sure is wet out there."

WAYS TO RECOVER FROM FUMBLES

11. Create a diversion. If the interviewer asks more than once whether you have any questions, chances are that he has formed an opinion about you and is trying to wrap it up. If you don't think that opinion is positive, ask for a glass of water. This will give you time to refer to prepared questions and start afresh. It also creates the impression that the interview's "second half" has just begun. If you can shine in the second half, you still have a shot at the position.

12. If you draw a complete blank to a question, ask the interviewer to rephrase it. You may not want to look stupid, but it is more damaging to stumble through a poor response. Say, "I'm not sure what you're asking. Which point would you like me to answer?"

13. If you do catch yourself rambling, ask, "Have I answered your question?"

DEAL BREAKERS

14. Excessive note taking. When a firm hires a manager, it wants someone who will take charge—not dictation. Jot down only those key points to which you want to respond.

15. Yes-man answers. Never say anything that you don't mean. Smart interviewers sense when they're being told what they want to hear—and they respond with tricky follow-up questions.

16. Clichéd responses to "What's your biggest weakness?" Interviewers have heard too many people say that they "pay too much attention to detail." Prepare in advance for these types of questions.

Helpful: When you admit to past mistakes, show that you learned something.

17. Not looking professional. Make sure your shoes are shined. Carry a briefcase, not a folder.

18. Not taking a business card. A common mistake candidates make when sending thank-you notes is misspelling the interviewer's name.

Best Time for A Job Interview

The best time for a job interview is in the morning. More than two-thirds of executives surveyed say they prefer meeting applicants between 9 am and 11 am. Only 5% prefer interviewing after 3 pm.

Survey of 1,400 chief financial officers completed by Accountemps, staffing company, Menlo Park, CA.

Dress Conservatively For Success

Appearance matters far more at interviews now. Conservative dress gives the impression of reliability. Medium to deep gray is the best suit color. Women should consider skirted suits instead of pantsuits. Accessories matter, as well—cuff links and expensive watches sometimes work against an applicant.

Paul D. Storfer, founder and president, InScope Corporation, a human resource management firm, Purchase, NY.

How to Handle an Interviewer Who Asks an Inappropriate Question

If an interviewer asks you a question you think is improper, stay calm. Ask politely, "Why did you ask that?" It is illegal for job interviewers to ask candidates improper or discriminatory questions, such as, "Are you a US citizen?"…"Do you have any disabilities?"…"Have you ever filed a workers' compensation claim?" Sometimes there is an acceptable reason for asking, in which case it doesn't constitute discrimination.

Examples: The interviewer may want to know *will you be able to pass security clearance …will you be able to perform a job that requires heavy lifting?*

If the interviewer is not able to give you a job-related reason for the question, ask, "Is that question relevant to the job?"

Michael Poskey, vice president of Zerorisk HR, Inc., a Dallas-based human resources risk-management firm.

Helpful Job Search Advice

If you are not hired for a job, ask the interviewer questions to help in your continuing search. Find out what factors led to choosing another candidate…what you could have done to raise your own chances…whether there are other openings in the company for which the interviewer would recommend you.

Consensus of career coaches, reported in *The Wall Street Journal.*

Better Work as a Temp

If you're planning on doing some temp work, be sure you sign with the best agency…

●**Choose a small local agency for more personal attention...**or a large multinational one for a wide range of job choices.

●**Ask other temps which agencies they like...**and ask professional trade groups in your field if they know agencies that specialize in your type of work.

●**Sign up with three to five agencies,** and try the positions they offer. Narrow the agencies down to one, so that the staff gets to know you.

●**Other things being equal, choose an agency with benefit packages,** which may include an annual paid vacation, a 401(k) plan and group health insurance. You may have to pay for the insurance yourself, but you probably could not obtain comparable coverage on your own.

Kiplinger's Personal Finance, 1729 H St. NW, Washington, DC 20006.

How to Buy a Business With No Money Down

Edward Mendlowitz, CPA, partner, Mendlowitz Weitsen, LLP, CPAs, which is one of only 800 CPA firms nationwide approved to audit public companies, K2 Brier Hill Ct., East Brunswick, NJ 08816. He is also author of *Introducing Tax Clients to Additional Services* (American Institute of CPAs).

Today, buying a business with no money down is easier than ever. The competition for bank loans and venture capital is way down due to a weaker economy. The cost to borrow money is the lowest it has been in more than 40 years. Better still, as companies cut back to their core operations, thousands of high-quality businesses are being sold.

HOW LBOs WORK

Often in a leveraged buyout (LBO), a company is sold to one or more of its senior managers, who put up little or none of their own money. Instead, they use the company's assets as collateral. The lender is then repaid—typically over a period of five years—from the company's after-tax profits.

The process is similar to taking out a home mortgage. Most of the purchase price comes from the mortgage lender, and the home is used as collateral.

Just as with a mortgage, your financiers can foreclose and take over your business if you fail to pay them back.

FINDING A BUSINESS

If you enjoy your job and like your industry, consider buying your employer's company. You know the business, and its owners know you. You may be able to get financing from the owner, especially if he/she is eager to unload a unit that is performing poorly or doesn't fit in with his long-term goals.

If your employer isn't willing to sell, look at a competing company or one in an industry with which you are familiar.

Don't assume that a business is too big. If a lender likes your plan, it will finance a deal of almost any size.

Since the loan will be backed by collateral, choose a business that has physical assets, such as machinery and inventory, instead of a service business, such as a consulting firm.

Best LBO candidates: The manufacturing and distribution companies.

STUDY THE NUMBERS

There is a core to every business. Before you even look at the financial statements, get down to that core and see if buying that business makes sense.

●**Find an accountant**—preferably one with experience in LBOs.

●**Review the financial statements** of every acquisition candidate. As a potential buyer, you have the right to demand all of the company's financial records. If the company won't produce the documents you need, walk away from the deal. To be sure you're getting a good deal, review more than one business possibility, even if your first choice is to buy your employer's company.

●**Project future profits.** To obtain financing, you will need to establish why the business will become a profitable entity under your stewardship. The business does not have to be profitable today. *Examples...*

●A division may be burdened with overhead costs associated with its parent company's home office. Once the division becomes a separate entity, that overhead will be eliminated.

●Corporate managers earn salaries above the industry norm. Once the sale has been completed, you can cut salaries and give valued employees a share of the profits.

●The business may be weak as a stand-alone but strong when combined with a company you already own. A client who owned a manufacturing company purchased a competitor that had a relationship with a big corporate customer. By buying the competitor, he secured this important account.

FINDING A LENDER

To obtain financing, prepare a written plan demonstrating that you know the business very well and can steer it through the initial stages following the acquisition—when debt is high. Show that you will be able to assemble a team that can handle all areas of the business. Once the lender likes your plan, it will review your credit history before approving the deal.

Example: One of my clients runs a trucking company that distributes food products to 500 supermarkets. He purchased a company that manufactures ice cream. Under the former management, the ice cream company was losing both market share and money. The client got financing by showing that under his ownership, the ice cream company would immediately "inherit" 500 new customers—pushing sales to as much as the business could handle.

STRUCTURING THE DEAL

Unless the business's former owner provides financing, you will need to borrow from banks and/or venture capital groups.

Helpful: Consult with a banker who knows both you and the company. If the bank isn't interested in the deal or it wants another party to put up capital as well, it will point you to a venture capital firm. Very likely, the bank has its own venture capital group.

In return for a share of the business, the venture capital firm will put up 10% to 80% of the capital, and the rest comes from the bank.

At the end of the investment period, you will need to cash out the venture capital firm.

Possible "exit strategies"…

●**Use profits from the business** to buy out the venture capital firm's equity interest.

●**Do a new LBO.**

●**Sell the company,** and use the proceeds to repay your backers.

●**Take your company public.** In the initial public offering (IPO), the venture capital firm sells its shares to cash out its stake. You also may be able to sell off a small portion of your stake in the company.

MISTAKES TO AVOID

Mistake #1: Not realizing how much borrowed money is really costing you. If you buy a business and finance 80% of the purchase price at 10% interest, your average yearly cost of capital is 8% (80% of 10%). Business profits must grow by at least 8% a year to cover interest payments.

Mistake #2: Buying a business that requires heavy capital spending. Because the deal is being financed with borrowed money, avoid businesses with high up-front costs. If a business requires expensive new machinery to become competitive, pass it by.

Mistake #3: Not doing enough due diligence before you buy. Don't look only at reported sales and profits. Dig deeper. Find out how items were sold. Maybe the seller temporarily raised prices to make the income statement look more attractive to a buyer. Result? Dollar sales may be up, but unit sales are flat or down.

Make a Fortune As an eBay Entrepreneur

Dennis L. Prince, Rocklin, CA–based author of several books about eBay, including *Starting Your Online Auction Business* (Prima-Tech/Premier) and *How to Sell Anything on eBay and Make a Fortune!* (McGraw-Hill). On-line, he buys and sells movie memorabilia and vintage toys and games.

About 160,000 people earn much or all of their income selling items on eBay, the user-friendly on-line auction site. These sellers have advantages over other retailers— they don't have to rent retail space, hire sales clerks or keep regular hours.

Still, the eBay entrepreneurs work long and hard. The process of listing a single item can take 15 minutes or more for less-experienced sellers—but eBay's elite class of power sellers whittle this down to a minute or two.

An established full-time eBay business generates an average annual gross income of $60,000, though incomes can run much higher. I know one seller who has an annual gross income of $250,000 and has hired employees.

To run a successful eBay business…

TARGET A NICHE

When you focus on a field, you build expertise in that area. You know what's in demand, the prices items are likely to fetch and how to write product descriptions that lure buyers.

Example: One seller can gross between $10,000 and $20,000 every month by selling comic books. It's not a field that just anyone could step into and be successful in. He devotes 20 to 50 hours a week to it.

Another advantage to narrowing your focus is that once buyers have purchased from you, you're likely to sell to them again.

Example: When your specialty is antique kitchen items, collectors of old toasters soon will learn that you can be trusted and will seek out your auctions.

To decide what to focus on…

• **Make a list of the product categories you know well** and those for which you have an avenue to obtain merchandise inexpensively.

• **Do eBay market research on those categories.** The preceding 30 days of eBay sales are archived on the site. Determine prices and the percentage that goes unsold. Track a minimum of three months of data before investing heavily in inventory—longer, if the category is seasonal.

• **Proceed only if you can sell items for at least 40% above your purchase price.** A narrower margin won't provide a reasonable profit with eBay fees, the cost of lost and damaged shipments and other expenses.

• **Avoid fads.** Prices on trendy items, such as Beanie Babies and Cabbage Patch dolls, invariably tumble. You could be stuck with a pile of inventory that is worth significantly less than what you originally paid for it.

• **Don't just assume that an underserved niche is an opportunity.** If no one is selling a particular item on eBay, it may be because no one's buying. Don't stock up on inventory until you're sure that there's enough interest to support a business.

BUILD INVENTORY

To find merchandise…

• **Buy off-season,** when there are great deals on clothes, sports equipment, decorations and other seasonal items. Store merchandise until the following year.

• **Look for liquidations.** Check under "Liquidators," "Importers" or "Wholesalers" in the *Yellow Pages,* or use these terms in a search engine. If you can get good deals on products in large quantities, you should be able to auction individual units profitably.

Example: Chris P. grosses close to $2,000 a month selling clothing overstocks. He sticks with brand names, such as Levi's, and popular goods, such as blue jeans. He devotes about 15 hours a month to the business.

Important: Be selective. Items usually don't reach the liquidators unless they already have failed to sell at retail prices. Stay away from outdated technology, such as computers and cell phones. Avoid goods that aren't brand names —these may be of inferior quality.

• **Make products yourself**—saleable handmade products, including quilts, novelty T-shirts with catchy slogans or distinctive designs, even paintings and sculpture.

CREATE CUSTOMER LOYALTY

• **Be honest.** Descriptions and photos need to depict the product accurately and disclose problems. If a buyer isn't satisfied, allow a return or provide a replacement without argument.

• **Send a follow-up e-mail** after shipping the merchandise to make sure the buyer is satisfied. Ask if he/she would like to receive periodic e-mails listing current inventory. If you have a Web site featuring similar products, include the URL.

Example: A movie memorabilia dealer I know has built traffic at his Posterpalace.com site through eBay customers.

• **Strive for positive feedback.** When a buyer or a seller has a positive experience with a transaction on eBay, he rewards the other person with a short, positive comment posted on the site. If the experience doesn't go well, he may leave a negative comment. Tell buyers that you're giving them positive feedback. This reminds them to do the same for you.

MORE SMART MOVES

● **Give buyers a credit card option.** Sign up for a business account with the third-party on-line transaction firm PayPal (instructions are on eBay). You'll attract more bidders and receive your money faster. You'll also lose fewer sales. Buyers sometimes back out after they sleep on their purchases. PayPal bills immediately, leaving customers little time for second thoughts. PayPal fees are 30 cents* per transaction, plus 2.2% of the sale price.

● **Trim packaging expenses.** Order free shipping materials, such as express and priority mail cartons, tubes and packing tape, on-line from the US Postal Service at *http://shop.usps. com.* They will be delivered right to your door.

● **Track competitors.** You might learn about a product subsector that's more popular than you imagined...or notice something in an item's description that you hadn't thought to include.

● **Keep scrupulous records of all your expenses and income.** The IRS is becoming increasingly interested in eBay sellers.

*All prices subject to change.

Making Your Home-Based Business a Success

Jay Conrad Levinson, creator of Guerrilla Marketing International, based in San Rafael, CA, *www.guerrillamar ketingbombshells.com.* Mr. Levinson is author of *Guerrilla Marketing for Free: Dozens of No-Cost Tactics to Promote Your Business and Energize Your Profits* (Mariner).

Owning a home business can be lucrative and fun. But numerous start-ups fail simply because the owners don't market their product or service effectively. *You can do better...*

CONTACTS ARE A GOLD MINE

Nearly everyone over age 50 has a large pool of friends and contacts. You may never have thought of them as people who could assist your business, yet many of them will be eager to do just that.

Make a list of the people with whom you have regular contact, as well as those you know only casually. Call them and explain briefly the type of business you want to start or are already running, and tell them what advantage your business has.

Example: You offer personalized service that a large company could never afford.

Ask if they're interested in your product or service or if they can refer you to people who would be. If the contact is unsure, ask what type of additional information he/she needs. Make notes of the information your contact asked for, and include it in your brochure and other marketing materials.

Most business owners are surprised at the positive responses. If a friend isn't interested in, say, your home repair service, he may know of someone who is. Or he just might know of a new realtor in town who is looking around for someone with your specialty.

CLUBS ARE A STRONG SUIT

Civic and community organizations will often invite small-business owners to speak on topics of interest to their members.

Examples: Investment consultants are always in huge demand. Or if you tutor children, some organizations will be eager to hear your ideas on how kids can improve their grades.

As a rule, clubs invite older people to speak because they're more likely to have the experience that members value.

When you speak to a club, *don't* make a direct sales pitch. Hand out company information afterward, and collect names of people who seem interested.

Exception: Some organizations will hold networking sessions for the purpose of letting small-business owners pitch their products.

Local chambers of commerce are usually good sources of information about organizations that invite owners of home businesses to speak to their members.

FREE NEWSPAPER ADVERTISING

In addition to speaking to local groups, write articles or columns for local papers on the same types of subjects you would speak about to local clubs. Offer to write articles free of charge. Include your name, phone number and Web site address at the end of the articles.

Essentially, that's free advertising. And once the article is published, you can get even more mileage by reprinting it and using reprints in mailings to prospective customers.

In addition to the big daily newspapers in your area, be sure to approach the growing number of neighborhood papers and even the "alternative" publications that are often aimed at younger audiences. Many civic and social organizations have newsletters that welcome articles on topics of interest to their readers.

LOCAL BULLETIN BOARDS

Community bulletin boards are another free —and overlooked—way to disseminate your company's message. They can be particularly effective if you select bulletin boards in locations frequented by likely prospects.

Example: Notices for a home-decorating service posted on bulletin boards in areas with a high concentration of new home owners.

STRATEGIC ALLIANCES

It often pays to team up with other home-business owners or even with owners of larger, established businesses for the purpose of swapping names of prospective customers.

Examples: A photographer or tutor could team up with a children's bookstore whose customers are parents...or a home-based insurance broker could form an alliance with a real estate agent who targets similar customers.

The best strategy is to start an alliance on a trial basis, say, for just six months. If it works, extend it. But there's no point in maintaining an alliance in which you give to your partner the names of many prospective customers but receive few in return.

VALUE AND LOYALTY

The big advantage of a home-based business is its ability to provide a personal touch and, through it, develop loyalty. *How to do it...*

- **Use your customers' names when contacting them.**
- **Offer free services,** such as consultations, seminars and demonstrations.
- **Respond personally by phone** whenever possible.
- **Write customers within a month after purchase.** Ask if they're happy with it or have any questions. Don't try to sell them anything at that time.
- **Use questionnaires to collect data** about customers. Ask about other places they shop, the products they like and what their ideal is in the type of service or product you're offering. Use their answers to custom-tailor your marketing message.
- **Maintain contact with your customers** by sending interesting information to them.

Example: If you know a customer hopes to vacation in Florida, send him an article you run across about a new hotel in Boca Raton.

USING THE INTERNET

The Internet has become all but indispensable in marketing a home business—if only because you can lose credibility by not having a Web site.

The cost of setting up and maintaining a Web site has plummeted. Today, many Internet service providers (ISPs) maintain modest sites for customers for only a small fee. Some do it free.

Don't let someone sell you a costly Web site. All that most home-based businesses need is four or five Web pages that explain clearly what the business does, why it does it better than competitors and how you can be contacted.

Web sites save you money in other marketing areas.

Example: Instead of printing an elaborate brochure or putting large ads in publications to explain your business, you can now buy smaller ads that ask readers to visit your Web site for more information.

Of course, when you speak to groups or write articles, mention your Web address. In this way, you save money on advertising and gain the advantage of learning the names—or at least the e-mail addresses—of prospective customers when they access your Web site.

How it works: On your Web site, offer to send additional information or a free special report to Web browsers who reply by e-mail. Someone running a home pet-care business, for example, might provide information on feline nutrition.

Depending on how much time you have, you can even offer a monthly e-letter to people who register for it on your Web site.

Once you obtain all the names and e-mail addresses of people who request this type of information, you can periodically send them other reports, as well as specific information about your products or services, especially special offers.

Cost saver: If you need any help with your Web site, phone a local high school or college and ask to talk with a student or teacher in the computer area. Students usually charge a small fraction of the fee that commercial computer service firms charge—and they frequently do a better job.

How to Stay Connected— Even When You Work from Home

Gil Gordon, telecommuting consultant in Monmouth Junction, NJ, *www.gilgordon.com.* His clients include Fortune 500 companies such as Citigroup, Johnson & Johnson and Merrill Lynch. He is author of a variety of books on telecommuting, including *Turn It Off: How to Unplug from the Anytime-Anywhere Office Without Disconnecting Your Career* (Three Rivers).

Almost 30 million Americans work from home. It can be wonderfully flexible but also isolating and distracting. *How to solve the most common problems...*

●**Isolation.** When you're off-site, it's much harder to make yourself indispensable and it can be downright lonely. How can you ensure that you are valued by colleagues and clients without regular contact? *Solutions...*

●Develop allies. They will keep you in the loop about developments with clients or at the office, including any changes in corporate culture or procedure.

●Meet with people who can help your business. If you waste time running errands, it could be a sign that you crave human contact. Arrange to meet clients in person. If you're telecommuting, schedule face time with your manager on a regular basis. Use this time to elicit feedback about your performance. You don't want anyone to keep quiet about problems with your work just because you're in a remote location. Make sure everyone treats you as part of the team.

●Join a professional association, and attend its meetings. You can network with peers, stay on top of key trends and derive emotional support from other solo workers.

●Create a satellite "office." Get out of your physical work environment one afternoon per week. Bring paperwork to a local coffee shop or the library. Exchange work spaces with a telecommuting friend for an uninterrupted day.

●**Unstructured workday.** If you lack discipline, it is difficult to make productive use of your time.

Example: An important report is due tomorrow, but after taking the dog to the vet and paying bills, it's 4 pm. Result? You finish the project after midnight. *Solutions...*

●Set specific goals. Don't earmark 30 minutes to "make phone calls." You're liable to make only the calls you want to make, not the ones you need to make. *Better:* Plan to make five necessary calls. Jot down what you hope to accomplish with each one.

●Develop rituals. Take a few minutes each morning to move from a "home" mind-set to a "professional" one. Check e-mail...outline priorities for the day.

Create an end-of-day transition, too. Turn on your home-office answering machine and decompress...take your dog for a walk...work out at the gym...have a drink with your spouse or a friend.

●Reward yourself. Create work-rest rhythms to replace the watercooler breaks available at the office. *Helpful:* Set a timer, and take a five-minute break each hour or a 10-minute break every 90 minutes. Do something that relaxes you—return a friend's call...surf the Internet...read the newspaper...meditate (something you can't do at most companies).

•**No boundaries set between home and work.** Your spouse assumes that you can deal with the plumber because you are "home all day anyway"…your neighbors ask you to sign for their UPS deliveries. *Solutions…*

•Prevent intrusions by clearly defining which household responsibilities—if any—you are willing to take on during the day. *Example:* Tell your spouse you will accept deliveries but not run midday errands.

Also, post a daily schedule on the refrigerator indicating when you may and may not be interrupted.

•If you get a late-night idea, don't rush to your home office. Jot down the idea on a piece of paper and leave it for the morning—just as you would do if you had a traditional office job.

•**Lack of professionalism.** You and your business will be judged by what others hear over the telephone. When you sometimes miss making that easy sale or get passed over for a promotion that you believe you deserved, you may be projecting an unprofessional image that is undermining your business. *Solutions…*

•Install a separate business line. Assure colleagues that you want them to call.

•When an important colleague or customer calls, use the person's name several times in the conversation. People just love to hear their own names. The repetition makes them feel that they have your full attention.

•Update voice mail frequently. Keep clients and coworkers aware of your schedule. Promise to return calls within a specific time.

•Avoid background noise. They are all too common in most homes—barking dogs…TV… screaming children.

•Refrain from making sarcastic comments, even in jest. Joking or teasing coworkers and regular clients might be fine when you are face to face. When you fall out of daily visual contact, your words are more easily misinterpreted.

•**Colleagues resent that you work from home.** Some might even hesitate to call you as a result. The best defense is to make contact hassle-free and communicate frequently no matter what happens. *Solutions…*

•Have your home-office business phone number added to the corporate speed-dial system.

•Prepare a backup plan to meet deadlines in case your computer crashes or a blackout renders your cordless phone useless. It might be as simple as using a battery-powered laptop computer or a corded phone…having an alternate e-mail account that you can access from another computer…knowing how to send/receive faxes on your computer if your fax machine fails. Most computers now come with free fax software.

USEFUL RESOURCES

For strategies on telecommuting, visit the International Telework Association & Council at *www.workingfromanywhere.org.*

For questions about home-office deductions, call 800-TAX-FORM or go to *www.irs.gov/forms pubs* for publication 587, *Business Use of Your Home.* If you qualify, check with a tax adviser or an accountant.

Nine Steps to Protect Your Home-Based Business From the IRS

Sandy Botkin, Esq., CPA, president of the Tax Reduction Institute, 13200 Executive Park Terrace, Germantown, MD 20874, *www.taxreductioninstitute.com.* He is a former IRS attorney as well as a senior tax law specialist and author of the best-selling *Lower Your Taxes Big Time!* (McGraw-Hill).

Having a home-based business can produce big tax savings. Not only will it provide many new deductions, but any losses it incurs can be deducted against other income, such as salary—providing a tax subsidy that can help you get the business through a period of start-up losses or later hard times.

You get this tax break even if your business is only a part-time sideline, such as consulting in your regular line of work, or a hobby that you've decided to turn into a business.

How a home-based business can pay off tax-wise—and how to protect its tax subsidy from the IRS…

•**Low- and zero-tax income.** By legitimately hiring your children and other family members who are in lower tax brackets and deducting their pay, you can move family income into lower tax brackets.

●**Home-office deduction.** You may be able to deduct previously nondeductible expenses of home ownership, such as a portion of utility, repair and insurance costs.

●**Travel expenses.** You can legally deduct pleasurable travel.

Examples: Travel expenses to business seminars in places like Las Vegas…business trips to cities in which you have friends or relatives.

Key: The primary purpose of the trip must be for business. Any incidental fun, however, is permitted.

●**Tax-favored benefits.** You may become able to deduct larger retirement contributions, more medical costs and other benefits.

●**Meals and entertainment.** Business owners have many more deduction opportunities in this area than employees.

●**Driving deductions.** When home is a workplace, previously nondeductible commuting can become deductible driving between two places of work.

Examples: Driving between home and another office or to a restaurant for a business-related meal.

BIGGEST SAVER

The biggest tax benefit from a home-based business may be an operating loss that these deductions, plus other business costs, combine to provide.

Business losses incurred in self-employment or through a pass-through entity, such as a partnership or S corporation, are fully deductible against other income—such as salary from a regular job and investment income. So these losses will effectively turn the business into a tax shelter.

Even better, you can carry business losses back two years to get refunds of taxes you've already paid.

You can also carry losses forward for up to 20 years—so even if losses exceed the income now available for them to be deducted against, no valid business deduction will ever be lost as long as you run your business with the appropriate "profit motive."

THE IRS CHALLENGE

When you own a home-based business that is unincorporated and is producing deductible losses, expect the IRS to question it. The critical IRS claim that you must be ready to meet is that your business is not a business at all, and, therefore, cannot produce deductible losses.

If the IRS succeeds with this claim, it won't need to bother examining your deductions on an item-by-item basis. All of them in excess of the amount of income your activity has generated will be disallowed in one fell swoop.

Key: The determining factor as to whether or not your activity qualifies as a business is whether you have a genuine *profit motive*. You do not have to actually make a profit—but you must be able to show a reasonable *intention* to make a profit.

Myth: Many people believe that to qualify as having a business, one must make a profit in three out of five years.

Reality: If you make a profit in three out of the first five years, the IRS assumes you have a profit motive. But even if you never make a profit, you can still show that you have a profit motive.

In fact, the courts have found businesses to be profit motivated after losing money for periods as long as 12 or more years in a row—making all their losses deductible.

HOW TO PROTECT YOURSELF

By taking the right steps, you can virtually ensure that your business will be safe from IRS challenge. *Nine steps that will help to prove profit-making intent…*

●**Run your business like a business.** This is first and foremost. To show that you have a real business, you must run it in a businesslike manner.

How: Keep full business books and records. Obtain local business licenses. Have a listing in the business pages of the phone book and print business cards. Consult with established experts about how to make the business succeed. Keep a business-expense diary and so on.

●**Have a written business plan**—and keep it up to date. Draw up a plan for how your business will generate money in the future.

Include projections of income and expenses into future years. Describe your marketing plans and other strategies. Then *update* the plan as you go along in light of the results you get. If you lose money, change the plan to improve results in the future.

Critical: Many court decisions have turned on whether a business plan was kept updated or not. When real businesses lose money, they change the way they operate—so be sure to keep improving your written business plan, too.

• **Conduct research.** Examine the opportunities that exist in the line of work you choose before starting the business. Keep records of the research to show the IRS. If you have personal experience in the field, such as from a former job, note that, too.

• **Work regularly in the business.** If a business is a part-time activity, it's better to work at it for 45 minutes every day than one full day once every two weeks. Record all time worked in your business diary.

• **Keep business and personal funds separate.** Have separate bank accounts, and do not pay for personal expenses from your business account.

• **Keep your expenses proportionate to income.** If you have $5,000 of income from a sideline business, do not then spend $15,000 on travel to a business convention. Expenses must be reasonable in light of your income.

• **Be careful what you say.** Don't tell anyone your business is a "tax shelter" or make any other statements that may indicate that you run it with a tax-saving, rather than profit-making, motive.

• **Change the way you market your business** if you aren't making money.

• **Consult with experts** and be sure to follow their advice.

STRATEGY

You can keep the IRS from questioning the profit motive behind your business for five years after you start it.

How: By filing IRS Form 5213 within three years after starting the business. By the time the five years are done, you may be running profitably and so be safe from an audit—after having deducted years of losses without audit risk in the meantime. But be careful, filing this form may be risky.

Why: Filing the form puts the IRS on notice that you have a loss-making business to examine—so by filing it you may be asking for an audit. Also, if your activity is still losing money after the five years, the form authorizes the IRS to disallow *all* five years' worth of your loss deductions. Otherwise it can generally go back only three years.

Therefore, the best strategy may be to not file the form, operate with a real profit motive and follow the nine steps mentioned here to prove it.

If you do so, you may be overlooked by the IRS entirely. However, if you do end up facing an audit, you will be reasonably sure of proving your profit motive and protecting your business's status.

Much Smarter Home-Office Deductions

Generally you would deduct a percentage of your rent, insurance and other costs that relate to your entire home that corresponds to the percentage of it that is used as an office. So if you used 20% of your home for the office, you would deduct 20% of these costs.

But if a particular expense is incurred disproportionately in your office, you may be able to deduct the larger amount.

Example: If your office is 20% of your home, but you incur 40% of your home's electrical cost in it—due to electrical equipment, an air conditioner, etc.—you could deduct the 40%.

Remember, though, you have to be able to prove the larger amount.

Lisa N. Collins, CPA/PFS, vice president and director of tax services, Harding, Shymanski & Co., PC, Evansville, IN.

Best Ways to Deduct Business Start-Up Costs

Sandy Soltis, CPA, tax partner, Blackman Kallick Bartelstein LLP, 10 S. Riverside Plaza, Chicago 60606.

Before your business is operating, your expenses aren't tax deductible. Therefore, when you start a new business, don't hesitate. Go into operation as quickly as possible.

The "best case" for expenses incurred before you are in business is an election to amortize such expenses over no less than 60 months. This election must be made on the company's first tax return.

Worst case? Certain expenses can't be amortized over 60 months. And failure to make a timely election erases the amortization opportunity altogether.

As a result, business start-up costs that you cannot amortize must be capitalized, in which case such costs might not be deducted until you sell or abandon the business.

BEGINNER'S COURSE

Start up expenses, according to the Tax Code, include costs that you incur before your business actually begins.

Money spent on the following activities might be considered start-up costs…

• **The investigation into creating a business** or buying one.

• **Preliminary market research.**

• **Search for office space.**

• **Rental expenses.**

• **Supplies purchased** before business operations begin.

• **Advertising and promotional expenses.**

• **Salaries and wages** paid before the business starts.

• **Other expenses** that would be deductible if the business were operating.

Flip side: Expenses incurred while you're still trying to decide what business to go into are personal and nondeductible.

Example: Outlays for trips to evaluate potential investments or businesses won't qualify as start-up costs, so there's no tax recovery.

UP AND RUNNING

Once your company is open for business, outlays aren't considered start-up costs. Instead, they are operating costs, which might be deductible expenses.

Opportunity: You can be in business before you have any revenues. Take action so that your company is in business as soon as possible. Don't wait until you have paying customers.

Example: You decide to create a system that makes it easier for doctors to track patient histories. Chances are, you won't receive any revenues for years.

Fortunately, you can be in business long before you sell your system to hospitals or to medical groups.

How to do it: Advertise in industry publications and send out press releases. Have business cards printed. Actively solicit future sales. Hire employees.

These and other steps will show that you are truly operating a business.

Example: You have created a waterproof "thigh holster" for campers' snacks, to be sold through sporting-goods stores. When you have the displays prepared and visit sporting-goods stores asking them to carry your displays, you're in business. That's true even though it may take months before sales start coming in.

Strategy: If you incorporate your business, hold a directors' meeting right away and keep minutes. Those minutes should state for the record that you're in business and list all the steps already taken to generate revenues.

Similarly, if you form an LLC, hold a meeting of the members or elected managers.

Key: For all business structures, keep careful records of all your efforts to bring a product or service to market. Such records may be vital in showing that you actually were in business as of the date certain expenses were incurred.

RAPID WRITE-OFFS

When your company is in business, many of your outlays will be fully deductible.

Moreover, the purchase of otherwise depreciable business equipment can be deducted ("expensed") under Section 179 of the Tax Code —up to $102,000 in 2004. This break applies if your total purchases for the year don't exceed $410,000 in 2004. It phases out, dollar-for-dollar, above the $410,000 threshold.

Strategy: A Section 179 election can be made only for the year equipment is placed in service, not necessarily when payments are made.

Thus, you can buy equipment at year-end on a credit card or installment sales agreement and take a full deduction, with no cash outlay.

Opportunity: These expensing deductions can't exceed your taxable income from business. However, you can deduct these expenses against taxable income from the active conduct of any trade or business, including wages. If you're married, you can deduct them against income reported on a joint return, including your spouse's earnings.

Strategy: Many new businesses are short on capital. In this situation, you can lease equipment and deduct the leasing costs.

You may be able to lease with the option to buy at the end of the lease. This option often makes sense, but only if the equipment has a useful life that is significantly longer than the lease term.

Strategy: Lease your business car rather than buy it. The deduction of the lease cost will generally exceed the depreciation allowance that could be claimed if the car were purchased. The more expensive the car, the greater the tax advantage of leasing.

LOSS LEADERS

In the first year of your new business, deductible expenses might exceed taxable revenues. With some business structures, you can report a loss and deduct it against other income.

Example: You go into a Web site design business in late 2004, taking in $25,000 in revenues. However, you spend $60,000 on utilities, rent, etc. Thus, your business, which you run as a sole proprietorship, reports a loss of $35,000 for the year.

However, you were ready to design Web sites for customers the first day you moved into your office and placed your equipment into service. Therefore, your outlays are largely deductible in 2004.

Caution: The IRS will look closely at such losses, especially if (1) they go on for several years, and (2) the activity involved is one that might be an enjoyable hobby, such as travel photography.

Strategy: Retain records showing that you have acted in a businesslike manner and had the goal of making a profit.

CUTTING YOUR LOSSES

What should you do in the event that your start-up business fails?

Loophole: When you put money into a specific business (not a mere search for a business opportunity), you can then deduct the expenses incurred as a capital loss or an ordinary loss, depending upon the facts and circumstances of your investment.

Trap I: Expenses incurred to generally investigate the possibilities of going into business or to purchase a nonspecific existing business are considered personal costs, and they are not deductible.

Examples: Costs included as a capital loss might include any professional fees incurred to establish a corporation as well as ordinary operating expenses of the corporation.

Trap II: While capital losses can be used to offset capital gains, only $3,000 worth of net capital losses may be deducted in a single year. Any unused losses can be carried forward to future years.

However, the costs of equipment purchased for a failed business cannot be used to figure your capital loss. Instead, your taxable gain or loss on such assets will be determined when you sell or otherwise dispose of them.

Keeping thorough records will help you maximize your tax benefits, as always.

Deduct Abandoned and Used-Up Equipment

Sidney Kess, attorney and CPA, 10 Rockefeller Plaza, New York City 10020. Mr Kess is coauthor/consulting editor of *Financial and Estate Planning* and coauthor of *1040 Preparation, 2004 Edition* (both from CCH). Over the years, he has taught tax law to more than 710,000 tax professionals.

Firms that carefully document all equipment acquisitions often fail to record how they dispose of equipment that they no longer need.

Key: When a business "junks" equipment before the end of its tax depreciation period, the equipment's entire remaining undepreciated cost can be deducted immediately.

Common mistake: Firms that don't record when equipment is disposed of may carry the "phantom" equipment forward on the tax books after it has been disposed of—which needlessly postpones deductions.

Good idea: Examine the list of equipment the company is currently depreciating and check it to see if it all is still in service. If not, there may be deductions waiting to be claimed. This also has an impact on property taxes imposed in some states. Check with your adviser to see what your state property tax rules are.

Most Rewarding End-of-Year Planning Strategies for Business

Larry Torella, CPA, tax partner at Eisner LLP, 750 Third Ave., New York City 10017. He is author of Eisner's annual year-end tax-planning guide.

End-of-year tax planning is more complicated than ever because of the tax law changes—for businesses and individuals —and the increased threat of the alternative minimum tax (AMT). Routine year-end planning strategies might not hold up for you this year. To develop the right year-end moves, step back and review your situation carefully.

INITIAL PLANNING STEPS

To plan effectively, you need to know where you are now, tax-wise, and where you expect to be next year. Look at your business income and your personal income—the moves you take with your business will affect your personal tax position. *Consider these questions...*

●**Is this a good year for me?** For my business? What do I project for next year? A two-year approach is essential for planning. You don't want to shift income into a higher-tax year, for example.

●**Am I subject to the AMT this year?** Next year? This will help you determine the true tax rate on your income.

Remember: Owners of pass-through entities (S corporations, partnerships and limited liability companies) report their share of the business's AMT adjustments and preference items on their personal returns. That increases their AMT exposure accordingly.

●**If I do nothing now, what will my taxes be this year?** Next year?

PLANNING IN GOOD YEARS

If this year has been a good one, review the steps you can take now to minimize your taxable income. Many strategies involve accelerating deductions (taking deductions now that might otherwise be taken next year). But if next year looks like it might be even better, think about not accelerating them all.

The same strategy applies to income, where the aim is usually to defer it from this year to next. But deferral may not be wise if next year is going to be better than this year. You may be in a higher bracket next year and pay more tax than you would if you had taken the income now—not to mention the benefit of having the money in hand sooner.

●**Accounts receivable and payable.** Cash-basis businesses can control somewhat the year in which they will report income and expenses. They can delay year-end billing for work so that payment is received in the following year and by paying outstanding bills to take deductions this year. Whether this general strategy should be followed depends on your two-year income projections.

Example: You are subject to the AMT this year, paying a rate of 26% or 28% on your top dollar of income, but you don't expect this next year when you will be in the 35% regular tax bracket. In this case, it makes sense to collect as much income as possible this year so that it's taxed at only 28% instead of 35% next year.

●**Business equipment.** You have until the last day of the year to place in service a new computer, office furniture or machinery that can be fully written off up to $102,000.

Need to buy more? Take advantage of the new 50% bonus depreciation. No matter how much you spend on equipment, you'll be able to deduct more than half its cost (bonus depreciation plus the regular depreciation allowance).

Strategy: If income is good but cash is tight, you can finance the purchase and then claim the full write-off.

●**New car.** If you are planning on buying a new car, the increased bonus depreciation for 2004 may be added incentive to act now. The dollar limit for first-year depreciation on a new car is now $10,610 (there's currently no dollar limit on the SUVs weighing more than 6,000 pounds, but Congress may close this loophole).

●**Bonuses.** Think about declaring year-end bonuses for key employees. Accrual-basis businesses can deduct the declared amount for 2004 as long as payment is actually made by March 15, 2005.

Caution: Bonuses to any S corporation and personal service corporation shareholders or to more-than-50% C corporation shareholders are deductible only when actually paid.

●**Dividends.** Profitable corporations may decide to distribute their earnings as dividends to shareholders. While dividends are not deductible by the corporation, they are now subject to a low 15% tax rate in the hands of shareholders. Paying out dividends avoids accumulated earnings problems with the IRS. These result when earnings and profits in excess of the reasonable needs of your business (plus the exemption amount of $250,000, or $150,000 for most of the service-based corporations) are retained by the corporation. Owners face the accumulated earnings tax penalties.

●**Retirement plans.** If your business does not yet have a retirement plan, consider setting one up by December 31. As long as you sign the paperwork, you have until the extended due date of your return to make the contributions. Tax law changes in recent years make it easier to choose a plan. For example, you no longer need both a profit-sharing and money-purchase plan to maximize contributions and can use the simpler profit-sharing plan.

●**Charitable contributions.** Accrual-basis C corporations can authorize their contributions by year-end, which are deductible this year if paid by March 15, 2005.

Charitable contributions by any business can be used to get rid of the nonmoving inventory. Generally, the deduction is limited to fair market value (FMV) reduced by gain that would be realized if the item had been sold instead of donated (essentially cost). But C corporations that donate inventory to public charities for the ill, the needy, or children get to deduct cost plus half the gain (not to exceed twice the cost). This enhanced deduction opportunity also applies to donations of any scientific property used for research purposes.

PLANNING FOR BAD YEARS

If this has been a bad year, don't despair. You can benefit from your tax losses and improve your cash flow by taking year-end steps.

●**S corporation shareholders.** Make sure that you have sufficient basis in your stock and debt (money you loaned to the corporation) so that you can deduct corporate losses that are passed through to you. *If you don't have enough basis, consider...*

●Lending new money to the corporation to build up basis through increased debt.

●Recasting outstanding loans to the corporation that you've guaranteed so that you become primarily liable. Ask the lender to revise the loan agreement to reflect your new status.

●**Adjust estimated taxes.** If things have not gone as well as expected, you may be able to skip the fourth installment of your estimated taxes (due January 17, 2005). You can use the funds set aside for this purpose to boost your business instead.

● **Apply for a quick refund.** If your business has a net operating loss this year that you can carry back, you can obtain a quick refund of prior years' taxes. You may apply for the refund as soon as you file the 2004 return. Complete the required form (Form 1045, *Application for Tentative Refund,* for individuals or Form 1139, *Corporation Application for Tentative Refund*) along with your return and submit it as soon as possible.

12 Secrets to Keeping Customers

Jack Mitchell, the CEO of Mitchell's of Westport and Richard's of Greenwich, independent high-end clothing stores in southern Connecticut that together gross $65 million a year. He is also author of *Hug Your Customers* (Hyperion), *www.hugyourcustomers.com.*

Customers buy more from businesses that treat them as friends, not invoice numbers. This is true whether your business is a law firm, a retail store or a manufacturing company. *Secrets to "hugging" customers…*

GET PERSONAL

The number-one reason customers are unhappy is that they fail to tell sellers what they want. Developing a relationship will open the door to better communication and satisfaction.

1. Hire a phone receptionist. It will give your company a personal touch that no automated switchboard can match. If you cannot afford a dedicated receptionist, ask your associates to take turns answering calls.

2. Compliment your customers. When they're wearing something that's attractive, tell them so. It will make them feel noticed and special.

3. Politely engage customers in conversation. Ask about their recent activities, family news, etc. instead of asking, "May I help you?" If a customer says he/she just wants to browse, ask, "May I hold your bags up front?"

4. Ask first-time customers their names. Later, remember to greet them personally.

5. Don't just write up the order when customers say they're interested in a particular product or service. If appropriate, politely ask why he wants it. The answer can help you to steer him toward other products.

6. Don't let customers buy the wrong products. You can make him a customer for life by talking him out of something he doesn't need.

7. Hire warm, friendly and honest associates. They should be confident and competent in their abilities and take obvious pride in serving customers. Offer bonuses and other incentives.

8. Collect information about customers. To gauge how a customer might use your product without seeming nosy, start conversations that will reveal aspects of his life. Ask about where he lives, his profession, members of his family, favorite activities, etc.

Caution: Probe—but don't pry. Gather information on an ongoing basis. Don't pursue your inquiries when the customer is reluctant to talk. Assure him that all the data you collect will be kept private and will be used only to give him access to special sales or services.

Additional payoff: By knowing more about your customers' buying patterns, you can then match inventories more closely to purchases.

9. Save information in a computer database. Make the customer profiles available to your salespeople. The salesperson should call up a familiar customer's profile when that person walks in—or before meeting with a client.

10. Follow up all major sales with a phone call—to check on the customer's satisfaction.

11. Keep in touch. Contact your customers by mail on their birthdays, anniversaries, holidays or other special days.

12. Customize your sales approach. With customer profiles, companies can direct customers and their family members toward appropriate products. For example, if you have a customer who has just purchased a new house, suggest moneysaving products.

Give big customers extra-special service. In small businesses, 80% of sales come from 20% of customers. Notify top customers about new products before offering them to others.

20

Kids, College And More

Financial Aid for Your Kids…No Matter How Much Money You Make

The cost of higher education has reached incredible levels…and certainly will go even higher. But if you follow this advice, you probably won't have to pay "list price" to send your kids to college.

There are two ways to make college more affordable…

●**Tax savings.** The Internal Revenue Code is studded with a variety of tax incentives for college education.

●**Financial aid.** Colleges arrange for loans, jobs and outright grants to help students and their parents manage all the bills.

Key: Know the trade-offs between the Tax Code and financial-aid formulas so you have the lowest net cost possible.

TYPES OF AID

The biggest mistake made by families during the college application process is not filling out standard financial-aid forms because they believe they won't qualify.

Reality: Not all of college aid is based on financial need. Most colleges also offer "merit-based aid."

Merit aid often takes the form of tuition discounts. It should be applied for.

Example: College ABC lists $15,000 as its annual tuition. Your son (who is a good student) applies to ABC, which decides to compete for his enrollment.

He might be offered a $7,500 "scholarship," effectively a 50% cut in tuition, if he chooses ABC. This scholarship is offered regardless of his family's financial circumstances.

Rick Darvis, president of College Funding, Inc., 121 N. Main St., Plentywood, MT 59254. Cofounder and director of the National Institute of Certified College Planners, he is the author of *College Financial Aid—The Best Kept Secret in America* (College Funding, Inc.). His Web site is *www. solutionsforcollege.com.*

Note: Even though merit aid isn't based on a family's finances, many colleges won't offer it to students who haven't applied for financial aid.

Bottom line: Most students wind up paying much less than the posted tuition price.

SHIFTING ASSETS

A few elite colleges do not offer merit aid; those schools offer only need-based aid.

Even if you're determined that your child will attend such a university, you should not give up on financial aid.

Families that apply for financial aid at these institutions are assigned "expected family contributions" (EFCs) based on income and assets. For parent and student, the income that you report is based on a special worksheet. Assets held by parents enjoy more protection, while the assets held by children are expected to be used for college costs.

Example: Working through the financial-aid forms, your EFC is set at $25,000 this year. If your child is accepted at a college where total costs are $20,000, no need-based aid will be offered. However, if your child goes to a college where costs are $30,000, you would be eligible for $5,000 worth of aid.

Key: The more expensive the college chosen, the more likely you will qualify for need-based aid. That's especially true for years when you'll have two or three kids in college.

Strategy: If you believe you will qualify for need-based aid, keep financial assets in your own name. And, load up on investments that won't be counted, such as life insurance, annuities and tax-deferred retirement plans. Also, be aware that home equity and farm equity are not counted at most schools.

Impact of 529 plans: These plans allow tax-free buildup and tax-free withdrawals for higher education. Depending on the type of plan, it may be counted as a parental asset for determining an EFC, or distributions may reduce the student's need-based aid.

Strategy: If you think you'll qualify for financial aid, transfer a 529 account to a non-parent (such as an aunt or a grandmother) before filling out the financial-aid form.

Caution: Beware of prepaid tuition plans, which reduce financial aid dollar for dollar.

REDUCING INCOME

Besides reducing your assets, to get need-based financial-aid, you should also legally trim your reported income.

Timing: For each academic year, the prior year's income is counted. So, for the 2005–2006 school year, for example, your 2004 income will be used to determine financial aid.

Holding down your adjusted gross income (AGI) will not only reduce your tax bill, it will also drop your EFC by as much as 47%.

Example: You run a business as an S corporation. You're allowed a $102,000 business equipment write-off. You buy $102,000 worth of equipment that you were planning to buy anyway which reduces your AGI in 2004 by $102,000.

Payoff: Depending on your income level, you might save 30% in tax by reducing your AGI. In addition, the AGI reduction will increase your family's eligibility for need-based aid by as much as 47% under the financial-aid formula depending on your family's financial and household situation. Your total benefit (tax savings plus increased college aid) could be 30% plus 47%, or 77%.

Another way to reduce your AGI and enjoy a double benefit is to maximize contributions to a retirement plan. If you are in business, you can contribute (and can deduct) up to $40,000 to a profit-sharing plan this year and even more to a defined-benefit plan. Individual taxpayers can reduce AGI by deferring income or accelerating expenses.

FIVE-YEAR PLAN

Even after some tax planning, your income and assets may be so substantial that no need-based aid is likely. Be sure to use the Tax Code as fully as possible.

Strategy: By shifting investment income and capital gains to your children, you might save thousands of dollars in tax. Those tax savings will make it easier to pay for college.

Even if you hope to receive college aid, it's not necessary to forgo income-shifting tactics altogether.

After the student's final financial-aid form has been filed, in January of his/her junior year of college, income shifting may save tax with no impact on financial aid.

Example: Your daughter plans to start college in the fall of 2005. If she graduates in the spring of 2009, five calendar years will span her college career—2005 through 2009.

If need-based aid is a possibility, refrain from shifting income until you fill out the form for her senior year (2008–2009). The form can be filed on January 1 of her junior year.

The time to shift is on January 2 of her junior year, no further financial-aid forms must be filed. You can begin shifting income to your daughter and save taxes without relinquishing any aid.

Example: You can give your daughter appreciated assets to sell. Under the current tax law, you and your spouse can give her $22,000 worth of stocks, with no gift tax consequences at all.

After the gift, your daughter may be able to sell the shares and owe only 5% tax on the gains, not the 15% you would have owed.

Even better: Under current law, low-bracket taxpayers will owe *no* tax on capital gains realized in 2008.

No matter what your financial circumstances, learning about college funding techniques can provide valuable lessons.

Financial-Aid Smarts

Raymond D. Loewe, CLU, ChFC, president and owner, College Money, a college finance advisory firm, located in Marlton, NJ, *www.collegemoney.com.*

Home equity has no bearing on college financial aid if your child is applying to state schools. On the Free Application for Federal Student Aid (FAFSA) form used by most state schools, your home is not counted as an asset, so reducing home equity in order to reduce the total value of your assets is not necessary.

More information: *www.fafsa.ed.gov.*

Home equity *does* count, however, on the Profile form used by most private schools—so borrowing and depleting your home equity can lead to greater financial assistance.

More information: Visit *http://profileonline. collegeboard.com.*

Financial-aid forms are due during January of the student's senior year in high school. Figure out ahead of time which forms each school requires for financial-aid consideration so you can decide whether or not you want to reduce your home equity.

More from Raymond Loewe…

Why You Shouldn't Use US Savings Bonds For College

Don't use US savings bonds to pay for college tuition. *Reasons…*

●**The bond's owner must be at least 24 years old** at issue date to get tax-free interest, so children and young adults won't qualify for this benefit.

●**Owner–parents who want to use the tax-free feature** of these bonds to pay for college must watch income levels carefully. Joint filers start to lose the tax-free benefit when adjusted gross income (AGI) in 2004 is $89,750 ($59,850 for single filers)…the benefit disappears completely at $119,750 married ($74,850 single).

●**Interest is figured into financial-aid forms,** lowering the chance of getting need-based assistance even if the bonds are in the parent's name.

●**The bonds' rate of return is unlikely to keep pace** with the rise in college costs.

Avoid Tax and Investment Losses with 529 Prepaid Tuition Plans

Doug Brown, president and CEO, Tuition Plan Consortium, Box 429, Albuquerque, NM 87103, *www.indepen dent529plan.org.*

Section 529 savings plans may not be your best education savings vehicle. Your account will grow (or shrink) depending on how specified investments perform. So you may not have enough to pay for colleges expenses.

Alternative: 529 prepaid tuition plans offer the same federal (and, in many cases, state) tax advantages as 529 savings plans *and* they protect you against investment losses.

HOW THEY WORK

With 529 prepaid tuition plans, you effectively buy a certificate that entitles you to a certain amount of future tuition.

Example: During the 2004–2005 academic year, tuition at State C's state university runs $12,000 per year. You invest $6,000 (50% of a current year's tuition) in State C's 529 prepaid tuition plan, naming your newborn daughter, Jan, as the account beneficiary.

By the time Jan is an 18-year-old freshman, tuition at that state university has increased to $48,000. (That would be an 8% annualized increase in tuition.)

Therefore, the 50% certificate you buy for $6,000 this year would *still* entitle Jan to a half year's tuition, worth $24,000 in the 2021–2022 academic year.

You have protected Jan's college savings against steep future tuition increases without exposing that money to the uncertainties of the financial markets. Yet you retain the tax advantages of 529 plans.

As in all 529 plans, earnings inside the plan are exempt from federal income tax and withdrawals also avoid that tax if the money is spent on qualified higher education expenses. Many states also extend tax breaks to 529 plans.

While tax-free withdrawals are scheduled to expire after 2010, experts think that Congress is likely to extend the benefit, so 529 plans may well retain their status as a favored tax shelter.

LEARNING THE LIMITS

Although they offer principal protection, 529 prepaid tuition plans have certain shortcomings compared with 529 savings plans.

●**Limited to tuition.** Money accumulated in 529 prepaid tuition plans can be spent only on tuition (and mandatory fees).

With 529 college savings plans, on the other hand, money can be withdrawn, tax free, for additional qualified expenses, including room and board. [See Sections 529(c)(3) and 529(e)(3) of the Tax Code.]

Solution: If you would like to accumulate amounts in addition to the cost of tuition, put enough into State C's 529 prepaid tuition plan to lock in full payment for four years' tuition. In addition, contribute to a 529 savings plan, naming your daughter Jan as the beneficiary. (The limit on the maximum amount that can be contributed each year to a 529 plan varies by state.)

●**Limited to in-state schools.** Most 529 prepaid tuition plans are only for the sponsoring state's public universities. In a few states, money can be spent for private universities—but still within the sponsoring state.

Note: Less than half the states currently offer prepaid tuition plans.

●**Refund rules.** What happens if you put money into a 529 prepaid tuition plan and then your child decides to go to a college that's not covered? In general, you can get your money back. But you probably will receive a scant return on your investment, or no return at all. Each state has refund rules of its own for 529 plans. For information on your state, check out *www.savingforcollege.com.*

●**Rising costs.** In recent years, some states have faced financial stress. One result has been the imposition of a premium on 529 prepaid tuition plans.

Example: In State D, the annual cost of tuition at public universities is now running $10,000. But, to lock in a future year of tuition, you might have to pay $11,000 or even $12,000 up front.

Solution: A new independent 529 plan is designed to remedy some of the disadvantages of state-sponsored plans. TIAA-CREF will administer this plan and manage its investments.

● **Private schools.** The independent 529 plan includes more than 200 private universities, including some of the nation's top colleges.

Money in this plan can be used for any of these schools. There is no need to make a selection in advance.

Example: When your son Larry is a newborn, private university E charges $20,000 a year for tuition. This school participates in the independent 529 plan, so you contribute $20,000 to lock in a year's tuition.

Eighteen years later, tuition at E is $80,000. If Larry is accepted there, he can cash in the certificate for a year's tuition. What if Larry isn't accepted at E? Or if he decides he would rather attend F, where he is accepted? Larry can use his tuition certificate at F, providing F is a participating school.

Example: F's tuition was $25,000 when Larry was a newborn and during that time, you contributed $20,000 to the plan. Larry would be entitled to 80% ($20,000/$25,000) of the prevailing year's tuition.

Assuming current law is still in effect, no federal income tax will be due.

● **Cost control.** All of the colleges participating in the independent 529 plan are required to discount their tuition by at least 0.5% per year.

Example: You make a contribution to this plan for your daughter Kate when she is eight years old. Ten years later, Kate enrolls in private university G, which provides a 0.5% tuition discount through the plan. Kate will be entitled to a 5% tuition discount (0.5% times 10 years) when she applies her independent 529 plan certificate to tuition at G. This enables Kate's parents to buy one year's tuition now, at less than it currently costs—which will be *much less than* what tuition will cost at the time Kate is ready to attend college.

This discount may offset, or even exceed, the value of state tax breaks, which are offered in many 529 plans but not in the independent 529 plan.

What if Kate decides to attend H, which does not participate in the plan? You will be entitled to a refund of your contributions, plus or minus up to 2% per annum, depending on past investment performance.

Great Scholarships On the Web

Paul J. Krupin, a government researcher with the US Department of Energy, Kennewick, WA. He is also author of the Magic Search Words *series of books, including* Magic Search Words: Scholarships *(Direct Contact). He started the series to help people use the Internet search engines more effectively. His Web site is* www.magicsearchwords.com.

Every year, millions of dollars of free money for college is left unclaimed because students just aren't aware of it. The Internet is a storehouse of information on scholarships and grants for students of all ages—but you have to know the best ways to find it.

Most of the scholarships are for either $500 or $1,000, though some offer as much as $10,000 per year. Some students are awarded several different scholarships. Nearly every college or university offers full scholarships that cover tuition and living expenses.

WHAT TO DO

Start your search at *www.google.com*. This popular search engine constantly updates its listings on scholarships, grants, paid fellowships, etc.

● **Plug in "money words."** Start with *scholarship*. Then search related money words, such as *grant...fellowship...assistantship*, etc. These will lead you to more revenue sources.

● **Search with word strings.** When you type more than one word in the search field, the listings will be more specific to your particular needs. Just enter the search words with a space between each word—you don't need to include "and" or a plus sign.

Example: Scholarship graphic design San Francisco 2005. The location you include can be either where you live or where you want to go to school.

Change one word at a time after your initial search. In the previous example, replace the word *scholarship* with *grant* or *graphic design* with *art*.

Helpful: Make a list of key words and their synonyms to include in your scholarship search.

●**Bypass commercial sites.** Typing *–.com* in the search field streamlines your search by eliminating paid-for scholarship search services.

●**Search your interests.** No matter what you like to do—play tennis, skydive, act, quilt—there are probably scholarships available. Pair your interests with the word *scholarship* in your search engine.

●**Search the sites of major foundations, associations and companies.** Many provide scholarships. *Some examples to search under…*

  ●Acting…
    ☐ Donna Reed Performing Arts scholarships
    ☐ Irene Ryan Acting Competition

  ●Athletics…
    ☐ National College Athletic Association or NCAA scholarships

  ●Business…
    ☐ IBM scholarships
    ☐ Rotary International scholarships

  ●Conservation…
    ☐ Soil and Water Conservation Society scholarships and awards
    ☐ World Wildlife Fund

  ●Science and technology…
    ☐ DuPont Challenge Science Essay Awards Program
    ☐ Intel scholarships
    ☐ Microsoft scholarships
    ☐ Military science scholarships
    ☐ National science scholarships

Going to a Good College Just Got Cheaper

College partnerships allow students to earn degrees from private universities at lower cost. Students transfer to specific private universities after graduating from a two-year community-college program.

Examples: Cumberland County College in New Jersey has a transfer agreement with Drexel University in Philadelphia. Maricopa Community College in Arizona has agreements with Arizona State University and the University of Arizona.

The average tuition at a two-year school is about $1,905 per year, compared with an average of $19,710 for a private university.

Information: *www.finaid.org/otheraid/partnerships.phtml.*

Mark Kantrowitz, publisher, FinAid.org, a financial-aid Web site, Pittsburgh.

Beware of Paying College Tuition by Credit Card

Some parents pay for college tuition by credit card to obtain the frequent-flier miles or to get other card rewards.

Snag: Many colleges now have hired third-party contractors to process such charges—with the contractors adding a fee that offsets or exceeds much of the value of the miles.

Find out about *all* the fees that may be involved beforehand.

David Weliver, freelance writer, *SmartMoney,* 250 W. 55 St., New York City 10019.

How to Cut Dormitory Costs

Invest in near-campus housing for your child to avoid the high cost of college dormitories. Find a house or condo within a few miles of campus in a safe neighborhood. It should be large enough for at least four tenants—one of whom will be your child. After picking a property, estimate potential rent and expenses, then make a bid that would enable you to cover your costs and have some cash left over. Do basic landscaping and repairs, then furnish the property with inexpensive, durable furniture. Charge reasonable rents, appropriate for the area, and insist on formal leases. You can pay your child a management fee to collect rents and maintain the property. Plan to sell the property when he/she finishes college.

Vita Nelson, comanager, MP63 Fund, which invests in the stocks of 63 companies that have dividend-reinvestment plans, Rye, NY.

More Parents Are Homeschooling

More than 1.5 million US children are now homeschooled—and that figure is increasing by 15% a year. Homeschooled students do better on standardized tests than public- and private-school students.

Information: National Home Education Network (*www.nhen.org*)...American Homeschool Association (800-236-3278, *www.americanhome schoolassociation.org*).

Laura Derrick, president, National Home Education Network, Box 1652, Hobe Sound, FL 33475.

Learn Anything You Want to Know On-Line

Janet Moore, chief learning officer, The Sloan Consortium, based in Needham, MA, and Angela Lovett, CEO and founder, World Wide Learn, based in Calgary, Canada.

People who want to take classes on anything from Chinese cuisine to advanced mathematics are no longer limited to the courses at nearby colleges or other institutions. The Internet makes it possible to learn from expert instructors the world over.

Even better: You can usually access your course at any time of day you choose from the comfort of your home.

All you need is basic computer knowledge and access to the Internet. If you don't have the equipment, it may well be available at your local library. Many libraries offer quick courses in using a computer.

Cost: Many courses are free. This is especially true for those leisure-time activities and courses that are offered by social and professional organizations to their members.

Classes in business management or Web-site design often cost less than $1,000, while top vocational schools charge $1,500 to $2,500 a course. Courses leading to a degree at a well-known university typically cost $900 to $3,600.

Be aware that there are pitfalls...

•**Unsuitability.** On-line learning may not suit you. Learning via a computer can be frustrating for anyone who enjoys the camaraderie of a classroom.

•**Rip-off peril.** Many less-than-reputable organizations are selling second-rate courses that are taught by unqualified instructors.

HOW TO BEGIN

The majority of American colleges and universities provide on-line programs for academic credit. Many other types of institutions also provide noncredit courses, including technical, business and vocational schools.

Example: Herkimer County Community College (315-866-0300, *www.hccc.ntcnet.com*) offers an on-line degree in travel and tourism.

In addition, colleges and other organizations also offer courses in hobbies and fine arts.

Examples: The University of Hawai'i (808-956-5666, *www.hawaii.edu*) offers extensive on-line instruction in music.

When you sign up for a course, you pay a fee and receive a password that allows you to access the course's Web site. You might also receive written material or textbooks, but most of the information you're expected to learn is accessed via the Internet.

These courses differ widely, but most of them require you to read or listen to a certain amount of material and then check what you've learned either by self-testing or by submitting answers to the instructor via e-mail.

Because students are linked to the Internet, teachers can illustrate points in spectacular ways.

Examples: Courses in art can show you close-ups of some of the world's finest paintings. Music courses let you listen to a chamber orchestra in Paris.

And if you want to see or hear something again, it's easy to replay it on your computer.

Tests: In most nondegree courses, students open an e-mail containing the test, take it and send it to the instructor for grading. Teachers follow up by asking students to solve problems that are difficult for anyone who hasn't thoroughly absorbed the material.

Tests for degree courses, especially those at prestigious universities, are rarely held on-line. Instead, students go to a nearby location—usually a local university—where the test is supervised in a traditional classroom setting.

There is no camaraderie in the traditional sense, but many courses include an on-line bulletin board or chat room. These let students discuss the subject matter among themselves or ask the instructor questions that have not been adequately covered during class.

CHOOSING A SCHOOL

Several Web sites list courses offered by legitimate institutions.

Examples: The Sloan Consortium, a group of more than 500 leading US colleges and universities at *www.sloan-c.org,* and World Wide Learn, a site that lists hundreds of on-line learning centers, *www.worldwidelearn.com.*

The on-line learning department at a local university can also provide advice. Or you can contact the trade organization associated with the field in which you want to take a course.

Examples: For interior design organizations, check the Foundation for Interior Design Education Research (*www.fider.org*)...or for theater schools, try the National Association of Schools of Theatre (*www.arts-accredit.org*).

For a general listing, enter a course description in an Internet search engine, such as *www.google.com.* By entering "on-line course in real estate," for example, you'll find dozens of organizations that offer instruction. Check to see if the professor/instructor is certified by a state board that licenses professionals in that field, such as a state licensed real estate broker, or

check to see if the school is certified by a regional accreditor.

Important: If you plan to use the course toward a degree or to further your career, take courses only at an institution that is accredited by one of the following six regional academic associations...

●Middle States Commission on Higher Education (215-662-5606, *www.msache.org*).

●New England Association of Schools and Colleges (781-271-0022, *www.neasc.org*).

●The Higher Learning Commission of the North Central Association of Colleges and Schools (312-263-0456, *www.ncahigherlearningcommission.org*).

●Northwest Commission on Colleges and Universities (425-558-4224, *www.nwccu.org*).

●Southern Association of Colleges and Schools (404-679-4500, *www.sacscoc.org*).

●Western Association of Schools and Colleges (415-506-0234, *www.accjc.org*).

Helpful: The Council for Higher Education Accreditation (202-955-6126, *www.chea.org*) lists institutions approved by other accrediting groups at its Web site.

If you are not using the on-line course to get a degree or to advance your career, accredited institutions are still a useful way to ensure that you pay for a quality course. Many well-known organizations and companies, such as AARP at *www.aarp.org/nrta/learning* or Barnes & Noble University at *www.barnesandnobleuniversity.com* also offer quality programs.

Many individuals offer courses on the Web as well, including experts in areas such as gardening and screenwriting. Be careful.

Example: Before taking an on-line course in screenwriting, ask whether the instructor is a member of the Screenwriters Guild of America and what films he/she has written. Then check out the answers by going to The Internet Movie Database at *www.imdb.com,* which lists films and detailed information about them.

Rule of thumb: Stay away from an on-line course if the institution's Web site is filled with ads for products and services—they may indicate that the organization is not as concerned with education as it is with quick profits.

21

Safe and Secure

What's Really Dangerous In the World Around Us... And What's Not

Life in America in the 21st century is safer in many respects than ever before. The diseases that were once mass killers have been all but eradicated. Life expectancy keeps rising and infant mortality keeps declining. However, this great progress has been accompanied by the appearance of various new risks.

Examples: AIDS...West Nile virus...SARS ...genetically modified food...mad cow disease ...weapons of mass destruction.

We hear a lot about these new risks every day. As a result, many people believe that the world is more dangerous for humans than it has ever been. Some of us live in constant fear —needlessly. By learning about different risks we face, however, we can put them into realistic perspective.

WHAT IS RISK?

To understand how significant a particular risk is, we must ask ourselves four questions...

● **How likely is the event to occur?** The higher its probability, the greater the risk.

● **Is there a hazard associated with the event?** If something to which we are exposed is not really hazardous, it is not a risk.

Example: Microwaves from microwave ovens. In a microwave oven that's functioning properly, the microwaves are kept safely inside, and you are not exposed.

● **How serious are the possible consequences?** The more severe the possible outcome, the more serious we judge the risk.

● **How much exposure do we have to it?** No matter how dangerous something may be, it is not a risk to us if we have no exposure.

David Ropeik, director of risk communication, Harvard Center for Risk Analysis in Boston. He is a coauthor, with George Gray, PhD, of *Risk: A Practical Guide for Deciding What's Really Safe and What's Really Dangerous in the World Around You* (Houghton Mifflin).

Extreme example: Being consumed by a shark while swimming is certainly not a risk in the state of Kansas.

Taking all four factors into account, risk is the probability that exposure to a hazard will lead to a negative consequence.

EVALUATING RISK

Scientists use the techniques of toxicology—the study of poisons—to determine how dangerous certain substances are likely to be to people. The results are often uncertain because the effects of small quantities of these substances on human beings may be quite different than they are on animals given high doses under lab conditions.

Whenever the Food and Drug Administration, the Environmental Protection Agency and other government agencies regulate the use of drugs or exposure to environmental pollutants, they are extremely cautious and only permit human exposures far lower than those found to harm lab animals.

Another risk evaluation method, that's used by epidemiologists, is to search for statistical connections between different exposures and outcomes.

Example: How many people who drank from a certain water supply developed a certain disease.

But the results of such studies may not be definitive because the relationship between the first event and the second may just be coincidental, or some factors ignored by the study may be more important than those that were considered.

Even when it *is* possible to measure a risk scientifically, people must decide for themselves whether the risk of harm from a particular activity outweighs the benefit they expect to derive.

Example: The easiest way to get somewhere is often to drive yourself. For people age 70 or older, driving becomes more risky because of slower reflexes, poorer vision and greater susceptibility to injuries.

Fear versus analysis: Many people are more afraid of some kinds of risk than others that are objectively less hazardous. And, these preferences seem to be deeply ingrained in human psychology.

Examples: Most people fear newer risks (SARS) more than the familiar ones (flu)…man-made risks (radiation from cell phones) than the natural ones (sunlight)…risks they choose themselves (their own smoking) than those that are imposed on them (other people smoking)…gruesome risks (shark attack) rather than less terrifying threats (heart attacks).

To minimize risk, analyze it objectively, rather than simply relying on instinct or emotion.

Example: There is a much lower risk involved in flying long distances than in driving. A good number of travelers who drove instead of flying because of fear of terrorism in the wake of 9/11 died as a result of car accidents.

RISKS PEOPLE OVERESTIMATE

●**Nuclear power.** Much of the public is fearful of radiation from nuclear power plants. Studies of survivors of the atomic bomb attacks on Hiroshima and Nagasaki show that radiation is a weaker carcinogen. The survivors—90,000 people—were followed for approximately 60 years. Scientists estimate roughly 500 cancer deaths in that population were the result of excess radiation exposure.

Under normal operating conditions, essentially no radiation is released by nuclear plants. And 20 years after the most serious nuclear plant accident ever in the US—the Three Mile Island meltdown—no negative health effects were found.

If you live near a nuclear plant: Be familiar with evacuation routes…keep a kit of basic first-aid supplies…know where to tune in your radio for emergency notification, including medical advice.

●**Pesticides.** Pesticides are toxic to *pests*. The dose that humans get when they use pesticides according to directions is too small to be harmful, although there is risk for workers exposed to excessive levels of pesticides. The level of pesticide residue found on fruits and vegetables is so low that its effect on health is negligible.

To further reduce exposure: Rinse fruits and vegetables under running water…throw away the outer leaves of leafy vegetables…

cook or bake your foods (heating can degrade some pesticides).

RISKS PEOPLE UNDERESTIMATE

•**Falls.** They are the most common accidental cause of death in the US, particularly for the elderly. In 2000, 13,000 people aged 65-plus (including 11,300 over 75) died from complications resulting from falls.

To reduce the risk of falls: Keep eyeglass prescriptions current...avoid medications that cause dizziness...remove loose rugs, electric cords and other tripping hazards...put antiskid mats in bathtubs and showers...install handrails and improved lighting on stairways.

•**Medical errors.** A 1999 study by the Institute of Medicine of the National Academies discovered that preventable medical errors kill between 44,000 and 98,000 US hospital patients annually.

Also, many fatal errors occur in outpatient clinics, doctors' offices and at home. These errors include wrong and illegible prescriptions ...overdoses and other prescription errors... mistakes in using medical equipment...failure by medical providers to wash hands.

What you can do: Speak up about your concerns...make sure prescriptions are filled correctly...keep a list of all medications and the reasons they were prescribed...ask about harmful interactions between medications... before any operation, mark the area that is to be operated upon.

Example: If you're having surgery on your left knee, mark YES on your left knee and NO on your right knee.

Are Your Children Safe at School?

Is your child's school safe from terrorism and other dangers? Don't assume "it cannot happen here." Parents should find out about the crisis-prevention and -resolution plans for their children's schools. Also make sure that a police officer has been assigned to the school.

Critical areas: Emergency communication systems...lockdown procedures...staff training ...locations where students can stay until their parents pick them up.

Important: Also ask your children about safety issues. Then inform school officials—in writing—of problem areas.

Curt Lavarello, executive director, National Association of School Resource Officers, Sarasota, FL.

Terrorists Will Always Be a Threat—Preparations That Make Sense

Angelo Acquista, MD, author of *The Survival Guide: What to Do in a Biological, Chemical or Nuclear Emergency* (Random House), and the former medical director of the New York City Office of Emergency Management. He is attending physician at Lenox Hill Hospital in New York City.

The most important thing you and your family can do to survive a terrorist attack is to arm yourself with information. It's essential that you understand the many limitations of nuclear, biological and chemical weapons (often referred to as NBC agents).

The most dangerous terrorist weapon is fear. If you empower yourself with knowledge, you have taken away one of their weapons.

CHEMICAL WEAPONS

Blister agents, including mustard gas...pulmonary agents, such as phosgene...and nerve agents, such as Sarin (GB), VX, GF and Tabun (GA), are probably the easiest weapons for terrorists to get their hands on. Many of the nerve agents, for example, are really just insecticides and pesticides.

But understand that chemical weapons have significant limitations. Environmental factors inhibit their activity—they can't be vaporized and spread through the air on cold days...and they dissipate rapidly on hot or windy days.

Your best protection: Soap, water, fresh air and time can combat most types of chemical exposures.

Caution: Routine use of gas masks is not recommended for the general population. They are a waste of money. Most people don't know how to use them correctly—and the chance of having one with you when you need it is slim. If not used properly, they can suffocate you.

Similarly, the nerve agent antidotes, such as *atropine* and *pralidoxime,* are dangerous if not administered properly, and they are only available by prescription.

Remain vigilant. While many agents are tasteless and colorless and therefore hard to detect, others have odors—a musky or sweet pungent smell, the smell of newly mowed hay or grass, almonds or garlic.

Watch yourself and those around you for symptoms that may develop, such as an acute onset of severe headache, blurry or double vision, profuse runny nose, watery eyes, drooling, uncontrollable urination or defecation.

If you suspect that you are a victim of a chemical attack...

• **Leave the area—move upwind.** Avoid mass transportation because of contamination by others. Seek shelter in a room without windows (or cover up windows, doors and vents with plastic sheeting).

Caution: Don't seal things too well or you will suffocate.

• **Cover your mouth and nose with wet fabric.** Remain calm, and take shallow breaths.

• **Don't lie down.** Most chemical agents are heavier than air.

• **Close your eyes**—as long as it does not hinder your ability to escape. When you can, rinse your eyes for up to 15 minutes using as much water as you can.

• **Wash yourself off with soap and water.** Do this as quickly as possible.

BIOLOGICAL WEAPONS

You have probably heard about the lethal effects of biological agents such as smallpox, anthrax, plague and Ebola—but not much about the therapies and cures that exist for some of them. Biological agents have varying incubation periods—usually between three and 10 days—before symptoms appear.

Once an initial cluster of patients is diagnosed, antibiotics can be given to people in the cluster area to significantly decrease the number who will get the disease. Although there is no antibiotic to treat smallpox, once you are exposed you do have up to four days from exposure to get a vaccination, and that will lessen the severity of the disease.

Recommended protection: You don't need to stockpile antibiotics, such as Cipro. These lose their effectiveness if not stored properly (plus they're expensive and don't work against viruses). A paper face mask with a rating of N95 will keep out polluted dust and some of the microbes, such as anthrax spores, and may decrease exposure to the smallpox virus. An N95 mask costs only one dollar.

NUCLEAR WEAPONS

There are three kinds of nuclear attack that terrorists could use—a dirty bomb, a nuclear reactor leak and a nuclear detonation. There is currently no evidence that terrorists possess nuclear bombs.

A dirty bomb is a combination of conventional explosives, like dynamite, along with a weak radioactive substance that can spread over only a three- to five-block area. The radioactivity from a dirty bomb is too weak to cause any acute or chronic illness (the only real danger is from the dynamite). Radioactive iodine, a dangerous substance, is unlikely to be released by a dirty bomb, so there is no need to take the antidote *potassium iodine.*

Radioactive iodine would be released by a damaged reactor, so in this case you *would* take potassium iodine. One dose lasts for 24 hours, so you wouldn't need an additional dose unless there is ongoing radiation. You have three to four hours after exposure to take potassium iodine—you can get potassium iodine pills at a pharmacy without a prescription.

Caution: Potassium iodine can cause reactions by those with certain skin disorders, thyroid disease and allergy to iodine. Don't take potassium iodine unless you have been told to take it by emergency personnel.

In the unlikely event you are exposed to radioactivity from a nuclear attack, there are three basic ways to protect yourself…

•**Time.** Decrease the time you are exposed to the radioactive source.

•**Distance.** Get as far away as possible from the source.

•**Shielding.** Seek shelter and create as thick a barrier as possible between you and the radioactive source. Go to the basement if you can.

AN EMERGENCY ACTION PLAN

Here are some simple things you can do now to be prepared…

•**Designate an out-of-state relative for every family member to call** in an emergency. This person can act as coordinator, passing on instructions to everyone who calls.

•**Discuss with your family what to do in case of an evacuation.** You should pick two places to meet—one outside your home and the other outside of your neighborhood to be used if necessary.

•**Obtain your community's emergency and evacuation plan.** Familiarize yourself with it. This is especially important if you live within 30 miles of a nuclear reactor.

•**Take your first aid kit and supplies** (described below) along with you if you have to leave the area.

Assemble your family first aid kit and supplies now. *To your routine first aid kit, add…*

•An emergency preparedness manual. You can download *The 9-1-1 Guide* (*www.911guide. com*) that will tell you when to use the items in your first aid kit, how to use them and why you're using them.

•Flashlights and extra batteries and bulbs.

•Hygiene supplies, such as soap, antiseptic, scissors, toothpaste, toothbrush, etc.

•Household bleach, which can effectively decontaminate surfaces.

•N95 face masks for all family members.

•Rubbing alcohol and hydrogen peroxide.

•Betadine, eye wash, syrup of ipecac and laxatives in the event of poisoning or chemical agent release.

The 911 Pack—a next generation first aid kit, which has items to deal with newer threats, in addition to the standard items—can be viewed and ordered at *www.911guide.com/index.html.*

Cost: From $99* for a one-person basic pack to $249 for a four-person complete pack.

Other supplies: The US Department of Homeland Security (*www.ready.gov*, 800-237-3239) recommends that you also have…

•A three-day supply of water—one gallon per person per day (and extra water for any pet).

•A three-day supply of nonperishable food, such as peanut butter, sealed crackers and other foods that are sealed and require no heating or refrigeration (and food for your pet).

•Prescription drugs regularly taken, such as insulin and heart medication.

•A battery-powered radio.

*All prices subject to change.

More from Angelo Acquista…

Are You Prepared?

For additional Web sites with sensible ideas regarding emergency preparedness and response, be sure to visit…

•**Centers for Disease Control and Prevention** at *www.bt.cdc.gov/index.asp.* It offers a Chemical/Biological/Radiological Hotline at 888-246-2675.

•**Federal Emergency Management Agency (FEMA)** at 800-480-2520 or *www.fema.gov.* It offers a booklet called *Are You Ready?*

•**American Red Cross** at *www.redcross.org.*

Don't Be a Victim of Crime: Advice from a Bodyguard to the Stars

Pat Malone, a protective services consultant based in Cleveland. He has served as a bodyguard for the Philippine government, the Saudi royal family and a number of American celebrities. He teaches hand-to-hand combat, close-quarter battle and defensive and survival tactics to law-enforcement agents and members of the military.

No one ever believes that he/she will become the victim of a violent crime. Statistics, though, can't be ignored. A violent crime is committed every 15 seconds, someone in the US is murdered every 20 minutes and there are 30 to 50 serial killers in the US at any one time, according to the FBI.

Here's some practical advice on how to protect yourself in an emergency...

BEST DEFENSE

•**Carry a cell phone,** and preprogram it to dial the police emergency number, usually 911. A cell phone shows that you are prepared—and criminals avoid prepared targets.

When you suspect a situation might be dangerous, immediately call for help. If you hit the preprogrammed 911 button and can't talk, the police still might be able to find you. Many police departments have electronic locators.

•**If you don't have a cell phone, fake it.** Reach into your purse or pocket, and pull out your compact or wallet. Cup it in your hand, put it to your ear and pretend you're talking. If the criminal thinks that you are calling for help, he may leave you alone.

A poor defense: Pepper spray, mace or a weapon. You won't have time to look for it if you're caught off guard. Even if you do try to use it, the criminal may be able to withstand the weapon and turn it on you.

IF YOU'RE APPROACHED

•**Planning is vital.** Nearly everyone without a plan hesitates and loses the first critical seconds that he needs to escape.

Result: The victim is at the mercy of his assailant.

•**Try to escape if you are confronted by an armed person**—whether you are male or female, old or young. Don't argue or plead with your assailant. Take out your wallet and drop it on the ground. Set down your purse. Take off your watch or jewelry. Then run, making as much noise as you can to attract attention.

Your assailant most likely is a robber, not a killer. If he wanted to kill you, he would have shot you first. He probably will grab the goods and make his escape. Even if he has a gun, he probably won't shoot...and if he does shoot, he will be too stressed to aim properly.

•**If a stranger tells you to get in a car—don't.** Do all you can to resist.

Every violent criminal says, "Do what I say, and I promise I won't hurt you." Don't believe it. Once a criminal decides to move you, he is no longer just a robber. He has something else in mind, probably rape or murder.

If he grabs you, you probably won't be able to kick or punch him. Instead, try to gouge out his eyes.

Many criminals are high on drugs or alcohol. Unless you cause severe pain, he might not feel it or he might be able to withstand it.

If you can't reach his eyes, bite him as hard as you can—he *will* let go.

When he loosens his grip, pull free and run. Yell, "Fire!"—not "Help!" This will attract more attention.

•**If you are locked in a car trunk, kick out the taillights,** stick your arm out the hole and wave like crazy. The driver won't see you, but others might.

Also: Some car trunks have an internal release. Become familiar with your own car *before* an emergency.

PREVENTING TRAGEDIES

Of course, it is best to avoid dangerous situations. *The basics...*

•**Even if you think you are safe...pay attention.** Criminals *really are lurking.* When a criminal sees someone who is distracted, he will strike...and act before you are aware that there is any danger.

•**Trust your instincts.** If a situation makes you uncomfortable, get out fast. Your intuition often is right.

•**Project the image that you're alert and ready for action.** Keep your head up, and walk briskly. *Women*—if you're on the street or in a parking lot and someone catches your eye or looks you over—look right back at him. Sending the message that you see him and won't be surprised is a good deterrent.

•**Don't be nice to strangers.** We all have an inclination to help others. Criminals know this and take advantage of it. Don't let anyone stop you to ask for change, directions or the time.

•**Avoid places that are potentially dangerous.** Don't drive through a bad neighborhood to save time. Take the elevator, not the stairs. Use ATMs inside buildings whenever possible. Exterior ATMs expose your back to people on the street while you are distracted, making you an easy target.

Parking lots and garages can be dangerous places. Don't walk into an empty parking garage alone. If you notice a single man sitting in the car next to yours, don't go to your car. Come back when the man has gone or call the police.

Don't park next to a van or between two sport-utility vehicles. Before getting in your car, look under and inside both your vehicle and the one next to yours. Once in your car, don't sit there with the window open, chatting on your cell phone. Immediately lock the doors, start the car and leave the area.

Self-Defense on the Road

Never pull off the road at a remote location for an unmarked vehicle. Just because it flashes lights at you, doesn't mean it's a police car. Wrongdoers sometimes attach roof lights to cars to imitate police cars and deceive victims into stopping in locations where they will be vulnerable.

What to do: If you have a cell phone, call 911 or the local police number and report what is happening. Or drive to a shopping mall, police station or other busy location and pull over there.

Note: In some states, it is against police policy to use unmarked police cars to stop vehicles for routine traffic violations. To be safe, learn the law in your state.

TravelSmart, Box 397, Dobbs Ferry, NY 10522, *www. travelsmartnewsletter.com.*

Cell Phone Alert

Cell phone calls to 911 cannot be traced by 82% of public safety call centers. Cell phone companies have started to add recognition technology, but state and local governments do not possess the funds and coordination to follow through.

USA Today, McLean, VA.

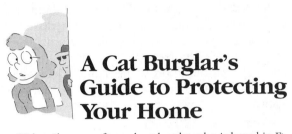

A Cat Burglar's Guide to Protecting Your Home

Walter Shaw, a reformed cat burglar who is based in Ft. Lauderdale, FL. He currently is producing a movie based on his life. His home-safety DVD, *It Took a Thief to Stop a Thief,* is available on his Web site, *http://allfornothin.com.*

I have spent most of my career stealing from people just like you. I was a member of the "Dinner Set" burglary ring for a dozen years. We stole about $70 million worth of jewelry—for which I spent 11 years in prison.

No one is better qualified to tell you that most people don't do enough to protect their homes from burglars.

Mistakes people make most often....

Mistake #1: **Installing—but not using—alarms.** Nearly all of the houses we robbed had expensive alarm systems—and more than half the time, the alarms weren't turned on.

Set the alarm even if you are only running out for 15 minutes. A sophisticated burglar will watch neighborhoods and learn when residents go to work or run errands and how long they are likely to be away. He/she is ready to move the minute you leave.

Get a zone alarm system that has room-by-room control. You can leave the bedroom alarm on when you're spending the evening in the living room, for example. We often burglarized homes while people were having dinner.

The best alarms offer multiple layers of protection, like motion sensors, heat sensors, light sensors, etc.

Mistake #2: **Posting detailed alarm signs.** Don't display signs that identify the alarm company. Burglars can buy information on how the systems are wired—and how to bypass specific versions.

Better: Buy signs at home-supply stores that read, *This house is protected by an alarm system.* As long as it doesn't give specific information, it can be a good deterrent.

Mistake #3: Leaving lights on. A light that stays on all the time is no more of a deterrent than a dark house. Use timers that turn lights on and off in different parts of the house at different intervals. Home-improvement and electronics stores sell motion detectors that turn on lights or appliances if someone enters the house.

Cost: About $20 each.

Mistake #4: Hiding valuables in the bedroom. It's the first place burglars look. We used to spend 15 minutes or less in each house we robbed. More than half of that time was spent in the bedroom, checking the usual hiding places—the underwear drawer…under the mattress…high closet shelves, etc.

Keep money or jewelry that you rarely wear in a safe-deposit box. Hide other valuables in places where burglars don't think to look—in the garage, for example, or above removable ceiling tiles. Or hide valuables in the freezer or in fake soup cans made for this purpose.

Don't hide all of your valuables in one place. A burglar is less likely to get everything if you put things in different locations.

Mistake #5: Getting a big dog. A 100-pound Rottweiler or German shepherd might look scary, but burglars know better. Most big breeds, unless they're trained as guard dogs, aren't barkers. What you want are "yappers," small dogs that make a lot of noise. Breeds such as Chihuahuas are better deterrents than large dogs.

Mistake #6: Hiding windows with landscaping. Tall bushes and shrubs allow burglars to jimmy windows without being seen. Keep bushes trimmed to below window level.

Also, don't count on cactuses or other thorny plants to prevent entry. Professional thieves routinely wear gloves and two layers of clothes —and they carry cutting tools to remove any thorny obstacles.

Mistake #7: Having newspaper and mail delivery stopped. When you ask to have your paper or mail stopped, you don't know who gets the information. Have a neighbor pick up newspapers and mail. Ask friends to drop by at different times of the day. The more activity burglars see, the less likely they are to target your house.

Mistake #8: Counting on chain locks. They are useless. The screws that hold them only go about one-half inch into the door or frame. They pull out with very little pressure.

Secure every exterior door with deadbolts. Use three—one each at the top, middle and bottom—of exterior doors. Install them directly across from hinges for more strength.

When an Intruder Breaks In—and You're at Home

Chris E. McGoey, founder and president of McGoey Security Consulting, in both Los Angeles and San Francisco. He is a security expert who has trained people in crime prevention for more than 30 years. Mr. McGoey is a frequent industry speaker who has appeared on national TV shows, including *60 Minutes, 20/20* and *Dateline NBC.* His Web site is *www.crimedoctor.com.*

It's 2 am. You are awakened by a loud noise downstairs. More noise. Someone is in the house! Your heart pounds…and your mind races. What should you do? Grab a baseball bat and creep into the hall to investigate? Call the police and wait? Try to escape?

This is a terrifying situation that happens to thousands of people. Each year, about 16% of American households experience a property crime. Occasionally a criminal breaks in while someone is at home—so it pays to know what you should do.

PREVENT A TRAGEDY

Make a plan—now. There is no single best strategy. Some people can climb out a window and run for help…others live or sleep on the upper floors and are unable to flee for physical reasons. If you're able to safely escape and get help—do it.

ONCE AN INTRUDER IS INSIDE

•**Be very quiet and just listen.** How many intruders are there? Are they ransacking the house? Are they making their way toward you?

●**Don't argue with your spouse about what to do.** This alerts the intruder to where you are.

●**Don't leave your bedroom with a bat or a flashlight.** A surprised intruder is likely to react violently.

●**Get to a safe place.** A safe room is one of the best options. Unlike what you have seen in the movies, it doesn't have to be large and filled with gadgets. An interior closet with a sturdy door that opens out is just fine. Put a deadbolt lock on the inside of the door and, most important, recharge your cell phone in there every night. Then, if you do hear someone in your home, you can go in the closet, lock it and call the police. Even if the intruder takes a phone off the hook to prevent you from calling for help, you will be able to call the police. You should be safe until the police arrive.

If you don't have a safe room, gather your family in a room, lock the door and then barricade it with furniture and other heavy objects. Choose the most secure room with the best door and lock, and stay there.

●**Be sure that you have a charged cell phone.** Program your automatic-dial phones to call 911. It's difficult to push even three buttons when you're panicked and your hands are shaking. Tell the police dispatcher your address and situation in a few sentences. Be specific.

Example: "Someone has just broken into my house. It sounds like one person. I don't know if he has a weapon. He's downstairs in the living room. I'm upstairs in the master bedroom with my wife."

Leave the phone line open so the dispatcher can listen to what is happening.

●**If the intruder reaches the room and turns the doorknob, call out,** "I've called the police." Just by doing so, you might scare him/her away.

ENCOUNTERING THE INTRUDER

●**Remain calm and be cooperative if you are confronted by the intruder.** How you behave in the first 30 seconds can set the tone for all that follows. When violence does occur, it almost always does so within these first few moments of confrontation.

Speak in as normal a voice as you can. Make no sudden moves. Tell him that you will cooperate. Put your hands out—palms up—to show that you do not have a weapon. Carrying any kind of weapon raises the chance that you will be hurt.

●**Avoid direct eye contact.** The intruder may interpret this as aggressive behavior and worry that you'll be able to identify him later.

The outcome of a break-in depends on the intruders. Most burglars will flee unless they are surprised or confronted.

Home-invasion robberies—a small but growing trend—can last for hours and are always violent. They are carried out by thugs who try to intimidate home owners into divulging safe combinations and bank ATM personal identification numbers, and handing over credit cards that can't be reported stolen while the owners are being held hostage.

●**Create a distress code with your burglar-alarm company.** If you are being held and your alarm has been triggered, you can signal trouble when its representative calls to authenticate the alarm. Your signal might be, "No, I can't meet you tomorrow." Or just don't pick up the call, so the company will send the police.

THE WEAPONS OPTIONS

It's your right and personal choice to own a firearm—but statistically, it's a bad way to stop a robbery. People generally aren't willing to shoot when they need to. Guns are used for self-protection in less than 2% of home-intruder crimes. Also, you would need to keep the gun loaded and nearby for it to be effective. That's a recipe for tragedy if children live in or visit your home. A gun is four times more likely to be used in an unintentional shooting than for self-defense.

If you do have pepper spray (*oleoresin capsicum,* or OC), only use it if you need help to escape. Facial contact and inhalation of the spray will induce up to 45 minutes of coughing, choking, nausea and temporary blindness. Even residual fumes can make your hiding place unbearable and can be hazardous to people with respiratory and heart conditions.

Your local police department can tell you if you legally can buy pepper spray in your state and where to learn how to use it. However, I do not recommend keeping any weapon on hand if children live in or visit your home.

IF YOU FIGHT

Never initiate aggressive action unless you believe that you are in a life-threatening situation. Escape almost always is the better option.

If you do decide to fight back, look for an opportunity when the intruder lets down his guard. Use a hard object to strike his eyes or throat as fast and hard as you can. Don't worry about inflicting an injury. Run as soon as he is stunned, and yell to get someone's attention. The intruder would rather escape than become the center of attention.

PREVENTING TROUBLE

Many break-ins can be avoided. Prevention begins with strong doors. Most burglaries and break-ins occur through the front door (34%) or the back door (22%).

Install steel-covered solid wood doors that are at least 1.75 inches thick. Make sure the doorjamb is steel as well. Any glass panels in or near your doors should be made of unbreakable glass.

How to Protect Your Most Important Papers

Ramona Creel, president of OnlineOrganizing.com in Atlanta. The company was named best organizing service for 2003 by the National Organization of Professional Organizers.

If a fire burned down your home, would it destroy your insurance policies? If you suddenly became incapacitated, would your family be able to find your living will? If the IRS claimed that you didn't make a payment, would you be able to prove that you had?

You're not truly prepared for a disaster unless your important documents are secure.

STORAGE OPTIONS

●**Fireproof safe.** Select a safe that can withstand temperatures of up to 1,700°F for at least one hour. If you wish to protect computer disks or videotapes, use a "media safe," which keeps internal temperatures particularly low. Avoid the "fire-resistant" lockboxes—these won't protect papers in a sustained fire.

Fire safes are available at such retailers as Lowe's, Office Depot, Staples, The Home Depot and Wal-Mart. You can get one with about two cubic feet of space for about $300. The affordable, reliable brand names include Sentry Safes at *www.sentrysafe.com* and FireKing at *www.firekingoffice.com.*

A home safe is best located in a basement, where temperatures remain coolest in a fire… there's no risk that a heavy safe will fall through a fire-weakened floor…and burglars often don't bother to search. If your area is prone to floods, make sure the safe is waterproof.

Keep the home safe door locked at all times, regardless of the inconvenience. Otherwise, it is simply an expensive cubbyhole. Remember to give a copy of the combination to a trusted relative or your attorney.

●**Bank safe-deposit box.** The safe-deposit box is located off-site, reducing the risk that a disaster will destroy both your home *and* your vital documents. Expect a safe-deposit box to cost from $20 to $200 a year, depending on where you live and the box size.

A safe-deposit box is inconvenient for documents that you refer to frequently, unless you store copies at home. It also is inappropriate for any papers that might be needed quickly and unexpectedly—such as wills and insurance policies—because banks are not open at night and on Sundays. Also, the box may be sealed when its owner dies so that tax authorities can assess the contents.

Important: The contents of a bank safe-deposit box are not covered by FDIC insurance. If valuables are stored along with important documents, consider adding a rider to your home insurance policy.

●**Relatives, accountants and attorneys.** Improve the odds that your documents will survive a disaster by storing duplicates at another location. Ask a relative to hold a sealed folder for you…or ask your attorney or accountant to keep copies of crucial documents.

●**Filing cabinets and cardboard boxes.** You can't store everything in a safe or a safe-deposit box—there just isn't room. Use these for any items that can be replaced fairly easily, such as financial statements.

WHAT TO SAVE AND WHERE

●**Personal records.** Birth certificates, adoption papers, citizenship records, marriage certificates, divorce documents, military service records, passports and Social Security cards can be replaced—but only with considerable effort, expense and delays of up to six months.

Where to store: Safe or safe-deposit box. If you'll need to refer to any of these documents frequently, make some photocopies. For example, children's birth certificates often are needed to register kids for school and other activities.

●**Tax returns.** You should keep tax returns forever and the supporting documents for six years. The IRS usually isn't permitted to audit returns that were filed more than three years earlier, but a number of exceptions can extend that deadline.

Where to store: Safe or safe-deposit box. If there isn't room for the supporting paperwork, store it in a file cabinet or a labeled box. If an accountant does your returns, have him/her retain copies for you in addition to storing the returns yourself.

●**Insurance policies.** Retain the initial policy you received when coverage began and the most recent addendum.

Where to store: A safe is a better choice than a safe-deposit box, which is inaccessible at odd hours, when you may need to refer to the policies.

Helpful: Keep a list of policy numbers and insurance company phone numbers in your safe for quick reference. Also keep a copy in your wallet. Half of all policyholders can't remember which insurance company provides their home, car, life, umbrella, liability and health coverage, much less what their policy numbers are.

●**Wallet contents.** If your wallet is lost or stolen, you'll want a copy of its contents. Next time you're near a copy machine, photocopy

the front and back of your credit cards, driver's license, insurance cards, etc.

Where to store: Safe.

●**Household inventory.** Your insurance provider will require proof of loss if your home is robbed or destroyed. Photograph or videotape your possessions, including valuables, everyday items and the insides of closets and cabinets. Keep appraisals of art, antiques and jewelry.

Where to store: Safe or safe-deposit box.

●**Legal documents**—wills, powers of attorney and trust documents.

Where to store: Safe and with your attorney.

Important: These should not be kept in a bank safe-deposit box, which might be temporarily sealed when the box owner dies.

●**Funeral instructions and deeds** to cemetery plots.

Where to store: Safe—not in a safe-deposit box, again because the box might be sealed up when its owner dies. You also should keep any funeral instructions and a copy of the cemetery deed with a trusted relative.

●**Emergency contact numbers.** Keep a list of the names and telephone numbers of your friends, neighbors, relatives, attorneys, doctors, veterinarian, employer, banks and investment companies. Your address book or an organizer might be stolen or lost in a disaster.

Where to store: Safe.

●**Investment records,** like CDs and stock certificates.

Where to store: Safe or safe-deposit box. Your monthly and quarterly investment account statements can be kept in a file cabinet, then discarded when they're replaced by year-end summary statements. Retain annual statements and transaction confirmations in a file cabinet for as long as you own the investments. IRA and 401(k) contribution records and copies of beneficiary designations should be kept forever in a safe or safe-deposit box.

●**Property information,** such as the deed to your house, mortgage agreement and title to your car.

Where to store: Safe or safe-deposit box. Keep all repair and maintenance bills in a file cabinet for as long as you own the house or car. When you sell, they will show potential buyers that you've been conscientious about upkeep of the home. Home-maintenance bills also may be useful when calculating the capital gains tax.

For other purchases, keep the warranties and receipts in a file cabinet for as long as the warranties are valid.

●**Photo albums.** Family photographs are not replaceable, so protect the negatives.

Where to store: Safe.

How to Prepare For a Blackout

Nancy Dunnan, a financial adviser and author in New York City. Ms. Dunnan's latest book is titled *How to Invest $50–$5,000* (HarperCollins).

Buying batteries for flashlights and radios and plenty of candles seems pretty basic, yet thousands of perfectly bright people forget to stock up on both. And, candles won't do much good unless you also have matches.

The Federal Emergency Management Agency has some excellent information at *www.fema. gov.* Click on "Library" and then on "Preparation & Prevention."

Regarding telephone service, you need to get a land line that uses electricity from the local phone company. Cordless phones that plug into electric outlets will not work without power.

Also make sure you charge extra batteries for any cell phones. (A cell phone charger that plugs into the cigarette lighter in your car can keep batteries charged if you lose power.)

Regarding your car, as soon as you hear a storm is coming your way, head for the nearest gas station and fill up the tank—pumps work electrically. And, if your garage door is electrically operated, open it. Lift it just enough so you can manually push it the rest of the way should you need to get to your car.

A final, not-so-ordinary tip: Know where your nonelectric can opener is stashed. And

stock up on canned baked beans and other canned goods. Many are very tasty, hot or cold.

More from Nancy Dunnan...

How Serious Is Identity Theft?

Identity theft has been in the news for good reason—according to a database maintained by the Federal Trade Commission (FTC), in 2003, more than 161,000 identity theft complaints were filed with federal, state and local law enforcement agencies and private groups. That's nearly double the number in 2001.

Because of the rising number of incidents, the FTC has issued specific advice about how to protect yourself...

●**Review all bank and credit card statements** very carefully.

●**Call the issuer when you're missing a monthly statement.**

●**Cut up expired credit cards.**

●**Check your credit report once a year** with the three major agencies.

●**Do not give out your Social Security number,** without good reason.

For details on how thieves work, visit *www. consumer.gov/idtheft.* Also, you should review *Identity Theft: Reduce Your Risk.* Download it for free at *www.pueblo.gsa.gov* or order the print version, also for free, from 877-382-4357.

Identity Theft Protection

Frank W. Abagnale, president, Abagnale & Associates, document-security and fraud-prevention consultants in Washington, DC, and author of *The Art of the Steal: How to Protect Yourself and Your Business from Fraud* (Broadway). His life was the subject of the film *Catch Me If You Can.*

To better protect yourself from identity theft, destroy compact discs (CDs) that have your personal information—Social Security number, bank or investment account numbers, bank or credit card PINs or other information—before you throw them out.

If you keep personal information on CDs: Consider buying an embossing machine, which makes CDs unreadable. They are available at office-supply stores.

Cost: About $50—much cheaper than CD shredders, which can cost as much as $1,200.

Reminder: Also shred sensitive documents, such as preapproved credit card applications, which a thief could divert to his/her own address, enabling him to open accounts in your name…and bank deposit slips, which he could use to deposit an uncovered check and withdraw cash from your bank account.

You can buy a crosscut document shredder for personal use for about $120.

Free Help If You're an Identity Theft Victim

Recover faster from identity theft by getting free counseling at Call for Action's consumer hot line, 866-434-6854. Counselors will provide phone numbers of law-enforcement agencies and instructions for recovering from identity theft. To avoid becoming a victim, you can request a free brochure on prevention strategies from Call for Action by calling 800-847-2511, or download it from *www.callforaction.org*. Click on "Identity Theft Resources."

Notorious Ex-Hacker Reveals the Latest Scams

Kevin Mitnick, formerly one of the world's most notorious hackers. He spent five years in prison for computer hacking–related charges and then began promoting computer security after his release in 2000. He is cofounder of Defensive Thinking, a computer security consulting firm in Las Vegas and on the Web at *www.defensivethinking.com* and coauthor of *The Art of Deception* (Wiley).

A favorite department store calls to confirm your credit card number, or a Web site asks you to select a user name. Both are perfectly common situations—and potential cons.

Every day, high-tech con artists trick some of us into revealing personal account information, computer passwords—even secret corporate files. In 2003, about 10 million Americans fell victim to identity theft. *The latest high-tech cons to watch out for…*

● **Caller-ID con.** Paul receives a call from a credit card company saying that he has been preapproved for a great credit card offer. Paul just assumes the call is legitimate because his phone's caller ID confirms the source, so he provides his date of birth, mother's maiden name, Social Security number and other confidential information.

Problem: Utilizing a widely available telephone switch, a con artist arranged for Paul's caller ID to display the name of the credit card company. The con artist just as easily could have made it Paul's bank, a store he frequents —even the White House. Surprisingly, the ability to post phony caller IDs is an unethical but not illegal use of the technology.

How to protect yourself: Don't trust caller ID. When someone asks for sensitive information, insist on calling him/her back and look up the number.

● **Bogus Web site con.** Susan receives an e-mail at work that includes an attractive offer for a popular piece of merchandise. The e-mail includes a link to a Web page that prompts her to select a user name and password.

Problem: Like many people, Susan uses the same password for all of her on-line accounts. The offer and site turn out to be bogus, but the con artist who sent the e-mail now has Susan's password. And, with that and her work e-mail address, he can access her company's computers. He also might gain access to Susan's Web-based investment accounts or other password-protected personal data.

How to protect yourself: Use a different password for each Web site and each on-line account. Make sure all passwords incorporate letters and numbers. This makes it difficult for hackers to guess them with programs that run through the dictionary. Never keep a list of passwords in an obvious place, and if you use *Windows,* don't let it save your passwords.

Note: The closed padlock image that appears at the bottom of your Web browser when you log onto a Web site indicates that the site has been certified as secure. This is a good sign that the site administrator has been vigilant about security issues.

●**Mislaid disk con.** Michael spots a computer disk on the floor of his office's restroom. The label says *Confidential Payroll Data* and carries the company logo.

Problem: Such a "mislaid" disk can be a computer-age Trojan horse left deliberately by a hacker employee or visitor. Once Michael loads the disk onto his computer, the hacker can gain access to his files. Worse, the disk unleashes a virus that crashes the company network.

How to protect yourself: Assume that a "lost" disk was left deliberately. Never put such a disk in your computer. Throw it away, or turn it over to your firm's information-services department.

●**Stolen data.** Alan gets a call from his company's payroll department. There has been a computer problem, and his paycheck will be delayed by a week unless he can help replace the lost information.

Naturally, Alan is willing to help. He is asked for his Social Security number, whether he uses direct deposit and, if so, the name of his bank and his account number. This con is especially prevalent at large corporations—hackers realize employees are unlikely to know the names of everyone in the payroll department.

Alan wouldn't give out such information to strangers, but the caller knows his name and seems to work for the company. Such information is available from company directories. Hackers can find the directories on-line or even by digging through the company's trash.

How to protect yourself: If you receive a call like this, take the caller's name and say you will call right back. Then dial your company's switchboard, and ask to be connected to the person in question. Consider it a red flag if the caller will not provide a name and call-back number. If you can't find the caller, notify your office manager so that he can alert everyone at your company.

If you own or manage a business, make it clear to all employees that it is always OK to say "no" to any phone request for confidential information.

Important: Hanging up and calling back might not be enough to stop the most sophisticated con artists. They might be savvy enough with phone systems to have your call rerouted to their phones. For more certainty, get up from your desk and speak to the caller in person or ask to speak with someone you know in that department.

●**Helpful technician con.** Karen is at her desk when she receives a call from someone in her company's information-services department. Would she read him the number on the jack to which her computer is connected? Most large companies label Internet access ports. Of course, she complies.

Days later, after Karen has forgotten about the first call, someone else calls to see if her Internet connection is working well and leaves his number. She soon does have problems and calls back—and gives the man her user name and password.

Problem: Karen's helpful computer technician has just stolen her confidential information. It was he who caused her computer problem by calling her company's information-services department and asking for her port to be shut down temporarily for testing. Most information-services departments wouldn't question such a request. Once the con artist has obtained Karen's user name and password, he then will call the department back and request that her port be turned back on.

How to protect yourself: When asked to confirm confidential information, ask the caller to read the requested number in his file to you. If he says he doesn't have it handy, say you'll get back to him in a minute with the information. Then call your information-services department to make sure you are talking to a real technician. Never let down your guard.

Even if you work from home, this con can be used by someone posing as a technician with your Internet service provider.

New Identity Scam Uses IRS Forms

The IRS warns that scam artists are sending out fake bank correspondence that includes phony IRS forms—often numbered W-9095, W-8BEN or W-8888—that request confidential financial and personal information.

The correspondence falsely says you must fill out the forms and fax them back to a provided number for tax purposes—such as to avoid having tax withheld from income earned in your accounts. The scammers will use this information to steal from your accounts.

Safety: If you get such correspondence, call your banker. Also, visit the IRS's "dirty dozen" tax scams Web page at *www.irs.gov.*

New Tax Scams Target Military Families and E-Mail Users

IRS News Release IR-2003-63.

There are two new tax schemes of which you need to beware. If you witness these scams in action, call the Treasury Inspector General's fraud hotline at 800-366-4484.

•**A caller posing as an IRS employee** says that because the family has a member serving in the military, it is entitled to a $4,000 tax refund. The caller even provides a genuine IRS toll-free phone number to appear legitimate, then requests a credit card number to handle the postage fee—and proceeds to make false charges on the credit card.

•**An e-mail that appears to be from the IRS** directs the recipient to a Web page that requests personal financial information that is used to commit identity theft.

Safety: Know that the IRS never requests credit card numbers over the phone, does not charge for sending out a refund and does not request personal information by e-mail or via Web sites.

ATM Cons

ATM skimming devices are set up by crooks to get confidential customer information and drain victims' bank accounts. Some devices fit over ATM controls and record personal identification numbers and other data, then produce a message saying that the ATM is not working. Other devices let the ATM work normally but record information during transactions.

Self-defense: Carefully examine the ATM before you use it, and don't use it if something looks wrong—for example, the faceplate is misaligned...don't use an ATM with unusual signage, such as *Swipe your ATM card here before inserting it in the card reader*...always check bank statements promptly for unusual charges.

Greg McBride, CFA, senior financial analyst for Bankrate.com, 11811 US Hwy. 1, North Palm Beach, FL 33408.

What to Do If Your Charge Card Is Stolen

Thieves will try small transactions to test the validity of stolen bank or charge cards and account numbers.

Examples: Buying a few gallons of gasoline or other small items.

If the transaction does go through, the thief knows the card is not yet on the stolen list and will make more expensive purchases. He/she knows that usage of a "hot" card is limited, so he may time the transactions for Friday night because no action will be taken on the card account until the following Monday.

Self-defense: Immediately report any missing card. Reconcile bank statements as soon as you receive them. Report and resolve unrecognized charges immediately. Access your accounts via telephone or the Internet to review the latest transactions.

Hal Morris, veteran Las Vegas–based consumer affairs journalist who writes widely about scams, schemes and other rip-offs.

Beware: Your Personal Information Is on the Web

Marjory Abrams, editor of *Bottom Line/Personal*, Boardroom Inc., 281 Tresser Blvd., Stamford, CT 06901.

Earlier this year, 1,800 New York University students received an e-mail message informing them that their Social Security numbers had been posted on the Internet. This highly publicized violation of privacy—which stemmed from flawed internal security measures that have since been tightened—surprised and troubled students and nonstudents alike.

The NYU situation did not surprise privacy consultant John Featherman. According to John, people only have to "google" their names—that is, enter them in the popular search engine—to see the extent to which their privacy is compromised on the Internet. *When I looked up myself and the members of my extended family, I readily found…*

●**Information on volunteer work,** charitable gifts and religious affiliations.

●**Real estate** transaction amounts.

●**Signatures** on political petitions.

●**Postings** to news groups.

●**Even the birthdays** of some of our kids.

According to John, my search only scratched the surface. He notes that many types of sensitive personal information now are available over the Internet—especially to people who are willing to pay for it. Such fee-based services as Informus, Infotel and Lexis-Nexis extract information from driver's licenses, court proceedings, voter registrations and public documents. Even

crime victims' and witnesses' statements may end up on the Internet.

Legislation and public pressure may limit the availability of personal data. But John says that the Internet is a haven for identity thieves and other predators.

First step in protecting yourself: Try to get information about yourself deleted from the Internet. John advises consistently and aggressively searching for your name and asking the offending Web sites to have it removed. (Many will do so upon request.) And, do likewise with on-line phone directories, such as *www.switchboard.com* and *www.411.com*…sites of organizations to which you belong…and other sites, such as *http://anybirthday.com*.

Smarter searching: Look up all the variations of your name—nicknames, with/without middle initials, maiden name, etc. And, put all the variations in quotes to get an exact match. If your name is a common one, try it with and without your state.

More strategies from Beth Givens, director of Privacy Rights Clearinghouse…

●**Be stingy about information** you give out over the Internet. Don't trust the Web sites that promise prizes or rewards in exchange for personal information.

●**Be aware that any message posted** to a public news group or forum is available to anyone—including nonmembers. People may be able to retrieve your name and e-mail address. Use a pseudonym as well as a separate e-mail address to mask your identity.

Another problem with postings: Most public postings are archived in searchable files. Before you post any message, ask yourself whether you want potential employers or other people to be able to read it in years to come.

●**Use encryption software** to keep on-line communications private. You can download the program titled *Pretty Good Privacy* free at *www.pgpi.org*.

●**Raise a fuss if your Social Security number is used** for identification purposes. Many institutions still do this routinely. Request that they use your driver's license number instead.

•**Do not use computers in cybercafés** or other public places to access bank accounts, pay bills or handle sensitive information.

Things may look bad in the cyber-privacy arena—but perhaps not as bad as they could be. I heard about an on-line database that purports to contain more than 220 million US driver's licenses, photos and all. Curious, I looked myself up in the database—which turned out to be a "prank" Web site. It contained no real information and showed a photo of a monkey face. Score one for privacy—for now.

How to Keep Your Medical Information Private

John Featherman, personal privacy consultant and president of Featherman.com in Philadelphia.

Charles B. Inlander, president, People's Medical Society, Allentown, PA, and author of *Take This Book to the Hospital with You* (St. Martin's).

The medical privacy form is the long-awaited result of the *Health Insurance Portability and Accountability Act of 1996* (HIPAA), intended to protect privacy, not take it away (*www.hhs.gov/ocr/hipaa*).

Below, Charles Inlander gives some examples of medical privacy problems....

•**Drug companies** obtaining patients' names for marketing purposes.

•**Insurers** telling employers about employees' health problems.

•**Embarrassing messages** concerning diagnoses or other confidential matters left on patients' answering machines.

•**Medical information** given to the media without the patient's consent.

•**Names of organ donors** released to the organ recipients without their consent.

The rules went into effect on April 14, 2003. Now, most health-care providers, health insurers and others who have access to your records are required to send you an explanation of how they use and disclose your medical information. Small health plans (those with annual receipts

of no more than $5 million) had an extra year to comply.

Released information is limited to the minimum amount needed for the purpose of the disclosure. For example, physicians may send an insurer information about injuries from an accident—not the patient's entire medical file.

Advice from John Featherman...

Never sign blanket waivers. And, review privacy notices before receiving services. You can change them to limit information released to the specific date, doctor and condition. Patients have the right to ask for even more privacy restrictions. *Some examples...*

•**Requesting that all mail from the doctor** be sent to your address of choice.

•**If hospitalized,** requesting that your name, general condition, etc. not be included in the patient directory.

•**Seeing a copy of your file** before it is sent to a third party. Make sure it contains only relevant information.

A health-care provider does not have to agree to your add-on requests—but it must abide by any agreement that it makes with you.

Other newly mandated rights...

•**You may inspect and copy your medical records**—and request corrections to errors that you find. You can't demand them.

•**You may request a listing of what medical information has been sent out about you**—and to whom.

Lest you feel too safe, Mr. Featherman explains that many entities are exempt from the rules—law-enforcement agencies, life insurance companies, auto insurers whose plans include health benefits, workers' compensation providers, agencies that deliver Social Security and welfare benefits, Internet self-help sites, cholesterol screeners at shopping centers or in other public places.

More from John Featherman...

Share a Computer? Protect Your Privacy

If you share a computer with anyone—perhaps your children at home or a coworker at the office—take the following precautions to protect your personal data from prying eyes. Check your "Help" file for instructions.

●**E-mail.** When using Web-based e-mail, select the option that tells the site to automatically delete your e-mail address from its memory when you close your browser.

●**Web surfing.** Erase your Internet history log before ending an on-line session.

●**On-line shopping.** Disable the automatic form-completion feature—this fills in a whole address or query based on the first few letters.

●**Files.** Enable password protection on files and folders. Empty the recycle or trash bin on your desktop and e-mail program before leaving the computer.

●**Software.** Consider software that lets you block Web sites, downloads and chat rooms. Set up different profiles for different users.

Best: Norton Internet Security at *www.symantec.com.*

Cost: $69.95.*

●**Public terminals.** Never enter personal information when using terminals in libraries, airports, etc.

*All prices subject to change.

Cover Your Tracks On the Internet

Kim Komando, Phoenix-based computer and Internet expert. She is host of The Kim Komando Show, *a weekly technology call-in program broadcast by more than 400 radio stations worldwide,* www.komando.com.

You leave an easy-to-follow trail when you wander around the Internet—but if you want to maintain your privacy, you easily can do so on your PC. Please note, however, that this involves deleting temporary Internet files and your history.

Instructions vary for Mac users. Consult your Web browser's help file.

USING INTERNET EXPLORER 5.50

●**Under "Tools,"** select "Internet Options" and then "General."

●**Under "Temporary Internet Files,"** click "Delete Files." Then select "Delete All Offline Content" and click "OK." Next select "Settings," "View Files." Finally, you need to select and delete all cookies.

●**Under "History,"** click "Clear History." Next to the "Clear History" button is a number box marked "Days to keep pages in history." Set it to one, and your history list will be purged every 24 hours.

USING NETSCAPE 7.1

●**Under "Edit,"** select "Preferences."

●**Select "History"** under "Navigator" and set "Remembered Visited Pages" to one day.

●**Select "Cache"** under "Advanced" and click "Clear Cache."

Workplace Security Basics

To stay safe at work, be sure to follow these helpful strategies…

●**Find out if access to the facility is tightly controlled** and if there are any unguarded entrances. All entrances should be locked and require either a key or a security code for entry.

●**Stay alert in the parking lot,** your office and your work area so that an intruder can't surprise you. Know how to draw attention to yourself if needed—simply screaming may not be enough. Pull the fire alarm, break a window, etc.

●**Verify visitors' identification** before permitting them on the premises.

●**Be careful what you say about coworkers outside the office**—plans to work late, appointments, vacation plans, etc.—and to whom.

Neal Rawls, corporate security chief and former police officer in West Palm Beach, FL, and author of Be Alert, Be Aware, Have a Plan *(Lyons).*

Index